THE
NATIVE
AMERICANS

THE
NATIVE
AMERICANS

The Indigenous People of North America

CONSULTANTS
COLIN F. TAYLOR
WILLIAM C. STURTEVANT

SMITHMARK

A SALAMANDER BOOK

This edition published in 1996 by SMITHMARK Publishers,
a division of U.S. Media Holdings, Inc.,
16 East 32nd Street,
New York, NY 10016

1 3 5 7 9 8 6 4 2

SMITHMARK books are available for bulk purchase for sales
promotion and premium use. For details write or call the manager
of special sales, SMITHMARK Publishers Inc.,
16 East 32nd Street,
New York, NY 10016;
(212) 532-6600

ISBN 0-8317-7335-9

All correspondence concerning the content of this book should be
addressed to Salamander Books Ltd,
129–137 York Way,
London N7 9LG,
England

CREDITS

Designed by DW Design, London
Filmset by SX Composing
Maps by Andras Berezney
Printed in the United States of America

This book was originally published in three illustrated volumes: *The
Native Americans, Native American Myths and Legends* and *Native
American Arts and Crafts.*

CONTENTS

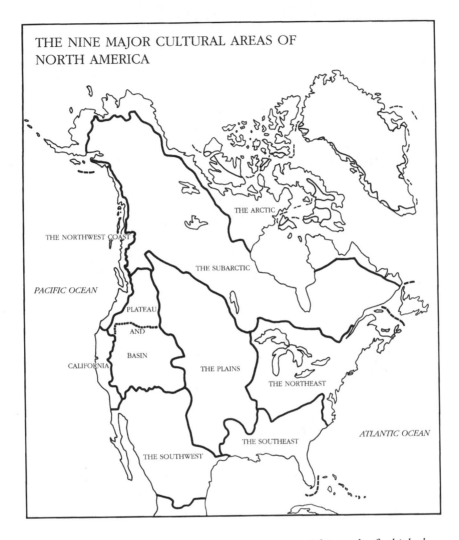

THE NINE MAJOR CULTURAL AREAS OF NORTH AMERICA

THE ARCTIC

THE NORTHWEST COAST

THE SUBARCTIC

PACIFIC OCEAN

PLATEAU

AND

BASIN

CALIFORNIA

THE PLAINS

THE NORTHEAST

ATLANTIC OCEAN

THE SOUTHEAST

THE SOUTHWEST

The more cultural areas of Native North America, within each of which the aboriginal cultures are broadly similar. More detailed maps of these areas are shown in at the beginning of chapters for each geographical region.

INTRODUCTION

A hundred thousand years ago the world was suffering from the last part of the Ice Age: great ice sheets covered much of North America, and sea levels fell dramatically revealing land corridors. During this time Neanderthal man developed fire for warmth and cooking. *Homo sapiens sapiens* evolved around 35,000 years ago, a big-game hunter with a sophisticated tool kit and great intellectual capacity. Though less robust physically than Neanderthal man, he was more adaptable to climatic variations. Families lived in substantial dwellings and buried their dead with grave goods. Evidence for *Homo sapiens sapiens* first occurred in Africa, Asia and the Near East, where they absorbed and replaced the Neanderthal populations. Several millennia later they appeared in Australia and Siberia. At the time when Europe was under glaciation, Northern Asia was cold, dry and free of glaciers.

The date of man's arrival in America is open to discussion, though archaeological evidence from sites suggests a date after 14,000 years ago. *Homo sapiens sapiens* (fully modern man) was the first to inhabit the Americas during the latter part of the Ice Age. Anyone living in the region needed to have the right technology: warm clothes and shelter, strategies for food storage, a means of traveling over snow and ice and a mobile way of life.

Geologists agree that for two long periods between 45,000–75,000 and 14,000–25,000 years ago, the Bering land bridge was exposed. The first Americans migrated from Siberia over the Bering Strait. Research has shown that common linguistic and cultural traditions survive to this day on both sides of the Bering Strait, and fauna and flora are almost identical in these land masses.

Central Beringia was dry land for several thousand years. It was a cold place, with strong winds and thin snow cover, believed to be treeless, but with enough vegetation and grasslands to support the late Ice Age mammals (mammoth, bison, wild horse and caribou). The study of fossil pollen grains has indicated that the vegetation may have been areas of steppe or tundra where reindeer roamed. Beringia may have been a refuge for animals and humans during the cold intervals of the last glaciation, and when conditions changed the animals moved on followed by the humans.

Around Beringia 11,000 years ago the inhabitants had adapted to a variety of different environments: maritime, tundra, river valley and mountain. Thus during the Ice Age there were several cultural groups living in northeast Asia, with diverse lifestyles under different environmental conditions. Of those groups, some scholars say it was only the big-game hunters who crossed over on the land passage between the ice masses following the animals south into America, and later evolved according to the landscape, climate and available resources.

The sea levels rose about 14,000 years ago and by 9,000 years ago the land bridge had vanished. It is generally accepted that the American Indians migrated from Siberia.

At Paleo-Arctic sites by the Yukon and in Alaska, there is evidence of post-glacial occupation around 11–12,000 years ago. Artifacts (small cores and microblades and bladelets) have been discovered similar to those found near Lake Baikal in Siberia. At such settlements people stayed in tent-like houses and lived by hunting, fishing and gathering wild fruits.

The skulls of Indians found by the great mounds were examined and compared with modern recent Indian and Mongolian crania. It was claimed that they were the same peoples, and that the first Americans were descended from Asian origins. Biologists have discovered that there is a relationship between the teeth of humans from North China and those from North America. Apparently there was a single early migration of hunter-gatherers who evolved by cultural differentiation. Two further migrations took place later, and gave rise to the Athapaskans and the Eskimo-Aleut populations.

According to Christy Turner, an expert on the physical characteristics of prehistoric man's teeth, the earliest penetration of Alaska by Asians took place over 14,000 years ago. They were followed a few thousand years later by two waves of immigrants from Siberia: the ancestors of modern Athapaskan Indians and northwest coast peoples; and the ancient Eskimo-Aleut.

Various bodies of research have divided the American peoples into three distinct pre-European groupings: the Paleo-Indians (Puebloans, Pimas,

Pai); the Athapaskan speakers (Apache and Navajo); and the Eskimo-Aleut. Neither the Athapaskans nor the Eskimo-Aleut penetrated deep into the Americas: the Central and South American Indians were Paleo-Indians. All three peoples came from northeast Siberia, but there were three language groups: Amerindian (most North American and all South American languages were part of one Amerind family); Na-Dene; and Eskimo-Aleut. According to certain scholars these three linguistic groups correspond to the three waves of migration. The Amerindian group arrived before 11,000 years, the Na-Dene around 9,000 years ago and the Eskimo-Aleut around 4,000 years ago.

There is more linguistic diversity in extreme northwest America where there are more contrasting environments than in the recently deglaciated northeast. It is suggested that the Eskimo-Aleut, Na-Dene and Algonquian languages spread from the periphery of the ice sheets into the newly unglaciated lands. The later two migrations limited their settlements to the north and northwest coast without penetrating further into the interior of the Americas.

The period between the first proposed crossing by man approximately 14,000 years ago, and the arrival of the so-called Clovis peoples around 11,500 years ago, is a subject fiercely discussed by archaeologists. There are widely accepted and precise dates for Clovis artifact sites throughout the Americas from around 11,500 years ago.

The following passages set out a few of the sites around which this controversy rages.

In the western United States, there may have been settlement of the US Pacific coastal and inland regions in the very early post-glacial period, 14-13,000 years ago, for humanly made stone fragments have been found. In California, on Santa Rosa Island, there were temporary encampments where hunter-gatherers butchered mammoths and settled for a few days during their seasonal migrations. This site is firmly dated around 7,500 years ago, though claims have been made for much earlier settlement. Pre-Clovis man may have occupied China Lake sites in California, but the stratigraphy is questioned by scholars. Other sites on the high plains of Colorado and in Texas may have been visited by pre-Clovis man but scholars have put forward a plethora of arguments against this.

In the eastern United States, Meadowcroft Rockshelter on Cross Creek by the Ohio River was one of the earliest occupied sites in North America, from which were found 45 species of mammal, 68 birds and 30,000 plant fragments. The environment there was stable for 11,000 years, and the rock shelter is known to have been used from 700–12,000 years ago, though archaeologists claim it was used much earlier.

In southern Florida, the area was cooler and drier than it is today; Paleo-Indian sites at sink-holes are today submerged below sea level, but may date from before 11,500 years ago. There the peoples camped for short periods while hunting game and may have exploited huge territories using pre-Clovis artifacts.

Although not directly relevant to this book, it is interesting too to note archaeological evidence of human occupation in Central and South America. In Central America archaeologists such as MacNeish are convinced that human occupation in Mexico can be dated back to 20,000 years ago, though the most reliable record begins 11,000 years ago, when the hunting groups are found to the south of the Rio Grande with Clovis-type points. In South America very early settlement dates of 14,000 years ago have been given for Pikimachay Cave in Peru, but these are highly controversial. In Brazil beautifully painted rockshelters have been found, mostly dating to between 7,600 and 8,000 years ago.

Evidence from artifacts for humans inhabiting the Americas prior to 14,000 years ago is open to debate. Scholars argue that the 'early' artifacts are intrusive, accumulations are natural, the association between mammoth bones and flakes is tenuous, or that dating materials are excavated from earlier levels and radiocarbon readings are inaccurate. It is agreed that after 12,000 years ago Paleo-Indians settled in South America, bringing with them their stone technology from the North.

Clovis peoples were hunters who followed the migratory paths of the larger mammals. They camped by rivers and streams where big game came to drink, and in the winter they stayed in rock shelters. People collected wild foods including fruits, berries, vegetables and nuts, to supplement their diet. They also ate the meat of both large and small mammals as is indicated by the discovery of these bones from their occupation sites. They were expert stone workers and artisans, renowned for producing beautiful translucent stone points with fluted bifaces, known as Clovis points.

These Paleo-Indians arrived approximately 11,500 years ago and within a few centuries spread to the North American coasts and as far south as Mexico. On the Great Plains of America, Clovis culture stone artifacts have been found, in direct association with bones of large extinct Ice Age mammals.

While it is generally accepted that Clovis people came from north of the ice sheets and migrated south as the glaciers melted, the problem for archaeologists is to trace their origins. The mystery exists because they appeared at sites with their fine, highly developed stone tools, for which there appears to be no precedent. Scholars believe that the Clovis point was developed on the Plains and not in the Arctic (Alaskan points are different). Clovis points have been found in the Canadian provinces, throughout the United States, on the Great Plains, in North America, Mexico and South America.

The Clovis people (the big-game hunters) flourished on the Plains for about 500 years, then around 11,000 years ago abruptly vanished. They were replaced by a multitude of different hunting and gathering peoples. Various reasons have been put forward to explain their disappearance. It was suggested that the climate had changed resulting in reduced water availability. Consequently animals clustered around the remaining springs, were easy prey and were over-hunted.

However, Paul Martin claimed that when the first Americans arrived they found themselves in an extremely favorable environment, with large herds of mammoths and other mammals who were not wary of hunters. As a result the human population exploded, and the rapidly expanding human population quickly depleted the slower breeding mammal groups. As big game became scarce the hunters moved on across America, and once the big game became extinct a population crash followed. Martin developed a computer projection that suggested that Paleo-Indians arrived in Panama by 10,930 years ago, and at Tierra del Fuego by 10,500 years ago. He suggested that the populating of the entire continent south of the ice sheets took a mere 1,000 years.

After the disappearance of the Ice Age mammoth, the people who had preyed on them turned to bison (buffalo) hunting, and for over 10,000 years the successors of Clovis pursued bison on the Plains. By 10,500 years ago, bison were the most dominant species found at all archaeological sites in the region. Bison survived because they adapted to feed on grassland in post-glacial times.

Mass bison drives took place: in Colorado the Olsen-Chubbock site held 152 carcasses in a canyon into which bison had been stampeded 8,500 years ago. Such bison hunts were communal affairs that may have been conducted once annually. When the bow and arrow reached the plains in AD 500, communal bison hunting reached its greatest prehistoric intensity.

11

In 1547 horses were introduced by the Spanish, and their use brought about dramatic change: bison herds were further reduced, the nomadic population grew and placed greater demands on the farm produce of sedentary populations. Tensions surfaced, different cultural values took hold and raids were prevalent. During the nineteenth century, Europeans with their muskets joined the bison hunt and herds were decimated. In the twentieth century great efforts have been made to save the bison, which were largely successful, and there are now herds on the Plains again, although not in the large numbers there used to be.

In the far north, the environment could only support a small population, so people moved regularly depending on the season. Na-Dene speakers came first. They were forest hunter-gatherers and spread south and west and into the interior, where they became known as Athapaskan. Later some split off, moved south and became the modern Navajo and Apache. The Eskimo-Aleut came after the Paleo-Indians, before the land bridge was severed (though some say that they arrived by boat). They are the most Asian of North Americans, and their language has Siberian roots.

The Eskimo spread over thousands of miles of mainland and probably split away from the Aleut about 4,000 years ago. Ties weakened as each group adapted to different environmental conditions. The Eskimo hunted using skin kayaks, traveled by dog sled and occupied land from the Bering Strait to Greenland between the tenth and eleventh centuries AD. Their predecessors hunted caribou and musk oxen on land, walrus and whale in the sea. They dug their houses into the ground to protect them against the arctic winter, with trapdoors to shield them against the cold. The Aleut were maritime hunters and fishermen, excellent boatmen, hunting seal, sea lion and otter on the open seas.

The first wave of settlement to the newly exposed northwest coastal regions were forest hunter-gatherers from Alaska, distinct from the Eskimo-Aleut. The climate and sea levels stabilized 5,000 years ago: there was a predictable supply of maritime food and more elaborate hunting and foraging societies developed in which wealth and social status assumed a vital importance. Powerful individuals came to the fore, and it was they who regulated ceremonial life and controlled commodities.

People lived in villages all year round in substantial log houses, and used canoes to move between settlements such as early sites on the Queen Charlotte Islands. Another coastal site was excavated at Ozette in Washington state where a mud slide buried a whaling village 500 years ago, and all household artifacts were preserved in mud. Baskets, nets, fish hooks and looms were found in cedar longhouses which had been divided into small rooms using low walls and hanging mats.

The Native American Indians occupied the entire American continent whether rain forest, desert, plains or arctic by the time Europeans arrived on the scene. In the desert and woodland areas, the first inhabitants had been dispersed bands living in seasonal camps, though more intensive foraging developed from 9,000 to 4,500 years ago, with people returning to the same location year after year. Maize cultivation developed 1,500 years ago: the cycle of planting and harvesting reduced people's mobility and greater storage was needed. Trade networks also developed.

The Eskimo-Aleut had settled on the islands and coasts of the central Canadian Arctic by the twelfth and thirteenth centuries, and the climate had warmed. Norsemen traded in the area in AD 1000 and remained until a new wave of Westerners penetrated the land in the sixteenth century.

In the eastern woodlands, the farmers of 4,000 years ago developed a preoccupation with burial: Adena people built earthworks and ceremonial compounds. The Hopewell burial mounds were even more elaborate than those of the Adena, and a flowering of artistic tradition came about. The Mississippian Culture emerged around AD 700, with both farmers and hunter-gatherers. The population grew to around 10,000 peoples and powerful chieftains ruled the valleys. This was contemporary with Mexican civilization when heavily fortified communities with temple mounds and plazas were built. These were seen by the Spanish in the mid-sixteenth century.

In the Pacific coastal regions most societies lived by hunting and foraging up until European contact. In seventeenth-century Mississippi the Cherokee were living in the north, with 100 settlements of around 60,000 people. In California people lived off the land and sea, and with rich resources large, permanent villages grew up ruled by local chiefs, and the population grew.

In Arizona in the Southwest around 2,000 years ago the Hohokam people began planting their crops to coincide with the rainfall patterns: they dug terraces, canals and dams to control water flow. By AD 900 the Anasazi (ancestors of the Hopi, Zuni and other Pueblo Indians) were farmers living in multi-room structures in New Mexico.

Today ethnologists generally divide North America into nine culture groups, mostly based on geographical location, for the early peoples adapted their skills to suit environmental conditions. This book offers the following breakdown: Southeast; Southwest; Plains; Plateau and Basin; California; Northwest Coast; Subarctic; Arctic; and Northeast.

The arrival of the Europeans changed the face of the entire continent and the lives of its indigenous peoples irredeemably. Vikings, English, French and Spanish explored the coasts of America and then settled there permanently. Colonists, missionaries, and explorers arrived, spreading disease, destruction and disruption which affected the traditional Indian way of life. Within a few mere centuries the old Indian way of life had been swept away forever.

Change came slowly. After World War II, increased awareness of the multi-cultural nature of society came about. Popular interest in the country's various ethnic groups surged, and the market for Indian arts and crafts soared, a market partly kept buoyant by the poor economic situation in the reservations and the Indians' ability to adapt their work to the preferences of their customers. Today Native American Indian artifacts and the people who produce them receive world-wide acclaim. Such artifacts and the importance of their original function within Indian society are now more widely appreciated than ever.

THE SOUTHEAST

The Indian cultures of the Southeast in the nineteenth century and the first half of the twentieth century were the products of a long period of change, disruption, and destruction – almost genocide, although the destruction was not the direct result of conscious state policies. Thousands of years of cultural development in this region were rudely diverted and truncated by the arrival of Europeans in the early sixteenth century. Little can now be known about what the lives of the southern Indian people were like when the invaders arrived, for the first literate observers left few records, and none for most of the region, and the archaeological evidence cannot answer many important questions. Native traditions cannot help, for the details of an old way of life cannot be preserved by word of mouth alone over 400 years in a society undergoing very rapid social and cultural change. However, the scale of the cultural and biological disaster that was visited on the Southeastern Indians has recently become clearer from advances in archaeological interpretations, filled out by scraps of information from the thin documentary record left by the first Europeans.

Certainly this was a naturally favored region. It is in the warmest part of the northern temperate zone, and south Florida is actually subtropical in climate. Most of the Southeast falls within the broad coastal plain bordering the Atlantic and the Gulf of Mexico. In this low-lying area the rivers meander and deposit fertile alluvial soils. In the broad valleys were many oxbow lakes and vast swamps of cypress and cane. Fields were easily cleared in the bottom lands along the rivers, and their productivity was rapidly renewed by the silt from seasonal floods. Fish were plentiful especially in the river backwaters, and migratory water fowl were easily taken. In some areas such as along the lower Mississippi River fish and water fowl provided

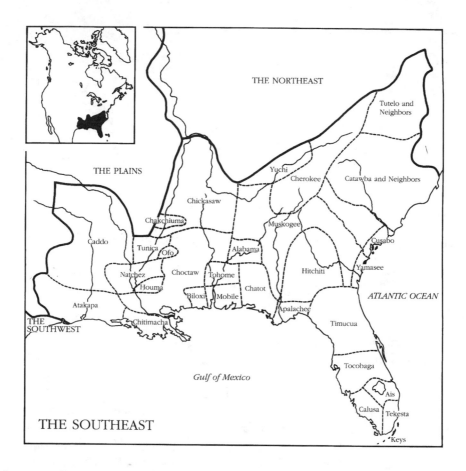

This map shows approximate territories of tribes and tribal groupings at about 1600 in Florida and along the Atlantic coast, and about 1700 in the rest of the region. After that, all tribes lost territory, many disappeared, many moved west, some new tribes arose.

at least half the protein in the Indian diet. Other animal food came from white-tailed deer, raccoons, and other mammals. Wild plant foods – nuts, fruits, berries – were a very important resource. Cultivated corn, beans, squash, sunflowers, and gourds were a major source of food everywhere except in south Florida, where, at least on the southwest coast, fish and shellfish were so plentiful that they allowed the Calusa to develop a complex sedentary society of a sort that normally depends on agriculture. The northeastern part of the area includes the Piedmont above the fall-line, and the low mountains of the Appalachian highlands. The environment here was different but also favorable. The valleys are narrower, but still fertile, and fish abounded in the river shoals. The economic cycle in general depended on growing crops and fishing during the warm season, then hunting deer during the cooler season.

What one sees now in the region is far different from the aboriginal situation. The forests and canebrakes are gone, many rivers are dammed and swamps drained, and the soil is much degraded and eroded from exploitative commercial farming of first indigo, then tobacco, cotton and corn. The passenger pigeons are extinct, and other birds, fish, and most wild animals are far less plentiful than they were even at the beginning of the nineteenth century.

The radical, disastrous changes in Indian life occurred before most of the environmental degradation. In the early period precipitous depopulation was the result of the introduction of European diseases, such as smallpox, to which the Indians at first lacked immunity. In many communities half or more of the inhabitants died within a period of weeks. The social and psychological effects of this disaster can scarcely be imagined, in general and in the loss of the bearers of knowledge and tradition. Later, after immunities to the new diseases had been established, the Indian societies were further disrupted by the complex effects of European and Euro-American intrusion: trade, new kinds of warfare, enslavement, the usurpation of food supplies, of goods, and then of land, epidemics of new diseases, and finally actual replacement of the Indian populations by people of European and African origins.

A good deal is known about Southern Indian cultures over the last 100 to 150 years, but probably less than in any other region of the continent can this knowledge be taken as indicative of the ways of life before European influence was felt. The first shocks came in the middle of the sixteenth century. The first good written descriptions of Southeastern Indians

ABOVE: *Cow Creek Seminole women, c.1917. Their skirts were strips of cotton cloth in contrasting colors. Patchwork was just beginning at this time. The central figure has coin silver brooches.*

date from more than 200 years later at the end of the eighteenth and the beginning of the nineteenth century, after massive realigning and restructuring of the societies had taken place. Really thorough records (and representative museum collections, and extensive series of photographs) begin still another century later, at the end of the nineteenth century and the beginning of the twentieth after most of the surviving Indians in the Southeast had been deported to quite different cultural and natural surroundings in Indian Territory west of the Mississippi (present Oklahoma).

The list on pages 19 and 20 includes all the tribes mentioned in the text.

The first contacts of Europeans with Southeastern Indians are unknown. The first recorded visit was by Juan Ponce de Leon, who landed in Florida, probably in the Calusa area, in 1513. But the hostile reception the Indians gave him strongly suggests that they had previous experience with some Europeans who left no other record. Other brief contacts followed, in Florida and along the Atlantic coast, which left very scanty records although they probably had serious effects on the Indians: European diseases were probably introduced, and more Indians learned how dangerous the strangers could be. Finally, in 1539-43 came Hernando De Soto's long incursion far into the Southeast. He arrived at Tampa Bay with some 700 men, 200 horses, a herd of hogs and a huge quantity of weapons and supplies, and proceeded inland north across what is now Georgia and South Carolina, into Tennessee, then down through Alabama, back north again and across northern Mississippi, across Arkansas, then south again to the lower Mississippi River in Louisiana. This expedition was a disaster for De Soto and his men, and even more a disaster for the Indians he met, hundreds of whom he and his men killed and kidnapped, and for many others, surely many thousands, who died from the diseases introduced.

The several contemporary written descriptions of the De Soto expedition are sufficient to give us a narrow window on the aboriginal societies of the Southeast, but these records are frustratingly brief and imprecise. Archaeological research provides more information, but of rather different sorts, and there are many problems in identifying specific archaeological remains with the poorly localized descriptions in the De Soto accounts. In recent years archaeological theory has suggested reasonable integrations of these two kinds of data, in part by looking at much later societies in the Southeast and by considering comparable societies in other parts of the world.

ABOVE: *A cabin home on the Cherokee Qualla Reservation, North Carolina, 1888. The cabin belonged to Ayunini, who stands at the right. He was a key informant to the anthropologost James Mooney.*

ABOVE: *A group of Mikasuki Seminole poling canoes. Flat-bottomed dug-out canoes were commonly used by most Southeast tribes.*

SOUTHEASTERN TRIBES

Ais. A small tribe on the east coast of south Florida, numbering perhaps 1,000 in 1650 and extinct by the 1720s. They grew no crops, being mainly dependent on fish. There is no evidence whatsoever on the Ais language.

Alabama. Their language, belonging to the Muskogean family, is very close to Koasati, the two being perhaps dialects of a single language. The Alabama population was less than 1,000 in 1704; after 1763 they were dispersed, some joining the Seminoles and Creeks and most going to Texas with the Koasatis. By 1910, there were only about 300 Alabamas in addition to those among the Creeks.

Apalachee. Speakers of a Muskogean language, missionized by the Spanish, their population was perhaps 5,000 in 1676. They were destroyed in the eighteenth century by English and Creek raids, a few survivors joining the Creeks.

Atakapa. The population was about 1,000 in the early eighteenth century, and the group was extinct by 1900. The Atakapa language was an isolate, that is, without demonstrable relationship to any other language.

Biloxi. Amounting to perhaps 1,000 people in 1650, the Biloxi spoke a language belonging to the Siouan family. By the end of the nineteenth century there were very few identifiable survivors, in Louisiana, Oklahoma and eastern Texas.

Caddo. This term includes several tribes, mostly in three confederacies, all speaking the Caddo language which is the southern branch of the Caddoan language family of which the other languages were spoken on the Plains. The Caddo population may have been 8,000 in 1700; by 1910 there were only about 550 Caddos, in Oklahoma.

Calusa. This was a non-agricultural chiefdom in south Florida, which may have included as many as 10,000 people in the 1560s. By 1750 there were none left. So little of the Calusa language was recorded that its affiliations are unknown.

Catawba. This tribe of the South Carolina piedmont is the descendant of several small tribes that joined together in the seventeenth and eighteenth centuries. Speakers of several different languages were probably involved, but only Catawba, a language of the Siouan family, survived into the twentieth century.

Chakchiuma. A small tribe, now extinct, probably speakers of a Muskogean language (perhaps actually Choctaw).

Chatot. Another small tribe, also probably speakers of a Muskogean language, driven by the Creeks to Mobile and then Louisiana. They probably merged with the Choctaws in Indian Territory (Oklahoma).

Cherokee. The largest Southeastern tribe from the eighteenth century until the present, speakers of an Iroquoian language. Some survive in their Appalachian homeland in western North Carolina, while most today live in Oklahoma.

Chickasaw. Numbering about 8,000 in 1650, they were removed to Oklahoma where they live today. The language is a variety of Choctaw, although the two groups have always been politically different.

Chitimacha. The population may have been 4,000 in 1700, while less than 100 survived in 1930. The language is an isolate, not known to be related to any other.

Choctaw. Speakers of a Muskogean language, they numbered about 15,000 in 1650. In 1930 there were about 18,000, mostly in Oklahoma but some in Mississippi and Louisiana, their original homeland.

Creek. English name for the political Confederacy centered on the Muskogee and including the Hitchiti and others.

Cusabo. A small tribe, totaling 535 in a 1715 census and now extinct, whose language is entirely unknown.

Hitchiti. A Muskogean language, spoken by seven or so large towns incorporated into the Creek Confederacy.

Houma. A small tribe in Louisiana, numbering 600-700 in 1700 and about the same in 1930. The language, now extinct, perhaps belonged to the Muskogean family.

Keys. The inhabitants of the Florida Keys seem to have been politically independent of their larger neighbors. Nothing of the language they spoke was ever recorded. They were extinct by the end of Spanish Florida in 1763.

Koasati. A Muskogean tribe numbering perhaps 250 in 1750, of whom in 1910 there were about 100 in Texas and one town among the Creeks in Oklahoma. The language is very close to that of the Alabamas, perhaps even the same.

Lumbee. Now one of the largest Southeastern tribes, numbering about 30,000 in 1970, the Lumbee are descended from the Cheraw and other Indian neighbors of the Catawba, as well as from Black and White refugees from the European frontiers. By the eighteenth century no Indian language survived among them. In most respects they are culturally the same as their White and Black neighbors, although socially and politically they are definitely Indian.

Mikasuki. About two-thirds of the Florida Seminoles speak Mikasuki, which is the same language as Hitchiti, as did many Seminoles in Oklahoma formerly.

Muskogee. This is the dominant element in the Creek Confederacy. The language, in the Muskogean family, is also spoken by about one-third of the Seminoles in Florida, and by most of the Oklahoma Seminoles.

Natchez. Numbering about 4,500 in 1650, the survivors were eventually amalgamated with the Creeks and Cherokees. The language is an isolate, not known to be related to any other.

Ofo. Speakers of a Siouan language, they were driven south from the Ohio River region by the expanding Iroquois.

Seminole. This tribe originated in the eighteenth century, when settlers from the Creek Confederacy moved into Florida. The Seminole Wars of the 1830s and 1850s resulted in most being deported to Oklahoma, while a minority survived in southern Florida.

Tekesta. A small, non-agricultural tribe inhabiting the Miami region, they became extinct in the eighteenth century. Their language is entirely unknown.

Timucua. A large group of northern Florida tribes, they numbered some 13,000 in 1650 (and many more a century earlier). The language, well recorded by Spanish missionaries, is not known to be related to any other. The last few Timucuas left Florida when the Spanish withdrew in 1763.

Tocobaga. A small tribe, nearly totally unknown, of the Tampa Bay region in Florida.

Tohome and Mobile. Two groups that evidently spoke a variety of Choctaw.

Tunica. Numbering perhaps 2,500 in 1650, less than 50 survived in 1910. Their language, although well recorded, is not related to any other.

Tutelo. Speaking a Siouan language, they numbered some 2,700 in 1600, but by 1800 the descendants had joined the Iroquois in Canada.

Yamasee. Perhaps speakers of a Muskogean language, they numbered about 1,200 in 1715, but soon fled to Spanish Florida where they had disappeared by 1763.

Yuchi. A tribe originally in the Appalachian highlands, they numbered about 1,500 in 1650, and by 1930 only about 200 among the Creeks in Oklahoma. The Yuchi language is an isolate, unrelated to any other.

A reasonable reconstruction of the aboriginal Southeast when Europeans first arrived shows many chiefdoms spread all across the interior and reaching the coast in several places. These were complex societies, each with a capital town containing massive earthworks in the form of mounds supporting temples and council houses, often surrounded by large canals and usually stockaded. Each chiefdom normally included several smaller towns with only one or two mounds, subordinate to the principal town. The largest of these chiefdom capitals was at Cahokia, in present Illinois across the Mississippi River from St Louis. This is well outside the historic Southeast, for one of the consequences of early contacts with Europeans was a retraction of the area covered by chiefdoms. Cahokia seems to have reached its height by about 1250, after which its population declined. At its maximum Cahokia covered more than five square miles and may have had a population of some 10,000. This was surely the largest town north of central Mexico, and in it was the largest artificial structure in North America. The central earth mound here rose in four terraces to a height of 100ft (30m), where a large building was built on the flat top, while the base of the mound measured about 700 to 1,000ft (215 to 305m) and covered sixteen acres. More than a hundred other mounds were grouped around plazas. Most were platform mounds supporting public buildings and per-haps the houses of leading people. There were also conical burial mounds. The central 200 acres of the town were surrounded by a large wall of upright logs set in a deep trench, with watchtowers and gates spaced along it.

Another chiefdom had its capital at Moundville, about sixty miles southwest of present Birmingham, Alabama, on the northeastern edge of the territory of the Muskogees in later times (whose ancestral capital it may have been). Moundville covers 300 acres on a bluff on the Black Warrior River. Here are twenty major mounds on two sides of a rectangular plaza covering some eighty acres. These mounds are more or less pyramidal, although with flat tops, and the largest rises almost 60ft (18m) above the level of the plaza. On the tops of these mounds were buildings, probably both temples or ceremonial structures, and houses for the rulers. A wall divided the plaza from a nearby settlement area, and the whole was sur-rounded by a palisade. High-ranking individuals, probably especially the holders of ritual offices, were buried in about half the mounds along the edges of the plaza. These burials were often accompanied by those of infants and of skulls or heads without bodies. Houses were built outside the plaza but within the surrounding palisade. Controlled from Moundville were about twenty smaller settlements, most of them with one small mound apiece, which were located within the valley for a few miles north and south of Moundville. In addition, the Moundville center dominated hundreds of small residential hamlets. It has been estimated that Moundville drew labor from as far as forty-five miles away, and much tribute especially from the secondary centers within ten miles or so.

Another, smaller archaeological site represents a chiefdom in what was later Cherokee country; it may itself have been subordinate to a larger site well to the south. Toqua, on the Little Tennessee River about thirty miles southwest of Knoxville, contains two flat-topped mounds, one 24ft (7m) high resulting from eight enlargements after it was first raised, and the other, about 300ft (90m) distant, only 6ft (1.8m) high and built in two construction stages. Both served as burial mounds as well as supporting structures. The village, consisting of some forty households, covered about fifty acres.

Construction of such large sites must have required well-organized labor. There is other evidence that these were hierarchical societies, each under a high chief ruling in a large town, which was surrounded by smaller towns and villages headed by subordinate chiefs. The chief and his relatives were considered to be descendants of the sun. The chiefs had great power and prestige, with many perquisites in the form of special insignia and possessions. They were surrounded by retainers, offered tribute and deferred to by their subordinates. Each chiefdom was expansionist, fighting with its neighbors. There were graded ranks within the nobility, while most of the populace were commoners. Everyone belonged to one of a set of clans, each of which included both nobles and commoners. These were totemic in that each was associated with a tutelary spirit, usually an animal, and members were considered to share character and behavior with this totem. The clans were matrilineal – each person's membership in the mother's clan was acquired at birth. The clans were exogamous, that is, marriage within the clan was prohibited. But the clans were not organized groups, and every clan was spread through many villages, with each village inhabited by members of several clans.

Although each clan was quite egalitarian – most members were equals – the clan as a whole was ranked. There were two sets or sides or moieties, the clans in each in a ranked series. Furthermore, one side seems to have been considered superior to the other. The chiefly offices were hereditary, certainly matrilineally, and offices of lesser rank were also hereditary, probably most of them matrilineally but perhaps another set inherited patrilineally, from father to son. However, nobles seemingly could only marry commoners, and the children in each generation were of lesser rank than the noble parent, becoming commoners after four or five generations.

The political and social systems surely varied from chiefdom to chiefdom, they were quite complex and the few literate Europeans who were in a position to observe them in action certainly did not understand them very well. One striking example that was quite thoroughly investigated by a Jesuit missionary in the 1560s was that of the Calusa in southwest Florida. Here the high-chief was differentiated from the rest of the society by an exception to the incest rules: he was required to marry his full sister (to the distress of the missionary). This custom is known from only a few other societies anywhere in the world, all of them with high social and political stratification and all very concerned with inherited rank. Royal full-sibling marriage is especially appropriate where the nobility is exogamous and no child can inherit the full rank of the noble parent.

For a late expression of the social stratification once typical of much of the Southeast, we may summarize French reports of the death and funeral of a high ranking Natchez chief.[1] The Natchez had two social classes, nobility and commoners. Within the nobility there were three ranks, Suns, Nobles and Honored People. These were exogamous: all could only marry commoners. Class membership and noble rank were acquired from the mother at birth, except that the children of fathers of Sun and Noble rank belonged to the next lower rank rather than inheriting their mothers' commoner rank. While rank in general was hereditary, some commoner men and their wives could achieve Honored rank through special merit. The king or highest ranking chief was known as the Great Sun, and he was succeeded in office by the son of his sister. There is much evidence for the deference and special privileges afforded to this man. The other high civil, military and probably religious offices were also filled by Suns. When any Sun died, his or her spouse was willingly sacrificed – one could say committed suicide – to accompany the spirit of the dead to the afterworld.

In 1725 a man named Tattooed Serpent died. He was the Great War Chief and a much-beloved brother of the Great Sun. As soon as he died, the news was relayed by death cries from village to village. His body was laid out on a cane bed in his house, probably on a small mound near the town plaza, dressed in his finest and with his face painted vermilion. His weapons were tied to his bed and around it were arrayed all the calumets (peace pipes) he had received during his career. All his other belongings were taken out of the house and packed to be buried with him. A special red-painted pole was hung with forty-six cane rings representing the number of enemies he had killed.

The first day the mourners fasted (this was a means for gaining spiritual strength among most Southeastern Indians). Those who were to accompany him into the afterworld were prepared. There were eight of them; the Great Sun himself would have joined them but was dissuaded, with difficulty, by the French. These eight people were the Tattooed Serpent's principal wife and his second wife, five officials or servants (one called by the French the First Warrior or Chancellor; a Noble woman who was a doctor and a special friend; the deceased's Head Servant, perhaps the same as his Pipe Bearer, and his wife; and the warclub maker); and a woman who would have been sacrificed at the death of an earlier Sun had she not then been a hostage of the French. Another man who had escaped a previous sacrifice but whose French protector had left was brought forth by thirty warriors, but since he was still reluctant to die he was dismissed by the Tattooed Serpent's principal wife as unworthy to accompany her and the rest to the other world. This was described to the French as a place without hunger, death or war, where the weather was always fine. For two or three days there were dances rehearsing the sacrifices to come on the fourth day after the death. Those who were to die were finely dressed, their hair daubed red and each carried a large conch shell. Each was escorted by eight male relatives wearing red head feathers: one carried a warclub, one the victim's sitting mat, one the cord to be used for strangling, one the skin for blindfolding, one a clay dish holding six pellets of tobacco (or perhaps it was a stronger narcotic), one a small drinking vessel of water and finally two men who were to draw the strangling cord tight.

Those who were to die and their attendants paraded from the Tattooed Serpent's house to the front of the temple on a mound at the plaza, issuing death cries. The Chief Priest came out of the temple with a message from the Creator. The celebrants then separated into two bands led by the two wives, and the principals each sat on their mats, giving the death cry in unison, and then danced in place while their attending relatives danced behind them. This dance was repeated in front of the Tattooed Serpent's house, and the War Dance and other dances were also performed.

On the second day the dances were repeated. This time those who were to die each carried a red warclub and a bundle of red cords. Two women relatives of the man who had been dismissed by the principal wife volunteered to die in his place and were accordingly strangled, not only freeing him from the obligation but promoting him to Noble status.

The final day was marked by fasting and smoking tobacco (both to gain strength). The end began when the Master of Ceremonies, his torso painted red and wearing a red feather head ornament and a belt or skirt of red and black feathers, carrying a red baton with black feathers, entered the Tattooed Serpent's house and raised the death cry, which was repeated by the crowd gathered in the plaza. The body emerged on a litter carried by six men, preceded by the Master of Ceremonies and the oldest War Chief who carried a calumet and the pole with forty-six hoops. The litter was followed by those who were to die, and their attendants. These attendants by this service were raised from commoners to rank as Honored People and were relieved of the obligation to die when another Sun died. After circling the house, the procession slowly looped across the plaza. At each loop, they walked over the body of an infant sacrificed by his parents (by this both releasing them from the duty to be sacrificed at a future Sun's death, and raising them from commoners to status among the nobility).

When the procession reached the temple, the chests containing the possession of the Tattooed Serpent were taken inside, for burial with him. Those to be sacrificed seated themselves on their mats in a semicircle facing the temple. All gave the death cry. They swallowed the tobacco pellets with water, numbing their faculties. The leather blindfolds were placed over their heads, then the cords were looped around their necks. The ends of these were strongly pulled by the relatives assigned this task, quickly strangling them.

One account says that five more were then strangled in the plaza: the 'nurse' of the Tattooed Serpent, a doctor from a nearby town and three old women.

The Tattooed Serpent and his two wives were buried in a trench inside the temple. The Noble woman doctor and the 'Chancellor' were buried on the mound but outside the temple. The others were carried on litters back to their home villages for burial in the temples there. Finally, the Tattooed Serpent's house was burned.

It is hardly surprising that several eighteenth-century French observers recorded these obsequies in great detail. While they said little about the Natchez beliefs that justified and maintained them, one can hardly doubt

27

that the ideology strongly supported a hierarchical social system. A few years later the Natchez attacked the French, who retaliated and nearly destroyed them. The survivors eventually joined the Creek and Cherokee Indians, and little is heard about them until the end of the nineteenth century and the beginning of the twentieth. The elaborate social system had by then been totally replaced by one much like that of the Creeks.

The economic base which supported the dense populations and their elaborate social and political systems can be envisioned by considering the economic activities of the Choctaws at a later period. An excellent idea of Choctaw subsistence in the late eighteenth century is given by the materials collected in Mississippi in 1823–5 by Gideon Lincecum, a frontier physician who apprenticed himself to a Choctaw medical practitioner and also wrote down and translated long historical traditions told by an aged Choctaw man named Chahta Imataha.[2]

In the eighteenth century the Choctaws had less territory than their neighbors, and were probably more dependent on agriculture. This was so productive that they were able to export corn. As in all the aboriginal Southeast there were important seasonal differences in Choctaw subsistence. In midwinter the fields were prepared for planting. On new plots, after a ceremony with dances, the underbrush and smaller growth was cut and larger trees were girdled. The dried brush was then no doubt burned, the ashes spread on the field providing the only fertilizer used. Planting was done in the spring, when the soil was turned and holes for planting the seeds were made with a digging stick, which was a short hardwood pole with a point that had been sharpened and hardened by charring in a fire. While the heaviest labor of clearing was done by men, the rest of the work was shared by men, women and children. In much of the rest of the Southeast, however, agricultural labor after clearing was almost entirely women's work. The most important crop was corn. Also planted in the same plots were beans and squash. Crops of lesser importance elsewhere in the Southeast, and probably for the Choctaw too, were sunflowers, marsh elder and gourds. By the late eighteenth century the Choctaws had added peas, watermelons, sweet potatoes and fruit trees.

After the crops were well established, it was still necessary to protect them from squirrels and crows, but most people could scatter to streams and lakes for fishing and turtling and collecting wild fruits, nuts and berries. These included persimmons, plums, hickory nuts, chestnuts, walnuts, pecans, acorns (probably leached after grinding), cherries, grapes and mulberries. Fishing methods included a kind of communal fish drive in shallow water, the use of a trap made by sewing a hide cover with a draw-string over a long tube of hoops, muddying the water in a pool of a river (perhaps, although Lincecum does not say so, including the use of buckeye or devil's shoestring as a plant poison to stun the fish), shooting fish with bows and arrows, and finally catching them with metal hooks gotten from the French.

When the corn first ripened in early summer, all gathered for the Green Corn Festival. Fishing, hunting waterfowl and gathering were then resumed until it was time to return in the fall for harvesting and storing the ripe corn. The men then left for a period of hunting in the fall and early winter, while the women, children and old people collected nuts and fruits in the woods. In the middle of the winter the hunters returned and the cycle began again with clearing the fields.

For hunting, men used bows and arrows before they acquired guns from Europeans. The most valued game was deer, which were killed in quanti-ties. Decoys made from the skin and antlers of a buck's head were used along with special deer calls. Bears were killed in cane brakes, especially for their fat. Boys as well as men hunted smaller game too, including turtles, alligators, rabbits, raccoons, turkeys, quail and prairie chickens. A favorite boy's weapon was a cane blowgun, some 7ft (2m) long, with darts having thistle down at the butt ends. Meat was sun-dried and also smoked and dried on racks over fires.

There were many different corn recipes. Green corn was roasted on the cob, and green corn kernels were slowly boiled with meat, with some lye added, to make a popular dish. Ripe corn kernels were pounded into flour in a wooden mortar and pestle. The Choctaw mortar was made of an upright hickory log about 2ft (60cm) high and 1 to 1½ft (30-45cm) in diameter, with a hollow up to 1½ft (30–45cm)deep charred out of the upper end. The pestle was a hickory pole about 5ft (1.5m) long with a weight about 1ft long and 6in (15cm) in diameter left on the upper end, and a round shaft about 2in (5cm) in diameter narrowing to a point at the bottom. Corn kernels could be ground after parching, or else they were boiled, dried and parched before grinding. For sifting and cleaning the ground corn, there was a set of three baskets made of plaited cane: a shovel-shaped fanner, a shallow squarish sieve, and a large flat container. Hominy was made by pounding dried kernels to remove the husks, then boiling the cracked pieces (the grits) for twelve to eighteen hours in lye water. This was a favorite food called *tanfula* in Choctaw, that was customarily kept in each house ready to serve to all visitors. It was adopted by non-Indians under the name Tom Fuller. There were many kinds of bread made from corn meal, simply baking it, or letting it ferment slightly to make a sour bread, or mixing corn meal with ground sunflower seeds for the dough, or stuffing corn dough in cornhusks and baking them in hot ashes, or wrapping corn dough mixed with beans or hickory nuts in cornhusks and boiling these, or grating green corn and mixing the meal with hot water. A special dish served by the bride's parents at a wedding was made from juice from strained, cooked grapes, in which small bits of corn dough were boiled. A lightweight, nourishing travel food for hunters and warriors (used all over eastern North America) was made from parched kernels ground in the mortar and carefully sifted. This could be eaten as a cold cereal by simply adding water to dampen a handful of the flour. The importance of cornbread in the traditional non-Indian cuisines of the American South is a legacy of the Indians.

Over most of the South documentary records are silent for about 100 years following the mid-sixteenth century, and for much of the area detailed records only begin some hundred years later than that. This was a crucial period of change, when the aboriginal chiefdoms broke up and were replaced by the towns, tribes and confederacies that can then be followed into modern times. Archaeological evidence tends to confirm that this period witnessed massive depopulation, due mainly to the spread of European diseases, with accompanying social and political reorganization, major movements and displacements of populations and the loss of many elements of culture. The number of populated sites decreased drastically. There were shifts in the tribal balance of power, accompanying demographic changes that proceeded at different rates and to different degrees in various regions. Many sites that had been occupied for centuries were abandoned. The construction of mounds and other major earthworks ceased. The marked differences between settlements in size and, presumably, power and authority, disappeared. In the late seventeenth century the Iroquois wars associated with the fur trade in the North had a domino effect to the South. The introduction of large numbers of firearms by the French, Dutch and English engaged in the fur trade resulted in Iroquois expansion and the flight of many of their enemies to the South. With the founding of Charleston in 1670 new disruptions entered the area from the east, with English capture and purchase of Indians for the slave trade in the

West Indies, and the development of a massive commerce in deerskins for export to Europe. It was during this period that the Creek Confederacy arose from the broken chiefdoms, in response to these outside pressures. Another result was the total destruction of the aborigines of Spanish Florida, who lacked guns to defend themselves against the Creek and English invaders. During the eighteenth century Florida was resettled by Creek colonists, whose descendants became the Seminoles when their connections to the Confederacy ceased.

After a century or so, the Southern Indian situation again changed radically. As non-Indian settlement expanded, especially in Georgia and Alabama, the Indians were pushed aside and their lands and fields usurped. Finally in the 1820s and 1830s nearly all were deported to Indian Territory – present-day Oklahoma. Many died during this so-called 'Removal'. A few managed to avoid the deportation: some Seminoles survived in south Florida, some Cherokees in western North Carolina, a few Creeks in far southern Alabama and many Choctaws in Mississippi. Some tribes entirely escaped Removal: the Catawba in South Carolina, the Tunica and Chitimacha in Louisiana, and the Lumbee and other mestizo populations in the Carolinas.

In Oklahoma the deportees reorganized and established new tribal governments, especially those that became known as the Five Civilized Tribes – Cherokees, Choctaws, Chickasaws, Creeks and Seminoles. During the Civil War many of these were divided and suffered heavily. Their governments reconstituted afterwards, and then the Five Civilized Tribes lost much land to non-Indians in the 1880s and 1890s. The tribal governments lost most of their remaining sovereignty with the arrival of statehood for Oklahoma in 1907.

The Creek Confederacy was (and still is) based on so-called towns. These are social and political units more than residential ones, quite equivalent to what are called tribes elsewhere. Each town was made up of the people affiliated with a ceremonial center, a square grounds (in modern Oklahoma parlance, a stomp grounds). They often lived quite far from the center, in scattered hamlets and homesteads. The number of towns varied over time, as towns could both split, when one faction established a new, separate square grounds, and merge, by two towns agreeing to share a single square grounds. From the middle of the nineteenth century until the 1930s, there were between twenty-five and thirty Creek towns, the total depending partly on how one counted closely associated towns. Most of these were Muskogee-speaking, but some five or ten were Hitchiti-speaking (or had been until recently when they adopted Muskogee for internal as well as external use). There was also at least one town each of other languages: Alabama, Koasati, Natchez and Yuchi. However, Muskogee was the general language of the Confederacy, through which speakers of other languages communicated with other Creeks and with outsiders.

The towns were divided into two groups, sometimes called 'sides', usually characterized as White and Red. The White or 'peace' towns were preeminent in civil affairs, while the Red or 'war' towns were conceived of as dominant in military matters. The White towns were said to control executive affairs of the Confederacy, the Red towns legislative and judicial ones. According to Creek traditions, the White towns controlled the Confederacy until the time of the American Revolution. From then through the Civil War period the Creeks were frequently drawn into war so the Red towns ran the Confederacy. After 1865 the White towns again were dominant.

The most important Creek towns around 1900 were the following:

White	*Red*
Kasihta	Coweta
Hitchiti	Tukabahchee
Abihka	Laplako
Okfuskee	Atasi
Okchai	Kealeychi
Ochiapofa	Chiaha
Tulsa	Osochi
Lochapoka	Alabama
Tuskegee	Eufaula
Koasati	Hilabi
Wiwohka	Hothliwahali
Wiogufki	Talmuchasi
Tokpafka	
Nuyaka	
Okmulgee	
Asilanapi	
Yuchi	
Pakana	

The affiliation of a town as either White or Red was not permanent, however. A town changed sides if it was defeated for four successive times by a town on the other side in the important match ballgames. These were the southern Indian form of the team game played between goals that is known as lacrosse in the North. In the southern form, often called 'stick ball' in English, each player used a pair of rackets rather than the single racket used in lacrosse. Like lacrosse, it was a very rough sport. The Creeks conceived it as a substitute for war, sometimes calling it 'the younger brother of war', and explaining that it kept the peace within the Confederacy.

The Creek Confederacy was modeled on the town organization, for the members of each town were also organized into two 'sides'. Here the social units of the dual organization were the clans. Every individual was born into the clan of his or her mother. There were fifty Muskogee clans, of which twenty-three were also Hitchiti clans. Most had animal or bird names, while a few were named for plants, and there were also Wind, Medicine, Salt and Arrow clans. They were totemic in the sense that the members had a special relationship to the clan species or phenomenon, but they did not trace descent from these totems. The clans had members in various towns, which offered hospitality to visiting clan members. Among the most important functions of clans was punishment for murder, for the victim's clan members took vengeance on the murderer or another member of the murderer's clan. There was no overall clan organization. Rather, within each town the clans filled special functions and provided the incumbents for town offices (not always the same ones in different towns). Each town was an independent, self-governing body headed by its micco or chief, chosen from a specific clan, usually a White clan since his duties were peaceful. Usually there was also a vice-chief or 'twin chief', and a set of assistant chiefs (sometimes from several different clans). There was also a body of sub-chiefs, usually from the micco's clan. Another set of officers directed work in the fields and on public buildings, and ran the Black Drink ceremony. These, the assistant chiefs and a set of respected elders known as 'beloved men' formed the town council. All of these were, in most towns, from White clans. Each town also had officials from the Red clans – three grades of war officials, who gained their positions from warlike deeds, rather than inheriting them. They dealt with war and the inter-town ball games. The highest grade of warriors also served as town police.

The Creek Confederacy as a whole was governed by a council made up of town chiefs, who met at irregular intervals and not necessarily as a body. It was a loose confederation rather than a state-like organization, at least before Removal, and seemingly served mainly to keep the peace between its member towns. It did not, however, unite them in war against any outside power.

The principal ritual of the Creeks was – and for many still is – the annual Green Corn Festival or busk (so-called from its name in Muskogee, *poskitø*). This varied in different towns and changed somewhat over time, but in essentials was the same among all the Creek towns and was very similar among their relatives the Seminoles. Similar festivals were shared by the Cherokees, Choctaws and probably other southeastern Indians. One of the best accounts we have is by John Howard Payne (actor, playwright, author of *Home Sweet Home* and supporter of the Cherokees in their failed struggle against Removal). Payne attended the Tukabahchee busk in 1835 in Alabama, just before the Removal. His conclusion to his detailed description indicated real understanding of what he had observed, very unusual for an outsider at that period.

> 'I never beheld more intense devotion; and the spirit of the forms was a right and religious one. It was beginning the year with fasting, with humility, with purification, with prayer, with gratitude. It was burying animosities, while it was strengthening courage. It was pausing to give thanks to Heaven, before daring to partake its beneficence.'[3]

Each town held its busk at a special square grounds, referred to in Muskogee as the 'big house', and evidently serving as a world symbol. The old Tukabahchee square grounds described by Payne were in a secluded location, where there were two adjacent rectangular grounds. The main square had on each side a shelter, called a 'bed', some 40ft (12m) long, with openings of about 10ft (3m) at each corner between the beds. Each bed was divided into three compartments, each seating a particular clan (or group of linked clans), while in front specific seats were occupied by particular town officials (without regard for their clan affiliations). Outside one corner of this square was a large semi-subterranean council house with a conical roof, on the edge of the second square which contained a ritual tall pole that served as a goal in a ball game played between men (with rackets) and women (without). On two sides of this ball square there were cornfields, on another side was an earth ridge, while the fourth side was formed by the back of one of the beds that faced the other square. In the center was a mound formed from dirt taken from the square grounds each year before a fresh layer was spread to consecrate the grounds in preparation for the busk. Outside one corner of the ball square was another mound, formed from the ashes of the central fire. The square grounds complex with its ritual structures is reminiscent of the massive ritual structures in and around the plazas of the earlier chiefdoms, and it certainly represents a much simplified descendant serving similar functions.

The Creek busk inaugurated the new year, and it was timed to coincide with the first ripening of the town's corn, for it was forbidden to eat the new crop before the busk. The ceremony was a form of renewal, of the people's relations to the spiritual world, as also to the world of plants and animals, and to other people. A feature that repeatedly struck outside observers is the amnesty afforded to those who had committed crimes (except murder) during the previous year. An important part of the ceremony was the ritual lighting of a new fire, which was distributed to all the households to relight the fires that had been extinguished as the houses were swept and cleaned. The same new fire was used to light the ceremonial fire in the center of the square grounds, where the ritual medicines were prepared.

At Tukabahchee the busk lasted eight days, with the pattern of ceremonies on the second four days being similar to the pattern on the corresponding first four days. On the first day the square grounds were cleaned, and participants and visitors gathered there. The second day was a feast day, with dances at night including a woman's dance that much impressed Payne. That night the men (only) slept in the square grounds. The third day was perhaps the peak of the busk. The men fasted all day, the new fire was lit with a fire drill and men took two medicines including the emetic Black Drink. The vomiting in the square that followed was compared by Payne to a libation; it was a form of ritual purification. Young men and boys were scratched with needles on their limbs, to fortify them. The Feather Dance was performed by men carrying poles with feathers attached, signifying peace. Various dances named for animals followed, and social dances filled the whole night. On the fourth day the new corn was eaten for the first time, as part of a feast. The sacred, ancient copper plates, a palladium unique to Tukabahchee, were brought out and reverently displayed. A mock battle known as the Gun Dance was performed, accompanied by women singers. In the evening the town council met. The fifth day was devoted to a ritual deer hunt. On the sixth day there was another feast, when salt was used for the first time in the year (it was felt to be weakening and deleterious). The women danced again, wearing the typical Southern box-turtle rattles attached to their calves. At the end the Old Dance was performed, by men alone, to free the feasters from all ritual restrictions. The seventh day was again devoted to fasting. On the eighth day the chief gave a final speech and the people dispersed.

In several ways the busk reflects the Southeastern Indian emphasis on maintaining good health and on curing. Perhaps this is a result of the demographic disaster suffered by their ancestors. In traditional Southeastern cultures there was no sharp distinction between religious and medical beliefs, rituals and practice. More is known about traditional Cherokee medicine than any other in the region. This is partly because Cherokee doctors made use of Sequoyah's remarkable invention of a syllabary for writing Cherokee. Although he was not literate in English, he was aware of the general nature of writing, or at least of the possibility of representing speech by marks on paper. After several years of experimenting with writing Cherokee, he introduced the results in 1819. He had invented a set of eighty-five symbols, of which five represent vowels, one represents the sound *s*, and the rest stand for syllables each made up of a consonant plus a vowel. The system was practical, and a great many Cherokees soon could write their own language. Because the system was not introduced by missionaries (as were other writing systems for North American Indian languages), it was readily used for the fundamentally non-Christian purpose of recording the secret magical formulas used for curing. Cherokee doctors made collections of medical charms, prayers and formulas. These provided an entree for study and description of Cherokee medicine, even though the records themselves are quite abbreviated and allusive in order to keep them secret from competing doctors.

According to Cherokee theory, illness was caused mainly by the spirits of animals, who, according to tradition, had invented diseases in order to take revenge on humans for killing and abusing them. Other diseases were caused by human and animal ghosts, spirits such as the dwarf-like Little People, and witchcraft. Dreams were sometimes a symptom or omen, and perhaps earlier a direct cause. Diseases were named for their causes, not according to their symptoms. A doctor diagnosed by first inquiring as to the location of the pain. Then the patient was asked whether any prohibitions or taboos had been infringed, and whether the patient had had any indicative dreams or omens, even over the preceding several months or two or three years. The doctor often had to suggest many possibilities that might fit the symptoms, and there were any number of possibilities for the same symptoms. If the interviewing still failed to reveal the cause, the doctor could resort to divination through the movement of beads he held between the thumb and forefinger of each hand. Discovering the cause of the sickness was necessary in order to choose the procedures to effect a cure.

Doctors cured by a combination of herbal remedies and the singing or recitation of magical formulas. Usually the formulas recorded in the Sequoyah syllabary indicate the cause, then often belittle the disease spirit, then threaten it with a rival spirit, who is invoked to drive it away. Frequently the formulas involve color and directional symbolism as well. Several hundred medicinal plants were recognized by skilled Cherokee doctors. Their appropriateness for curing often depended on some similarity in name or appearance to the causative agent of the disease, and sometimes on a perceived similarity between the plant and the symptoms of the disease (according to the ancient folk medical doctrine of signatures). The herbs were collected only as they were needed for a specific case, then usually boiled in water. The medicine might then be rubbed on the patient, sometimes into scratches made on the skin, or alternatively the doctor might blow it over the patient through a cane tube.

The effectiveness of Cherokee medicine is of course impossible to measure, since it depended partly on psychosomatic factors and partly on the pharmacological properties of plants (most of which have never been scientifically tested). However, Cherokee medicine was certainly at least as effective as European and European-American medicine of a century and more ago.

MYTHS AND LEGENDS

The culture of the Southeastern Native American is like a great shattered bowl. Historians and anthropologists assemble the broken shards, knowing they will never be able to recreate the original, but sometimes their efforts produce discernable themes and patterns which provide a momentary insight into the diversity and harmony that once existed. Charles Hudson, author of *The Southeastern Tribes*, noted that our lack of knowledge about the region's original inhabitants is due largely to the fact that many of them were killed, their societies disrupted and their cultures greatly changed before educated people thought them worth studying.[4]

There is evidence that this social and cultural breakdown was beginning even before De Soto's exploration of the region in 1540. De Soto found villages that had been abandoned, emptied by epidemics. The majority of the Southeastern tribes ceased to exist during the next 200 years. The wars and forced migrations of the 18th century obliterated hundreds of tribes, and others found themselves shuttled to and fro, often decimated to the point that they were forced to take refuge with a neighboring tribe. Such assimilations were completed with remarkable ease: Waxsaws and Cheraws joined the Cherokees, Choctaws mingled with Creeks, and Creeks with Seminoles. Historians noted that even though the tribes spoke different languages, the world view was essentially the same.

The mythical cosmology of America's Southeastern tribes is markedly consistent. Their myths describe a three-tiered world: the Upper, which contains deities and spirits; the Middle, which is the abode of Native Americans, along with most of the animals; and the Lower, which is inhabited by evil spirits and abnormal life forms. Mortals are thus trapped between the good and the bad, aspiring upward but frequently falling victim to the dark forces lying in wait.

All life forms are defined by their proximity to the opposing worlds. Birds are powerful forces of good, while snakes and turtles live close to the Lower World. In an earlier time, gigantic hawks and eagles lived in the Middle World with mankind, and plants and animals had the power of speech; however, when mankind became deceitful, the great birds returned to the Upper World. Finding themselves victims of mankind's greed and violence, the animals withdrew and refused to communicate. Thus, the plant and animal life that now lives on the Earth are poor imitations of the divine forms which once thrived.

To the tribes of the Southeast the Earth is a great island floating in a boundless sea. Four cords hanging from the great crystal sky vault (located between the Upper and Middle worlds) are attached to each of the cardinal directions. Their mythology states that 'no one remembers who suspended the island,' but many of the creation stories end on a fatalistic note. In time, the cords will weaken and fall, the island will sink and the dark waters will bring death to all life.[5]

ORIGIN MYTHS

Before the time of man, there were only two worlds: the Upper and the Lower. Eventually, the great birds, animals and insects that lived in the Upper World came to feel that there was not enough room, and their dissatisfaction caused them to look for another home. Water Beetle offered to explore the Lower World which was a great ocean. Diving beneath the water, Water Beetle found soft mud on the bottom. Returning with the mud, Water Beetle began to build a great mound which became the island of the Middle World.[6] (To the Cherokee it was Water Beetle, to the Creek and Uchi it was Crayfish.)

The animals of the Upper World refused to inhabit the island until the soft mud became dry. Great Buzzard was sent to hasten the drying by flapping his wings over the island. Sometimes he flew so low, his great wings struck the soft mud, creating valleys and great mountain peaks which would one day become the home of the Cherokee.

When the animals descended to live on the Earth, the land was in darkness, so the Sun was brought from the Upper World to provide light. The animals had trouble in determining the distance between the Sun and the land and only found the right position after seven attempts.[7] Each day, the great stone vault of the sky rises twice: once in order to allow the Sun to enter, and again at the onset of night when the Sun departs.

■ The Coming of Fire
The nights, however, were cold and the Moon gave neither warmth nor light. The animals appealed to their relatives in the Upper World for help and fire came in a great flash of lightning. The animals saw it strike a hollow sycamore tree on an island far out in the great water. Who should go and bring back the fire? The animals conferred and Raven offered to go. The smoke and heat blackened his feathers, but he returned without the fire; so it was too with the Screech Owl, the Hooting Owl, the Black Racer and the Black Snake. Each was marked by the fire, but they failed to grasp a burning ember. Then, the little Water Spider offered to go, and she succeeded where the others had failed, for she wove a tusti bowl and placed it on her back to carry the fire.[8] Variations of this Cherokee story exist throughout the Southeast with a different assortment of animals attempting to retrieve the fire.

■ Creation of Mankind
Myths dealing with the creation of the human race are rare in Southeastern mythology. Some stories simply conclude that no one knows where they (people) came from. However, a fragmented Cherokee myth says that a being which they called Someone Powerful created the first man and woman from the mud of the Lower World. Hence, humanity is a mixture of Darkness (Evil) and Divine Spirit (Good). When the first man and woman awoke, Someone Powerful told them to walk around the island on which they lived. With the completion of each circuit, the couple discovered a new gift: corn, beans, a dwelling, etc. At first, the acquisition of food was effortless and life was good. Then Someone Powerful told the man to strike the woman with a fish. He did so, and seven days later she gave birth. Every seven days, another child was born which became an adult in seven days. In a short time, this world (Middle World) became crowded, so Someone Powerful decided that the woman would bear one child each year, and that becoming an adult would take much longer. It has been so ever since then.[9]

The creation myths of the Creek and Choctaw, however, seem to have been influenced by the mythology of Western tribes. In both cultures, the human race emerges from a great hole in the ground. Their flesh is pale and damp and they bask in the sunlight until their skin darkens. Then they

40

begin migrating eastward in separate groups, thus accounting for the different tribes. The Cherokees, according to this, become lost and wander to the North; the Creeks and Chickasaws travel to the East and South; only the Choctaws remain near their origin.

A variant notes that the tribes migrated because 'the Earth began to swallow them.' However, their migration is fruitless since the Earth develops arms that reach for hundreds of miles. The Choctaws are safe because they cluster about the devouring giant's feet where he cannot reach. It is noteworthy, however, that in all creation myths, the Native American is created from the damp mud of the Lower World and warmed by the divine Sun, thus becoming a composite of the two opposing worlds.[10]

■ The Flood

Like all preliterate culture throughout the world, the Southeast has numerous deluge stories. In the majority, a man and his wife become aware of the approaching flood due to some form of supernatural warning. Variations include an avenging spirit from the Upper World (Caddo), a prophetic frog repaying a kindness done him by a human (Alabama) and a speaking dog (Cherokee). Usually, the man and his wife are told to build a raft, make a great earthen jar or climb inside a huge hollow reed. As the waters subside, various birds are sent to find land (usually the woodpecker or dove) and the couple undertake the task of repopulating the earth, frequently with supernatural assistance.

ALL-POWERFUL SPIRITS

Although the world of the Southeastern tribes contains an awesome variety of supernatural beings, there is no doubt that those which appear with the greatest regularity are the Little People and the Immortals. The Cherokees call them the *Yunwi Tsunsdi* and the *Nunnehi,* and both supernatural beings appear in the myths of the Choctaws, Creeks and Catawbas, although with different names.

■ The Little People

The Little People bear a marked resemblance to the Irish Leprechauns, or 'wee folk.' They are mischievous, given to pranks and delight in the company of children. However, when angered they can be most terrifying and deadly. Like the Cherokees, the Catawbas have numerous stories about children stolen by the 'little wild people,' and all Southeastern cultures have stories that attibute magical powers to them. According to the Cherokees, they are about 2½ft (76cm) tall and have long hair. Although usually described as unclothed, some stories describe their 'white clothing.' One Cherokee myth describes an annual festival of little folk who meet in the spring on a great flat mountain-top, and their white clothing makes the mountain appear to be covered with snow.[11]

Invariably, to see them is an omen of approaching death. A number of Southeastern myths tell of Cherokees who have become lost in a mountainous wilderness; discovered by the Little People, they are escorted to villages where they have a number of magical encounters. Snakes become belts, and necklaces and terrapins are transformed into seats. Food appears magically, but if the Cherokees attempt to carry it home it turns to dust and ashes. Frequently, after leading their lost visitors within sight of their home, the Little People caution them not to tell where they have been until three weeks have elapsed. Often, the lost Cherokee ignores the warning and dies shortly afterward.

The Little People sometimes train children to be medicine men. The Choctaws call the Little People *Kwanoka'sha* and relate a story in which a stolen child (usually a sickly one) is conducted to a cave in which three spirits test the child's worthiness to be a healer. The child is offered a choice of three things: a knife, poisonous herbs and 'herbs of good medicine.' Selection of the knife indicates a cruel nature; if the poisonous herbs are selected, the child lacks discernment and cannot cure others; if the good herbs are selected, the child is trained for three days and told never to repeat what has been learned and not to use the new-found healing powers until attaining adulthood.

■ The Immortals

Although occurring in many Southeastern cultures, the Immortals are most fully described by the Cherokees. Usually invisible, they disregard natural law and live where they wish: beneath the waters of lakes, in the sky or beneath the earth. A mound called Nikwasi near Franklin, North Carolina, was allegedly built over one of their towns.[12] 'Clear smoke' from their townhouse rises from a rock fissure in nearby Tuckaseigee, and a number of regional stories deal with the curative powers of the warm vapor. The Cherokees describe these *Nunnehi* as gourd-headed, hairless and tall. Since they love to dance, the *Nunnehi* frequently disguise themselves as women and attend Cherokee festivals. There are a number of comical stories dealing with men who become enamored of the disguised *Nunnehi* and attempt to follow them home. The *Nunnehi* walk into a lake or a rock cliff leaving their bewildered suitor behind.

The *Nunnehi* are benevolent spirits who are saddened by the suffering incurred by the mortal Cherokees and, occasionally, they offer assistance. A well-known story relates how the *Nunnehi* once attempted to move the Cherokees to their own world where they would never sicken or grow old. (A variation of this myth warns the Cherokees about the coming of the white man and urges them to join the *Nunnehi* in a world beyond the white man's reach.) These stories relate how the *Nunnehi* came to all the Cherokee villages and told the inhabitants to fast for seven days and seven nights. The *Nunnehi* returned on the seventh night and led all those who had fasted to a nearby mountain (now called Pilot Knob) where the villagers passed through the solid rock and into the realm of the *Nunnehi* .[13] Since the majority of the Cherokees had not kept faith with the *Nunnehi* and had not completed the fast, they remained behind. Since that time, the Cherokees have waited in vain for the *Nunnehi* to return.

HERO CREATURES AND MONSTERS

To the Southeastern Indian, his world (Middle World) was often the battleground for the endless war between the divinities above and the evil forces beneath the earth. Symbolically, this war was depicted by the hawk and the serpent. Although mortals felt a kinship with creatures of the Upper World, they frequently found themselves to be the victims of both hawks and serpents. The Alabama, Natchez, the Cherokee tell stories of the *Tlanuwa,* or Great Hawk; and the Cherokee, Creek and Coasati of the *Uktena,* or Great Serpent.

■ The Great Hawk

The *Tlanuwa* built nests on mountain peaks near villages and great rivers. The gigantic birds preyed on children, carrying them back to feed their young. A popular story tells of a young man who was carried to the nest of the Great Hawk, but managed to escape by riding one of the half-grown chicks into a tree-top.

A variant on this particular theme has a grandmother who rescues her grandchild from the nest and hurls the young birds into the river where they are consumed by the water serpent, the *Uktena.* (In one variant she magically 'creates' the serpent by dropping a rope into the river.) The returning parents find the nest empty and see the *Uktena* consuming their young. Enraged, both birds attack the serpent, dragging it from the water, and while one Great Hawk holds it aloft its mate slashes the serpent into pieces. (This story is used to explain how a series of unusual rock formations in the Tennessee River came into being. They were created by pieces of the *Uktena* falling into the river) Having lost their brood, the birds ascended to the Upper World and never returned.

■ The Great Serpent

The *Uktena* permeates Southeastern mythology. There are minor variations in his appearance: in Cherokee mythology he is horned with a great flashing jewel in his head and seven bands of colour around his neck; in some versions the serpent has 'antlers like a stag', or is winged, making it possible for him to function in water, on land, or in the air. Among the Creek, Uchi and Hitchiti the serpent becomes a 'tie-snake' and preys on children and fishermen.

Strangely enough, the shaman who finally destroyed the *Uktena* was not a Cherokee but a Shawano – a hated enemy of the Cherokees. In exchange for his life, *Aganunitsi* (Grandhog's Mother) promised the Cherokees that he would kill the serpent and bring the magic crystal embedded in its skull back to the Cherokees where it would heal the sick, make the rivers teem with fish and cause the corn to grow. The shaman was as good as his word. Shooting an arrow through the seventh band of color encircling the *Uktena*'s head, *Aganunitsi* pierced the serpent's heart. Then, he called all the birds in the world to come and feed on the snake's flesh for seven days. Finding the magic stone among the *Uktena*'s bones, he returned to the Cherokee village. As promised, the 'flashing crystal' brought prosperity to the Cherokees, but the shaman was less fortunate. Because a drop of the serpent's blood struck him, a red-eyed snake grew from his head. He became a slave to it and the magic stone, killing to feed them.

The extensive number of stories about the Great Serpent, and the frequent references by early travelers in the Southeast to the wide-spread belief in his existence, suggest that the *Uktena* had acquired something akin to totem status. He is incised on conch shells, pots and gorgets. Similar carvings among Florida tribes depict a serpent with a cougar's head, and the corresponding myths about the Great Water Cougar are variations of the *Uktena* myths. When Sir Alexander Cumming visited the Southeast in 1730, he encountered frequent references to the 'healing crystal' that had once been in the *Uktena's* head and talked to medicine men who claimed to possess it. Medicine men among the Seminole, Creek, Choctaw and Cherokee tribes *still* speak of the healing crystal which can prophecy, cure disease and end barrenness in women. Throughout the Southeast there is considerable mystery associated with the 'healing crystal.' Tribal shamans believe that the stone will lose its power if non-Indians know where it is located. In some traditions, the crystal must be fed fresh blood every seventh day or it becomes an avenging spirit, searching in the night for the medicine man who has neglected to feed it.

HOLY PLACES, SACRED SITES

For the tribes of the Southeast, the homes of deities and mythical creatures were numerous and familiar. Each deep pool, rounded hill and rocky mountain crest carried a story. Deeply incised scars on boulders in a river bore mute witness to a mythical battle, and warm air rising from a fissure in the earth denoted the presence of a *Nunnehi* town beneath the ground. The mountains, valleys and streams of eastern Tennessee, northern Georgia and western North Carolina are teeming with dozens of significant places.

■ The Nikwasi Mound

According to Cherokee tradition, the Nikwasi Mound near Franklin, North Carolina, is one of the many sacred sites associated with the *Nunnehi* (Immortals). In ancient times, the Cherokee came here to ask the *Nunnehi* for assistance in warfare. If their prayers were answered, the *Nunnehi* would emerge from beneath the ground with magic weapons and join the Cherokee in battle. James Mooney, the noted authority on Cherokee culture and myth, recounted the story of such a battle. According to oral tradition, the Cherokees of Nikwasi were attacked by a superior force. When defeat seemed certain, a mighty force of *Nunnehi* streamed from the mound and became invisible as they rushed to the attack. The bows and tomahawks floated across the battlefield, and the terrified enemy force fled. However, the spears and arrows of the *Nunnehi* pursued them, swerving around rocks and trees. When the enemy force was reduced to six warriors, they fled to the head of the Tuckaseigee River, turned around and in despair pleaded for their lives. The Cherokees named the place *Dayulsunyi* (Where They Cried). The *Nunnehi* spared the six warriors and returned to vanish into the mound.

Because of the ancient traditions associated with the mound, the Cherokees frequently choose the site for important tribal meetings. Local legends recount stories of hunting parties who have camped near it only to be awakened in the night by the sounds of drumming and chanting.

■ Mounds and Effigies

The temple mounds near Cartersville, Georgia, are among the most impressive in the Southeast. Containing some of the finest examples of Southeastern art, the Etowah Mounds undoubtedly functioned as a ceremonial center. Gorgets, necklaces and carved statuary recovered from this site contain representations of falcons, eagles and snakes which suggest associations with Southeastern mythology.

Numerous sites along the Tuckaseigee River are associated with the *Uktena,* and each bears a name specifying its significance. A rock ledge was a sleeping place, and misshapen rocks still bear the scars of the *Uktena's* battle with the *Tlanuwa.* Cohutta Mountains, Georgia, was not only the place where the *Uktena* was finally killed, but is also the location of an ancient 855ft long (261m) rock wall which many historians feel is a replica of the mythical serpent. One of the most impressive serpent effigies is in southern Ohio. Built atop a steep bluff, this earthen structure represents the body of a snake which undulates for 737ft (225m). The body of the snake is about 20ft (6m) wide and 4–5ft (1.2-1.5m) in height with a coiled tail and a carefully detailed head.

Several rock bluffs along the Tennessee River are identified as nesting sites for the *Tlanuwa,* the most noteworthy being the one near Chattanooga, Tennessee. An effigy mound in Georgia (Rock Eagle) consists of rocks which have been piled in the shape of a great bird, perhaps an eagle.

■ Thunder Beings and Daktu

Whiteside Mountain in Jackson County, North Carolina, is associated with the Cherokee Thunder Gods and the monster spearfinger, the witch who constructed a stone bridge on its summit which she traditionally crossed in order to prey on Cherokee villages.[14] Deep pools in the French Broad in North Carolina and Toco Creek, in Monroe County, Tennessee, are associated with the *Daktu,* the giant fish that used its tail to slap Cherokee hunters into the water where the fish swallowed them. There are variations of this story throughout the Southeast which involve a hero who cuts his way out of the *Daktu*'s stomach with a mussel shell.

A family of Thunder Beings, similar to those that lived on Whiteside Mountain, occupied a home behind Tallulah Falls in Rabun County, Georgia, from where they produced terrifying sounds when fishermen came too near.

REVERED ANIMALS

The fragments of oral tradition that have survived, stress the ancient bond which exists between man and animals. Tradition and custom indicated that the harmonious balance between the two could only be retained through mutual respect. Man must hunt and kill animals in order to survive; and animals accepted their inevitable death provided that their sacrifice was properly acknowledged. Many of the early settlers commented on the 'curious custom' they sometimes observed among the Southeastern Indians: hunters who had slain a deer or bear would kneel by the dying animal and ask its forgiveness. 'My family is hungry,' the Indian would say. 'I regret taking your life, but I must feed them.'

■ Bear, the Brother

The Cherokees and Creeks have an old story about a time in the dim past when their people were almost destroyed by a famine. After repeated treks into the forests, the elders called a great meeting in the townhouse. 'This may be the end of us,' said the elders, 'for we can find no food.' In the Cherokee version, the people gathered in their clan towns to discuss the famine. In recent times there are seven clans, but at this ancient time there were eight.[15] It was the members of the eighth clan that came to the elders with a solution: 'We have decided to die that our brothers may live,' they said. Then, they turned and walked into the forest. Several days later they returned, but they were almost unrecognizable. Long, black hair grew all over their bodies – they had become bears. The starving villagers shot them and ate them.

One hunter, finding a family of bears in the woods, felt that he could not kill them. 'You are my brothers,' he said. 'It is not right that I should kill you.' The bears approached and spoke to him. 'It is meant that you should kill us,' they said. 'Our bodies will nourish you, and our souls will not die, but will return to the Upper World where they will be clothed in flesh again so that we may return and give you our flesh.' And so it was that hunters would kneel by the slain bear and say, 'Thank you my Brother.'

Among the Alabama, the sacrificial bear is white, and although there is no famine, the close bond between the hunter and the hunted is always stressed.

Success in hunting is due not to skill but to the power of the animal which grants the hunter the ability to find and kill the animal. If a hunter is unmindful of an animal's sacrifice and fails to show proper respect, the animal's spirit will send sickness and disease to him.

■ The Corn Maiden

In the plant world the close tie with mankind is even more pronounced. The Southeastern Indians believed that for every sickness or disease visited on them by the animal world, there was a corresponding plant or herb that would cure them. In addition, there are numerous stories about food plants that illustrate the same kinship. The following is an extract from the story of *Selu,* the Corn Maiden.

Selu, the first woman, gave birth to two sons. They were mischievous boys who were always hungry. 'We are hungry and there is nothing to eat,' said the boys. Finally, *Selu* told her sons that she would go in search of food. She left with a basket, and in a short time returned. The basket was filled with corn. She made a bread and baked it and the sons were delighted. Each day, she left the house and returned with corn. 'I wonder where she is getting that corn,' said her sons. 'Let us follow her and see.' And so, the two boys followed their mother, and when they saw her enter a little cabin they peered between the logs. Inside, they saw *Selu* place the basket on the ground. Then, she shook herself violently and the basket filled up with corn.

Returning home, the sons said nothing until she had baked the bread and they had eaten it. 'We saw you, mother,' they said. 'We know where you got the corn.' *Selu* smiled sadly. 'I am sorry that you spied on your mother,' she said. 'Now that you know the secret, I must die. After my death, you must drag my body through the field. And after I am gone, corn will grow in the field. From this time on, you must work for your bread.' Then, she lay down and passed away.

There are numerous variations of the *Selu* myth. The Cherokee and Creek sometimes amend it with a version that requires the sons to kill and dismember their mother, scattering bits of her body in the field. The sons are told that they should not be reluctant to kill her since her body will produce food for everyone. In the Choctaw version, corn is brought by a crow after the waters of the Great Flood have subsided.

RITUALS AND CEREMONIES

One of the most popular legends among the Southeastern tribes was the story of Stone Man. This monster is a classic example of the supernatural beings described by the historian, Frank G. Spek: '. . . Monsters clad in stone, bone, metal, or scales are very characteristic of the region. The monster is usually a cannibal, and is finally slain by persons or beings who have learned the secret of its only vulnerable spot.' In addition, the Stone Man legend gives an explanation as to where the ceremonies, dances and rituals of the Southeast came from: they were gifts from Stone Man.

■ Stone Man

According to the Cherokee, Stone Man's body was covered with slabs of rock, but the Yamasee claim that he had made himself a great coat out of small pieces of flint after seeing a hunter kill a deer with a flint-tipped arrow. In his hand he carried a magic staff which enabled him to cross ravines. When he pitches his staff into the air, it became a stone bridge , and when he was safely on the other side the bridge vanished and the staff returned to his hand. Stone Man also used the staff to find human livers – his favourite food. Stone Man was a shape-changer, and would frequently travel into villages disguised as an old woman.

In an effort to defend themselves against Stone Man, the villagers asked their shaman to help them. The shaman told the villagers that Stone Man could be destroyed by 'moon-sick' (menstruating) women. When Stone Man was seen approaching the village, the elders sent seven such women to lay by the path. As Stone Man passed each successive woman, he grew weaker; and at the seventh, he fell to the earth, vomiting blood. The women rushed forward with seven basswood stakes and, pulling aside the stone covering, drove the stakes through his body.

When Stone Man did not die, the villagers built a great fire on top of him. Stone Man told his captors that he did not fear death since he knew his spirit would survive. Further, he said that he bore them no ill-will, and would teach them songs and rituals which would aid them in hunting, planting and war. Then Stone Man began to sing and the villagers memorized his songs. He muttered magic incantations that would cure sickness and the villagers learned them all. Finally, when his voice no longer rose from the fire, the villagers raked the ashes and found a lump of red 'wadi' paint which they used afterward to paint their faces when they spoke the words and performed the ceremonies that Stone Man had given them.

■ Purification

Many ceremonies, songs and ritual dances deal with purification and cleansing. Others celebrate the balance and harmony between mankind, animals and plants. The complex tobacco rituals recorded by James Money concern cleansing, divination and conjuring. The Green Corn Dance, one of 12 seasonal celebrations of thanksgiving, involved ritual cleansing of homes and public buildings, and extended to physical and mental purification.

Perhaps the most well-known Southeastern purification ritual is the Black Drink Ceremony. Among the Cherokee, Creek and Choctaw, the drink was brewed from a species of holly and acted both as a stimulant and a diuretic. Consuming large amounts invariably produced vomiting and perspiration.[16]

Going to Water denotes a Southeastern purification ritual which was most commonly conducted prior to traditional ballgames. Performed in conjunction with the scratching of each player with a ritual cob with seven rattlesnake teeth, the ceremony was performed in sacred streams. Each player received over 300 scratches on his body, and then waded into a stream at a point that allowed him to face the east. As the player washed the blood from his body, the shaman asked that the player be granted strength, agility and quick thinking.

Although no longer performed, historians generally consider such rituals to be remnants of a vast and complex system that existed prior to the coming of the white man. Then, the Southeastern tribes perceived everything in terms of balance.[17] The sole purpose of a ceremony was to restore or maintain balance. Everything was in opposition: Upper World and Lower World, north and south, man and woman. Charles Hudson states:

> 'The aboriginal Southeastern Indians would have understood traditional Chinese cosmology with its opposed Yang and Yin forces far better than they would have understood our own . . . philosophy that man should conquer nature by tampering with it in a thousand new and unheard ways.'[18]

ARTS AND CRAFTS

The story of Southeastern Indian arts and crafts is different from that of other Native Americans. When Europeans first penetrated the Southeast in the early-16th century, the Indians had reached a social, political and religious development more akin to the grand civilization of the Mesoamerican Aztecs than to other North American Indian groups. Between about AD 1000 to AD 1540, the Mississippian Period, the Southeastern Indians' political order consisted of large and small chiefdoms presided over by a priestly elite who could command the construction of large temple mounds and other impressive earthworks. This system was supported by intensive riverine corn agriculture and maintained through warfare.

The Mississippian way of life suffered swift deterioration after European contact. European diseases, to which the Southeastern Indians had no natural immunity, were deadly foes causing a sharp population decline, the destruction of the chiefdom political order and social dislocation as people relocated and reorganized. During this time, the better-known historic Southeastern Indian groups such as the Cherokee, Choctaw, Catawba, Creek, Chickasaw and Seminole formed out of the wreckage of the chiefdoms. Their societies bore little resemblance to the past.

Following on the heels of the introduction of disease, an equally profound force for change occurred when the Southeastern Indians were incorporated into the European economic system through trading deerskins. Throughout the 17th and 18th centuries, the Southeastern Indians regularly encountered, lived among, were dependent upon, intermarried with and, occasionally, fiercely resisted whites. By the 19th century the cotton agriculture and the plantation economy came to dominate the Old

South. Unlike the deerskin trade, the plantation economy did not need the Indians; it needed their land. No longer necessary to the market system, the Indians became an obstacle, and this ultimately led to Removal, when almost all of the Southern Indians were forcibly relocated to Western territories.

Southeastern Indian art reflects their history. The highest artistic achievements of the Southeastern Indians undoubtedly occurred during the Mississippian Period. The people who lived during the Mississippian Period displayed a pageantry and rich ceremonial life unparalleled anywhere in Native North America. Mississippian accouterments are lavish, eloquent and highly crafted. Mississippian art is explicitly iconographic. Design motifs, although varying stylistically, are elements in what is termed the Southeastern Ceremonial Complex. These motifs include the bi-lobed arrow, the falcon-man, the forked-eye design, sun circles, crosses and swastikas, winged serpents and animals with mythological or social significance such as the bear, woodpecker, raptorial bird and rattlesnake.

This artistic expression, so closely tied to ceremony and elite authority, declined along with the chiefdoms after European contact.[19] In the Ceremonial Complex, art was inextricably associated with religious, social or political life. During the Historic Period, Southeastern Indian ceremonial life took a more egalitarian turn and did not require the trappings of a priestly elite. In the Historic Period, European trade provided most of the material items of daily life.

■ Ceramics

Southeastern Indian ceramic art during the Mississippian Period was unsurpassed in North America. Southeastern Indians did not possess the potter's wheel, and women, who were the masters of this medium, used coiling and hand modeling to fashion their wares. Although there are no descriptions of Mississippian potters at work, contemporary Catawba potters still practice a variant of the coiling method, and it is reasonable to suppose that Mississippian women followed similar procedures.

In the coiling technique, lumps of clay are rolled on a board until they form rounded fillets of uniform thickness and length.[20] Each piece of rolled clay is pinched together to form one long, continuous fillet which is then wound around and up to form the rough shape of the vessel.[21] The ware is then smoothed and further shaped and the walls thinned with a spoon-shaped gourd rind or mussel shell.[22] After allowing the ware to air dry,

Catawba potters finish the surface by using a smooth mussel shell or kitchen knife to scrape the inside and outside of the ware and to cut and smooth the rim.[23] Handles, spouts, lugs, pedestals, legs, necks and so on are hand-molded and attached separately. Before fire-drying, the potter polishes the surface with a worn, smooth pebble.[24] Catawba women prize their polishing stones; the more worn and smooth ones are considered irreplaceable and are often handed down from generation to generation.

Mississippian ceramics were made in an interesting array of forms. Utilitarian wares, usually undecorated, vary from small bowls to cooking and storage pots that hold up to six gallons. Ceremonial and mortuary objects have elaborate decorations and forms. Some of the most outstanding ceremonial forms are the human and animal effigy bottles and bowls, especially the noticeable 'dead head' effigies which obviously represent a dead person.[25] The bottles were shaped into full figures of animals or into a usually kneeling human form. The bowls have miniature ceramic human or animal heads attached to the rim.[26] Other ceremonial bottles are globular bottles with relatively long necks and decorated with geometrical or curvilinear incising or polychrome painting. Many of the ceremonial containers are incised or painted with Southeastern Ceremonial Complex motifs such as the sun circle, the hand and eye motif, and the winged serpent.[27] All of the archaeological and ethnohistorical evidence points to a drastic decline in ceramic art after the arrival of Europeans and, especially, after the Indians had access to metal pots, pans, bowls, cups and dishes. The historic groups continued to make ceramic utilitarian wares, but not in such quantities and certainly without the mastery of their ancestors. Ceremonial ceramic wares ceased being made. Around the turn of the 20th century, with an increase in tourist trade and collector interest, Catawba and Cherokee women returned to ceramic manufacturing as an art form.[28]

■ Stonework

The stonework of the Southeastern Indians, like their ceramic art, reached its height during the Mississippian Period. Stone working was almost certainly a man's domain. Mississippian men knew the attributes and limitations of a vast variety of stone for sculpting and chipping. Men quarried local stone sources such as chert, steatite, greenstone, shale, quartz, granite, diorite, slate, hematite, limestone and marble.[29] Especially valued high-grade stone was traded throughout the Southeast.

The primary techniques in stonework were chipping and grinding. The chipping technique was used mostly in the manufacture of cutting tools. Flakes were struck from the stone being shaped with another stone or a piece of deer antler to give it the desired form and thinness. Smaller flakes were removed by applying pressure with smaller tools to refine the shape and sharpen the edges.[30] In the grinding technique, the stone to be worked was simply pecked and ground into shape and then polished with sand mixed with oil or water.[31] To fashion the more intricate stone objects such as effigy pipes, men used a soft, easily carved stone such as steatite, and then used stone chisels, drills and scrapers to carve highly detailed forms with deeply incised lines.[32] The pipe holes were then drilled and the pipe polished.

Although many tools for daily life were made of stone, stonework became a true art form in the production of ceremonial and religious objects. Chipped-stone war clubs, blades and batons are so finely crafted, delicate and unmarred, that they could not have been used in actual hand-to-hand combat. Grinding produced some marvelously sculpted objects, the most noteworthy being the kneeling-human mortuary figures carved out of limestone, sandstone or marble. These figures, which may have represented mythical or real ancestors, were kept in the charnel houses which were the repositories of the elite dead; some were interred in high-status burials.[33]

The chunky game, played well into the Historic Period, required a ground-stone gaming piece or chunky stone. These pieces are discoidal stones, sometimes with concave centers on both sides; the finer ones are highly polished and perfectly round. Chunky stones, although probably used frequently, are works of art in themselves, showing a gracefulness of line and beautiful symmetry.

After European contact there was a dramatic decline in stonework.[34] Southeastern Indians readily replaced stone tools with European-made metal tools and weapons. Men continued to make stone tools, but these did not have the same attention to detail and craftsmanship as those from the Mississippian Period. After all, the flintlock gun was now the weapon of choice.

Men, however, never completely lost the artistry of grinding and carving. Chunky stones from the Historic Period are as finely crafted and beautiful as those from the Mississippian Period. Tobacco pipes played an important role in Historic Period Southeastern Indian ceremonial life, and a great deal of care and attention went into the artistry of Historic Period steatite pipes.[35] The Cherokee were famous for their fine tobacco pipes. Historic Period pipes are usually carved with an animal effigy on the stem. Animal figures on the pipes are often bears, although panthers and frogs are also common. Pipes occasionally have a reclining human carved on the stems or, reportedly, even men and women in explicit sexual poses.[36]

■ Metal and Shellwork

During the Mississippian Period, shell and metal, primarily copper, were scarce in the Southeast, and that which was available was traded throughout the area. Traders brought copper from the Lake Superior region and from the Tennessee Valley, and shells from the coastal areas were commonly traded to interior peoples.

The techniques used in copperwork were fairly simple. The coppersmith placed a copper nugget on a piece of buckskin laid over a hard surface, and hammered out the nugget with a hammer stone and then cut it into shape.[37] A smooth cobble or piece of stone was then used to smooth further the surface on both sides. Shellwork was usually done on a large conch shell (*Busycon perversum*). The conch shells were hollowed out for use as cups or dippers, or the smooth interior portions of the shell were cut into circles for use as gorgets which were worn around the neck, over the breast or collarbone.

Shell and copper objects are almost all ornaments – beads, necklaces, hairpins, masks, gorgets, earspools, headdress emblems and so on. Except for the jewelry, these ornaments were used as part of ceremonial or religious dress or as grave offerings to accompany the elite dead. Sheet copper, laminated over celts, axes, earspools or other stone and wood objects, have been discovered in elite burials. Sheet copper also was cut into silhouettes of war clubs, bi-lobed arrows or feathers that were worn in the ceremonial headdresses of the elite.[38] Coppersmiths devoted special skill and time embossing figures of men in various poses and dances on copper sheets. The most prominent of these are the copper plates from the Etowah site in Georgia in which a falcon-man is depicted in full ceremonial regalia and brandishing a war club. These plates appear to have been intended only as grave offerings to the elite dead.[39]

On gorgets, designs were incised on the smooth interior using sharpened stone awls and needles. Shell cups and dippers usually were engraved on their outside portions. Some shell gorgets and cups have incised designs representing human figures like those on the copper plates but most of them represent rattlesnakes, woodpeckers, spiders or mythological beings such as the underwater panther and the winged serpent.[40] Gorgets may have been worn as political or military insignia. For instance, the Citico gorget, which depicts a coiled rattlesnake-like being, is only found in those Mississippian Period archaeological sites that once comprised the chiefdom of Coosa.[41] The shell cups and dippers were probably used to serve Black Drink, a herbal tea drunk as a sacrament at political and religious events.[42]

With the abrupt disruption of the Mississippian ceremonial and political life, copper- and shellwork virtually ceased.[43] Historic Period Southeastern Indians appreciated fine metals and purchased trade ornaments such as crescent-shaped gorgets, hairpins, arm bands, turban bands, earrings and rings. The Southeastern Indians continued to drink Black Drink throughout the Historic Period, but shell cups and dippers were replaced by European metal ones.

■ Basketry

Southeastern Indian basketry is perhaps the only craft that continues from the prehistoric past until the present.[44] River cane (*Arundinaria tecta* and *A. macrosperma*) is the preferred material for basketry.[45] Despite the difficulty in cutting and processing river cane splints, the women never forfeited the distinct shiny gloss of river cane for easier material. The sheer abundance of river cane also probably contributed to its popularity, since a woman would not have had to search far for her supplies.[46]

To prepare cane splints, a stalk is split lengthwise, usually into four splints. The shiny outer material is then pulled from the coarse inner fiber. The inside of the splint is then scraped of any remaining inner fiber and trimmed along the edges to a uniform width. The famous Chitimacha basketry has distinctively narrow, delicate cane splints, a technical feat in itself.

The women employ primarily two types of weaving techniques – checkerwork and twilling – both of which were used in prehistoric times.[47] In checkerwork, a number of splints are placed side by side to make the warp; weft splints are woven in one at a time, over and under, at right angles, until a mat base is formed. Then all the splints are turned up to form the warp of the sides.[48] Twilling is a diagonal weave in which each element of the weft is woven over two or more warp splints at an oblique angle.[49] The most difficult and skillful twilling technique is the double-weaved twill, in which the weave is doubled over at the rim and continued inside the basket. In this way so-called double-weave baskets are made.

Southeastern Indian basketry is noted for its mastery of color and design. Cane splints are colored with vegetable dyes made from black walnut and butternut for a deep brown or black, puccoon root for a red or orange, bloodroot for a redbrown, broom sedge for a burnt orange, and yellowroot for a deep yellow.[50] A variety of geometrical and curvilinear designs are formed by varying the width and color of cane splints and the number of over and under turns. Because of their intricate designs, the most famous basket makers in the Southeast are the Chitimacha women of southern Louisiana and the Cherokee women of North Carolina. Chitimacha women weave distinct, colorful design bands that criss-cross or curve over the whole of the basket.[51] Cherokee women prefer simple geometric lines forming squares, triangles, diamonds, and crosses over the whole basket.[52]

Women make small baskets with handles, sieves for sifting hominy, hampers, and mats for sitting, sleeping, or as wall hangings.[53] The most striking basket form of the Southeastern Indians is the burden basket. These are large, sturdy baskets with a flared opening. They were carried on the back with a leather tump-line attached to the sides and placed across the chest or forehead. Choctaw, Chitimacha and Creek women fashion 'cow nose' or heart-shaped baskets, which are small, triangular baskets remarkably similar to the pouches of the Ceremonial Complex.[54]

■ Fabrics and Clothing

Daily clothing for Southeastern Indian men and women was a simple affair. Women wore knee-length skirts and men wore breechclouts, and both usually went without upper garments. They wore leggings which are long, wide pieces of single cloth wrapped around each leg and suspended by garters from a belt. In cold weather, men and women wore 'matchcoats' which were cloak-like garments worn draped over the shoulders. Europeans often compared textiles from the late-Mississippian Period through most of the Historic Period to finely-made European fabrics. These textiles were made from various types of animal fur, grasses and bark, particularly the inner bark of the mulberry tree which produced a fine, pliable cloth similar to linen.[55] Animal skins from deer, bison, bear and smaller animals were used to fashion moccasins and matchcoats.[56] Handmade textiles were either dyed with vegetable dyes or painted with mineral paints. Skin matchcoats were sometimes painted with geometric designs, animals or military exploits.

As soon as European textiles became available in any appreciable quantity, men and women substituted them for handmade textiles.[57] Buckskin continued to be used through most of the 18th century for moccasins, but the Southeastern Indians soon preferred European woolens for their matchcoats. Men eschewed European-style pants until the 19th century; but they quickly adapted the knee-length, military-style European jackets and shirts and began wearing these blousy, open shirts as part of their daily and fancy wear.[58] These shirts were decorated with colorful applique strips along the bottom, and often they were covered with various ornaments of beads, silver, ribbon and so on. Women began using European textiles for their skirts and began wearing calico bodices in the late-18th century. Both skirts and bodices were fully ornamented with beads, bells, rattles and ribbons.

After Removal, most Southeastern Indians began wearing American-style dress, except for the Seminoles. Those Seminoles who escaped Removal moved into the Florida Everglades where they remained isolated for a long time. American-style clothing was not readily available to them, and Seminole women made ankle-length skirts, bodices with capes and military-style men's shirts into the 20th century.[59] After the manual sewing machine became available, applique gave way to the patchwork garments which have become the national dress of the Seminole.[60]

In Seminole applique, single strips of printed cloth are sewn directly onto the garment. In patchwork, patterned cloth is first torn into long strips which are then sewn together to produce a band of striped cloth. The band is then snipped into several pieces which are arranged side by side or offset and sewn together into a long band. This technique allows for an astonishing variety of designs, and a woman usually uses several bands of varying designs in making one garment.[61] The bands are then sewn together to form a whole piece of cloth that can be cut into patterns and sewn. The final product is a very colorful patchwork garment with a variety of intricate, detailed designs.[62]

■ **Beadwork and Featherwork**

Except for the delicate feather wands and fans, beads and feathers were used as clothing decorations or for personal adornment. Southeastern Indian women produced finger-woven, tasseled sashes, belts and garters, and they did so in the Mississippian Period as evidenced by the engraved figures on shell gorgets and copper plates. Sashes and belts constituted part of their clothing throughout the Historic Period as well, and to the present day the

Choctaw and Creek are noted for their beaded belts.[63] Sashes were worn over one or both shoulders, crossing diagonally or criss-crossing across the chest and tied at the waist with tassels and cords hanging down, often below the knees. In the late Historic Period, belts worn about the waist served to fasten the buttonless military-style shirts. Women also made finger-woven garters with which to fasten leggings and the fancy, beaded, men's pouches (their clothing usually did not have pockets).

In finger-weaving, yarns are attached to a single bar and the threads are intertwined by the fingers alone.[64] This technique only allows for the manufacture of relatively narrow strips of cloth, hence the predominance of sashes and belts made with this technique. With beaded sashes and belts, beads are slipped onto the threads during the weaving process. Designs are constructed by varying the color of threads and weave. In examining the design motifs of belts and sashes, two style areas emerge. The Eastern style area, typified by the Seminole and Yuchi, is characterized by simple, all-over geometric designs of diamonds, Vs, Ws and crosses. In the Western style area, comprising the Choctaw, Chickasaw, Koasati and Alabama (the latter two were both historic Creek groups), curvilinear designs are laid out in a panel against a monochrome background.[65]

Without doubt, feather matchcoats were the finest featherwork products from the Southeast.[66] Basically, these were made of woven or mulberry cloth nets into which hundreds of feathers were twisted or tied. Turkey feathers, which have opalescent brown, red, purple and blue hues were the preferred feathers. The feather down, of course, made these cloaks particularly good outerwear during cold weather.[67]

Finally, feather wands and fans were made from the Mississippian Period through the Historic Period. These wands were usually made of eagle feathers arranged fan-like and fastened at the quills with a leather handle or attached to a fan frame or a carved sourwood rod.[68] The eagle was a revered emblem of peace, and eagle feather fans were frequently used during ceremonial occasions and dances.[69] Fans made from other feathers such as turkey apparently were used as everyday fans.

■ Woodwork

Because wood preserves poorly in the acidic Southeastern soils, one can only estimate the importance of this medium to the Southeastern Indians. Although some wooden artifacts have been found elsewhere, the largest cache of Mississippian wooden artifacts are from the Key Marco site in

Florida, from which many utilitarian and ceremonial wooden objects have been recovered from the saltwater marsh muck. Of these, the painted masks and tablets, animal figurines and naturalistic animal heads are the most noteworthy.

Masks and figurines were carved and chiseled from a single piece of wood using shell chisels, sawfish-tooth blades and stone scrapers and drills. They were then smoothed with sand or sharkskin to remove all traces of tool scars.[70] Wooden animal heads sometimes were made of several pieces. For instance, a deer head has detachable ears and an alligator has a separate lower jaw that articulates with the upper jaw. These wooden pieces are painted, incised and inlaid with shell.

How the people of Key Marco understood or used the animal figurines and heads is unknown since, for the most part, these are not representative of the Southeastern Ceremonial Complex. However, masks were worn by Southeastern Indians in various dances and ceremonial affairs from the Mississippian Period through the Historic Period. Some were used as decoy masks for hunting, in which a hunter donned an animal skin and mask and mimicked, with astonishing fidelity, the movements of his prey. Some decoy masks also were used in performing hunting dances.

Masks also were used to impersonate mythical beings, other humans or to characterize esteemed personal traits such as bravery and fierceness in war.[71] The falcon-man motifs of the Southeastern Ceremonial Complex clearly depict masked creatures. The rattlesnake-dance masks of the Cherokee reportedly indicate the dancer's bravery since he would be obviously unconcerned about the rattlesnake carved on the forehead.[72]

Historic Cherokee masks are the most well-known. Cherokee masks may seem crude in comparison to those from the Northwest coast or from the Northeast. Certainly the detail is missing. However, the Booger Dance masks show a finesse in caricature that is truly artistic. The Booger Dance was a burlesque dance performed by the Cherokee of North Carolina that re-enacted the arrival of white people. The Boogers wore masks representing what the dancers perceived as grotesque attributes of white men.[73] These masks were carved with grimaces and leering smiles and topped by shaggy, unkempt hair and mounds of facial hair. One mask, made in the mid-20th century by Will West Long, depicts in perfect caricature a quite distressed Indian.

REFERENCES

SOUTHEAST

1 These accounts are quoted in translation on pp. 139-57 of John R. Swanton's 'Indian Tribes of the Lower Mississippi Valley and Adjacent Coast of the Gulf of Mexico,' *Smithsonian Institution, Bureau of American Ethnology Bulletin* 43, 1911.

2 T. N. Campbell, 'Choctaw Subsistence: Ethnographic Notes from the Lincecum Manuscript,' *Florida Anthropologist* 12(1): 9-24, 1959.

3 John Howard Payne (introduction by John R. Swanton), 'The Green Corn Dance,' *Chronicles of Oklahoma* 10:170-95, 1932.

4 Hudson, 1976:4.

5 This fatalistic theme bears a marked similarity to the attitude reflected in Norse and Germanic mythologies in which the world hangs in the limbs of a dying tree. Eventually, the tree will fall and the world will be destroyed.

6 Mooney, 1972:239–40

7 The number seven is undoubtedly the most significant in Cherokee culture. This significance is related directly to Cherokee cosmology and arises from the identification of seven directions: east, west, north, south, up, down, and here (where the speaker is standing).

8 Mooney, 1972:241.

9 It is interesting that in Cherokee mythology, the creation of man and woman comes *after* the creation of animals. Consequently, the Middle Earth was a paradise inhabited by divinities until mankind appeared and despoiled it.

10 George Lankford, editor of *Southeastern Legends*, notes that there is considerable evidence that the mythology of some Southeastern tribes was influenced by the 'emergence' tradition of the south-west. Specifically, these are myths that explain the origin of tribes by their having emerged from a hole in the Earth. Variations of this myth are common among the Creeks, but unknown by the Cherokees and Yuchi. Lankford, 1987:112.

11 According to a popular (non-Indian) story, a gathering of little people was witnessed atop Chimney Rock in 1806 by a number of witnesses who later signed sworn statements. They were dressed in white and flew to and from the mountain crest in large numbers.

12 The remains of a large number of mounds are scattered throughout western North Carolina. Some historians note that in some instances the Cherokee's oral tradition claims that a number of mounds, such as the ancient one located on Governor's Island in Swain County, were not con-structed by the Cherokees, but by another race of people.

13 Mooney, 1972:335–336.

14 The witch Spearfinger, like her male counterpart Stone Man, killed Cherokee children for their liv-ers. Despite her magical powers, she was lured into a trap and killed by the Cherokees when a small bird revealed her 'vulnerable spot' to be her hand (where her heart was hidden).

15 Modern Cherokees are still aware of their clan. Many anthropologists feel that the clan concept was a sophisticated way of avoiding inbreeding. The seven clans are: *Ani-waya* (Wolf), *Ani-Kawi* (Deer), *Ani-Tsiskwa* (Bird), *Ani-Wadi* (Paint), *Ani-Shani* (Blue), *Ani-Gatigwi* (Potato) and *Ani-Gilahi* (Long Hair).

16 When Henry Timberlake witnessed the Black Drink Ceremony at Chota in 1761, he noted that a Cherokee woman, called the *Ghighau* or Blessed Woman, prepared the drink: 'She took out the wing of a swan, and after flourishing it over the pot, stood fixed for near a minute as she mumbled an ancient chant, then reached again into the deer-skin pouch. She withdrew branches of yapon shrub which she cast into the boiling water of the twenty-gallon pot.'

17 The belief system in the Southeast often stressed the need to avoid the mixture of opposites. Fire was not meant to mingle with water, nor birds with snakes. Unnatural blendings produced impurity. The tradition of extinguishing fires at the year's end is based on the belief that the fire had become impure through association with mankind and must be born again anew.

18 Hudson, 1976:319

19 Contemporary artists and craftspeople, submitting to market demands for 'traditional' crafts, have, however, relearned old techniques.

20 Contemporary Catawba women dig clay from local clay pits noted for the purity and consistency of the clay. After the clay is prepared the potter breaks off suitable quantities and either uses them immediately or wraps them in damp cloth or leaves for storage (Fewkes, 1944:73).

21 Fewkes, 1944:113. Catawba women use ring coiling, rather than true coiling. They lay rings one on top of another to build a cylinder (Fewkes, 1944:78).

22 Fewkes, 1944:83.

23 Fewkes, 1944:88.

24 Fewkes, 1944:83. The Southeastern Indians did not possess the kiln. Catawba potters gradually dry their wares by placing them progressively closer to an open fire, finally placing the whole piece on the coals. (Fewkes, 1944:89).

25 Haberland, 1964:195.

26 Animal effigies were representations of various animals common in the Southeastern Ceremonial Complex. It is unknown what or whom the human effigies represented.

27 Fundaburk and Foreman, 1957:168-183.

28 Harrington, 1908:401-403; Speck, 1920:63. Contemporary Catawba trade pottery is especially noted for its fine craftsmanship.

29 Mississippian men usually extracted stone from local quarries by chiseling out large chunks. They then chipped them into suitable sizes.

30 Fundaburk and Foreman, 1957:116. In fashioning the rough shape of a chipped stone tool the stoneworker held the stone to be worked in a piece of buckskin in his palm and struck it with a cobble or the butt end of a length of antler.

31 Fundaburk and Foreman, 1957:116. In the grinding technique, the stone worker pecked and fractured the stone using a cobble of harder stone so that it gradually wore off the surface of the former. To refine the surface, the stoneworker used a grinding technique in which a harder stone was rubbed against the softer stone, wearing the softer stone and giving finer lines to the form and smoothing the surface. Finally, the object was polished to a high sheen using an abrader.

32 West, 1934:387-388. Mississippian men made a variety of carved effigy pipes, some in the shapes of animals, most predominantly the owl, bear and frog. The most distinctive and outstanding Mississippian effigy pipes, however, are the human effigy pipes.

33 Brose et al., 1985:104

34 Contemporary Southeastern Indians do not practice much stonework, except in the tourist demonstration villages. But in the past few decades, the Eastern Band of Cherokee in North Carolina have revived this art form. (Leftwich, 1970:119).

35 Witthoft, 1949:54-55.

36 Witthoft, 1949:47.

37 Cushing, 1894:100. Copper plates were usually cut into the outline of the figure or design intended for the finished product. Southeastern Indians, up to the present day, value bilateral symmetry in their designs.

38 Haberland, 1954:200.

39 Hamilton et al., 1974:5.

40 Haberland, 1964:199-200.

41 Hally et al., 1990.

42 Hudson, 1976:372-373.

43 The Creek people of Tuckabatchee owned a number of metal plates in the form of celts similar to those of the Southeastern Ceremonial Complex (Hudson, 1976:400). These plates were only brought out during the Green Corn Ceremony. They were taken to Oklahoma during Removal and have been, over the years, interred in the graves of beloved men and women (Howard, 1968:65-74).

44 Only remnants of Mississippian and early Historic Period baskets have been recovered, but these show good craftsmanship and design.

45 Choosing the right cane requires an intimate knowledge of cane and its growth patterns. Generally, basket-makers choose stalks of cane about two years old, the diameter of a thumb and with long, straight shafts between knots.

46 In recent years river cane has become scarce, forcing basket-makers to use substitutes such as white oak and honeysuckle. See Leftwich, 1970.

47 Mason, 1904:221-229. Basket making has two basic techniques – weaving and coiling. In recent years some Southeastern Indian women have begun making coiled baskets out of coiled pine needles or certain types of grasses.

48 Leftwich, 1970:30.

49 Speck, 1920:80.

50 Dixon and Domjanovich, 1992:41; Leftwich, 1970:29. Vegetable dyes are processed by first pulverizing the roots, bark or leaves in a mortar and pestle, and then mixing the powder with water and boiling it. Cane splints are placed in the boiling water and occasionally stirred to ensure an evenness of color.

51 Turnbaugh and Turnbaugh, 1986:102.

52 Leftwich, 1970:51; Turnbaugh and Turnbaugh, 1986:106.

53 Porter, 1990:84.

54 Porter, 1990:86. In the 1920s and 1930s Chitimacha, Choctaw, Creek and Cherokee women, although never having abandoned basketry altogether, began producing a variety of forms for the tourist trade.

55 Carr, 1897:401. These materials were pounded and separated and then hand-spun either with a hand spindle or by simply spinning the pieces together on the knee and pulling with the other hand. European eyewitness accounts from the 18th century also describe women using suspended, two-bar looms for producing broad pieces of cloth and as using finger-weaving for narrow sashes and belts (Dockstader, 1967:54, 61).

56 Carr, 1897:401. Animal hides were soaked, scraped and treated with pulverized animal brains to make them soft, supple and of a uniform, desired thickness.

57 The outstanding fashion era for the Historic Southeastern Indians occurred in the late-18th, early-19th centuries, just prior to Removal. At this time, Southeastern Indian men and women reckoned fashion and clothing as a true expression of aesthetics and national identity, combining colors, materials, and ornamentation in fancy wear to achieve an overall appearance of color, coordination and elegance to their costumes.

58 Wood, 1981:52.

59 Downs, 1979:38-40; Sturtevant, 1967:161.

60 Sturtevant, 1967:171.

61 Downs, 1979:34-35.

62 Seminole men's clothing until around 1930 consisted of knee-length big shirts, which were, in effect, knee-length dresses, and Seminole men usually went bare-legged until around 1930.

63 Medford, 1975:46.

64 Dockstader, 1978:57.

65 Goggins, 1967:173. Interestingly, the Western style motifs closely resemble prehistoric pottery

designs. It is uncertain whether these designs have been continual or were copied later.

66 Southeastern Ceremonial Complex falcon-men representations show men wearing feather capes in the form of falcon wings. A fragment of textile from the Spiro Mound in Oklahoma clearly has a wing design, but whether or not others were made of feathers is not known.

67 Part of the Mississippian ceremonial dress included feather headdresses with copper emblems. Feathers rarely preserve however.

68 Medford, 1975:42; Speck, 1951:39.

69 Speck, 1951:39-44, 94.

70 Gilliland, 1975:47-48.

71 Speck, 1951:1-13.

72 Speck, 1951:63.

73 Speck, 1951:24.

THE SOUTHWEST

The Southwest has no specific limits or definite boundaries but can be conceptualized as the states of Arizona and New Mexico in the United States and Sonora and parts of Chihuahua in Mexico. Small parts of Colorado, Texas, Utah and Sinaloa are included in the region. Spanning two modern nation states, this is yet one culture area, characterized by a common arid environment and a multi-cultural present that is the result of a multi-cultural past. Newcomers to the Southwest of European, African and Asian ancestry meet and mingle with Native Americans to produce a distinctive and rich society. While close to a hundred groups make up the Southwest, it is the Native Americans who give the region its distinctive flavor and who provide its cultural foundations. Unlike other regions of North America, over twenty-five Native American groups have survived the onslaught of European expansion and been able to remain on their traditional homelands with some complement of their distinctive customs as enclaved cultures. These groups represent almost three-quarters of the Native American cultures that inhabited the region at the time of the first Spanish explorations.

The Southwest as a region is rooted in the land and in ancient traditions. The land is varied – high rugged, snow capped mountains, fruitful river valleys, sweeping grasslands and arid deserts. The vast but often harsh landscape required many ecological adaptations. It also engendered a love of place that is so common among indigenous peoples. This love of place, the feeling of oneness with the land, conceptualized as Mother Earth, permeates Southwest Native American thought and culture as strongly today as it did 300 years ago. The land lives and all peoples respect her. Southwest Native Americans are of the land; they do not exploit it. It is this orientation that helps distinguish them for the descendants of European peoples.

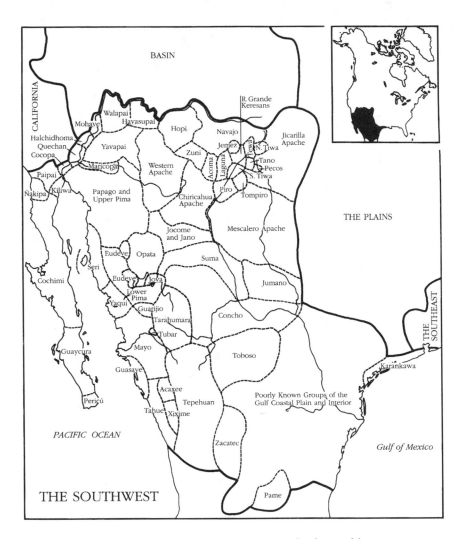

Map labels (clockwise / by region):

BASIN

CALIFORNIA

Walapai
Havasupai
Mohave
Hopi
Navajo
R. Grande Keresans
Jicarilla Apache
Halchidhoma
Quechan
Cocopa
Yavapai
Zuni
Jemez
N. Tiwa
Acoma
Laguna
Tano
Pecos
S. Tiwa
Paipai
Maricopa
Western Apache
Nakipa
Kiliwa
Papago and Upper Pima
Chiricahua Apache
Piro
Tompiro
THE PLAINS
Jocome and Jano
Mescalero Apache
Eudeve
Opata
Suma
Seri
Cochimi
Eudeve
Jova
Lower Pima
Yaqui
Guarijio
Jumano
THE SOUTHEAST
Guaycura
Tarahumara
Concho
Tubar
Mayo
Toboso
Guasave
Karankawa
Pericú
Acaxee
Tepehuan
Poorly Known Groups of the Gulf Coastal Plain and Interior
Tahue
Xixime
PACIFIC OCEAN
Zacatec
Gulf of Mexico
THE SOUTHWEST
Pame

ABOVE: *This map shows approximate territories of tribes and language groups at the earliest periods for which there is reliable evidence: the sixteenth century for the Pueblos (the groups from Hopi to the Piro to N. Tiwa), the seventeenth century for the extreme southwestern part of the area, and the eighteenth century for the Apache, Navajo and groups on the far northwest edge. After these dates, many tribes lost territory, some disappeared and a few gained territory.*

This does not mean that all Southwest Native Americans societies are alike, or that they are all homogeneous or never-changing. Each has a distinctive culture, one that is the result of a long historical development. All Southwest Native American cultures are independent, composed of dignified and self-reliant peoples who have wrested their living from local and regional resources. Their cultures today are a legacy of the past, the present and the future. In the Southwest, as nowhere else in North America, all that is vital in life remains as it was and as it will be.

Native Americans came to the Southwest at least 12,000 years ago. In these early times people were hunters and gatherers of wild plants. Following a nomadic way of life, they lived in small family groups and hunted first large game, like mammoths and bison, and later as the environment changed, small animals such as deer and rabbits. When this transition occurred it signaled a new adaptation and way of life and we have given them a new name, the Archaic or Desert peoples, in recognition of this change. These peoples, whose cultures emerged around 6000 BC, began to experiment with growing food around 2500–3000 BC.

Slowly the peoples of the Southwest developed distinctive cultures; those living in the mountainous regions are called the Mogollon, those on the Colorado Plateau, the Basketmakers and Anasazi, and those in the western and central parts of the region, the Patayan, Sinagua and Salado. (Unfortunately almost nothing is known about the prehistory of northwestern Mexico.) Each group became horticulturists growing corn, beans and squash supplemented by hunting and the gathering of wild foods. Each adapted in different ways to their special environments. Around 300 BC migrations brought new groups into the Southwest from Mexico. These individuals quickly developed a culture, known as Hohokam, that was based on agricultural traditions. Living in central and southern Arizona they built extensive irrigation systems, refined tools and monumental architecture. Each of the four groups centered around a geographical area – desert mountains and plateau. (Unfortunately almost nothing is known about the prehistoric groups living in Sonora either.) Except for those people who lived in areas that could not support agriculture, all these prehistoric peoples lived in permanent and semi-permanent villages. Some were so large and complex that they resembled small towns with extensive and complex organizations.

The fourteenth and fifteenth centuries were a time of great population movement which has not yet been explained. Following a large drought, old regions were abandoned, the largest trading centers no longer used. Groups aggregated and settlements were frequently abandoned. The main Southwestern groups who developed into the peoples we recognise in the Southwest today – the Puebloans, the O'Odham (Pima) and the Yumans – settled in what is now called their traditional homelands. Heralded in an extensive series of clan or migrations legends, each group has a rich oral history about this period. Other groups moved into the region from the north – the Navajo and the Apaches. From the east came Plains peoples who would trade with the native peoples. Occasionally groups from the Great Basin would meet with the settled peoples in the north and along the rivers. Harassed by drought again and the new roving tribes, groups such as the Anasazi moved on to mesa tops and east to the Rio Grande, but as a region, the Southwest was characterized by much interaction and cultural borrowing.

Finally came the Europeans, first the Spanish and later the English-American. The frontiers of the Spanish and English conquests of the New World met and overlapped in the arid Southwest. When the Spaniards arrived in the mid-sixteenth century, they found the entire region inhabited by numerous groups. Some of these peoples were town-dwelling farmers called Puebloans, others were seminomadic hunters and raiders; still others lived in small bands surviving by hunting and gathering. The peoples spoke a bewildering variety of languages and followed numerous ways of life. Yet all were similar in that they differed markedly from the level of political and economic organization the Spanish had encountered in central Mexico. Without the domination of agriculturally based empires like that of the Aztecs, peoples in the Southwest were politically independent and socially and economically self-sufficient farmers; all but a few hundred people on the coast of the Gulf of California and in the northern end of the Sierra Madres Mountains knew how to raise corn, beans and squash. While they differed on the extent to which agriculture was the primary mode of food production or a supplement to hunting and gathering, these peoples were quickly distinguished from the buffalo hunting peoples of the Plains to the east, from the seed-gatherers and rabbit-hunters of the north and the acorn-gatherers of California. Sporadic and small-scale trade in the form of surplus and luxury items was mutual rather than a matter of controlled tribute in food staples and people. No society maintained military or political control over another. This did not mean that groups did not form temporary alliances for warfare, but warfare was not conducted for conquest and subjugation. People fought for revenge or to gain new agricultural lands, displacing older inhabitants.

The Spanish quickly began to settle the Southwest but their advance was stopped by the Apache. Wherever they went, the Spanish established a conquest culture with programs designed to 'civilize the savages' and impose a new world view. Backed by military force and identifying civilization with specific Spanish customs, missionaries, soldiers and settlers introduced Castillian (which became the lingua franca of the region), detached houses placed around a central plaza, men's trousers, new concepts of time and work, the notions of empire, politics and Christianity. They also established a system of forced tribute, forced labor as servants, farm workers and miners, and extensive slave trade with peoples from all over the region sent to the silver mines in Mexico. They introduced some beneficial items as well – new foods and livestock, especially sheep and horses, and silversmithing. The Spanish and later Mexican policies of concentrating the small nomadic bands in Chihuahua led to the consolidation and extinction of many groups. These changes were so drastic in Mexico that some groups, like the Opata, could no longer be distinguished from the Spanish or Mexican population by the mid-1700s. Other groups welcomed these changes. To others they meant nothing; groups that were isolated because of geographical barriers, like the Seri and the Tarahumara, remained relatively untouched. Others reacted violently. Changes were enforced on the people so brutally that by 1680 the Pueblos were rising in revolt and successfully drove the Spanish from the Rio Grande region. While the Spanish eventually re-conquered the area, they never overcame the Apaches, the Tarahumara, the Upland Yumans or the Yaquis. It was not until the late 1880s that these groups ceased to be military threats and the final Mexican settlements occurred in northwestern Mexico. By this time, the Mexicans were interested in political and economic control, not in religious conversion. Thus groups were not forced to change and it was individuals who assimilated. Many individuals voluntarily left their native communities to find work in Mexican towns.

Anglo-Americans took over the northern half of New Spain from the Mexican government in 1848. With their settlement of the region they, like the Mexican government in the south, erected great obstacles to the retention of the old way of life for Native Americans. The most important of these was the imposition of the reservation system which isolated groups on sections of their traditional homelands and policies of forced assimila-

ABOVE: *Lieta, a Pima woman, from the Gila River Reservation, Sacaton, Arizona, 1902. She exhibits a style of face painting obsolete by this time but which was reconstructed for the photograph.*

tion. Native Americans were provided with agricultural technology and sent to schools far from their families. As dependent nations, these groups were given new forms of government – constitutional tribal governments that exercise inherent and sovereign powers but are limited by treaties, statutes and agreements with the federal and state governments. They were placed in a dependency role, had a set of values superimposed with no consideration of their desires. Paternalism has meant that economic development and self-determinancy were limited, but it has not meant that any groups have died out because of government policies.

Changes in economic possibilities have also meant many changes in Native American life. The destruction of the traditional subsistence strategies and new trading patterns pulled Southwest Native Americans into the nation-state's market economy. Craft objects, formerly created for home use and minor trading of surplus goods by barter, began to be produced as supplemental or major sources of income. Craft production became important in the economic strategies of many families, even though there was a low hourly return for the labor involved. Weaving, basketry, painting, silversmithing and pottery allowed economic flexibility. People also began working for wages, on farms, on the railroad, in mines as well as in the cities.

While European groups became politically dominant, brought hardship and deprivation, had the force of laws and military might to make the old ways of life impossible, they did not eradicate all cultures. This does not mean that there were not demographic changes; many epidemic diseases raged through the Southwest and took their toll. For example, in 1883 half of the population at Hopi died from smallpox and in the 1918 influenza pandemic over half of the Jicarilla Apache and close to one quarter of the Navajo died. Since the 1920s, however, the populations have slowly and steadily increased. Other Native American groups were destroyed through internal warfare – such as the Halcidoma. But more than any other region in North America, the Native peoples have remained. They have changed, of course. There is a misconception that since Native Americans no longer follow a 'pure' aboriginal culture (i.e. one 'uncontaminated' by Europeans) they no longer exist. This is not true. Native American cultures in the Southwest are vital and vibrant. Native peoples co-exist as part of the culture of the Greater Southwest and as distinctive members with unique ways of life. They are still rooted in the past and in the land. Based on earlier lifestyles, joint ancestry, ecological adaptation, economies and linguistic

ABOVE: *Apache hunters, one in knitted socks probably issued by the Army. Note the typical Apache costume of headband and high mocassins. The arrows are much longer than those of the Plains Indians.*

affiliation, we can define four basic groups of Native Americans living in the Southwest. The following pages look at the groups of the Southwest who existed in the 1600s and have survived into the present. For the core has persisted and groups – the Puebloans, the rancheria peoples, the band peoples and the hunters and gatherers – remain distinct.

In northern New Mexico and Arizona, on the Colorado Plateau and along the Rio Grande River and its tributaries, the Puebloan peoples were most in evidence – numbering over 40,000 individuals – living in ninety villages. Today there are only thirty; the others have been abandoned because of drought, disease and warfare. Called Pueblo Indians by the early Spanish explorers because of their distinctive architecture – permanent, compact, multi-chambered houses made of stone and adobe – these peoples were the descendants of the Anasazi and Mogollon peoples. Pueblo means 'village dweller' and this designation accurately reflected Pueblo life. The Pueblo Indians did not constitute a tribe; each Puebloan culture was a village that functioned as an autonomous political entity. This does not mean that these groups lived in a vacuum. They traded with one another, recognized common ancestry, occasionally intermarried and shared many similar values and world views.

The Puebloan peoples speak many different languages. The largest language group is *Tanoan*, part of the Kiowa-Tanoan language family. Tanoan consists of three main languages – *Tiwa, Tewa* and *Towa*. The people of Taos, Picuris, Sandia and Isleta speak dialects of Tiwa. At San Juan, Santa Clara, San Ildefonso, Pojoaque, Nambe and Tesuque, Tewa is spoken. Tewa is also spoken at Hano in Hopi country because many Tewa families migrated from the Rio Grande valley about 1700 following the re-conquest of the area after the Pueblo Revolt. Jemez is the only pueblo today in which Towa can be heard. In the past the inhabitants of the famous pueblo of Pecos were also Towa speakers but the village was abandoned in the early 1800s.

Living dispersed among the Tanoan speakers are the *Keresans*. Along the Rio Grande and its tributaries are the Keresan villages of Cochiti, Santo Domingo, San Felipe, Santa Ana and Zia; farther west are Laguna and Acoma. Even farther west is the pueblo of Zuni where *Zunian* is spoken. Zuni is part of the Penutian linguistic stock and is unrelated to other languages in the Southwest. (Other Penutian speakers live in California.) Finally there are the Hopi in northcentral Arizona. Hopi consists of a series of villages located on three mesas on the Colorado Plateau. *Hopi* is a

ABOVE: *A Navajo war captain wearing a war hat of tanned leather and carrying a lance and rawhide shield. This photograph was taken near Keam's Canyon on the Navajo reservation, 1892–3.*

74

language that belongs to the Shoshonean branch of the Uto-Aztecan language family. Thus Hopi is related to Piman, Ute and Paiute in the Southwest and many language groups in central Mexico.

The Pueblos are divided into two main subgroups based on location and ecological adaptation. The Eastern Pueblos (Tanoan and Keresan speakers), who live on the Rio Grande and its tributaries, have a permanent water source enabling them to practice irrigation agriculture. The Western Pueblos (Hopi, Hopi-Tewa, Zuni, Acoma and Laguna), lacking a steady supply of water, rely on dry farming. The difference in water supply affects many aspects of culture from food procurement to religion. Economically all Puebloans are agriculturalists. Many also raise small herds of sheep and cattle, produce art – such as weaving, silversmithing, jewelry, katchina dolls, pottery and baskets. (Most Pueblo Indians, like everyone else in the Southwest, are wage earners today. This means that many must live off their land or move to the large nearby cities of Albuquerque, Santa Fe, Gallup, Flagstaff and Phoenix. All return home for important ceremonies.)

With the Pueblo Indians religion transcends and permeates all aspects of life, including interaction patterns with the land, with other peoples and with the supernaturals. All aspects of Puebloan life – arts, crafts, economics, social structure and the family – are inextricably interwoven and integrated under a single world view. From the simple tenet that people must live in harmony with nature, the Pueblo Indians have developed rich cultural traditions that are expressed in poetry, legends, song, dance and art. In this way central values are given outward expression. For example, many of the designs on pottery are derived from motifs connected with ceremonial life. Architecturally the center of a village, both physically and symbolically, is a special chamber called *kivas*. Here private and communal rites are performed daily and at appropriate times throughout the year. Prayers are given for blessing and to ensure the germination and maturation of crops and to give thanks for good health. Through religion all else is given significance.

Secular and ecclesiastical authority are sharply delimited in the pueblos. Each village is a tightly and highly structured theocracy, organized around an elaborate ceremonial life. Based on their ancient patterns, this theocracy, whose head is called the *cacique*, is kept secret within the village. To the outside world the secular political structure is more evident. In the eastern Pueblos, the secular organization is in the hands of a *governor* who is appointed or elected each year. These governors were given canes of office

ABOVE: *War captain and chief hunter of the Pueblo of Nambe, New Mexico, 1880. He wears a bear claw necklace, a powder horn and pouch. His blanket of rabbit skin predates the use of woollen blankets.*

by President Lincoln in the 1860s and these have become valued symbols of office. The governor has several assistants called *principales*, a group of elder statesmen whose lifelong experience enables them to integrate wisely civil and religious matters. In all the pueblos there is a hunt chief and a war chief or war priest.

Tewa pueblos are composed of two social divisions, what anthropologists call moieties. Membership in a moiety is through the father, though a woman may change her moiety affiliation if she marries a man of the opposite group. Each moiety has political officers. During half of the year, the governmental and ceremonial duties of the pueblos are in the hands of the Summer People, while the Winter People (the other moiety) are in charge of obligations for the other half-year. Within each moiety there are certain religious societies, but other societies cross-cut and meld the kinship divisions. Among the Keresan peoples, social organization is more unified. There is but one cacique per village and he is aided by a council composed of the heads of religious societies who all serve for life.

In all the pueblos the family is the cornerstone of life. While in the Tewa communities the extended family of either the father or mother is emphasized, at Zuni and Hopi it is the mother's that serves as the basis for the society. Puebloans, when compared to other groups in the Southwest, are non-individualistic and innovations are accepted or rejected by group decision, by consensus and persuasion. While all Puebloan peoples share many common values, ideas and traditions, each is distinct. A Pueblo village is closely united and a highly systematized organization. Each village favors marriage within its own group. There are variations in the ceremonies of each group, and the pottery and stylistic designs are distinctive. Good examples of such outstanding pottery and stylistic designs one Puebloan group – the Zuni.

At the time of Spanish contact, the rancheria groups – the Cahitans, Tarahumarans, Pimans and Yumans – comprised the largest subgroup in the Southwest, over 150,000 individuals or approximately three-quarters of the peoples in the Southwest. They lived in widely spaced settlements along rivers or in well-watered mountain and desert areas in southern Arizona and northern Mexico. Relying on irrigation and flood waters, rancheria peoples were farmers. The extended family, rather than the village, formed the basic social unit; each family owned a house and fields dispersed along the river as much as half a mile apart. Kinship was generally bilateral or patrilineal. Nevertheless, the members of each settlement still thought of themselves as a community, moved as a unit, and symbolized their unity by placing a community house in the center of each settlement. Rancheria peoples frequently had more than one village, shifting from one settlement to another depending on the season of the year. All rancheria peoples are very interested in social gatherings, disdaining structured situations and displays of wealth, however. They are sensitive to the maintenance of form and custom in social intercourse. While this meant there has been a weak development of religious leadership – the important religious leaders were shamans rather than priests, and political leaders were senior men who were influential speakers – there is a respect for all who have knowledge and wisdom. This has led to a highly developed native literature in myth, song, folk stories and formalized oratory. Among the most famous for these skills are the Huichol.

The rancheria groups belong to two basic linguistic groups – the Uto-Aztecan and the Hokan. The Uto-Aztecans rancheria speakers can be divided into four basic language groups: Pima, Cahita, Opatan and Tarahumaran. The Pimans live in southern Arizona – Upper Piman, Tohono O'Odham, Sobaipuri – and in Mexico – the Pima Bajo and Tepehuan. The Cahitan speakers (the Mayo and Yaqui), the Opatan speakers (the Opata, Eudebe and Jova), and the Tarahumaran speakers (the Tarahumara, Warihio and Concho) live in Mexico in mountainous areas and along major rivers. The Hokan speakers live in Arizona and upper Baja California and are known as the Yumans. The Upper Yumans – the Walapai, Yavapai and Havasupai – live in the upland region of western and northern Arizona while the lowland Yumans – the Mohave, Halchidoma, Yuma, Cocomaricopa, Cocopa and Cochimi – live along the Colorado River and its tributaries. Moving constantly because of intertribal warfare, some Yuman groups all but killed each other off by the early nineteenth century. The Maricopa eventually moved in with the River Pima in the area around Phoenix because they had been displaced from the Colorado River.

In Mexico the mountain-dwelling Tarahumara are well-known. Living in shelters ranging from caves in rugged cliffs to stone masonry houses, they planted small cornfields in mountain valleys in the summer and retreated to the lowlands in the winter. Like other rancheria groups the Tarahumara also utilized wild plant foods. Only recently have the Tarahumara been affected by the outside world: the first railroad into their region did not exist even as recently as ten years ago.

On the plains and lower valleys to the west live groups like the Huichol, the Mayo, and the Yaqui at the mouth of major river systems, some of the richest farmland in all of Mexico. Favorable agricultural conditions permitted more concentrated settlements than the mountainous and desert regions and the Yaqui and Mayo developed tribal organizations for warfare and defensive purposes. So successful were the Yaqui that they were the only group in the region who were not conquered by the Spanish. Interestingly, the Yaqui were also the only group to request missionaries and voluntarily to become Christians. However, they changed much of the ritual and the meanings and developed what is essentially a new religion, Sonoran Catholicism. This is a mixture of Spanish, Mexican and traditional beliefs and customs. The central ritual is the Eastern ceremony that lasts for forty days, culminating with the destruction of evil by good in a mock battle the day before Easter Sunday. This ritual, like many others still conducted by Southwestern groups, is done to ensure that the world will continue.

The Yaquis have another distinction in the Southwest. After years of warfare they were finally defeated by the Mexicans who occupied their territory in the late 1880s. At conquest the Mexicans deported most of the people to the Yucatan peninsula to work in forced labor camps. Some of these individuals escaped and came to the United States, building several communities in southern Arizona. The Yaquis sought and were given political refugee status and allowed to stay, even after the Yaquis, were allowed to return to their homeland in the mid-1920s. One of the reasons they were given political asylum was because of their distinctive religious ceremonies.

Farther north were the O'Odham (Pima) peoples who lived in more compact settlements than the Tarahumara. The Pima have a long history which reaches back into the archaeological past of southern Arizona and northern Mexico. The Pima word for themselves is *O'Odham*, meaning The People. The Pimas can be divided into four basic groups – the River Pima who live along the rivers in central Arizona, the Tohono O'Odham (formerly called the Papago), the Pima Bajo who live in Mexico, and the Sobaipuri who lived in southeastern Arizona and were driven out by the Apache and Spanish. The survivors of this group have intermingled with the other Piman groups. All Piman groups were agriculturalists; in fact, the River Pimans were so successful that they supplied much of the food for the U.S. Army during the Western campaigns of the Civil War and for Anglo-American settlers moving to California during the Gold Rush of the 1860s. The River Pimans also served in the Civil War as the only Union forces in the Arizona territory; they successfully defeated Confederate troops and kept the lines to California open. After the war they served as scouts in the Apache wars. The River Pimans remained prosperous until Anglo settlers in the town of Florence, upriver from them, appropriated their water thereby making agriculture no longer possible. The river ran dry at planting time and many people starved. Unfortunately it took the U.S. Congress until 1924 to recognize that their rights have been ignored and allot them water when the Coolidge Dam was built. It took many more years for the Pima to recover economically and socially. The Pima refer to this period as the 'Forty Years of Famine'.

Along the Colorado River lived another group of rancheria peoples, the Yumans. Like the Cahitans they had a permanent water supply and hence could have more densely settled homesteads. They also were organized as a tribe for warfare and had a strong tribal sense of identity. In civil matters, however, the local group made decisions. As groups also they relied more heavily on wild plants for their houses, clothes and food supplements than the Cahitans and their material culture was more like that of the Pimans and their neighbors to the west in California. The River Yumans were tied closely to the annual cycle of river flooding. Since their homes were periodically washed away, they had no cultural incentive for the accumulation of wealth. Even today, the Cocopa, for example, disdain ostentatious displays of wealth. A person's goods are destroyed at his or her death. Even the goods of relatives and friends are placed in the burial fire at death and again in the anniversary festival, the most important religious ceremony. In the Historic Period the River Yumans were joined by a group from central California, the Chemuehevi, who have adopted a lifestyle similar to that of the Mohave.

A final group of Yumans, the Upland Yumans, can be placed either with the rancheria peoples or the non-agricultural peoples because their homelands lacked enough water for permanent farming. The Upland Yumans – the Walapai, Yavapai and the Havasupai – lived primarily by hunting and gathering on the upland areas of western and northern Arizona. Living a lifestyle that was similar to other hunting and gathering peoples, the Walapai had a limited technological base and lived in small groups that moved often in an established round. The Havasupai lived on the Colorado River in Cataract Canyon, next to the Grand Canyon, and have adopted many Hopi traits. The Upland Yumans had little interaction with the Spanish and Mexicans except for meeting an occasional explorer searching for minerals. Today the Yavapai and Walapai live on small reservations and herd cattle or work for wages. Through extensive intermarriage and because of their forced internment on Apache reservations many Yavapai have become intermingled culturally with the Western Apache. By 1900 the Yavapai began to drift off the San Carlos Reservation and return to their traditional homelands in areas that had not been claimed by Anglo-American miners.

Everyone has heard of the Apaches yet few know much about them except for stereotypes, the 'warlike raiders and marauders' of so many movies. But this is a one-sided view. While the Apacheans were fierce raiders and were feared with good reason, they also had and have rich cultures that have remained unexplored. The Southern Athapascans or Apacheans were newcomers to the Southwest, arriving just before European contact. Related to other Athapascan-speakers in the North, most Apacheans lived in small units based on extended families and followed a semi-nomadic existence; their residences were temporary and seasonal. Local groups composed of several matrifocal extended families formed bands, the largest level of political organization. There were no tribes, as conceptualized by Hollywood producers and writers of pulp fiction. Today each group refers to themselves as a nation, however.

The Apaches can be divided geographically into eastern and western groups. In the east are the Jicarilla, Mescalero, Lipan (forming, in fact, a Southern Plains group), and Chiricahua Apaches; in the west are the White Mountain, Carrizo, San Carlos, Fort Apache, Pinal, Arivaipa, Apache Peaks, Mazatzal, Tonto and Cibecue bands who together are referred to as the Western Apache, and the Navajo. All share a basic world view, religious orientation and mythological cycle. Ceremonies are given to cure illness, to set the world right and to ward off possible evils. All groups are matrilineal and have elaborate and important puberty ceremonies for girls. In the Mescalero ceremony, for example, the family constructs a large, brush tipi or wickiup in which the girls dance to a series of ritual songs. This ceremony is under the direction of a shaman or medicine man, called a singer. In the second part of the ceremony, called the Sun Greeting, the girl is introduced as an adult following a period of fasting and instruction by elders.

The Athapascan-speaking peoples were the last major Native American group to come to the Southwest and the last major group to be brought under Anglo-American political control. Originally natives of northwest

81

Canada and Alaska, the Athapascans moved into the Southwest during the late 1300s-early 1400s, right before the arrival of the Spanish. By 1600 there were probably 15,000 Apaches in the Southwest. When they arrived as small bands of migrating peoples, they were undifferentiated. The groups quickly spread into the areas around the Pueblo villages and claimed areas as their traditional homes with identified sacred locales. Some groups mingled with Plains tribes – the Lipan Apache moved into west Texas and displaced the Comanches; the Mescalero and Chiricahua Apache moved into the area east of the Rio Grande Valley; the Jicarilla and Navajo moved into the northern part of New Mexico while the Western and other Chiricahua Apache moved into the old Western Anasazi and Mogollon homeland.

Apacheans lived by hunting and gathering. When they reached the Southwest they added to this economic base raiding and agriculture. All quickly acquired either Plains, Puebloan or rancheria customs as well as a reputation for fierceness. They also readily took to the horse. Much of the history of the Southwest revolves around Apache raids for goods and Puebloan, Piman, Spanish and Anglo-American retaliation and counter-raiding. By AD 1700 much of the Southwest was an armed camp with fluctuating alliances based on economic expediency. The Jicarilla Apaches were united with the Spaniards in their wars against the French and the Pawnee. Joining the Jicarilla were the Utes and the Tewa, especially the people of Taos, to fight the Comanche and Kiowa of the Plains. Other Apaches raided Pueblo villages to such an extent that the Pueblo communities moved to high defensible ground; many Piman communities had stockades and permanent guards. Other Apache groups raided into Mexico to such an extent that entire areas were abandoned. Because of retaliation and these economic patterns, the Apaches, in turn, lived in protected highlands, canyons and mountain valleys. They kept small communities that could be moved quickly and the situation remained thus for over 200 years until the last Apache group was defeated in the mid-1880s.

Apachean raiding was not done by a tribe but by local groups. This pattern can be loosely equated with guerilla warfare. The goal was not to kill; in fact, Apache men gained no status from killing and never took scalps. They gained status from successfully bringing back food and horses to their families. The object was to avoid encounters with the enemy. Those who led raids were men who felt the possessions in the encampment were in short supply. Apache tribes had no recognized leaders; bands and local groups did. These influential men and women had prestige because of their wealth, their abilities and personal influence. The Apacheans made a sharp distinction behaviorally between raids and warfare. A war party was formed to avenge an Apache casuality, led by a relative of the slain individual. In general, Apache attitudes toward warfare contrasted sharply with those of Plains groups; there were no warrior societies and there was no enthusiasm for standing ground in a hopeless situation or counting coup. Legendary figures like Geronimo, Naiche or Cochise became famous because of their ability to elude the U.S. cavalry. The ascendancy of tribal leaders occurred only after Anglo-American political institutions were introduced.

Some Apachean groups practiced very little agriculture and lived almost like Plains groups. The Jicarilla Apache (from the Spanish word for little basket weaver) lived in the northern part of New Mexico and the Mescalero (gatherer of agave) lived in the south-central part of the state. Both groups ranged on to the Plains and hence have many cultural traits that reflect contacts with groups in Texas. For example, the Jicarilla and the Mescalero traditionally lived in tipis. (Other Apaches, who lived in forested mountain dells, built shelters of brush, called wickiups.) After a defeat by Kit Carson and the U.S. Army in 1868 the Jicarilla were placed on a reservation with the Mescalero, but the two groups constantly fought and the Jicarilla were given their own reservation, in their traditional homeland, in 1887.

The San Carlos Apache began herding in 1884 when the U.S. Government issued live cattle for beef rations. Men became cattlemen while women supplemented the family income by gathering wild foods and producing baskets for sale. As often happened, parts of the reservation held excellent grazing land and Anglo ranchers quickly began to encroach. By the late 1890s the Anglo-owned Chiricahua Cattle Company quietly obtained through its influence with the army permission to graze a herd of 2,000 head at Ash Flats. Other Anglo ranchers encroached illegally on San Carlos land and shot Apache cattle. By 1900 the situation was critical, a range war was imminent and the army was called in. However, it was not for another ten years that the situation was brought until control.

With the end of their traditional economies based on raiding and hunting, all Apache groups developed a flexible economy in the twentieth century partly based on livestock – cattle and sheep.

The Navajo call themselves the Dineh – 'The People'. The word Navajo is a Tewa term 'Navahuu' which means cultivated field in an arroyo. The Pueblos and early Spanish chroniclers of the early seventeenth century distinguished the Navajo from other Apaches living west and south of the Rio Grande because they were 'very great farmers'. This success in agriculture was also noted by U.S. Army reports 150 years later. Today we think of the Navajo as sheep herders and weavers but this did not happen until after they became agriculturalists. Like other Apacheans the Navajo raided Spanish and Puebloan settlements for sheep and horses. They quickly developed an economy and life that was based on herding, agriculture and raiding and because of this they led a semi-nomadic life.

When the United States Government annexed Navajo territory in 1849, the Navajo were feared as a warring, raiding group of bands. They were not organized into a tribe – each community and kin group was independent. For many years the government tried to stop the raids in order to allow settlement by Anglo and Mexican ranchers, but the constant raids on Navajo families by slave traders who wanted to ensure that the territory was in a constant state of flux to make capturing Navajo easier meant that warfare continued.

During the Civil War, the U.S. Government wanted to keep New Mexico and Arizona territories in the Union and ensure that the lines of communication to California remained open. To do this they felt they had to stop Apachean raids, particularly that of the Mescalero Apache and the Navajo. The campaign against the Mescalero lasted five months in 1862. The Mescalero were moved to a new military post on the Pecos River called Fort Sumner (or Bosque Redondo). The location on the edge of the Great Plains lacked firewood, good drinking water and arable land.

In 1863 Colonel Kit Carson was commissioned by General Carleton to round up The People and move them to the new military reservation in east-central New Mexico. The military sent out peace negotiations to a few bands and local leaders telling them to move; if they refused, the general orders were to remove them forcefully. Most of the Navajo who lived in widely scattered local groups never heard the ultimatum and General Carleton made no attempt to locate them. Instead he sent Carson to destroy the Navajo economic base. Joined by Utes and Pueblos and New Mexican irregulars, Carson undertook a scorched earth policy that destroyed cornfields and orchards, hogans, water holes and livestock. Over a thousand of The People were killed, wounded or captured. The Navajo had nowhere to hide and little to eat; they surrendered in 1864.

By 1864 over 8,000 Navajo had surrendered and begun the Long Walk, one of the bleakest events in Navajo history. Over ten per cent of the captives died on the way to Fort Sumner. The journey was one of hardship and terror. There were no wagons; people walked over 300 miles. People were shot if they complained of being tired or sick; women in labor were killed.

Not all the Navajo went on the Long Walk. Many were sold into slavery or hid in inaccessible locations like the Grand Canyon or moved in with other groups. Those who lived at Fort Sumner recounted their experience as a time of despair and deprivation. Army arrangements were inadequate; there was little food and no blankets. Shelter was inadequate also, epidemic disease rampant. Confined with their traditional enemies the Mescalero Apache, tempers flared and disputes were common. Droughts and poor agricultural land doomed the reservation to failure. The horror of the Long Walk and the imprisonment at Fort Sumner remained pivotal events in the history and consciousness of The People.

When the Navajo were allowed to return to their homeland five years later they quickly re-established their way of life as herders and horticulturalists. They did no more raiding; instead they developed new economic pursuits – craft production and wage labor. In crafts the Navajo are famous as weavers and silversmiths. The tribe prospered and grew so that today they are the most populous group in North America and all cannnot live on the land. Unfortunately, sheep and horses became so prevalent that the fragile land became overgrazed. By the 1930s the land could no longer support the livestock and the federal government ordered the stocks to be reduced, a tragedy for the Navajo.

Navajo ceremonies, like other Apachean ceremonies, are performed not calendrically but when necessary to restore health and secure blessings in order to ensure survival. In the Navajo universe there are two classes of people – Earth People (or human beings) and Holy People (supernatural beings who are holy, powerful and mysterious). The Navajo believe that the universe functions according to certain rules that both they and the Holy People must follow. If these rules are followed there will be safety, plenty and a world that is harmonious and beautiful. If rules are not, if disease and accidental injury affect an individual, ceremonies are held in which the Holy People are asked to restore the delicate balance of the universe. In these ceremonies, which are very complicated and intricate, sandpaintings are made and prayers recited. Sandpaintings are impermanent paintings made of dried pulverized materials that depicted the Holy People and serve as a temporary altar. Over 800 forms of sandpaintings exist, each connected to a specific chant and ceremony. Sandpaintings are made inside the hogan; the hogan was considered to be the center of family life.

There are a few tribes who live in extremely marginal environments and on the fringes of the Southwest culture area who never developed agricultural ways of life. In the north, these included isolated groups who lived near the arid Great Basin – the Utes and the Paiutes, in the region – some of the Shoshonean speakers who moved from California to become farmers along the Colorado River, the Upland Yumans (already mentioned), in the south the Chemehuevi and a group of Sand Papago, a subgroup of the Tohono O'Odham already discussed, the Seri and groups living in Baja California. There were never more than a few thousand people who existed at this level of economic development. The most well-known are the Seri.

Producing none of their own food and following a nomadic and semi-nomadic lifestyle, these groups lived in small bilateral bands. Moving often, they possessed small inventories of material cultures, living off the land for all their needs. For example, the Seri, the smallest group in the Southwest, relied heavily on marine products as did groups in Baja California. They also hunted deer and rabbits, and gathered the abundant cacti fruits, greens and seaweed seeds of the desert coast and adjacent islands. Even today these groups eke out a poverty-level living by fishing and turtle hunting on the desert shores of Baja California.

In anthropology it is usual to discuss the Utes and their relatives the Paiutes in the Great Basin and Plains culture areas. Both of these groups speak a Uto-Aztecan language of the Shoshonean stock and were thus in the distant past related to the Hopis.

These groups were so isolated and few in number that they were affected very little by Spanish expansion. It was only in the mid-1800s and later that European incursions changed their ways of life.

These four basic cultural groups of the Greater Southwest can be recognized in modified form today. Even after three hundred years of European contact, three-quarters of the groups have managed to preserve a sense of individual cultural identity and a feeling for the land that is recorded in rich oral traditions. Indian groups have not, however, completely retained their pre-contact cultures, nor have they reacted uniformly to the attempts of Hispanic, Mexican and Anglo-American societies to assimilate them. All exist as part of either the Anglo-American or the Mexican socio-economic system and incorporate a mixture of traditional customs and European patterns. Thus, while they are distinct cultures, they are no longer separate societies. They maintain their ethnic identities in various ways, such as producing distinctive forms of art and retaining feelings about, and interaction patterns with, their environment. It is this sense of continuity with the land that has helped them survive years of subjugation to conquest cultures. Zunis, for example, say that Anglo-Americans and Mexican-Americans have no respect for the land and abuse it rather than work with it.

Southwest Native Americans have retained 'identity systems that have as an important element the symbol of roots in the land – supernaturally sanctioned, ancient roots, regarded as unchangeable', according to noted Southwesternist Edward Spicer. Such a perspective provides these groups with strong mythological sanctions for their residence, their right to live in the Southwest and their views of the land. The land is not something that can be controlled and changed; it is something of which all human beings are a part.

American Indian thought is integrative and comprehensive. It does not separate intellectual, moral, emotional, aesthetic, economic and other activities, motivations and functions. Beauty is in the nature of things as well as in people, and it is the natural state of affairs. The land is beautiful by definition because the supernatural beings designed it to be a beautiful harmonious, happy and healthy place. For beauty to be maintained the Navajo, for example, feel it must be expressed in actions such as the creation of art or conservation. The land supports life, it is beautiful because of this and must be preserved. Housing and village layout reflect the visions of the land and the universe.

Native Americans face many challenges. They live both on isolated reservations and in cities, for they are members of and must survive in two worlds. While European expansion has transformed much of Native American life it has done so unevenly and differentially. But never completely. Native Americans today are struggling for economic and political independence – self-determinancy in a situation where they face poverty like other rural poor. It is a paradox that once self-sustaining and healthy populations find themselves living under poor conditions in a land of plenty. But Southwest Native Americans will adapt, as they have done in the past for the core of their lives, their relationship to the land, has been preserved. No culture is static, even though we tend to portray indigenous peoples as homogeneous and frozen in time and space. But Southwest Native Americans do not regard themselves as deprived members of society. They retain a strong sense of who they are and their special place in the multi-cultural Southwest. They recognize that they have much to offer others if these others will but listen. This rich exchange will continue into the future.

MYTHS AND LEGENDS

Myths and legends have played, and continue to play, an extremely important role in the lives of the Native Americans of the Southwest.[1] People say the myths have been, and still are, a reflection of their culture, presenting an enduring system of values on which they continue to base their lives. Some regard the myths as a complete source of learning, and although the myths have their pragmatic or serious side, many are also a source of entertainment. Told by elders on long winter nights,[2] they can produce awe or wonder, amusement or terror. Though the stories are often for the benefit of children, any adults present listen too.

Today the myths are a basis of learning and are integral to Southwestern ceremonial life.[3] The practice of sandpainting, which the Navajo are famed for, has no ceremonial meaning unless accompanied by a recitation of the appropriate myth. Myths affect normal, everyday life too: when Morris Opler recorded Jicarilla Apache myths in the 1930s, he noted that bad behavior was explained by saying, 'He doesn't know any better. The poor fellow never had a grandfather to give him the stories.'[4] Children were taught obedience by telling them a tale which showed them the consequence of their bad behavior, and adults continue to regard such stories as a source of moral guidance. Similarly, many Hopi stories praise the work ethic, which is a central component of their culture, or they demonstrate the terrible consequences which can occur because of dissension and loss of respect for the elders of the tribe.

The oral tradition of myth-telling has meant that although legends have preserved their form across long periods of time, several versions of the same tale can exist. Cottie Burland, writing about Navajo myths in the 1960s, suggested that the storytellers may have felt inspired to make alterations where they felt clarification was needed. The cultural dynamic is also seen in the alteration of traditional tales to include modern influences and objects.[5]

The survival of so many myths and legends today is a testament to cultural resilience in the face of over 400 years of active onslaught. Indeed, the myths have played a major role in keeping the culture alive. Between the suppression of native religion and the punishment of its leaders by Spanish colonials and the eventual extension of religious freedom to Native Americans in 1934, the myths were a link which provided a fundamental expression of native spiritual belief. Today they form the basis of inspiration for the economically vital production of arts and crafts which are sold to tourists.

In the Southwest the ceremonies and rituals performed today are the same or similar to those performed for centuries, and are done by the same cults, clans and societies. Although the Roman Catholic Church is an important spiritual force, native beliefs still provide the vital basis of people's spirituality.

ORIGIN MYTHS

The emergence myths are the most sacred and the most secret to many of the Southwestern peoples. A general emergence myth might be told to children, while the real story may only be revealed when a person is initiated into the *kiva*.[6] As a result, traditional religious leaders are opposed to the origin myths being recorded. The Tiwa people at Isleta pueblo have been brought up in the knowledge that telling the sacred stories to strangers shortens their lives. Among the Cochiti it is taboo to tell whites the stories even if they are accepted and valued as friends. This secrecy surrounding the origin myths is for several reasons. The Navajo regard their origin myths as having great power: the telling can heal the sick, initiate an aspirant to religious experience and unite people with nature. The Hopi insist details of individual clan origins, as revealed in the origin cycle of stories, are secret and are the property of the clan concerned. This secrecy is respected and regarded as a source of strength. In the past, confidences have been exposed in books by scholars and this led to even greater reluctance to divulge them.

■ Multiple Worlds

The origin myths are the longest and most complicated of the legends.

90

Both the Navajo and the Hopi tell of the existence of several worlds. To the Hopi the present world is the fourth, while to the Navajo it is the fifth.[7] Their worlds are stacked like plates, floating one above the other, and the emergence involves climbing from one to the next. Similarly, in the Zuni creation myth the people travel through four underground cave-wombs before emerging to the Upper World of Knowledge and Seeing. The idea that the preceding worlds were too small or became flooded or contaminated by witchcraft is a common thread. The move to the next world is usually essential and often in the form of an escape. The Navajo stack four mountains on top of each other[8] and then plant a reed which they climb up to get from the third world, which had flooded, to the fourth.

■ The Creators

The worlds themselves are usually made by a Creator who wishes them into existence, or makes them using substances from their own body. In a Papago myth the Earthmaker, or Earthdoctor, creates the world from sweat and dust rubbed from his skin. He and other creators also use this recipe for making humans. Among the Navajo, *Estanatlehi,* or Changing Woman, creates people using corn dust and water mixed with skin from her breasts. In Pima legend the Magician, or Man Maker, decides to make humans of clay and builds an oven; however, Coyote interferes, first telling Man Maker that the people are ready prematurely (whites) and then persuading him to leave them in the oven too long (blacks). White people and black people are made and put overseas before Man Maker gets it right and creates the Pima.

Explanations for the existence of whites occur in other myths. In Navajo myth they are sent along with war and pestilence by *Atse Hastiin* and *Atse Asdzan,* or First Man and First Woman, who are jealous of Navajo prosperity. In the Yaqui creation myth, the *Surems,* little people who hate noise and violence, are told of the coming of the whites. Given a choice between going away and staying to face the future, some of the *Surems* go, but the ones who stay grow tall and strong and eventually become the Yaqui and fight off the whites when they arrive.

People who have been created invariably need to be taught how to do things. The Apachi deity *Usen,* after creating the people, teaches them how to find herbs to make medicine when they become ill. *Montezuma,* creator of the Papago, teaches the people to hunt and to grow maize. The original creator of the world or the people often disappears and this led to them

91

being named Vanishing Creators by Ruth Underhill.[9]

The most common reason for the destruction of past worlds and peoples is that they have been bad. In Navajo myth, First Man and First Woman send monsters to destroy people who anger them by claiming that happiness is their own creation. In Papago legend the first people quarrel with Montezuma who creates a new human race which destroys the first. An Apache tale tells how misbehaving people are destroyed by a flood, as does Pima legend too.

ALL-POWERFUL SPIRITS

The most powerful spirits are often shared by several cultural groups, and have similar names and characteristics. There are numerous spirits of nature, such as Rainbow Maiden and the spirits Thunder and Hail who control nature. In addition there are several notable spirits who are supremely powerful, but are more specifically related to one people.

■ *Masauwu*

Masauwu, the Hopi deity of fire and death, rules the whole Hopi world, both the surface of the Earth and the underworld. He is terrifying and mighty, wears a bald and bloody mask upon his head and is clothed in raw animal skins. Every night he walks around the edge of the world carrying a flaming torch. People cannot bear to look at his face; if they do they are likely to die of fright, since he has the face of death. A more recent Hopi story tells of how Dr. Fewkes, a Smithsonian archaeologist and ethnographer, was visited by *Masauwu.* Dr. Fewkes was studying ceremonies in the village of Walpi in 1898 and during the sacred part of the *Wuwuchim* Ceremony, he was told to go and stay in his house as *Masauwu* was due to arrive. There he was terrified by the god, who had turned himself into a straw and entered through the keyhole. According to the Hopi this was the reason for the departure of Dr. Fewkes back to New York, not the dose of smallpox which he claimed!

■ *Usen* and Earth Mother

Some creators vanish, but others are a continuing source of power. The Apache deity *Usen* is an all-powerful god. Even so, other Apache gods are of considerably importance, such as the *Gahan,* or Mountain Spirits, who have power to help or harm people, and White Painted Woman, the mother of the Twin Brothers. Both she and the Twin Brothers have parallels throughout the Southwestern cultural area. To the Navajo she is known as *Estanatlehi*, or Changing Woman, and to the Hopi she is Hard Substances Woman. She is most often seen in the role of Earth Mother. In all three cultural groups she is mother to the Twin Brothers and often re-populates the world after disasters.

■ Twin Brothers, Spider Woman and Coyote

The Twin Brothers, whose father is usually the Sun, are known by various names including Twin War Gods and the Beloved Two. Most often they play the part of heroes, and their activities are usually crucial to the pros-perity of humans. Similarly, in Papago myth there is a god called *Iitoi*, or Elder Brother, who was created by Earthmaker. He was the first born, when the sky came down and met the Earth. Elder Brother helped Earthmaker to shape the people and the world, and is a protector of the Papago. While the twins are powerful in their own right, the Sun is often there to help them. The Sun is regarded as a father, or Father Sky, to many groups in the Southwest and Hopi babies are still presented to the Sun God *Tawa,* who is told that a new life has begun.

Another powerful spirit is Spider Woman, variously referred to as Spider Old Woman, Grandmother Spider, Spider Lady, Grandmother or Grandma, and one people may know her by several of these names. The Hopi name for her is *Gogyeng Sowuhti* and she appears either as an old woman or as a small spider. The Hopi regard her as living medicine: she often gives medical advice, comes to the aid of people in danger, is kind and can always cope with any situation.

In contrast Coyote has power but is indiscriminate in its use. His actions bring both good and disaster. Coyote has similar characteristics in all of the Southwestern cultural groups, and is known as a trickster or buf-foon. His exploits make him more of a mythical hero than anything else, but he is often integral to Creation and can use his power to perform good deeds. In Navajo myth he is the catalyst forcing people to move from one world to another, and often he is responsible for the stars being scattered in the sky.

■ The Kachinas

Kachinas are at the center of Hopi religious life and are also particularly important to many other peoples of the Southwest. They are perhaps the most well-known supernatural spirit beings. The kachinas have varying origins and purposes but overall have the well-being of the people at heart. The Hopi believe that when good people die they become kachinas and are associated with clouds. Rainfall is extremely important for agriculture in the arid Southwest, and the kachinas are seen as the bringers of rain. The Zuni know them as *Koko,* or Raw People. They are associated with rain, and with the ability to give people the good things in life including longevity, fecundity, power, strength of will and good fortune. However, rather than being powerful in their own right, the Kachinas are often seen as beings who communicate people's wishes to the gods.

HERO CREATURES AND MONSTERS

The inhabitants of Jemez pueblo feared a monster called *Tsakapi'yadya* who caught people and ate them, and kept all the game animals. Villagers asked the Twin Boys to help them, and after four days preparation they all set out to the monster's home, but half-way there the Twin Boys told the villagers to turn back. When the twins arrived the monster was very nice, it complemented them on their strength, bravery and singing, and offered them food. It said they would have a competition to see who could shoot an arrow to a mountain in the south, and told them to bet their lives on it. The twins appeared doubtful and said that they could not shot an arrow so far, but the monster insisted. The older twin agreed so long as the monster took the first shot. The monster shot his arrow to the base of the mountain. But the twins shot their arrows right over it, then killed the monster using a small piece of petrified wood. The monster's body fell into the canyon breaking into many pieces. The twins rescued people the monster has imprisoned, freed the captured animals and they all went back to their homes.

The origin of monsters vary. In some myths they are not explained, but are seen as having always been there; in others they are the gods' off-spring, or have been created by the gods as a punishment when people have been bad. Where there are monsters there are usually heroes to kill them and put an end to their reigns of terror. However, the exploits of the culture hero Coyote are usually humorous, such as the recent Apache tales of how he outwits the whites.

■ Child of Water

Monsters occur most frequently in origin myths. In the Chiricahua Apache myth, recounted by Geronimo, the beginning of the world was full of monsters which were continually killing humans. Many monsters were killed in the battle between the beasts and birds. Eagle killed one of the most hideous monsters, who was impervious to arrows, by flying high and dropping a boulder on its head. Afterward there were still some monsters left including a most horrific dragon who had four coats of scales and ate all the children. Only one child, whose mother hid him in a cave, survived. One day the boy, Child of Water, went out hunting with his uncle. The monster smelled their cooking and after he and Child of Water had wrestled over the meat, Child of Water challenged him to a contest which he won by penetrating the four scales above the monster's heart with four arrows. Thereafter people lived and prospered.

■ Terror in the Navajo Worlds

Monsters play a large role in the Navajo emergence myth. The water monster *Tieholtsodi* floods the third world after Coyote kidnaps his two children, but when people escape to the fourth world *Teholtsodi* follows and floods that too. At last, when the people are emerging into the fifth world, they discover the children and throw them back to the monster who disappears and the floods retreat.

There are more monsters to contend with in the Navajo fifth world, sent by First Man and First Woman to punish the people. They include *Yietso* who, along with his children, eats human prey; *Delgeth*, a flesh-eating antelope; The People Who Kill by Lightning in Their Eyes; and The Kicker, a giant who kicks travelers off mountain trails.

■ Flesh-Eating Monsters

Many monsters have flesh-eating predilections in common. This is a characteristic of the Papago monsters, Killer Eagle and *Ho'ok*, both of whom are killed by Elder Brother. Most monsters are killed by being outwitted: *Ho'ok* is trapped in a cave and smoked to death; Killer Eagle has his head chopped off by Elder Brother who enters his cave disguised as a fly.

The people of Acoma pueblo tell the story of the hunter *Kasewats* who came home to discover that his wife had been taken by *Sko'yo*, a giantess. To find her he went to the spring his wife had been snatched from and made a lot of noise. The same giantess came, snatched him up and carried him to her home where he found his wife with many other frightened people whom the giantess was fattening up. *Kasewats* then tricked *Sko'yo* and killed her. He freed the people and returned home with his wife. This is a typical myth where intelligence overcomes force.

HOLY PLACES, SACRED SITES

The most widely held view among the Native Americans of the Southwest is that the land itself is a living being. The Zuni regard it as a spiritual relative; everything which makes up the landscape – the trees, the rocks and clouds – are seen as being interconnected. The Navajo call this *hozho*,[10] which translates as balance or harmony, and they strive to maintain this harmony. Within the whole landscape particular features are regarded as especially sacred. The overriding importance of water is reflected in the reverence felt for springs. The Zuni see many aspects of the landscape, for example buttes, lakes, geological formations and religious trails, as important and offerings are left at these sites, and prayers made for them. The land is dotted with shrines, places which may be significant to many people or only to individuals, but this does not diminish their sacredness. Zunis consider the Middle Place to be the heartbeat of the world. After they came into the world they searched for it for many years, and eventually found it near the center of Zuni pueblo. It is equidistant from four oceans, and is believed to be the center of their six directions.

■ Places of Emergence

Many places are holy in mythology and continue to be sacred today. The Hopi place of emergence, known as *Sipapu,* is located at the bottom of the Grand Canyon. According to myth, the Hopi dead go to a house below this opening. At this place is a yellow pool located at the confluence of the Colorado and Little Colorado rivers in the Grand Canyon, 60 miles (96 km) east of Oraibi. The Hopi say their ancestors could talk freely with the Creator through *Sipapu,* but today the opening is almost always closed, due, they say, to mankind's departure from the correct path. In Navajo legend the dead also return to the place of emergence, while in Zuni myth the spirits of the dead go to the confluence of the Zuni and Little Colorado rivers. This is different to the Zuni place of emergence which is thought to be either in the Grand Canyon or the Moúave Desert.

Eight important shrines mark the extent of traditional Hopi territory: to the north is *Tokanave,* or Black Mountain, which the whites call Navajo Mountain; the second is on the Supai Trail west of Grand Canyon Village; there is one at *Kawestima* with some ruins which lie to the north of Kayenta; one near Williams, Arizona, called *Tesaktumo,* or Grass Hill; one on the San Francisco Peaks; one on Woodruff Mountain south of Holbrook; the seventh is at a place called *Namiteika,* near Lupton; and the last is on the Apache Trail on Mogollon Rim. The Hopi regard all land between the shrines as being theirs. They say the shrines mark some of the last staging points in their migrations to the three mesas.[11]

■ Places of Deeds

Mythology provides explanations for some of the stranger elements in the landscape. A prominent mountain called Cabezon (the eroded plug of a volcano) is known to the Navajo as *Tse Najin,* or Black Rock. According to mythology, it is the head of the giant *Tieholtsodi* who was killed by the Twin War Gods (*Nagenatzani* and *Thobadestchin*) on Mount Taylor. They struck off the giant's head, which rolled and bounced to its current resting place. Nearby lava beds are said to be the coagulated blood and gore from the giant's body. Canyon de Chelly is the site of Spider Rock, the home of Spider Woman, and today it forms part of the Navajo Reservation. Visitors to the canyon are requested to treat it with 'reverence and respect'. According to the Navajo, Spider Woman lives on the top of the tallest of two needles with make up Spider Rock. The top of the rock is white rather than red, and this whiteness is said to be bones of naughty children captured by Spider Woman and carried off to Spider Rock where they were devoured.

The directions of the compass are important and are usually associated with sacred colors. Before the Tewa people emerged from Sand Lake, the Two Little Boy War Gods were created. They were sent from the lake to report what they could see. They shot off their arrows, and the direction that the first arrow went was established as north and this was associated with the color blue. The other directions and colors followed: west was yellow, south red, east white, the zenith above was speckled and the nadir below black.

REVERED ANIMALS

Animals in myth may act as messengers, guards, advisors and servants. Mythological animals are essentially human. They think, speak and act like humans but also have the abilities of their animal forms. Some are major deities such as Coyote and Spider Woman, but other common sacred spirit animals include bears, antelopes, deer, eagles, badgers and wolves. Eagles are particularly important and their feathers were used in ceremonies, though now these have largely been replaced by turkey feathers. The Hopi believe that there is another land up in the sky where eagles go to breed before returning to Earth. They believe that children can be transformed into eagles and are cared for by eagle parents.

Animals not only act like humans but really are human under their skin. People entering *kivas* tell how animals remove their skins and hang them up like clothes. In Hopi myth the animals all have homes and when they need to rest they go and live there in their human form, though sometimes humans stumble upon them. A Yaqui man hit a snake which was lying across his path; later, he came to a village and was taken to the chief, beside whom was a young woman wearing a bandage around her waist who accused him of hitting her in the stomach.

■ **Helpers**

One of the most common animal roles is as helpers. Many emergence stories show animals are important in getting from one world to the next. In one version of the Navajo origin myth, Turkey is the last in the queue to climb up the reed from the third world to the fourth. When the flood waters reach his feet, he gives the signal to climb. Badger and Locust are important, in getting from the fourth world to the fifth: Badger digs away at the earth to get from the fourth world and Locust outwits the challenge of four colored swans, so that all the people are let into the fifth world. Similarly, in Hopi myth four birds are sent out to investigate the world above.

The living, as well as the dead, become animals but sometimes this is done by trickery. Once a Tewa man's wife and friend set out to get rid of him. The friend was a witch and invited the man to see a new dance, to which he asked all his witch companions. They all leapt through a hoop and turned into coyotes, then leapt back and returned to their human form. The man was encouraged to go through the hoop and he too turned into a coyote, but the witches took the hoop away before he could jump back through it. Similar metamorphoses take place in several stories but usually the humans are eventually recognized as such and helped to return to their human form while the perpetrators get punished. In the Tewa story the witch agrees to make a new hoop, and afterward dies of shame.

■ **Destroyers**

Animals are not always helpful or benevolent. One Navajo story tells how

Frog and Turtle intend to catch some human women but people from their village catch up with them and attack them. Frog and Turtle, while acting like humans, use the advantages of their animal forms to escape. When hit, Frog hides in Turtle's shell which doesn't break, and when put in an oven, Frog puts the fire out with water from his mouth. In White Mountain Apache myth the actions of Big Owl are always destructive.

■ Clans

Many clans and societies in the Southwest region are named after animals, who may be thought of as direct ancestors. A Hopi male ancestor married the daughter of a snake chieftain and their descendants became the Snake Clan. To members of this clan, snakes are seen as relatives and are never killed. Snakes are widely revered, and both the Zuni and Hopi believe that they take messages to the gods. The Hopi, of course, also perform the famous Snake Dance in honor of Great Snake.

In Zuni mythology sacred animals guard the cardinal six directions. Mountain Lion guards the north, Badger the south, Bear the west, and Wolf the east, while the sky is looked after by Eagle, and the inner earth by Mole. Hoofed animals are associated with certain directions and also with kachinas, as Zuni kachinas may become hoofed animals when they die. Likewise people who die return as animals: girls and uninitiated boys are said to become turtles or water snakes.

RITUALS AND CEREMONIES

Ceremonies are conducted to maintain or restore harmony. This is true of both the kachina and the sandpainting ceremonies and rituals which may benefit all people or just an individual. Ceremonial life is integral to native culture. Hopi ceremonies are described as being intertwined with daily life to the extent where one could not exist without the other. There are many different types of ceremonies: some are arranged calendrically and only performed at certain times of the year, while others occur whenever they are thought necessary. Many Southwestern ceremonies have their origins recounted in myth. White Mountain Apache legends about the Water, Hawk and Snake ceremonies are regarded as holy and are seen as being of much greater importance than the emergence myths.

Stories recount the origins of ceremonies and give direct inspiration on how to conduct them. One Jicarilla Apache legend describes the contest between Killer of Enemies and One Who Wins and is used as the basis for the purification ceremonies conducted for people who have come into contact with the dead. Anyone who has been so contaminated needs to be brought back to the 'life-side'. The ceremony involves a singer who takes the role of Killer of Enemies and fights the forces of evil personified by One Who Wins. Songs and prayers recount the bitter contest which was finally won by Killer of Enemies.

◼ The Hopi Snake Dance

Several ceremonies are believed to have been brought to the people by heroes. The Hopi Snake Dance was discovered by *Tiyo*, or The Youth. Myth tells how *Tiyo* set out to find the source of the Colorado River. Eventually, with the help of Spider Woman, he was shown the source of the river by Great Snake, and after he had proved himself Tiyo was initiated into the Snake Clan. Finally he returned home with his wife Snake Maiden and taught the Hopi how to perform the Snake Dance. The Snake Dance is still performed today and public performances attract huge crowds. It is said that the Snake Priest at Walpi still uses the original *tiponi* (medicine bundle) that was made by *Tiyo*. The Snake Dance is performed by initiates of the Snake and Antelope clans and requires two weeks of ritual preparations. Snakes are caught from the four directions and are made 'brothers' in the Snake Society, before they are taken back to the desert carrying the Hopi prayers for rain. The ceremony is most famous for the Snake Dancers' ability to hold snakes in their mouths without being bitten.

◼ The Kachinas

The kachinas are of prime importance in many rituals including those of the Zuni and Hopi, and at Acoma pueblo. The Hopi feel they are spirit essences who show their presence by rainclouds or mists and they stay with the Hopi for seven months every year until July. Then after 16 days of rituals they return to their homes in the San Francisco Peaks, near Flagstaff. Kachina dances restore and maintain harmony in the spirits of all living things and are held from late winter until the end of the July rituals. The dances are offered to the Creator for people's health and welfare, and in thanks for good crops. In myth the kachinas were actual beings sent by the gods until they had taught the ceremonies to the Hopi priests. Today, dancers are members of the Kachina Cult. There are many different types of kachina, including clown kachinas who are naughty and provide entertainment between the ceremonies.

■ Sandpainting

The Navajo perform many rituals to maintain harmony between humans and the spirit world, such as songs, chants, and the creation of sandpaintings. Like the Hopi Snake Dance, sandpainting was taught to the Navajo by a mythical figure. A young woman called *Gilspa* found the Snake People's village where she was tutored by Snake Man, and when she returned to her people she taught them the ceremonies she had learned. There are said to be hundreds of different Navajo sandpaintings, each of which is accompanied by its own song. The Apache are reputed to have around 50 different types. Traditionally, the sandpaintings are made on the floor of the *hogan,* dwelling, by the *hataali,*[12] or singer, out of cornmeal, sand, charcoal and pollen and can take several hours to complete. Their beauty and their depiction of the spirits' power attracts the spirits themselves. The actual power of the spirits is then used in ceremonies which may last over a week. At the end of the ceremony, done either for the benefit of an individual or for the greater good, the paintings are destroyed. Commercial sandpaintings contain errors so as not to offend the spirits.

ARTS AND CRAFTS

The American Southwest has one of the most harsh and difficult climates of any area on the North American continent, yet for thousands of years it has supported a culturally active and spiritually integrated Native American population. The arid climate has naturally produced religions which are fixed upon water, control of water and snakes, frogs and clouds. Long cotton tassels on white dance sashes evoke the rain falling from the high clouds.

The greater part of this area is arid or semi-arid, with extreme variations from high forested mountain ranges, from which springtime run-off of the heavy winter snows provides an important part of the waters of the Rio Grande, the Colorado and the Pecos. A major part of the area is plateau, steep-sided sandstone mesas, deep canyons with intermittent streams and scattered clumps of piñon and juniper trees. The southern half of the area is marked by broad areas of nearly level, hot, dry desert separated by steep, rocky mountains of limited extent which break up the flat land.

This varied Southwestern habitat offered its prehistoric occupants – the Anasazi, Hohokam and Mogollon, Basketmakers and Mimbres cultures – an enormous variety of resources, many of them to be found only in very restricted zones. This encouraged the development of greatly differing lifestyles, each adjusted to the resources available and taking advantage of several different micro-environments. To take advantage of this diversity, the peoples of the Southwest were knit together by interlocking networks of economic and social relationships.

These ancient cultures all produced pottery, basketry, weaving, carving in wood and some small carvings in shell and stone, some of them very beautiful and sophisticated. The study of the Southwest and its arts and crafts is influenced by the knowledge that the present Indians are the descendants of those who made the great cities in the desert such as Chaco and Mesa Verde. In the Southwest it is possible to observe in use the same loom that was used prehistorically, the same sash, the same basket . . . and this also gives insight into the meaning of these things within their original culture.

Crafts in the Southwest have maintained their high standards, techniques and esthetic vision, and are still an important source of income for Native American people. Many of them sell their arts and crafts to supplement their income. There is an artisan in almost every home, and the importance of their arts and crafts is appreciated. Until this century the finest objects were made for ceremonial purposes, for the gods, and to ensure the continuation of human life. Today often the very best of their arts and crafts are most frequently destined for collectors or museums.

Although their lives often reflect the stress of living in two cultures, the Indians of the Southwest maintain their traditional way of life, and it is possible to glimpse the way these people lived 500 years ago. A quiet moment at a ceremonial dance, with the drum beat which has gone on and on all day, and the long lines of dancers stretch back to earliest days of the Anasazi, when the plaza dancers heard the same songs and drums. The past is not distant here; there is an occasional pot shard, a broken bit of flint, or the discovery of a ruin, tucked away in a cliff to remind us that there were people here long ago.

The arts are one of the strongest and most visible links to this past. The bestselling articles are made in the old traditional ways. Everything is done by hand, and with materials available if one knows how to pray for them, where to find them, how to process them, and how to respect them.

■ Ceramics

Of all the arts of the Southwest, pottery may be the most definitive. It is still made using the same methods that have been used for thousands of years, and ceramics of great beauty and sophistication have been produced. The pottery of the Mimbres, Anasazi, Hohokam and the historic and contemporary pueblos are some of the best known of the crafts of the American Indian. There is a clear stylistic link between the present and the past in Pueblo pottery, and prehistoric designs are often reused; for example, the Mimbres-influenced pottery designs of Lucy Lewis in Acoma. This link is a central feature of the Pueblo world, serving both utilitarian and ceremonial functions and tying social life to the natural environment in a fundamental way. And Pueblo pottery accounts for probably 90 per cent of all Southwestern pottery and thus typifies the region.

In centuries past, many vessels were hand-painted with elaborate designs, and simple kitchen items – storage jars, pitchers and ladles, canteens, seed jars and serving bowls – were executed with the care and creative genius that characterize works of art. Like many traditional craftspeople, Pueblo potters have a remarkable ability to instill in a common household object a life and spirit of its own, and the so-called utility wares are exemplars of this quality.[13] Traditionally, pottery has also been viewed as possessing power and the ability to take on the attributes of the substance it holds. Thus water, a sacred element, transfers its power to the pottery vessel that holds it: 'Water contains the source of continued life. The vessel holds the water; the source of life accompanies the water, hence its dwelling place is in the vessel with the water.'[14]

Potters have a respected place in contemporary Pueblo society:

'Despite the changes which have engulfed the Pueblo world, there remains the underlying world view that recognizes a spiritual dimension to every phase of life, to all common objects and everyday activities. This world view is expressed by the still vital ceremonial calendar and is embodied in items fashioned by hand from the materials provided by the earth.'[15]

To make a pot (or a figurine, spindle whorl, charm or fetish), an Indian woman goes to her traditional clay source, which every pueblo has, and then to her own part of the source and digs out as much clay as she needs. She then dries it and puts it through a sieve or screen to get rid of the rocks and roots. After the clay is clean, she will add some sort of temper, old pot shards, volcanic earth or ground mica, which keeps the clay from expanding too fast and cracking, and then add water so that the clay is workable. Pots are made not on a wheel but by coiling ropes of clay one on another and then pinching them together. The clay is then smoothed, often with a piece of gourd, so that no joints are visible. The clay is then sanded and smoothed again. This may end the process or, at this point, the slip, or a paint made from clay and usually of a different color, is applied, and quickly the burnishing begins. The slip is a fine clay dissolved in water so that it is really like a paint. Slips can be of red or white clay. Production methods differ little between pueblos; the temper of the clays may differ but the main visible difference is in the decoration and thickness of the walls of the pots.

Polishing pottery is a long and tiresome process. Small polishing stones, sometimes dinosaur gizzard stones frequently found in the arroyos or dry stream beds, are used to press and stroke the surface of the new pot until it begins to gleam. These small, smooth stones are treasured and passed down from generation to generation. Once the polishing is started it cannot be stopped, so the effort required to polish a large pot takes a small team of people. If the pot is to be painted, then it is not polished. Before firing, it will be covered with a slip and it can then be decorated and polished.

The pot is then fired. Sheep manure provides a good fuel, burning evenly and slowly. The ashes retain their initial form and hold the heat of the fire. Some potters today in very windy locations like Acoma, high on a mesa, are using electric kilns which are easier to control. Firing is the most delicate part of the potting process, and pots are usually fired in the morning when there is little wind.

There were no glazes in the Southwest but the lack of a glaze was not considered to be very important. It was understood that the pottery would let the water evaporate slowly. The clay gives the water a sweet taste, and many Pueblo people think that the best water comes from these pots, called ollas, which keep the water cool and tasty.[16] There are, as mentioned, many decorative variations in the Pueblo pottery of the Southwest. If a black ware is desired, the fire is smothered after it has burned down, and covered with sheets of tin or any fireproof material so that the heat and smoke are held in the fire and forced into the body of the pottery. Today this black ware is made in New Mexico by San Ildefonso and Santa Clara pueblos, but pre-historically this sort of pottery was more widespread. This black ware is burnished to a metallic sheen and had almost disappeared but was revived by Maria Martinez of San Ildefonso, and today her lustrous black pottery is highly prized by collectors. Maria and her husband Julian, who decorated her pots when she began to make pottery for sale, became the best known of many teams of potters whose production was designed for the market.

The relationship between market desires and the potter's designs is recurrent; tourist tastes have strongly influenced pottery designs: for example, the decorative use of floral motifs which have been incorporated into pueblo designs, particularly those of the Southern pueblos, Acoma, Laguna, Zuni, Zia, Santa Ana, San Felipe and Cochiti. Many of the designs which now seem traditional may have been adapted from things which the

19th century potters saw on imported crockery – flowers, parrots and bands which separated areas of the pot – in order to make the pottery more saleable to outsiders.[17] More traditionally, the decoration was distinctive if a pot was to have some role in an internal ceremony, often including water symbols, frogs, tadpoles and clouds. Since men were in charge of religion they may have produced and painted all the pottery for kiva use, or, as Dillingham suggests, occasionally it was made by a woman who had been struck by lightning and lived, thus qualifying her to make kiva pottery.[18]

The shapes of pots have evolved gradually. The olla, or water vessel, was designed to be balanced on the head of a woman carrying water from a stream or spring to her house. It generally has a shoulder, which spreads the weight of the water, and a narrow neck, to keep the water from spilling and evaporating. Other types of pottery produced continuously are seed jars, small globe-like pots with very narrow openings, canteens, which were introduced by the Spanish and, occasionally, effigy jars. Prehistorically the Anasazi produced mugs and pitchers, but those shapes, like the black pottery, had disappeared until these forms were revived for tourists.[19] A later, unintended effect of the popularity of the pueblo pottery was that the pottery library at the pueblos was depleted by institutions such as the Smithsonian who purchased enormous amounts of material and shipped it into museums. In cultures where innovation is not greatly valued, this produced more changes than might have occurred otherwise, since it removed the collective memory bank of the potters of a pueblo.[20]

The Pueblos share a way of life, a world view and a landscape, but they speak half a dozen languages and live in more than 30 villages. Although several pueblos may share a language, internally they may have different societies and clan structures, so that they are not alike in organization. There are, naturally, several distinct styles of pottery.

Down along the Rio Grande the Tewa pueblos of San Ildefonso and Santa Clara are known today for their black and red wares. San Ildefonso, the home of Maria Martinez, produces mostly black pottery, but earlier this century when Maria was a young woman, she produced a fine black on white ceramic ware. Today no one in San Ildefonso makes the black on white pottery which was once so common. Maria's switch to black on black, a reduction-fired clay which is burnished and then painted which leaves certain areas matte, has become the standard for San Ildefonso. Similarly, no white-slipped pottery is made at neighbouring Santa Clara.

The Tewa pueblo of San Juan produced pottery which was mostly undecorated; today's new style is really a reinterpretation of ancestral shards, combining incised lines in unslipped tan on a middle band between a polished top and bottom. In northern New Mexico the Tiwa-speaking pueblos of Taos and Picuris are the home of an unslipped micaceous ware which usually comes in the form of a lidless beanpot. This is used for cooking stews and beans, and the clay is thought to impart a special, delicious flavor.

In the early part of this century potters from the Tewa pueblo of Tesuque made pottery which was black on white and looked like that being made at the same time in San Ildefonso. In the 1940s and '50s it produced a lot of low-fired work painted in unfired, bright commercial tempera paint to appeal to tourists visiting nearby Santa Fe. Paradoxically, it remains a conservative pueblo maintaining a rich ceremonial life.

The Keresan pueblos to the south of Santa Fe make a thinner-walled ceramic which is slipped white and decorated with black and red. This is called polychrome because it has several colors. The Keresan-speaking pueblos of Cochiti, Santo Domingo, Santa Ana, Zia, Laguna and Acoma all produced large bowls and ollas. Their pots all have a red band at the base, then a design area which is white with black and red designs, often birds and flowers. The top band is either a continuation of the middle panel or geometric.

In Cochiti, Helen Cordero invented, or more accurately revived, a figure called a story-teller. She remembered her grandfather singing to his children and began to produce sitting figures with open mouths and many small children sitting and listening to the story or song. Helen Cordero, like Maria Martinez and the Hopi Nampeyo, has opened many economic doors for the pueblo potters. Story-telling figurines are changing rapidly and may be considered folk art. Very popular, they have been copied extensively.

Santo Domingo is a few miles south of Cochiti and it is a very conservative pueblo. Even recent designs are likely to be variations of designs which were popular in the 1700s. These designs are described as simple geometric. Santo Domingo leaders forbid the representation of the human figure and other designs are not allowed on pottery for sale. Santo Domingo pots continue to be used on feast days and in the kivas, but today's production is limited.

To the west were, and are, more great potters, in the three Keresan-speaking pueblos of Zia, Laguna and Acoma, and in Zuni. These have much in common; all use white slip and black and red decorations. The clay around Acoma is special, dark and dense, and it has a tendency to pit, which has made some modern Acoma potters resort to commercial clay. The pottery of Acoma has been especially enhanced by looking at the designs of their ancestors in the Mimbres valley. Prehistorically the potters of this western part of New Mexico excelled at black on white designs, and the tradition is carried on today. In the past 20 years Acoma has developed this distinctive style, and the distinguished potter Lucy Lewis and her descendants have inspired a younger group of potters to continue their traditions and innovations.

Zuni is a separate language although Zuni pottery appears to be closely related to the Keresean model. Historical Zuni-related pottery is called Tularosa Black on White and St. Johns Polychrome, although at other sites there are polychrome pieces which have a glaze decoration. After the Pueblo Revolt in 1680, the Zunis consolidated in one pueblo which is called Zuni. Historical Zuni ware has a white slip and three bands of design. The Zuni designs of this century have concentrated on the rosette and deer with what is called a heart line, from the mouth to the heart of the deer. Zuni ceramics were in decline earlier this century, but are currently being revived and young Zunis are making pottery again, although most today make jewelry.

Hopi pottery from about 1300 was not distinct, but there was an artistic explosion in the 1450s which produced black on white and black on orange wares. These early Hopi designs are characterized by sweeping curvilinear motifs, birds, animals and human representations. The free designs are different from all other pottery designs in the Pueblo world, with the possible exception of the Mimbres in western New Mexico.[21] The Hopi have always used coal to fire their pottery and are the only group to do so, although it crops up all over the Pueblo world.

The Hopi pottery renaissance is partly due to a woman named Nampeyo who lived a century ago in the Hopi village of Hano and was extremely skilled at making symmetrical vessels. In 1890 Nampeyo saw some of the pot shards from the excavation of black on yellow pots being excavated at Sikyatki and was inspired to reproduce these fragments as pots. Sikyatki Polychrome uses unbalanced design areas, dynamic color fields, stippling, engraving and other textures. Nampeyo was a Tewa whose ancestors moved to Hopi as a result of Spanish pressure in New Mexico in the 17th century, so her pottery is Hopi/Tewa. Today the Hopi pottery she revived is characterized by its golden slip and polychrome decoration, elements derived from Sikyatki. Nampeyo's great fame came from her elegant design sense, which took elements of the past and reused them on contemporary pottery. Today there are many potters at Hopi who have been inventive and produced very simple variations of the traditional designs.

Other pottery in the Southwest is not as well known. The Athapaskan Navajo and Apache did make some early pottery but it is impossible to identify today.[22] Although the Pueblos continue to dominate pottery today, there is an increasing production of some unslipped, pinched rim pottery made by the Navajo. The Navajo are also making low-fired ceramic figurines of Navajo going about their daily life. These figures are very lively and appealing and are being sought by folk-art collectors. Apaches, too, have produced some ceramics, but their efforts so far have been limited to undecorated pieces, red slipped canteens and other small pieces.

The Pima and Papago of Arizona produced a red ware pottery using the paddle and anvil and the coil technique, although they are much better known for their basketry. Their neighbors the Maricopa made a red and black ware using coils. Maricopa ware shows some Mexican influence; they paint black designs around the necks of the pots in unbanded designs. The Maricopa, and the other Rancheria tribes including the Yuma, the Cocopa and Mojave, also make clay figurines which wear clothes and beads.

■ Jewelry

Among humans the urge to ornament is universal. In the Southwest, body paint was probably the most common ornament in the past, with jewelry scarce but popular. Most of this jewelry was made of stone or shell, the latter obtained by travel or trade which contributed to a wide distribution of marine-shell varieties. The only non-marine shell used was the terrestrial snail (gastropod). All other shells were worked to some extent; the most common use was to make beads from the small olivella shell. Shell was made into beads, rings and bracelets by abrading it against a harder surface. Objects of ornaments are rare before AD 500 and become more popular in later periods. In the southern parts of the area there are some copper bells which were probably traded up from Mexico. By 900–1200 there was an increase in jewelry in the Southwest: stone and bone rings, copper bells, turquoise, jet and stone pendants, stone and shell beads and shell bracelets. In both the Hohokam and later in the Anasazi/Chaco area there was beautiful mosaic inlay. Shell was cut into the shape of birds and animals, and acid and wax etching was done on shell pendants.

Turquoise was the favorite stone of all Southwestern Indians and has many variant colors, from green to robin's egg blue, depending on the mine and the mineral composition. Because of this demand, it was traded over great distances; turquoise from the Cerrillos mines in New Mexico – controlled today by Santo Domingo Indians[23] – went into the inlaid Aztec masks from Tenochtitlan. The Santo Domingo Indians have a myth that when their people emerged from the underworld two other groups came with them, and that before they parted to go their individual ways, the Santo Domingo promised to make beads for the other Indians. To this day, they love to trade and whole families are engaged in the production and distribution of turquoise and beads of other materials.

The manufacture of these beads, called *hishi*, is still a very important skill. The shaping of turquoise, and other materials like shell or stone, into beads is done by rolling it on tufa or sandstone to smooth all the edges. The beads are then assembled into graduated necklaces or *jaclos*, a very old and simple necklace form that has been unchanged since prehistoric times. Beads found in the Anasazi burials at Chaco Canyon are indistinguishable from beads made now. Beads and amulets were holed in the center by the use of a pump drill; the string of rough beads was then rolled on a wet slab of sandstone. This time-consuming technique is still used because it produces beads which fit together in a comfortable way.

When the Spanish first came into the Southwest looking for gold, the Indians did not have a word for metal. They were, however, quick to appreciate the bright and enduring qualities of it, and small pieces began to appear as necklaces or rings, or as additions to a shirt although it was not worked until the middle of the last century.[24]

The Native Americans had to learn to work metal in the most primitive of conditions. The early techniques for silversmithing were very simple. Some coals were taken from the fire, and a torch was used to heat the silver. The coals caught the heat and acted as a small furnace melting the metal. As soon as the metal was hot, it was placed on an anvil and pounded into shape. As it cooled, it was reheated with bellows and reworked. The tools needed were an anvil, a hammer, several die stamps for decoration, some silver, some solder and a fire.[25]

The original Navajo bellows were made of goat hide and served to keep the coals glowing.[26] Decoration was added after the piece was shaped. Often differently shaped dies were stamped into the silver. If the die was cut too deep, it could slice through the silver, so the artist had to be careful. Many of these dies were originally made in Spain or Mexico to stamp Mexican leather saddles, bags and costumes. The Navajo discovered that the dies worked beautifully as silver decoration but they also learned to make their own dies using files to cut designs. The early Navajo silver work was very straightforward, and is characterized by its pure sense of design.

The influence of Mexicans who occupied New Mexico and Arizona was strong, their love of ornament being adopted by the Navajo. This is evident in several examples: the concha belt, the squash blossom necklace, the naja and the use of ornamental buttons were all related to the Mexicans. The Navajo found that coins pounded into a domed shape and with a loop soldered to the back made both a decoration and a purchase at the trading post. The conchas, which means shells in Spanish, were originally round or oval silver plates which were larger than buttons and were attached by straps. These were used to decorate belts, spurs, or a jacket, and the shape and design of the concha belt were fixed as early as 1880: 'The grand prize of the dandy Navajo buck is his belt . . . this is of leather completely covered by immense elliptical silver plaques.'[27] Navajos owned concha belts long before they learned to make them. The Utes, Comanches, Kiowas and other Southern Plains Indians with whom the Navajo feuded wore belts strung with plaques of copper, brass or German silver (a non-ferrous alloy of copper, nickel and zinc), and a Navajo might take a belt from a slain enemy or, in peacetime, obtain it in trade. Even before their capture and exile in the 1860s at the Bosque Redondo, the rich Navajos wore concha belts. White influence has reduced the size of the conchas and other forms alternate with traditional ones. Today these belts are very popular both with the Native Americans and the visitors to the area.

Another design element which the Navajo borrowed from the Mexican is the naja which is a crescent-shaped ornament used to decorate the center of a horse bridle. It appeared on Navajo horses about the same time as concha belts became common. The naja may derive from the Moorish crescent moon, or another Moorish symbol, the hands of Fatima. Crescent-shaped figures were also popular with the Plains Indians, and the Navajo may have found it in their hunting and raiding there. The design of the naja occurs all over the world, but the most likely source for the Southwest is the Spanish/Moorish route. The naja was a popular pendant and for the Navajo was used almost exclusively, although the cross was also used, sometimes in combination with a naja, the cross symbolizing the morning star.

111

In addition to decorating the horse bridle, the naja is part of every squash blossom necklace. The squash blossom is a fertility symbol for the Pueblo people, and the name has become associated with this necklace although the actual flower in the necklace is a pomegranate blossom, which is also a fertility symbol. The pomegranate was a popular bead shape on Mexican trouser and jacket ornaments and has been a favorite Spanish decorative motif for centuries. The combination of pomegranate-shaped ornaments with a naja, spaced with shaped silver beads, has a hybrid beauty. This design, along with the concha belt, has come to be thought of as distinctively Navajo.

By the 1890s the Navajo had begun to add turquoise to their jewelry and were setting turquoise in simple bezels. Some of the first traders to the Navajo even imported turquoise for their silversmiths. The trader Lorenzo Hubbell at Ganado was selling fine Persian turquoise to the Navajo in 1890.[28] Hubbell also often supplied the Navajo with Mexican pesos which were pure silver and easy to work as in 1890 there was a prohibition against defacing United States coins which had previously supplied the silver necessary to make jewelry. The Navajo silversmiths were supplied partly by the traders and partly by their old trading partners in the Pueblos.[29] In addition to making and selling jewelry, the Navajo love to wear jewelry which they make. The display of wealth in the form of necklaces, belts, bracelets, rings, earrings, buttons and silver-decorated horse bridles was, and is, important to the Navajo culture.

Among all the pueblos, the pueblo of Zuni is most noted for its jewelry. The Zuni probably learned to make jewelry from the Navajo. In 1880 they were making simple forms but by 1910 they had evolved the style which is recognizably Zuni. In contrast to the Navajo, the Zuni generally had more modern jewelry tools, which they got from their trader C. J. Wallace. Their work is more intricate and uses more and smaller stones than that of the Navajo. The tools included fine pliers which are essential to make the small bezels for the small turquoise stones which characterize Zuni jewelry in the style known as Needlepoint.

The other important tools were the vise and the emery wheel, which makes polishing turquoise and silver much easier. The small rows of turquoise stones in Zuni bracelets may be inspired by rows of kernels of blue corn (a crop with sacred significance). Zuni jewelry is usually lightweight and the silver serves as a base to hold the turquoise rather than as an important design element. Commercial from an early stage, the sale of their jewelry has made a big difference to the economic well-being of Zuni.

In the late 1930s the Hopi began to make jewelry, but there were not many silversmiths until after 1946. The work done before that is not distinctive from that of the Zuni or Navajo. The best-known Hopi jeweler was Charles Loloma from Hotevilla. He used secret settings of different stones – turquoise, coral, sugulite and obsidian – to make colorful bands inside the curves of his rings and bracelets, so that they could only be seen by the wearer. His design sense was very strong and clear and today many of the Hopis make jewelry which is inspired by Loloma and his teachings. Other pueblos make some jewelry, but most of the production is from Zuni, Hopi, Santo Domingo and, of course, the Navajo Nation.

■ Weaving

Prehistorically textiles were made by a number of ingenious processes from whatever suitable plant or animal fibers came to hand. After cotton was introduced these processes were still retained. Non-loom techniques can be divided into two categories: finger-weaving of the single element which requires no tools or only simple devices and that using netting and looping, and coil without foundation, or warp-weft weaves involving two sets of elements worked at right angles to each other. It is interesting to note that knots had great ceremonial and cultural importance, and are carefully rendered in the murals of the *kivas* at Pottery Mound and Kuaua.

Surprisingly large and complex textiles can be made with these simple processes. Non-loom warp-weft weaves are made without a loom with heddles. These were favored by the basketmakers to make narrow bands, sandals, soft bags and fur or feather robes. This process involved winding a sturdy yarn continuously around two supports. The yarn between these loops was separated and treated as warps. More complicated weaves such as tapestry weaves were employed by the Anasazi Basketmakers for apron fronts, tump-lines and other bands. The Anasazi and Mogollon sites also produce warm, weft-twined blankets of fur or feather cord. In these the warps are established by winding one continuous fur or feather cord back and forth. Pueblo weaving on looms goes back to at least AD 700 when cotton first began to appear in the Southwest. The loom was introduced from Mexico, and by 1100 vertical looms were found all over the Southwest. The vertical loom of the Pueblos was used exclusively with cotton yarns, creating a distinctive form known as Beautiful Design which consists of embroidered colors on a white cotton background.

There was a division of labor between the Pueblo men and women in weaving, the men producing most of the weaving. Men wove on their looms in the *kivas* (although they also made non-loom ceremonial belts and tump-lines). A Hopi groom's male relatives were expected to weave his bride's wedding dress. Groups of women working together made fur and feather blankets, which were non-loom weaving. The use of the upright loom with heddles has now almost died out in the pueblos, but there is still non-loom weaving, now done by men.

The Navajo probably learned to weave from the Pueblo Indians no more than 300 years ago – although they weave wool rather than cotton using women rather than men – and today they are the best-known weavers. The Navajo textiles are closely related to Pueblo cultures in their use of balanced formal designs; indeed the distinctive banded design style of Pueblo blankets and shawls is an obvious influence on much Navajo work. The loom which they use, an upright loom, is related to the loom used by Pueblo men. The interchange between Pueblos and Navajo is hard to trace, but the twill and diamond designs appear in Pueblo weaving from long ago and the Navajo may have learned from the Pueblos and then later given the technique back. The woman's dress, or *manta*, for both Pueblo and Navajo is black wool with a red border, but blue at Zuni. It is woven in two pieces, joined at the side and fastened over one shoulder. Today the women wear a cotton calico undergarment, but on feast days the garment is worn as it was prehistorically. It may be that the diamonds in the weaving represent the different worlds in which the Indians lived and passed through to arrive in this, the world of living people.

The Navajo loom is made from any wood which is at hand. The main supports are two posts which are set upright in the ground. A set of beams is then lashed horizontally at the top and bottom forming a roughly rectangular frame.[30] Usually a woman weaves outside her home or *hogan*, in the shade of a tree. She weaves when there is time, when the baby is asleep, when the sheep are not demanding care or when the meal is over. It is a stop-and-start process. Navajo weaving is characterized by the use of what are called lazy lines. These are breaks in the weaving which are the result of a sitting woman weaving only as far as she can reach, then scooting over and weaving another section. They are so-called because they save energy for the weaver who is sitting in the shade, and not working her entire loom.

The Navajo value weaving highly and say that they learned to weave as a gift from Spider Woman. Baby girls are prepared with a special ritual for their future as weavers. In Navajo legend it is said: 'When a baby girl is born to your tribe you shall go and find a spider web which you must take and rub on the baby's hands and arms. Thus when she grows up she will weave and her fingers and arms will not tire from the weaving.'[31] In deference to such origin stories the women used to leave a hole at the center, like a web, but traders stamped out the practice and a 'spirit outlet' replaced it; this is a thin line or flaw from the center to the edge.

Early Navajo blankets were banded and serrated with limited amounts of red used carefully as a color accent. These are the early blankets which are woven to be worn with the stripes around the body. They are woven with a very tight weave, which makes them somewhat waterproof and warm; the colors derived from various hues in the wool (white, black, gray) and vegetable dyes (yellow, red, indigo). Because the Navajo were nomadic and far-flung in their remote region, we know little about the chronology of their weaving but it appears that by 1863 the level of technical sophistication in Navajo weaving was very high.[32]

The categories of First, Second and Third Phase Chiefs' Blankets are somewhat misleading. These handsome blankets were not worn by Chiefs, or even exclusively by men but there is no question that these blankets were valued highly (and ownership lent a connotation of power) and that weaving such a blanket was a mark of prestige. It appears that these Chief blanket patterns were woven concurrently with more complicated design patterns and other weaving which was for internal use and was not as fine.

In 1868 many Navajo were allowed to return to their homes from their imprisonment at Bosque Redondo and a small group of merchants moved onto the reservations to trade the Navajo's manufactured goods (jewelry and blankets) for items the Indians needed in their new economy. In an attempt to help the Navajo, two traders, Lorenzo Hubbell and J. B. Moore, and others began to suggest more commercial patterns which the Navajo might weave. They, and traders in other parts of the vast reservation, were responsible for the development and marketing of Navajo crafts, as well as changing the way it looked. Their trading posts were also another way of moving crafts to market and other posts began to appear on the Navajo reservation.

The new designs came from books showing oriental rugs, probably mostly Turkish, thought to be more in keeping with the then tastes of American consumers. The Navajo women looked at the pictures of the oriental rug designs, memorized them and wove them. These designs took the name of their regional trading posts and are called Crystal, Ganado (red, black, gray and white geometric designs), Tuba City (storm designs with lightning), Shiprock (which produced a distinctive *Yei* design of the Navajo gods in long dancing rows), the Two Gray Hills (noted for its very fine tight weave and black, gray and white wool), Wide Ruin (soft, natural colors) and others. There are more than a dozen different areas; the actual design, however, is always different because it is the product solely of the individual weaver. The rugs were more colorful than before and often had a border, an element missing in traditional Navajo weaving. Finally, the Navajo began to weave some of their stories and occasionally some of their religious ceremonial designs. Navajo sandpaintings, which were used in curing ceremonies, were woven into wall hangings. (These rugs, especially those woven in the 1930s by the great Hosteen Klah, are the core of the collection at the Wheelright Museum of the American Indian, and are quite rare – only a medicine man could weave them.)

Today many copies of old Navajo rug and blanket designs are being produced in Mexico, using cotton weft or inferior wool, but following Navajo colors and designs. These copies of Navajo rugs sell very well, since the cost of a fine Navajo rug has gone up, and fewer young weavers are entering the market. The traditional Navajo way of life, the language, tending sheep and living in isolation, and the importance of ceremonies are all under stress as the modern world makes more inroads on the reservation. There are signs of a weaving revival, but the time and patience required to produce a rug are not easily assimilated into the life of today's teenage Navajo. For the Navajo, the two skills of making jewelry and weaving blankets and rugs have formed the basis of present day Navajo arts and crafts. These are both arts which appeal to the nomadic soul, are useful and portable. In the Pueblos, however, weaving has almost stopped. The pueblos of Acoma and Zuni were weaving wool mantas, which are used to make dresses and can also act as heavy shawls, until after 1900, but the availability of ready-made clothes at the trading post hurt the Pueblo weaving trade. The fine diamond-weave designs on mantas with embroidered borders which were done for ceremonial use and are still used for dances are handed down as ceremonial heirlooms.

■ Basketry

Baskets represent a vital aspect of American Indian life from the standpoint of survival as well as artistic expression. Along with the working of stone and bone, basket-making was probably a basic technical skill of the first occupants of the North American continent. Because basketry materials are so perishable not many relics survive, but in the dry climate of the Southwest, especially in caves, many baskets and basket fragments have been preserved, with some radio-carbon dates going back more than 10,000 years.

There was a large prehistoric group in the Southwest called the Basketmakers during the period from 100 BC to AD 700. The technical level of their baskets is unsurpassed. From this period there are large storage baskets, sandals, aprons and mats, and practically every article which they used, which was not stone or bone, was a type of basketry. The extensive reliance on basketry declined with the introduction of ceramics about AD 700, but baskets were still used for washing grain and winnowing and for starting pots.

The earliest basketry technique is twining, where the moving elements, or wefts, twist around the foundation elements, or warps. Several thousand years later the coiling method came into being. In coiling a hard or soft core element, which makes the coil, is wound round and round in a spiral fashion and held in place by thin wrapping elements, the stitches. A third technique is plaiting, where the warps and wefts merely go over and under each other in a particular pattern which varies from simple to complex. Within these three basic groups large regional variations occur and significant differences can be used to identify each region and tribe.

Before any basket can be made, the weaving materials have to be gathered and prepared. This takes a great deal of time and knowledge, not only in the careful selection of choice raw materials such as willow, grass and reeds, but because the materials have to be gathered seasonally and to have reached a particular point in their growth cycle. Once the materials have been assembled, before weaving can be started there usually has to be some preparation in the form of cleaning, stripping, splitting or treatment by applying heat or liquids. These procedures are complicated and time-consuming. In some cases the roots of plants are specially treated by heat by being buried in hot sand for a day or so in order to make them more pliable and more durable. Occasionally the fibers may be twisted into cordage for warps or wefts. Stems, shoots and twigs are often split, necessitating great skill to produce long and even-sized elements. Colors and dyes have to be prepared, or the materials may be treated directly, for example, by being buried in mud.

When all the materials are prepared, the basket maker makes a decision about the size and decoration of the basket. Working out a design requires concentrated effort. Gathering materials may be somewhat routine, but thinking up the design takes more effort. It must be fitted to the size and shape of the basket; all the elements must work out evenly, so there has to be mathematical proportion and symmetry with accurate calculations. The weaver has to keep in mind all the details of the various elements of the pattern: where there are design elements, how they are placed and their relationship to each other as the weaving progresses. The variations in length, size and shape of the design and the spaces between require many permutations and intense concentration. In many cases the weaver cannot keep track visually because she (both historically and at the present, most basket weavers are women) cannot see the opposite part of the basket. For true quality work, the weaver cannot begrudge either time or patience. The finished basket is usually a marvel in geometric and mathematical perfection.

Baskets are versatile and are woven in many shapes. Woven water bottles were common all over the Southwest, many of them made by the Paiute and traded to the Hopi, Zuni and Navajo. These woven water bottles are covered with pinion pitch so that they do not leak. It is also possible to cook in a basket, by filling the basket with hot water and food, and dropping hot rocks into the basket. This method of cooking was still used by the Paiutes as late as 1900. The unbreakable and lightweight nature of baskets made them the best choice for portable cookware. Basketry may be the mother of pottery. Today a shallow basket is sometimes used to hold the clay as a pot is first begun. It is possible that the use of coils to make ceramic vessels came from the experience of using coils to make baskets.

The Hopi of Second and Third Mesa are probably the best known contemporary basket makers in the Southwest. (The other Hopi Mesas do not make baskets.) The Hopis weave by coiling or plaiting, using yucca over grass or shredded yucca bundles; they plait baskets either with yucca strips or with rabbit brush wefts and wild currant warps. The flat baskets best serve as trays or sifters – or as well plaques. Deep baskets with flared sides of rabbit brush and Native or aniline-dyed designs are also decorative and useful items for sale to tourists. The Hopi use coiling to make circular trays or plaques and storage baskets in various sizes. Hopi flat trays of wicker are used for carrying the sacred corn meal, and serving the flat piki bread. Some of the best of these come from the village of Old Oraibi.

When a Hopi girl is about to be married, she asks her female relatives to help weave all the baskets which will be required for her dowry. It may take several years to weave all the baskets. The requirement for this skill in a wife shows both the economic and ceremonial importance of basketmaking to the Hopi. Wedding baskets are important for the Navajo too, but they require only one basket for the wedding and it is an important part of the ceremony, not the dowry. This basket is a shallow bowl which is coiled with the basic colors of red, black and natural vegetation color.[33] The material is of sumac stitched over a three-rod willow foundation. This design band is said to illustrate the hills and valleys of this world and the underworld. There is a break in the design which is the path that spirits take between the two worlds. According to tradition the end of the coil must line up with this break: this provides an easy method of locating the opening which must face east during the ceremony.

Many other fine basket-making groups live in the Southwest. The Havasupai are Hokan-speaking Yumans who live in a secluded branch of the Grand Canyon which has beautiful waterfalls. They are known for their weaving which has continued to the present day. The Walapai are close relatives who live in northwestern Arizona, making baskets by coiling and twining. They frequently use sumac twigs since sumac grows all around their reservation. The Hualapais and Yavapais are similarly active.

A much larger group, the Apaches, are close Athabaskan relations to the Navajo and probably came into the Southwest with them. They are well-known for their excellent baskets. These were nomadic peoples who did not want to settle down on reservations; baskets were easy to move and did not break. Today they do live on reservations but their main craft remains basket-making, although that skill is not being passed on to the next generation. Apache basketry has been commercial since the 1880s, traditionally crafted from yucca, sumac and mulberry, made to simple and utilitarian designs, and colored with reds, yellows and blues. The three traditional types are round, shallow trays; tall burden baskets; and vessels made watertight with pitch.

There are two principal divisions in the Apache, a result of their nomadic past, each with several main bands: the Western Apache comprises the San Carlos, White Mountain, Cibecue and Northern and Southern Tonto; to the east are the Mescalero, Jicarilla and Chiricahua groups. The Western Apache traditionally practiced more farming and were culturally closer to the Navajo, the San Carlos Apache in particular having produced many examples of beautiful basketry.

The Jicarilla still weave some baskets, partly thanks to Lydia Pena, a remarkable weaver who has done a good job in restoring interest in basket-making among the tribes. She teaches classes and sells most of her produce, but it is hard work and it is difficult to price the baskets high enough to cover the time involved.

The work of the Western Apache is mostly coiled trays, large burden baskets and storage baskets. The designs are mostly geometric, but the use of human and animal forms is common. It is interesting to note that these most nomadic of the Southwestern Indians continued making baskets like burden baskets, for practical use in moving materials around, rather than using baskets for ceremonies or specific processing of food as was the case in the pueblos. This survival of baskets in such ceremonial use makes anthropologists think that basketry is very old in the Southwest, since the ceremonial use of objects is usually very conservative.

There are two groups of Indians in southern Arizona who are specially noted for their baskets, the Pima and the Papago. These people live in the very hot and arid desert and their basket work is closely related. Pima baskets are made from willow and devil's claw over a foundation of tule. Since the 1890s the Papago have changed material, and now yucca has replaced willow in Papago work, which makes it easier to distinguish between them. The start of the baskets is also different, the Papago basket start is a cross, and the Pima a plaited knot. Probably the most recognizable Papago basket is the burden basket. Today's Papago probably make more baskets than any other tribe with animal and plant forms as their favorite decorative elements. Since the Papago basket is pounded as it is woven, their baskets tend to be flatter and wider than a Pima basket. Pima baskets are close to Apache baskets in the excellence of their weave. Their designs are usually geometric patterns in swirls or a quadrant layout. Most designs are based on squash blossoms, whirlwinds or a maze. These are frequently shallow baskets which were used for winnowing seeds or ground wheat.

■ Sculpture and Leatherwork

There has been sculpture in the Southwest since prehistoric times. Soft stones have been carved, and figurines in stone, wood, clay and shell were common throughout the Anasazi times: there is a carved stone Hohokam ram which may have been a palette, or designed for some ceremonial use. One form of carving still much in evidence is the Zuni art of fetish making from minerals and semi-precious stone. The animal figures are very important in regional culture, being used in the hunt societies and as part of medicine bundles. Carved from turquoise or soft stone, the fetishes are usually small for portability and concealment. They often have bundles of sage or feathers tied around them. Today, fetishes have become popular charms for tourists.

One of the most notable losses during the early Spanish period was that the kachinas, the masked gods, disappeared from the Rio Grande pueblos, although they still appear in Zuni or Hopi. Many small carvings of the sacred kachinas have been made from dried cottonwood by the Zuni and the Hopi for the past few centuries.[34]

In the 19th century Zuni kachinas were often dressed in real cloth and leather, while Hopi kachinas had their clothing carved out of the wood. Zuni kachinas also usually have taller bodies, and their limbs are articulated. Today, the lines between Zuni and Hopi kachinas are somewhat blurred, and the situation is further confused because the Navajo have been making kachinas since 1985 for sale to tourists. The kachinas embody the spirit of many different ideas and things. For the Zuni and the Hopi the kachinas come to bless and to chastise people. It is important to know what kachina you are seeing, and so the dolls are made to teach the children to recognize and to invoke these special beings. This is especially true for girls, since boys will learn to recognize the kachinas in the *kivas*.

Kachina dolls today can be elaborately carved, but a century ago they tended to be simple. They have always been sought by collectors since they portray the rich religious life of the Pueblos in a tangible way. Simple, wooden kachina dolls were traditionally given to Hopi children as their first toys, the mother kachina, or *Hahay'iwuuti*, being hung over the cradle to bring good health. Today, the technical excellence of all the carvers has increased and most of the production of kachinas is for the market. There are many kachinas, and different ones appear seasonally. Spending half a year with the Hopi, the kachinas bring them rain and prosperity. Each kachina has different attributes and subtle changes in costume. It is important to all the Pueblos that the kachinas do not disappear, and the depiction of the kachinas is one way of reminding people of who the kachinas are, their special functions and, as important, who the Pueblo people themselves are.

As well as kachinas, gambling and gaming objectives were carved, ceremonial sticks prepared and painted, and figures created to form part of the altar screen in the *kiva*. *Tablitas*, or flat headdresses, were also made and painted for women's dances; the Butterfly Dance or the Corn Dance, for instance, may use different *tablitas*.

Another craft associated with the Apache in the last century was the manufacture of handsome, cut-leather shirts and dresses. Whole skins of deer or antelope were tanned, then fringed and pierced with circles or square holes in order to create designs made by the cutaway portions of the skin. The leather might be dyed and ornamented with shells or feathers to add beauty and/or protective medicine. Many fine examples of dresses and saddle bags are held in various museum collections.

REFERENCES

THE SOUTHWEST

1 The myths and tales of the Southwestern peoples have many points of similarity running through them, particularly the Western Apache and Navajo who have similar emergence stories, heroes, gods and goddesses. The number four is a broader example: it is the number of directions; the number of Hopi worlds and number of days they use to fast, to think about a problem or to undergo purification; the number is invariably four whenever anything needs to be counted in a myth (days, events, objects, etc); it is the number of nights taken to tell the Papago origin myth; and so on.

2 Some people believe winter is the only time that it is safe to tell the stories, the time when they are safe from lightning and the snakes are asleep. Such time-of-the-year taboos are not unusual: the Jicarilla.

3 The origins of the Navajo sandpainting ceremonies are related in legend; the Hopi myths describe either how their ceremonies were given by the gods to the clans before they emerged from the underworld or how they were revealed to mythical heroes during the course of their adventures.

4 Opler, 1938:Preface xii.

5 An example of 'modern influence' is the inclusion of whites in the myths; that having been said, it is thought that the Hopi myth of the good *bahana*, or white man predicted to come from the east, was pre-contact.

6 *Kivas* are over 1,000 years old and central to the cultural and ceremonial life of the Southwestern pueblos. The *kiva* is a social gathering place for the men of the village – women are usually excluded – as well as a religious place for the transmission of secret ritual knowledge and practice.

7 To the Hopi the four worlds follow the pre-Earth spirit world of boundless space they call *Topkela*. The first three worlds were destroyed to punish human misbehavior. The Fourth World, or *Tuwagachi*, is the current world we live in. The Navajo recall their story of creation and its multiple worlds in the lengthy Blessing Way ceremonial.

8 The Navajo have seven sacred mountains. Their traditional land is bounded by four of them: Blanco Peak, or *Tsisnaajina*, to the east; Mount Taylor, or *Tsoodzil*, to the south; the San Francisco Peaks, or *Doko'oosliid*, to the west; and Hesperus Peak, or *Dibentsaa*, to the north. These mountains were made from earth brought from similar mountains in the Fourth World.

9 An authority on the North American Indian, Ruth Underhill was associated for 13 years with the United States Indian Service and was Professor Emeritus of Anthropology in the University of Denver.

10 Navajo belief conceives the universe as being one in which good and evil are maintained in inter-related harmony. Mankind's problem, or duty, is to maintain that harmony, or *hozho*, and cere-monials help to achieve this.

11 Three mesas contain the Hopi villages. First Mesa has Walpi, Sichomovi and Hano; Second Mesa has Shungopovi, Mishongnovi and Shipaulovi; and Third Mesa has Old Oraibi, New Oraibi, Hotevilla and Bakabi, with the farming community of Moenkopi nearby.

12 The *hataali* conducts the ceremonial, having memorized the complicated rituals involving word-perfect recitation of hundreds of songs. Due to the complexity, singers tend to specialize in just a few ceremonials.

13 Dillingham, 1992:5.

14 Cushing, 1886:511.

15 Dillingham, 1992:8.

16 Before the Spanish arrived in 1598, some pueblos had developed a low-melting-point lead glaze which was used as decoration, not as a seal. When the Spanish returned after the 1680 Revolt, the use of lead glaze disappeared and the pottery of the southern pueblos and Hopi was slipped with a clay that fired to a matte finish, and decorated with red and black which is still in use today.

17 The American entrepreneur, Fred Harvey, brought good food and quick service to the travelers on the railroads which were pushing west. He also saw that he could make money selling Indian arts and crafts. His agent, Herman Schweizer, went around the reservation buying and sometimes com-missioning things which could be sold. The railroad of the late 1880s also led to a reduction in the size of many of the large vessels. Tourists wanted things of a size that they could pack to take home.

18 Dillingham, 1992:10. This is interesting because it indicates the strong sex-linked roles in these traditional cultures, that being struck by lightning is a clear transformational experience and that only then could one cross a sex line to perform tasks which were culturally assigned. That division, however, has broken down.

19 We believe there was a change in the shape of vessels when the Spanish introduced wheat. Bread dough needs a big open bowl to rise, and although the market for big dough bowls may have been steady under the Spanish, the American troops who arrived in 1848 were all bread, not corn tor-tilla, eaters, and the best known of the bread bowls, the Santo Domingo dough bowl, was prob-ably produced to make wheat and yeast bread for the tastes of the American Army. Information from David Snow in an unpublished manuscript.

20 Margaret Harding, an anthropologist at the Lowie Museum, University of California, brought back photographs of the insides of pots to Zuni in the mid-1980s. These were pots which had dis-appeared from Zuni when Frank Hamilton Cushing in mid-1880 had collected almost every pot in Zuni and taken them to the Smithsonian in Washington. Verbal communication with Margaret Harding in 1985.

21 Sturtevant, 1979:517.

22 Personal communication with David Snow, Southwest ceramic specialist.

23 They got control of the great turquoise mines from the pueblo of San Marcos, which emigrated to Santo Domingo when San Marcos was abandoned.

24 During the Bosque Redondo in 1864-68, one man, *Atsidi Sani*, or Old Smith, first began to work iron and fix the bridles for the soldiers and cowboys.

25 'All the smithing was done outside beside a campfire. Sometimes an apprentice would watch and help. If a young man has a father who is a silversmith, he will begin to help him with the work when he is about fourteen years old . . . As he grows older and becomes more experienced in work-ing metal, his father gives him more to do, and within a period of a year or two he is able to make silver by himself and sell it at the trading post.' Adair, 1962:76

26 It is thought the masterful Navajo learned the craft from the Pueblos who gained it from the Spanish; there was, however, metalworking among the Athapaskan kin of the Navajo in the north, so their knowledge may predate their migration.

27 Bloom 1936:226.

28 Adair, 1962:15.

29 Herman Schweizer had pre-cut turquoise given to Navajo smiths who were working for traders. The Harvey company sent the material to trading posts to be made into bracelets, beads and other jewelry.

30 A second pair of horizontal beams holds the weaving. These are laid on the ground and the warp, the vertical threads, is strung continuously in a figure-eight conformation between the beams. This is then raised and fastened inside the rectangular frame. It is not attached at the top beam, but is lashed to an intermediate pole, the tension beam. This intermediate beam creates a more even tension for the warp. The lower warp is then tied directly to the bottom of the frame. Then the heddles, which are used to raise and lower the weaving, are made. They open a temporary space, or shed, between the two planes of the warp threads through which the yarn passes. After the yarn has passed, the batten – a wide flat stick – is removed, and the yarn is beaten into place with a weaving comb or a firm stroke of the batten. Berlant and Kahlenberg, 1991:41-42.

31 O'Bryon, 1956:56.

32 Personal communication with Mary Hunt Kahlenberg, 1994.

33 The Apache say that they use the Navajo basket because once when an Apache chief was sick, a great Navajo medicine man helped his Apache brother with the curing ceremony. The patient recovered, and when the Apache thanked his helper and asked the secret of his power, the Navajo said the basket was important.

34 The kachina is made from the dried cottonwood root, the center of which must also be the center of the kachina.

THE PLAINS

The Great Plains form the very heartland of North America. A land of sun, wind and grass, they stretch north to south more than two thousand miles from the North Saskatchewan River in Canada almost to the Rio Grande in Mexico, while their east-west boundaries are approximately those of the Mississippi–Missouri valleys and the foothills of the Rocky Mountains, in all encompassing an area of some one million square miles.

During the eighteenth and nineteenth centuries, when contact with whites was first made, the Great Plains were largely dominated by Algonquian and Siouan linguistic groups, although others such as Athapaskan and Uto-Aztecan were also represented. The principal tribes included the Blackfeet, Gros Ventre, Sioux, Crow, Comanche and Pawnee.

The Northern Plains were largely dominated by Algonquians, the Central Plains by Siouans. These particular linguistic groups were not well represented on the Southern Plains although some Cheyenne and Arapaho formed strong military allegiances with the Kiowa and Comanche who dominated this region.

The population was relatively small; in 1780, for example, the Blackfeet (name used in this chapter; also called Blackfoot), one of the largest groups on the Northern Plains, were estimated at fifteen thousand, the Lakota ten thousand and the Cheyenne three and a half thousand, while the semi-sedentary tribes such as the Omaha, Mandan and Arikara on the Missouri River have all been estimated to have been less than four thousand in 1780.

Climate varies on the Plains; in general the limited rainfall produces a semi-desert-type terrain particularly to the west and south, where in places the arid conditions result in so-called 'badlands'. To the east, however, in the Mississippi and Missouri valleys, the rainfall is higher, often producing

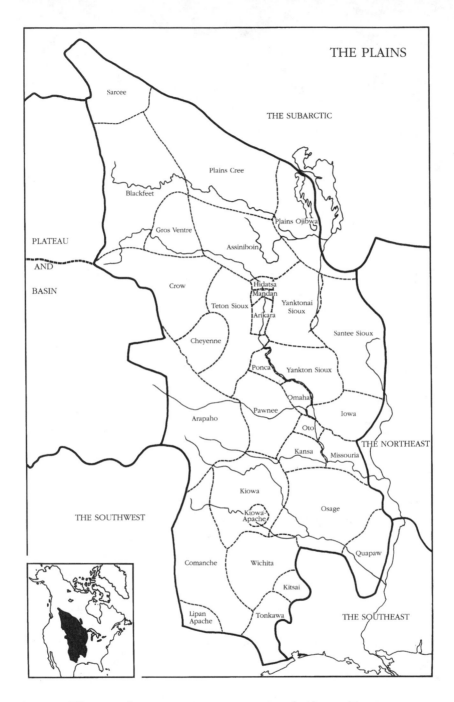

ABOVE: *This map shows approximate territories of tribes and language groups at about 1800. After that, all tribes lost territory and some moved.*

humid conditions and green prairie lands. In these areas the grass is tall and luxuriant; further west in such regions as the present-day states of North and South Dakota, Nebraska, Montana and Kansas this gives way to a short grass; while it is generally referred to as 'buffalo grass', it is in actuality a vital food resource for many Plains animals.

Plains animals exhibit characteristics which are indicative of the nature of the country in which they live. Thus, all can survive without water for extended periods, and all, except the wolf and coyote, are grass-eaters. Most are ultracautious and extremely difficult to approach and kill, such characteristics being particularly exemplified by the prong-horned antelope. Its acute sense of sight, great speed and ability to communicate danger by means of the white patch on its rump give it a high survival rating. In the nineteenth century and earlier, the antelope was found in vast herds across the Plains, possibly being even more abundant than the better known buffalo which, because of its size, first caught the attention of early white explorers.

The antelope was an important resource to both prehistoric and historic man on the Great Plains. When the Cheyenne, for example, first moved out on to the Plains in the late eighteenth century, they found evidence of antelope pounds – converging streams, bush or rocks terminating at a deep pit or ditch – which earlier pedestrian inhabitants had employed. The Cheyenne repaired and extended these, realizing that it was the most effective way of capturing such a wily creature. The antelope obviously greatly impressed the Plains tribes; not only were they a nutritious source of meat, but their horns were used in special headdresses or painted on ceremonial regalia while the skins were fabricated into garments – shirts, leggings and dresses.

The animal which most dominated the Plains, however, was the bison, better known as the buffalo. Although archaeological evidence and early explorers' descriptions indicate that this animal was formerly widely distributed in North America, by the mid-nineteenth century it was largely confined to the Plains region where it roamed in immense herds, the total population of which has been conservatively estimated at sixty million. The bull buffalo stood almost 6½ft (2m) high at the shoulder and weighed 2000lb (about 900kg); unlike the antelope, buffalo had poor eyesight and although their sense of smell and hearing was well-developed they could often be approached downwind by a cautious hunter.

Early pedestrian man on the Great Plains commonly hunted the buffalo in a similar way to the antelope, stampeding the herds in to a V-shaped drive leading over a cliff edge. Evidence of such early drives is noted in the Introduction; one site in southern Alberta was used by Paleo and Historic Plains Indians until about 1850, when the buffalo herds began to disappear. Called by the Blackfeet *Estipah-Sikikini-Kots* – 'Where-he-got-his-head-smashed-in' – it was also a place of great ceremonial and ritual importance, where practical action in the trapping of buffalo was accompanied by appeals to higher powers, evoking the spirits of the mountains, winds and the raven, the latter considered by the Blackfeet to be the wisest of birds.

Thousands of buffalo were killed annually at such sites by stampeding the animals, often so many at one time that it was impossible to utilize all the fresh meat and, while much was subsequently dried and made into pemmican for winter use and the hides used for tipi covers, there was the inevitable waste. Thus, in December 1809, when the fur trader-explorer Alexander Henry came across a recent pound kill on the Vermilion River (in what is now present-day Alberta), he was quick to observe that 'The bulls were mostly entire, none but the good cows having been cut up'.

Who the *archaic* Plains pedestrians were is conjectural. However, it is almost certain, as was discussed in the chapter on the Plateau and Basin (pp. 179–205) that several tribes such as the Kutenai, Flathead and particularly the Shoshoni commonly traveled on foot to the Plains region to hunt buffalo. Some archaeological evidence suggests that several bands may even have lived on the western fringes of the Plains 'for several thousand years'.

It was not, however, until the acquisition of the horse from the South and the gun from the East that a full flowering of historic Plains culture emerges; further, while the horse gave great mobility and enhanced the general quality of life – the elderly were no longer abandoned, tipis could be larger and more goods and food transported – the gun enabled the pedestrian Blackfeet and Cree to match and finally force the equestrian Shoshoni to abandon the Plains country. A decisive encounter which demonstrated the superiority of the gun, even against an enemy which had horses, was dramatically described by an aged Piegan chief, Saukamappee, to the explorer David Thompson in 1787. The battle, which occurred about 1740 (probably in present-day Saskatchewan), was between the Shoshoni and combined Assiniboin Piegan, the latter considered a frontier tribe of the Blackfeet Confederacy who, armed with a few guns (but no horses), were thrusting their way into the Northern Plains. Saukamappee first briefly explained how conditions had rapidly changed in perhaps just over a decade:

> 'By this time the affairs of both parties had much changed; we had more guns and iron-headed arrows than before; but our enemies the Snake Indians and their allies had Misstutim (Big Dogs, that is, Horses) on which they rode, swift as the Deer, on which they dashed at the Peeagans, and with their stone Pukamoggan knocked them on the head, and they thus lost several of their best men. This news we did not well comprehend and it alarmed us, for we had no idea of horses and could not make out what they were.'

Saukamappee then described the formation of the combined Piegan and Assiniboin war party, the preliminary war ceremonials and the tallying of their weaponry by the War Chiefs. In all they had some ten guns with plenty of ammunition and powder between them and those so armed were 'now considered 'the strength of the battle'.

After a few days march they were confronted by a large war party of Shoshoni; Saukamappee continued:

> 'When we came to our allies, the great War Tent [was made] with speeches, feasting and dances as before; and when the War Chief had viewed us all it was found between us and the Stone Indians we had ten guns and each of us about thirty balls, and powder for the war, and we were considered the strength of the battle. After a few days march our scouts brought us word that the enemy was near in a large war party, but had no Horses with them, for at that time they had very few of them. When we came to meet each other, as usual, each displayed their numbers, weapons and shields, in all which they were superior to us, except our guns which were not shown, but kept in their leathern cases, and if we had shown [them], they would have taken them for long clubs. For a long time they held us in suspense; a tall Chief was forming a strong party to make an attack on our center, and the others to enter into combat with those opposite to them; We prepared for the battle the best we could. Those of us who had guns stood in the front line, and each of us [had] two balls in his mouth, and a load of powder in his left hand to reload. We noticed they had a great many short stone clubs for

129

Above: *Kill Spotted Horse, an Assiniboin warrior, c.1898. The eagle feather headdress is of quite an unusual style, the feathers being set well back from the brow so as to lie close to the head.*

close combat, which is a dangerous weapon, and had they made a bold attack on us, we must have been defeated as they were more numerous and better armed than we were, for we could have fired our guns no more than twice; and were at a loss what to do on the wide plain, and each Chief encouraged his men to stand firm. Our eyes were all on the tall Chief and his motions, which appeared to be contrary to the advice of several old Chiefs, all this time we were about the strong flight of an arrow from each other. At length the tall chief retired and they formed their long usual line by placing their shields on the ground to touch each other, the shield having a breadth of full three feet or more. We sat down opposite to them and most of us waited for the night to make a hasty retreat. The War Chief was close to us, anxious to see the effect of our guns. The lines were too far asunder for us to make a sure shot, and we requested him to close the line to about sixty yards, which was gradually done, and lying flat on the ground behind the shields, we watched our opportunity when they drew their bows to shoot at us, their bodies were then exposed and each of us, as opportunity offered, fired with deadly aim, and either killed, or severely wounded, every one we aimed at.

'The War Chief was highly pleased, and the Snake Indians finding so many killed and wounded kept themselves behind their shields; the War Chief then desired we could spread ourselves by two's throughout the line, which we did, and our shots caused consternation and dismay along their whole line. The battle had begun about Noon, and the Sun was not yet half down, when we perceived some of them had crawled away from their shields, and were taking to flight. The War Chief seeing this went along the line and spoke to every Chief to keep his Men ready for a charge of the whole line of the enemy, of which he would give the signal; this was done by himself stepping in front with his Spear, and calling on them to follow him as he rushed on their line, and in an instant the whole of us followed him, the greater part of the enemy took to flight, but some fought bravely and we lost more than ten killed and many wounded; Part of us pursued, and killed a few, but the chase had soon to be given over, for at the body of every Snake Indian killed, there were five or six of us trying to get his scalp, or part of his clothing, his weapons or something as a trophy of the battle. As there were only

RIGHT: *Quanah Parker, principal Chief of the Comanche, shrewd politician, Peyote religion proselytizer, and his wife Tonasa, in about 1892.*

BELOW: *Crow warriors dressed for dance, c.1890. Note the large brass bells tied just below the knee; with drums and singers, these added to the dance rhythm.*

three of us, and seven of our friends, the Stone Indians, we did not interfere and got nothing.'

Under such pressures, the Shoshoni tribes gradually retreated from the Northern Plains, a process which was accelerated as the Blackfeet, Assiniboin and Cree progressively acquired more guns due to the expansion of the fur trade and also changed their warfare tactics, now successfully raiding the Shoshoni for horses.

In contrast, while the Shoshoni traded with the Spaniards in New Mexico, obtaining articles of clothing, iron kettles, metal bridles, stirrups and mules, the Spanish policy was not to trade firearms to Indians. This put the Shoshoni at a decided disadvantage, as one of their distinguished chiefs, Cameahwait, complained to Lewis and Clark, 'But this should not be, . . . if we had guns, instead of hiding ourselves in the mountains and living like the bears on roots and berries, we would then go down and live in the buffalo country in spite of our enemies, whom we never fear when we meet on equal terms'.

While the time-scale and pressures varied, similar patterns were replicated across both the Central and Southern Plains. Thus, into this vast area moved Algonquian and Athapaskan-speaking tribes from the north and east – the Blackfeet Confederacy, Cree, Arapaho, Cheyenne, Sarcee and Kiowa-Apache. From the east and southeast came the Siouan tribes – the Nakota, Lakota and Dakota, Crow, Hidatsa and Mandan and from both west and southeast the Pawnee, Arikara, Comanche and Kiowa. They brought with them a diversity of cultures which, due to the impact of a new environment had, by about 1800, led to a commonality of basic lifestyle enhanced and mixed by trade and warfare, but often retaining much of their former ethos.

On the Northern Plains much, particularly that relating to horse nomadism, was obviously adopted from the former dominant occupants, namely the Shoshoni who, as Lewis and Clark observed in 1805, had 'within their own recollection' formerly lived on the Plains, but had been 'driven into the mountains by the Pawkees, [Piegan] or the roving Indians of the Sascatchawain'. Lewis and Clark's vivid descriptions of the Shoshoni fit much of what was to become typical of the nomadic historic Plains Indian: an emphasis on warfare as a means of achieving high social status, a coup-counting hierarchy, scalping, the use of the horse in all aspects of their lives, short bows – typically about 3ft in length (less than a meter) for

ABOVE: *Powder Face, an Arapaho chief, 1870. His crooked lance indicates membership of the Arapaho Spear Society – one of the warriors who was expected never to retreat in battle.*

effective use on horseback, given high elastic qualities by a backing of sinew – otterskin bow-and-arrow cases, small circular buffalo hide shields endowed with supernatural powers of protection derived from their ceremonials of fabrication and painting, and the use of highly dangerous stone-headed clubs. Likewise, much of the horse equipment, such as stirrups, saddles and bridles, was clearly similar in style, some of which was undoubtedly strongly inspired by the Spanish. For example, the common pack saddle was modified and given a high flat-topped pommel and cantle and, while popular with Shoshoni women at the time of Lewis and Clark's visit, it later emerged as a classic Crow woman's style of saddle. Further, the elaborate horse collar which became such a well-known feature of Crow horse equipment, seemingly had its roots in the Shoshoni custom of suspending 'at the breast of his horse the finest ornaments he possesses'.

One important factor which led to the success in the emergence of Historic Plains Indian nomadism was undoubtedly the development of the tipi. It is unclear as to the type of dwelling actually employed by the earlier Plains Shoshoni; possibly it was a small-scale conical shaped dwelling covered with pieces of elk or buffalo skins. However, the true tipi – which consisted of a large semi-circular cover pulled over a conical frame of straight poles and having a facility for regulating the draft of smoke from the central fire generally by the adjustment of the distinctive ears or wings at the top – was observed by Spanish expeditions to the Southern Plains as early as the middle of the sixteenth century. Since dogs were used for transportation at that time, it is probable that these dwellings were small, possibly no more than 8ft (2.5m.) in diameter. The inspiration for such habitations may well have been based on the conical wigwam which was found throughout the boreal regions of both the New and Old World for, as one scholar has pointed out, these tipi dwellers observed by the Spanish (probably Athapaskan-speaking Plains Apaches) had only recently migrated from the vicinity of the Northern Plains.

The tipi was generally pitched with its back toward the prevailing westerly wind direction, its wide base and sloping sides giving high stability to the sometimes sudden and strong winds which occur on the Plains. While all tipis were similar in appearance, there were some definite tribal variations, classification being broadly based on the number of foundation poles. In the areas where the winds were particularly strong, a three-pole foundation was used, while in more protected areas – near the mountains or wooded river valleys – a four-pole foundation was favored. Thus, such widely spaced tribes as the Blackfeet on the Northwestern Plains and the Omaha in the Southeast employed the four-pole base whilst the Assiniboin to the east of the Blackfeet on the windswept Plains of what is now Saskatchewan and Manitoba, and the Kiowa on the Southern Plains, tended to the three-pole type. The Crow favored the use of elegant, unpainted tipis, and the Lakota those which were embellished with both realistic and geometrical paintings, but perhaps the most impressive were some of those belonging to the Blackfeet which, even as early as 1809, were described by the fur trader, Alexander Henry, as heavily embellished with pictographs of animals and birds, both real and mythological.[1]

The designs on tipis were believed to secure for their owners protection against misfortune and sickness, and definite conventions were employed in the painting of symbolic motifs which were clearly understood by the custodians of the particular tribe's religious tradition, but not necessarily by the common man. Thus, for the Blackfeet what might be called the Maltese Cross was traditionally symbolic of the Morning Star – endowed with powers to protect those entitled to employ the motif – and was painted in red at the rear top of the tipi. Ownership of a sacred painted tipi, together with all that it entailed, was an outward display of high social standing within the tribe.

High status, however, also pivoted firmly on success in warfare, the capturing of enemy horses rather than killing being a major objective in the Historic Period; appeals to higher powers for help in these matters attempted to evoke the spiritual forces which would help attain the goal. Much of the Plains Indian cosmos centered on observed animal powers – the strength of the buffalo, the speed of the antelope, the bravery of the eagle and weasel, and so on – but there was also a recognition of an intangible power of the universe which manifested itself in varying forms from one linguistic group to the next and was embedded in ancient beliefs which, while modified by the Plains environment, can be traced back to the original Woodland homelands of several Plains tribes.

Widespread was the concept of three parallel worlds. Under the surface of the lake on which the earth floated, were powerful spirits which had control over animals and plants on land and in the water, while above the earth beyond the dome of the blue sky, lay the realm of the upper world. This world was dominated by spirits which matched those of the underworld, among the most powerful of which were the Thunderbirds who, by the flashing of their eyes and flapping of their wings, produced the lightning and thunder. A perpetual state of war existed between the sky and water spirits and while the sun was often closely associated with the Thunderbird, it was considered that it and the moon were the energy sources which controlled the day and night and the seasonal 'cycles'. On earth, the spirits of the four winds changed the seasons, their energies both sustaining and perpetrating the life 'cycle'. For hundreds of years, the symbolic and religious artwork of the Woodland tribes gave free expression to these great powers.

These ancient concepts were modified and interpreted in various forms by the Historic Plains Indians, environmental factors undoubtedly having considerable influence on the changes that were made. Thus, the Eastern Sioux replaced the underwater panther, so important to the Woodland tribes, with symbols of an underwater horned monster which had the ability to emerge from the lakes and live in trees, and further west among the Blackfeet the symbol of such powerful underwater spirits was the tadpole, its use on the costume of the owners of the prestigious Beaver Bundle being explained by a Blackfeet myth which associated the frog with the Blackfeet culture hero, Old Man, who defeated the terrible underwater enemies of mankind. The metamorphosis associated with the frog and its ability to move freely from water to land clearly has parallels with Eastern Sioux mythology.

A complex intertribal trade network was anciently developed in the Plains region and while there was little incentive for trade between tribes who had similar lifestyles, that between the hunters and horticulturists was beneficial to both sides. Thus, the nomadic tribes could offer dried buffalo meat and other products of the chase such as tanned deer and buffalo hides, numerous articles of apparel and buffalo hide tipis (used by the village tribes on their hunting expeditions), and in exchange the horticulturists offered corn, beans and pumpkins. With the introduction of the horse and European goods, it is probable that the newcomers to the Plains adopted the established trade patterns of those pedestrian nomads whom they displaced, and simply extended the activities. Among the best documented of these relates to the Cheyenne and Crow, the former trading to Missouri River tribes – the Mandan, Hidatsa and Arikara – the latter mainly with the Hidatsa and Mandan. Such trade expeditions must have been colorful and spectacular affairs. For example, when the fur trader, Charles Mackenzie, traveled to the Hidatsa villages in 1805, he witnessed the arrival of over two thousand Crow Indians on a trading expedition (Mackenzie, in Masson, 1889:360). Dressed in all their finery and subsequently pitching a village of three hundred tipis adjacent to the earth lodges of the Hidatsa, the trade was elevated to the status of an elaborate ceremonial. After smoking the pipe of friendship, the Hidatsa laid before the Crow trade goods which consisted of two hundred guns with one hundred rounds of ammunition for each, a hundred bushels of corn, together with quantities of axes, clothing (probably European) and kettles. In exchange, the Crow gave two hundred and fifty horses and large quantities of buffalo robes, leggings and shirts. The trade was lucrative to both sides. Thus, the Crow sold their horses to the village tribes at double the price that they fetched at the Shoshoni Rendezvous, while the village tribes doubled the cost again to the Cree and Assiniboin who brought in European goods from the northeast. Recent research suggests that the rapid movement of trade goods across the Plains appears to have been facilitated by a middle rendezvous between Western and Eastern Crow bands – the so-called Mountain and River Crow. This network efficiently distributed guns from the English Hudson's Bay trading posts (situated in present-day Manitoba and Ontario), through the Hidatsa/Mandan villages via Assiniboin and Cree, across the Plains via the River and Mountain Crow to be traded to the Nez Perce and Shoshoni for horses and Spanish horse equipment such as saddle blankets and bridles. While the frontier of the gun thus moved west and south, that of the horse rapidly moved to the north and east.

Costume styles were clearly influenced by trade patterns of this sort, well beyond the regions of the Plains, and involved more than just commodities. One ancient and ever-expanding network almost certainly introduced cultural influences from the Lower Mississippi Valley via the Mandan and Hidatsa villages on the middle Missouri River. This increasingly led to an integration of early Northern Plains ritual, cosmology and art, with that of the cosmic structure and ceremonialism of the southeast. The spread was undoubtedly via Assiniboin Indians who lived in the region of the Qu'Appelle Souris and Assiniboine Rivers of present-day Manitoba, so that Mississippian cosmology was incorporated in the world-view and rituals of the Plains buffalo hunters. As one observer recently put it, 'The role of Sun and his son, Morningstar, the cosmic struggle between thunderbirds and water monsters, virility derived from the elk spirit, and many other concepts can be traced to the southeast'. Thus, unlike the well-documented trade of goods across the Plains, the major import from the Lower Mississippi was one of a spiritual nature. Additional evidence for this assumption is provided by petroglyphs painted and etched on cave walls and cliff faces found in the Plains region which, after about 1730, changed markedly from animal pictures (suggesting spiritual relationships between artist and animal spirits), to scenes of warfare. 'A new way of life emerged, made up of fragments of the old world-view changed to function in new contexts, increasingly motivated by the achieving of war honors and acquiring material wealth, to be ostentatiously displayed in warfare and tribal ceremonies. Much of this colorful paraphernalia and ceremonialism undoubtedly originated in ancient times, but owed its survival to a reinterpretation of symbolism in terms of warfare'. Coupled with this emphasis, there was also cultural elaboration due to abundance of natural resources and adoption of the horse leading to a shift of regional culture from horticultural villagers to equestrian nomads.

The warlike spirit of many, if not *all*, Plains tribes was clearly motivated by something more than material wealth because a typical Plains Indian family did not require vast herds in order to supply material wants; indeed, considering their nomadic way of life, such apparent wealth could well be a hindrance rather than an asset and, in the main, it is to the Plateau tribes that we must look for individual ownership of several hundred horses. While generosity could enhance a man's status, it was, above all else, the acquisition of *war honors* – an inherited craving for distinction and glory – which seems to have been the basis of Plains warfare. Analysis of the possible nature of cultural ethos input relating to warfare from the Southeast shows that here war was considered to be a social institution and that warlike exploits were necessary for social advancement. The essence of much typical Plains warfare, such as counting coup on a live enemy with a harmless stick, was reported on for the Illinois Confederacy in the early 1700s.

Taking a scalp signified more than the death of an enemy[2] and ancient traditions dictated that the deed brought with it several exacting obligations. Thus, in the early eighteenth century, one missionary reported of the 'Nations of Louisiana' that those who for the first time had taken a scalp or made a capture 'do not sleep at their return with their wives, and do not eat any meat; they ought not to partake of anything but fish and thickened milk. This abstinence lasts for six months. If they fail to observe it, they imagine that the soul of him whom they have killed will cause them to die through sorcery, that they will never again obtain any advantage over their enemies, and that the slightest wounds they may receive will prove fatal'.

Customs were obviously no less rigid – but with a different emphasis – among the pedestrian nomads who occupied the Northern Plains at about the same time. Thus, the Piegan Chief, Saukamappee, told of the return of a successful war party carrying more than fifty enemy scalps.[3] There was much discussion among the warriors as to the symbolic meaning of those taken from the enemy who were found dead under their shields because no one could say that he had actually slain the enemy whose scalp he held; there was less doubt about the others, the War Chief finally decreeing that those who had taken 'the trophy from the head of an enemy they had killed, said the Souls of the enemy that each of us has slain belongs to us and we have given them to our relations in the other world to be their slaves, and we are contented'[4].

While initial encounters of Plains Indians with the white man were generally friendly, particularly in Canada, the systematic slaughter of both beaver and buffalo, brought about by the demands of the fur trade together with the influx of white immigrants into and across the Plains region after about 1840, caused a progressive deterioration in relationships between the various groups of established Native Americans and the newly arriving Europeans. An earlier, unfortunate encounter between two Piegan warriors who were killed by Meriwether Lewis during his epic voyage as co-leader of the Corps of Discovery after the Louisiana Purchase of 1803, caused relationships to be hostile between Blackfeet and Americans for many years. Further aggravation occurred with the American Fur Company's policy of sending white trappers into Blackfeet country rather than, as in the case of the Hudson's Bay Company, 'depending upon the Indian supply'. Not until 1846, when Alexander Culbertson – who was married to the daughter of a Blood chief – established Fort Benton near the junction of the Marias and Missouri Rivers, were relationships stabilized, at least in part, with the fierce Blood, Piegan and Siksika who comprised the Blackfeet nation: thus from that time for some thirty years, trading in buffalo hides, a commodity which the Blackfeet could easily supply, was carried on, a commerce which was considered highly beneficial to both sides.[5]

The lucrative returns of the fur trade spelled the death knell of the Plains tribes as the demand for buffalo hides grew. One English observer, William Blackmore, who traveled through the valley of the Platte River in 1868, reported seeing immense herds of buffalo which extended for a distance of over one hundred miles. The Plains were 'blackened with them' and at times the train on which he was traveling was brought to a standstill to let them pass. Some five years later, in the autumn of 1873, Blackmore was to travel over virtually the same ground. This time he was confronted with an entirely different scene, the whole country being whitened with bleaching buffalo bones and in some areas 'there was a continuous line of putrescent carcasses, so that the air was rendered pestilential and offensive to the last degree . . . The professional buffalo skinners had moved in.' Subsequent investigations by Blackmore revealed that even as early as 1872 the number of buffalo which were being slaughtered for their hides alone was at least a million per annum. The professional hunters formed lines of camps along the banks of the Arkansas River and *continuously shot buffalo* night and day as they came down to drink.

The wanton slaughter alarmed and appalled the Plains Indians. The *New York Herald* reported on 16 November 1877, that Sitting Bull was said to have observed:

'It is strange that the Americans should complain that the Indians kill buffaloes. We kill buffaloes, as we kill other animals, for food and clothing, and to make our lodges warm. They kill buffaloes – for what? Go through [the] country. See the thousands of carcasses rotting on the Plains. Your young men shoot for pleasure. All they take from dead buffalo is his tail, or his head, or his horns, perhaps, to show they have killed a buffalo. What is this? Is it robbery? You call us savages. What are *they?*'

Not only were the Plains tribes being deprived but, in addition, Blackmore pointed out, the settler who always looked to the buffalo for a winter supply of meat could no longer depend on their appearance and, like the Plains Indian, bitterly opposed the slaughter solely for their hides.

Adding to the decimation of the buffalo was another problem – the immigrant movement to Oregon. By 1845, it was a common sight to see the distinctive covered wagons wending their way along the Oregon Trail, which commenced in eastern Kansas, followed the Platte River across Nebraska and on to Fort Laramie in Wyoming. In western Wyoming it cut through the Continental Divide following the Snake River to Idaho and then into Oregon, terminating at The Dalles on the great Columbia River which led to the Pacific Ocean. Part of the Oregon Trail – in Nebraska and Wyoming – cut across the hunting grounds of the Oglala, one of the largest and most powerful of the Lakota sub-tribes. By the summer of 1850, lured by tales of a land (now called California), where neither snow nor illness existed, and 'the black soil of Oregon was

141

bottomless', thousands of immigrants 'cascaded up the valleys of the Platte and the Sweetwater'.

This large influx of immigrants not only frightened away or destroyed game in the areas through which they passed but, more alarmingly, brought diseases to which the Plains tribes had little or no resistance. Within the space of a few years the Plains Indian and his environment was suddenly and frighteningly subjected to severe pressures, 'even the seemingly limitless bison of the Great Plains, grew suddenly less abundant and in places disappeared from their customary haunts . . . Alcohol drained the vitality from those attracted to the settlements and travel routes . . . Tribal ranges, . . . shifted constantly as groups dispossessed or shouldered aside encroached on others'. The situation was rapidly getting out of hand. Protection of both immigrants and the indigenous population now became a vital Government concern and to control a potentially explosive situation urgent measures were considered: the outcome was by both treaty and militarily.

Two major treaties were drawn up with the Plains tribes in the early 1850s: the Fort Laramie Treaty[6] in September 1851 which led to negotiations with representatives of the Lakota, Cheyenne and Arapaho, Crow, Arikara, Assiniboin, Gros Ventre and Mandan, and the Fort Atkinson Treaty of July 1853 which attempted to stabilize relations with the Southern Plains tribes such as the Comanche, Kiowa and Kiowa-Apache. In the case of the Laramie Treaty, boundaries for the tribes were defined and Head Chiefs appointed, such as Conquering Bear, a Brulé Lakota. Generous presents, with promises of more to come, were an important part of government policy[7] when encouraging chiefs to become signatories; it caused, together with the appointment of the 'paper chiefs' (as they became known), great discord, particularly with non-treaty factions. The military build-up in anticipation of potential problems with this latter group, was partially achieved by purchase or garrisoning by the army of the old and established fur-trade posts. Thus, Fort Laramie, purchased by the government from the American Fur Company for $4,000, now became a strategic military post; indeed, even before the 1851 Treaty, it had been garrisoned (in August 1849) by two officers and fifty-three men. A similar pattern was swiftly replicated across the Central and Southern Plains. While the established fur posts took on a strategic military function, others, such as Forts Riley and Larned, were purpose-built by the military for protection of another famous route to the south of the Oregon Trail – the

Santa Fe Trail. Additionally, protection of the route from San Antonio to El Paso, and deep in the heart of Comanche, Kiowa, Mescalero Apache and Tonkawa territory, was achieved by the establishment of military forts, such as Clark (1852), Hudson (1851), Stockton (1852) and Bliss (1849), near or on the Pecos and Rio Grande rivers. An uneasy peace was established, but it would be less than a decade before, from Mexico to Canada, Comanche, Kiowa, Arapaho, Cheyenne, Sioux and other tribes, would present a formidable opposition to further expansion, and which for almost a generation would impede the advance of the American frontier.

Dangers and attitudes were succinctly summed up by a popular immigrant camp-fire refrain:

'The Injuns will catch you while crossing the Plains.
They'll kill you, and scalp you, and beat out your brains.
Uncle Sam ought to throw them all over the fence,
So there'll be no Red Injuns a hundred years hence.'

A slow war of suppression of the Plains Indians began, strangely enough, with a cow, so thin and emaciated that it had been abandoned by its Mormon immigrant owner. Desiring a piece of rawhide and perhaps a questionable meal in the bargain, High Forehead, a Miniconjou Sioux who was visiting at Conquering Bear's camp, shot the animal dead on the afternoon of 18 August 1854 'to make restitution or satisfaction for any wrongs committed . . . by any band or individual . . . on the people of the United States . . .'.

The immigrants demanded compensation and although Conquering Bear immediately offered a horse in payment, Lieutenant Hugh B. Fleming considered the matter so trivial that no decision was reached that night. Probably the matter would have rested there, but next day Lieutenant John Grattan strongly supported the immigrants and claimed the right to command a detachment of infantry to arrest the offending Indian.[8] Reluctantly, Fleming agreed to the proposal, instructing Grattan to receive the offender, and in case of refusal by Conquering Bear to give him up, to act upon his own discretion, and 'not to hazard an engagement without certainty of success'.

Grattan, along with Sergeant W. Faver, twenty-six infantrymen, two musicians and a terrified interpreter (one Lucien Auguste) rode toward the Lakota encampment. Twice Grattan was forcibly warned of the potentially

143

dangerous situation. Obridge Allen, a professional immigrant guide, rode up and pointed out to Grattan 'that the Oglalas had begun driving in their pony herds – typical Indian preparation for battle'. Shortly after, James Bordeaux, an experienced and shrewd trader at that time trading directly with the Lakota, observed to Grattan, 'Why don't you let the old cow go. It was laying there without food or water and would soon die; it was too lame to walk; its feets [sic] was worn through to the flesh. It was shot by some boys who wanted a piece of skin'. Grattan told Conquering Bear that he had come to take High Forehead back to the Fort. Reported Man-Afraid-Of-His-Horses, 'The Bear said to me, "You are a brave, what do you think of it?" I said to him, "You are the chief. What do you think?".' Then Conquering Bear told Grattan that High Forehead was 'a guest in his village and not subject to his authority.' Although Grattan was made further offers of ponies to pay for the cow and was urged to delay any action until Major John W. Whitfield, the Indian agent, arrived, he ordered his troops into the Brulé village announcing that he would 'go himself to High Forehead's lodge'. He halted some sixty yards from High Forehead's lodge which stood near that of Conquering Bear's, and then he ordered the howitzers primed and positioned his men on either side of the cannon.

The parley now became increasingly bitter and even the diplomatic Conquering Bear was beginning to lose patience with the arrogant Grattan. Reported Man-Afraid, 'The Bear said it was hard as it was a poor cow and that today the soldiers had made him ashamed that he was made chief by the whites and today you come to my village and plant your big guns . . . For all I tell you you will not hear me. I would strike you were I not a chief. But as I am chief and am made so by the whites will not do it.'.

Within a short time, the frustrated Grattan broke off the parley and, moving toward the troops, gave a command that the Indians did not understand. Two or three shots were fired and one warrior was hit. Bordeaux then heard the chief's shout to the warriors not to fire, that perhaps this was just a shot to protect the honor of the troops and they would leave. Grattan, however, was now convinced of the need for a further demonstration and ordered the infantry to fire a volley. Arrows began to fly from the bowmen on the flank and Grattan's command, few if any of which had any experience of Plains Indian warfare, suddenly scattered in panic. Grattan himself crashed to the ground struck by arrows; when his body was found later, it had twenty-four arrows in it. One had gone completely through his head and he could only be identified by his pocket watch. Within a short time the entire command, except one, was wiped out. The sole survivor was Private John Cuddy who, although badly wounded, had crawled into the wild rose bushes. Cuddy died two days later without giving any account of the battle.

The clash underlined the vast differences between the two cultures, and it served as a warning to other would-be 'paper-chiefs'. The uneasy peace was over. The Grattan Massacre, as it became known, heralded the beginning of spasmodic and often brutal wars which were only finally and tragically terminated almost forty years later, in December 1890, with the massacre of Big Foot's Lakota on a tiny creek in South Dakota, which the world now knows as Wounded Knee.

As early as 1834, hostility by the Comanches towards white settlers who were moving westwards from Arkansas into the Plains of Kansas and Texas initiated the formation of a Dragoon Expedition led by Colonel Henry Dodge, to lay the foundation for a peace treaty. They arrived at the enormous village of some six to eight hundred tipis which was pitched in the vicinity of the confluence of the Washita and Red Rivers (in present-day Texas). Dodge explained to the Comanche the friendly motives of the expedition; that he was sent by the President of the United States and hoped that a system of trade could be established 'that would be beneficial to both'. The expedition proved a success and the following year agreements were ratified.

Problems, however, were looming for the Comanche, as Cheyenne, desirous of trading at Bent's Fort, moved south and joined the Arapaho. Together, these two tribes forced the Comanche, Kiowa and Plains-Apache to accept the Arkansas River as the northern boundary of their domain. Two years later, however, realizing the potential dangers of approaching well-armed eastern Indians and whites into the Southern Plains, *The Great Peace* alliance was formed; not only did it ensure that the Cheyenne and Arapaho now had plenty of horses (from the horse-rich Comanche), and that the Kiowa and Comanche had access to guns and ammunition (via the northern trade), but it also led to a formidable barrier to any further encroachment by whites from the east. The Comanches had every reason to be wary of the whites and even this great alliance did not protect them. In March 1840, for example, twelve Comanche chiefs met with Texas commissioners, hoping to conclude a peace treaty; the Texans, however, demanded that the Comanches gave up their white prisoners. On refusing, troops were brought into the council room and in the ensuing fight all twelve chiefs, together with twenty other Comanches, were slaughtered.

After the annexation of Texas to the Union (in 1845), the federal government made attempts to develop a consistent and fair policy toward the Southern Plains tribes. In 1847, a tactful and patient agent – one Robert S. Neighbours – was appointed as special agent for the Indians of Texas, and for several years his friendly influence maintained an uneasy peace on the Southern Plains. However, an unratified treaty made with the Kiowa and Comanche in April 1863 led to further discontent and Comanche, Kiowa, Cheyenne, Arapaho and some Sioux caused the routes to Denver and south as far as the Santa Fe Trail to become unsafe: immigration stopped 'and much of the country was depopulated'.

Retaliation by Colonel J. M. Chivington, heading a state militia of Colorado Volunteers, led to the massacre and rout of a peaceful Cheyenne village at Sand Creek, some one hundred miles southeast of Denver, under Black Kettle, White Antelope and Left Hand. While the latter two chiefs fell under the hail of bullets, Black Kettle miraculously survived but the barbarity and savagery of the militia – men, women and children were scalped and mutilated in a brutal manner – shocked the American people and the Sand Creek Massacre, as it came to be called, precipitated a policy of continuous harassment by the more militant Cheyenne Dog Soldiers[9] led by Tall Bull and White Horse, whose ranks were swelled by Northern Cheyenne under Roman Nose and Lakotas under Pawnee Killer. By June 1867, with Denver virtually isolated, the warriors advanced and attacked Fort Wallace, just northeast of the now infamous Sand Creek site. An ensuing engagement gave an Englishman, Dr William A. Bell, an insight into the brutality of Plains warfare and the incident made famous forever a fellow countryman, one Sergeant Frederick Wylyams. According to Bell, Wylyams, who was educated at Eton, while 'sowing his wild oats had made a fatal alliance in London and gone to grief'. Wylyams had then left for America where he enlisted in the U.S. Army; he was with Captain Albert Barnitz's G. Troop of the Seventh Cavalry when Bell met him. Wylyams had hoped to gain a commission and thereby get back into the good graces of his family; it was not to be. As the cavalry followed a small band of Indians beyond a ridge, they were suddenly confronted by a large body of warriors. Bell records, 'They halted a few minutes . . . then, like a whirlwind, . . . they rushed on the little band of fifty soldiers . . . Saddles were emptied, and the soldiers forced back over the ground towards the fort . . . the Indians pressed heavily cutting off five men, among them Sergeant

Frederick Wylyams . . . one by one the soldiers fell, selling their lives dearly.' The Indians were finally repulsed by Captain Barnitz's better armed cavalry and the bodies of the fallen five discovered. The shocked Dr Bell later recorded, 'I have seen in days gone by sights horrible and gory – death in all its forms of agony and distortion – but never did I feel the sickening sensation, the giddy, fainting feeling that came over me when I saw our dead, dying and wounded after this Indian fight. A handful of men, to be sure, but with enough wounds upon them to have slain a company, if evenly distributed.' The sergeant's body had been savagely mutilated and, with scientific objectivity, Bell described in detail the different signs which each tribe had left on his body so that their presence in the battle was thus recorded; he felt that there was little difficulty in recognizing the meaning of some of the wounds. 'The muscles of the right arm, hacked to the bone, speak of the Cheyenne, or "Cut Arms", the nose slit denotes the "Smaller tribe" or Arapaho; and the throat cut bears witness that the Sioux were also present. There were therefore amonge the warriors Cheyenne, Arapaho and Sioux. It was not till some time afterwards that I knew positively what these signs meant, and I have not yet discovered what tribe was indicated by the incisions down the thighs, and the lacerations of the calves of the legs, in oblique parallel gashes. The arrows also varied in make and colour according to the tribe; and it was evident, from the number of different devices, that warriors from several tribes had each purposely left one in the dead mans body.'[10].

A Special Governmental Joint Committee, which published *Condition of the Indian Tribes* in 1867, pointed out that the major problem with these southern tribes was due to extensive white intrusion into their territory. This led to the Medicine Lodge Treaty near Fort Dodge, Kansas, in October 1867; it was a genuine attempt by the Government of the day to reconcile the vast differences which existed between the interests of both. The great Indian village of some eight hundred and fifty tipis and five thousand Indians – Cheyenne, Arapaho, Comanche, Kiowa and Kiowa-Apache were represented – was finally assembled in the vicinity of Medicine Lodge Creek, so-called because the Kiowa had recently celebrated their annual Sun-dance nearby and the medicine lodge was still standing at the time of the conference.[11] The some one hundred whites, commissioners, interpreters, clerks and newsmen were escorted by a battalion of the Seventh Cavalry under Major Joel H. Elliott. The impressive assembly has been described in recent times as one of the 'largest and most colorful gathering[s] of Indians and officials ever witnessed on the plains' and 'free food and plenty of coffee were provided to ensure that the Indians did not wander away'.

Although the treaty was signed by such famous chiefs as Little Raven (Arapaho), Black Kettle and Little Robe (Cheyenne), Satank and Satanta (Kiowa), Wolf Sleeve (Kiowa-Apache) and Ten Bears (Comanche), and the attacks on whites ceased for several months, intertribal warfare continued unabated. Cheyenne and Arapaho raided the Osage and Kaw, while the Kiowa and Comanche raided the Navajo, Caddo and Wichita. Later, they began forays to the farms and settlements of the Chickasaw[12]. As one of their number wryly observed: 'The wolf will respect a treaty as much as Mr Wild Indian'.

The problem stemmed from several misunderstandings and difficulties, a pattern which was to be repeated in later negotiations with tribes on the Central and Northern Plains. The treaty had stipulated that in return for safe traffic across the Plains, agencies and schools would be built, and farming tools, seeds, doctors, instructors and artisans provided. At the new agencies, rations and annuities were to be regularly distributed and arrangements made so that unscrupulous agents and traders did not cheat the Indians. The government, however, was slow in meeting the stipulations of the treaty and it later emerged that many of the Indian signatories did not fully understand their obligations, or if they did, found it difficult to control the younger warriors, particularly those of the Comanche and Kiowa, who still raided into Texas which, since its annexation in 1845, made its people citizens of the United States. Traditionally, raiding south into these areas had been the Kiowa and Comanche warriors' path to wealth and glory and the continued hostile action of the southern tribes led to demands for more effective military protection.

The death of Roman Nose at the Beecher's Island battle in September 1867, and the slaughter of Black Kettle together with over one hundred men, women and children, by Custer at Washita in November 1867, the progressive decline of the buffalo, superior weapons and the Cavalry's ability to strike the village communities in winter, wore the tribes down. By the early 1870s, the principal Kiowa and Comanche war leaders – Satank, Satanta and Kicking Bird – were dead; new leaders – such as Feathered Lance of the Kiowa and the able Quanah Parker of the Comanches – sensing the inevitable, turned to negotiation and many visited the Great Father in Washington.[13]. By 1875, warfare on the Southern Plains was all but over;

less so, further north, where smoldering apathy over broken treaties was being rapidly replaced by open hostility.

The Fort Laramie Treaty, which was finally concluded in November 1868 with Red Cloud's signature together with those of some two hundred leaders of the Lakota – Brulé, Oglala, Miniconjou, Hunkpapa, Blackfeet, Sans Arc and Two Kettle – as well as Santee and Yanktonai, conceded all of Red Cloud's demands which 'for the army, it was an unpalatable but not indigestible prescription'. This was withdrawal of the army from the Bozeman Trail, abandonment of such forts as Fort Phil Kearny and C. F. Smith, and the granting of hunting rights on the Republican River and in Nebraska and Wyoming. It also reserved the Powder River country as 'unceded Indian territory' on which no white might trespass without Indian consent. As with the Medicine Lodge Treaty the previous year, it provided for the building of schools and the issuing of rations and annuities. On several counts the Laramie Treaty was a success; it ended the eponymously named Red Cloud War which had shed so much blood on both sides particularly with the annihilation of Fetterman and more than eighty men on the 21 December 1866 and the later Wagon Box of 2 August 1867 where, although white casualties were not so high, some of the men never fully recovered, mentally or physically, from their ordeal.[14]

The government-sponsored expeditions to the Black Hills in 1874 and 1875 to investigate mineral wealth led to a largely unfounded rumor of extensive gold deposits. The Treaty of 1868 had defined the Great Sioux Reservation to encompass a vast area west of the Missouri River of what is today the state of South Dakota; this included the *Pa Sapa* or 'Black Hills', an area considered sacred to the Lakota. By late 1875, a Gold Rush had commenced; encroachment into Lakota territory was a violation of the 1868 treaty and the army attempted to keep the miners and others out. Inevitably, the task was impossible. As Senator Hurlbut noted in July 1876: 'I say to you there is not power enough in this Government to stop the progress of this [our] conquering race . . . you cannot repress . . . the people of this country . . . there is not power enough to stop the migration of our people'.

By February 1876, a new war with the Lakota was on, precipitated by Sitting Bull's refusal to leave the Powder River country and register at one of the agencies, the ultimatum being initiated by none other than Ulysses Grant himself, President of the United States: 'If they neglect or refuse so to remove', said Congressman Chandler in July 1876, 'they will be reported to the War Department as hostile Indians, and that a military force will be sent to compel them to obey the orders of the Indian Office.'[15]

A winter campaign by Brigadier-General George Crook, who led ten companies of cavalry and two of infantry into Powder River country against Sitting Bull and Cheyenne allies in March 1876 was quickly abandoned due to severe weather conditions. On return, a spring campaign, larger and better organized, was planned by Brigadier-General Alfred H. Terry. On 29 May 1876, Lieutenant-General P. H. Sheridan reported to General W. T. Sherman in Washington, DC, on 29 Nov 1876, on the projected three-pronged campaign under Terry and Crook. 'Brigadier-General Terry moved out of his command from Fort Abraham Lincoln in the direction of the mouth of Powder River . . . The total strength of his column is about nine hundred men . . . General Crook will move from Fort Fetterman with a column about the same size. Colonel John Gibbon is now moving down north of the Yellowstone and east of the mouth of the Big Horn with a force of about four hundred . . . each column should be able to take care of itself, and to chastise the Indians, should it have the opportunity . . . I presume the following will occur: General Terry will drive the Indians towards the Big Horn valley and General Crook will drive them back towards Terry; Colonel Gibbon moving down on the north side of the Yellowstone, to intercept . . . the result of the movement of these three columns may force many of the hostile Indians back to the agencies . . .'

Unknown to these three forces, one of the largest concentrations of Plains Indians ever known in the Historic Period was rapidly building up along the valley of the Little Big Horn, drawn by the charismatic Sitting Bull of the Hunkpapa and Crazy Horse, undoubtedly one of the most distinguished War Chiefs the Oglala ever produced. A village of some fifteen hundred tipis containing between twelve to fifteen thousand Indians – mainly Sioux and Cheyenne – was strung for three miles along the banks of the Little Big Horn River. Sitting Bull's message had traveled far; a few weeks previously, he had invited the powerful and influential Blackfeet chief, Crowfoot, in Canada 'to join the Sioux in their fight against the Americans and after victories over both the Americans and Crows, the Sioux would join the Blackfeet in Canada to eliminate the whites.[16]

The predicted retreat of the Indians from Crook's forces was foiled by Crazy Horse's attack on the morning of 17 June. Crook was camped on the headwaters of the Rosebud with more than one thousand officers and men and some two hundred and sixty Shoshoni and Crow scouts. The Indians struck without warning – Crook was playing a game of cards and his men were having breakfast. The ensuing battle lasted six hours; unhindered by consideration of their women and children who were camped some seventeen miles further north, Crazy Horse's forces employed unusual offensive tactics leaving Crook's column severely depleted of ammunition and with nearly one hundred dead and wounded. Most importantly, Crook was eliminated from the three-pronged campaign.

Four days later, on the afternoon of the 21 June, Terry, Gibbon, Custer and Brisbin held a council of war on board the *Far West*. Later that day, Mark Kellogg sent what was to be his last despatch to the *New York Herald*; in his dispatch he outlined the next step of the historic campaign. Custer would 'start with his whole command up the Rosebud valley . . . and follow the Indians as long and as far as horse flesh and human endurance could carry his command . . . [he] proposes to live and travel like Indians; in this manner the command will be able to go wherever the Indians can. Gibbon's command has started for the mouth of the Big Horn'. Custer's Seventh Cavalry consisted of some 31 officers, 586 soldiers and in addition 33 Indian scouts and 20 employees and citizens. As Custer bade farewell, Gibbon apparently called out, 'Now Custer, don't be greedy! Wait for us!' Custer made the ambiguous reply 'No, I won't'.

At 12.05 on Sunday, 25 June, Custer divided his forces into four columns and prepared to attack. Major Marcus Reno with 131 men was to parallel Custer's movements; Captain Benteen with 113 men to the southwest and Custer with five companies (in all some 215 men), followed a line of hills leading to the lower end of the Indian village. At the Washita battle in November 1868, Custer had divided his forces in a similar way, attacking the village simultaneously from different points and hence maximizing confusion. At 3.15 Reno struck the *southern* portion of the great Sioux-Cheyenne encampment – Sitting Bull's Hunkpapa. As the writer Stanley Vestal has noted:

> . . . 'under a towering cloud of dust, they caught the glint of gun barrels, saw the flutter of a guidon, the blue shirts of the troopers . . . . Lead whistled overhead, smacking the tipi poles. The soldiers were coming on the gallop straight for the Hunkpapa camp. In that camp all was confusion. Old men were yelling advice, . . . women and children rushing off afoot and on horseback, . . . fleeing from the soldiers . . . grabbed their babies, called their older children, . . . The

Hunkpapa stood their ground bravely . . . Every moment reinforcements came up and the firing grew constantly heavier . . .'

Several weeks earlier, during Sun-dance ceremonials on Rosebud Creek,
Sitting Bull had experienced a dramatic vision; it foretold of a great triumph for the Sioux with many dead soldiers falling into camp. Inspired by
the promise and imagery, the Hunkpapa stood their ground. 'Instead of
running, the Indians ahead multiplied until there was a solid front before
the village.' Reno's force was now pushed into a defensive position, the
command was being rapidly surrounded by Sioux and Cheyenne warriors
and began to retreat in a free-for-all. 'The fight was not at all in accordance
with my ideas' said Thomas H. French of the 7th Cavalry. 'The so-called
charge from the valley was almost a rout. I became sick and disheartened
with what was going on . . .'.

Cut off by a maze of bluffs which caused the timing to be misjudged,
'Custer's luck' had run out; his regiment was fragmented and each potentially exposed to separate defeats before they could again be united. Had
Reno's initial charge been sustained, victory may have ensued, but for Reno
the odds seemed too great: shortly after ordering his men to dismount, he
then gave the command 'Retreat to your horses men!' Confusion reigned:
'I thought that we were to charge headlong through them all, – that was the
only chance. To turn one's back on Indians, without being better mounted
than they, is throwing away life. When he [Reno] started to that hill he had
told me, not one minute before, that he was going to fight – this was in
reply to a question of mine', said French. While Reno was in retreat, some
three and a half miles away Custer attacked the other end of the village.
Like Reno, he too was confronted by a mass of Sioux and Cheyenne warriors, this time Hunkpapas under Gall, Oglalas and others under Crazy
Horse, and Cheyennes under Lame White Man; they repulsed his charge.
Within minutes, Company L under James Calhoun, their horses stampeded by Crow King and his warriors, was annihilated. The other four
Companies, C, E, F and I, many soldiers now dismounted, stood their
ground on the higher bluffs. Before 5 o'clock, however, Custer and his
entire force was completely surrounded and in less than an hour they were
all dead. 'Custer's Field' was discovered on the morning of Tuesday 27
June and as Captain Edward S. Godfrey later recorded, it was 'a scene of
sickening ghastly horror': Sitting Bull's prophesy had been fulfilled.[17]

The great Indian encampment rapidly dispersed; villages of that size could not be sustained, the grazing was soon exhausted and game driven away. Many returned to the agencies but most of the non-treaties under Sitting Bull, Crazy Horse, American Horse, Dull Knife and Little Wolf remained in Powder River country; their free life on American soil, however, was rapidly coming to a close. As Congressman Maginnis stated in July 1876:

> One repulse does not give enemies final victory . . . the blood of our soldiers demand that these Indians shall be pursued . . . [they must] submit themselves to the authority of the nation . . .

By late summer 1876 a two-pronged campaign against the Cheyenne and Lakota started to take effect; it extended well into the winter of 1877. At Slim Buttes, 8 September 1876, Mills and Crook attacked American Horse's village; the chief was killed and the village destroyed. At Red Cloud and other Sioux agencies, Crook subdued the Indians by a display of strength. Crook deposed Red Cloud, whose sympathies with the non-treaties were all too apparent. At Willow Creek, 25 November 1876 (south of the Big Horn Mountains), Ranald S. Mackenzie destroyed Dull Knife's village, thirty Cheyennes were killed and seven hundred ponies captured.[18] At Cedar Creek, Yellowstone River, 20 October 1876, Colonel Nelson A. Miles parleys with Sitting Bull who demands peace on the old basis (freedom to roam and hunt). Miles later recorded, that Sitting Bull 'spoke like a conqueror and he looked like one'. Wolf Mountain, Big Horn range, 8 January 1877, Miles attacks the Lakota under Crazy Horse, . . . village destroyed and Crazy Horse withdraws. March 1877, Sitting Bull and some nine hundred followers retreat to Canada. Lame Deer, west of Tongue River, 7 May 1877, Miles attacks and captures Miniconjou village, chiefs Iron Star and Lame Deer killed. Red Cloud Agency, May 1877, Crazy Horse surrenders.[19] Fort Robinson, Nebraska, 7 September 1877, Crazy Horse resists arrest and is bayoneted by a guard: 'My father, I am bad hurt. Tell the people it is no use to depend on me any more now'. Fort Robinson, Nebraska, January 1879, Dull Knife's Cheyenne starved into submission, break from army barracks, sixty-four killed and fifty wounded.[20]

There is little doubt that at this time it was Sitting Bull who epitomized the free and independent Plains Indian but the road ahead was to be particularly difficult as game became scarce on the Canadian Plains and gradually hundreds of Lakota crossed back to the United States to join friends and relatives at the agencies. By 1881, Sitting Bull had less than two hundred followers and finally, on 20 July 1881, at the head of his small band, he rode into Fort Buford, Dakota Territory, and surrendered: 'the final surrender of his cherished independence was a hard blow to his pride, and he took it hard. He was much broken'.

For two years Sitting Bull was held as a prisoner-of-war, finally returning to his people on the Standing Rock Reservation in 1883; the signs were ominous . . . Sitting Bull's return coincided with the last great Indian buffalo hunt. The immense herds had gone forever.

The continued influx of settlers and the building of the railroads exerted more pressures. The Great Sioux Reservation was increasingly viewed as standing firmly in the way of any further expansion westward and the settlers continuously insisted that the Indians move aside. In 1889, after much wrangling and questionable promises by the government, vast areas of the Reservation were signed away, a move bitterly opposed by Sitting Bull.[21] The winter of 1889-90 also heralded epidemics and with frightening suddenness the full realities of Reservation life became starkly apparent: Lakota political organization was shattered, their religious ceremonials were suppressed, the hunting economy abolished and now even their children taken away to distant schools to learn the ways of the white man. Thus, all the old values became meaningless so that the conditions necessary for self-fulfillment and the attainment of happiness no longer existed. The Lakota had reached an *anomic* state, a situation which was common to virtually all other tribes throughout the Plains, and elsewhere, as they were forced to adapt to a new way of life.

Wovoka's message of the *New World* to come was simple and clear. The Son of God would punish the white man for his injustices towards the Indians, he would wipe them from the face of the earth, the dead would be restored to life, the buffalo and other game would return, 'dance four successive nights . . . you must not hurt anybody . . . when the earth shakes [at the coming of the new world] do not be afraid. It will not hurt you'. As W. H. Prather of 1 Company, 9th Cavalry, wrote in *The Indian Ghost Dance and War*:

> 'They swore that this Messiah came to them in visions sleep
> And promised to restore their game and Buffalos a heap.'

The people danced – they called it the Ghost or Spirit Dance – and the earth indeed shook for shortly thereafter rifles and Hotchkiss guns also thundered.

'They claimed the shirt Messiah gave, no bullet could go through,
But when the Soldiers fired at them they saw this was not true
. . .
A fight took place, 'twas hand to hand, unwarned by trumpet call,
While the Sioux were dropping man by man – the 7th killed them all . . .'

On 15 December 1890, Sitting Bull crashes dead to the ground, bullets in his head and chest; 29 December, Big Foot together with some one hundred and forty-six men, women and children of the Miniconjou Lakota, dies on the Wounded Knee Field.[22] 'Do not be afraid,' Wovoka had said; 'It will not hurt you.' But the nation's hoop was broken and scattered, there was no longer any center, the sacred tree was dead – the conquest of the Plains Indian had become a reality. Wovoka's *new* message rang loud and clear, 'My children, today I call upon you to travel a new trail, the only trail now open – the White Man's Road' Samuel N. Latta, Indian agent for the Upper Missouri, summed up about 1860:

'A powerful and warlike people, proud, haughty and defiant – well over six feet in height, strong muscular frames and very good horsemen, well dressed, principally in skins and robes; rich in horses and lodges; have a great abundance of meat since buffalo, elk, antelope and deer abound in their country. They say they are *Indians* and do not wish to change their mode of living.'

MYTHS AND LEGENDS

The historic Plains tribes – the buffalo-hunting, tipi-dwelling, equestrian nomads – arrived comparatively recently on the Plains, moving into the region with the introduction of the horse in the mid-18th century. While the Plains culture lasted for no more than a century (1780–1880), it was forceful, dynamic, innovative and resilient. And during this period, there were many changes, some of surprising rapidity.[23]

There seems to be something within the unique environment of the Great Plains which causes a people to live with such vivid intensity and an awareness and wonder of the things around them. The Plains Indian was so much in daily association with his environment and so dependent upon it, that not only animals but plant life and even some inanimate objects were believed to have a spiritual existence. There was an awareness of a great power – the energy of moving force of the universe – which, in the sacred language of the Lakota shamans, was called *Skan* or *To* and the blue of the sky symbolized its presence. This was distinct from physical power and it could act in different ways for good or evil. It was against this background that ritual and ceremonial of the Plains tribe was set – the harnessing of this power to best effect, both at the individual and tribal level.

The importance of mythology was paramount in Plains Indian ceremonialism and the description of any ceremonial was invariably in terms of myth; such myths explained the topography of the Plains, with its lakes, mountains, badlands and majestic prairies, with repeated reference to the warpath, buffalo and quest for supernatural powers. Perhaps the most widespread are the versions of Old Man Coyote myths which relate to the origin of the Earth and Man: human heroes, too, are popular, animal figures often being transformed into humans (and perhaps back again) at various stages of a myth.

Myths expressed a fundamental pattern of conduct which regulated, and to a certain degree regimented, the population, the ceremonies being dramatizations of the sacred myths, and so, at least in theory, the complex details of a ceremonial continued unchanged through successive generations.

ORIGIN MYTHS

The creation of the world from a sample of mud, brought to the surface by a diving animal, frequently occurs in the mythology of the Plains tribes.

■ *Napi* or Old Man

The Blackfeet sages referred to the time when there was nothing but water, together with *Napi* or Old Man, the original culture hero, who sat on a log with four animals[24] pondering the possibility of something beneath the water. He persuaded them to dive down and explore; only the muskrat returned, bearing a sample of mud, which *Napi* took, rolling it in his hands while it grew rapidly before falling back into the water, assuming such dimensions that he was able to stand on it. He then released a wolf which ran across the partially dried mud, and whenever it stopped a deep indentation appeared, producing a valley. His further movements gave rise to the mountains and plains, while water flowed into some of the indentations to produce the lakes and rivers. The role of animals in the origin of the world was commemorated in the elaborate ceremonial of the Beaver Bundle which contained, at least in theory, representations of all the animals associated with Blackfeet cultural history – all except the frog which was excluded since it could neither sing nor dance!

■ First Creator of the Mandans

While the Mandan origin myths also make reference to diving animals and the formation of the Earth, the origin of the tribe itself was explained in terms of emergence from underground. Emerging, for example, from the butte of the Black Tailed Deer,[25] they brought corn up with them. Their chief at that time, Good Furred Robe, taught one group, the *Awigaxa*, special songs for success in growing corn. He also had a special robe that, if sprinkled with water, would cause the rains. The Mandans moved progressively north, and in one particularly dry year two men, First Creator and

Lone Man, appeared. These two culture heroes were credited with the origin of the Buffalo Dance, telling the tribe that whenever there was a shortage of food they should perform this dance to call the buffalo to the vicinity of the village. Mandan legend relates that there was a progressive development of the ancient and simple Buffalo Dance which led to one of the most complicated of Plains ceremonials, the *O-kee-pa* Ceremony.

■ **Pawnee Sky Powers**
While most of the Plains tribes explain their origins in terms of emergence from the earth, the Pawnee credit *Tirawahat,* the One Above, supreme and changeless, with making all things. He gave the stars great power, in particular the Morning Star whose younger brother was the Sun. In the east were those stars representing men and ruled over by the Morning Star and Sun; in the west were those stars like women, with the Evening Star and Moon as their rulers. The lengthy myth results in marriages between the Morning Star and the Evening Star and, after reconciling their differences, between the Sun and the Moon. Children were born to each couple and placed on Earth, who in turn married, populating the Earth.

The obstacles in the myths symbolically represented the sicknesses and troubles that humans experienced throughout life, and the teachings were that only by elaborate ceremonials, invoking the helping powers of the Morning Star and Sun, could these evils be overcome. Such myths led to the development of a complex sacred bundle system which was believed to have been given in ancient times by various of the heavenly powers, hence linking the powers to Earth-bound Man.[26]

■ **Underwater and Sky Powers of the Crow**
The Crow Indians' version of the origin of Earth and Man combines underwater and sky powers. Thus, Medicine Crow, the informant for this myth, related that many years ago there was no earth, only water, and the only creatures were ducks, and *Isà'katà'te,* or Old Man. One day, Old man came to meet the ducks, saying, 'My brothers, there is earth below us. It is not good for us to be alone,' and instructed a red-headed mallard to dive down and bring up some earth, but he was not successful. Then a pinto duck, blue-feathered duck and hell-diver were ordered to do the same thing but only the latter was successful, emerging with a little mud in his webbed feet. So, in company with the successful duck and with mud in hand, Old Man, traveling from the east, spread the mud around, thus making the

Earth. Traveling across the Plains, they found a medicine stone, *bacò'rit-si'tsè*, which Old Man said was the 'oldest part of the Earth,' able to reproduce itself, thus explaining why there are stones to be found all over the Earth. Finally, they saw a human who Old Man said had been a star but was now Earth-bound, but on approaching him he transformed himself into a tobacco plant – regarded by the crow as the first plant on Earth. Medicine Crow then explained that it was believed that the stars had assumed this form and if the tobacco was taken, raised in the spring and appropriate ceremonials performed – the Tobacco Society rituals – all the needs of the people would be met.

ALL-POWERFUL SPIRITS

The mythology of the Plains Indians provides valuable data on their culture, insights into their religion and into the way they viewed the powers associated with the spirit world. It also enables interpretation of much ceremonial of their often elaborate regalia.

■ The Adventures of Scar Face

The Blackfeet Scar Face myth, which makes reference to the powers of the Morning Star, the Sun and the Moon, concerns the adventures of a poor young man referred to as Scar Face because of a long ugly scar on his cheek. He was in love with the daughter of a chief but she was unwilling to marry him unless he could find a way of removing the scar. Desperately seeking supernatural aid to this end, he leaves for the Land of the Sun, a journey encountering many adventures and culminating in the killing of seven large white geese and seven aggressive cranes, the heads of which Scar Face took to the Sun. Thus, the Blackfeet explain the origin of scalping – proof that an enemy had been overcome – by reference to this mythological episode.

So impressed was the Sun with these feats of courage that he presented Scar Face with a fine costume embellished with weasel skins. The shirt had a quilled disk on the chest and back, symbolic of the Sun, and seven black stripes painted on the sleeves to represent seven of the birds, while the leggings were embellished with seven bands, symbolic of the defeat of the other birds.[27] Scar Face subsequently married the chief's daughter and became one of the most successful of Blackfeet ceremonialists.

■ The Spirit World of the Crows

The Crow Indians' concepts of supernatural powers are explained in the myth relating to *Eehtreshbohedish*, Starter of All Things or First Worker, who was said to be composed of the many vapory elements that existed before the world was formed by him. They said that First Worker gave to *all* things both a purpose and a power, which was referred to as *Maxpé* or medicine. It could be bestowed upon individuals by a supernatural helper to assist them throughout their earthly life, but they did make a distinction. For example, in their most important ceremonies, such as the Sun Dance and Tobacco Society rituals, the Crows offered prayers directly to First Worker.

■ The Lakota Concept of Power

The stand these people took toward the rest of mankind was to regard themselves as superior, but before the awesome forces of nature they presented themselves as humble and weak supplicants, yearning to gain – through a vision or dream – some of the powers which daily they observed around them. The Lakota perceived an all-pervading force, *Wakan,* the power of the universe, which was manifested in the blue of the sky or in the brilliant colors of the rainbow. Then there was the terrifying crash and reverberation of the thunder and associated destructive power of the lightning. All these, together with the wind and hail to name but two, were viewed as potential sources of power which, if symbolically harnessed, could be used to personal best effect. Thus, most of these powers were appealed to in the Sun Dance and Spirit Keeping ceremonials. The totality of the creative force of the Lakota universe was *Wakan-Tanka,* the Great Mysterious. Although it was recognized that *Wakan-Tanka* could at the same time be both one and many, it was only the shamans who attempted a systematic classification with the *Tobtob Kin,*[28] a system not fully comprehended by the common man. The shamans also said that *Wakan-Tanka* could communicate with humans through the *Akicita Wakan*, or Sacred Messengers. Those who had had visions sometimes drew what they had experienced, and both realistic and conventionalized representations of such messengers and spirits are found on Lakota accouterments, such as shields and warshirts;[29] the key to their interpretation lies in an understanding of the *Tobtob Kin.*

■ The Pawnee Universe

In Pawnee mythology it was *Tirawahat* who reigned supreme. The blue of the sky was associated with *Tirawahat* and he was ever-present in all things, particularly the storm. Pawnee mythology relates that in winter the gods withdrew from the Earth, the first thunder in the spring being a signal that they had once more turned their attention to it; thus commenced the Thunder and other ceremonies in succession. This first thunder was believed to be the voice of *Paruksti,* the deity who was a messenger of *Tirawahat;* and so as *Paruksti* traveled above the land with thunder as his speech, the Earth was reawakened and life rekindled. His return was celebrated by the commencement of the Thunder Ceremony, which traditionally ushered in the ceremonial year, and thanks were given by the people to the all-powerful spirits for renewal, the growth of crops, the birth of animals and birds, and the return of the buffalo – the cycle of all life on Earth.[30]

HERO CREATURES AND MONSTERS

In common with other regions, heroes in Plains culture came in many guises but more often than not drew directly from the animals in the world around them. Coyote was considered particularly powerful, for instance, in Crow mythology, being credited with attaining life by his own efforts. He transforms from animal to man and back depending on the circumstances.

■ Old Man Coyote and Summer

In this tale, the summer and winter are kept in different colored bags which are owned by Woman with the Strong Heart, but all she would release to Crow country was the winter, while the South always had summer. Despairing of the climate, Old Man Coyote tells a youth that he is going after the summer and obtains four male animals to help him – a deer, coyote, jack rabbit and wolf – and he assesses how far they can run. In order to arouse sexual passions, Old Man Coyote changes himself into an elk and arriving at Woman's tipi, exposes himself; on hearing shouts, Woman leaves her abode and Coyote takes the opportunity to slip in. When Woman returns, she is confronted at the door by Coyote who subdues her by rubbing medicine paint on her face. Coyote then carries of the bag containing summer, running with it until he is tired when the jack rabbit, deer and finally wolf carry it in turn. On reaching Crow country, wolf opens the bag and agreement is reached that each country should now have a summer and winter.

■ The Little People

Dwarf-like creators are a common ingredient in Plains mythology, in particular the Crow named Pryor Creek as *Aratace,* or Arrow Stream, at the request of a mythical dwarf who wanted arrows shot into the clefts of so-called Arrow Rock as an offering to him. offerings are still made today to a spirit who guided the last great Crow chief Plenty Coups, on his first mountain-top vision.

Not all Little People were exclusively benevolent, however. The Dakota and Lakota Tree Dweller, *Canotina* or *Canotili,* was a powerful spirit who generally appeared as a little man and dwelt in the forest ready to confront solitary hunters. He was generally malevolent and to be avoided for he caused people to be lost in the woods. His appearance struck terror in humans, since if they actually saw *Canotina* one of their close relatives was said to be doomed to die.[31]

■ Blackfeet Star Myths

The chief characters in the Blackfeet star myths either appear as heavenly bodies or become such at the end of their earthly careers. A number of these myths explain the acquisition of tipi designs, the origin of buffalo-calling and ceremonial episodes such as those associated with the Sun Dance. Generally, animals take an important part in these rituals, being persons in disguise and identified in descriptions as Otter Woman, Crane Woman, Beaver Man and Elk Woman. The latter refers to the medicine woman who was principal leader in the Sun Dance and, in Blackfeet mythology, dug a forbidden turnip out of the sky.[32]

■ Power of the Morning Star

In Pawnee mythology, Morning Star is a leader of men, helping with the creation of the universe. Morning Star travels with his brother, the Sun, to the land of the western stars in an attempt to overcome the power of the Moon who has killed all previous approaching man-stars. This hero figure uses the power of a sacred bundle and an associated war club to overcome the obstacles Moon puts in his way and thus enter the women star village.

■ Water Monsters

Water Monsters figure prominently in Sioux mythology, the Lakota refer-ring to them as *Unktehi,* their greatest powers being in water where no other forces could trouble them. They were thought to make the floods which they spewed out of their mouths, and they were said to catch people or animals and to eat them. Their power was in their horns and tails which they could push out or draw in as they wished. They were in a continual state of war with *Wakinyan,* the mythological Thunderbird. The subordinates of the *Unktehi* were said to be serpents, lizards, frogs, ghosts, owls and eagles.

HOLY PLACES, SACRED SITES

The Great Plains, as stated earlier, was a place of outstanding beauty, desolation and privation, and – given the right season – abundance. In common to all was the fact that they were nature's gift and few man-made sites existed.

■ The Home of the Sun

One of the most fascinating structures in the Plains region associated with the early occupants of the area is the Medicine Wheel, located in the Bighorn Mountains of modern-day Wyoming.[33] It is a circular outline of piled stones, approximately 69ft (21m) in diameter but flattened on one side. It was discovered by Euro-Americans in the 1880s and is documented as a vision quest site by the Crow Indians. This was *not* the original use of the Medicine Wheel, which dates from not later than 1700, and it is speculated that some of the earlier ceremonies of the Mountain Crow, close relatives of the Hidatsa, were practiced there when they were a sedentary people. Crow informants referred to it as the 'home of the Sun,' rather firmly tying it in with the Sun Dance and the Mandan *O-kee-pa.* The Medicine Wheel is now more than a remnant from the past for many Native Americans; as one Crow spiritual leader explained, 'this Medicine Wheel is our church . . . it is a United Nations for Indian people.'[34]

■ Pryor Mountains: Crow Vision Quests

Vision quest sites were located on eminences in terrain such as that Guthrie described for the Crow in Montana and northern Wyoming:

> 'An enormous world, a world of heights and depths and distances that numb the imagination . . . the mountains are loftier . . . the streams are swifter . . . the wind fiercer . . . the air sharper . . .'[35]

Among the best know of these, exclusive to the Crow for their favorite fasting place, are the Castle Rocks, just south of Billings, Montana, on the northeast edge of the Pryor Mountains. Here, fasters would sit in a small

U-shaped stone structure, facing the Morning Star which was considered to have great supernatural power. According to the Crow chief, Two Leggings, the Castle Rocks had additional sacred associations, being the home of the Little People, mythical beings who had great physical strength and supernatural powers. Similar sacred sites for the Lakota are Bear Butte and Harney Peak in the Dakotas, still favorite sites for vision quests.[36]

■ The Dakota Badlands

East of the Black Hills are the South Dakota Badlands, an area known to be rich with the fossil remains of extinct animals. The Lakota said the Badlands was the home of *Wakinyan,* the mythological lightning or thunder spirit. Petroglyphs and pictographs depict him as a great bird but sometimes he assumes a partly human shape. On war whistles or warshirts, he is represented by a zig-zag line to evoke communication with that awesome power. The lightning was said to be the flashing of his eyes and the thunder his voice, his awesome power apparent in the large treeless zones of the Lakota domain, where animals and humans were struck not infrequently, while his voice reverberated through the sacred *Pa Sapa,* Black Hills, and the canyons of the Badlands.

■ Dog Den Butte

The third day of the Mandan *O-kee-pa* Ceremony, The Everything Comes Back Day, comprised most of the bundle owners of the village. Animal rites were performed. Mandan mythology relating that these originally belonged to the Buffalo People who were created in the vicinity of Heart River by Lone Man and who were, together with all other animals on Earth, imprisoned by *Hoita* or Speckled Eagle, in Dog Den Butte. *Hoita* then put on, for the first time, the Buffalo Dance in Dog Den Butte and called all the buffalo away from the villages. Every living thing was brought in and the people faced starvation. Eventually the cooperation of *Hoita* was obtained and he set the animals free.

■ Chief Mountain

The highest mountain on the Blackfeet Reservation in Montana has origins in *Napi* or Old Man, whose powers were being tested continually. Challenged by the Great Spirit to demonstrate his strength, Old Man made the Sweet Grass Hills and then brought Chief Mountain to its present location and named it.

■ **Sacred Enclosure of the Mandans**

It should also be emphasized that there are less spectacular sacred places of which today only the initiated are really aware, and of all these the sacred cedar is paramount. First Man, the mythological Creator of mankind, founded the *O-kee-pa* ceremonial and established the custom of leaving an open area within each village for dancing, thus every Mandan village traditionally had an open plaza reserved for ceremonials. At the center stood a cedar post which was painted red and symbolically represented not only the body of First Man but also tribal ancestors. This sacred enclosure was a central pivotal point for the *O-kee-pa,* symbolizing the integrity of the Mandan as a people. Today, this ancient and holy shrine, sometimes referred to as The Ark of the First Man, is still located within the traditional territory of the Mandan tribe.[37]

REVERED ANIMALS

In common with many Plains tribes, the Lakota recognized that all living creatures and plants derived their life from the Sun. A deeper knowledge of each animal was greatly desired because not only was it believed to have been taught its ways by *Wakan-Tanka,* the Great Mysterious, but also that all animals were of benefit to one another. The acquisition of some of their powers was possible by a dream or vision of one of them, whereupon the creature was adopted as a helper and part of it worn on the person.[38]

■ **The Powers of the Elk**

A dream of an elk and acquisition of elk power was of particular significance among young men. In much of Plains mythology reference is made to the many desirable attributes of the elk – beauty, gallantry, lightness of foot and great physical strength. The elk was also considered to live in harmony with its surroundings and was blessed with a long life. Above all, however, the male elk was known to have great influence over the opposite sex. It was observed that the elk would stand on a hill and call or whistle, bringing the females to its side. This intangible power was greatly desired and the *flageolet* (a type of flute) was used to imitate the elk call. Sioux, Blackfeet and Plains Ojibwa mythology all have myths for working the charm with a *flageolet,* and additionally the Sioux made use of a special courting blanket which usually displayed the painted figures of an elk, a spider and whirlwind.[39]

■ Crow Love Medicine

Among the Crow, the elk was considered to be primarily the giver of love medicines, generally associated with personally owned bundles, which had been taken as a result of the grief caused by unrequited love. Such medicine power was not confined to one sex and both men and women possessed these various medicines, seeking to attract the person of their choice.

■ Buffalo Power

While the elk emerges as a symbol of love and gallantry, it is the buffalo which, above all, is woven into ceremonials and figures most prominently in Plains legends. Its origins are explained in terms of emergence, such as this Omaha legend:

> 'The buffalo were underground. A young bull browsing about found his way to the surface . . . the herd followed . . . As they went they came to a river. The water looked shallow, but it was deep. As the buffalo jumped in, the water splashed and looked gray in the air. The herd swam on and over the stream, where . . . they found good pasture and remained on the earth.'[24]

In most of the complex ceremonials, the buffalo was recognized as the life-giving gift of the higher powers. The mythology associated with the rare white buffalo epitomizes the revered animal mythology. White buffalo were particularly swift and wary and for this reason, together with their rarity, they were difficult to secure. When a white buffalo was killed, the fatal arrow was purified in smoke from burning sweetgrass, and before the animal was skinned the knife was similarly purified; no blood was to be shed on the hide. Only men who had dreamed of animals were allowed to eat its flesh and only a woman who was noted to have lived a pure life could tan it. In an annual ceremonial of the Omaha, the albino was represented by the skin of a small white buffalo with the horns and hoofs intact. It was considered one of the tribe's most revered objects and symbolic of the tribe's continued survival.[41]

■ The Blackfeet Beaver Bundle

The place of revered animals is perhaps no better illustrated than in the mythology associated with the Blackfeet Beaver Bundle which invokes the power of the legendary figure Weasel Woman – the name based on observations of the weasel's bravery and therefore a patron of warriors. Weasel Woman's husband was the owner of a Beaver Bundle, the most complex and ancient of all Blackfeet medicine bundles. Owners of Beaver Bundles were often referred to as *ijoxkiniks,* 'those having the power of the waters,' and they were obliged to show no fear of water in any form. A very important duty of the Beaver Bundle owners was to take on the role of buffalo-callers,[42] during which the power of Raven was invoked, calling the buffalo down to the vicinity of the village. Raven was considered the wisest of all birds, its superior abilities being recorded in the myth referring to the contest between it and the Thunderbird, when Raven made it so cold that the only way the Thunderbird could keep from freezing was by constantly flashing his lightning. He finally conceded defeat!

RITUALS AND CEREMONIES

Among the most important of Plains Indian religious practices was the quest for personal supernatural power, which was usually acquired by the visitation of a guardian spirit in a dream induced by fasting, praying and perhaps self-mutilation. The guardian spirit could be almost anything, animate or inanimate,[43] but was often the Moon, Morning Star or a bird or animal invested with supernatural power. The vision quest generally took place in complete solitude on a high eminence and could last up to four day,[44] usually being preceded by a ceremonial sweat bath; this purifying of the body in sage or sweetgrass smoke removed the human odor which might be offensive to the spirits.

■ The Circle of Life

A recurring theme in Plains Indian ceremonialism is that of regeneration and harmony expressed by the symbolism which the Sioux associated with the circle or hoop. To them it emphasized the relationship between mankind, the buffalo and all the rest of the universe, which was perceived as existing in cyclic harmonious balance. The Sun Dance of the Lakota, as well as their other major ceremonies such as the Spirit Keeping and *Hunka,* emphasized this theme, and the mythological figure of the White Buffalo Maiden who represented the Buffalo tribe and gave the Lakota the ceremonial pipe was intricately woven into these ceremonials. By correctly observing annual ceremonials, the unity of the people was maintained and the great hoop of life remained intact; if this hoop was broken, the people would be destroyed.

■ The *O-kee-pa* Ceremony

The Mandan believed, in common with most Plains tribes, that many animals and birds and even some inanimate objects, possessed some spirit power which they called *xo'pini*. Such power, they said, could be transferred to individuals by involvement in certain rituals, the most important of which was the *O-kee-pa* which, prior to the virtual extermination by smallpox of the Mandans as a tribe in the summer of 1837, was without question the most complicated and colorful of those performed on the northern plains, probably strongly influencing the nomadic tribes such as the Lakota, Blackfeet, Kiowa and Cheyenne in their developments of the Sun Dance. The *O-kee-pa,* a four-day ceremonial performed at least once every summer, acted out the mythological history of the tribe. It was a dramatization of the creation of the Earth, its people, plants and animals, together with the struggles the Mandan endured to attain their present position, and in addition it enabled key participants to renew the coveted *xo'pini.* One of the most striking episodes was when young suppliants were suspended from the ground by splints through the muscles of the chest or back, the sight of which, one observer reported in 1832, 'would almost stagger the belief of the world.'[45] Naturally, this act took courage and caused the tribe to speak of them as brave men and to look to them for leadership.

■ Sacrifice to the Morning Star

While the torture episode in the Mandan *O-kee-pa* is a dramatic example of penance, that of the *Skidi* band of Pawnee was perhaps the most extreme, embracing as it did the sacrifice of a young girl. Analysis of Pawnee mythology leaves one in little doubt of the great powers associated with the Morning Star which was viewed as a personification of manliness and conceived as a great warrior who drove before him in the sky the other stars, identified as people in Pawnee mythology. The sacrifice, however, was actually considered as the symbolic overcoming of the Evening Star by the Morning Star and their subsequent union from which sprang all the life on Earth, the young girl being perceived as a personification of the Evening Star. When she was ritually killed – by an arrow through her heart – the life of the Earth was symbolically renewed. Human sacrifice was an unusual custom among Plains Indians and there was increasing opposition among the Pawnees to its performance. In 1818 the custom was finally abandoned.

■ Black Elk's Lament

Annual ceremonialism and ritual, so vital in the ethos of the Plains tribes, was progressively suppressed during the early reservation period. The effect was devastating and it led to the Ghost Dance ceremonial and tragedy at Wounded Knee in December 1890. The despair was captured in Black Elk's now famous lament:

> You see me now a pitiful old man who has done nothing, for the nation's hoop is broken and scattered. There is no center any longer, and the sacred tree is dead.[46]

ARTS AND CRAFTS

Perhaps more than any other peoples, the Indians of the Great Plains of North America – the Blackfeet, Sioux, Crow, Kiowa and Comanche to name a few – have captured the imagination of the world. Resplendent in costume, picturesque in appearance and romantic in their customs, these equestrian nomads roamed the prairies and plains living in tipis and hunting the buffalo. The fundamentals of the culture, however, were due largely to two momentous imports of the white man – the horse, which came from the Spanish settlements in the Southwest, and the gun from the French in the Northeast.

A characteristic of Plains culture was to put great emphasis on the inter-relationship between ceremonial, costume, adornment and song – a holistic world view where everything was linked in a complex pattern of mythology and ritual: as one Blackfeet ceremonialist put it 'My clothes are my medicine.'[47] Throughout the region, women displayed a high degree of skill in the preparation of animal hides for use in the fabrication of many household objects, clothing and dwellings. This craft gave a decided common thread to the culture: the emphasis in artwork, however, differed considerably among the areas. Thus, northern and central Plains tribes did some exquisite porcupine quillwork while on the southern Plains such work was almost entirely absent. Later, with the introduction of beads in the early-19th century, definite identifiable area – even tribal – styles were developed. Likewise, skill and emphasis in such fields as carving, pipe-making, feather-work and pictographs varied from one part of the Plains to the next. Nevertheless, in all cases the end product reflected the concern and skill and dedication of the craftsman or craftswoman to produce an object which was a thing of beauty and in harmony with its environment even though the work might often be carried out under the most adverse conditions.

■ Porcupine Quillwork

Although sometimes considered a gastronomic delicacy, the most important use of the porcupine in North America was as a source of material for
quillwork. The North American porcupine, *Erethizon dorsatum*, was commonly found on the northern and western Great Plains and the quills were
a significant trade item to those tribes who did not have direct access to the
animal.[48] The pelage of the porcupine is a dense woolly undercoat and
white-tipped guard hairs and quills on the heads, back and tail. The quills
are white stiff hollow tubes with brown to black barbed tips and those used
for quillwork range in size from about 2–5in (30–140mm) in length and
.04–.09in (1–2mm) in diameter. In addition to porcupine quills, bird
quills were also occasionally used, particularly by those tribes on the
Missouri River, such as the Hidatsa, Mandan and Arikara and, perhaps to
a lesser extent, by the Santee and Yankton Sioux and Ojibwa along the
upper Mississippi River.[49]

Archaeological evidence suggests that porcupine quillwork has long
been practiced in North America, the main evidence for this coming from
the region of Utah and Nevada where artifacts preserved in caves show the
use of quills as a bonding element; such items date to c.500 BC, while moccasins decorated with quillwork and dating from the 13th and 14th centuries have been reported from archaeological sites.[50] It has been suggested
that quillwork possibly had its origins in Asia, with examples of woven mats
and baskets found in Asia exhibiting the same basic weaving and sewing
techniques as used in quillwork in North America.[51]

Highly formalized quillworkers' guilds have been identified among such
tribes as the Cheyenne and Arapaho,[52] and these guilds used certain designs
which were considered sacred and could only be produced by the initiated
women. Similar customs appear to have prevailed among the Blackfeet,[53]
whom it has been reported, traditionally at least, put considerable emphasis on the religious significance of quillwork.[54] Guilds appear to have been
less formalized among the Siouan tribes such as the Lakota, Mandan,
Hidatsa and Crow but several of these tribes – in common with the Plains
Algonquian – explain the origin of quillwork in mythological terms.[55]

In preparing the quills for use, artisans first softened them by the application of moisture, generally in the mouth, and they were then flattened by
being drawn between the teeth or finger nails; while some elaborately
carved bone or antler quill flatteners are to be found in the collections, it is
probable that they were actually ceremonial in function. In early days, the

sources of dye were various roots, berries and mosses, but later, colored trade cloth was used when cloth and quills were boiled together, the color from the cloth penetrating the quills. Commercial dyes obtained from white traders were increasingly used after 1870.

Some 16 porcupine quill techniques were used by the Plains tribes, of which eight were very common and in combination they can frequently be utilized to determine both the tribal origin and age of a particular specimen. The tools used were relatively simple and in addition to the possible use of a quill flattener, a woman quillworker used a bone marker, awl, knife and sinew threads. The marker either simply impressed the surface or was dipped into a colored fluid and then used as a pen. The sinew thread was used to secure the quills to the hide. Wrapping techniques on rawhide strips were common and widely used in the decoration of hair ornaments and pipe-bags, both being particularly favored by the Sioux. Woven quill-work was used by the Cree and possibly in early days by the Blackfeet, and it also occurs on at least one shirt from the Santee Sioux now in the Nathan Jarvis collection in the Brooklyn Museum. The technique is of particular interest since it utilized a small loom, the exquisitely finished work having the appearance of being made from fine cylindrical beads. More specialized methods such as the plaited technique and quill-wrapped horsehair were particularly well-developed by the Crow and appear on shirts, leggings and moccasins, and although such work was also found on similar items collected from the Hidatsa, Mandan, Arikara and Nez Perce, in most cases this was probably due to trade with the Crow.[56] With the wholesale introduction of beads to the Plains tribes in the mid-19th century, quillwork was displaced as a decorative medium. However, fine traditional costumes decorated with quillwork were still being produced in limited quantities as late as the turn of the century on both the central and northern Plains, the Hidatsa in particular excelling in this skill. An exhibition of contemporary Sioux quillwork was assembled in 1974 at the Sioux Museum in Rapid City, South Dakota, and since that time, a number of Sioux quillworkers have found a 'ready market for their wares.'[57]

■ Beadwork

Until approximately 1830, porcupine quillwork predominated over bead-work even though beads were introduced to the Plains tribes in the early 1800s. Thus, when the trader François Larocque traveled to the Crow in the vicinity of the Yellowstone River in 1805, he reported that they already possessed small blue glass beads which had come from the Spaniards in the southwest and probably via Shoshoni intermediaries. The Crow were so fond of these beads that they were willing to give a horse for one hundred of them; in consequence their high value at this time limited their use to the edges of porcupine quillwork strips. This, however, was the beginning of the so-called 'Pony Beadwork' phase on the Great Plains.

Pony beads – so called because they were transported on pony pack trains – were large, somewhat irregular china and glass beads which were made in Venice and were about one-eighth of an inch (3mm) in diameter. The colors were limited, blue being the most popular but white, black and red were also used. By 1840 these beads were being used in great profusion often in combination with a colored cloth and they were applied to pipe-bags, moccasins, leggings, shirts and buffalo robes. On clothing, the bead-work was generally carried out on a separate band, perhaps 3–4in (8–10cm) wide and then sewn to the shirt or leggings, although on buffalo robes, the bands could be up to 8in (20cm) wide. Patterns consisted of tall triangles, bars, squares and diamonds and often reflected the designs used in earlier quillwork. The pony beadwork period lasted until about 1855 when a smaller type of bead became popular; referred to as 'seed' beads they varied in size from three-sixteenths of an inch to one inch (.5–2.5cm) in diameter and gradually displaced the pony beads as a working medium.[58]

Two main methods of sewing beads to a surface were employed by the Plains tribes, the overlaid or spot stitch which was popular on the northern Plains and the lazy stitch which was much favored by the central Plains tribes. In the overlaid or spot stitch, the technique was similar to that used in quillwork: here, a thread of sinew was strung with a few beads which was then attached to the surface by another thread sewn across it at intervals of every two or three beads. If a broad surface was to be covered, line after line was attached with the lines laid close together. In the lazy stitch, a number of beads were strung on a thread of sinew which had been fastened to the skin, and then a perforation was made to attach the sinew at the end of the row of beads. As in the overlaid stitch, the perforation did not completely pass through the skin but ran just below the surface so that no stitches appeared on the back of the work. The same number of beads were again strung on the sinew which was carried back to the starting point and passed through another perforation adjacent to the first one. Varying colors could be introduced and so arranged as to produce a design.

The tribal differences both in technique and style may be illustrated by reference to the beadwork of the Blackfeet on the northern Plains and that of the Sioux on the central Plains.[59] Almost without exception, the Blackfeet employed the overlaid stitch, patterns being built up of scores of small squares or oblongs which were united to form larger patterns with the borders which were invariably an arrangement of different colored squares or oblongs. The large figures were generally squares, diamonds, triangles or slanted bands with long, stepped sides. The inspiration for this style of beadwork seems, at least in part, to have derived from earlier quillwork designs, particularly in woven quillwork.[60] Floral designs were also used by the Blackfeet possibly influenced by the Cree and Ojibwa and, with the increased use of seed beads in the late-19th century, floral designs on moccasins became common. As J. C. Ewers has observed, 'Photographs of Piegan Indians in the 1880s indicate that moccasins beaded in flowered patterns were then about as common as ones decorated with geometric designs.'[61] Additionally, floral designs were commonly used on saddles, saddle bags and martingales; less commonly they appear on men's shirts and leggings. In contrast, the Sioux seldom used floral designs – the lazy stitch which they almost exclusively employed in their beadwork tending to restrict the patterns to blocks, crosses, tall triangles and particularly after c. 1880, figures with thin lines, terraced and forked, which were spread out on a white or, less commonly, blue background. The inspiration for this type of work, it has been suggested, came from the patterns which appeared on Caucasian rugs brought in by white settlers.[62] About 1890, some craftswomen began embroidering live figures such as men, horses and elk – markedly different to the earlier traditional geometrical designs – and these figures were commonly worked on men's vests and pipe-bags.[63] Crow beadwork is particularly distinctive, the style appearing more massive than that of other tribes with large triangles, hourglasses and lozenges in various combinations. A definite characteristic of Crow beadwork was the outlining of many of the patterns with white beads setting them off from the background. A similar type of beadwork also prevailed among the Nez Perce and Shoshoni, the inspiration coming, at least in part, from those designs which commonly appeared on painted parfleches.[64] Men's and women's dress clothing, containers, robes and blankets, moccasins as well as riding gear, were commonly decorated with this distinctive style of beadwork.[65] In marked contrast to those tribes on the central and northern Plains, the beadwork of such tribes as the Kiowa, Comanche and Southern Cheyenne on the southern Plains, was generally restricted to single lanes – perhaps seven or eight beads wide – along the edges of leggings, shirts and women's dresses. The work was always of a high quality, the beads being both small and carefully selected, presenting a neat and expertly finished artifact. Some exceptions were the exquisite fully beaded bags and awl cases which, particularly among the Kiowa, invariably exhibited a distinctive glassy red-bead background.

■ Carving and Engraving

The large carved house posts, totem poles and the like so common and well-developed by the Indians of the northwest coast of America, found virtually no place in Plains Indian carving, the majority of which was rendered in the miniature. An exception to this was the use of human effigy spirit posts carved by Plains Cree and Ojibwa. These were observed as early as 1799 by the fur trader, Peter Fidler, in the vicinity of the Beaver River in what is now eastern Alberta. The posts were generally life-size and had crudely carved heads being referred to as *Mantokans* which derives from the Algonquian *maniot*, a term used for the mysterious life powers of the universe. Peter Fidler said that they were erected by Indians in the hope that 'the great *Menneto* will grant them and their families health while they remain in these parts'.[66] While the nomadism of most typical Plains tribes does go a long way to explaining the desire for small three-dimensional artwork, even among the semi-sedentary Plains tribes such as the Mandan, Hidatsa and Omaha of the Missouri River, no large carved sculpture was found.[67]

Prior to the arrival of the Europeans, the production of carved artifacts was carried out by the use of stone implements although bone and pieces of copper obtained in trade might have been used. While appearing primitive, they were clearly more efficient in the hands of a skilled craftsman than might be imagined; thus the shaping of lance and flint arrowheads – the so-called Folsom and Clovis points – by early Plains inhabitants, demonstrates that great skill and workmanship was possible without the use of iron tools.

It can only be speculated as to how much wooden carving the early Plains tribes produced since wood rapidly deteriorates in the ground and no archaeological sites on the Plains have yielded wooden effigies; however, stone carvings of catlinite (a soft red stone) produced prior to the 15th century, have been found and some of the finest Plains Indian carvings were of catlinite.[68] Additionally, shell and bone effigies which may date as early as AD 1000 have been found in sites associated with the ancestral Mandan.[69]

By the middle of the 19th century, and probably earlier, wooden carved animal effigies were associated with medicine hunts, tree-dweller ceremonials and war medicines. War clubs, courting flutes, pipe-stems, Sun Dance dolls, children's toys and effigy horse figures were also carved and widely distributed across the Plains.[70]

Horse effigies were often depicted on mirror-boards and pipes, but the most elaborate carvings of horses were used in victory dances and were highly symbolic. Thus, when Walter McClintock visited the Blackfeet in 1898, he observed 'One of these dancers named Rides to the Door carried the carved wooden figure of a horse to remind people of his bravery and skill in raiding enemy horses'.[71] Such effigies had wide distribution being used by the Sioux, Crow, Hidatsa, Ute, Blackfeet, Gros Ventre, Blood, Assiniboin and Cheyenne.[72] A famous carver of horse effigy dance sticks was the Hunkpapa Sioux, No-Two-Horns, and a particularly fine carving (one of several extant) by this man is now in the Medora Museum, North Dakota. It seems to have been made to commemorate an event in the Custer Battle when No-Two-Horns' horse was wounded seven times and died in action. The wounds are indicated on the carved horse by triangular areas of red flowing from a wound at the apex of the triangle. No-Two-Horns was also known to be adept at other types of carving, producing dolls and miniature weapons for his grandchildren.[73]

In addition to carving, several items used by the Plains tribes were engraved, such as the riding quirts or roach spreaders of elk antler. This was a material which was relatively easy to work and could be shaped and finished with simple tools. When used for quirts, there seems to have been some preference for the prongs which protruded forward on each side of the main rack just above the skull.[74] Such prongs could be made into handles with the minimum of effort; in turn these handles were not infrequently engraved with war exploits, life figures, geometric and curvilinear patterns, the process being carried out by use of an awl or knife point while deeper lines were made with the cutting edge of a knife blade or a file;[75] roach spreaders were engraved in a similar way. Before about 1870, they were usually made of a flat plaque of antler and often displayed military exploits and were carefully shaped matching the contours of the roach base. Later, they were made of wood, metal or rawhide. Roach spreaders had a multifold purpose – to spread the roach farther apart, support the plume holder such that the eagle feathers stood out from the back of the roach, and to beautify the roach further with the engravings which were on it.

Horn spoons with elaborately carved handles displaying effigies of snakes, beaver, bighorn, birds and elk were much favored by the Western Sioux, particularly during the second half of the 19th century and, after the buffalo were virtually exterminated in the 1880s, the effigy spoons were made of cowhorn from those animals slaughtered as rations for Indians on the reservation. Typical is an elk-head spoon of cowhorn on which the handle is bent at the end, the elk head facing the same direction as the bowl of the spoon; the carver has taken pains 'to show the animal's open mouth and lightly incised nostrils and eyes, as well as its spreading horns.'[76] Elk power was associated with sexual prowess by many Plains tribes. As the English sportsman, John Palliser, observed in 1847, 'In the breeding season the wapiti chants the most beautiful musical sound in all the animal creation; it is like the sound of an enormous soft flute, uttered in a most coaxing tone.'[77] Thus, in seeking elk power, the Sioux fabricated elaborately carved flutes of cedar wood which not infrequently displayed a carved elk head at one end in the act of calling his mates.

■ Pipes

The ceremonial use of tobacco was widespread in North America and had supernatural associations; the ritual of smoking was said to lift one's thoughts to the spirits above, linking earthbound man with the sky above. Pipes used by the Plains Indians were made of various workable stones – limestone, steatite and chlorite – but the most favored was a red stone quarried in the area of present-day Minnesota and referred to as catlinite after George Catlin who first visited the quarry in 1835 and who brought a sample of the stone back for scientific analysis. This pipestone was known to the Indians of the region from prehistoric times and prior to c. 1700 was in the territory of the Oto and Iowa. After this time, the Sioux took over the quarry and by the mid-19th century they were its sole owners, the stone rough blanks or finished pipes then being traded to other tribes.[78]

North American Indian pipes have been divided into two major categories depending upon their form: one style is tubular in which the smoke travels in one plane, the other is elbow in which it travels in two planes.[79] Both types were found on the Plains in the Historic Period. More recently this classification has been extended to the five most common forms – the tubular or straight pipe, the modified Micmac pipe, elbow pipe, prowed pipe with flaring-bowl, and the calumet or inverted T-shape.[80] A number of these pipes were particularly elaborate, exhibiting effigies of animals and humans; some of the finest in the category were made by the Sioux and Pawnee. George Catlin expressed the opinion that the Pawnee were probably the 'most ingenious' of all the Plains tribes in the production of such articles. Effigy bowls were of high artistic quality with imaginative designs, the likenesses of humans and animals usually being carved so that they faced the smoker; some made social comments such as the effects of liquor on Indians.

The carving of a pipe from catlinite or other stone was a formidable task and, before the introduction of steel tools by Europeans, the stone was fashioned using flint or other hard materials, the bowl being drawn on the stone and the excess cut away; the holes for tobacco and stem were a particular problem as Catlin observed: 'the Indian makes the hole in the bowl of the pipe, by drilling into it a hard stick, shaped to the desired size, with a quantity of sharp sand and water kept constantly in the hole.'[81] The bowls were then finally shaped and polished with flint, quartzite and fine sand, and buffalo tallow and other animal fats gave the finished piece its polish.

The modified Micmac style of bowl was so named because it was the Micmac of Nova Scotia who were first observed by Europeans using this type of pipe. The style traveled west in trade and was a distinctive shape having a bowl not unlike an inverted acorn upon a keel-like base. The Plains Cree, Crow, Assiniboin and, in particular, the Blackfeet, utilized pipes of this type although there were many variations on the basic style.

Ewers found this modified form of Micmac pipe still being made as late as 1947 and he obtained an example of such a pipe from his Piegan informant and interpreter, Reuben Black Boy, who had fabricated it a short time previously. It resembled a pipe first illustrated by Carl Bodmer more than a century earlier (1833) and was referred to by the Blackfeet as a 'real pipe'. The technique of manufacture had, however, changed markedly – Reuben was now using a pencil to outline the shape of the bowl, a wooden vise to clamp the slab, a hacksaw to rough out the bowl, a carpenter's brace to drill the holes, a wood rasp to get the final shape and the exterior was smoothed with commercial sandpaper. The final blackening of the bowl, however, followed more traditional lines. Reuben built a fire of green buckbrush and, placing a stick in the pipe-stem hole, he held the bowl over the fire for about 15 minutes. After the stone had cooled, he rubbed the surface with his hand, giving it an even, shiny surface.[82]

Most of the pipes so far described had stems which, for ceremonial purposes, could be up to 3–4ft (1–1.3m) in length. The stems were made of ash, oak or hickory, the pith in their center being burned out with a hot wire. An alternative was to split the stem lengthwise, scrape out the pith and then glue the pieces together. Flat pipe-stems were most popular on the central Plains while round ones were used on the northern Plains. Some had open work 'puzzle stems' where only the carver knew the true pathway of the smoke as it zig-zagged from bowl to mouthpiece, by-passing the decorative and symbolic designs which were carved on the stem. Other stems were of the spiraling variety where rounds stems were carved with a knife and file, sometimes a double spiral being produced. The stems were not infrequently decorated with porcupine quillwork, generally in the so-called braided technique with additional decoration in the form of horsehair, feathers, beaks and paint. Although both bowl and stem were considered to be endowed with sacred power, the pipe itself was not considered activated until the two parts were brought together and, when not in use, stem and bowl were taken apart and stored in a bag, beautifully embellished with beads and porcupine quills.

■ Featherwork

As early as the mid-16th century, a crown of feathers came to indicate Indian identity in most of the Americas.[83] Such headdresses generally consisted of a simple band with the feathers of the wild turkey, hawk, heron or eagle attached so that they stood upright around the head. Similar to this early style was the headdress of the Blackfeet of the northern Plains which, by the profuse combination of eagle feathers and ermine skins, turned the ancient and simple headband style into an imposing form of warrior and society regalia. This style, referred to as a 'straight-up bonnet', was said to have originated with the ancient Bulls Society of the Blackfeet.

Headdresses of this type were made from a piece of thin rawhide or heavy tanned skin six inches (15cm) or so in width and of sufficient length to fit the wearer's head. It was then folded along its long dimension and holes were cut in the edge of the fold through which the eagle feathers were passed.[84] Some 20 to 30 feathers were attached to the band either by cutting the feather quill and tucking it back into itself so as to form a loop or, alternatively, pushing a small wooden pin into the hollow quill of the feather. The feathers were then fixed in place by the use of a lacing thong which went through the quill loop or over a groove in the wooden pin. A second thong usually passed through the quill about halfway up the feather which held it in place and gave shape to the bonnet. The headdress was then covered with red cloth which was decorated with brass studs or, occasionally, beadwork. Long ermine fringes were hung from the sides and back and additional decoration, in the form of narrow strips of rawhide wrapped around with porcupine quills, were sometimes attached to the quills of the eagle feathers with small fluffy plumes at the base of each. Finally, the ends of the band were joined by tying them together at the back and carefully adjusting so that it fitted snugly on the head. Such headdresses were worn on ceremonial occasions, in dances and parades. They were also worn in battle but this was considered a particularly brave act since it made the wearer exceptionally conspicuous and a more than likely target for enemy fire.

The use of the straight-up headdress progressively decreased after c.1895 and by the 1940s very few such bonnets were then worn, having been replaced by the Sioux style of flaring bonnet.[85] Elderly Blackfeet explained this by saying that the straight-up bonnet was considered very sacred regalia and that few people had the right to wear it.[86]

The Sioux-style warbonnet contrasted with the Blackfeet style, having a cap of soft buckskin which fitted loosely to the head. To it were attached feathers to form a circle but unlike the Blackfeet style where the feathers were fixed rigid and upright, the feathers were at an angle, flaring both upward and backward from the wearer's head and having freedom of movement.

The development of the Sioux-style flaring bonnet can be traced through early travelers' accounts of the Plains tribes beginning with the French explorer, La Verendrye, to the Mandan in 1738 who referred to feather headbands; while later, in 1811, the English explorer, Brackenridge, refers to Arikara headdresses with the feathers arranged as a kind of crown.[87] It seems that by 1820 the flaring style of warbonnet was well-developed, clustering among tribes who put emphasis on coup designation by the use of eagle feathers, such as the Dakota, Arikara, Pawnee, Hidatsa, Mandan, Crow and Omaha. There were slight variations within the style, but of them all, the Sioux version – where the feathers swept back from the brow and the middle side feathers were approximately 45 degrees to the vertical – typifies the style. Some 30 or more feathers were used, the foundation being a buckskin cap. The feathers were first carefully prepared and most important was the formation of a loop at the bottom of the feather. This was either made by cutting the quill as one would for a pen and tucking the quill back into itself or alternatively binding leather or rawhide strips to the quill leaving a loop at the bottom. The feathers were further embellished with buckskin or colored cloth at their base together with several fluffy plumes while the tips were decorated with horsehair. The feathers were then laid out in the order that they would appear on the bonnet, the two longest and straightest being at the center. Then they were laced to the cap by running a buckskin thong through the loop and pairs of slits cut in the cap. Another thong was run through the feathers part way up the quill, holding the feathers in place and enabling the bonnet to be set so as to become a balanced and uniform spread. A 'major plume' was then attached to the center of the cap, originally in the form of a power amulet such as the skin of an animal or bird. In later years – 1870 onwards – it was replaced with a long stripped quill cut and embellished in a certain way to distinguish the owner. The headdress was completed by the addition of a quilled or beaded brow band with rosettes on each side from which were hung ermine and colored ribbons.

Traditionally, the flaring style of bonnet could only be possessed and worn by the consent of a man's fellow warriors – by an individual who had gained both war honors and the respect of the leading men in the community. Among the Omaha each feather stood for a man, the tip of hair fastened to the feather and dyed red, representing the man's scalp-lock. Before a feather could be fastened on the bonnet, a man had to count the war honor which actually entitled him to wear the feather and so enabled him to prepare it for use in decorating the bonnet. When the warrior counted his honors he held up the feathers which were to represent them, saying 'In such a battle I did thus'.[88] Thus, the wearing of a warbonnet by a privileged individual did not refer exclusively to that individual's feats of arms, rather it signified the best warrior and underlined the interdependence of men.

■ Buckskin Garments

While the most typical garment for Plains Indian women in the mid-19th century was a one-piece sleeveless dress, a closer study of women's costumes indicates that despite this general pattern there were considerable variations in tribal styles. Thus, on the northeastern Plains an early style was the 'strap dress' which consisted of two long pieces of buckskin sewn at the sides and held up by straps over the shoulders with the addition of separate cape-like sleeves which were connected by thongs across the front and back. Another early style on both the northern and central Plains was the 'side-fold dress' which consisted of a wide rectangular piece of hide folded on one side, the other being sewn with the top turned down to form a type of cape. A hole was made for the arm on the folded side and the dress was sewn or laced at the shoulders. By 1830, however, both these styles of dress were beginning to go out of fashion being replaced by the 'two-skin dress' probably due to influences from the Plateau tribes farther west. This was made by sewing two deerskins together with the hind legs at the shoulders, a few inches – which included the tail – being folded down.[89] Thus, the natural shape of the tanned hide was retained – a good example of how the form of a costume is determined by the material used. Piercing, trimming, additional inserts and mode of decoration on this basic garment were often indicative of tribal origin. On the southern Plains, however, among such tribes as the Southern Cheyenne and Arapaho, Kiowa and Comanche, three skins were used in the construction of a woman's dress. Here, two deerskins were cut straight a few inches below the forelegs, these skins became the skirt of the dress, a third skin being folded lengthwise and sewn to the other two skins at the waist. A hole was cut into the top of the fold to allow the head through. The Southern Cheyenne and Arapaho tended to decorate such dresses with bands of beadwork about 3-4in (7-10cm) wide on both the shoulders and across the chest while the Kiowa and Comanche often painted their dresses and used only a limited amount of beadwork at the edges.

In the fabrication of clothing, a common practice among Plains Indians was maximum use of material at hand with minimum wastage. In this respect, the style of leggings used by men was no exception. Hides from the white or black-tailed deer or prong-horned antelope were commonly used in the manufacture of leggings. An excellent contemporary account of Plains-style leggings was given in 1805 by the explorers, Lewis and Clark:

> 'The leggings are generally made of antelope skins, dressed without out the hair and with the legs, tail and neck hanging to them. Each legging is formed of the skin entire and reaches from the ankle to the upper part of the thigh and the legs of the skin are tucked before and behind under a girdle around the waist. It fits closely to the leg the tail being worn upwards, and the neck highly ornamented with fringe and porcupine quills, drags on the ground behind the heels. As the legs of the animal are tied round the girdle the wide part of the skin is drawn so high as to conceal the parts usually kept from

view, in which respect their dress is much more decent than that of any nation of Indians.'[90]

Such styles of leggings were widely used on the central and northern Plains but farther south tribes such as the Kiowa and Comanche began to make leggings which were more tailored than those used farther north. The most popular form of skin legging in the second half of the 19th century, was the so-called 'tab and fringe' style. Here, the legging was fashioned from a single hide folded lengthwise to form a double flap, after a tailored leg seam had been sewn. The flap was then cut into a fringe leaving a whole portion near the top; referred to as the 'tab' this was generally tastefully decorated with paint and beads.[91]

Embellished buffalo robes, certain styles of headgear, special forms of leggings and, in particular on the central and northern Plains, the ceremonial shirt, were all important ways of communicating an individual's position within the social and political strata. Thus, among the Pawnee, the wearing of the skin shirt was 'one of the outstanding symbols of high status. . . . very few men were privileged to wear them' and even able chiefs might be excluded.[92] The sacred character of a special style of hair-fringed shirt among the Sioux was emphasized by the elaborate rituals developed relating to its conferment and, as late as the reservation period when such shirts were being made for collectors, special rituals were still performed during both its fabrication and transferral.[93] Traditionally, the Sioux ceremonial shirt was made of two deer, bighorn or antelope skins; about one-third of the top was cut off each skin which was then folded to make the sleeves, the lower two-thirds becoming the front and back of the shirt. The head portion from each skin was then used as a decorative flap on the front and back. The sides of the shirt were generally left open and the sleeves sewn from the wrist to the elbow only. Most of these shirts have quilled or beaded bands over the shoulders and often two – generally narrower – bands down the arms. These were invariably, although not exclusively, worked separately on a leather base and then sewn to the shirt. Human hair fringes were attached to the edges of these shoulder and arm bands which represented the war deeds – or perhaps a mark of allegiance – of the members of the Chiefs' Society or individuals who sanctioned the wearing of such garments by outstanding leaders.[94] A typical garment in this class was worn by the Oglala leader, Red Cloud, and others when they visited Washington in the 1870s.[95]

■ Petroglyphs and Pictographs

The communication of ideas by means of petroglyphs and pictographs is of ancient origin in North America. Petroglyphs have been defined as pictures 'upon a rock either in situ or sufficiently large for inference that the picture was imposed upon it where it was found'.[96] Pictographs, on the other hand, were pictures upon skins, bark, pottery and later on woven fabrics such as linen cloth and muslin as well as paper, the latter producing, in the late-19th century, a proliferation of so-called ledger-book art.[97]

Recent studies of Plains petroglyphs – now popularly referred to as Rock Art – have identified two major styles, Ceremonial and Biographic, the first being of considerably greater antiquity than the second.[98] A variety of techniques were employed in producing the petroglyphs but most commonly the rock surface was scratched or alternatively the surface was pecked with a small sharp-edged stone, both methods removing the darker weathered surface.[99]

Pictographic work on hides was generally carried out using 'brushes' made of the spongy, porous part of the buffalo's leg bone, one edge of which was sharpened to make narrow lines while the flat side was used to spread color over larger surfaces.[100] Colored earth and clay and some vegetable materials were used for paints, these being ground into a powder and mixed with a gluey substance which was obtained from boiling hide scrapings or the tail of a beaver. As with petroglyphs, painted art work on skins was both geometric and representational; generally, the former was done by women and the latter by men.

One of the most popular geometric designs used by women was the so-called 'box and border' and much favored by the Sioux and Arapaho. This exhibited two distinctive features – a continuous border which surrounded all four sides of the hide together with an enclosed rectangular, decorated field, usually located just above the center of the hide and always elongated horizontally. An associated style was the 'border and hourglass' pattern; here, the central pattern tended to be variable in detail but its essential form was always broad at the ends and constricted in the middle – a form suggestive of an hourglass.[101] It is suggested that such designs were stylized representations of the buffalo showing its internal structure, as Hail has observed, 'It was easy for the people of hunting cultures to visualize internal organs, as they were accustomed to butchering their kills and distributing the parts. This is true especially of women, since they were responsible for cutting up the meat that the hunters brought in. The joys of a full stomach and relief from the fear of starvation for her children would be part of her pleasure in drawing these designs'.[102]

The earliest documented painted robe showing extensive detail of inter-tribal warfare among the Plains tribes and obviously in the category of an autobiographical treatise, was collected by Lewis and Clark from the Mandan in 1805. It was reported that the pictographs depicted a battle fought about 1797 between the Mandan and Minnetaree against the Sioux and Arikara.

Analysis of robes of this type leads to the conclusion that the subject matter of early Plains Indian representative painting was overwhelmingly that of humans and horses, while the episodes recorded put emphasis on the stealing of horses or the counting of coup on the enemy.

Horses were represented in a variety of ways, a stick-like leg with a hooked hoof – actually representing a hoof print – being typical of hide painting done prior to 1850. Later, horses are shown in a more realistic way, the eyes, phallus, tail and sometimes the mane being depicted while the running horse was conventionalized to forelegs extending forward and hind legs backward.[103] Early depictions of human figures were knob-like heads which were generally devoid of features although hair-styles were not infrequently shown. Arms and legs were stick-like with simple triangular and rectangular bodies. There were several notable exceptions to this early style – in particular the work of the Mandan chief, Matotope (c. 1833) whose pictograph technique was possibly influenced by white artists.[104] In the second half of the 19th century, there was considerable refinement of human proportions, an abundance of detail, increase in richness of colors, some experimentation with spatiality and the appearance of new themes and subject matter.[105]

■ Rawhide

Rawhide has great strength and versatility and because of these qualities it was highly prized by Plains Indians and used in a variety of ways.

The preferred hide for making rawhide was that of the buffalo and although elk, moose and domestic cattle hides were used, particularly during the reservation period, buffalo was considered to be more elastic and fibrous and 'long use of a piece of buffalo rawhide made it somewhat like heavy, firm cloth'. There were considerable variations in the production of rawhide but the end product was always the same – a clean hide devoid of fleshy material and hair which, on drying, was white and opaque. A widespread technique was to stake the hide out by putting pegs through slits cut around its edge and to use a chisel-like bone (later metal) tool called the 'deflesher' to remove fat and tissue from the inner part of the hide.[106] The hide was then turned over and, with an adze-shaped tool, the hair was carefully scraped away. Finally, it was thoroughly washed and left in the sun to dry and bleach.

While rawhide was used in the fabrication of such items as shields, drums, knife sheaths, saddles, cruppers, horseshoes, burden straps, hats, doors of tipis, mortars, decorative and symbolic cut-outs and even cradles; its commonest use was in the production of the parfleche[107] which was a flat rectangular and expandable case in which clothing, food and other materials were placed for storage and transportation.[108] Parfleches were generally made in pairs from a buffalo hide which had already been cleared of fat and tissue during the rawhide production process. The flesh side of the staked-out hide was marked out using peeled willow sticks of different lengths defining the parfleche shape and the geometrical patterns which were to be painted on it. A bone 'brush' was used to draw the outlines of the patterns which were generally in a single color; the larger areas were then filled in with the desired colors. The surface was then covered with a thin coat of glue or size which gave a gloss to the paint and protected it from wear and tear when in use.[109] After the paint and glue had dried, the hide was turned over and the hair removed in the usual way: finally, the parfleche was cut out from the rawhide to the desired shape. Regardless of tribal origin, most of the patterns on parfleches consisted of geometrical designs made up of rather massive rectangles, squares, triangles and hourglass-type figures. There were, however, some definite tribal variations, thus the Blackfeet frequently used curved lines, the Crow put emphasis on using straight lines and the Sioux used a mixture of both. Some of the finest parfleches were made by the Cheyenne whose designs were unusually delicate and the combination of colors particularly distinctive.[110]

■ Moccasins

With the exception of the sandal-wearing tribes of the Southwest and Mexico, moccasins were universally worn throughout most of North America. The true moccasin – the term originating from eastern Algonquian dialects – was a type of footwear in which the 'soft sole and the upper, or part of the upper, are continuous, passing upwards from under the foot, forming a well-constructed foot covering which always has a back seam.'[111] There were considerable variations within this basic style but typical for the Plains Indians in the early-19th century, is Larocque's (1805) description of Crow moccasins, which he said were 'made in the manner of mittens having a seam round the outside of the foot only without [a] pleat'.[112] The Blackfeet referred to this earlier one-piece soft-soled moccasin style as the 'real moccasin'. Since soft-sole moccasins wear out quickly in the harsh Plains environment, a modification in the form of an additional piece of leather was sometimes added to the sole but the basic pattern survived to at least the beginning of the reservation period (c. 1870), being preferred for winter wear when buffalo hide with hair inside was used.

Around the middle of the 19th century, another style progressively came into use. This was the two-piece moccasin which had a rawhide sole with a soft buckskin upper. Although this style came to have wide distribution on the Plains, even toward the end of the 19th century, some tribes – notably the Crow – were still using both types. As the army officer, Captain W. P. Clark, observed in the 1880s, 'the Crows make their moccasins of one piece sewed at the heel, though some have separate soles'.[113]

On the southern Plains from around 1860 onwards, a high-topped style, particularly popular with the Kiowa and Comanche, was in use; a tube legging was attached to the moccasin, the seam being covered by a single lane of beadwork. The moccasins were always of the hard-sole variety and these, together with the attached legging, were painted yellow or green. Heavy German silver discs were usually attached to the leggings and the edging beadwork exhibited intricate patterns worked in small seed beads.

A floral design was invariably worked on the instep of Kiowa high-topped moccasins, a feature seldom used by their close allies, the Comanche.[114]

REFERENCES

THE PLAINS

1 Blackfeet tipis of this type might use as many as twenty buffalo hides for the cover supported on a foundation of some twenty poles, 25 ft (over 8m) in length (those of the Crow could be even longer). See Laubin (1957) for the basic study of the Plains tipi.

2 Scalping, however, was *not* necessarily fatal. Several cases have been reported where scalped victims have survived the ordeal. Catlin, for example, sketched an individual 'who had been scalped and recovered from the wound' (Catlin, 1841, vol.1:240). Perhaps the most bizarre episode, however, was that of the brakeman, Edward Thompson, on a Union Pacific Railroad freight train which was traveling across Kansas in 1868. The train was derailed by a combined force of

Cheyenne, Arapaho and Lakota warriors. Plunged into the darkness, he was felled by a bullet; later, he reported that although the bullet knocked him down, it 'did not render him unconscious and that his greatest trial in that terrible night was the necessity of shamming dead and not daring to cry out when the Indian was *slowly sawing* at his head covering with a *very* dull knife'. The rescue party later found the scalp and it was put into a bucket of water. On arrival in Omaha, an effort was made by surgeons to sew it back in place, but without success (see Taylor, 1975:93 and Dodge, 1876:400, in ibid, 1980:23).

3 This was related to the explorer, David Thompson, in 1787. It refers to an episode in Saukamappee's youth and took place about 1730.

4 Note also here, as with the Louisiana people, the emphasis on the belief that the spirit or soul of the scalped person 'was somehow in and of human hair' – a concept which also prevailed among the Sioux (Hassrick, 1964:84).

5 Fort Benton was originally named Fort Clay, founded after the abandonment of Fort McKenzie in 1844 and Lewis in spring 1847. Renamed at Christmas 1850 in honor of Senator Thomas Hart Benton of Missouri who was a strong supporter of the fur trade, the first steamboat arrived a decade later (July 2, 1860). River traffic was maintained until the late 1880s when the new railroads took over most of the freight. Although the Missouri was navigable to St Louis, it had to be continually dredged and cleared of snags.

6 The actual campground for this important Treaty was some thirty-four miles down the North Platte river at Horse Creek in present-day southeast Wyoming.

7 In return for safe immigrant travel up the Platte, west to the mountains, the United States government agreed to 'make an annual payment to the Sioux in goods valued at $50,000 per year for fifty years, to be delivered in the Fort Laramie area . . . should any of the Indian nations, party to this treaty, violate any of the provisions thereof, the United States may withhold the whole or a portion of the annuities mentioned in the preceding Article from the nation so offending, until, in the opinion of the President of the United States, proper satisfaction shall have been made' (McCann, 1956:3-4).

8 The following account of this tragic encounter is based on the superb research of Dr Lloyd E. McCann (1956) of Butler University, Indianapolis, Indiana, being based on data in House and Senate executive documents; a narrative of Man-Afraid-Of-His-Horses, now in the National Archives; and an interview with Red Cloud by Judge E. S. Ricker at Pine Ridge, South Dakota, 24 November 1906. It demonstrates so much of the attitudes and prejudices which existed at this time and gives unusual insights into the diplomacy and fair play of mature Plains Indian leaders. Conquering Bear, who emerges as a man of exceptional ability and tact, was mortally wounded in this encounter.

9 The Cheyenne had a legend which told 'how, after a disastrous encounter with some other tribe, they all decided they would become terrible fighters and so become great men'. The formation of the *Hota'm ita'niu*, 'Dog Men' was a living reminder of that legend. The 'Dog Soldiers', as they became known to the whites, considered that they were the watchdogs of the Cheyenne people. (See Vestal, 1948:63.)

10 Bell and Wylyams had arranged earlier on that fateful day to work together and print some photographs which Bell had taken en route. The shocked Bell later observed 'so I had to print off my negatives alone, and to take a photograph of him, poor fellow, as he lay; a copy of which I sent to Washington that the authorities should see how their soldiers were treated on the Plains' (Bell, 1869:vol.1,64)

11 The town of Medicine Lodge, Barber County, Kansas, now stands on the site.

12 This important tribe of the Muskhogean linguistic stock were originally located on the Mississippi near present-day Memphis, Tennessee. Under white pressure, together with the Choctaw, they began to immigrate west of the Mississippi as early as 1822.

13 Indian delegations were usually treated well and often given the opportunity of publicly presenting their side of the picture. Newspaper reports generally gave sympathetic coverage of such
events, pointing out the difficulties confronting both races. Typical was the Cheyenne, Arapaho
and Wichita delegation, led by the head chief of the Arapaho, *Ohnastie*, or 'Little Raven', who
arrived early in the summer of 1871. As the *New York Times* expressed it (1 June 1871) 'Their
main purpose was to meet the "Great Chief of the American Nation" and to have their reservation boundary lines clearly defined.' They were 'astonished by our cities; such a gathering of men
all in one place . . . they do not understand our railways, telegraphs, etc. They know such things
are done, but they cannot understand by what power, etc . . . they have no words in their language to comprehend all they see.' (For further details of this visit and also that of Red Cloud's
in 1872, see Taylor, 1975:106-7.)

14 It was, however, a victory paid for dearly by the Lakota whose tactics were to ride down the enemy
before they had time to reload. Unknown to Red Cloud, new Springfield breech-loaders had been
recently issued to the troopers and more than sixty were killed and 120 wounded under the with-
ering fire power during a battle which lasted more than four hours. Such heavy casualties were
devastating to small population Plains tribes. Leaders were supposed not to lose any men 'if he
could possibly help it' (Pakes, 1989:21). For an excellent up-to-date analysis relating to the nature
of Plains Indian warfare, see ibid.

15 After the 1868 Laramie Treaty, the Lakota divided into three main factions: agency Indians
wholly dependent on the Government; those who stayed at the agencies in winter and left in
spring to live in Powder River country, and finally those who permanently shunned the agencies,
preferring their own free life in the Yellowstone and Powder River regions. This third group 'was
regarded by the army as the principal barrier to white encroachment' (Taunton, 1977:7).

16 Crowfoot refused to join, almost certainly due to the fair-minded and honest treatment which
the Canadian Plains tribes received at the hands of the North-West Mounted Police, which was
founded in 1873 on the recommendation of Colonel W. F. Butler (Butler, 1891:378-9). Sitting
Bull and Crowfoot later became firm friends and Sitting Bull was to name his son in honor of the
Blackfeet chief.

17 For a detailed analysis of the aftermath of this historic encounter, see Taunton (1986).

18 This particular battle was graphically documented by Captain John G. Bourke, U.S. Army. Third
Cavalry. He describes in great detail the complete destruction of the Cheyenne village (which
consisted of some two hundred tipis) and hence 'wiping off the face of the earth many products
of aboriginal taste and industry which would have been gems in the cabinets of museums . . .
Never were orders more thoroughly executed . . .' (Bourke, 1890:29). It was a pattern replicated
many times by the U.S. Army in their subjugation of the Plains Indian.

19 Apparently, Crazy Horse and Sitting Bull had discussed surrender on a number of occasions but
Sitting Bull said 'I do not wish to die yet' (Vestal, 1957:182).

20 Recent researches by members of the University of South Dakota and the Dull Knife Memorial
College, have put a new perspective on the escape route followed by the Cheyennes supporting
the oral history of the tribe (see McDonald, McDonald, Tallbull and Risingsun, 1989:265-9).

21 This reduction of the Great Sioux Reservation is considered in great detail by Utley (1963:40-
60).

22 A general sentiment among those tribes who adopted the Ghost Dance religion was that their
domination by the white race would soon end 'and that a beautiful new world was coming in
which everyone would live forever' (Smith, 1975:74).

23 When white contact was first made with the Plains tribes in the 18th and 19th centuries, the
region was dominated by Siouan and Algonquian linguistic groups, although the Uto-Aztecan and
Athapaskan were also represented. On the northern Plains were such tribes as the Blackfeet, Cree,
Gros Ventre and Plains Ojibwa; the central Plains were dominated by the Sioux, Crow, Mandan,

189

Hidatsa and Arikara; while the southern Plains were occupied by the Comanche, Kiowa, Wichita, Pawnee and Kiowa Apache. (For a fuller discussion see Sturtevant and Taylor, 1991:62–63.)

24 These were an otter, duck, badger and muskrat.

25 This site was referred to by recent Mandan informants as the 'center of the world'. (Paul Ewald interviewed by the author, July 1976.)

26 The ceremonies which were connected with the bundles evoked two basic ideas – offering or sacrifice.

27 Patterns worked within the quill or beadwork on these garments were often representations of the Morning Star. Such patterns also occur on the regalia of the linguistically related Cheyenne who, in their ancient *Massaum* Ceremony, used the Morning Star symbol. See, Grinnell, 1923, Vol. II:305; Petersen, 1988:140.

28 The *Tobtok Kin*, four times four, unified the spirit powers as well as the physical aspects of the Sioux cosmos, assigning a definite power quantum and function to a matrix of beings. It embraced all the benevolent gods, each of four classes and four in each class, as one whole.

29 For example, on regalia that was said to have belonged to Crazy Horse, and is now in the Museum of the American Indian and The Smithsonian Institution, are emblems of the Thunderbird, dragonfly and forked lightning that refer to thunder powers – the ability to strike and kill, invulnerability and direct communication with high powers.

30 'They sang this song above, they have spoken.
They have put new life in the earth.
Paruxti speaks through the clouds.
And the power has entered Mother Earth.
The earth has received the powers from above.'
(First song of the Pawnee Thunder Ceremony – Linton, 1922:10.)

31 Images of Tree Dwellers were made by the Sioux. These were generally man-like figures perhaps no more than 8in (20cm) high. They were placed within a cylindrical tube made of cottonwood which had been split lengthwise so that the contents could be removed easily.

32 Other Star Myths, such as those of the Seven and Bunched Stars, underline the acute observations that the Blackfeet made of the heavens and refer to the North Star, Great Dipper, Ursa Major and the Pleiades.

33 The Medicine Wheel is now a National Historic Landmark. It is nearly 10,000ft (3,000m) above seal level. The majority of the stones are limestone and its estimated age is between AD 1200 and AD 1700.

34 Chief Joseph of the Nez Perce was said to have fasted at the Medicine Wheel after his gallant but abortive retreat to Canada in 1877. Chief *Washakie*, a Shoshone, gained his power there to help him guide his people through the torment of reservation life, and an early chief of the Crows, Red Plume, was said to have received eagle feathers and medicine at the Wheel to protect his people from harm.

35 Guthrie, 1947:284

36 Joe Medicine Crow referred to the vision site as *Ala-xabna* or 'where to lay down'. (Joe Medicine Crow interviewed by the author, July 1993.)

37 I am indebted to the late Paul Ewald of New Town, North Dakota, who, following an introduction by the Tribal Headquarters of the Three Affiliated Tribes (Mandan, Hidatsa and Arikara), took me to the various places sacred to the Mandan in the historic period.

38 Plains Indians observed that deer could endure thirst for a long time, the hawk was the surest bird of prey, the elk gallant and brave, the frog watchful, the owl had much night wisdom and gentle ways, the bear fierce and the possessor of many herbs for the good of man, the kit fox active and wily, the crow direct and swift in flight, and the wolf hardy.

39 Sioux flageolets, having five holes, were often carved with the head of a bird or elk while Blackfeet

and Ojibwa instruments were generally less elaborate, having four and six holes, respectively.

40 Fletcher and La Flesche, 1911:147

41 This hide was stolen in 1898 from the elderly keeper, Walking Sacred One (Fletcher and La Flesche, 1911:284). In 1991 it was finally returned back to the tribes (see *Wall Street Journal*, August 27, 1991).

42 Special buffalo-calling backrests appear to have been used by these Cree men (Brasser, 1984:56–63).

43 It was generally agreed that the more hazardous the quest site and the more that the person fasting was made to suffer by the spirits or by the elements, the more likely he or she 'is to have pity taken on him by the supernatural powers and the greater will be the power that he receives' (Conner, 1982:86).

44 Joe Medicine Crow said that the Crow vision quest site was referred to as *Bi-li-shi-sna*, meaning 'water they do not drink' (Joe Medicine Crow interviewed by the author, July 11, 1993).

45 Catlin, 1841:Vol.I:157

46 Neihardt, 1932:276

47 Waugh, 1990:70

48 Best and McClelland, 1977:4

49 Feder, 1987

50 Loud and Harrington, 1929:24. Libby, 1951:276. Martin, Quimby and Collier, 1947.

51 Some of the earliest extant examples of quillwork are to be found in the European museum collections, such as the elaborately quill-embellished shirt now in the Ashmolean Museum, Oxford (Turner in MacGregor ed., 1983:123-130) and the collection of early moccasins and headdresses in the Musée de l'Homme, Paris (Fardoulis, 1979).

52 Grinnell, 1923, Vol.I:163. Kroeber, 1902-07.

53 Ewers, 1945:29.

54 Dempsey, 1963:52.

55 Possibly the earliest account of porcupine quillwork from the Plains region was by Dr. Samuel Lathan Mitchell, who has described in great detail an Assiniboin quilled wapiti skin collected before 1817. (Fenenga, 1959:19-22. Orchard, 1926:64).

56 Taylor, 1962, 1981. Quillwork on bark, very common among the Micmac and Ojibwa, was not found on the Plains; however, the use of moosehair while firmly associated with Woodland tribes was, on occasions, also utilized by the Plains Cree.

57 Bebbington, 1982:30

58 The pony bead still continued to be used in Idaho, northwest Montana and eastern Washington even as late as 1900.

59 Lanford (1990) has recently put forward ideas relating to the origins and precursors of symbolic and decorative beadwork motifs among the Central Plains groups.

60 Pohrt (1989) has further references relating to North Plains beadwork.

61 Ewers, 1945:38

62 Lyford, 1940:71

63 Lessard (1991) has a detailed discussion of pictographic Sioux beadwork which includes identification of the producers.

64 Lowie, 1954:143

65 A discussion of the origins of Crow Indian beadwork designs appears in Wildschut, 1959, and more recently in Feder, 1980.

66 MacGregor, 1966:116

67 Robert Ritzenthaler's survey (1976) of Woodland sculpture demonstrates that carved objects were rarely more than a foot (30cm) in length and that woodworking was carried out by men. Several parallels have been found between Woodland carving and that from the Plains (Ewers,

1986:11).

68 Ewers, 1986:12 and 15

69 Ewers, 1986:41.

70 Ewers, 1986:18 pictures a human effigy Tree-Dweller Medicine, said to have been for some 200 years in the Wabasha (Santee Sioux) family. It is 6in (15cm) high and of painted wood.

71 McClintock, 1937:13

72 West, 1978:64.

73 West, 1979:295 and 299.

74 Pohrt, 1978:63.

75 Pohrt, 1978:63

76 Ewers, 1986:177.

77 Palliser, 1969:146-47.

78 From time immemorial, the area was considered to be neutral ground and anyone could visit the quarry in peace and mine the stone (Catlin, 1841, Vol.II:169). The pipestone and finished product was widely traded, pipe bowls of catlinite having been found in 17th century Iroquoian sites. The Pipestone National Monument was established in 1937 and the exclusive right to the use of the quarry by Native Americans only was established.

79 Douglas, 1931.

80 Ewers, 1986:50.

81 Catlin, 1841, Vol.I:334. Experiments show that such work was very time-consuming. To drill a cone-shaped hole some 1in (25mm) deep into catlinite employing the method described by Catlin took one hour. (West, 1934, Vol.I:341-42).

82 Ewers, 1963:42 and 50.

83 Sturtevant, 1992:28.

84 Golden or 'calumet' eagle feathers were the most prized for headdresses. These came from the immature bird and were white with dark brown or black tips. Such feathers were considered exceedingly valuable. (See Denig, 1930:589).

85 Ewers reported that when the Sioux-style bonnet was introduced among the Blackfeet in about 1895, it became so popular as to replace the traditional Blackfeet style almost entirely. (Ewers, 1945:61)

86 Ewers, 1945:61.

87 Taylor, 1994:23.

88 Fletcher and La Flesche, 1911:447. (See Taylor, 1994:91-99 for a more detailed discussion relating to the symbolism).

89 The cutting, lacing and beadwork embellishment associated with the Blackfeet woman's dress has been considered by Conn (1961:114-117). (See also Ewers, 1945:42).

90 Lewis and Clark, 1904, Vol.II:129. Further descriptions and a discussion of the various styles of leggings used on the Northern and Central Plains are in Taylor (1961).

91 Cooley, 1983.

92 Weltfish, 1977:375.

93 Wissler, 1912(b):40.

94 Taylor, 1989:247.

95 238 human hair and 68 horsehair locks embellish this shirt which is now in the collections of the Buffalo Bill Historical Center, Cody, Wyoming.

96 Mallery, 1893:31.

97 Petersen, 1971 and 1988.

98 Conner, 1971, and Keyser, 1987. In pre-reservation times, petroglyph sites were regarded as special places and imbued with spiritual power.

99 Some petroglyphs were colored with earth paints enhancing the image, but unless the petroglyph

was protected this coloring faded.

100 A number of bone 'paint brushes' have been found in early Pawnee and Mandan sites (Ewers, 1939:36).

101 Ewers, 1939:9-10.

102 Hail, 1983:40.

103 Ewers, 1939:19-21.

104 Taylor, 1973.

105 Arni Brownstone has recently compared traditional Blackfeet pictography and 19th century European painting, identifying two distinct pictorial systems. (See Brownstone, 1993:29.)

106 A favored source for making metal defleshers was the sawn-off end of the old northwest gun.

107 The term 'parfleche' is of doubtful origin but it appears in French narratives as early as 1700 and is probably from some old French root, possibly from *parer* 'to parry', *fleche* 'arrow' in reference to the shield or body armor of rawhide.

108 See Spier, 1931:82, for a definition of the parfleche.

109 A beaver tail was often boiled to make a sticky glue. (See Ewers, 1945:17).

110 Morrow, 1975:78. Torrence, 1994.

111 Webber, 1989:4 , considers the theories of the development of the moccasin.

112 Larocque, 1910:27.

113 Clark, 1885:259. For a detailed analysis of Crow, Sioux and Arapaho moccasins, see Wildschut 1959; and Kroeber 1902.

114 Wissler's (1927) studies of moccasin decorations cover the 25-year period 1890–1915 and considers both partially and fully quilled and beaded moccasins and their distribution.

PLATEAU AND BASIN

The plateau area stretches from central British Columbia, south and across the United States border, eastern Oregon and Washington, then across the majority of the northern half of Idaho and straddles the Continental Divide into northwestern Montana. It is laced by rivers – the names of several suggesting both their character and products, the Clearwater, Boulder, Salmon, Beaverhead and Cascade – and the Blue and Bitterroot Mountains which skirt the Columbia Plateau – the most dominant geographical feature of the area and through which runs the great Columbia River which, together with the Fraser in the north, is the lifeblood of the land and its people. The area, covering approximately two hundred thousand square miles, is one of great contrast and beauty being marked by forested mountains, deep valleys and canyons, clear rushing streams, open meadowlands and, to the south, bordering the northern rim of the Great Basin, windswept plains and desert regions dotted with sagebrush and rock.

The rivers are rich in fish resources, particularly salmon which migrate from the Pacific via tributaries of both the Fraser and Columbia; other fish also abound such as sturgeon, lamprey eel, whitefish and trout. The clear, cold waters, with their high oxygen content, support much life in comparison to the warmer and often murky rivers of the Great Plains. While the area was largely devoid of buffalo, there were many elk, deer and mountain sheep as well as otter and beaver.

The Plateau was dominated by two major linguistic groups: in the north, occupying the inland areas of present-day British Columbia, were the Salishan-speaking Shuswap, Lillooet, Thompson and Okanagan, while across the border into present-day Washington and Idaho lived the Kalispel, Coeur d'Alêne, Spokane, Colville, Sanpoil and Flathead. In the middle Columbia ranged the Sahaptin-speaking Klikitat, Yakima, Umatilla, Walla Walla, Palus, Nez Perce and Cayuse. Other linguistic stocks were also represented, such as the Kutenai in the northeast who spoke a language of their own, but now shown to be distantly related to Algonquian, and in the west – although their cultural traits tend to identify them more with the tribes of the Pacific coast – the Chinookans on the lower Columbia. Associated with this latter language was the foundation of the so-called Chinook jargon, the Indian trade language of the Columbia River region, its use extending to the Pacific coast and reaching from California up to Alaska.

While gathering and hunting were important to the Plateau people, their principal subsistence depended on the salmon which were speared, netted, gorge-hooked or trapped, the latter method being by the use of weirs constructed of willows and boulders across the smaller streams. The spearing was a way of obtaining quantities of large salmon and these were caught from specially built platforms which projected over the water, or from jutting ledges of rock. The platforms were generally built above the weirs which impeded the movement of the fish. One magnificent painting by the Canadian artist, Paul Kane, vividly illustrates the various techniques used by the Spokane in the vicinity of the Kettle Falls on the Columbia River in what is now northeast Washington state. Clearly, in 1846, when the sketches used for the painting were made, the Indians highly valued this bountiful area; sadly, they lost it a century and a quarter later with the building of the Grand Coulee Dam across the Columbia whose backwater (as has happened with several other dammed rivers in the United States) has flooded forever this ancient Indian site.

The spears depicted by Kane, which were identical to a type used by the Nez Perce further south, consisted of a three-pronged gig attached to a shaft some 8ft (2.5m) in length. Through each prong, which was made of a flexible wood such as hackberry, were pointed bone pins; these projected inward and away from the end of the prongs. The spear was not thrown, instead it was jabbed down into the water, the spread of the three prongs adding to its efficiency; it was a favorite style for night fishing, the light of pitch torches being used to attract the salmon. Another type of spear which had a detachable head was also used by the Nez Perce; here, the point was of heavy bone (cut from the thickest part of an elk leg bone) with a socket of elderberry wood, the whole being bound firmly together and attached to the shaft some 11in. (30cm) from the head. When the salmon was speared,

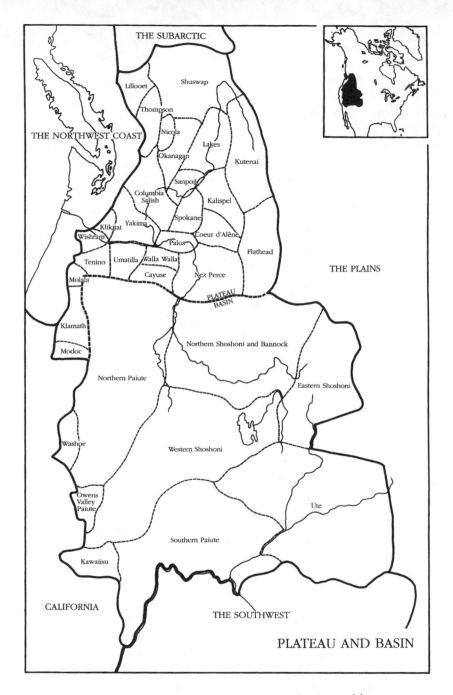

The map labels include:

THE SUBARCTIC

THE NORTHWEST COAST

Lillooet
Shuswap
Thompson
Nicola
Lakes
Okanagan
Kutenai
Sanpoil
Columbia Salish
Kalispel
Klikitat
Yakima
Spokane
Wishram
Coeur d'Alène
Palus
Flathead
Tenino
Umatilla
Walla Walla
Molala
Cayuse
Nez Perce

THE PLAINS

PLATEAU
BASIN

Klamath
Modoc
Northern Shoshoni and Bannock
Northern Paiute
Eastern Shoshoni
Washoe
Western Shoshoni
Owens Valley Paiute
Ute
Southern Paiute
Kawaiisu

CALIFORNIA

THE SOUTHWEST

PLATEAU AND BASIN

ABOVE: *This map shows approximate territories of tribes and language groups at about 1850, and somewhat earlier in the western and eastern edges of the Basin. After that, all tribes lost territory and some moved.*

the head loosened from the shaft; fish, head and shaft were now easily pulled in by an attached braided cord. While much of the fish caught was eaten fresh, a great deal was dried on scaffolds and smoked for winter use.

The Nez Perce, as with many other tribes on the Plateau, attended the great Dalles Rendezvous which was held every fall on the Columbia River where it cuts through the Cascade Mountain range.[1] For several environmental and historical reasons, The Dalles became one of the most important centers for a lively trade throughout the summer, reaching its peak in the fall. In the vicinity of The Dalles lived the Wishram and Wasco, both of whom spoke Chinookan dialects, and were identified as noted middlemen between the Plateau and Pacific coast tribes; they hosted many groups who came to their villages during the fall trading fair.

In order to obtain the goods they required, each tribe tended to specialize in producing or acquiring materials which they knew would trade well at The Dalles. Thus, the Nez Perce, several bands of which hunted on the Montana and Wyoming Plains to the east, brought along buffalo robes; others, such as the Klamath, specalized in camas bulbs, a widely used sweet and nutritious vegetal food; dentalium and other shells were brought in from the Pacific coast by the Wishram and Wasco. Although the Rendezvous appears to have been established long before white contact, according to the explorers Lewis and Clark, who visited The Dalles in January 1806, 'the circumstance which forms the soul of this trade is the visit of the whites'. From such contacts, Lewis and Clark reported, Plateau people obtained access to somewhat outdated 'British or American muskets, powder, ball, and shot, copper and brass kettles, brass tea-kettles and coffee-pots, blankets . . . scarlet and blue cloth . . . brass wire [and] knives'. Clearly, the Plateau people became increasingly dependent on European goods which ultimately became essentials rather than luxury items.

The habitations of the Plateau Indians varied in style and emphasis, at least four distinct types having been identified. Traditionally, the northern Plateau tribes such as the Shuswap, Thompson and Okanagan, used semi-subterranean earth lodges; occupied by one or two families, they were constructed by excavating the dry sandy ground to a depth of some 6.6ft (2m) and were about 13ft (4m) in diameter, although sizes varied considerably. Poles were laid across which were covered with grass and earth to a depth of 4in. (10cm) or so and the entrance was generally, but not always, from the top, via a simple ladder. Further to the south amonge the Nez Perce, similar habitations tended to be used by women before and after childbirth,

197

ABOVE: *Chief Joseph of the Nez Perce, photographed in 1901. The mottled feather in his hair is from the tail of a maturing golden eagle.*

and during the menstrual period, while a smaller sudatory lodge was used by boys above fourteen years of age.

A favorite habitation, however, used by many tribes on the Plateau both in winter and summer, was the conical lodge, formed by stacking seven to nine poles around a tripod and then covering the frame with mats woven from cattail (*Typha latifolia*) or tule (*Scirpus lacustris*). Such habitations gave the appearance of the Plains tipi, although on average they were somewhat smaller. For winter living these lodges were covered with two to four layers of mats and generally sunk about 2ft (60cm) into the ground with the earth stacked around. On occasions, such habitations could be very large; Lewis and Clark reported seeing an ancient circular house ring some 30ft (10m) in diameter, the rimmed circumference being about 3ft (1m) in height and the center sunk more than 3ft into the ground.

There were also communal long houses: Lewis and Clark in describing their visit to Neeshnepahkeook or Cut-nose, a Nez Perce chief, refer to the entire village of some thirty-eight families occupying two large houses. 'At a little distance from us are two Chopunnish houses, one of which contains eight families, and the other, which is by much the largest we have ever seen, is inhabited by at least 30. It is rather a kind of shed built, like all the other huts, of straw and mats in the form of the roof of a house, 156 feet long and about 15 wide, closed at the ends, and having a number of doors on each side. The vast interior is without partitions, but the fire of each family is kindled in a row along the middle of the building, about ten feet apart'. The upright supports of these lodges separated the ridge poles by several inches so that an aperture extended the whole length of the lodge, thus serving as a smoke vent.[2] Poles were then leaned onto the horizontal ridge poles and long mats attached to these in a shingle-fashion; earth was packed against the lower part of the mat which was generally protected from decay with a covering of dry grass. The mats were carefully selected. Those of cattail were simpler in construction than those made of tule. The former were not very effective in repelling rain, thus although generally of the same size, approximately 4 × 10ft (1.2 × 3m), the more exposed surfaces were covered with tule mats. As a safeguard against the wind, more poles were often leaned up against the mats and during cold weather – especially with the smaller habitations – the interior was lined with skins.

The Okanagan and other tribes further north also utilized a similar long house, but it was, according to one observer, a temporary shelter that was made to accommodate people at gatherings and at the fishing places. They

ABOVE: *Interior of a Shoshoni lodge, 1878. The standing woman wears a striped Witney 'point' blanket. The baby is in a typical Shoshoni cradle: fine beaded saddle bags hang behind the figures.*

were favored when communities camped together because they required a lesser number of mats than the conical tents to accommodate the same number of people. It is probable that Lewis and Clark, therefore, were describing a temporary Nez Perce camp. This is consistent with the observations of Mylie Lawyer who related that the long house (which she referred to as the *Lah-pit-ahl Ain-neet*) was popular when large groups of people got together, 'a gathering place for social, religious and war ceremonials'.

As mobility increased with the introduction of the horse, those tribes on the eastern side of the Plateau region such as the Pend d'Oreilles, Flathead, Colville and some of the Nez Perce bands, made forays to the Plains buffalo country. There they traded for buffalo hide tipis which tended to displace the mat covered conical tent, being far more convenient for hunting and trading expeditions.

Prior to the introduction of the horse during the early eighteenth century, the Plateau was settled with small and independent bands generally on, or near, the many rivers and streams which characterized this region. As has been outlined, in adapting to their environment, they had shaped out a pattern of living – undoubtedly established over a period of several thousand years – which pivoted on the extensive use of fish and other food resources, wide travel, mutual interdependence and trade, and a limited war complex.

Travel to the great trading fairs held at such places as The Dalles, Kettle Falls and Celilo Falls, was mainly by means of canoe, portaging past dangerous rapids such as those on the Upper Clearwater. The style of canoe varied. In the north, tribes such as the Shuswap, Thompson and Okanagan used the sharp-snouted 'sturgeon-nose' type which was made of cedar bark; the same style, which Kane also illustrated, was also used by the more southerly Coeur d'Alêne and Kutenai. Rafts of tule lodge mats, rolled into bundles lashed together and pointed at each end like canoes, were also used on occasions. Tribes to the eastern part of the Plateau area, such as the Kalispel and Pend d'Oreilles, were particularly well-known as expert canoe people and while these crafts resembled in shape those of the northern Salishan tribes, they differed in having the ends cut off square. J. A. Teit has suggested that this style was due to Iroquois influence, some of whom, employed by fur traders, 'made bark canoes of the eastern or Iroquois shape on Flathead Lake'.

The Nez Perce (south of the Pend d'Oreilles in the valleys of the

Clearwater), seem to have favored the simple dug-out type of canoe which was made from a single log and hollowed out by fires; it was propelled by either paddles or poles and might vary between about 16–42ft (5–13m) in length. The former importance of water travel to the Nez Perce may be indicated by the Crow name for these people, *A-pu-pe*, which means 'to paddle'. However, even as early as 1806, canoes were scarce in the Nez Perce camps which Lewis and Clark visited, and some large villages were 'entirely without them'. The horse, it seems, was now the major mode of travel and as with the Plains Indian it brought great cultural changes to all the Plateau people. Lewis and Clark were greatly impressed by the number of horses owned by many of the tribes whom they came into contact with during their travels through the Plateau region and, compared to the Plains Indians at this time, their wealth in horses was immense. The explorers reported that fifty to one hundred horses per individual among the Nez Perce was quite common, and forty years later it was reported that as many as fifteen hundred horses might be owned by Cayuse and Nez Perce family units, while reports for the Crow – considered to be the wealthiest among the northwestern Plains tribes – gives an average of seven per lodge in 1805 and fifteen in 1830.

The traditions of the Flathead and Nez Perce credit the Shoshoni as furnishing them with their first mounts; the Shoshoni in turn said that they obtained them from their kinsmen, the Comanche, who, as early as 1705, raided the horse-rich Spanish settlements in what is now present-day New Mexico. The subsequent horse trade was thus via a very complex route stretching from such places as Santa Fe, probably west of the Continental Divide to the Snake River and Shoshoni Rendezvous, whence to the country of the Nez Perce, Flathead, Pend d'Oreilles, Kutenai and Kalispel. Tribal traditions of this last tribe – typical of many – records the first appearance of the animal: 'Some people saw the horse's tracks where it had passed over some sand. They called other people, and discussed what kind of animal had made the tracks, which were strange to them all. Some thought it might have been a horse, as they had heard about them. Other people lower down, near the river bank, saw the man approach on the horse at a lope. They observed that he was smoking, and that he seemed to be quite at his ease. They watched him enter the river and swim across on the horse. They gathered around and examined the animal with much curiosity'.

An amusing story related by the Okanagan refers to the initial efforts to ride this strange creature; the main fear it seems was falling off! 'The first horse [we] obtained was very gentle. The first person who mounted it rode with two long sticks, one in each hand, to steady himself. Another man led the horse slowly, and the rider shifted the sticks (as one does with walking sticks) as they went along.'

Much of the Plateau region was fine horse country, the natural barriers protecting the animal from wandering too far and also from would-be thieves, while the well-watered valleys, such as the Wallowa and Grande Ronde,[3] provided nutritious forage and shelter in winter. The horse also fitted well into the established seasonal movements of the Plateau people. By careful and selective breeding, such tribes as the Nez Perce and their close relatives, the Cayuse, built up enormous horse herds. Eliminating the poorer stallions by castration, the Nez Perce became justly famous for the superior speed and endurance of their horses, among the most distinctive of which was the traditional war-horse, which came to be known as the Appaloosa.

It was Meriwether Lewis, in 1806, who first made a definite reference to what was almost certainly the forebear of the Appaloosa, describing a few of the Nez Perce horses as being marked with large spots of white, irregularly scattered and intermixed with the dark brown or other dark shade. Later, in 1820, Alexander Ross of the Hudson's Bay Company observed that the Nez Perce preferred entirely white horses which were painted for war 'drawing a variety of hieroglyphic devices, the head and neck were dappled with streaks of red and yellow; the mane dyed black, the tail red, clubbed up in a knot and tied short . . . and the rider as well as the horse was so besmeared with red, blue and yellow ochre, that no one could tell what the natural color of either was.' At this time, however, next to white, those horses which were speckled or white and black were in most demand, being used by distinguished warriors in preference to any other and being valued at two or three times the worth of other horses. They were more than just handsomely marked, being generally larger and heavier than the average Plateau breed, sure-footed and possessing great endurance; they also matched well the varying Plateau country, capable of traveling with equal ease through heavy timbered or mountainous terrain. While the Appaloosa became indelibly associated with the Nez Perce, it is possible that the name derives from Palus, a tribe closely associated with the Nez Perce and Cayuse, the latter breeding a distinctive type of pony.

With the acquisition of the horse into Plateau culture – probably around the first quarter of the eighteenth century – the basic mode of travel was considerably modified, resulting in increased interaction between more distant tribes such as those on the Plains to the east, in particular the Blackfeet and Crow. It also led to an expansion on the already long established seasonal activities, in particular the scope for trade, which was greatly enhanced by an ability to transport quickly and easily large amounts of trade commodities; not surprisingly, the horse itself also became a highly valued trade item.

Unlike the Plains, neither the dog nor the travois were popular on the Plateau as a means of transporting equipment and while the Plateau tribes became adept horsemen, most of the horse equipment which they used, such as pack and riding saddles, bridles, cinches, whips and ropes, were adopted along with the horse from the Shoshoni. Nevertheless, when the Plateau people made their own horse equipment, it displayed some distinctive features. Men's saddles, in common with those used by the Plains Indians, were generally of the pad-type with the four corners of the saddle embellished with quill or beadwork; women's saddles, on the other hand, had a high pommel and cantel, generally with a hook or spike at the front with hanging triangular shaped flaps beautifully ornamented with trade cloth and beads. The stirrups were made of bentwood covered with rawhide, those used by the Flathead, Pend d'Oreilles and Nez Perce women being particularly distinctive in having beaded pendants attached to the bottom. Wide cruppers and horse collars were also used, the latter again exhibiting heavily embellished flaps similar to those used on stirrups. This attractive horse equipment was also used by the Crow and has been particularly associated with that tribe. However, the style may have been copied by them from the Plateau people, the roots of which can in turn be traced to the Spanish settlements of New Mexico and Texas. The Nez Perce women's horse equipment and mode of riding was sufficiently distinctive for the Presbyterian missionary, Henry H. Spalding, to observe that their saddles were an 'improvement upon our side saddle if we consult the ease of the woman' and the Nez Perce woman always used a blanket or robe which was 'thrown over the saddle covering the lower part of the person,' wrote A. C. Fletcher in my opinion the more modest way of riding as also the more natural & comfortable'.

With the acquisition of the horse, tribes such as the Coeur d'Alêne, Spokane and Nez Perce began to visit the Plains for buffalo hunting and trading. The goods which passed from east to west were chiefly catlinite and pipes of the same material, clothing, buffalo skins and robes. While both Plains and Plateau people tended to make the same items, there was an emphasis on *quality* goods, it being recognized that one group was more skilled than the other in the production of certain items. For example, while the Plateau made headdresses, they considered that the finest were made by the Sioux,[4] and the Crow robes – of the softest tan and embellished with beaded or quilled bands – were greatly sought after: 'Often a horse and, in addition, a well-made leather shirt, was paid for one of the best kind of robes', noted J. A. Teit. Porcupine quillwork, beaded and quilled pipe-bags, moccasins and parfleches were all items made in quantity and *quality* which the Plateau tribes desired from the Plains people. This trade had a profound impact on their clothing styles, particularly that which was worn for ceremonial and dress occasions.

While the trade in horses from the Plateau to the Plains was a major activity – and even the rare Appaloosa was occasionally traded – the Plains Indians also desired such items as salmon oil, pemmican, cakes of camas and berries, hemp and hemp twine, shells, certain types of beads, pipes of green soapstone, eagle-tail feathers, mountain-sheep horn and horn spoons, and woven bags. One of the most coveted items, however, was the highly perfected Plateau bow which the Plains tribes considered was greatly superior to those of their own make. Among the finest of these bows were those made from mountain-sheep horn, being a particular speciality of the Nez Perce.

The traditional dress of the Plateau was of soft tanned skins from the antelope, elk or deer, generally without the hair. The men wore soft-soled moccasins, leggings and breechcloth, shirt and a robe, while the women wore moccasins, calf-length leggings, a long dress and a robe. The women's dress of the Coeur d'Alêne was very similar to that worn by the Nez Perce. Two deerskins formed the body, a third was for fringing and shaping. J. A. Teit wrote: 'The upper parts of the skins were folded down on the outside of the dress, forming a kind of false yoke at back and front. They were sewed to the body of the dress throughout, or stitched here and there with thongs. Pendants and tassels were often attached to the edges of the fold. The hair of the tailpiece was clipped in lines, and the end of the tail generally, but not always, cut off. Usually the sleeve parts were left open underneath, but sometimes they were stitched or tied here and there with thongs. Generally three rows of inserted fringe or thongs extended around the skirt below the waist. Single rows were also placed on the back and front of the dress below the yoke, but only rarely . . . Often all or the lower part of the yoke piece was beaded or quilled in lines following the contour of the edge of the yoke, or the dress itself was beaded immediately below the yoke . . . Most dresses reached to the ankles, . . . Some had several lines of quillwork across the breast and back of the body and many had long fringes following the edge of the yoke.' The leggings were also of tanned hide; they reached to the knee and were generally fringed on the outer edges. Most could be opened at the sides and wrapped around the leg and then fastened with tie strings, one string going around the leg above the calf to hold the leggings in place. They were often heavily beaded on the lower part with a narrower band extending up the outside of the legging.

Although Teit has identified five moccasin types which were worn by the Coeur d'Alêne and adjacent tribes, the most popular and traditional type with wide distribution on the Plateau was constructed so that both the sole and upper were of one single piece of deerskin with the main seam extending around the outside of the sole starting on the inner side near the big toe and terminating a few inches beyond the heel seam. Near the base of the heel seam were additional strips of buckskin to enable the moccasins to be easily removed and an extra single piece of hide was sewn around the top producing flaps which could tuck under or be attached to the leggings. The summer soft-soled moccasin fitted snugly to the foot, but those made for winter use were looser, not infrequently being made of tanned hide – deer, antelope or buffalo – with the hair left on the inside.

After sustained and extended contact with the Plains tribes toward the end of the nineteenth century, a two-piece rawhide-soled moccasin became increasingly popular, particularly among the more eastern Plateau people such as the Kutenai, Flathead and Nez Perce, and ultimately it all but replaced the ancient soft-soled type. Lewis and Clark likened the costume of the Nez Perce to that of the Shoshoni, extending on the idea of not only a general similarity in clothing styles throughout the Plateau region, but also to the Great Basin. However, deeper analysis indicates that there were considerable differences. For example, in his studies of Nez Perce women's dresses, C. Wissler concluded there were 'a number of distinct cuts for the contour of the yoke and the bottom of the skirt. Yet, there is very little variation within the tribe, . . . [each tribe] followed a definite form for the bottoms of their dresses, making it clear that they had a fixed mode, or style for the cut.'

Two particularly fine women's dresses – almost certainly Nez Perce and probably among the earliest now extant from this tribe – were collected by the Presbyterian missionary, Henry H. Spalding, who sent them to his brother in Oberlin, Ohio, in 1846. Each dress, Spalding said, was valued at three horses[5] and the dentalium shells which embellished one of them he described as 'very costly' . . . and the shells removed 'From a single dress were once taken to the mountains by a man who lives near, & sold in small parcels for $1600.00 sixteen hundred dollars. A young lady (Red one) in one of these dresses, upon a firey horse well equiped [sic] with saddle & crouper [sic], makes a fine appearance.' Spalding's vivid description continues, referring to objects which were so typical of Nez Perce accouterments of the period when natural materials were utilized to their best effect – both for service and decorative embellishment. The elk teeth on the other dress and the cradle which he also sent, were, he explained, from the 'Buck elk, two from an animal, after & before certain ages'.[6] He refers to the woven fiber bags for which the Nez Perce are justly famous: 'The bags are made of the hemp of the country & used for packing roots, etc.' Such bags were indeed coveted trade items; in the older types, the warp and weft threads were of hemp (*Apocynum cannabium*) and the false embroidery material was of bear grass (*Xerophyllum tenax*) which was dyed in soft natural colors and combined in such a way as to produce attractive geometrical patterns across the surface of the bag.[7] A distinctive flat-topped hat that was commented on by the explorers Lewis and Clark in 1806, without a rim and utilizing similar techniques of weaving to that for the bags, was also made and worn by Nez Perce women; it has been described as the highest form of Nez Perce textile art and 'the gayest portion of their dress'.

While Plateau culture was profoundly affected by the horse and the extensive contacts which they subsequently made with the Plains tribes to the east, the tribal domains remained largely intact and Plateau intertribal warfare was minimal.[8] Less so with forays to the Plains, where for almost one hundred years the majority of the Plateau tribes were arrayed in war against the Blackfeet and Crow (although at times there was an uneasy truce). The Kutenai, Flathead and some of the Northern Shoshoni, in particular, viewed the Blackfeet and Crow as intruders into the western Plains region which for centuries they had used as intertribal buffalo country. Tribal traditions collected by Wissler and Teit[9] from Blackfeet and the Plateau in the early twentieth century, confirmed the report of the explorer, David Thompson, who, when traveling in the region of present-day Calgary, Alberta, observed: 'All these Plains, which are now the hunting ground of the above Indians (Blackfoot), were formerly in full possession of the Kootenaes, northward; the next the Saleesh and their allies, and the most southern the Snake Indians.'

Armed with guns which they obtained from the Cree to the east, the Blackfeet forced the Kutenai, Flathead and Shoshoni to abandon their former hunting grounds, and some of the bands who had previously lived east of the Rockies were all but exterminated, others retreated to the Plateau. The Shoshoni were so badly decimated that for more than half a century none were 'seen on the northwestern plains north of the Yellowstone'. This devastating experience had a positive and lasting effect; it greatly strengthened the interdependence ethos which was so much a part of the Plateau culture and added another – the war complex.

The Flathead invited the Coeur d'Alêne and other Salishan tribes to join them as partners when traveling to their former Plains hunting grounds, the result being a great war alignment of tribes (Plateau versus Plains). The latter were weaker in this respect because of the constant warring which occurred among the Plains people themselves (for example, the Crow and Blackfeet were almost constantly at war with one another). Thus, expeditions across the mountains were relatively commonplace, and parties of Coeur d'Alêne, Spokane, Kalispel, Pend d'Oreilles and Nez Perce hunted in territory now claimed by the Blackfeet and Crow. Initially, a rendezvous was made in Flathead country, then three or more large parties would travel to the Plains keeping in touch with one another during their travels. The worst enemy were the Blackfeet, but even with them the Plateau tribes would form a truce so that trading could take place for a few days. 'No one on either side was to quarrel, fight, or steal horses; but all were to be friends for the allotted number of days, and all were to play games and trade as they felt inclined,' J. A. Teit wrote. 'The conduct of the people during these periods of truce was in great contrast to their attitude at other times, when each side was always ready to attack or repel an attack. Sometimes . . . less than a day passed before one side made an attack on the other. The Blackfoot are said to have been the worst offenders.'

Some lasting friendships were, however, made particularly by the Nez Perce bands who commonly traveled to the Plains following the Lolo Trail[10] across the Rocky Mountains into present-day Montana and Wyoming, there to barter with a western branch of the Absaroka – the Mountain Crows. As early as 1806, Lewis and Clark referred to these contacts although they reported that of the seven groups of Nez Perce (whom they referred to as *Chopunnish*) only two traveled to the Missouri. In the 1860s, it seems to have been small bands such as those led by Looking Glass, who had the reputation of being a great wanderer, that forged and maintained these links.

The effect on these Nez Perce bands was that it led to the adoption of a number of Plains traits, particularly those of a material culture nature and it served in the second half of the nineteenth century to distinguish more clearly between two groups of Nez Perce, those who were strongly influenced by the missionaries and therefore were increasingly giving up their traditional religious, tribal customs and lifestyles, and those who wished to maintain their independence and ethos. Henry Spalding, for example, instructed the Nez Perce 'to give up their native dress before they could receive the rewards of salvation and the power of Christian spirits' and many native materials 'were abandoned or destroyed, mostly by burning'[11]. Divisions increasingly became apparent; as the Nez Perce agent, John Monteith, reported in August 1872: 'The tribe is about equally divided between Treaty and those who term themselves Non-Treaty Indians. The Non-Treaty portion with very few exceptions reside on the outside of the Reserve along the Snake River and its Tributaries. They never ask for assistance . . . .'.

Although convenient from the white man's standpoint to regard the Nez Perce as one single body, this was entirely inconsistent with the traditional social organization of these people – the tribe consisted of both Treaty and Non-Treaty bands, each with its own leader. Regardless of the appointment by government officials of Lawyer as 'Head Chief of the Nez Perces Nation', the bands largely acted independently.

By the mid-nineteenth century, the Plateau country became increasingly subjected to white settlement and, in an attempt to avoid conflict, the Stevens Treaty of 1855, among others, defined Nez Perce territory. Agreement was reached with little dispute, the Treaty being signed by Lawyer, a highly respected leader and direct descendant of Chief Twisted Hair who had so well received Lewis and Clark half a century previously.[12] Forty-seven others also signed; the anticipated difficulties, it appeared, had thus been resolved, but sadly, not for long. Five years later, in 1860, a trader named Elias D. Pierce discovered traces of gold deposits on the reservation and by the end of that year, Pierce had set up camp with some thirty-three recruits. The intention was to mine the following spring.

Anticipating a further influx of miners, another Treaty attempted to reduce the Reservation further. This time, an agreement could not be reached and the Lower Nez Perce – which included Looking Glass' band – walked out of the negotiations, refusing to sign. It was again left to Lawyer and others to negotiate and this time the lands of the Lower Nez Perce – largely the Non-Treaty faction – were ceded by Lawyer and the Band Chiefs closely associated with him. This included the Wallowa Valley, a traditional homeland of *Tu-eka-kas* or Old Joseph, as he was known to the whites; there were deep regrets and concern on both sides. As Agent Monteith observed in 1872: 'It is a great pity that the valley was ever opened for settlement. It is so high and cold that they can raise nothing but the hardiest of vegetables . . . It is a fine grass country and raising stock is all that can be done to any advantage. It is the only fishery the Nez Percés have and they go there from all directions . . . If there is any way in which the Wallowa Valley could be kept for the Indians I would recommend that it be done.'

This report was written some months after Old Joseph died, who on his deathbed charged his son never to relinquish the Wallowa and Grande Valleys: 'Always remember that your father never sold his country.' As *Hein-mot Too-ya-la-kekt*,[13] better known to the world as Joseph, later commented: 'I buried him in that beautiful valley of winding waters. I love that land more than all the rest of the world.'

In 1872, Monteith had also reported that while at that time there were no white houses yet built in the Wallowa Valley, some were to be built 'this fall' . . . [Then] the question will have to be settled soon to those Indians living outside the Reserve . . .'

In 1877, General Howard's[14] adjutant, Major H. Clay Wood, considered the legality of the 1863 Treaty and concluded: 'In my opinion the non-treaty Nez Perces cannot in law be regarded as bound by the treaty of 1863, and in so far as it attempts to deprive them of a right to occupancy of any land its provisions are null and void. The extinguishment of their title of occupancy contemplated by this treaty is imperfect and incomplete.' Nevertheless, as more whites, believing they were within their rights, moved into the valley, the situation became obviously tense. One historian who considered the status of these incoming settlers was led to the conclusion that a number were 'human parasites of varying degrees of undesirability'. He quotes Major Wood's authoritative study of the Nez Perce problem, who had observed: 'I could fill page after page in portraying the number and nature of outrages the Indians and their families were subject to.'

In a final council meeting between Joseph and Howard, a show of military force finally caused capitulations: the Non-Treaty Nez Perce agreed to leave the Wallowa and Grande Ronde Valleys. Howard reported 'We have put all non treaty Indians on reservation by using force and persuasion without bloodshed.'

An unrealistic time limit of thirty days for the move to be completed added to the consternation and deep resentment of the Nez Perce, and young *Wahlitits*, whose father had been murdered by a white man some three years earlier, decided to seek revenge. As one historian put it, 'a taunt about Eagle Robe's death that was the match that lit the fuse'. On Wednesday, 13 June 1877, *Wahlitits* and two young companions killed Richard Devine: the next day they killed Henry J. Elfers, Robert Bland and Harry Becktoge. The trio were joined by seventeen others from White Bird's camp and, plied with stolen liquor, the rampage continued. Detailed analysis clearly demonstrates that the prominent leaders – Joseph, his brother *Ollokot*, Looking Glass and *Too-hool-hool-zote* – had no part in these incidents and that their attempts to deliver the culprits were foiled by unscrupulous volunteers. As Agent Monteith reported to General Howard, 'the fact is there is a certain class here who are afraid there will not be an Indian war'. In less than a week the die was cast and a war with the Non-Treaty Nez Perce was on.

The first major conflict, at White Bird Canyon on 17 June 1877, caused great consternation in the ranks of Howard's force under Captain David Perry, when approximately seventy warriors, a historian wrote, 'quickly and completely routed a column consisting of four officers and ninety-nine men plus ten or eleven armed citizens. Not only did the Indians whip them soundly, but they wiped out one-third of the cavalrymen and chased the remainder for about thirteen miles' and in 'one salutary demonstration, the Nez Perce showed that not only would they fight but that they could fight with the skill, courage and determination that would have been creditable to the best troops in the Army'. Sobered by this humiliating defeat, Howard now mustered a more than five hundred strong artillery-supported force. The chase of some two hundred and fifty Nez Perce warriors together with their families numbering about five hundred women and children had commenced . . . it took nearly four months and seventeen hundred miles across rugged terrain to stop them just forty miles short of their final intended destination, Sitting Bull's camps in Canada. Howard undoubtedly regretted penning the following information to Division Headquarters on 15 June 1877: 'Other troops are being brought forward as fast as possible . . . [I need] authority for twenty five Indian scouts . . . Think we shall make short work of this.'

Although supported with these further reinforcements, the Nez Perce again turned the tables on Howard; they encircled the troops and pushed on to the valley of the Clearwater and then dug in for protection. This time, however, on 11 July, assisted by the howitzers, four companies of cavalry, six of infantry and five of artillery acting as infantry, in total some four hundred and forty men exclusive of his staff, Howard, after twenty-four hours of siege, routed the Nez Perce; an enormous amount of property was abandoned and as one elderly Nez Perce woman related, 'many, many, had been wounded'. So harrowing was this attack, and probably anticipating what the future would hold, Joseph was prepared to surrender at this point, but differences of opinion existed in the Nez Perce camp in regard to a Treaty of Peace, with White Bird, Looking Glass and *Too-hool-hool-zote* voting to make for the buffalo country. The precedent of hanging had already been established for leaders who were involved in uprisings and this was a major fear among the Nez Perce, thus while at the Clearwater they lost so much which was vital to their subsistence, they refused to capitulate and picking up the one hundred and fifty mile long Lolo Trail, they headed through the Bitterroot Mountains toward Montana. Traveling through the Bitterroot Valley, exhausted but still defiant, they camped on the banks of the Big Hole River. There at dawn on 9 August, they were attacked by the two hundred-odd force under Colonel John Gibbon who, under orders from Howard – now lagging sadly behind somewhere on the Lolo Trail – had ridden out from Fort Missoula to try to head off the fleeing Nez Perce.

The Battle of the Big Hole on 9 August resulted in a terrible massacre of some eighty Nez Perce, fifty of whom were women and children: 'Many women and children were killed before getting out of their beds,' a report said: 'In one lodge there were five children. One soldier went into it and killed every one of them.' Andrew Garcia later related what his wife – who as a seventeen-year-old girl was in the Nez Perce camp – told him of her terrible ordeal: 'The bullets came through [my father's] Gray Eagle's lodge like hail and rain, and hit one of Hoot Owl's women in the head, killing her dead, and another bullet hit one of Hoot Owl's sons in the breast, so that he fell down and lay there. With this rain of bullets coming through the tepee and the noise of the soldiers' guns, with the warriors and white men's yells, . . . the scream and shrieks of the squaws and children . . . Then

[we] all tried to get out of the tepee at once, . . . but the soldiers were there . . . Hoot Owl and his other woman and two of the small children were shot dead, and [my] father shot in the belly, . . . [my] sister . . . now fell dead with a bullet through her head . . .' *In-who-lise* was struck in the right shoulder and fell down near the creek bank: she recovered with a soldier standing over her and tried to get up by grabbing his leg – the surprised soldier pushed her back with the butt of his gun, hitting her in the mouth injuring her lips and teeth.

Although the initial phase of the attack was successful, the tide of battle unexpectedly turned. One scholar of the Nez Perce has dramatically described that moment: 'Soon, at one end of the camp could be heard the voice of White Bird, and at the other, that of Looking Glass. In tones that stood out above the sounds of the fight like the notes of a bugle call, these two chiefs rallied their warriors and turned what had started as a rout into a desperate fight.' After the Nez Perce managed to regain their camp, Gibbon later recorded: 'Few of us will soon forget the wail of mingled grief, rage, and horror which came from the camp four or five hundred yards from us when the Indians returned to it and recognized their slaughtered warriors, women, and children.'[15] More than forty women and children and some twenty-six warriors were dead and others would die later of their wounds – including *In-who-lise*'s father, Gray Eagle – to be buried on the Trail. But the Nez Perce would not give up, they pushed on for another thousand miles – Camas Meadow on 20 August where *Ollokot* and twenty-seven Nez Perce warriors stalled Howard's men by stampeding his horses and mules . . . 13 September, Canyon Creek, where Nez Perce marksmen stopped four hundred Seventh Cavalry troopers under Colonel Samuel Sturgis while the women and children escaped with the horses[16] . . . A respite at Cow Island, 23 September, where a raid on an Army cache, deposited because the Missouri was too low to get it to Fort Benton, provided much needed supplies[17] . . . and finally, 30 September, on to the Bearpaw Mountains, camping on Snake Creek, only forty miles from the Canadian border. With Howard – now dubbed by the Nez Perce as General Day After Tomorrow – and Sturgis judged to be some two or three days march away, the remnants of the Nez Perce clearly considered themselves safe. They were wrong.

On 18 September after receiving a report – which took five days to arrive – from General Howard and Colonel Sturgis that the Nez Perce had 'left them hopelessly in the rear', Colonel Nelson Miles, together with some three hundred and fifty men, rode from Fort Keogh on the Yellowstone traveling northwest towards the Bearpaw Mountains arriving within a few miles of Snake Creek on 29 September. Early on Sunday 30 September, their movements shielded from the Nez Perce by a blinding snowstorm, they attacked the village; the result was unexpected and a devastating repulse with some twenty per cent of Miles' force put out of action. As Captain Snyder later recorded: 'Our loss today Capt Hale & Lt Biddle & 23 enld [enlisted] men killed and 4 Officers & 40 men wounded. Indians still hold their position.'

But one major objective had been achieved in that attack – the majority of the Nez Perce horse-herd was captured.

The next day, 1 October, under a flag of truce, Joseph attempted negotiations with General Miles; by now many of his relatives, friends and council members were dead or lost, including both Looking Glass and Joseph's brother, *Ollokot*, who had been killed the previous day. This left only the defiant White Bird and Joseph as the key leaders. Joseph stayed in Miles' camp overnight, the Nez Perce held Lt Jerome as a hostage; the next day, each man returned to his own camp, a stalemate had been reached.

According to one contemporary observer – Lieutenant Charles Erskine Scott Wood, Howard's acting aide-de-camp – the Nez Perce had literally honeycombed a portion of the site of their camp, and other transverse gulches, with subterranean dwelling places and communicating tunnels.[18] In addition, they were using their dead horses as fortifications as well as a source of food: 'Here they held their own, refusing all offers of surrender, and saying in effect: If you want us, come and take us.'

With the loss of most of the horse-herd, however, the possibility of yet another flight towards the Canadian border and freedom was out of the question.[19] Winter was now setting in and the freezing weather with rain and snow caused suffering on both sides. Howard and a small escort arrived on the evening of Thursday 4 October and the next day the terms of surrender were agreed, a message being conveyed by two Treaty Nez Perce who had daughters in Joseph's camp. There was little room for maneuver, Howard pointing out that his whole command was only two or three days behind him. This force, together with that of Miles', would have thus combined to a total of at least six hundred fighting men – to be arrayed against no more than one hundred able Nez Perce warriors, who had the added responsibility of protecting the women and children.[20] Promises were made of good treatment and Joseph asked if his people would be allowed to return to Idaho. 'He was told that he would unless *higher authority* ordered otherwise.'[21] Joseph's final answer summed up the desperate experiences and now the plight of the remnant Nez Perce, its poignancy, eloquence and dignity being a remarkable tribute for all time to the people that he represented, for it was the end of an era:

'Tell General Howard I know his heart. What he told me before – I have it in my heart. I am tired of fighting. Our chiefs are killed. Looking-glass is dead. *Too-hul-hul-suit* is dead. The old men are all dead. It is the young men, now, who say 'yes' or 'no' [that is, vote in council]. He who led on the young men [Joseph's brother, *Ollicut*] is dead. It is cold, and we have no blankets. The little children are freezing to death. My people – some of them – have run away to the hills and have no blankets, no food. I want to have time to look for my children, and to see how many of them I can find; may be I shall find them among the dead. Hear me, my chiefs; my heart is sick and sad. From where the sun *now* stands, I will fight no more forever!'

The Nez Perce 'are among the most amiable men we have seen. Their character is placid and gentle, rarely moved to passion' . . . 'the Shoshonees are not only cheerful but even gay; . . .in their intercourse with strangers they are frank and communicative, in their dealings perfectly fair, . . . [nothing] has tempted them into a single act of dishonesty.'[22]

*

Although there is no abrupt natural barrier change as one moves south from the Plateau to the Great Basin region, the declining influence of the two great rivers, the Columbia and Fraser, upon which so much of Plateau culture depended, becomes increasingly apparent. Lying as it does between the Rocky Mountains to the east and the Sierra Nevadas to the west, with only limited and widely varying precipitation – particularly to the west and south – the Great Basin with no rivers draining to the sea, includes the southern parts of Oregon and Idaho, all of Nevada and Utah, and the western halves of Wyoming and Colorado. It is a region characterized by mountains which tower above the flatlands, but the terrain varies markedly. In the central and southeast areas of this region, where the Colorado River has carved immense canyons whose towering walls exhibit richly coloured sedimentations, saltbush and sagebrush deserts dominate, while to the north and east in areas which are drained by the Snake and Green rivers, there are wide sweeping grasslands of varying composition and, at higher elevations, scattered open forests of conifers and alpine-type herbland.

In this vast, diverse area covering some quarter of a million square miles, lived a predominantly Shoshonean-speaking people[23] whose territory once also extended to the Northern Plains and south almost into Mexico. In the northeast – at times overlapping with the Plateau Nez Perce and Flathead – were the Shoshoni and Bannock, to their west the Paviotso or Northern Paiute, while to the south of these tribes were the Western Shoshoni, Paiute and Ute. Unlike the Plateau people there was a great difference between the lifestyles of these various tribes, particularly after the acquisition of the horse by the more eastern Shoshoni and Ute, the latter using pack-horses, although apparently not yet riding them, as early as 1650.

Recent archaeological analysis of ancient camp sites in the more northern parts of the Great Basin – in the vicinity and to the west of the Great Salt Lake in Utah – gives some important insights into early Indian lifestyles, which are probably typical for much of the central and western Basin area. Here the environment varied from salt marshland to alpine herbland and the individual camp sites from large and well-ventilated caves to small and open camps. Of particular interest is that more than eighty per cent of these sites were located between an elevation of about 5,250–7,550ft (1,600–2,300m), only eleven per cent were located below 5,250ft; for obvious reasons, the indigenous population generally avoided open desert with its lack of protective cover, and its intense heat and high aridity. Above 7,550ft (2,300m) game was often unpredictable and limited, and winters severe. Clearly, the Basin people managed successfully to strike a balance between these environmental extremes.

Unlike the Plateau to the north where natural resources were generally predictable and abundant, leading to a subsistence economy which pivoted on intertribal trade, that of the Basin was largely characterized by a people whose lifestyle has led them to be described as 'superb resource generalists'. Roots and seeds were a major food resource for these people; however, the prong-horned antelope was to be found scattered throughout the region and these, together with the more abundant jack-rabbit, were an important food resource, the annual family gatherings in the autumn enabling these animals to be captured by use of communal drives. In the east, the Northern Shoshoni and Bannock had the luxury of buffalo which, prior to c.1840, were to be found west of the Continental Divide. After this date, bereft of this resource locally, it was necessary for these tribes to travel annually to the Plains region – a hazardous venture in territory of gun-armed tribes – or accept the harsher alternatives of the more central and western Great Basin environment, where brush wickiups replaced the comfortable hide tipi for shelter, and a largely foraging economy that of hunting.

These central and western Shoshonean groups – largely occupying what is now Utah and Nevada – were, particularly in the mid-nineteenth century when first described by whites, referred to as 'Digger Indians', a derogatory term, drawing attention to their extensive use of a pointed stick which was used to pry roots and wild vegetables from the ground. These people, variously designated as Gosiutes, Northern Paiute, Panamint, Kawaiisu, Chemehuevi (Southern Paiute) and Weber Utes[24] were loosely grouped according to the major type of food utilized, such as sunflower seed, root, pine nut, squirrel, sheep and even earth or dust eaters. A remarkably adaptable and practical people, they represented a culture sustained in the arid regions of the Great Basin for thousands of years, largely shut away from the outside world and little influenced by the Plateau or Plains people to the north and east. In order to survive, they utilized an immense range of plant and animal resources, some of the major root crops being camas, bitterroot, caraway, onion and Indian potato. Salad plants were miner's lettuce, sweet cicely, violets and certain brackens. Fruit, seed and nut crops which occurred in the foothill and riparian zones, were chokecherries, currants, oregon grapes, blue elderberries, amaranths, chenopods, sunflowers, acorns and pine nuts, the latter generally referred to as *piñon*, being among the most important for a large part of the region and a focus of great activity by groups in late summer and early autumn, particularly in the central Great Basin.

The complex subsistence technology, developed in order to render the *piñon* crop both edible and suitable for storage, commenced with the collecting of the green cones with the aid of harvesting poles, which were then transported in large conical-shaped woven baskets[25] for pit roasting which caused them to open; now piled up, the cones were beaten, or individual cones tapped, to release the seeds which were then lightly parched in a tray making the shells brittle – a combined flat metate and huller, together with winnowing, finally separated the seed and husk. The seeds were then given a final parching in trays: they could now be used in this raw state or ground into a meal from which a gruel was prepared. Alternatively, the meal was molded into cakes which were then dried in the sun and in this form they were stored in lined ground pits for winter use, a vital step for survival given the unpredictable nature of the Great Basin, since studies have shown that 'good nut years are irregular: no definite cycle exists'. The Great Basin people, however, held the belief that a bumper crop occurred every seven years and in this respect they were indeed correct, since it has been recently recognized that even in a single valley, local environmental factors were such that synchrony of production from one grove to another never occurred.

The *piñon* subsistence complex also involved ceremonialism – prayers before the season, dances at the harvesting and special prayers of thanksgiving over the first seeds. Ceremonials of this sort are still (even in the late twentieth century) practiced, remaining 'as one of the key features of Native identity'.

In addition to the communal antelope and rabbit hunts, there are descriptions of grasshopper drives. The first priest to visit the Western Shoshoni in the mid-nineteenth century, Pierre Jean De Smet, refers to an area which swarmed with grasshoppers and was often visited by the local Indians (probably the Gosiutes who lived some one hundred miles to the west of the Great Salt Lake). He relates a fascinating firsthand description: 'They begin by digging a hole, ten or twelve feet in diameter by four or five feet deep; then, armed with long branches . . . they surround a field of four or five acres, more or less, according to the number of persons who are engaged in it. They stand about twenty feet apart, and their whole work is to beat the ground so as to frighten up the grasshoppers and make them bound forward. They chase them toward the center by degrees – that is, into the hole prepared for their reception. Their number is so considerable that frequently three or four acres furnish grasshoppers sufficient to fill the reservoir or hole.'

The Gosiutes preserved some of these grasshoppers for future use by crushing them into a paste which they then dried; for more immediate needs they were either made into a soup or the largest selected for roasting at the campfire. In later years, white settlers would view the presence of such myriads of grasshoppers as bordering a plague, but to the indigenous population they were clearly seen as another natural subsistence resource, quite in keeping with the unstated but widely practiced ethos which characterized the Great Basin area – if it moves it can probably be eaten! There was, however, in all this an element of conservation and environmental manipulation; widespread, for example, was the avoidance of killing female animals during the gestation and rearing seasons and the Northern Paiute and Northern Shoshoni speared only male trout or salmon on the spawning beds or runs. Complex fish weirs were used to control migrating fish; the Washoe of the Pyramid Lake region cut the upper branches of browse plants to encourage deer herds to remain in the vicinity during the winter months and, at times, antelope were kept penned and killed as needed while some plant life was improved and conserved by selective harvesting and pruning.

The scarcity and unpredictable nature of food resources in the Great Basin region led to the development of a World View which put emphasis on respect for plants and animals so vital for survival in an often hostile environment. In the gathering of plants, for example, prayers were offered to the plant spirits and the Northern Paiute commonly buried a small stone or bead in the hole left vacant by a lifted root, while slain animals were often placed with their heads facing east or body parts, such as the eyes, glands and gall bladders, laid out or buried. Special terminology which may be used in an accompanying address reflected the respect shown for the animal and at the same time it was an appeal to the spirit powers that the food resource would be sustained.

The power to cure disease frequently derived from the animal spirits, while more than three hundred plant species, burned, crushed and powdered, were used medicinally. Great Basin mythology was also replete in references to plants and animals, the latter's adventures and misadventures explaining such things as the creating of the earth and its people, the formation of the seasons, food taboos and the establishment of social behavior. Of particular interest, as recently pointed out by one anthropologist who has studied Great Basin culture in depth, is the naming of constellations after animals and associating these in turn with 'tales of their adventures and misadventures in the sky'.

The Great Basin religion put strong emphasis on immortality. After death, the Western Shoshoni said the human spirit went to the land of the Coyote, who together with Wolf his brother, had created the world; not until Wolf had revived and washed the spirit was its place correctly established. So strong was the belief in immortality that on occasions sutteeism was practiced; one 1861 eyewitness account refers to the killing of a Shoshoni woman in Carson Valley, Nevada, so that her spirit could accompany that of her husband to the land of the Coyote. Death and regeneration was a recurring theme in Great Basin religion. The anthropologist, Robert

H. Lowie, for example, recorded the dream experiences of a Northern Shoshoni who reported that ' . . . my body dropped, cold and dead. I looked at it for some time; it made no movement at all . . . The Sun told me I would be restored to life . . . I don't know how I returned. Suddenly I was back alive . . . On another occasion, I went up to the clouds. The people I met there were nothing but skeletons . . .' Another student of the Shoshoni reports that the predominate way supernatural messages were received was through 'unsought dreams' and in this respect the experiences of the Paiute holy man, Tavibo, and later his son, Wovoka, fit the Great Basin shamanistic pattern, but they are modified by Christian teachings.

The great communal drives for the antelope and jack-rabbit were also invariably associated with religious ceremony. Certain men were credited with the power to lure the game, their dance being accompanied by ritual and song. Restrictions were associated with such rituals; for example, among the Paiute, women were excluded as were menstruating women among the Western Shoshoni, the belief being that the calling powers would thus be weakened.

The jack-rabbit was a source of both food and clothing to these interior Basin people and fine garments for winter use were fabricated from strips of the skins; but they were expensive, up to forty skins being required for a single robe. It was thus a garment owned only by the most prestigious, and the majority sufficed with a few skins wrapping the feet and legs as protection against the harsh terrain. In summer, the men wore only a breechcloth and the women a double-layered skirt woven from a fiber derived from sagebrush.

Except for the annual get-togethers, the majority of the year was spent by small family groups ranging tribal territory, and in addition to root and vegetable gathering, they snared and netted small animals, birds and fish. During spring and summer, housing consisted of temporary shelters or windbreaks made of reed mats and branches. A common form of pottery was a flat-bottomed cylindrical-shaped vessel with holes in the rim for suspension[26] and this, together with matting, stone metates, digging stick, twined and coiled basketry and open hooded baby carriers, made up the typical family household utensils. In winter, shelters were more substantial, some being subterranean with an opening through the mound-like roof which served as both door and smokehole; clusters of such habitations, when viewed at a distance, have been described as resembling a prairie-dog town.

Such was the lifestyle which epitomized Great Basin culture: unchanged for thousands of years, a constant search for food and reduction of essentials to the minimum – an environment where survival of the fittest had a very real meaning.

Not all of this region, however, was so harsh and unremitting. To the east and north, as has already been described, the terrain changed and while in common with the Northern Paiute (Paviotso), Paiute, Washoe and Western Shoshoni, there was still considerable dependence on a foraging existence, the lifestyle of the Northern and Eastern Shoshoni, together with that of the Ute (who between them ranged southern Idaho, western Wyoming, eastern Nevada and much of Colorado), differed to a marked degree. This was a shift from bare essentials and was now enhanced by intertribal trade which included Plains as well as Plateau tribes, access to buffalo country, a more complex social organization and ceremonial warfare and, from the early seventeenth century, contact with the Spanish Southwest which brought the greatest luxury of all – the horse.

The establishment of Spanish rule by Juan de Oñate in New Mexico in the period 1597-1610 led to the importation of several hundred horses to the region, within comparatively easy reach of Ute bands, particularly those in the vicinity of the San Juan river in present-day southern Utah and Colorado. These people soon acquired a knowledge of the horse and by the mid-seventeenth century used them, together with the dog, as pack animals. Ute tribal territory took in the majority of the Colorado Plateau which differed sharply from the interior Great Basin further west, having high average rainfall, giving well-watered valleys and grasslands; it was ideal pasture land for the horse and a resource rapidly exploited by the pedestrian Ute. The Pueblo revolt in 1680 and the establishment of missions by Father Eusebio Kino in central Arizona among the Pima and Papago led to a further source of horses – acquired by both theft and trade – and by 1730 the horse had reached the Northern Shoshoni, who, rapidly adapting to an equestrian lifestyle, expanded their territory deep into the buffalo country of the Northern Plains and at least as far as the Belly River[27] in southern Saskatchewan. One group split off from the Eastern Shoshoni probably to be nearer the southern source of horses. Here, armed also with guns which they obtained from the French, they claimed the country from the Platte to New Mexico driving the Apaches south and, turning on their former allies the Utes, by 1755 had crossed the Arkansas. With both gun and horse they, together with the Kiowas, dominated the southern Plains for more than a century; history knows them as the Comanches,[28] a Spanish rendering of a Ute word, *Cumanche*, 'enemies'. The Comanche never, however, completely severed their former Great Basin links and continued to visit back and forth, and some bands such as the Yamparika Comanche still had a taste for root vegetables, partially clinging to a Shoshoni foraging subsistence, but predominately now buffalo meat eaters, living in tipis – dashing and free.

By contrast, Shoshoni equestrian life on the Northern Plains was less successful. Archaeological evidence suggests that as pedestrian hunters they at least made extensive excursions into Plains country 'before the birth of Christ', and it was thus territory familiar to them; but the moving frontier of the horse from the west virtually coincided with that of the gun from the east and this, together with the devastating smallpox epidemic of 1781, gave the Shoshoni but transient equestrian residency.

In less than a generation, under pressure from the well-armed Piegan who spearheaded Blackfeet[29] dominance of the Canadian Plains, the Shoshoni progressively retreated to the safety of the Rocky Mountains. For all their outward appearance, however, these Eastern Shoshoni retained much of their Great Basin culture – mythology, religion, forager economy, social organization and a widely intelligible language – and although it has been rigorously debated,[30] there is much in one contemporary observation which attempted to distinguish between the Eastern and Western Shoshoneans: thus, when the former 'acquired a horse . . . he (became) a Shoshoni; if he found himself deprived of it, he was once again a Shoshoko (Walker or Digger)'.

Ironically, in just less than a century after the Shoshonean retreat from the Plains, it was to be reverberations from their peaceful Shoshoko kinsmen which led to the final collapse of the warlike spirit – epitomized by the Lakota – of the Historic Plains Indian.

On New Year's Day 1889, during an eclipse of the sun, Wovoka, a Paiute holy man, ill with a high fever, had a vision; later, he related that 'When the sun died' he was taken up to heaven and saw God and all the people who had died a long time ago. Wovoka claimed that he was told by God that he must go back to earth and preach goodness, industry and peace to the Indians. If they followed his instructions they would be reunited with their relatives and friends who had died. A new world would be created where there would be no more death, sickness or old age.

Much of Wovoka's experience reflected the Great Basin shamanistic pattern outlined earlier. It was, however, somewhat modified by Christian doctrine.

An important phase of the new faith was a dance for the Indians. It came to be known as the Spirit or Ghost Dance, spreading to the Great Plains where each tribe put their own interpretation on Wovoka's teachings. In the case of the warlike and independent Lakota, it precipitated the tragedy of Wounded Knee and the death of Sitting Bull, both in 1890 – and inscribed forever in the annals of American Indian history the name of a gentle, Great Basin Paiute, whose vision reflected an immense and widespread yearning for a past life which was now rapidly disintegrating under the impact of the European-American.

MYTHS AND LEGENDS

The Plateau and Basin region, constituted by two culture areas rather than one, is most difficult to summarize. Indeed, anthropologists long believed that neither the Plateau nor the Great Basin had any distinctive cultural features of their own but were amalgamations of the customs of those around them. (And it is true that Plains influence can be detected in both areas,[31] and in the Basin some peoples shared features with adjacent California cultures.)

Also, since traditionally the people of the region, especially those of the Basin, were hunter-gatherers, and anthropology as a social science discipline arose during a period much infected with hierarchical notions of race (with 'civilized' Caucasian city-dwellers at the top, downward through agricultural and pastoral peoples), these tribes were considered 'primitive' and uncomplicated. The Shoshonean-speaking peoples, who showed notable ingenuity in surviving for countless generations in the extremely hostile aridity of Nevada and Utah, were designated by incoming whites as 'Digger Indians', a derogatory term that referred to their practice of digging for roots and wild vegetables. In fact, of course, the cultures of these peoples were highly complex and, due to the marked geographical variation across the region and the sheer number of different tribes, extraordinarily diverse. The contrast between the canoe-owning Kutenai in the far North, into present-day British Columbia, and the Chemehuevi, a Southern Paiute group who used to roam the Mojave Desert and now reside mostly on the Colorado River Reservation, could hardly be greater.

Despite such differences, all Plateau and Basin peoples believed, above everything, in the sacredness of all life. They held these views in common with most other Indians, but perhaps with greater passion or, at least, intensity of expression, and in treaty negotiations with whites they frequently voiced reverence for the Earth. It is therefore not surprising that important inter-tribal religious movements, such as the Ghost Dance,[32] originated in the region, or that they had a richness of origin myths for their staple foods. In the Plateau these told of the genesis of the need for hunting and fishing, and included stories of the theft of salmon. In the Wishram version, Coyote freed the fish from two old women who kept them in a lake, appearing to them as a baby boy and secretly digging a channel between their lake and the Columbia River. The old women were then turned into swallows. In the Basin the equivalent myth was that of the theft of piñon nuts.

It is important to remember that all cultures are dynamic. Here it is possible to give only a sample of the variety of beliefs and practices of this range of peoples, and no inkling of the changes that have occurred over time.

ORIGIN MYTHS

The peoples of the Plateau and Basin, in common with those of other cultural areas, explained the origin of the world out of primeval waters. In most stories the Creator, while floating on the water, called on the animals to fetch mud from the bottom and the Muskrat, Chickadee, Toad, Turtle, Beaver, Duck and Mink were among those who were successful in various versions. The Creator then flattened and stretched the mud to create a new earth. In one Shoshoni and Bannock version the sky and people were also formed from this mud. As with much Indian mythology, the occasional existence of many versions of a myth among one tribe shows that each was not believed as a single truth, but as one reasonable explanation among several.

In a Northern Paiute version, the flood was decreed by the Creator to follow a great fire. After the world dried, the people began to make war and the Creator went away southwards with his wife. In one Northern Shoshoni version, the flood resulted from Coyote's desire to wash the world, and in another, Wolf and Coyote in the Upper World created land by throwing soil down into the world ocean below. For the Kutenai and the Flathead, Chief Eagle of the Mountains fired an arrow to stop the flood rising, thereby leaving behind what is now called Flathead Lake.

■ The Scattering of Tribes

The predominant Plateau myth concerning the dispersal of people depicted Coyote defeating a giant monster who had swallowed all the

225

animals. In Kalispel mythology the creature was actually a huge whippoor-will. In the Nez Perce story, Coyote deliberately allowed the monster to swallow him; while in the Flathead and Kalispel versions he was carrying a tamarack tree with which to block the monster's mouth, but was swallowed involuntarily. The tree took root where the monster threw it away, near what is today Arlee, Montana.

After being sucked in, Coyote severed the monster's heart and instructed the animals to run out through the creature's openings as it died. The last animal to escape varied in different versions, but included Woodtick, Ant and Muskrat. Coyote then created the Indian tribes by scattering the monster's body. In the Nez Perce story, Fox reminded Coyote that he had not made any people in the valley where they stood. Coyote created the Nez Perce from the blood on his hands sprinkled with water, explaining they would be few in number, but very strong.

In other myths humans originated from the offspring of Coyote and two women whose supposed vaginal teeth he broke. When Coyote was sent away with the children in a container, he opened it out of curiosity and the ancestors of all Indian tribes jumped out.

■ Fire

Usually fire was obtained by theft from a guarded montain-top or from the sky, very often masterminded by Coyote; occasionally Rabbit was the hero (Southern Paiute), or more frequently Beaver (Nez Perce, Cayuse, Sinkiuse). In all these versions, the central character tricked the guardians of fire (for example, Coyote let his headdress trail in it and then ran away when it caught light) and all the animals were vital in relaying it to safety, many of them being killed by their pursuers along the way. In alternative Nez Perce versions, fire was kept in the sky by the Creator, but a small boy managed to shoot it down with an arrow onto an abalone shell; or Coyote's son was kicking a tree stump around in such a way that it split and made fire.

ALL-POWERFUL SPIRITS

In the Basin area, and to a lesser extent in the Plateau, most powerful spirits were elements of nature and not separate deities. The most important deity, as such, of both sets of people was the Creator, who was usually known as Our Father. In the Basin this was often the sole supreme being, whereas in the Plateau other powerful spirits were sometimes mentioned.

Among the Cayuse, *Hon-a-woat* was the Great Spirit; among the Lillooet, he was Great Chief; among the Washoe, he was This Man Up Here.

Our Father was important not only to indigenous religions, but also to such inter-tribal movements as Peyotism, a religion centered upon the ritual consumption of the mind-altering peyote cactus.[33] Peyotism, which spread to Basin peoples in the last two decades of the nineteenth century and reached its peak in the 1940s, included among its paraphernalia a Father Peyote fetish. The Eastern Shoshoni and others had a Father Dance in which they gave thanks to *Tamapö* and prayed for his continued blessings; it was also a plea to keep children healthy against the smallpox.

Some debate exists about whether the Our Father concept was influenced by contact with Christianity, but it seems likely that it was of aboriginal origin. In any case, the fact that *all* of these myths have been translated, and altered from oral to written forms, means that precise meanings can never be ascribed.

■ Wolf

Wolf was sometimes an interchangeable substitute for the highest god. The Eastern Shoshoni called him *Pia Apö*, or Big Father, and called Coyote *Tei Apö*, or Little Father. Among the Northern Paiute the Creator was *Nümüna*, or Gray Wolf. Wolf was regarded as the creator of people and the solar system, and was also known as Father by some Northern Shoshoni and Bannock, the Ute, some Southern Paiute and some Western Shoshoni, who believed the power of a wolf gave cunning and strength.

■ Sun

'All the products of the Earth are children of the Sun, born of the Earth.'[34] This is how Kate McBeth, a missionary, explained the Nez Perce view of the world. They would ask for the blessings of Father Sun and Mother Earth, and before every meal the food vessel was silently turned, in imitation of the Sun's rotation.

Among the Kalispel, Flathead, and Coeur d'Alène, *Amotken* was the Big Spirit Above, or Highest Mystery; other names for him were Sky Chief, Power of the Upper World, and He Who Sits on Top of the Mountain. The creator of the Sun, Earth and other worlds, *Amotken's* symbol was the Sun, and myths told of *Amotken's* son, *Spokani*, being the Sun and the Moon. In the spring, when the first bitterroot and camas were dug, the chief would offer prayers to the Creator, to the Sun and to the Earth before the harvest was eaten. The daily morning prayers of the Kutenai were addressed first to the dawn, for the young of the family, and then to the Sun, for children outside the family.

■ Master of the Animals
Most of the peoples of the Plateau and Basin had a spirit which they identified as having power over the animals, especially those which they sought for food. The Ute and Southern Paiute believed that bears, mountain sheep, elk and deer were controlled by a snow-white being who lived high in the mountains.

■ Thunder
Thunder was a spiritual entity for many tribes, and frequently less powerful only than the Creator. Among the Wishram and Wasco, Thunder was a large bird which caused lightning when it spat. The Northern Paiute told of Thunder Badger, who lived in the sky, and when he felt that the land was too dry, put his head down to the ground and dug, sending clouds up in a flurry and thundering curses at the earth.

HEROES AND MONSTERS
Coyote tales were found over much of North America, and they dominated the legends of the Plateau and Basin. Coyote was a trickster figure, but he was also a creator, and often he was the younger brother of the more responsible Wolf. The stories in which Coyote figured tell of his exploits during the course of his journey eastward along the Columbia River from its mouth. The task he was given by the Creator was to prepare the Earth for the imminent event of the coming of people. Although he heroically rid the land of evil monsters, he also inadvertently made many errors which were both amusing and tragic, and he ordered the world in ways that were not always the most logical or just. Coyote tales are simultaneously comic and solemn. He died many times, but was always brought to life by Fox in order to continue his duties. Although Coyote's adventures could be traced to particular locations along the river, their chronology was irrelevant. Thus, several stories exist concerning Coyote and women, some of them his wife – but in one Flathead and Nez Perce version his wife was Mole, in a Northern Paiute one she was Weasel and in another she was the wife of Thunder and was stolen by Coyote. In the mythology of the Kalispel, Flathead, and Coeur d'Alène tribes, Coyote labored to overcome the

malevolent actions of *Anteep,* the wicked chief of the Lower World.

Coyote was at once a hero and a comic figure. He created the world as people knew it and was therefore revered as a creator and transformer, but he was also depicted as both a cunning trickster and a greedy fool. At times it was his avarice, stupidity, curiosity, or lack of foresight which were blamed for the hardships of humans, such as hunting, childbirth, winter, and death.

■ The Water Monsters

Water Babies featured in the legends of most of the peoples of the Plateau and Basin. Neither sex was specified in the original languages, but they were usually depicted by those who had seen them as female, and they were typically solitary. They were generally described as small people with long hair, and they were responsible for the creation of hot springs. For most tribes, they were evil creatures who stole unguarded babies at night and pulled people into rivers and lakes. In the Plateau, the Nez Perce saw them as benevolent, and a child was expected to offer discarded teeth to them; the Northern Paiute had the same custom, but the offering was made instead to Old Sage Woman. Among the Northern Paiute, the water babies were sometimes regarded as messengers to the Lower World.

Other water monsters were told of, such as the Washoe great bird of Lake Tahoe (present-day California), the giant water serpent in Pyramid Lake and the white water buffaloes in Bull Lake (both present-day Nevada). Some tales ascribe the primeval flood to the vengeance of a water baby (Washoe) or water ogre (Shoshoni).

■ Giants, Cannibals and Dwarf Spirits

Giants and cannibals occurred in many stories. Sometimes they had only one leg or eye, or their eyes glowed with supernatural brightness. The Washoe feared a one-eyed giant who lived in the Pine Nut Mountains near the Carson Valley, Nevada. Other tribes often had legends in which mountains were inhabited by giants: the Kalispel, Flathead, and Coeur d'Alène told of the *Natliskeliguten,* or Killers of Men; the Northern Paiute told of *Nümüzo'ho,* or Crusher of People. Stone manos, metates and mortars were all said to have been created by *Nümüzo'ho* and displaced to the edges of lakes which he jumped into when the world was burning. The Wishram told of a cannibal woman called *Atata'tiya* who was outwitted by a girl and boy.

In much of the Plateau and some of the Basin, a dwarf spirit was the master of the animals. He was described as a little green man who fired invisible arrows which caused sickness in both humans and animals. Although many tribes had a taboo against saying his name, in the Plateau he was not always seen as an evil spirit, but one who actually helped hunters and good shamans.

HOLY PLACES, SACRED SITES

The Wallowa River runs through the Wallowa Valley in northeastern Oregon. It is not only where Old Joseph was buried, it is also the spiritual heartland of the Nez Perce, and its loss to the United States in 1863 was one of the contributory causes of the Nez Perce War of 1877. Chief Joseph spent the last years of his life campaigning for its return to his people.

Lake Waha (meaning 'beautiful'), situated in the mountains above Lewiston, modern-day Idaho, was one of the places to which Nez Perce children were sent for their spirit quests.

Many of the flood stories mention a local high point which either remained above the water or was the first dry land to emerge, and for the Nez Perce tribe this point was Steptoe Butte in the southeastern part of present-day Washington state.

■ Ancient Wishram Shrines

For the Wishram, *Nixlu'idix,* today called Wishram, was where Coyote found the woman chief *Tsagigla'lal* and told her that the world would soon be changing and women would no longer be chiefs. She was changed into a rock to watch over the people at this place. A petroglyph face, with huge eyes, marks this spot on the Columbia River, upstream from The Dalles.

Not far away from Wishram, or *Nixlu'idix,* is a cave on the river bank called *Tca'mogi* whose entrance is under water at high tide. There is also a big rock in the water at *Waca'k'ukc,* nearly a mile below the village of *Cqô'anana.* Both of these sites were sacred to the Wishram and children were sent there on vision quests.

■ Plateau Sites

Near Elko, British Columbia, the images of three spirits are found on the cliff. To the Kutenai they represented *Kukluknam* (Weariness), *Kukisak* (One Leg) and *Kaklokalmiyit* (There Is No Night to Him); the latter being the highest and most difficult spirit to obtain. The Kutenai also believed that in the future the dead would return to the shores of Lake Pend Oreille, Idaho, where rocks above it are marked with sacred paintings.

Medicine Tree in Bitterroot Valley is now in Montana State Park south of Darby. Here, according to the Flathead, Coyote killed an evil mountain ram, leaving its horns imbedded in the tree. People left gifts at the site for the Creator.

Volcanic Mount Hood, Oregon, is where the Cayuse claim that fire was guarded by demons before Beaver and Woodpecker masterminded its theft. Woodpecker still continually taps trees with his beak to show people where fire may be found. The John Day River is said to have been created by the path of melted snow which Beaver left behind him as he ran.

To the Kalispel, *Kaniskee,* or Spirit Lake, Idaho, was a feared place at which the loveliest bride of each moon was believed to be in danger of being stolen by witches. The accompanying tale involved the tragic death of two sweethearts from enemy tribes drowned when forced to meet in secrecy. The Coeur d'Alêne had the same story about Hayden Lake, Idaho.

■ Sacred Places in the Basin

In Malheur Cave in southeastern Oregon, which was also called Water Cave by the Paiute, water babies, Indian-crushers and cannibals were said to have lived and been responsible for the piles of rocks found there. These evil creatures were banished by the Creator to the earth-hole near Sucker Lake (Pyramid Lake, Nevada). Malheur Cave is now a meeting place for various Indian fraternal orders.

For the Paiute, Mount Grant, near the southwest end of Walker Lake, Nevada, was the first mountain to emerge from the primeval deluge. This mountain was also the place to which Sage Hen retreated with fire to save it from the surrounding water by fanning her wings.

Dinwoody Canyon and Bull Lake, Wyoming, are holy places marked with pictographs. Like other sacred sites, especially caves, these places were believed by the Eastern Shoshoni to be former entrances to the subterranean pathway which led to the Lower World.

REVERED ANIMALS

The practice of sponsoring was widespread in the Plateau; the sponsor could be an individual, a family or a band of families, who took charge of inviting other families, building any necessary structures, preparing the food and hiring any necessary singers for a dance dedicated to an animal by the first man to dream of it during the year. Often the need for the dance, or the appropriate time for it, was revealed to the sponsor in his dreams.

■ The Bear Ceremony

The bear had an important role for the Kutenai and their springtime dance was held to secure immunity from attack by grizzly bears which were soon to emerge from hibernation.

The Ute also held a Bear Dance, in late winter, which was a line dance and thus unusual for the Basin, although the Bear Dance itself was fairly common in the eastern area of the Basin. Bear was believed to give sexual and hunting prowess.

■ Bluejay and the Winter Spirit Dance

Bluejay, an important figure for the Northwest Coast, was central to the religious life of the tribes of the southern part of the Plateau, such as the Sanpoil, Spokane, Kalispel, Coeur d'Alène and Colville. He had a uniquely important and complex role for the Flathead, including healing, and had a vital part in the Winter Spirit Dance, the major ceremony of all these tribes, which was held at the winter solstice.

The dance lasted several nights, for the purpose of spirit singing, power contests and shamanistic performance. It was sponsored by an individual shaman, or a non-shaman who possessed a guardian spirit, but participation was open to all who possessed a spirit, and attendance was open to the whole community. One of its features was the initiation of novices, and this involved the difficult task of extracting the youth's spirit song. The young man did not know the identity of the spirit who had given his song until it was interpreted for him by a shaman. Sweat lodge purification took place for three days before the ceremony, and it was accompanied by a feast or gift-giving, or both.

Gift-giving was one of the more variable features; for instance, it was not obligatory for the Sanpoil but was for the Wishram, although the Sanpoil tended to give bigger things while the Wishram only gave little tokens. The Flathead and Southern Okanagan did not give to people at all but to the spirits, the gifts being hidden in the forest. Generally, gifts were hung on a special center pole. Typically, sponsors gave more than others and shamans more than laity. Among the Sanpoil, strangers were the first to be given gifts and the best gifts went to those who danced the hardest. In all cases the act of giving bestowed power on the giver.

During the dance, anyone whose guardian spirit was the bluejay – and there might be several – was transformed utterly: his face was painted black, he discarded clothes, spoke unintelligibly or not at all, and perched in the rafters of the ceremonial lodge, all to the accompaniment of fiercely shaken deer-hoof rattles.

■ Horse

The horse was very important to the peoples of the Plateau and to those in the north and east of the Basin. Although it soon became more integrated into Plateau cultures, the horse was probably introduced through trade with the Basin's Shoshoni, the peoples in the Basin having had earlier access to horses through their proximity to the missions in California and the Southwest. The Basin habitat, however, was not conducive to supporting the animal because it needed the foods on which the peoples themselves depended, hence there was resistance to the horse found among the Western Shoshoni, Washoe and others. In some cases, however, dominant tribes deprived weaker ones of the horse, in the manner in which the Shoshoni prevented the Gosiute from obtaining any.

In the Basin, the horse was most integrated into the cultures of the Northern and Eastern Shoshoni, and the Bannock. It was not highly incorporated into their religious life, however, as it was for many peoples of the Plateau. There, the horse was of prime religious significance to the Nez Perce and Cayuse.

RITUALS AND CEREMONIES

The central element of the religions of the region was the acquisition of spirit power through visions. The Plateau followed the Plains pattern, in that it was vital for a man to have at least one spirit helping him through life. In the Basin it was not as crucial, and it was generally true to say that visions were not sought there with such fervor as in the Plateau, and sometimes not at all. In the south and southwest of the Basin, spirit power came from spontaneous dreams – more like the pattern of California and the Southwest. The Ute believed shamanistic power to come with life, and did not usually seek it, although some Ute shamans, unlike others in the Basin, did undertake vision quests. The Bannock and the Eastern and Northern Shoshoni were more like the tribes of the Plains.

In the Plateau, all boys and some girls were sent into the wilds to seek visions. Their return was celebrated with a feast, but they would not be

233

asked about their experience and did not tell of the vigil's outcome until adulthood, maybe 10 years later. Vision quests continued among some peoples for years, the distance and difficulty of the child's quest increasing with age, sometimes into adulthood, until the desired spirit appeared. Each man's spirit would inform him of individual food taboos. The Flathead revealed their spirit only at such a time as it was needed. A man's spirit song was learned from him at his death, when others would sing it for him.

■ Shamans

Throughout the region, there was a strong belief in the efficacy of dreams and the power of prophesy. The Spokane did not start fishing at the beginning of the season until a man, whose special role it was, dreamed a predictive dream that was then verified.[35] Individuals who had certain spirit power became shamans, responsible for using their powers for the rest of the tribe and capable of healing, harming or controlling the weather. In the Basin, there was a certain ambivalence toward the power of the shaman, and resistance to becoming one. This was partly because it was not known at first whether the person's power would take a beneficent or malevolent form. People rarely sought to achieve the power of a shaman unless they already were one; if power was offered and refused, a person became ill.

In return for his duties, the shaman was often made a rich and very powerful member of the tribe, although shamans of the Kalispel and Flathead sometimes refused payment for their services. A shaman would not begin practicing his power until he was around 50 years of age. The Basin was fairly unusual in that there were an equal number of men and women shamans; in the Plateau, women were capable of receiving power, but only practiced on their own sex.

■ Round Dance

Round dances were the most important, and sometimes the only, ceremony of the Basin peoples. They were held at times of thanksgiving, such as the piñon harvest, the first rabbit drive in the autumn or the first antelope hunt of the spring. The Northern Shoshoni and Bannock held one in the early spring to ensure the return of the salmon, and another at the arrival of the salmon. They also held dances in the autumn or any other time of adversity.

The dances took place in a clockwise direction around a pole or tree, each person joining hands with those on either side, stepping to the left and bending the right knee; most lasted about four nights. The dances were primarily for pleasure and an opportunity for courtship, but in some places they also had a rainmaking function. It was a variation which became the Ghost Dance.

■ Mourning Cry

Some of the Basin tribes held an annual mourning ceremony known as the Cry. It ended formal mourning by the relatives of those who had died during the year and it included the ritual washing of the mourners, who had abstained from cleansing themselves since the death as a sign of their grief.

For the Southern Paiute it was the most important ceremony of the year. It took place in the fall among the Owens Valley Paiute, and was generally practiced by those on the border with California cultures; the Washoe may also have performed it. Generated in the south of the Basin, it was sometimes mixed with the Bear Dance of the eastern groups referred to before.

ARTS AND CRAFTS

The Plateau and Great Basin culture areas cover a vast and diverse area of the interior of western North America. The traditional Native cultures of the Plateau evolved in the upper Columbia River Basin in the present states of Washington, Oregon, Idaho, Montana and adjacent sections of the province of British Columbia between the Rocky Mountains on the east and the Cascade Mountains on the west. Numerous tribes, including the Wasco/ Wishram, Cayuse, Umatilla, Yakima, Palouse, Spokane, Nez Perce, Coeur d'Alêne, Kutenai, Kalispel, and Flathead all lived in the Plateau area. This location enabled them to draw artistic inspirations and materials from the Native people of the buffalo plains east of the Rockies as well as from the maritime cultures west of the Cascades. They did this both through extensive trade networks with other Native people and with Euro-Americans, as well as by extensive travel themselves. Central and eastern Plateau people, particularly the Nez Perce and Flathead, regularly made the difficult and dangerous journey east across the Rockies to the buffalo plains of Montana to hunt and trade. The people practiced a lifestyle that revolved around hunting, fishing and gathering wild foodstuffs on a seasonal cycle, and they were consummate horse people after the mid-18th century. Trading and direct inter-tribal contacts with other culture areas resulted in Plateau arts and crafts that are a unique synthesis of equestrian and maritime cultures. Native Plateau artisans worked with a wide range of materials and media to produce objects of utility and beauty.

The Great Basin is an even larger area between the Sierra Nevada Mountains on the west, and the Rocky Mountains on the east. It is centered geographically in the present states of Nevada, Utah, Oregon and Idaho. The traditional cultures of the Great Basin are diverse, varying from the desert-dwelling hunter-gatherers in the south and west to the big-game hunting, horse-mounted nomads in the north and east. Great Basin ethnography is sometimes confusing because groups of people with the same tribal name developed widely varying cultures. The Northern Shoshonis, Northern Paiutes (Bannocks) and the Utes of the semi-arid and mountainous areas of eastern Idaho, western Wyoming, eastern Utah and eastern Colorado developed a nomadic horse culture that was very similar to those of the Great Plains. They lived principally by big-game hunting and often ventured on to the plains after buffalo. By contrast, the Washoe, Paiute, Western Shoshoni, Goshute, Southern (Utah) Ute and other desert dwellers of southern Oregon, western Idaho, Nevada and western Utah never became horse nomads. Theirs was a naturally harsh and difficult arid environment which was one of the last areas of North America to be dominated by the Euro-Americans. The desert dwellers had the ingenuity to live and prosper there for generations, and through most of the 19th century continued to practice their ancient pattern of seasonal hunting and gathering, relying upon a wide variety of animal and plant foods. Their possessions tended to be few and light and this in turn had a significant impact upon their arts and crafts.

In both the Plateau and the Basin traditional arts and crafts were produced primarily by women. Basketry, porcupine quillwork, parfleche decoration, hide-tanning and clothing were all produced almost exclusively by women. Objects of stone, wood and horn, realistic hide painting and weapons were produced primarily by men.

■ Beadwork

The Plateau people already valued and used glass beads acquired in trade even before the time of their first recorded contacts with Euro-Americans in the early-19th century. The earliest surviving pieces of Plateau beadwork date from the 1830s and are heavily embroidered with predominantly black-and-white beads .1–.2in (3–4 mm) in diameter. These beads, now called 'pony' beads, were manufactured largely in Venice and were acquired in trade from other tribes or from Euro-Americans.[36]

Plateau pony beadwork produced before 1850 was usually executed in only a few primary bead colors, including translucent sky blue, white, black and rose (a translucent red with an opaque white center), although a variety of other colors such as shades of green, shades of blue, pink, translucent cranberry and yellow were occasionally used. The beads were usually sewn onto a hide backing with animal sinew thread or sometimes with native fiber cordage. The geometric designs were simple and bold with strong color contrast. Womens' dress yokes, moccasins, shoulder and sleeve strips on men's shirts, men's legging strips, blanket or robe strips, cradle boards and a variety of horse gear were among the items commonly decorated with early pony beadwork. The visual impact of pony beadwork with its simple designs and strong color contrasts could be dramatic. About 1840 an observer noted that a 'young lady . . . in one of these dresses, upon a fiery horse well equipped with saddle & crouper, makes a fine appearance.'[37]

By the middle of the 19th century Plateau women began to use fewer of the larger pony beads and incorporated smaller, .04–.08in (1-2 mm) in diameter, glass 'seed' beads. Seed beads were also manufactured primarily in Venice, and were used in a much wider range of colors than pony beads.[38] The small size and color variety of seed beads, used alone or in conjunction with the larger beads, allowed Plateau women to create more delicate and complex designs than was possible with pony beads alone. By at least the mid-1840s they were creating beadwork employing curvilinear designs. The earliest Plateau curvilinear beadwork in the 1840–60 period usually employed outlined, symmetrical designs based upon a double-curve motif on a hide or dark fabric background.[39]

There were several bead-sewing techniques most commonly used. The lane stitch or 'lazy' stitch was used, for example, on the broad bands on women's dress yokes and on narrow bands outlining beaded panels. A stitch was taken in the foundation material, a sufficient number of beads was strung to cover the desired width and a second stitch was taken to secure the row. These stitches were continued side-by-side to complete the band of beadwork. Curvilinear beadwork was done in a two-thread applique or spot stitch. Beads were strung on one thread, and a second thread was stitched between every second or third bead to secure the beadwork to the foundation. A third major technique was the 'Crow' stitch in which bands of lane stitch were completed and then secured to the foundation by a second thread that looped around the lane stitch at right angles between every four to six beads.

Lane stitch produces slightly humped or ridged rows of beadwork while the spot stitch and Crow stitch both produce smooth, flat beadwork. Lane stitch and Crow stitch were both used to produce geometric designs, while the spot stitch could be used for either geometric or curvilinear designs.

By about 1860 curvilinear beadwork was very popular on the Plateau.

Bold, colorful symmetrical abstract floral designs were set against a light color background that was beaded in the same contours as the adjacent curved motifs. The texture of the background bead rows produced a subtle radiating or halo effect around the primary beaded designs. By the end of the century very realistic floral designs predominated, with outlined, filled-in designs set against a fully beaded background in horizontal, not contour, rows. On many late-19th and early-20th century beaded pieces, particularly women's flat handbags and men's vests, realistic often asymmetrical bead designs included not only floral but also animal figures.[40]

At the same time that Plateau women were perfecting the use of curvilinear, floral and animal designs, they were also perfecting what has come to be known as the Transmontaine style of beadwork. This term reflects the fact that this distinctive beadwork style was produced by women on both sides of the Rocky Mountains, principally by the Crow along the Yellowstone River and by many of the Plateau tribes in the upper Columbia River, the foremost probably being the Nez Perce.[41]

One of the hallmarks of this style in its fullest development is the optical ambiguity created between what is a design element and what is 'background'. This is much like the line drawing which may first appear to be a vase and may then appear as the profiles of two faces. Transmontaine beadwork designs are closely related to painted parfleche designs, discussed below. The same design elements, design layout and to a certain extent the same colors were used in both painting and beading, at least in the 1860-1900 period. A wide variety of objects was beaded in the Transmontaine style, including large bandoleer bags, otter bowcase and quiver sets, men's shirt and legging strips, cradle boards, horse equipment, gun cases, moccasins and men's flat mirror bags.[42]

The beadwork traditions of most Great Basin people have never been thoroughly studied and are poorly understood. The available evidence indicates that little or no porcupine quillwork was produced in the area and that beadwork was not a major art form among the western, desert-dwelling tribes. The women of the eastern Great Basin tribes – the Shoshoni, Bannock and Ute – were active beadworkers, although only among the Ute was beadwork as prominent as it was in the Plains and Plateau. There are some surviving pieces of Ute pony beadwork which probably date from before 1850, and it is probable that the Great Basin beadworkers went through the same transition from pony to seed beadwork as did the women of the Plains and Plateau.

Late-19th century photographs of Shoshoni and Bannock people often show little or no beadwork, even though the people are wearing a variety of other types of ornamentation. The beadwork that appears is often executed in simple, blocky designs on light backgrounds. Historic photographs also show Shoshoni and Bannock people using curvilinear beadwork (usually on an open hide or cloth background), and occasionally with beadwork in the classic Transmontaine style common to Crow and Plateau beadworkers. It may be that Shoshoni and Bannock women produced beadwork in all three of these styles in the last half of the 19th century.

Ute women were prolific beaders who had regular contact with people from the Great Basin, the Plains and the northern Rio Grande Pueblo areas. The best known Ute style was characterized by bold, simple geometric designs in only a few colors on a light, usually white background. This style, which lasted from about the 1820s until the 1890s, is very reminiscent of early geometric design pony beadwork of the Plains and Plateau. Ute women worked first in pony beads and then in seed beads by the 1860s, and used both lane-stitch and flat-stitch techniques. Shoulder and arm strips on men's shirts, men's legging strips, women's dress yokes, women's leggings and men's tobacco bags all were commonly decorated in this style.[43]

Ute women were also fond of the Transmontaine style of beadwork, and Ute people sometimes used pieces 'imported' from the Crow or Plateau. However, Ute women also practiced this style of beading in small but significant numbers of pieces. Ute beadwork in this style usually incorporates a Transmontaine-style panel bordered by distinctly Ute panels in multi-row geometric lane stitch. Men's tobacco bags were often decorated in this fashion. Ute women also produced curvilinear beadwork, usually in symmetrical abstract floral motifs with cloth or hide for the background. This technique is most often seen on distinctive Ute cradles with wicker hoods, but also on other items such as horse gear and moccasins.

■ Porcupine Quillwork

Decoration with porcupine quill embroidery was a uniquely Native American art form. While early descriptions of Plateau decorative arts mention the use of quillwork, it is clear that Plateau women largely, but not completely, abandoned quillwork by the mid-19th century. Little is known about early Plateau quillwork that would distinguish it from early quillwork from other areas.

One rare quillwork technique that persisted late into the 19th century in the Transmontaine (Plateau and Crow) art area was quill-wrapped horsehair. Quills were wrapped around parallel bundles of horsehair about one-eighth of an inch (3mm) in diameter and sewn between the bundles as they were attached to the hide backing. These quill-wrapped bundles were sewn side-by-side to form decorative strips. Simple blocky designs were produced by altering the colors of the quills, or by wrapping with colored yarn instead. These strips, always edged with a single lane of beadwork, were used for the decorative strips on men's shirts and leggings, for blanket or robe strips and occasionally for moccasins.[44]

Plateau women may also have used other techniques of porcupine quill decoration, particularly multiple-quill plaiting. This technique involved weaving multiple flattened quills together to form decorative bands an inch (2.5cm) or more wide. Usually two such bands of plaiting were worked parallel to each other and were bordered with a single lane of beadwork on each edge, just like quill-wrapped horsehair. Some extant pieces of early quillwork, primarily blanket or robe strips and mens' legging strips, consist of quill-wrapped horsehair rosettes separated by rectangles of multiple-quill plaiting.

■ Hide Painting

The women from most Plateau tribes produced quantities of storage containers made from parfleche, which was cleaned, dehaired but untanned hide, usually buffalo or elk.[45] The most common parfleche containers were envelopes folded from large rectangles of hide, but smaller flat envelopes and tubes with closed ends were also produced.[46] The outer surfaces of parfleche containers provided a smooth, hard surface which was decorated in two different ways. In the first, designs were painted onto the wet, skin-side surface of the hide while it was stretched flat.[47]

A second, possibly older technique of parfleche decoration on the Plateau employed the dark-brown epidermis on the hair side of buffalo hides. Designs were cut or scraped just through the surface of the wet hide, and when the hide dried the cut lines opened to show the lighter layer of the hide underneath. The design consisted entirely of light and dark areas of hide, and usually no paint was used. When buffalo hides were not available, the women used elk or other hides and darkened the epidermis with animal blood before incising the design. Traditionally the incised parfleche was used for food storage, while the painted parfleche was used for storing clothing and food supplies. Surviving incised parfleches are now extremely rare.[48]

The horse-mounted nomads of the Great Basin – the Shoshoni, Bannock and Ute – shared the painted parfleche container tradition with the people of the Plains and Plateau.[49] The Northern Shoshoni parfleches were made of buffalo, elk and later, of cattle hides, and were very similar to those of the Crow and Nez Perce. Shoshoni women usually painted a three-panel or nine-block design layout using straight lines, blue outlining of the design elements and a major central geometric design element. Ute parfleches were made of the same materials but the painting was different. Thin brown or black lines outlined the design elements; designs were composed of blocks within blocks; squares filled the rectangles; and overall designs were not enclosed by a border.[50]

■ Fiber Arts and Basketry

A variety of baskets and other fiber objects played an important part in the lives of the Plateau people.[51] The two Plateau basketry types most well known today are the 'cornhusk' bag and the 'Klickitat' basket, both of which were produced by the women of several tribes in the area. The cornhusk bag was a flat basket originally woven from native hemp cordage by a simple twining technique. Decoration was applied by false embroidery using dyed grass as well as cornhusks and later, wool yarn. The earliest bags were large rectangles up to 2×3ft (60cm×1m) with an opening at the top that closed with a drawstring, and were used primarily for food storage. Designs on these early bags were repeated simple geometric forms in soft natural browns and tans, typically arranged in horizontal bands across the bag. Decoration was almost always different on each side of the bag.

In the latter part of the 19th century, as traditional food gathering and storage became less important, cornhusk bags were produced in smaller sizes that were more square than rectangular and which were used primarily for women's decorative hand bags. Brighter dyed natural materials and wool yarn were used for the false embroidery, and commercial twine began to replace native hemp cordage. By the end of the 19th century, designs became more complicated, employing symmetrical geometric forms and realistic figures such as humans, animals and plants. The earlier practice of asymmetrical designs on the two sides was retained, as was the uniqueness of virtually every bag design.[52]

Women from many Plateau tribes wove tall round baskets using the wrapped twining technique. The designs were usually rather simple colored bands, although more elaborate designs in false embroidery were used. The Wasco/Wishram round baskets were often decorated with distinctive stylized human and animal figures very similar to those used in woven beadwork. Plateau women also produced coiled spruce-root basketry, usually decorated by imbrication. While these are usually referred to as 'Klickitat' baskets, they were produced by several other Plateau tribes including the Yakima and Nez Perce. The designs were usually executed in simple natural colors, but in elaborate geometric as well as stylized realistic designs. In the southern Plateau coiled baskets tended to be rounded oblongs with two small 'ears' or lifting loops on the top rim. In the northern Plateau the coiled baskets were similar, but tended to be more globular and rectangular in shape, sometimes with lids.

Basketry has been called one of the technological hallmarks of the Great Basin,[53] and the extremely arid conditions in much of the area have preserved samples of highly developed basketry from prehistoric periods. This aboriginal skill in basketry continued throughout the Basin in the Historic Period, although production and use tended to decline among the northern and eastern tribes that adopted the horse.[54]

Traditional Great Basin basketry was produced in several well-defined forms that reflected their utilitarian role in a hunter-gatherer society. Wild plant foods – especially seeds, berries and pinenuts – were important parts of the diet of the Great Basin people, and specialized basketry forms were developed to gather, process, store and consume them. The largest baskets were conical burden baskets, usually twined, which women carried on their backs using an attached tump-line or carrying strap across the shoulders or forehead. While gathering wild plant foods, women used a smaller conical or rounded gathering basket to do initial collecting, dumping it into the burden basket as it filled. Elongated, fan-shaped seed beaters were used to dislodge seeds and berries for gathering, while flattened trays were used for nut and seed gathering, sorting, winnowing, parching, cleaning and serving. Basket bowls were used for mush cooking (using hot rocks) and eating.

Tightly woven water bottles waterproofed with evergreen pitch were widely used throughout the area. Great Basin women also wove and wore basketry hats much like those worn on the Plateau, but usually covering more of the head. Finally, most Great Basin cradles were made of twined willow rods, usually with a curved rod sunscreen and were often covered with buckskin.

243

■ Other Arts and Crafts

The Native people of the Plateau and Great Basin traditionally produced for themselves everything needed to sustain their life and economy. They continued to do so on a significant scale even after widespread trade allowed the substitution of Euro-American materials for many native materials. Tanning large animal hides for clothing and other uses, for example, was a constant chore at which most Plateau and Basin women were experts even after the general availability of cloth in the mid- to late 19th century. Even where cloth replaced hides for clothing, the garments were still largely handmade by the women.

The Plateau and horse-mounted Great Basin people produced a wide variety of horse equipment such as saddles, stirrups, ropes, halters and cruppers. Canoes built on a bark-covered wooden frame were extensively used on the Plateau. These canoes were covered with cedar, birch, white pine and other barks, and had a unique long, pointed 'sturgeon nose' shape. Plateau people commonly made containers for temporary and more permanent use out of folded bark sewn with cedar root. Plateau people made extensive use of the horn of the bighorn sheep, carving and shaping it into bowls, ladles and hunting bows. Several varieties of local stone were carved into cooking vessels and pipe bowls used with wooden stems. The earliest pipe bowls were straight tubes, while the later ones were a curved elbow shape, sometimes embellished with lead inlay.

Most Great Basin people wove light, warm, twined rabbitskin blankets out of thin strips of hide with the hair left on, and also made robes of multiple small animal skins sewn together. Mountain sheep horns were used to make short, strong sinew-backed bows. Ladles and bowls were made from sheep and buffalo horns. Large vegetable-fiber hunting nets and rush, feather-covered duck decoys have been found preserved in several caves, and were still in use into the 20th century. Small stone, wood and clay figurines have also been found. The Great Basin is also an area rich in representational and geometric rock art produced since prehistoric times by painting and by inscribing into the rock surface.

REFERENCES

PLATEAU AND BASIN

1 This was some seventy-five miles southeast of a now particularly famous landmark – Mount St. Helen's, Washington.

2 Mylie Lawyer, an elderly Nez Perce, direct descendant of Chief Lawyer and residing at Lapwai, said that during the Nez Perce wars of 1877 the makeshift shelters were of a single lean-to type (M.L. to C.T., 1969).

3 In present-day northeast Oregon.

4 (i) Teit reports that the Crows obtained these from the Sioux to trade to the Plateau people.
(ii) Mylie Lawyer had many items of Sioux make which were family heirlooms.

5 Spalding estimated that the dresses would sell for '$50 or $60 a piece' in the 'southern states'.

6 These milk teeth were highly prized by the Crow who used them to decorate their women's dresses: because of their rarity, imitation ones were made of bone.

7 More recently made bags are generally false embroidered with corn husk (hence the modern term 'corn-husk bags'), colored with either soft-toned native or the brighter (trade) aniline dyes and perhaps the addition of colored yarn. The end-product is, however, still highly attractive and the process is a time-consuming exercise. At Lapwai in 1969, Ida Blackeagle's daughter, Josephine, showed me a partially completed corn-husk wallet. It measured about 7in. (18cm) wide and she said that it took her mother 'about one hour' to do a one-inch full-width section. Such bags were not infrequently exchanged with the Crows for the rawhide parfleche.

8 Wissler, 1910:17, and Teit, Boas ed.,1930:304-5.

9 These tribal domains appear to have been established over a period of several thousand years. Unlike the Plains Indians, the Plateau people have no legends of ever living anywhere else.

10 An ancient Indian route across the Continental Divide from Idaho into Montana.

11 Mylie Lawyer reiterated this fact. The missionary/school teacher, Kate McBeth, was said to have had an enormous bonfire (c.1875-6) to destroy 'leather materials'.

12 Lewis and Clark were very well received by the Nez Perce band led by Twisted Hair which formed the basis of particularly friendly relations between the Nez Perce and Americans in the years to come. Of interest is the fact that the explorers left American flags at various places and sent one to Twisted Hair as a token of friendship (Lewis and Clark, Coues ed., 1893, vol.II:610). Research specifically on Nez Perce material culture in 1969 suggested that there was some preference by this tribe for the use of both stripes and stars in their 'decorative' work on such items as bags, shirts, women's dresses and horse equipment. The Nez Perce were greatly influenced by the flag design and incorporated it in their artwork as a mark of esteem to the explorers. At Yakima, the trader and collector Roger Ernesti showed me an unusual Nez Perce shirt which emphasized the star symbol. It had fringes of blue trade cloth, the white selvedge edge of each fringe being cut into a V shape. When the shirt was shaken, it gave the appearance of dancing stars.

13 Thunder Traveling to Loftier (Mountain) Heights.

14 Brig. General Oliver O. Howard, who was assigned to the northwestern command in 1876, was sometimes referred to as the Christian General (it was maintained by his men that he hated fighting on Sundays). Howard, who had distinguished himself in both the Civil War and on a mission to Cochise in 1872, was a man of strong humanitarian principles and largely in sympathy with the Non-Treaty Nez Perce.

15 Two years later, Garcia and *In-who-lise* returned to the Big Hole Battlefield – a site now scattered with human remains. They finally located the disturbed grave of Gray Eagle and reburied his bones. More than fifty years later, in 1930, Garcia returned to the site and found the lance head which he and *In-who-lise* had agreed to leave intact as a tribute to its former owner (Garcia, Stein ed., 1799:270).

16 Nez Perce sharpshooting was both effective and selective; cornered at the Clearwater, the elderly *Otstotpoo* advised not to bother with the common soldier, suggesting instead 'Shoot the commander!' (McWhorter, 1940:70). It was a technique employed time and again with great effect throughout the four-month retreat.

17 This area is still remote and difficult for access. A visit by the writer to the Cow Island site in the summer of 1986 gave an opportunity to examine the deep rifle pits which are still to be found, dug during the Nez Perce–Seventh Infantry contingent skirmishes (under First Sergeant William Moelchert) on the night of 23 September 1877.

18 Some twenty years ago, it was still quite easy to locate remnants of these fortifications and also the rectangular hospital area where the troops were buried. One surprising fact was the obvious close proximity of troops and Indians, perhaps no more than 1,969ft (600m) separated them.

19 Howard's mandate from General Sherman was a *carte blanche* to follow the Nez Perce wherever they went but *not* into Canada.

20 One of these children was Josiah Red Wolf (*Heemeen Ilp Ilp*), a boy of five at the time of the retreat. In 1969, I visited this ninety-seven-year-old veteran at the Sommerville Rest Home near Lapwai, Idaho (courtesy of Marcus Ware of Lewiston). Red Wolf was then the sole survivor of the 1877 war; it was a sobering and privileged experience to be in the company of a man associated with an historic event which took place almost a century earlier.

21 The emphasis is mine since this was a significant statement. Although it is clear that the officers of the day – Howard and Miles – made this promise in good faith, the complexities of politics prevented its implementation. After several years' exile in Indian Territory, Kansas, Joseph, together with some one hundred and fifty Nez Perce, were settled on a Reservation in Washington – some 300 miles (483km) north of his beloved Wallowa Valley. He was granted but one visit to his father's grave in the summer of 1900 and died in Nespelem four years later – it is said, of a broken heart.

22 Lewis and Clark, Coues ed., 1893: 1017 and 556.

23 It should be noted that both the Shoshoni and Bannock languages belong to the Numic branch of the larger Uto-Aztecan linguistic stock.

24 Some of the designations were localized, for example, Brigham Young's term for the Weber Utes was Cumumbahs.

25 The Great Basin people excelled at basket-making; some were rendered waterproof and could be utilized for stone-boiling meat or vegetables.

26 A very widespread style which was used throughout the Great Basin and reached both the Plateau and Plains regions.

27 A Blackfeet term for the South Saskatchewan River just to the west of present-day Regina.

28 The Central Numic dialect spoken by the Northern Shoshoni is comprehensible to the Comanche.

29 The Blackfeet Confederacy consisted of the Siksika, Blood and Piegan.

30 See, for example, Hultkrantz (1968).

31 The Eastern and Northern Shoshoni, Ute, Bannock and Northern Paiute all practiced the Sun Dance ritual but the essential Plains element of self-mortification was rare.

32 The Ghost Dance was a revitalization movement in the 1870–90 period which was influenced by the slightly earlier Dreamer Religion originated by *Smohalla*, chief of the Sahaptin-speaking Wanapum people related to the Nez Perce. *Smohalla* preached that white people's ways were eroding indigenous ones and violating nature, that the people would be led by the dead returned and that whites would go to a different place as a result. The Ghost Dance began in 1869 among the Paiute of Walker Lake, Nevada, who traditionally held an annual Mourning Cry for the dead; it recurred in its largest manifestation during the late 1880s under the influence of the Paiute prophet *Wovoka* or *Kwohitsauq* (Big Rumbling Belly). It culminated in the Wounded Knee massacre of 18990.

33 In one sense, Peyotism is akin to the Ghost Dance in providing a Pan Native American identity-

strengthening movement in the face of the overwhelming white culture.

34 Clark, 1988:23

35 Among the Nez Perce those who in their youth had visions featuring the Sun, Moon, fish-hawks or pelicans would become a shaman; only these spirits gave the power to cure. Among the Thompson, water had this power; elsewhere it varied widely, including night, mist, blue sky, thunder, eagles, crows, wolves, bats and objects connected with the dead.

36 In 1805 Lewis and Clark recorded that the people along the Columbia River were very eager to trade for blue and white beads. However, surviving pieces of beadwork reliably dated to before 1850 are very rare today.

37 Rev. Spalding, quoted in Wright, 1991:36.

38 While the popularity of seed beads increased as the 19th century progressed, they never completely replaced the earlier pony beads. In the 1840-70 period Plateau women often incorporated both in the same piece of beadwork.

39 The development of curvilinear beadwork on the Plateau may have been influenced by the beadwork worn by Eastern Indians who participated in the fur trade in the West as early as the 1820s.

40 Elk, deer, horses and even fish were most common in the earlier part of the period.

41 The Transmontaine style is characterized by the use of a wide range of bead colors to produce large diamond, hourglass and triangular design motifs in a flat stitch. Major design elements were often outlined in a single line of white beads or by a lane of dark blue beads or both, set against a light field. The Transmontaine style also makes extensive use of red wool cloth as a background.

42 Another distinctive beadwork style was produced by a small group of Wasco/ Wishram women on the western edge of the Plateau. Usually found on small flat bags, this work appears to be 'loomed' but was woven with a loose warp technique. Bead colors were usually very simple, with designs in one color of dark beads on a white background. Distinctive animal, human and skeletal human 'X-ray' designs were popular.

43 Classic Ute blocky-design seed beadwork after about 1870 is virtually indistinguishable from Jicarilla beadwork of the same period.

44 Experts disagree whether quill-wrapped horsehair was produced exclusively by Plateau women, by Crow women or both.

45 The natural range of the buffalo extended into the southern Plateau and northern Great Basin areas. Buffalo were found there in small herds until they were killed off in the 1830s.

46 One of the earliest surviving pieces of Plateau art is a painted, flat, fringed parfleche envelope collected in 1841 and now in the Smithsonian.

47 Liquid paint was made from powdered natural or trade pigments mixed with a medium such as glue. It was usually applied to the hide with a porous bone 'brush' or stylus. Alternatively, powdered pigments were mixed with a glue medium and allowed to dry into small cakes, which were used to draw directly onto the damp hide.

48 Parfleches filled with food, clothing and other articles were commonly given away in large numbers during inter-tribal events on the Plateau, such as marriages. This factor, plus the fact that many Plateau tribes have shared reservations for over a 100 years sometimes make distinct tribal styles of parfleche design hard to differentiate.

49 Shoshoni men also practiced the Plains tradition of realistic paintings on soft hides, depicting their war exploits.

50 The Southern Paiutes may have made some parfleches, but parfleche use was not prevalent among non-horse people.

51 Mats were made from tule stems twined and sewn together side-by-side with hemp cordage. These mats were used primarily for longhouse coverings, as well as for a variety of other household purposes.

52 Cornhusk bags filled with roots were common gifts at both inter- and intra-tribal occasions on the Plateau so it is difficult to identify a particular cornhusk bag design with any particular tribe. The

same materials and weaving techniques were used to produce a wide variety of other objects such as horse gear (saddle drapes and martingales), belt pouches and occasionally clothing.

53 Fowler and Dawson, 1986:705

54 Those people, principally the northern and eastern Shoshoni, Bannock and Ute, adopted Plains-style parfleche and tanned-hide containers for transport and storage.

CALIFORNIA

From the sub-sea-level sands of Death Valley, the continent's lowest point, to the peaks of the Sierras, where Mount Whitney rises as the highest point of the lower forty-eight states, California is a land of contrasts. Its nearly 1,200 miles (1,932km) of coastline makes such a dramatic swing that Eureka, to the north, is the nation's most westward city outside of Alaska and Hawaii. Yet, San Diego, at the southern end of the state, is farther east than Reno, Nevada. This is the face of the present-day California. Although modern names have been applied to the towns, rivers and regions of what was formerly aboriginal territory, the following paragraphs clearly emphasize the richness and variety of the land and why it was held in such esteem by the Indians of California.

Over millions of years, subterranean plates, volcanoes, glaciers, wind and water have shaped the countryside that helped form such features as the Great Valley, perhaps California's main topographic element. The Siskiyou Mountains are now a northern barrier that serves as a border between the Golden State and Oregon in an area where timber abounds, particularly in the northwest. Lava flows provide a surreal landscape in the northeast. Farther south, the Tehachapis, the Sierra, the San Bernadinos and other ranges divide 'the so-called Valley of Southern California, a broad strip of broken country near the coast, from arid wastes of the Mojave and Colorado deserts in the hinterland'.[1]

The Northern rivers, the American, Feather, Indian, Pit, Sacramento, and Yuba, owe much to Mount Shasta's annual melting snows for replenishment of their southerly flow. The San Joaquin, which shares the name of the valley it waters, runs northward from its source in the mountains of present-day Fresno County, being joined by the Calaveras, Consumnes, Fresno, Kings, Mokelumne, Stanislaus and Toulomne rivers, as well as by

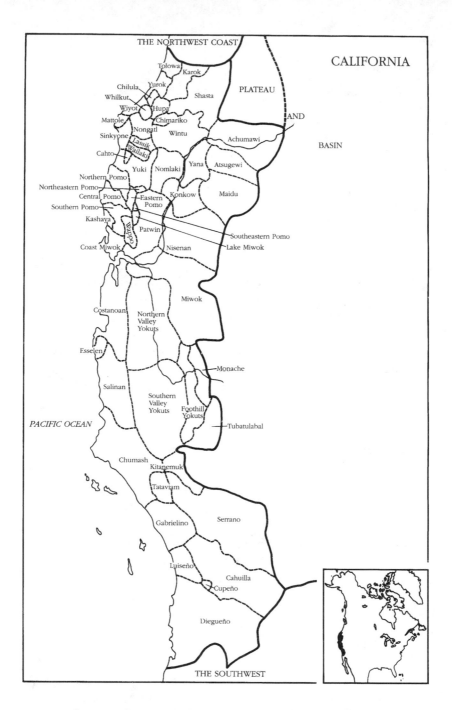

THE NORTHWEST COAST

CALIFORNIA

Tolowa
Karok
Chilula
Yurok
Whilkut
Shasta
PLATEAU
Wiyot
Hupa
AND
Mattole
Chimariko
Nongatl
Wintu
Sinkyone
Achumawi
Lassik
BASIN
Cahto
Wailaki
Yuki
Nomlaki
Yana
Atsugewi
Northern Pomo
Northeastern Pomo
Central Pomo
Eastern
Konkow
Maidu
Southern Pomo
Pomo
Kashaya
Wappo
Southeastern Pomo
Coast Miwok
Patwin
Nisenan
Lake Miwok

Miwok

Costanoan
Northern
Valley
Yokuts
Esselen
Monache
Salinan
Southern
Valley
Yokuts
Foothill
Yokuts
Tubatulabal
PACIFIC OCEAN
Chumash
Kitanemuk
Tataviam
Gabrielino
Serrano
Luiseño
Cahuilla
Cupeño
Diegueño

THE SOUTHWEST

ABOVE: *This map shows approximate territories of tribes and language groups in about 1800. After that, all tribes lost territory and some disappeared.*

250

a considerable number of other smaller streams.

The Klamath, Scott and Trinity drain the seaward slopes of the Coast Range with the Eel, Mad and Russian rivers carrying water north of San Francisco Bay, the marvelous 'harbor of harbors' so cherished by Spain. To this port's south run the Salinas, Santa Clara, Santa Maria and Santa Inez rivers. Proceeding still southward, the Los Angeles, San Diego, San Gabriel, San Luis Rey, Santa Ana, Santa Margarita, and Ventura rivers slow to a trickle much of the year or become dry beds until spring floods bring them back to life.

These various natural elements combine to form a half-dozen life zones: Arctic, Canadian, Hudsonian, Transition, Upper Sonoran and Lower Sonoran. The first areas exist, 'in the higher elevations of the Siskiyous, the Trinity Mountains, the Sierra, the San Bernardino and the San Jacinto ranges'. Next, the Santa Cruz Mountains, along with the upper portions of the Santa Lucias combine with 'all of the coast country north of San Francisco, the heavily watered northeastern counties and a long belt, between 2,500 and 5,000 feet [750–1,500m] high in the Sierra' to form the Transition zone. In turn, the foothills of the Sierras lie within the Upper Sonoran which also contain 'the lava plateaus of Modoc and Lassen Counties, the western slopes of the Sacramento Valley, the inner chains of the Coast Range and Valleys from Medocino County to San Francisco Bay, and all of the coastal region south of San Francisco' with the exception of those segments noted as part of the Transition zone. Finally, the Lower Sonoran consists of most of the Great Valley between Bakersfield and Red Bluff, 'all of the great arid desert regions southeast of the Sierra to the Nevada and Arizona lines, and several long narrow strips extending from the Salinas Valley south'.[2]

Each of the six environments support divergent flora and fauna. The high peaks of the Arctic-Alpine are treeless, but alpine buttercup, alpine shootingstar, blue and fragrant polemonium, Sierra primrose and steer-shead can be found at these lofty elevations. The Sierra rosy finch makes its regular home here. Hummingbirds and the gray and white Clark nut-crackers pass through as do the Sierra cony and white-tailed jack-rabbit. Bighorn sheep also once ranged in this land.

At slightly lower reaches, the Hudsonian zone shares lodgepole pine as a mainstay of ground cover with the Canadian zone. White bark, foxtail and silver pines grow higher up, mingling with mountain hemlock. Fowl and mammals, most importantly the alpine chipmunk, California pine

ABOVE: *A Karok, one of the most northerly tribes of California, in war costume of rod armor and helmet, with an animal skin quiver under his arm.*

grosbeak, mountain bluebird, Sierra cony, Sierra least weasel, Sierra marmot, white-crowned sparrow and wolverine, are found in the Hudsonian zone.

Besides lodgepole pine, the Canadian zone boasts yellow pine, Jeffrey pine, mountain pine and red fir. Cancerroot, ceanothus, several species of corallorrhiza, dwarf manzanita, herbaceous vegetation, Sierra puffball and snowplant carpet the floor. Blue-fronted jay, evening grosbeak, Sierra grouse, Sierra hermit thrush, Sierra junco, Townsend solitaire, water ouzel and western chipping sparrow soar above. Various types of chipmunk share the zone with mountain weasel, golden-mantle ground squirrel, Sierra chickaree, snowshoe rabbit and yellow-haired porcupine.

In the Transition zone, however, lie most of California's great forests, the most impressive of which, the redwoods, often intermingle with broad-leafed maple, California laurel, Douglas fir, madrona and tanbark oak. Other vegetation runs the gamut with several types of trees and many eatable plants being found to support the animal life and what was quite a complex food chain.

Black bear, bobcat, California ring-tailed cat, Columbian black-tailed deer, cougar, elk, fox, marten, mink weasel, mountain beaver, Pacific coon and packrat once roamed in numbers. Many reptiles and amphibians find the range a suitable habitat, as do an assortment of birds from chickadees to mountain quail. Moreover, coyote, muledeer, hawks and some sparrows inhabit the Canadian zone, as well as are distributed throughout some other zones.

The Upper Sonoran zone encompasses a great chaparral belt that was once the home of the California grizzly and the nearly extinct California condor. Blue and scrub oaks, California buckeyes, digger pines, ceanothus and species of manzanita and yucca grow, along with several other shrubs. Anna hummingbird, bell sparrow, bush tit, California and stellar jay, California thrasher, dusky poorwill, house finch, mourning dove, valley quail and yellow-billed magpie typify the feathered denizens of the zone. Land animals include antelope, brown-footed woodrat and brush rabbit, as well as the ring-tailed cat.

The Lower Sonoran zone offers its specialties, too. The Colorado Desert has bigelovia, a litany of cacti, California fan palm, echinocatus, mesquite, palo verde and screwbean. In the Mojave Desert grow other specimens with the Joshua tree (*Yucca arborenscens*) standing out among the plant life. Fremont cottonwoods and valley oaks flourish in still

ABOVE: *Cecilia Joaquin, a Central Pomo speaker from the Sanel community at Hopland, demonstrating the use of the seed beater to collect seeds in a close-twined burden basket.*

different parts of the Lower Sonoran.

The zone has a fair share of nocturnal animals as well. All sorts of rodents, kit fox, chipmunk, opossum, jack-rabbit and, in times past, tule elk, share the land with desert tortoise, lizards and snakes. In the air, blue grosbeak, cactus wren, hooded orioles, mocking-birds, phainopeplas and Texas nighthawks are plentiful, while the long-legged roadrunner remains earthbound, depending as it does on speed of foot rather than the ability to fly as the key to survival.

With both an array of potential food sources and also numerous climatic advantages, California proved an attractive magnet for early hunter-gatherer peoples. While no one knows for certain when *homo sapiens* first trod on California soil, some evidence points to the arrival of humans over 20,000 years before the present.[3] Despite the lack of definitive evidence as to origins, with the passage of the ages, it is certain that distinct groups emerged with highly developed territorial and cultural traits. Of these, 'about one half of California was held by Penutian-speaking people', a collection of 'small families which linguists believe were related because their languages employ some of the same grammatical tricks'.[4] In general terms, the diverse 'tribes' followed a lifestyle which took on a more uniform pattern than usually evidenced elsewhere among North American Indians. One of the chief similarities revolved around the consumption of acorn-based foodstuffs. Over the centuries, the first people to live in California unlocked the secret of turning the bitter, tannic acid laden product of the oak into 'a rich, nutritional food' which, as a soup, porridge or kind of bread, provided the mainstay of their diet.[5]

Two basic means allowed for this process to be accomplished. Either individuals pulverized and leached the nuts in sand or a basket or they could immerse or bury acorns in water or mud, and thereby not have to crush the nuts. Since the earth provided this source free for the taking, along with other plants and animals for sustenance, agriculture really did not evolve in early California.

Moreover the people varied their diets by hunting, gathering and fishing. They enjoyed resources which 'were bountiful in their variety rather than in their overwhelming abundance along special lines'. Thus, the fare contained venison, rabbit, gopher, lizard, snakes (including rattlers), ducks and small birds, depending on local availability. These might be obtained by snares, throw stones and such implements as could be fashioned from stone and other natural materials. Crayfish, molluscs, turtles and an assort-

RIGHT: *Four Diegueño men wearing traditional feather headdresses and black and white body paint; the two women in front wear calico skirts and plaid shawls.*

BELOW: *A Karok basketmaker, 1896. To her right is a space-twined pack basket used for packing acorns, fish and so on.*

ment of creatures from water and marsh might be procured in several ways with harpoons, nets, digging tools and poison-numbing among the means developed to take advantage of this type of bounty. Caterpillars, grasshoppers, maggots and snails added to the possibilities for protein.

Despite the broad-ranging approach to food, not everything was considered fit for meals, either because of religious beliefs or for practical reasons. For example, most northern groups would not eat dog, except the Yokuts, whose southern branch also 'relished the skunk, which when smoked to death in its hole was without offensive odor'. Conversely, these same connoisseurs of pole cats 'eschewed all reptiles, pronouncing them unclean'. Additionally, certain northern tribes rejected frogs, gopher snakes and water snakes. Usually, the majority of groups refrained from grizzly bear and coyote, mainly because these animals figured into many spiritual tenants. Sometimes brown bear was avoided, nor did 'birds of prey and carrion from the eagle down to the crow . . .' constitute common dishes.[6]

Thriving on the resources they found, California's Indian population rose, with estimates ranging from 133,500 to 350,000 inhabitants during the golden age prior to the arrival of the Spanish and others. Given even the higher figure, the average density represented only three people per square mile for those areas not considered an uninhabitable desert. These numbers would fall dramatically in the wake of later events so that 'the low point was reached between 1880 and 1900 with a recorded number of no more than 20,000 or perhaps 25,000 souls'.[7]

In their heyday, though, these culturally and linguistically rich groups came into contact with each other in several ways. A major means of association resulted through the trade which occurred on an inter- and intra-tribal basis. Routes and complex exchange systems grew up where a wide assortment of commodities-tools, food, clothing, pottery, slaves, sea shells and basketry-changed hands between and among players from as far away as western Canada and the mainland of Mexico.[8]

Baskets came to be particularly prized and remain an important part of continuity between the past and the present. Serviceable, aesthetically pleasing pieces, the baskets of California's first residents served utilitarian purposes and also demonstrated the extraordinary artistic talents of their makers. These objects likewise bespoke of the level of sophistication and diversity present among those people who made them. Examples from one of the best-known practitioners of the art, the Pomo, who lived in a rather compact unit in the Russian River valley, underscore some of the points about the importance of basketry to California's past.[9] The Pomo produced baskets which gained 'the name, among Americans, of being the finest in California; according to many, in the world'.[10] Relying upon ten or twelve types of material, with five being commonly employed, the baskets often took on an intricate nature.[11] Willow normally served as the warp for both twined and coiled examples. For the woof, *Carex* (sedge root), *Cercis* (redbud bark), *Scripus* (bulrush root), and digger pine root were used, with the first named medium being the most important basic ingredient. In turn, red patterns relied upon the redbud (used most commonly with twined leaves). Dyed bulrush gave black patterns, usually for coil work. Finally, digger pine fibers, in the main, were the woof for course twined baskets. Thus, by 'convention and habit . . . practically all the basketry of the Pomo' consisted of these five materials.[12]

The Pomo, unlike most other California basket-weavers who ordinarily worked in one or two techniques, employed upwards of a half-dozen approaches. Not only did the Pomo use twining, the norm for the most northern reaches and for the Achomawi, Atsugewi, Modoc, Northern Wintu and Shasta, but also they were adept at coiling, which generally dominated the remainder of the state. It seems the Pomo alternated between the two forms with equal ease and regularity.

When turning out coil pieces, the Pomo utilized both single-rod and triple-rod foundations. In the twined versions they perfected five weaves: plain, diagonal, lattice, three-strand twining and three-strand braiding, beside incorporating a wealth of inventive decoration and design elements.

While examples of Pomo basketry demonstrate some of the spectrum of this art so often associated with California's indigenous people, other indications of the cultural medley once represented by the state's Native American population might best be appreciated through a brief survey of several of the major groups who once carried out an array of lifestyles there. (For locations of the various groups mentioned in this survey see the accompanying map to this chapter on page 250.)

Starting to the far northwest, the Tolowa people speak an Athapascan dialect from whence their name came (a designation derived from the neighboring Yurok). Living in a dozen and a-half or so towns, this group sometimes feuded among themselves but a number of villages might unite if an expedition was mounted against the nearby Yurok or Karok. Such exchanges may have been infrequent, however, since the Tolowa seemed to be middlemen in the trade of dentalium shells from Vancouver Island, a highly regarded commodity which served as currency in the region. Evidently the Yurok looked upon the Tolowa as being quite wealthy.

Beside being purveyors of dentalium, the Tolowa became skilled boatsman, constructing canoes from redwood trees. They made ropes and cords from a species of the iris, practiced twined basket-making techniques and fabricated rattles from deer hooves for accompaniment to religious ceremonies, such as the girl's adolescence ceremony and dance. Other rituals included war dances, doctor-making dances, the Deerskin dance and the so-called 'salmon dance' which was somewhat akin to a new-year celebration which entailed 'the catching and eating of the first salmon of the season; after which fishing was open to all'.[13] Much later, in the last decades of the nineteenth century, they also added the Ghost Dance to their beliefs.

The Yurok and Karok flanked the Tolowa on the south and southeast respectively. The former group resided on the lower Klamath River and shared many traits in common with those around them as well as the inhabitants of the Pacific Northwest to Alaska. Living in more than fifty autonomous hamlets, the Yurok pursued fishing on the river and ocean along with hunting and gathering. They too made redwood canoes which could be bought for a pair of twelve-dentalium shell strings or ten large or sixty small woodpecker scalps. As can be deduced from this price structure, the Yurok had a sophisticated monetary system and, according to one source, they held wealth in high esteem. There was:

> 'Blood money, bride purchase, compensation to the year's mourners before a dance can be held . . . Every injury, each privilege or wrong or trespass, is calculated and compensated. Without exactly adjusted payment, cessation of a feud is impossible except through utter extirpation of one party, marriage is not marriage but a public disgrace for generations, the ceremony necessary to the preservation of the order of the world is not held. The consequence is that the Yurok concerns his life above all else with property. When he has leisure, he thinks of money; if in need, he calls upon it.'[14]

Other standard costs provide an idea about relative value in the society. An eagle skin brought only one small shell while the 'dowry' for a bride could be as high as ten strands of shells of various lengths. This indicated the status of marriage since a fishing spot fetched only one to three strings, a house five and a tract of land bearing acorns from one to five strings of shells. The last mentioned item, an acorn plot, indicates a concept of private land ownership. Indeed, in this individualistic culture, 'up to a mile or more from the river, all land of any value was privately owned; back of this, there were no claims, nor was there much hunting'.[15]

A number of other traits separated the Yurok from many other cultures. They observed inheritance practices, passing on much of their holdings to kinsmen. If an individual required ferrying across the water, the service customarily was granted free of charge. A shaman received considerable fees for services and those who entered the field might expect to make a considerable living. Class-consciousness existed to the degree that the Yurok made a definite distinction between rich and poor in their dealings.

Early Yurok clothing resembled that found throughout most of California. Young men regularly wore a folded deerskin wrapped around the waist while older men might go naked in warmer seasons. A buckskin fringed front piece and 'a broader apron or skirt . . . brought around to meet the front piece' served as the standard garb for women. Women also wore basket caps as the rule. When weather dictated additional covering, a cape or blanket of two sewn-together deer hides provided protection. Wealthier women sported extensive ornamentation. For footgear, a plain one-piece, front-seamed moccasin sufficed, being used most commonly by women when traveling, obtaining firewood or for dress occasions.[16]

This same physical description might be applied to the Karok, whose name comes from the adverb *karuk*, meaning 'upstream', their location in relationship to the Yurok. While outwardly very similar, the two groups differed in one major respect, their languages. The Yurok spoke an Algonquian tongue and the Karok belonged to the Hokan linguistic family.

Moreover, they could be distinguished from the culture found downstream in a number of other ways. For example, in the dance for adolescent girls, the men played a more prominent role than the males among the Yurok. Then, too, the Karok's 'world making' ceremonies were more defined. Finally, they prided themselves on the ability of their shaman, whom they claimed had no equal save among the Shasta and a few other groups located further over to the east.

This respect for the Shasta may have stemmed from a regular contact between the two peoples. Indeed, the nearby Shasta traded deerskins, obsidian and sugar-pine nuts to the Karok for baskets, canoes, dentalia, seaweed and tan-oak acorns.

Not all intercourse with outsiders stemmed from peaceful exchanges.

The Karok raided periodically, the women sometimes accompanying the men, possibly to cook and carry provisions. The warriors occasionally donned a hide helmet or headband, along with armor of rods or elk skin as they set out to do battle.

It seems that the Shasta did not turn their aggressions toward the northeast where the Modoc made their home, ranging across the present-day Oregon and California state lines. Had the Karok attempted this, they would have met stiff residence since 'the Modoc . . . probably possessed more tribal solidarity than the great majority of California Indians . . .'[17] Although the Modoc have been included in the map on page 100 as a Plateau tribe, it is suggested here that the boundary between the Plateau and California was not, in the mid-nineteenth century, as fixed as this. As with many hunter-gatherers, their boundaries were not restricted. For this reason, and because of the importance of the events surrounding the resistance of Captain Jack and the Modoc Indians, the Modoc and their final flourish are considered in greater depth in this chapter.

For all this, the Modoc suffered greatly at the hands of white encroachment. The steady increase in miners and settlers to their home eventually led to relocation on an Oregon reservation. In the mid-1860s, they began their short-lived, turbulent stay with the Klamath who spoke a Lutuami-based language, as did the Modoc. Friction increased between the two occupants of the reserve. The situation deteriorated even more with the killing of a Klamath shaman by one of the Modoc who would play a major part in subsequent events. Soon thereafter, some of the Modoc quit the confines of Oregon to head back to their former Lost River region in California under such leaders as John Schonchin and another key player variously known as Keintpoos, Kintpuash, or, more commonly, Captain Jack. It was Jack who had shot the Klamath healer thereby bringing about charges of murder. Under the circumstances, he saw the wisdom of returning to the traditional Modoc territory. This move, however, caused yet more conflict since 'just north of Tule Lake, white settlers had already moved in with their herds and had erected cabins'.[18]

Some four years passed with an uneasy attitude prevailing on both sides. Kintpuash, whose father had been killed by whites under Ben Wright in 1852, could not be persuaded to rejoin the Klamath. Failing to dislodge Jack and his compatriots, local citizens turned to the U.S. Army for assistance.

The local senior military officer in the area, Major John Green, attempted to speak to Captain Jack in September 1872 but to no avail. Within weeks, Green's superior, Brigadier General E. R. S. Canby decided to press the issue. He sent orders for the arrest of Captain Jack and two other important headmen, Black Jim and Scarface Charley. Miscalculating the effect of this directive, a detail set out in response to Canby's command. On the morning of 29 November 1872, Captain James Jackson, Lieutenant Frazier A. Boutelle and Assistant Surgeon Henry McElderry rode with some three dozen or so enlisted men from Company B of the First U.S. Cavalry into the Modoc camp. Jack, asleep in camp along with most of the other villagers, awoke to find armed men in their presence. The would-be captors' arrival led to bloodshed. An exchange of fire left casualties on both sides. The Modoc fled. A war had begun.

In the confusion, Jack escaped as did many others of the band. Splitting into at least two different parties, the Modoc ultimately regrouped in the region south of Tule Lake, which had been called by some 'hell with the fire burnt out'. Here, 'in this wild expanse of black lava, that nature had piled into a gigantic fortress', the Modoc made their stand. They knew every fissure, cavern and passageway. Patches of grass subsisted their cattle. Sagebrush and greasewood yielded fuel. Water came from Tule Lake.[19] The weeks which passed before the U.S. Government's forces arrived on the scene allowed the Modoc to prepare for the siege which ensued. Scarface Charley particularly would distinguish himself once the whites arrived to do battle.

Regulars and volunteers surrounded their foe. After their first attack on 17 January 1873, the troops found the Modoc to be tenacious freedom fighters. The opening engagement ended in a clear victory for the Lava Beds' defenders, despite the fact that they were outnumbered by an estimated seven to one. In defeat, the whites broke off to tend to their wounded and see to their dead.

Time passed. The Modoc held their own against cavalry, infantry, artillery and militiamen from Oregon and California. New tactics seemed in order. Kaitchkona (also known as Toby Riddle), Captain Jack's cousin, and a few other courageous individuals visited the entrenched Modoc in an effort to reach some sort of settlement. In addition, a peace commission dispatched from Washington, D.C., arrived with hopes of bringing an end to hostilities. For six weeks they tried to entice Jack and his people to the bargaining table but their efforts produced no results. By this time, Canby had come from his headquarters in Salem, Oregon, to assume field command. He sought to end the whole affair, moving his units closer to the Modoc stronghold. Captain Jack finally met with the general. This exchange allowed the Modoc to state their case. They wanted the troops to withdraw; they requested their own reservation on the Lost River; and they sought protection 'from charges of murdering a number of settlers'.[20]

Nothing came of this conference. Then, on 11 April 1873, Canby again went to speak with Captain Jack. On Good Friday, Canby and other fellow commissioners resumed negotiations. In the midst of the talks Captain Jack pulled out a concealed weapon and fired point blank into Canby's face. The wounded officer attempted to flee. Another Modoc fell on Canby and finished him with a knife. Two of Canby's party, the Reverend Eleazer Thomas and Oregon Superintendent of Indian Affairs, A. B. Meacham, went down in the killing frenzy. When the slaughter stopped, Canby and Thomas were dead and Meacham sustained wounds, not the least of which was the loss of his scalp.

Up to that point, the Modoc had gained considerable sympathy for their cause, with the military being painted as incompetent aggressors. Now, public opinion turned. Canby's successor redoubled efforts to dislodge the enemy. After considerable bloodshed and suffering, on 1 June 1873, the ill-fated Modoc survivors capitulated. A trial followed with Captain Jack and three others being given the death sentence. The remaining 153 Modoc received a different fate, relocation to Quapaw Indian Agency in present-day Oklahoma.

While this clash of cultures was well-known, the Modoc were not the only Native Americans to suffer at the hands of Europeans and Euro-Americans. From 1769, when the Spanish arrived to establish their first settlements in Alta California, a long, unfortunate decline in the Indian population and territory began. The first long-term contact started in the south with those groups living in the north being the last to face the consequences of meeting the new-comers.[21] They would not be exempt forever though, for as Captain E. D. Townsend, assistant adjutant general for the Pacific Division, confided in an 1852 entry to his diary:

'If the tale of these poor wretches inhabiting the more Northern parts [of California], could be impartially related, it would be a picture of cruelty, injustice and horror scarcely to be surpassed by that of the Peruvians in the time of Pizzaro. In their eager search for gold the whites have boldly penetrated and explored wilderness and mountains far beyond the reach of settlements. They have established themselves in many cases in large communities so that Tribes of Indians were left between them and the settlements. Aggression would naturally be of frequent occurrence on one side or the other, and the whites found it convenient to seize upon Indian lands, or to move them away for any cause, it was an easy matter to raise a quarrel in which the natives were made to appear in the wrong, and then an expedition would be fitted out against them which would butcher sometimes, thirty, fifty or a hundred men, women and children.'[22]

In these few terse sentences, Townsend summarized the fate of not only many California Indians but also that of numerous Native peoples all over North America.

Before this tide swept away the old ways, however, the diversity of California's native cultures flourished. The northern peoples went about their daily lives. There were the Achumawi, Atsugawi, Chimariko, Pomo (the main bands of which were the Northwestern, Central, Southern, Southeastern, and Eastern bands) and Yana, who all shared Hokan as the base for their dialects, as did the Shasta, whereas the Hupa, Cahto, Lassik, Mattole, Nongatl, Sinkyone, Wailaki and Whilkut had Athapascan as a base, just as was the case with the Tolowa. Another pair of people communicated in Yukian, the Yuki and Wappo, with a third practitioner of the language being a possible offshoot of the Wappo who were surrounded in a small enclave by the more numerous Eastern and Southeastern Pomo.

The remainder of the northern groups spoke in a root of Penutian. The Konkow, Lake Miwok, Maidu, Miwok, Nisenan, Nomlaki, Northern Valley and Southern Valley Yokuts, Patwin and Wintu fell into this category, as did the Coast Miwok and Costanoan.[23] These last two peoples might be looked at in more detail to obtain a better sense of several representative traits found among many of the other inhabitants of this part of the state, along with some of the unique characteristics which set them off from others who once lived in California.

To begin with, the Coast Miwok and Costanoan territories surrounded San Francisco Bay, the former being found on the north and the latter to the south and east, and occasionally in Marin and the islands of the Bay. Besides similarities in language, they shared many attributes which provide a means for comparison and contrast.

Starting with the Costanoan, for whom considerable enthnographic information exists, some eight major subdivisions have been noted. Each of the groups had 'separate languages, as different from one another as Spanish and English'.[24] Evidently, they had no common name for themselves but 'the label Costanoan had its roots in Spanish history [the term being taken from *Costanos* or coast people] and has long since established itself as a recognized language family'.[25] More recently, 'Ohlone' has been applied to the Costanoan. Descendants of this stock tend to prefer the newer reference.

In those earlier times, when the people had no commonly accepted single name, outer appearances nonetheless reflected their ties. Men and boys commonly went about naked while a grass or tule apron, which covered the front and back below the waist, constituted the clothing for women. When the weather dictated, capes or cloaks fashioned from deer, rabbit, water-fowl feathers or sea-mammal skins provided protection.[26] Even mud occasionally served 'as insulation from the cold – a custom not recorded among their neighbors, the Coast Miwoks'.[27]

The Costanoans regularly walked barefooted and without head coverings, except on ceremonial occasions. Painting and tattoos provided decoration and clan affiliation, the former practice being applied in patterns which made it appear as if the people wore striped tights. Pierced ears could be adorned with beads, feathers, flowers or grass while pierced nasal septums might hold a small bone, although the custom was not universal and seemed only to apply to men. Both sexes often added necklaces of beads, feathers, and shells (abalone and olivella) to their wardrobe.

For shelter, poles bent into a conical shape and covered in brush or tule sufficed. Occasionally, split redwood or redwood bark constituted the basic construction material. The building of balsas was another use for tule. Double-blade paddles propelled these light craft swiftly through the water.

These people produced other items as well. Baskets, frequently embellished with beads, feathers and mother-of-pearl were typical. Wild onion or soaproot brushes, mollusc shell spoons, wooden stirring paddles and various stone implements made many daily chores possible. Both self-bows and sinew-backed versions launched arrows with bone and stone tips.[28]

As with other material necessities, the Costanoan depended on nearby natural resources for food. The ubiquitous acorn, available from several types of live oak, served as the basis for flour to make mush and a form of bread. Other seeds could be roasted and ground into meal too, with chia, digger pine and holly-leaf cherry offering other forms of subsistence, and which, according to the early missionary, Francisco Palou, could be made into 'a sort of dumpling, ball-shaped and the size of an orange, which was very rich and savory, like toasted almonds'.[29] Strawberries, manzanita berries, and Christmas or the Toyon berry offered other treats in season. Roots, such as *amhole* (soaproot or Chlorogalum), along with wild carrots, onions and the herb chuchupate could be obtained too.

Besides vegetable matter, dog, grizzly bear, mole, mountain lion, mouse, rabbit, raccoon, skunk and squirrel could be taken on land, with snares serving to catch the smaller creatures. The Costanoan likewise hunted deer and did so with deer-head masks as disguises. They took seals too, although the means of hunting these mammals is uncertain. Quail, hawks, doves, ducks and geese could be had with nets and traps, depending on the type of the bird. Nets also brought in sturgeon and salmon. Shellfish, most notably abalone, clams and mussels, offered fine fare when gathered from December through April when they were safe to consume. Shark, swordfish and other salt-water species may have been killed with spears or taken by hook and line. Occasionally, when a whale washed ashore, the Costanoans held a feast for this specially prized meat.

The Costanoan considered certain food taboo for new mothers who abstained from meat, fish, salt and cold water for a number of days after giving birth. As young adolescents, females observed these same dietary restrictions. They held some sort of puberty rite as well, while males celebrated their entry into manhood by induction into what was known as a *datura* society.

Once of age, a young man might take a wife. He and his relatives provided a gift to the bride's family. Then, the couple started their life together with no further formalities. When an infant arrived, the mother nursed for about twenty weeks, during which time the wife and husband refrained from sexual relations. Padre Palou commented on the fact that he saw many of the couples living 'in the most perfect union and peacefulness, loving their children dearly, as the children their parents'.[30] In the event two people chose to end a relationship, they simply separated. Evidently, the children remained with the wife. For a woman who lost a husband, mourning involved such practices as smearing the face with asphalt or black ashes and the cutting of hair. When laying the dead to rest, the women used a stone pestle to beat their breast and heads. The deceased's belongings would be destroyed or buried, while the body might be cremated but sometimes was buried, especially where a person was poor.

In the main, the Costanoan made contact with Europeans in the late eighteenth century and soon thereafter provided the population required for the establishment of several Spanish missions founded to the south of the Golden Gate.[31] Conversely, the Coast Miwok (sometimes spelled Mewuk and Meewoc) traced their association with foreign visitors to a much earlier time. Beginning in 1579, some of these inhabitants of land north of San Francisco set eyes upon Sir Francis Drake's crew who had come ashore to repair their ship. They made presents of arrow quivers, feathers, skins and tobacco to the English and crowned Drake, treating him as a god. Descriptions by the British depicted them as tall, striking and strong people who regularly traveled at the run. They parted their long hair in the middle or tied it behind in a bunch, the men wearing beards but scant clothing, other than a deerskin loincloth on occasion.

The double apron favored by the Costanoan persisted among Coast Miwok women. Blankets or capes of rabbit fur and other small mammals resembled those of their southern and eastern neighbors. They likewise carried on the practices of tattooing, body painting and adornment with feathers fashioned into belts and wristlets. Clamshell disk beads sometimes added to the display but usually this material served as currency.

For food, the Coast Miwok shared a similar diet as described for the Costanoan. They added greens such as miners lettuce, monkey flower and watercress, and also may have consumed California buttercup and lupine either as greens or in seed form. Other seeds provided the basis for *pinole* or a mush. Wild cucumber or manroot and edible roots, most notably the bulbs of the wild hyacinth, found their way into the diet.

Coast Miwok diet taboos paralleled those of the Costanoan, but a new mother could have fresh fish and kelp. Sexual abstinence did not seem to last as long as with the Costanoan, however, although fathers halted their fishing and hunting activities for a brief period and did not smoke during the same time of abstinence.

These people tended to be monogamous and expected fidelity. When a spouse died, her or his goods were to be buried with them, unless many children remained behind. In that case, shell money would be kept back for the use of the family. This was important since all transactions required payment.

While a monetary system existed, the concept of land ownership was foreign to the Coast Miwok. Nevertheless, they regarded food-producing sources and fishing rights as private property to be respected. So strong was this concept that the Coast Miwok marked their belongings with some sort of personal ownership symbol. They were far from totally materialistic people, however, and supported intricate religious beliefs centered around dance, doctoring, fasting, offerings and prayer. Often they accompanied many of these ceremonies with music provided by bone whistles, bull-roarers, drums, flutes and rattles. When not engaged in religious practices or providing food, shelter or clothing, these first residents of present-day Marin County played games of skill and chance primarily aimed at adults, while children played with dolls and other toys.[32]

Leisure time for some other groups who dwelled along the coast cannot be ascertained with the same certainty. This particularly proved the case with the Esselen people who lived just south of the Costanoan. In fact, little information remains on these people who 'were one of the least populous groups in California, exceedingly restricted in territory, the first to become entirely extinct, and in consequence are now as good as unknown . . .'[33] Soon after contact with the Spanish, the people became part of the mission complex at San Carlos, eventually disappearing as a distinct, independent stock. What little data still remains about them stems from some knowledge about their language which was a generalized Hokan derivative.

So, too, did the Esselen's nearby Hokan-speaking relatives, the Salinan, suffer reductions in numbers after the arrival of the Spanish. In the period before contact with outside forces, the Salinan subsisted on birds, fish, reptiles and most mammals in their area 'with the single exception of the skunk, and possibly dog and coyote . . .'[34] A half dozen types of acorn, grasses, clover, berries, sunflower, pine nuts, chia, buckeye and wild oats could be had in their territory.

They took much from the Yokuts way of life in their beliefs, customs and industries since they frequently traded and carried on other forms of interaction with these people. While friendly with the Yokuts the Salinan usually considered the Costanoans as enemies. Finally, despite a common boundary to their south with the Chumash, the Salinan remained rather aloof from this fellow Hokan language group.

The Chumash far outnumbered the Salinan and ranged over a larger area. They, nonetheless, succumbed to the mission process which at first they willingly accepted. In fact, the Chumash may well have been the first natives of California to be 'discovered' by explorers flying the ensign of Spain. In 1542-3 Juan Rodríquez Cabrillo met the Chumash, who inhabited not only the coast but also some offshore islands making them 'more nearly maritime in their habits than any other California groups'.[35] Their canoes, *tomol* or *tomolo*, consisted of planks bound together with cords and then caulked in asphalt found readily around the beaches. Light and swift, the crafts could be powered by as few as two or three paddlers but at times larger versions could be propelled by eight men and carry an additional half-dozen passengers.

Besides these plank canoes, the Chumash made another important product, spear-throwers. They could be used on land or at sea, in the latter instance making it possible to harpoon seals and otters. Although these products set the Chumash apart to a certain extent from other California Indians, they did draw upon other native groups for inspiration, such as the Yokuts and the Shoshoneans of the southern part of the state for their basket-making.

The Shoshoneans formed a corridor on the eastern side of the state which ran almost the entire lower two-thirds of California. Another spur jutted out to the west below today's Santa Barbara and above San Diego. The various sub-elements consisted of such peoples as the Kitanemuk, Tubatulabal, Serrano, Gabrielino, Luiseño, Cahuilla, and Cupeño. Another common name assigned to eastern bands located toward Arizona and Nevada (and considered in the Plateau and Basin chapter) was Pah-Ute or Paiute. On the eve of the Civil War, some of these people crossed swords with the U.S. Army under Major James Henry Carleton. For some time, friction continued but eventually subsided as these Mojave Desert-based residents dwindled in numbers.[36]

The 'cousins' of the Paiute, living in what is now the greater Los Angeles area and extending down toward San Diego, the Gabrielino and Luiseño, did not clash openly with military forces of Spain, Mexico or the United States, 'although they had oft-times distinguished themselves in warfare with other tribes'.[37] One of the weapons the Gabrielino devised when they did engage in combat was the war club, 'which ranged from a heavy stick to a shorter form with a definitely marked cylindrical end . . .'[38] Additionally, they developed a curved stick, the *makana*, which they wielded with great effect against rabbits and birds as a sort of boomerang.

The Gabrielino were also innovative in that they had moveable stone mortars for the grinding of various plant foods rather than being restricted to bedrock mortar holes that they could not transport to enable relocation to another site when a village moved. The Luiseño also used moveable mortars alongside bedrock ones. The so-called portable variety actually constituted a large boulder of up to 200lb (90kg) which was hollowed out to form a recessed surface.

A small variation of the Luiseño mortar likewise found its way into the Diegueño society, one of the southernmost inhabitants of California, who, along with the Kamia, Yuma, Halchidhoma, and Mohave peoples living in an arc which ran to the east and then up the Colorado River, spoke Hokan dialects. Pottery-makers as well as basket-makers, the Diegueño employed other familiar aspects of California native culture, most significantly tule balsas which they paddled with double-bladed oars. They made pipes of stone and pottery too, the former types presumably being set aside for religious purposes.[39] They were known for their gourd and turtle-shell rattles that provided accompaniment to ceremonies but the Diegueño had no drums, nor did any other southern California group for that matter.

The Diegueño numbered among the first of California's Indians to be incorporated into the Spanish missions. While the impact of the experience took its toll, the intent was far more benign and humane that the conditions which resulted when the United States gained control of the region after concluding the Treaty of Guadalupe Hidalgo (1848), in the wake of the War with Mexico. The discovery of gold soon followed this transfer of title. With that event, pressure grew to remove the Native Americans to reservations, which:

'from their inception in 1853 until relatively recent times, is hardly a matter of pride. During the 1850s and 1860s, many of the officials placed in charge of Indian affairs were unfit for their posts. Too often, whenever a reservation contained valuable land, selfish whites were permitted to swoop in, and the Indians were driven on to rocky or sandy terrain.'[40]

In time, reactions against this deplorable situation led to reform movements. One champion of the California Indians' cause, Helen Hunt Jackson, wrote two books which attempted to bring the plight of these people to a sympathetic audience. Her publications, *A Century of Dishonor* and *Ramona*, released in 1881 and 1884, respectively, caused ripples to be felt in Washington, as did writings of Mary Hunter Austin and Marah Ellis Ryan, both of whom followed Helen Hunt Jackson's literary tradition most effectively.[41]

Redress came slowly. The Dawes Act of 1887 attempted to reverse the disintegration which escalated in the nineteenth century. Reduced to less than six dozen reservations, with as few as seventy people living on some in the 1960s, the battle to regain lost land went to the courts and Congress. One Federal commission awarded $29 million in exchange for the estimated 64 million acres which once sustained the state's Amerind population. Unfortunately, 'These legal victories came rather late . . . and have scarcely proved useful in salvaging tribal integrity.'[42] In fact, a mass exodus to cities, particularly Los Angeles and its environs, has depleted reservations even more than before such financial settlements took place.[43] In the urban environment, California Indians tend to be outnumbered by all others, including Indians from groups which originated outside of the state. Thus, the first people to tread this territory struggle to maintain an identity in the face of overwhelming odds. They confront the possible fate of Ishi, 'the last of the wild Indians' of California, whose passing ended an era.[44] Such a loss would affect not only the people of the many cultures who once thrived in California but also diminish us all.[45]

MYTHS AND LEGENDS

Prior to the coming of Europeans in the late18th century, California was one of the most densely inhabited areas of North America with an estimated population of 310,000. Archaeological evidence indicates human presence in the California area for perhaps as long as 26,000 years, and native traditions affirm long residence there. Once one of the most linguistically diverse areas in the world, the region was home to more than 60 'tribes'. Some of the languages spoken by people of a single tribe living as close to each other as neighboring river drainages were as different from each other as Spanish is from French.

The California culture area can be divided into three main regions: northwest, central and southern. Tribes in the northwest, such as the Yurok, Karok and Hupa, developed a rich culture which relied on plentiful salmon, plant foods (such as acorns), and animals, including deer. They were skilled woodworkers, producing dugout canoes, split-plank houses, sinew-backed bows and other objects. The women were fine basket weavers. Accumulated property (such as dentalium-shell beads) indicated wealth and was a means of acquiring status.

In central California people relied on the acorn as their principal food source, along with hundreds of other plant foods. Animals, including deer and elk, were also important to their diet. Homes consisted of the large earth-covered, semi-subterranean structures of the Nisenan, Valley Maidu, and Patwin in the Sacramento Valley; the brush-covered dwellings of foothill Maidu people; and the dome-shaped, tule-covered homes of some Pomo and Yokuts peoples. Women of all these groups developed coiled, and in some cases twined, basketry to a high art. Baskets became an obvious symbol of wealth, and village leaders insured their prestige at feasts by serving many large baskets filled with acorn mush. To honor the deceased, some baskets were made to be burned during mourning ceremonies.

In southern California, people adapted to a more arid environment. They lived in dome-shaped homes covered with brush, tule or grass, and women wove fine, coiled baskets. The Chumash, on the coast, had an elaborate ceremonial system and developed fine artistry in creating small steatite sculptures, beads and pendants, multi-colored rock art and ocean-going redwood plank canoes.

Native people still live in California today, some practicing native beliefs. World Renewal ceremonies held in northwestern California use new regalia, created by talented contemporary artists, along with the old. In central California, the Pomo, Patwin and Miwok people hold dances in newly created ceremonial roundhouses built at ancient village sites. And in southern California, too, groups such as the Chumash have worked diligently to revive ceremonies and ensure that their ways will not disappear.

ORIGIN MYTHS

Henry Azbill, an elder of the Valley Maidu people from Chico, recalled a story as it was told to him by his grandmother around 1900. Older tribal members commonly recounted the origin myths of their people, as in this way tribal history was passed on. Azbill retold *Sokeneh's* creation story in the 1960s:

'In the beginning *Helin Maideh* created the water and the misty air. He was alone with Turtle on a raft, and since he was lonely, he brought *Kodoyampeh* (World Maker) into being to keep him company. *Kodoyampeh* descended from the sky on a white feather rope and he had a face so bright that one could not look at it. After days of drifting on the water, *Helin Maideh* told *Kodoyampeh* that there should be earth and people, and he charged him with the task of creating them.

Kodoyampeh told Turtle to dive into the water and see what he could find. Three times Turtle dove, and found nothing. On the fourth day he made his dive and pushed deeper through changing colors of water until he felt something. He was gone a long time, and when he returned to the raft he seemed more dead than alive. When he was pulled on to the raft, small bits of mud were found under the nails of his hands and feet.

Kodoyampeh gathered the mud, rolled it into a ball, flattened it,

273

and placed it upon the water. The power of *Kodoyampeh*'s thought caused the little mud patty to swell and grow until it was the size of the world, with all the rivers, lakes and mountains. In order to keep the world from floating away, *Kodoyampeh* anchored it at the north, south, east and west with four ropes.

Helin Maideh had already created the animals, fishes, birds, and trees, and he said that there should be people. He told *Kodoyampeh* to cut two straight willow sticks, strip them of their bark and hold one in each of his armpits when he slept. If he felt anything unusual in the night, he was to act as if nothing was happening and under no circumstances was he to move. In the early morning he felt movements and fingers tickling him all over his body. He looked up and saw a man and a woman. he rose from his bed and sent them to bathe and then to come and eat. He gave them fire, instructed them how to live, and gave them songs to sing as prayers. There was no sickness and no death. Life was good.'[46]

Most origin myths of the California people begin with a world covered in water. In a Sierra Miwok version, Coyote helps to create the world. Usually known as a trickster, Coyote behaves himself in completing that task; later he became a comic, ribald character prone to making mistakes. According to the Maidu, it was Coyote who suggested that death would be good. When the first person to die was coyote's son, Coyote regretted his idea, but it had become a fact of life which he could not change.

■ Diegueño Creation

The Diegueño people of the south tell another version of creation. The world was covered with salt water like a big sea, and two brothers lived under it. They had to keep their eyes closed or the salt would blind them. The older brother went up to look around, but he could see nothing but water. As the younger brother followed him up, he opened his eyes and was blinded by the salt. Since he saw nothing, he went back down. The older brother decided to make little red ants, and from them he created land. Then he made birds, but they couldn't see their way to roost. he tried to make a light from yellow, red and black clays, but it was pale when he placed it in the sky. It became the Moon. He took more clay and made another object for the sky. It became the Sun. He then made a man and a woman from the clay.

ALL-POWERFUL SPIRITS

Warnings about the *hohape* were told to Southern Miwok children who wanted to swim in certain pools of the Merced River. The *hohape,* river mermaids who caused people to drown, are but one example of the many spirits who controlled the world of California Indian people. The spirits included all-powerful spiritual entities that controlled much of everyday life, and lesser spirits who inhabited and gave life to every valley and creek. California Indian people constantly gave thanks to these spirits through prayer, dances and offerings of food and beads.

■ The *Chingichngish* Religion

In southern California, the Luiseño-Juaneño, Gabrielino, and Tipai-Ipai practiced the *Chingichngish* religion, derived from the teachings of the shaman-like hero, *Chingichngish.* He dictated a moral code to live by and enforced it with spirits called 'the avengers'. These spirits, which included Rattlesnake, Spider, Tarantula, Bear and Raven, watched to see that people obeyed the laws, and they punished wrongdoers.

■ Nature Spirits

Among the Central Sierra Miwok, a class of nature spirits were called *suchuma.* They had the power to cause rain, violent windstorms or whirl-winds, and to roll rocks down on people. Miwok children were warned to stay away from spirits such as the *Nenakatu,* a two-foot tall, human-like creature with hair that hung to her heels.

The Miwok used the wormwood plant for protection from these spirits, to keep away ghosts and to purify and protect those who had come into contact with evil forces. Some Southern Miwok people wore pieces of root from a rare plant strung around their necks to protect themselves from supernatural sickness, in much the same way as Central Miwok people tied folded wormwood leaves onto string necklaces.

Some spirits lived in specific geographic locations that were often shunned by native people. In Yosemite Valley, Miwok and Paiute people avoided the areas around waterfalls because of the *nunu,* the spirits who lived there and destroyed people who ventured too close. In Central and Northern Miwok country, limestone caverns were thought to be the home of *Chihalenchi,* an evil, hair-covered man who ate people who ventured into the caverns, and of *Ettati,* a man-eating, snake-like creature.

Other spirits in certain locations were sought out by shamans, and it was from them that some shamans obtained their power. Maidu men, for instance, obtained shamanic power by swimming in certain places. After diving into a deep pool and losing consciousness, they were often able to communicate with animal spirits. When they came to, they would have been deposited on the shore by the spirits. Later, they would be able to speak with the spirits, dream of them and, after a long quest, obtain power and help in curing from them. These spirits were sometimes those of animals, but others could be those of deceased people. One Maidu shaman had as a helper spirit, a gold miner who had died 50 years before.

■ The Power of *Moki*

One of the most powerful spirits in central California was known as *Moki* by the Valley Maidu and neighboring Patwin, and *Kuksuyu* by the Nisenan and the Sierra and Plains Miwok. The Sierra Miwok believed that the Kuksuyu was a wild spirit who lived in the forest and could sometimes be seen on a moonlight night. A brave dancer who saw the spirit on such a night sang for him instead of running away. Subsequently, the dancer copied the spirit's costume and began impersonating it in dance ceremonies.

The Valley Maidu likewise believed the *Moki* was extremely powerful and potentially dangerous; some believed the spirit was actually the Creator itself. In dance ceremonies, the *Moki* was impersonated by a man dressed in an all-enveloping feather cloak. The dancer had to observe numerous taboos and strict rituals, for a mistake could be very dangerous for the dancer and other people present at the ceremony. So great was this spirit's power that just the act of touching the feather cloak would cause common people to become violently ill.

HERO CREATURES AND MONSTERS

Chief Richard Fuller warned family and friends of the monstrous snake which lived in limestone caverns in the Sierra Nevada mountains. Elsewhere, too, wonderful heroes and terrible monsters fill the mythological world of the California people. Characteristic of many such creatures is the Southern Miwok story of *Uwulin*:

'Long ago, the bird and animal people lived in Yosemite Valley, and they lived well. But then came *Uwulin*, a great giant from the north who began to eat people.

He was as big as a pine tree and his hands were so huge that he could hold 10 men at a time in each hand. He traveled with a great sack on his back into which he placed the people he had captured. His sack was so big that it could hold the entire population of a village. He caught so many people that he cut them into small pieces and made jerky of their meat. He hung the jerky to dry on a huge granite rock near the Merced River, and to this day that rock is stained with the blood from his making jerky.

The bird and animal people tried to kill the giant in every way, but they failed. Arrows and spears could not penetrate *Uwulin*. Finally, the bird and animal people asked Fly to help them. They told him to bite the giant all over his body to discover where he could be hurt. Fly searched for the giant and finally found him asleep. He bit *Uwulin* everywhere. The giant did not flinch until Fly bit him on his heel, which caused the giant to kick his massive leg.

Fly returned and told the bird and animal people of his discovery. The bird and animal people decided to make a number of long, sharp, deer-bone awls, like those used in making baskets. They arranged the awls with the points up along the giant's trail, so that he could not avoid them.

When *Uwulin* came down the trail, he stepped on many of the awls. finally, one pierced his heel where his heart was. He died immediately. The bird and animal people decided that they must destroy his body with fire, and they all carried wood and covered *Uwulin* with it. They watched his burning closely to ensure that no part of his body escaped the flames, for they feared that such a part could grow and let *Uwulin* come back to life.'[47]

■ The Story of *Oankoitupeh*

There are other stories of heroes and monsters, as in the Valley Maidu and Konkow stories of *Oankoitupeh* who was miraculously born to the daughter of the chief in dire times. He grew to manhood in four days and set about making the world right. He drained the Sacramento Valley by breaking away mountains where the Carquinez Straits are today, and he destroyed both a fierce, human-sized black eagle and a She-Devil that had been killing people. Finally, he traveled to the north and challenged the doctor *Haikutwotupeh* to gamble with him for the return of the people *Haikutwotupeh* had won from *Oankoitupeh*'s grandfather. *Oankoitupeh* won his grandfather's people back and restored every tribe to its original place.

■ The Cannibal Head

Throughout central and northern California, stories are told of a cannibal head that rolls about the countryside eating people. Most of these stories start when a man who has accidentally injured himself first wipes away the blood, and then starts to lick his wound. The blood tastes so good that he devours his entire body, leaving only his head and shoulders. From then on, he bounces and rolls around, searching for and eating people. In one Maidu version, the monster dies when he bounces into a river and drowns.

■ The *Antap* Religion

Among the Chumash, the Sun was the basis for the *Antap* religion. *Antap* consisted of a society whose members were primarily tribal leaders of wealth and power. By means of a lunar calendar, members of the *Antap* Society set the schedule for important ceremonies to renew the world, especially at harvest time and the winter solstice. Society members presided at ceremonies where the Sun was worshipped as a threatening male deity, and Wind, Rain and Fire as female deities. The powerful deities were somehow connected to the power and wealth of the *Antap's* members.

The stories of monsters are not limited to legendary times. Even today, some Miwok parents warn their children against going into the limestone caverns of the Sierra Nevada, for the huge, snake-like *Ettati* is said to be living there still.

HOLY PLACES, SACRED SITES

The Wukchumni elder *Tawp'naw* told this story in the 1930s as part of his people's creation story, and it illustrates how, to the Indian people of California, all of the land has a history making it sacred or holy. Many places were sacred because of their association with legendary events, while other sites were known to be home to spirits.

■ Rock Art

Chumash shamans produced elaborate rock art using native pigments at hundreds of locations. Many of these sites are in nearly inaccessible locations, while others are more easily accessible on large rock formations. One such site, where a mass of sandstone rocks rise 30-40ft (9-12m), was a solstice shrine called the House of the Sun. Among motifs found painted in the rock shelters there is a large red disc with lines radiating from it, perhaps denoting the sun. There is also a black circular design with a red outline which may represent an eclipse. Other images at this site, as well as at other Chumash sites, suggest mythological figures such as Bear, Condor and animals of every sort. Another rock art site near the Chumash village of *Tashlipunau* consists of work spread through four caves. The images include large circular motifs with concentric rings, zoomorphic and anthropomorphic figures, dots, bifurcates, and zig-zag forms. They are painted in black, white, yellow, cream, red, orange, green and blue-green. The orange and green paints have only been found at this site and it is possible that they were obtained by the Chumash when they sacked mission supplies in 1824. The use of paint in the pictographs may have been an effort to gain supernatural control over the Chumash's Mexican enemies.

■ Sacred Mountains

Prominent mountains were often considered to be sacred places. Mount Diablo, just east of San Francisco Bay, was held sacred by many tribes in central California. To the east of Mount Diablo, the Central Sierra Miwok claimed that the *Lileusi* Dance came from the mountain, while other Sierra and Plains Miwok people place legendary events such as the creation and acquisition of fire as taking place on the mountain. The Patwin people to the north declared that some medicine people went to Mount Diablo to pray for prosperity and health. The Nisenan (Southern Maidu) believed that the dead crossed the mountains on their way to the land of the dead and that spirits watched from Mount Diablo's peak for wrongdoing. Among some of the Ohlone (Costanoan) people, a site just below the summit was an area where people gathered for a major autumn ceremony.

Mount Shasta figured prominently in the lives of Wintu people, who believed that the mountain possessed benevolent spiritual power and was the 'main one' in the Wintu inventory of sacred mountains. When burying the dead, bodies were generally oriented toward the north and funeral orations directed souls on their journeys to Mount Shasta and the heavens. It was believed that the soul of a dead person went first to Mount Shasta before rising to the Milky Way, from where it would travel south and then east to the hereafter.

Wintu people today still consider Mount Shasta to be the sacred place it has always been to their people. Some Sierra Miwok and Ohlone people remember the importance of Mount Diablo in their spiritual background, and many Chumash people revere the sacred rock paintings of their ancestors.

With the rapid growth and development that has taken place in California in the last century, many sacred sites have been lost to native people. Most of the Gabrielino village of Puvungna, birthplace of the Chingichngish, founder of the Gabrielino religion, is covered by the campus of the California State University at Long Beach. The small portion of the site which had not yet been built upon was recently slated for development, but the site was saved after a vigil by Gabrielino people. Today, Indian people are fighting to protect their sacred sites.

REVERED ANIMALS

Like most California Indian people, the Maidu considered certain animals to be sacred. They believed that the eagle was a messenger to the Creator, and that by using eagle feathers in ceremonial dance regalia, or on a special flag to be hung in front of the ceremonial roundhouse on sacred occasions, one's prayers would be conveyed to the Creator. Among the Diegueño, the Eagle Ceremony was held to honor deceased leaders. A captured eagle was ceremonially killed by apparent supernatural means (which usually involved strangulation). Its wing and tail feathers were plucked for ceremonial regalia and its body carefully buried in a ceremony similar to that which would be held for a person. Skeletons of eagles, vultures and condors have been found in archaeological sites buried like humans; some of these burials date back 2,000 years.

■ The Supernatural Condor

The condor was the largest bird in California with a wingspan of nearly 10ft (3m), so it is not surprising that California Indian people considered it to be a special animal, capable of providing communication with the supernatural world. The condor appeared frequently in the legendary history of many California Indian people. Legends among widely scattered peoples (including Central Sierra Miwok, Wiyot, Valley Nisenan, many Yokuts groups, Western Mono and Chumash) related many supernatural and powerful acts performed by Condor during the early days of the world. The condor was considered a 'bird chief' among the Central and Northern Miwok, and some Central Miwok shamans acquired their power from the condor, allowing them to suck supernatural 'poisons' from their patients' bodies.

Dances honoring the condor, in which dancers represented the bird, were widespread in central California. Most of these dances among the Sierra Miwok, Patwin and Pomo involved a dancer wearing a condor skin with its feathers still attached. Southern Californians sometimes used condors in ceremonies similar to the Diegueño Eagle Ceremony and used condor feathers to create ceremonial skirts and feather-quill bands. Far to the north, Yurok, Karok and Hupa people sometimes pieced together several condor feathers to make what appeared to be one enormous feather, 20in (51cm) or longer, which was worn by participants in the White Deerskin Dance.

■ The Bear

In the 1970s, Northern Sierra Miwok elder Alice Pruitt admonished her grandchildren, 'A bear is just like a person. You don't want to eat him because you might be eating your grandfather.' Such views about bears, grizzly bears in particular, were held by many Miwok, Maidu and other California people. Some Sierra Miwok people believed that the spirits of deceased, malevolent shamans might inhabit a grizzly bear, and thus they avoided them. Some regarded the bear as almost human, and others thought it was a messenger spirit. Out of respect, they would not eat bear meat, but would use the hide as a robe, for bedding or for ceremonial regalia.

The Pomo greatly feared 'bear doctors' who, dressed in a bear disguise, waylaid and killed hunters and travelers for their goods. These bear doctors reportedly dug caves in a secluded, mountainous region. There, the doctor and his or her assistants would construct the special regalia which would imbue the doctor with the power of the grizzly bear. A similar belief in bear doctors was found among the Konkow and Maidu people, but they believed that bear doctors were sometimes so powerful that they were able to turn themselves into bears and did not need to resort to dressing in bearskins.

Although grizzly bears are now extinct in California, and the California condor is on the verge of extinction, many native people still revere the supernatural power of these animals' spirits. In the Sierra Nevada, the Maidu still perform the Bear Dance every spring in honor of the grizzly, and the Condor Dance has recently been revived among the Chumash. In many contemporary California Indian homes, elders and parents instruct their children in the importance of respecting the power of these animal spirits.

RITUALS AND CEREMONIES

Rituals and ceremonies were an integral part of the lives of California Indian people. Special ceremonial observances were held to mark the changing of the seasons, give thanks to the spirits and mourn the dead – although these ceremonies differed greatly from group to group throughout the region. Many of the rituals and ceremonies were given to humans in legendary times by the Creator or various spirits. Besides their ritual importance, ceremonies were also a social time for feasting and renewing ties with neighboring villages and other tribal groups.

■ The World Renewal Cycle

In northwest California, the Tolowa, Karok, Yurok, Hupa and Wiyot had an elaborate ceremonial life. Rites conducted by priests and their assistants were often secret, and part of the World Renewal cycle of ceremonies. Those held in public included two major dances: the White Deerskin Dance and the Jump Dance. In the White Deerskin Dance, a line of dancers held elaborately decorated hides from rare albino deer up on poles. The dance, which sometimes lasted as long as 16 days, celebrated the world's renewal. Through a display of regalia that got markedly more elaborate each day of the dance, it climaxed in a stunning display of wealth. In the Jump Dance, male dancers wore headbands made of woodpecker scalps and carried sacred dance baskets. These dances were each hosted by different ritual centers at distinct times of the year, and an extensive network of wealthy sponsors was required in order to organize and sustain the events, each of which might draw over 1,000 people.

■ Secret Societies

The term *Kuksu* describes a secret male dance society that flourished in most of central California, sometimes assisted by a similar women's dance society. The society performed dances, particularly during the winter months, to ensure prosperity and health. Boys were initiated into the society as adolescents and were taught the dances, regalia, songs and rituals that accompanied each of the ceremonial performances. The ceremonies were markedly different from one tribal group to the next, and sometimes even from village to village. Individual religious leaders had some leeway to practice their own ideas and beliefs while respecting long-established tribal beliefs about 'correct' ritual procedure. Among almost all of these central California groups, the donning of regalia and the act of dancing brought forth a manifestation of supernatural power. This power, while not evil in nature, was believed to be so potent that bad luck could strike those who did not demonstrate proper respect in handling dance regalia or in performing rituals. The impressive array of regalia used in the dances included headbands made from the scraped quills of flicker feathers, woven belts which incorporated scarlet woodpecker, and iridescent green mallard scalp feathers, and cloaks made of feathers from larger birds (i.e., eagles, hawks and herons).

■ The Whirling Dance

The Tipai-Ipai, Luiseño, Gabrielino, Cahuilla, Cupeño and others had an elaborate ceremony to commemorate the anniversary of the death of a chief or dance leader. Young condors or eagles were taken from their nests, raised and then used in a ceremony which culminated in the bird's death by strangulation or from pressing on the heart. The bird's wing and tail feathers were used to create a fringe at the ends of a net-skirt, worn in the Whirling Dance. Among the Tipai-Ipai, the Whirling Dance was part of an elaborate ceremony performed after the death of a member of the *Toloache* Society, and involved a single male dancer who carried two sticks and wore only the skirt, a head ring and plumes of owl feathers. The dancer's skipping and turning caused his feather skirt to whirl away from his body, giving the dance its name.

Today, some California Indian people still gather to practice old rituals. Among the Yurok, Tolowa, Karok and Hupa there has been a strong revival in the production of ceremonial regalia and the resurrection or continuation of ceremonial dances. In the central part of the state, an unbroken chain of seasonal dances continues in a few places, while in other communities certain dances and ceremonies which have been preserved in the memories of elders, have recently been reconstructed and reintroduced after a hiatus of 40 to 50 years. Since the 1970s there has been a revival of Chumash ceremonial life, many of them not seen for a century or so.

ARTS AND CRAFTS

The area now known as California was one of the most linguistically and culturally diverse areas in the world prior to 1800; more than 60 tribes, all with their own languages and material culture, made their homes in the California region. For the sake of this discussion of arts and crafts, the California culture area can be divided into several major regions which share similarities in their arts and crafts: northwest (including Yurok, Karok, Hupa, Tolowa, Wiyot and neighboring tribes), northeast (including Achomawi, Atsugewi and Shasta), central (including Pomo, Maidu, Yuki, Miwok, Yokuts, Patwin, Wappo and others) and southern (including Chumash, Cahuilla, Tipai-Ipai, Gabrielino, Juaneño, Luiseño, Cupeño, Serrano and Tataviam).

In northwestern California, people shared a rich culture which relied on salmon, animals (such as deer), and a great variety of plants. Women made fine twined baskets of hazel or willow shoots and conifer root, overlaid with patterns in black maidenhair fern stem and shiny yellow bear grass. The men were skilled craftsmen, producing dugout canoes, split-plank houses, finely incised antler purses and exquisite dance regalia.

In the northeastern part of the state, people had varied material cultures influenced by extreme variations in elevation, climate and vegetation in the region. From deserts, coniferous forests, swamps and meadows, the Achomawi, Atsugewi and their neighbors obtained a vast array of plant and animal resources to provide for their subsistence. They also produced a distinctive style of fine twined basketry, using some of the same, and some different, materials as people in northwest California. Their baskets were similar in appearance to those of the Klamath River, except that overlaid patterns were evident on both the inside and outside of the baskets. Men in this region made fine sinew-backed bows, which were an important trade item, and dance regalia, though it was not as highly developed an art as it was in the northwest. After the arrival of non-Indians, woven glass bead-work became firmly established in this area, and thousands of woven strips were made utilizing a limited repertory of patterns executed in hundreds of different interpretations.

People in the central portion of California relied on acorns as an important food source along with hundreds of other plant foods. Animals, including deer, elk, squirrels and various birds, were also important in their diets. The Pomo peoples made and used a great variety of twined basketry, primarily reserving coiled basketry for fancy baskets, often made as special gifts. Some of these baskets, fully covered with small, brilliantly colored feathers, have become the best known of Pomo arts. Coiled basketry for everyday use assumed more prominence among peoples to the east and south of the Pomo, including the Maidu, Patwin, Miwok and Yokuts. Men among the Maidu, Patwin and Pomo produced exquisite dance regalia, including flicker-quill headbands, belts woven of native hemp and ornamented with green and red feathers and white shell beads, and a myriad of feathered headpieces and cloaks.

In southern California, the Chumash on the coast utilized the wealth of the sea, while tribes living inland adapted to their more arid environments. Inland tribes used the various resources offered by the desert, including clay, which was formed into elegant and useful pottery vessels. In basketry, coiled baskets were made and used almost exclusively. Women from the Chumash, Cahuilla, Tipai-Ipai, Gabrielino, Juaneño, Luiseño, Cupeño, Serrano and Tataviam made elaborately coiled baskets which sometimes incorporated three colors. Men, apparently, executed the polychrome rock art characteristic of the Chumash region. A tradition of beautifully carved, steatite utilitarian ware and sculptures was centered in the Chumash-Gabrielino region.

■ Basketry

Basketry is perhaps the best-known art of California, and Native women have become well-known for it the world over. It is an ancient skill in California, and there are marked differences in baskets from different regions. Basket-making was primarily a woman's art; generally men made only a few coarse-twined baskets, like fish traps. Women took great pains to produce their baskets according to traditionally dictated methods and ideals, although each basket was unique and identifiable as the product of a specific individual.[48] Weaving skills took many years to develop, and young girls were encouraged and expected to participate in gathering and preparing basket materials as well as weaving. By the age of 10 or 12, most girls were capable of good basketry.

Baskets were indispensable in the lives of California Indian people and they were woven in a multitude of shapes, each designed to function in a special niche of the Native lifestyle. Specific baskets were made for cooking and food preparation, storage, carrying loads and cradling children.[49] Prized baskets, often made especially for the occasion, were given as gifts or burned or buried with the dead, and baskets were frequently burned during mourning ceremonies to honor the dead.

The study of basket form, manufacture and change over time does not extend far into the past, as baskets do not usually survive in archaeological sites.[50] Different styles of basketry developed in distinct areas, and people often regarded their own style as the 'correct' one. The words of the Karok woman, 'Imakyanvan (Mrs. Phoebe Maddux), in about 1930 embody this principle:

> 'Each new year ceremony my deceased mother would go to Clear Creek to attend the new year ceremony. She would pack upriver two pack basket loads of bowl baskets and openwork plates, and dipper baskets; she would trade them for blankets, Indian blankets, and upriver hats, and juniper seeds, for all kinds of things, upriver things. They used to give us those upriver hats sometimes, but we did not wear them, it does not look right on us.'[51]

Mrs. Maddux's comments describe not only how desirable her mother's baskets were as trade items, but also how these Karok women viewed the women's basketry hats from upriver tribes such as the Achomawi as not quite 'right'.

Weavers of northwestern California produced baskets in plain twining with decoration overlaid on the baskets' exterior. Mush bowls, twined with conifer roots on a foundation of hazel sticks, were embellished with a horizontal band of design in shiny yellow bear grass. More elaborate baskets, such as the dress caps worn by women, were further ornamented with shiny black maidenhair fern stem and woodwardia fern stem dyed to a rust color with alder bark. Only the most highly prized women's caps were further ornamented with additional overlay in yellow-dyed porcupine quills. The quills surrounded by the shiny black of the maidenhair fern stem made a striking contrast to the lighter yellow bear grass background.[52]

A handful of Yurok baskets collected by members of the Vancouver voyage in 1793 are preserved in British museums, but otherwise few baskets exist from this region from before 1890. After that date, the tradition of destroying an individual's possessions (and, therefore, baskets) upon their death fell increasingly into disuse, so more baskets survived. Additionally, women started to make baskets specifically for sale to non-Indians. Many of the baskets produced after 1890 for non-Indians were made with patterns and shapes specifically designed to make the baskets more salable, including motifs of realistic arrows and swastikas, and innovations such as pedestal bases and knobbed lids. In baskets made for their own use, as well as in most made for sale, women of this region still adhered to time-honored ideas of 'correct' patterns and basket forms. Some innovative weavers, such as Elizabeth Hickox (born in 1873), achieved a previously unrealized fineness and beauty by applying Karok patterns to a unique, lidded basket form. Her yellow-on-black baskets are among the finest from northwestern California.[53]

Baskets of northeastern California were produced in plain twining with a decorative overlay that shows on both the basket's interior and exterior. Like the Karok and Hupa to the west, women among the Wintu and Atsugewi wove their baskets on stiff warps of willow or other sticks. Some Achomawi women used twisted cordage (made from the sheath of the tule) for their warps, as did Klamath and Modoc people to the north, resulting in flexible baskets. By the early-1900s, some weavers were making changes in their baskets to make them more salable to non-Indians. Many women wove large baskets with patterns that had previously only been evident in smaller baskets. Others experimented with new forms (such as oval baskets) and/or patterns (such as eight-pointed stars and serrated diamonds, patterns that reached the area with the arrival of woven beadwork). Some weavers covered their completed baskets with loose-warp-woven beadwork, producing striking objects that were a blending of ancient basketry with more recently learned glass beadwork technique and patterns.

Women in central California wove both twined and coiled baskets. Colored patterns were produced by substituting colored weaving strands for the background color strands. Pomo women excelled in both twined and coiled basketry, and they also produced feathered baskets. In these baskets, small feathers – such as scarlet woodpecker-scalp feathers, bright-blue bluebird feathers, brilliant-yellow oriole or meadowlark feathers, and iridescent-green mallard duck-scalp feathers – were incorporated into the basket, held in with the basket's stitching. Thus, a completed basket's exterior was covered with a velvet-like coating of fine feathers. Such baskets were further embellished with abalone shell pendants and clamshell disk beads.

Many supreme Pomo artists created exquisite works of basketry art. While it was unusual for men to weave, both William Benson (1862-1937) and his wife Mary (c. 1878-1930) wove baskets of a quality rivaling the best produced anywhere; some of the coiled baskets had a stitch count of over 32 stitches per inch.

The Bensons, weaving for the non-Indian market, pushed basketry beyond the traditionally-accepted Pomoan style and made it into textile sculpture.[54] Similarly, other weavers such as Joseppa Dick (c. 1860-1905), produced exquisitely designed basketry with fine stitching (sometimes as many as 41 stitches per inch).[55] Cache Creek Pomo-Patwin weaver Mabel McKay (1907-1993) was renowned for her feathered and beaded baskets, and she taught the art of basketry to both Indian and non-Indian weavers, helping to ensure the art's survival.

Other central California peoples also produced excellent baskets; the Patwin and Maidu were renowned for their fine coiled baskets. The Patwin made baskets in both single-rod and three-rod coiling (like their Pomo neighbors to the east), but the Maidu produced only three-rod baskets. Farther south, the Yokuts and Western Mono made coiled baskets using a foundation of bunch grass stalks, and the Miwok made baskets using all of the above-mentioned coiling techniques.

Just after the turn of the century, Yosemite Valley, in Southern Miwok territory, became an important locale for the development of basketry into an art form produced solely for sale to non-Indians. Around 1910 weavers of mixed Southern Miwok and Mono Lake Paiute ancestry (Mono Lake Paiute people had come across the Sierra Nevada into Yosemite Valley) began to create a fancy style of three-rod coiled basketry with black-and-red patterns. The design style was encouraged by the Yosemite Indian Field Days, a rodeo-fair event held in Yosemite during summers of the 1920s; basketry contests at the Field Days spurred weavers to produce baskets with extremely fine stitching (sometimes exceeding 30 stitches per inch) and complex patterning. Individual women such as Lucy Telles, Carrie Bethel, Nellie and Tina Charlie and Leanna Tom were recognized as artists, and collectors eagerly sought to acquire their baskets.[56]

Women in southern California wove both coiled and twined baskets, though fewer twined baskets were made (they included winnowers, sieves, seed beaters and asphaltum-coated water bottles made by the Chumash). A wide variety of baskets, many very finely woven, were made with coiling. A highly developed design style evolved in certain Chumash groups; specific patterns and design placement were rigidly followed (for example, alternating colors of stitching on a basket's rim and the principal design band's placement on the upper part of the basket).

As early as the late 18th century, southern California Indian women began to make baskets for foreigners. Spanish officials stationed there often obtained Chumash baskets as gifts for visiting European dignitaries, thus excellent examples of Chumash basketry are contained in museum collections in Germany, Spain and England. By the end of the 19th century, when basket collecting became a fashionable hobby in the United States, southern California weavers again filled the demand by weaving thousands of baskets for non-Indian patrons.[57]

■ Ceremonial Regalia

Ceremonial dances were an important part of Native people's existence throughout California. Dances often manifested supernatural power; they were extremely complex performances and were usually considered prayers in visible form. A great array of carefully crafted ceremonial regalia was indispensable to these dances.[58]

In central California, dance regalia differed among dances. Flicker-quill headbands were used in most of them, however. These bands were made with salmon-pink scraped-feather quills of the common flicker (a woodpecker-like bird) and each band required the feathers from 20 to 60 birds. Many of the dances also required dancers to wear feather capes (most often men wore them on their backs). The capes were made from large feathers obtained from hawks, eagles, vultures, condors or various waterfowl.

In addition to flicker-quill headbands, a wide variety of headgear was worn in different ceremonial dances, with many styles reserved for specific spirit impersonators. Pomo women sometimes wore fur-covered forehead bands decorated with short, projecting quills. Each quill was ornamented with a small mat made of sewn flicker quills and beads. Both men and women wore feather bunches on their heads. These were made of feathers tied and coiled into a bristling tuft.

The Patwin, Valley Maidu and Pomo made a headpiece known as the 'bighead' which was worn by spirit impersonators in the *Hesi* ceremony. This was over four feet (1.2m) in diameter and made up of about 100 stripped willow shoots. The shoots were usually painted red and tipped with white waterfowl feathers, then thrust into a bundle of tule tied onto the dancer's head. The headpiece looked like an immense pincushion.

Elaborately decorated, woven feather belts were perhaps the most remarkable achievement in ceremonial regalia of central California. The belts, produced primarily by the Valley Maidu (Konkow) and Patwin, averaged six feet (2m) in length and about five inches (12cm) in width. They were woven of native milkweed or hemp fiber in a weft-face weave; included in the weaving were small, scarlet scalp feathers of about 500 acorn woodpeckers, and iridescent-green scalp feathers of some 100 male mallard ducks. These feathers were arranged in alternating panels, and the red panels were further ornamented with small olivella-shell disc beads which had been baked in ashes of a fire to turn them white. Such a belt was the most expensive item in the trade economy of central California, worth three large feathered baskets, several bearskins, or over 1,000 clamshell disc beads.[59] The belts, which were worn by men in ceremonial dances such as the *Hesi*, testified to the group's wealth and dedication to using their best when dancing to ask for the spirits' protection.

In northwestern California, featherwork was also an important part of dance regalia. Woodpecker scalps (from pileated, or less commonly, acorn woodpeckers) were considered a visible manifestation of an individual's wealth and they were used in a myriad of ways: headbands worn by men in the Jump Dance required more than 30 pileated or 200 acorn woodpecker scalps; albino deerskins carried in the White Deerskin Dance and otter-fur quivers carried in the Brush Dance were trimmed with them; most hairpins worn by male dancers and some women's basketry caps and braid ornaments were also ornamented with either entire scalps or individual tufts of scarlet feathers.

Women's dance regalia in northwestern California was elaborate, and produced its own music from the hundreds of shells and shell beads used in necklaces and as decoration on dance aprons. Women wore a front apron, which was often made of bear grass woven over buckskin cords and pine nuts or glass beads. This was worn with a back apron ornamented with bear grass and maidenhair-fern stem with an upper fringe of beads and abalone shell pendants, and a lower fringe of fine buckskin thongs. The rustling of the shells against one another produced a pleasing sound that is inseparable from the music of the dances on the lower Klamath River region.

Dance regalia in southern California was more limited than that to the north. Perhaps the most elaborate regalia in the region was produced among the Chumash and their neighbors. Skirts were made of strings twisted from native fiber incorporating eagle down, so that each string became a white, fluffy streamer; these were often tipped with sections of jet-black crow feathers or cinnamon-colored mature red-tailed hawk tail feathers. Men sometimes wore a high feather crown of magpie or roadrunner tail feathers surrounded with black-crow feathers and then with a band of white eagle-down tied across the brow. The headpieces also bore testimony to the owner's wealth and to the abundant bird life of the region, as only the center feathers from magpie tails were used in the headpieces, and more than 50 birds were needed to manufacture a single headpiece.[60]

Quill bands, similar to those of central California, were made by the Chumash and their southern neighbors. These bands differed, however, from the flicker headbands made farther north, as they were usually used as streamers and attached to poles at ceremonial sites, or worn as bandoleers. They also differed in that the section of stripped quills was narrow, averaging about two inches (5cm), and were solidly bordered by the unstripped feather. The bands were made of feathers not only from flickers, but also from crows and jays, as well as small feathers of pelicans and condors.

Also worn by Chumash men, and by the Cahuilla, Tipai-Ipai and neighboring groups, was a net skirt which had a lower edge fringed with eagle or condor feathers. The skirt, worn with a headband of owl fluffs and head plumes of stripped great-horned-owl feathers, comprised the costume for the Whirling Dance.

■ Beadwork

Beads were an important part of the economy of Native California long before the arrival of Europeans. Among the Yurok, Karok, Hupa and their neighbors, tusk-shaped dentalium shells (obtained in trade from the north) were a standard currency. Beads of bull-pine nuts and juniper seeds were used by women to decorate ceremonial regalia.[61] The Pomo and Coast Miwok just north of San Francisco Bay were the primary suppliers of clamshell disc beads to northern and central California.[62] The Pomo also produced highly valued, pink stone beads made from magnesite. On the southern coast near Santa Barbara, the Chumash produced olivella-shell disc beads as well as soapstone beads.

Glass beads were brought to California as early as 1542 with the explorer Juan Rodriguez Cabrillo, but they did not become common until they were distributed as a result of missionary activities between 1769 and 1800. By the first half of the 19th century, opaque, white glass beads and translucent green glass or white glass beads coated with a red exterior, along with less common green, blue and black beads, were widely used in central California.

It was not until sometime in the later half of the 19th century, however, that woven beadwork bands were first produced in California. Woven beadwork technique, and many patterns, reached California from the Wasco and their neighbors in the Columbia River region through interior groups in Oregon. The method of making woven beadwork bands using a 'loose-warp' technique was quickly assimilated by the Klamath, Modoc, Achomawi, Wintu and their neighbors, probably sometime around or just before 1870.[63]

Along with the technique of making woven beadwork strips, certain patterns and forms came to California from the Columbia River region. Eight-pointed stars, serrated diamonds and pairs of triangles linked together along a central dividing line were among the most enduring of motifs to be used in California. One form which was used in California with little change was the multi-tab, octopus bag of the Wasco. Produced entirely in woven beadwork, the Wasco bag was usually multi-colored with a variety of designs. The Wintu version of the bag was somewhat changed, incorporating a closing flap at the top (usually produced with red, black or blue designs on a white ground), and making use of only a few simple, but striking, geometric patterns.[64]

By the 1890s, Paiute people along the eastern flank of California were also producing woven beadwork bands, although they often made them using a bow loom. Their use of this style of beadwork facilitated the introduction of beadwork to groups such as the Southern Miwok and Maidu across the Sierra, although beadwork never gained a strong foothold with either.

Beadwork is still produced today by members of many groups in California, some of it still relating to the earliest techniques, but much more of it is wholly new.

■ Sculpture

The archaeological record in California provides ample proof of the antiquity of stone sculpture. While various types of plummet-shaped charms are known to have been produced since perhaps 2000 BC in central California, the most elaborate stone carvings were produced in the Chumash and Gabrielino areas.

A wide variety of effigies were produced by the Chumash, primarily from steatite (soapstone). Some were small models of plank boats. The little boats were highly prized charms for boat builders, ensuring good luck in fishing. The charms' owners sometimes kept several to be assured of fishing success. When the owner died, the small charms were buried with him.

Other sculptured effigies are representations of specific animals, but there is great variation in the degrees of realism with which they were made. Many of the charms represent whales; some clearly and accurately detail the mammal's anatomy, while others are more abstract representations, lacking fins, eyes and other details. Other effigies are phallic in nature, or represent fish, seals and birds.

In the northwest corner of California, the Yurok, Karok, Hupa and their neighbors produced a limited amount of utilitarian sculpture. Men carved sleek redwood canoes with elegant prows and sterns, each made from a single tree; the boats were the primary mode of conveyance on the Klamath River. Wooden trunks, carved from a solid block of redwood, were used to store ceremonial regalia and other valuables. Tubular pipes were made from dense yew wood, usually fitted with soapstone bowls. So exquisite was the workmanship on these pipes that early explorers marveled at their symmetry and thought they must have been turned on a lathe.

Antler provided another medium for sculpture among the peoples of the lower Klamath River. Sections of elk antler were scraped, carved, polished and incised to produce what the Native people called purses: small boxes with fitted lids used to store dentalium shell money. The section of the antler that attaches to the elk's skull was used to carve elaborate spoons that had intricately carved handles decorated with delicate cut-out patterns. These spoons were used by men to eat acorn mush and served as an elegant symbol of the people's wealth and prestige.[65]

■ Rock Art

Although rock art is found throughout California, it appears to be concentrated in specific areas. Both petroglyphs (patterns pecked, abraded or ground into stone) and pictographs (patterns applied to the stone with paint or pigment in one or more colors) are found, although there seems to be little overlap in the two techniques.

Rock art seems to be an ancient style of art in California, so old that in most areas Indian people ascribed the rock art to people who lived in the area before them or to legendary beings. One of the few areas for which information exists about the ethnographic use and production of rock art is among the Chumash.[66] Chumash rock-paintings were probably produced by elite shaman-priests. They seem to incorporate astronomical data as it was associated with Chumash cosmology and mythology. The production of such paintings, at least among some of the Chumash, was tied to the time of the winter solstice. One Chumash story tells of a neighboring Gabrielino sorcerer who caused a famine and many deaths by producing a painting on rocks of many falling men and women who were bleeding from their mouths.

Indeed, some of the finest rock art in North America is found in the Chumash area. In the mountains north of Mount Piños, in the territory of the Emigdiano Chumash, is the most elaborate extant Chumash rock art site: it comprises four shallow caves, each of which has walls covered with finely executed paintings of large circular motifs with concentric rings, anthropomorphic and zoomorphic figures, dots, bifurcated and zig-zag patterns in black, white, yellow, cream, green, blue-green, red and orange. The green and orange are unique, among the Chumash, to this single site. It has been speculated that the colors were obtained from Mexican sources during the revolt of 1824, and that the use of these 'foreign' colors may have been an attempt to gain supernatural power over the Mexicans during the revolt.[67]

■ Today

Many of the arts discussed are no longer produced in California, while some skills, such as basketry, survive among some groups. On the lower Klamath River, weavers such as Susan Burdick preserve and continue the fine weaving that characterizes the area, just as Konkow Maidu weaver Rella Allen and Maidu weaver Lily Baker make the traditional coiled basketry of their region.

Some skills, such as the manufacture of steatite carvings in southern California, had not been practiced for many years until they were revived in the past decade by William Pink (Cupeño) and L. Frank Manriquez

(Tongva-Ajachme[68]); they produced pieces of high quality that rival the best of prehistoric examples. Similarly, Hupa-Yurok artist George Blake's fine sinew-backed bows, elk-horn spoons and purses, and redwood trunks and canoes are among the finest extant examples of these objects.

Traditional artists demonstrate their skills to the public at special events and at recreated Native villages in many locations throughout California. Perhaps the best-known demonstrator today is Julia Parker, a Pomo woman who has demonstrated the traditional skills and basketry of her husband's Miwok-Paiute family to visitors to Yosemite National Park since 1960. An accomplished basket weaver, Mrs. Parker says:

'I always say I wouldn't be what I am and couldn't weave like I do without the women who came before me. I feel like a little bit of them comes out in me whenever I weave.'[69]

REFERENCES

CALIFORNIA

1 Federal Writers' Project, 1943: 9.
2 All information and quotations about the various environmental zones are taken from ibid.: 23.
3 Joseph and Kerry Kona Chartkoff, 1984, shed additional light on this topic.
4 Wissler, 1966: 202. The other main language families once extant in California were the Algonquian, Hokan (including the Isoman), Lutuamian, Shoshonean (also called Uto-Aztecan) and Yukian; Heizer and Whipple, 1971: 111. According to another source, some twenty-two linguistic families had existed at one time or another in the state, speaking 'no less than 135 regional dialects'; Rolle and Gaines, 1979: 21.
5 Wissler, 1966: 203.
6 The section on food came from Heizer and Whipple, 1971: 297-300.
7 Cook, 1976: 1, 199.
8 Davis, 1974, discusses this subject in some detail.
9 The group itself deserves more attention than just for its basket work. Some of their world views, for example, are of great interest, as indicated in Clark and Williams, 1954.
10 A. L. Kroeber, 1970: 244. To place work by Californian native basket makers in context, refer to Mason, 1976.
11 Merrill, 1980, explores this topic more fully.
12 Heizer and Whipple, 1971: 319.
13 Ibid.: 53.
14 A. L. Kroeber, 1970: 2.
15 Ibid.: 34.
16 Ibid.: 76.
17 Ibid.: 319.
18 Thompson, 1971-5. This publication provides a fine overview of this conflict and is recommended reading.
19 Utley, 1984: 171.

20 Members of the Potomac Corral of the Westerners, 1966: 196.

21 For more on this topic consult Cook, 1976a. Also refer to Heizer ed., 1974.

22 Edwards ed., 1970: 56.

23 It should be noted that gold discoveries in the acorn-bearing domain inhabited by the Miwok and Yokuts led to friction between the native people and the encroaching white miners. While space prohibits further discussion of this topic, the reader should consult Crampton ed., 1975, for an excellent account of this turbulent time.

24 Lang, 1979: 3. Generally speaking, this synopsis of the Costanoan and Coast Miwok was taken from this source as found on pp.1-56.

25 Ibid.: 7.

26 An early Franciscan missionary noted many of the Costanoan men were bald and bearded and made 'a habit of pulling out the hair of their eyebrows by the roots . . .'. The same source also mentioned observing capes of beaver skins and pelican feathers for the men and 'plaited tules' skirts for the women, 'for very few skins of animals are seen among them'; Bolton ed., 1926: 121.

27 Lang, 1979: 11.

28 Heizer and Treganza, 1972, provides more details about sources of materials for stone implement making.

29 Fray Francisco Palou, 'The Founding of the Presidio and Mission of Our Father St Francis', George E. Dane, trans XIV, *California Historical Society Quarterly* (June, 1953): 109.

30 Ibid.: 110. Palou was not the only missionary to provide important commentary about early California Indians. Many of the other padres did so, one important example of this type of information being found in Geiger and Meighan, 1976.

31 The northern Costanoans could be found at Missions San Francisco Assis, San Jose, Santa Clara and Santa Cruz, and the southern Costanoans made up the main numbers at San Juan Bautista, Soledad and San Carlos. Here, as elsewhere throughout New Spain, the mission, a key colonial institution sanctioned by the Spanish sovereigns to deal with the native people, 'had three fundamental purposes. They desired to convert him, to civilize him, and to exploit him', Bolton, in Bannon ed., 1974: 190. For more on certain aspects of native activities at these combined religious and civil complexes, see Webb, 1952.

32 To provide an overview and some context in this area, the reader should consult Cullin, 1975.

33 A. L. Kroeber, 1970: 544.

34 Ibid.: 547.

35 Ibid.: 550

36 Casebier's two monographs, *Carleton's Pah-Ute Campaign* and *The Battle at Camp Cady* (both published by the author in Norco, California, during 1972) provide details on this short-lived military operation.

37 Reid, 1926: 49.

38 A. L. Kroeber, 1970: 632.

39 The people in this region tended to manipulate both stone and bone by inlaying the basic materials with various patterns and designs. Burnett, 1944, delves into this subject at some length.

40 Rolle and Gaines, 1976: 24.

41 Tuska and Pickasski, 1983: 12-14, 190-91, 303-4, provides basic details about the work of these three authors.

42 Rolle and Gaines, 1976: 27.

43 Wax, 1971: 36, 216-17, 222, shares some useful statistics for more recent times.

44 Theodora Kroeber, 1976, traces this fascinating, bittersweet story.

45 For further reading, Heizer, ed., 1978, remains a must.

46 This story is a compilation from several versions told by Maidu elder Henry Azbill to the author between 1968 and 1973.

47 This version of the *Uwulin* story is from LaPena et al, 1993:1–2. The word *Uwulin* signifies 'eater'.

48 For perhaps the most complete discussion of ethno-aesthetics among Yurok and Karok basket weavers, see O'Neale, 1932.

49 For a discussion on the use of a variety of baskets in processing acorns for food, see Ortiz, 1991.

50 Bates, 1982:33-34, and Bates and Lee, 1990:39-40.

51 Harrington, 1932:128.

52 O'Neale, 1932.

53 Mrs. Hickox was actually the daughter of a Wiyot woman and a non-Indian man, although she identified as Karok. (See Fields, 1985.)

54 Their lives are detailed in McLendon, 1990.

55 For more on Joseppa Dick see Smith-Ferri, 1993.

56 Bates and Lee, 1990.

57 Dawson and Deetz, 1965.

58 Bates and Bibby, 1985.

59 These belts continued to be produced into the first quarter of the 20th century. Belts made in the late-19th century often used commercial cordage for the weft and glass beads for decoration. For additional information on the belts, see Bates, 1981a, Bates and Bibby, 1983, and McKern, 1922.

60 This style of headpiece was commonly used by Yokuts people, by people as far north as the Coast Miwok of the Bodega Bay region, and by people as far east as the Paiute of western Nevada. The use of these magpie headpieces does not seem to have spread farther south than the Chumash.

61 A discussion of the manufacture and use of pine-nut beads is in Ferris, 1992.

62 For clamshell disk and magnesite bead manufacture among the Pomo, see Hudson, 1897.

63 There is very little published on the spread of glass beadwork to California. Most of the known primary sources are cited in Bates, 1981b.

64 These octopus bags among the Wasco were probably produced in imitation of Cree-Meti bags, brought west during the fur trade in the 1830s and 1840s. See Schlick and Duncan, 1991.

65 For a lengthy discussion see Kelly, 1930.

66 Grant, 1966; Hudson and Underhay, 1978.

67 Lee, 1979.

68 L. Frank Manriquez uses these village names to identify herself, rather than the Spanish names of Gabrielino and Juaneño.

69 Bates and Lee, 1990:171.

THE NORTHWEST COAST

The Northwest Coast offers a mild climate with a wide array of food resources. Several distinctive cultures developed on the Northwest Coast from the Columbia River through coastal British Columbia to the top of the Alaskan panhandle. The cultures are very similar in some ways and remarkably diverse in others. People from all regions developed a rich ceremonial and spiritual life. They invested tremendous creative energy in artistic expression, including songs, dances, legends and spectacular, philosophically powerful art work.

There are several different languages indigenous to the Northwest Coast, each with its own subdivisions or dialects. Since there were no large political units outside of the individual village, the cultures are conveniently grouped today according to language. The southern portion of the Coast, including the mainland and lower Vancouver Island, is the homeland of the Coast Salish. The Nuu-chah-nulth people live on the west coast of Vancouver Island and were formerly called the Nootka, a name originally given them by Captain Cook. They are closely related to the Makah on the tip of the Olympic Peninsula in Washington state, and the national boundary that separates them is a relatively recent development in the history of the Northwest Coast. The Southern Kwakiutl villages are in northeastern portions of Vancouver Island and the adjacent mainland. Branches of the Northern Kwakiutl, who speak different dialects and have some different cultural characteristics from the Southern Kwakiutl peoples, live in the central portion of the British Columbia coastline. The language of the neighboring Bella Coola people is related to that of the Salish; they originally moved to central British Columbia from the south and adopted some cultural traits of central groups. Along the coastline and the lower Nass and Skeena Rivers to the north are the villages of the Tsimshian. The

Queen Charlotte Islands are the homeland of the Haida Indians, whose large seaworthy cedar canoes kept them from being isolated. A few centuries ago a group of the Haida moved northward and settled what is now the southern portion of Prince of Wales Island in Alaska. They are now known as the Kaigani Haida but have maintained communication with their relatives on the Charlottes; here, too, the national boundary is both recent and arbitrary. Tlingit Indians live along the panhandle of southeast Alaska; some also moved into inland British Columbia. Because this chapter focuses on the eighteenth and nineteenth centuries, past tense will be used; but it should be emphasized that Northwest Coast Indians still live on the coast today and are culturally and politically active.

Northwest Coast peoples enjoyed a relatively favorable natural environment compared to most other places in North America. While the entire region can get harsh winds and rain, only the portion in the north regularly gets freezing winters and heavy snowfalls. The yearly salmon runs offer a fairly reliable food resource; and there are a variety of other fish, shellfish, sea mammals and plants, roots and berries to supplement the diet and compensate for poor salmon seasons. However, the Native peoples were able to take advantage of these resources only because they developed very specialized knowledge and highly efficient tools for both harvesting and processing.[1] People stored food they harvested in the summer for consumption in the winter. Thus, like agriculturalists, they did not have to travel after food in the winter and could establish permanent villages.

Because of this environment, the region supported a relatively dense population compared to other places on the continent north of Mexico. While population estimates are always speculative, it has been suggested that there were over 46,700 Indians in coastal British Columbia in 1835.[2] Undoubtedly the population there was greater before white diseases were introduced. In 1880 the Native population of southeast Alaska was estimated at about 12,000, and again, the population was undoubtedly smaller than it had been before the arrival of Europeans.[3]

Traditionally people lived in numerous villages along the coastline and inland rivers. Often large extended families lived together in communal longhouses spread in a row along the beach. The villages were permanent settlements inhabited for generations or longer. People made excursions from them for hunting and fishing, trading, social activities and military raids. The village was the major political unit, and people identified first and foremost with the leadership in their village.

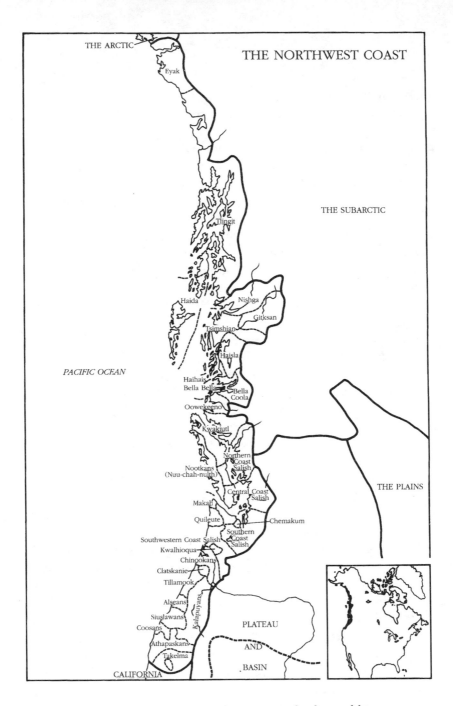

THE ARCTIC

THE NORTHWEST COAST

Eyak

THE SUBARCTIC

Tlingit

Haida

Nishga

Gitksan

Tsimshian

Haisla

PACIFIC OCEAN

Haihais
Bella Bella

Bella
Coola

Oowekeeno

Kwakiutl

Northern
Coast
Salish

Nootkans
(Nuu-chah-nulth)

Central Coast
Salish

THE PLAINS

Makah

Quileute

Chemakum

Southern
Coast
Salish

Southwestern Coast Salish

Kwalhioqua

Chinookans

Clatskanie

Tillamook

Alseans

Siuslawans

Coosans

Athapaskans

Takelma

Kalapuyans

PLATEAU

AND

BASIN

CALIFORNIA

ABOVE: *This map shows approximate territories of tribes and language groups in the early nineteenth century. After that, all tribes lost territory.*

The villages were always located along waterways, either the coastline or rivers closely connected to the coast. From the sea came food, but also materials that were used in manufacturing clothes and tools – skins from sea mammals, as well as bones, bladders and sinew. The great temperate rainforests were also vital to the cultures. Trees, especially cedar, provided the materials for large communal houses, sturdy canoes and a variety of utilitarian and ceremonial items.[4] Women used the inner bark of the cedar and the roots of cedar and spruce to weave highly functional baskets, capes, mats and cordage. Some of these baskets were woven so tightly that they could hold water.[5]

In addition to the food it yielded, the ocean was tremendously important for transportation. The coastline of the region is rocky and irregular, and land transportation was much less practical than travel by canoe. Again, it was the Indians' technological skill that made it possible for them to take advantage of this opportunity. They built large canoes, spreading them to a functional width with steam. In this method, water is placed in the bottom of the dugout log and hot rocks are dropped into it to create the steam. The sides of the canoe must be well balanced in width to create a stable and seaworthy vessel, and the entire process takes considerable work and skill. The canoes were vital for hunting and fishing, and also for trade and social exchange between villages up and down the coast. People from southeast Alaska may have traveled down the coast as far south as California for trade. In some Haida oral traditions there are stories of voyages to Hawaii, although these have yet to be corroborated by any archaeological record.

The Northwest Coast region was probably inhabited very shortly after the ice sheets from the last Ice Age uncovered the coast line – some 9,000 to 13,000 years ago. The land and water fluctuated for some time before reaching the configuration we know today. At first the human populations were nomadic, but as the flora and fauna came to resemble that of the present, they developed the food-storing technologies that make permanent villages feasible. Archaeological finds suggest that the cultural characteristics known in recent times were already highly developed at least fifteen hundred years ago and probably somewhat earlier than that.[6] Indians on the Northwest Coast traded with other coastal groups and with inland peoples prior to the arrival of Europeans, so they were by no means isolated. Substantial contact between Indians and Europeans began to occur in the last quarter of the eighteenth century. Thus, that time is often known as the

RIGHT: *John Hunter, a Nu-chah-nulth, in dance costume. His heavy robe is hide, probably painted with (mainly) black and red pigments.*

BELOW: *A Tlingit village in Alaska, c.1883. The siting of houses in this permanent village is typical, located on low benches slightly above the high water mark of sea or flood-level of rivers.*

beginning of the historic era, but Northwest Coast Indians had a vibrant history and kept oral historical records long before the arrival of the Europeans.

On all parts of the Northwest Coast, family ties were extremely important. People identified closely with extended families and with lineages, and in many places rank and political leadership were hereditary. Each lineage owned certain privileges. These ranged from the right to perform specific dances to the right to use resources in a certain geographic area. In most places on the coast there were various levels of social status, including people of high rank, people of lower rank and slaves who were captured in battle or purchased through trade.[7]

Among the Tlingit, Haida and Tsimshian on the northern coast, the society was matrilineal, and children inherited through their mother. Thus, a leader might be succeeded by his sister's son rather than by his own son, and boys were often trained by their maternal uncles. In the northern groups with matrilineal descent, social divisions based on kinship were especially important. For instance, the Tlingit divided themselves into two basic hereditary groups, known as moieties. One was known as the Raven, while the other was called the Wolf (or occasionally the Eagle). Everyone in society belonged to the Raven or Wolf moiety, and people could only marry someone from the opposite moiety. Thus, since the society was matrilineal, children always had the same moiety affiliation as their mother and a different one from their father. Each moiety was subdivided into smaller groups, which anthropologists often call clans or sibs. The Raven moiety had some twenty-seven clans.[8] Within each village, there would be a leader for every clan that lived there. Many clans had branches in more than one village, but leadership always remained local. Social organization among the Haida and Tsimshian was similar, with some clans also among the Northern Kwakiutl.[9]

Among the groups on the lower coast – the Southern Kwakiutl, Nuu-chah-nulth, Bella Coola and Coast Salish groups – inheritance came from both parents. Family ties and local kinship group relationships were still considered extremely important. As in the north, kinship families had recognized leaders who gave guidance about such matters as resource use and marriages.[10]

In all parts of the coast, ties between different kinship groups were politically and economically essential. These ties were solidified through trade, and often – as in Europe – marriages helped promote political and eco-

ABOVE: *Kwakiutl group gathered around blankets at a potlatch, photographed at Fort Rupert, Vancouver Island, before 1895.*

ABOVE: *Kwakiutl village, Fort Rupert, about 1888. Note the traditional windless cedar plank dwellings, one with a painted front (left) and several carved totem poles.*

nomic relationships between different kinship groups or different villages.[11]

Ceremonial gatherings also served to develop and reinforce these ties. There were many different types of ceremonial gatherings up and down the coast. Today they are often all referred to by one term – potlatch – which is a word from the Chinook trade jargon meaning 'to give'.[12] Actually, though, there was tremendous diversity in the nature and purpose of the ceremonies. They were very complex institutions combining social, cultural, spiritual, political and economic elements. Because of the diversity on the coast and the complexity of the celebrations themselves, it is difficult to discuss them without reducing them to a much too simplistic level.

In brief, potlatches were sponsored by a host who had saved food and material goods for the express purpose of the occasion. Guests were invited from other kin groups and other villages, and the celebrations could continue for days or considerably longer. During the potlatch, the host displayed and emphasized certain rights or prerogatives. For instance, these privileges might include the right to take the name, political title or other hereditary prerogatives of a relative who had recently died. In some potlatches parents or other relatives would confer certain prerogatives on their children. The prerogatives were expressed at the potlatch through dances, songs, oration and display of art.[13]

The guests from other lineages and other villages watched these claims to rights, acting as witnesses. The host fed them amply from the food he had stored, and gave them gifts from the material possessions he had accumulated for the purpose. When the witnesses accepted the food and gifts, it was understood that they affirmed the host's right to claim the privileges displayed during the potlatch. In effect, the witnesses were paid for publicly acknowledging these rights and for keeping the memory of the potlatch alive. People passed on stories of potlatches they had attended, creating a communal memory of the event and of the affirmation of the host's right to the privileges he displayed there. This system of witnessing, of communal memory and of oral tradition functioned very efficiently as a way of keeping records, and made a written language unnecessary.

Thus the potlatches were extremely important for validating rank and leadership. They were also vital for passing the rich cultural heritage from generation to generation, for during ceremonies children saw the songs, dances and art work that referred to the history and legends of their families and their people. The potlatches served an economic role, for they kept goods circulating in several ways. A leader saving for a potlatch would often

ABOVE: *Tlingit in ceremonial costume at a potlatch in Klukwan, Alaska. The man to the left wears an elaborately painted hide tunic over a trade shirt.*

ABOVE: *Tlingit potlatch dancers, Klukwan, in about 1900.*

306

loan goods, receiving goods of their value back with interest as the time of the celebration grew near. That leader then distributed goods to his guests in payment for their witnessing role. In return, high-ranking guests would aspire to reciprocate with their own potlatch, matching or exceeding the gifts of the former host. In preparing for that event, they would loan some of their goods. Thus, the potlatch system supported a cycle of exchange of material wealth. The host of a potlatch might be almost bereft of material possessions at the end of the gathering, but his wealth measured in honor would be greater.

Ceremonies took place in the winter months, when families were living on food they had stored during the summer and autumn. Freed from the necessity of traveling for food, they were able to take the time for large social gatherings. Thus the rhythm of life moved with the seasons, with different economic, social and cultural activities in different times of the year.

Whatever the season, Northwest Coast peoples surrounded themselves with artistic expression. There was no firm demarcation between 'art' and 'daily life', as tends to exist in Western cultures today. Northwest Coast arts were functional arts, adapted to perform a task or convey a message. The purpose of the art went far beyond aesthetics, and it was intended for much more than contemplation. Northwest Coast peoples decorated tools and utensils they used in daily life, and they created spectacular and dramatic masterpieces to display crests or for use in dances. Men carved wood, bone and antler and sometimes also worked in stone. Women wove with plant and animal fibers, decorating their vessels, mats and blankets with careful designs. While most adults developed skills in making articles for daily uses, it took specialized training to create monumental and ceremonial art. Thus, carvers of totem poles, masks and similar art works apprenticed with master carvers to learn the skills. They earned high reputations for their proficiency, and leaders commissioned art from these masters. In the Tlingit region, usually art was commissioned from an artist who belonged to the opposite moiety from the patron.[14]

Northwest Coast Indian art is well known today internationally. Most people associate the term either with the highly structured linear art of the northern regions of the coast, or with the dramatic and colorful dance masks of the Southern Kwakiutl. In fact, there is tremendous diversity in artistic expression up and down the coast, and it would be much more accurate to refer to Northwest Coast Indian arts in the plural. Regional artistic styles developed, and in some cases specific styles can be traced to individual villages. There are certain characteristics common throughout the coast, and others that differ regionally.

There were three principal forms of art made on the coast: two-dimensional design in the way of painting or light engraving; three-dimensional sculpture, usually woodcarving; and the production of baskets, mats, woven hats and textiles. Two-dimensional design appears on a wide variety of articles. Pigment for paints was made from minerals such as red ochre and copper mixed in a medium of fish roe; later artists adopted commercial pigments bought through trade. House fronts and canoes sometimes had motifs painted on them. Large storage chests were often painted, or both painted and engraved. Woven hats sometimes also had painted motifs, showing collaboration between female and male artists. Wood food bowls and grease dishes often had two-dimensional design engraved on their surface, and utensils such as berry spoons were also frequently painted or engraved. Ceremonial items such as masks were also painted. Two-dimensional design was practiced long before Europeans arrived on the Northwest Coast. Archaeological finds suggest that the technical, highly formalized styles found on the northern part of the coast were developing there at least a thousand years ago.

Three dimensional sculpture also included a wide range of articles, from wood carving tools to feast dishes and ceremonial masks – and, on some parts of the coast, the totem poles for which the region is famous. The tradition of sculpture extends back centuries and possibly millennia. Very expressive stone sculptures have been found in many regions of the coast dating back at least three thousand years.[15] Almost certainly these same artists were practicing in wood as well, but wood deteriorates more quickly than stone and is less likely to be preserved in archaeological sites.

Female artists made woven and coiled baskets, woven mats, hats, capes and textiles. After trade with Europeans started, they also practiced beadwork and appliqué, and outlined designs on commercial wool dance blankets by sewing rows of decorative pearl buttons. Until recently, these art forms unfortunately received less attention in the literature about Northwest Coast Indian arts, but they, too, required substantial skill and creativity. Like wood, basketry does not last well in archaeological sites except under unique circumstances, but there are still enough indications to suggest that Northwest Coast people have made baskets for thousands of years.

Each of these three primary art forms differed regionally on the coast.

The two-dimensional design made by northern artists – the Haida, Tsimshian and Tlingit – was quite different from that made by artists to the south – the Southern Kwakiutl, Nuu-chah-nulth, Bella Coola and Salish. Northern Kwakiutl villages, in a central position between these regions, produced some works resembling northern styles and others suggesting a southern influence. The two-dimensional art practiced by the Haida, Tsimshian and Tlingit artists follows the same very technical set of conventions. It is very difficult to tell two-dimensional art from these peoples apart unless there is documentation, or unless the work also has sculptural qualities. The very complex art style is known today as 'Northern Formline'.[16] Stated much too simply, artists depicted animals by using a series of standard conventions and combining them in fairly uniform ways. Basic outlines are defined by formlines which are curvilinear; right angles are rare. The formlines vary greatly in width, giving the designs a dynamic sense of fluidity and motion. The lines converge and diverge to form certain shapes that recur again and again. Thus, a somewhat oval shape, called today an 'ovoid', usually depicts eyes and joints in limbs or appendages. U-forms often indicate ears, snouts and wing feathers, and the fins and flukes of sea mammals and fish. There were very standard ways that artists combined the formlines to create these elements, and there were also standard ways in which artists placed the design within the shape of the field they had to decorate. Individual expression writ large was not the goal; but individual artists had personal styles that were all the more creative because of their subtlety.

Two-dimensional design in the more southern groups, by contrast, followed fewer standard conventions. Thus there is considerably more variety in style. It is usually not difficult to distinguish Southern Kwakiutl, Nuu-chah-nulth and Salish two-dimensional design from each other. Each of these groups had their own aesthetic and artistic goals. Unfortunately there is not much information about Southern Kwakiutl art in the eighteenth century. In the nineteenth century these artists experimented with elements from northern painting, varying them significantly to create a style that is distinctly Southern Kwakiutl. The early works from the Nuu-chah-nulth, found in archaeological sites and collected by late eighteenth-century European explorers, suggest a tradition emphasizing rows or bands of geometric elements and liberal use of circles and dots. Some of the curves suggest more northern elements. In the mid-nineteenth century, some Nuu-chah-nulth artists also began incorporating more northern elements into their art work. The lines and shapes in Coast Salish two-dimensional design have much in common with the northern graphic art, although again there are fewer standard conventions, more wide-ranging variation between designs and a highly developed aesthetic unique to Salish artists. It is possible that far back in antiquity there was once a much more uniform art style on the coast, and people in different regions chose to modify it in different directions.[17]

Sculptural styles differ substantially up and down the coast. In the north, where two-dimensional art is almost identical, sculptural styles vary considerably from language group to language group. The variations are even greater in the south, where each group has a particularly distinctive carving style and a unique genre of masks.[18]

Women up and down the coast were proficient at weaving baskets, mats, hats and capes from plant fibers. The inner bark of the cedar, cedar root, spruce root and grasses were most often used. Twining was the technique most prevalent, although women from interior Salish villages also made coiled baskets. Dyed grasses and other dyed plant fibers were added during the manufacturing process to form decorative designs, which were usually geometric. Types of designs and forms of baskets varied somewhat from region to region. In the eighteenth century, the Nuu-chah-nulth wove a very distinctive conical-shaped hat with whaling scenes. Along with their close relatives the Makah, they were the only Northwest Coast peoples to hunt whales, and these whaling hats are unique to that region.[19]

Women in some groups – particularly Coast Salish and Tlingit – also wove blankets from animal wool. Salish women used hair from small domesticated dogs as well as wool of mountain goat, often mixed with plant fibers.[20] Tlingit women made the famous Chilkat dancing blankets of mountain goat wool and cedar bark. These blankets show elaborate figures in Northern formline design, taken skillfully from a pattern painted on a wooden board by a male artist.[21] When commercial beads became available through trade, women also began using them for ceremonial items.

Ceremonial and monumental art played a variety of roles in traditional cultures. Like artistic style, these roles varied from region to region. In northern areas, much of the ceremonial art displayed crests identifying the lineage of the owner. Thus, a man wearing a mask of a bear would belong to the Bear sib or clan. In some ways, the crests served much as coats of arms in Europe. In other ways, they differed from coats of arms, for they also might refer to experiences that the wearer's ancestor – the person who founded the family – had had with an actual bear spirit.

In fact, much of the art refers to a primordial time when boundaries between human beings, spirits and animals were much more fluid than they are at present. During this time, animals could marry human beings, and sometimes spirits transformed themselves from animal form to human form. People who had experiences with animals and spirits in these ways could acquire the right to display an animal as a crest and to pass that crest on to descendants. Thus, a work of art that displays a crest may do more than signify genealogy. It may also speak of the history of the family and of the specific rights that family enjoys as a result of ancestral experiences. In effect, the art work makes visible all the invisible rights the family has – the rights to perform certain dances, sing certain songs, tell certain stories and claim a specific ancestral history. These rights were carefully guarded, and it was inappropriate for any member of society to perform a dance or sing a song to which he or she was not entitled.

Crests were displayed in a variety of contexts. Masks were carved in the form of crests and worn in dances. Ceremonial frontlets with crest designs were worn on the forehead. Chilkat blankets were woven with crest designs, and basketry hats had crest designs painted on them. Sometimes house fronts were painted with crest designs. Probably the most well-known form of crest display is the totem pole, which has become a symbol for the Northwest Coast today. Contrary to popular belief, they were not carved all over the coast, and were most prevalent among the lower Tlingit, the Haida, the Tsimshian and the Kwakiutl peoples. There has been some debate as to whether totem poles existed prior to the arrival of European traders with their iron tools. Almost all scholars agree today that totem poles were a well-established art form before Europeans arrived. However, it is also almost certainly true that the iron tools – as well as the ceremonial activities that were supported by the fur trade – increased the number of totem poles being carved.

There were many types of totem poles, varying in size depending on their function. When a high-ranking person died, often his successor, or other members of his family, raised a pole in his honor. The pole would display crest figures pertinent to his ancestry. Other poles, known as frontal poles, stood against the front of house displaying crests of a family living in it. Interior house posts, which were shorter than most memorial poles and frontal poles, supported the beams of the house. In some regions of the coast, especially among the Haida, human remains were placed in grave boxes at the top of mortuary poles. Mortuary poles tended to be relatively short, with one or two primary crest figures displayed. In places on the coast where people were buried, carved figures were often placed to mark the grave. Freestanding carvings of human beings, known as welcome figures, were sometimes placed on village beaches, especially in the lower half of the Northwest Coast, to welcome visitors.[22]

Totem pole raisings were accompanied by a potlatch. The guests who came acted as witnesses affirming that the family raising the pole had the right to do so. The potlatch accompanying a memorial pole would honor the person who had recently died, and would create a communal memory that that person had been so honored. Totem poles were commissioned from master carvers who had apprenticed to learn their skills and who had earned reputations as fine artists. Between the cost of the pole itself and the potlatch ceremonies surrounding the pole raising, each pole represented a considerable expense.

The art that displays crests also displays considerable wealth. Wealth on the Northwest Coast was measured by rights as well as by material possessions. Thus, art work displaying a crest suggested a much broader complex of entitlements belonging to the family that owned the crest. Not all art on the Northwest Coast displayed crests in this way, but other forms also spoke of rights and entitlements. Ceremonial masks also were worn in very prestigious dances that were inherited. People gained the right to participate in the dances and to claim the less visible wealth of their inheritance by going through initiations. The dances formed a part of this initiation. Examples of art associated with these dances are the dramatic masks used in ceremonies among the southern Kwakiutl and the Nuu-chah-nulth.[23]

The Southern Kwakiutl are particularly well-known for their Tseyka dances or winter ceremonies, known popularly as the Hamatsa dances. These dances, too, refer to ancestral experiences with spirits. The Hamatsa, or initiate, re-experiences the adventures of an ancestor who encountered the supernatural cannibal spirit Bakhbakwalanooksiwey. This spirit was attended by a number of fierce birds capable of eating human beings. The ancestor escaped and brought back to his family the right to perform dances he had learned from the encounter.[24]

During the winter ceremonies, the boundaries between human beings and spirits were temporarily transgressed, as were the boundaries between present and past and the boundaries between initiate and ancestor. The initiate relived the experiences of the first ancestor in his encounter with

Bakhbakwalanooksiwey. After a period of isolation, he returned to the village during the winter ceremonies in a wild state, and was tamed and restored to his former human state in a set of specific dances. Gradually the boundaries between human being and spirit, between present and past, and between initiate and ancestor were re-established.

During some of these dances, dancers wore large masks representing the cannibal birds that attended Bakhbakwalanooksiwey. These dramatic masks were carved of wood with great strands of red cedar bark draping from them. The masks have movable beaks that the dancer opened and closed by working a network of strings. The cedar bark strands hung thick, obscuring the dancer's body and hiding his hands as he moved the strings. The clap of the beak added both sound and motion to the dance.

The Tseyka ceremonies spoke of special privilege limited to people who inherited the right to those entitlements and who had gone through a specific initiation to gain the right to display them. The art work helped re-enact – or to re-experience – the ancestral experiences that conferred the privileges to the descendants. A ceremony with similar function took place among the Nuu-chah-nulth and the Makah peoples. They called it the Klookwana or the Klookwalli, respectively. In this ceremony, initiates were removed by supernatural wolves, and villagers participated in dances to help bring them back. These efforts eventually succeeded and the initiates returned to dance specific dances they had inherited. The dances were performed in set orders. In some of these dances, dancers wore carved masks representing wolves. In others, headdresses made of flat painted boards were worn on the forehead. These represented profiles of the wolf, mythological lightening snake or thunderbird. Again, in the Klookwana or Klookwalli, boundaries between human being and spirit, present and past, initiate and ancestor are temporarily transgressed.[25]

Some Salish peoples – those living on the Olympic Peninsula near the Makah – also participated in dances of this nature. Among the Salish living along the Puget Sound, other ceremonies took place that did not feature initiates. Nevertheless, they too spoke of the fluidity of boundaries. These ceremonies, known as Spirit Canoe ceremonies, were performed to cure people who were ill. Shamans or people in the community invested with special powers to communicate with spirit helpers, enacted a canoe voyage into the world below the earth where the souls of the dead stayed. The ceremony was intended to cause the spirit helpers of the shamans to make the actual journey and bring back the soul of the ill person. During the ceremony, distinctive wooden boards and carved figures were used to help evoke power and to bridge the boundaries between human beings and spirits. Because of their potency, these art works were kept in hiding away from the village when they were not in use.[26]

Coast Salish art often referred to personal spirit helpers, even when on utilitarian objects. Particularly in British Columbia, a very distinctive mask style was also used. This mask, known as the Sxwayxwey mask, was used by individuals at very personal times in their lives: births, marriages, deaths and at times when they took new names. Unlike other masks on the coast, these masks have blunt cylindrical eyes that extend from the surface of the mask. They also often use the technique of 'visual punning', incorporating bird designs into the features of a larger mythical figure.[27]

This technique of visual punning is prevalent up and down the coast, so it deserves more mention here. In 'visual punning', portions of one animal double as portions of another animal. Thus, the wings of an eagle may also portray the pectoral fin of a whale, enabling an artist to suggest shared identity.[28] Again, this artistic technique implies that boundaries can be very fluid. Two presences can occupy the same place at the same time, just as the dancer can exist in present and past at the same time.

The discussion above has often talked about initiates who gained the right to perform certain dances and claim certain privileges through inheritance. Some ritualistic art was also used by another small sector of society, the shamans or spiritual healers. These people had special powers to transcend the contemporary boundaries between human beings and spirits and to communicate with spirits directly. They used those powers to help heal ill people and to foresee events. Each shaman had a personal spirit helper or a series of helpers, and his or her personal collection of art work that was used to call on the power of these helpers. The shamans and their art work were often buried away from villages because of the danger of their power.

The art and ceremonial expression on the Northwest Coast was integrally connected to all parts of life. Utilitarian objects and ceremonial objects alike were decorated. The art was functional art, often used in the place of a written language to convey genealogy and to preserve historical memory. Similarly, the ceremonies kept experiences of ancestors alive and also made hereditary privileges evident. Certain art work both represented and facilitated the power of shamans to cross the boundaries between human beings and spirits and to call on supernatural powers. The ceremonial life was extremely rich and varied on the Northwest Coast. Despite strong cultural oppression on the part of non-native peoples who opposed native ceremonialism in the nineteenth century, many ceremonies have survived and are practiced today.

The earliest record of contact between Northwest Coast Indians and Europeans occurred in 1741, when the Russian explorer Chirikov harbored his ship briefly in the area in southeast Alaska near present-day Sitka. The next recorded contact was in 1774, when the Spanish explorer Juan Perez reached the Queen Charlotte Islands and traded with Haida Indians there. Perez was followed by another Spanish expedition the following year, and by the English captain James Cook in 1778.[29]

The Indians on the Northwest Coast were well accustomed to trading with other indigenous groups, and were interested in the materials the Europeans brought. In the initial years of exchange with Europeans, iron – especially iron with a blade – was particularly in demand. In return, Indians traded food and furs, especially the thick fur of the sea otter. Captain Cook's crew discovered that they could sell sea otter pelts for very high profits in China. This information became generally known in 1784 when the journals of that expedition were published, and investors began supporting trading voyages to the Northwest Coast. Very quickly, the Northwest Coast became a commercial center with Europe and the eastern United States, and the Indians on the Northwest Coast engaged in active trade in sea-otter pelts. By 1820, these small sea mammals had practically disappeared.

The maritime fur trade affected native lives in a variety of ways. It was not without its incidents of violence: the sailing ships were always armed with cannon, and misunderstandings arising from cultural and language differences could lead to tragedy on both sides. Fur traders accidentally introduced diseases such as smallpox, and since native peoples lacked natural immunities the diseases hit hard. Traders introduced firearms as well; it is still unclear whether these weapons increased deaths in intertribal warfare.

In a more positive light, the maritime fur trade introduced a great influx of material wealth into Northwest Coast societies in a short period of time. This new wealth helped support ceremonialism and cultural expression. There were probably more potlatches and more production of ceremonial art in the decades immediately following the advent of the maritime fur trade than there had been previously. The fur traders were for the most part transient. They did not appropriate native resources, and they had no wish to change Indian cultural or economic activities as long as Indians kept bringing furs. The trade may have disrupted social structures somewhat by making wealth accessible to a wider range of people. However, it did not attack native culture, and in some ways it supported it.[30]

This situation began to change as European and Euro-American settlers moved to the Northwest Coast. These settlers expected to be permanent residents, and they wanted land resources that belonged to Indians. These developments happened at different times in different parts of the Coast. Except for the Sitka region, where Russians had the settlement of New Archangel, Indians in southeast Alaska did not feel great pressure from non-natives until after Alaska was transferred to the United States in 1867. In southern British Columbia, pressure was felt somewhat earlier. In 1849 the British government started encouraging the colonization of Vancouver Island in order to keep the United States from claiming it. In the 1850s, some treaties were made with Indians in British Columbia. After that time, reserves were established without treaties. The white settlers and their government appropriated lands that belonged to Indians and restricted their access to these lands. Gunboats patrolled the coastline, ready to shell native villages if there were signs of insurrection. The first governor, James Douglas, had recognized native title to land, but his successors denied Indians ever had title. Entering the 1990s Indian land settlement issues in British Columbia remain unresolved.[31]

In southeast Alaska the situation was much the same. No treaties were negotiated and no reserves were set aside except for one which was formed after a group of Tsimshian Indians from British Columbia followed the missionary William Duncan across the border in 1887. From 1867, when Alaska was transferred to the United States, to 1877, the U.S. Army was stationed in southeast Alaska; in 1879 they were replaced by naval gunboats. In the 1870s, industrialists began moving into the region to establish canneries and mining concerns. Indians became wage laborers in these industries, working for relatively low pay and leaving villages to live in cannery or mining housing. Land issues in southeast Alaska were dealt with through a settlement in 1959 – following decades of pressure – and the state-wide Alaska Native Claims Settlement Act in 1971.

Along with the settlers, Christian missionaries came to the Northwest Coast. Russian Orthodox missionaries had been active among the Tlingit in New Archangel in southeast Alaska since the mid-nineteenth century, and in the last quarter of the century southeast Alaska also saw the arrival of Roman Catholic, Presbyterian and Friends missionaries. In British Columbia, starting in the mid-nineteenth century, missionaries from Roman Catholic, Anglican and Methodist denominations were represented. In addition to church services, missionaries ran schools for children and adults. Some, such as William Duncan, established 'model villages' separated from existing villages, where Indians lived in European-style houses and agreed to abandon traditional forms of cultural expression such as the potlatch.[32]

Indians on the Northwest Coast had mixed reactions to missionaries. Many were interested in access to the missionary teachings – especially because missionaries could help them learn English and other skills that would equip them to survive in the new Euro-American society that was developing around them. As white settlers appropriated native lands and white industries took over native fishing streams and food resources, it became harder for Indians to continue entirely in their traditional economy, and it was increasingly important for them to be able to work as wage laborers.[33] Missionaries could help them acquire these skills and could prepare them for functioning in a society where white people were ready to exploit them. While missionaries are often condemned for their paternalistic, condescending and frequently dictatorial attitudes, they cared whether Indians survived and they believed at the time that their actions were helping the Indians.

However, missionaries and government officials did much more than teach English. They also held that traditional native culture was at the best that of 'heathens' and was at worst depraved. They waged an active campaign to stop Indians from practicing their own cultural expression and from passing on their heritage to their children. They often forcibly removed children from their parents and communities, raising them in residential schools where they were punished for speaking their own language or celebrating their culture.

The potlatch was a particular target of missionaries and government officials both in British Columbia and in Southeast Alaska. They viewed it as a threat for a variety of reasons. Since they measured wealth only in material possessions, it seemed wasteful to give away summer earnings during winter ceremonies. Indian agents in British Columbia, who wanted Indians to become agriculturalists, would have greatly preferred to see the money spent buying farm equipment and seeds. Missionaries charged that children were taken out of schools during potlatches, while employers complained the ceremonies made workers unreliable.

However, probably the most fundamental reason for opposition to the potlatch was the recognition that those ceremonies kept native culture alive. It was the expression of native ceremonialism that passed on Native history and culture to young people. It was also the expression of Native ceremonialism that affirmed Native spirituality, native political systems and systems of hereditary rights – all of which seemed threatening to missionaries and government officials. The potlatch came to be viewed as the Native custom that was preventing Indians from becoming 'civilized' as defined by missionaries and government officials, and they felt they had to destroy the potlatch if Indians were to become both Christians and citizens.[34]

Thus, in both British Columbia and southeast Alaska, missionaries and government officials launched an active campaign against Native ceremonialism. In 1884, these efforts resulted in Canadian federal legislation outlawing potlatches. This law stayed on the books until 1951. Many Indians – and some white authorities – protested the legislation immediately, but to no avail. While it was not enforced regularly, the threat of prosecution – coupled with the other manifestations of cultural oppression the Indians faced – caused people to stop performing ceremonies in public. In some places on the coast, the ceremonies continued in clandestine fashion, always under the threat of prosecution. In other places, people gradually abandoned the ceremonies for the same reason.

In southeast Alaska, no legislation was passed outlawing potlatches. However, government officials and missionaries put strong pressure on Indians to stop potlatches, and many agreed to do so voluntarily.[35] Some felt that with white attitudes as they were they could not afford the prejudice that came from Native cultural expression. When they were trying to find ways for their children to live with a reasonable amount of physical and psychological safety, they could not risk the prejudice they faced from whites when they expressed their culture openly. In 1904, many Tlingit leaders in southeast Alaska agreed at the governor's request to stop holding potlatches.[36]

In addition to appropriation of lands and extreme cultural oppression, white settlement brought another devastating blow to Native societies and cultures. This was the introduction of diseases and of alcohol. These problems, which first developed during the maritime fur trade, increased exponentially with white settlement. As more whites came in to the region regularly, more diseases were introduced. Equally significant, Native peoples from a number of villages throughout British Columbia began to gather at one city, and an epidemic that broke out in that city could be carried throughout the region.

This in fact occurred in 1862, when a ship from San Francisco accidentally brought smallpox to Victoria. When Indians camped outside the city contracted the disease, white residents drove them away. They returned to their home villages, inadvertently bringing the germ with them. The tragic epidemic wiped out at least one third of the total Indian population in British Columbia, and in some areas along the coast line, villages were practically eradicated. In addition to smallpox, other diseases such as measles, influenza, tuberculosis, venereal disease and alcoholism had grave and disruptive effects on Native societies.[37] In a short period of time, every Native person almost certainly had friends and relatives who had died. Due to the social disruption, populations consolidated into a few villages in some places on the coast. The devastation made it easier for forces of cultural oppression to take their toll.

By the first decades of the twentieth century, the open expression of Native ceremonialism had been effectively suppressed by white authorities. In British Columbia Indians could and were prosecuted for continuing their ceremonialism. This was particularly true of people from the Southern Kwakiutl region, who continued their ceremonialism more actively than most.[38] The cultural oppression, along with the other forms of devastation that Indian societies faced, led to fewer and fewer ceremonies. Thus, there were fewer contexts in which traditional art was used, and fewer ceremonial art works were made.

Starting in the 1870s, museums in North America and Europe became very interested in collecting Northwest Coast Indian art.[39] Curators believed erroneously that the cultures would not survive and wanted to make a scientific record while it was still possible to do so. They sent collectors to the Northwest Coast to make 'representative' collections of the cultures. Collectors purchased art from Native peoples who no longer were using it in ceremonies and who needed the money. Frequently, too, collectors took art from graves without permission. In a few decades, vast quantities of ceremonial art and of totem poles were removed from the Northwest Coast.

During this period, except among the Kwakiutl and Salish peoples, very little ceremonial art was still being made. Some artists made works to sell to tourists and other non-Native peoples. Some of these works remained technically excellent, especially the baskets being woven by women for white collectors. Because women had fewer opportunities to earn wages in the white economy, they could afford the time it took to make baskets, and this activity was also compatible with child care. However, with so few traditional contexts for ceremonial art and with more opportunities to work in white industries, fewer and fewer male artists could afford the time it took to become skilled carvers and painters. Also, with the population decline, there were fewer masters left with whom to apprentice. Predictably, this situation worsened as the twentieth century went on. By the 1960s, when art historian Bill Holm studied the Northern Formline style, he could not find a practicing artist from the Bella Coola region who had learned in traditional methods.[40]

Despite the extreme cultural oppression and social disruption, though, Native peoples retained their sense of ethnic identity and their cultural values. Even when ceremonialism was suppressed, these values remained. Today, when civil rights and human rights are more widely acclaimed, Northwest Coast Native peoples are reviving their traditional ceremonialism and are again practicing their cultural expression openly. Artists are active again making traditional forms of art, both to sell to collectors as fine art and to use in their own ceremonies. Indians are also very well organized politically and are still seeking redress of injustices of the past. They are also playing a strong role in environmentalism, for the preservation of their culture is integrally tied to the preservation of the forests in their traditional homelands of the Northwest Coast.

MYTHS AND LEGENDS

The stories of the Northwest Coast peoples are the transporters of hereditary rights, ethical behaviors and appropriate interactions in the powerful interchanges between social, natural and supernatural worlds. The people had a distinctive and ingenious response to explaining the universe to themselves, to ongoing generations and to us, the outsiders. They did this with a wealth of stories, rituals and visual images that ignited imaginations and drove the dullest mind into action. Their myths are histories of human and ancestral events. Their rituals are the means to make visible these stories, to bring to life and to memory the complex constellation of relationships between humans, nature and the supernatural. Brilliant yet subtle, the stories are still being told. dominated for a while by other societies and thoughts, the stories still speak to the people, and transcending, time and space, to us.

For centuries the Northwest Coast people lived in a uniquely mild environment on the North American continent. The people had many diverse languages, but shared a similar maritime culture that is considered one of the world's most distinctive. They included the Tlingit, the Haida and Kaigani Haida, the Tsimshian (comprising the Gitskan, Nishga and Coast Tsimshian), the Salishan-speaking Bella Coola, the Northern Kwakiutl or Bella Coola), the Kawkiutl, the Nuu-chah-nulth (also called Nootka) and the closely related Makah, and the Coast Salish.

If we are to characterize the stories of the Northwest Coast, not in an effort to 'de-mystify' or to catalog them, but to provide a framework for them, then there are some aspects of their culture relevant to understanding the tremendous forces that inform and guide these people. Abundant with the stuff of life – ample food from the sea and land, cedar rain forests to furnish everything from cradle to coffin, and a temperate climate – the

Pacific Northwest ecology provided the appropriate setting for permanent villages of planked houses. These abundances also provided the leisure time to develop an amazing array of material culture. The visual and oral arts especially flourished and reflected the peoples' deep spiritual response to this generous environment. If the physical setting provided leisure and abundance, their spiritual life provided an environment of deep contemplation and explanation. One seems necessary for the other, a concept that may elude contemporary Western minds. For without contemplation of the laws of nature, human conduct is without moral laws or rules and thus is alienated from the supernatural.[41] This fundamental assumption in Northwest Coast spiritual life was probably never intended to be stated so simplistically, and this chapter's simplification of complex mythological and ritual structures is only intended to be a broad framework with which to view some of the ingenious and diverse responses to the synthesis of the social world with nature and the supernatural.

ORIGIN MYTHS

Among the thousands of myths on the Northwest Coast many origin stories begin with accounts of supreme beings living in an upper world. This world has many layers, fits like an inverted bowl over the curved Earth and is the residence of the supreme beings who have human forms and live in human-style dwellings. The Bella Coola call this *Nusmata,* or the 'place of myths; legends; stories'.[42] The stories are often told in the past tense, because the events took place so long ago.

■ A Supreme Being

Most of these cultures believe that the supreme being was not himself created, but always existed and is responsible for creating primordial life forms and the geographical features of the world, either singularly or by delegating the task to other lesser deities. Supernatural transformative creatures then created the world as we know it today. The Haida people, for example, speak of *Nanki'lsLas-lina'-i,* or He-Is-Going-to-Become-He-Whose-Voice-is-to-be-Obeyed, a nebulous creature who eventually became Raven and who formed the world by a complex recipe that is typically elusive and vague. The Yakutat Tlingit describe *Nas-caki-yectl,* or Creator, as the supreme but nebulous power of the universe that made all living things, including humans.[43] The Bella Coola people describe a 'supreme deity', *Atl'kwntam,* having no particular form, but who is addressed as 'highly respected one'.[44]

■ Primordial Darkness

The beginning of time was a period enveloped in darkness and was inhabited by humans, animals and ghosts. In the primordial darkness all three had similar cultures, forms and souls. Humans were decidedly less knowledgeable and less capable than animals or ghosts, though they did possess some power and had a potential to obtain it. Animals of the land and sea had more power because they had the ability to transform their human bodies into animal forms at will. In their natural realm, they lived within a ceremonial and social structure that paralleled that of humans. Ghosts triumphed over animals and humans because under cover of darkness ghosts were invisible and dangerous in their constant quest to devour souls as well as food.

■ Daylight and Fire

The first time of darkness ended when a transformative being, Raven, brought the first and most important gifts to the world: daylight and fire. Ghosts, who hated light of any kind, fled to distant darker regions and, though still dangerous, became less of a threat. Animals became more covert about transforming themselves into human forms. People generally acquired more power and wisdom and entered a relationship of reciprocity with plants and animals.

■ Birth of the People

Sometimes Raven found people, as he did on the beach at Naikun where, hearing muted sounds coming from inside a large clamshell, he discovered infant humans: the ancestors of the Haida of the Queen Charlotte Islands. In another story, this Haida Raven was said to have summoned four different tribes out of the ground: the Tsimshian, Haida, Kwakiutl and Tlingit.[45]

Other cultures, of course, have their own origin stories. Many of the Kwakiutl clans and families trace their origins to supernatural beings who in animal forms descended from the sky, out of the sea or from the underground to specific localities, removed an animal mask and became a human ancestor.[46] The Bella Coola's *Alt'kwntam* created four supernatural carpenters to create land features, plants and animals, and humans. The Salish trace their origins to the all-powerful *Swai-swei* rising out of the Fraser

River and creating the first woman and mother of all men.

These creation or origin stories attempted to answer universal human questions about where we came from and why. Origin stories acknowledge the beginnings of human consciousness while recognizing the quality of the eternal, of time without beginnings, of creators who themselves knew no creation. They are a handle for speculating on the trajectory of human endeavors, while forming explanations about the elusive and sometimes paradoxical worlds around us.

ALL-POWERFUL SPIRITS

Raven has many names on the Northwest Coast. He is *We-gyet* or *Txamsem* among the Tsimshian, *Yehl* among the Tlingit, *He'mask.as* (Real Chief) among the Bella Bella, *Kwekwaxa'we* (Great Inventor) among the northern Kwakiutl, and *Nankil'slas* (He Whose Voice is Obeyed) among the Haida. Raven was an instrument of the Creator.[47] In the beginning of time, he traveled around the world and throughout the cosmos, a hero finishing the job of creation. Although wisdom and integrity were not the wily Raven's strongest features, he often unwittingly became the benefactor to many human communities, bringing the first salmon, the first berries and other gifts such as the Sun, Moon, stars, the tides, rivers and streams.

■ The Sun and the Box of Daylight

Most Raven stories begin with an account of how he stole the Sun. First he impregnated the Sky Chief's daughter by turning himself into a conifer needle she swallowed in a drink of water. She gave birth to a boy who was really Raven in disguise. (In some stories, Raven simply appeared after the birth, scooped the child out of its skin and assumed the boy's identity.) The grandson of the Sky Chief grew rapidly and, as young children will do, the toddler became irritable and cried when he could not have his own way. The doting grandfather, like all grandfathers anxious to please, and perhaps just as anxious to placate the screaming child, gave him the box containing the Moon. The box was broken open and the Moon escaped into the sky. The crying resumed and the next toy proffered was a larger box containing the Sun: the Box of Daylight. Seizing the prize he came for, the child transformed back into Raven and escaped through the smoke-hole of the chief's great house. (Some story-tellers claim that this is why the Raven's feathers are the color of soot, for in the time before the liberation of light, Raven was a white bird.) Raven traveled around the world, opening the Box of

Daylight, not only bringing light to the spirits of the world, but giving many of them the physical forms that they have today.

■ **Thunderbird**

All the First Nations of North America tell stories of Thunderbird, of its monumental size and power. A swift death-bringer, Thunderbird's awesome supernatural power is represented by two 'horns' on top of its head. This being is so enormous that extinct volcanoes cradle its nest. Called *Hagwelawremrhskyoek,* or Sea-monster Eagle, by the Tsimshian, this giant bird swoops from the sky and devours whales. When the bird blinked, lightning flashed, and thunder crashed from the flapping of his great wings. In the Coast Salish (Comox) Thunderbird Dance, a small amount of gunpowder was ignited near the ceremonial house entrance to represent the flash of his eyes.[48] For the Tlingit, seeing or even hearing a Thunderbird made a person wealthy.[49]

■ **The Whale**

Of all the groups on the Northwest Coast, only the Nuu-chah-nulth hunted whales, the 'salmon of the Thunderbird'. In their stories, Thunderbird had Lightning Snakes under his wings that he hurled down to kill a surfacing whale. The whalers painted the image of Lightning Snake on the prow of their canoe, then concealed it with black paint: the power of Thunderbird's lethal weapons was thus transferred to the hunters.[50]

HERO CREATURES AND MONSTERS

Monumentality is a feature of Northwest Coast material culture exemplified by the towering crest poles in front of huge planked houses. These gabled dwellings not only housed many families, they were metaphorically large enough to contain the cosmos during the winter ceremonials.[51] Monumentality is also a feature in the description of all-powerful spirits of the coast including those amalgamations of natural forms that we call 'monsters'. Many of these monsters can assume any shape. Often, monsters provide people with monumental wealth, but sometimes they are also the source of almost unthinkable fear and danger.

■ **The Trickster**

Raven's importance to the world as the transformer-hero is paralleled by his role as the supreme trickster. In his voracious search for food and sex,

Raven is a transforming monster, a randy jester and frequently a shamed fool. In some stories Raven loses or injures parts of his anatomy while attempting to steal food or sex; in others, he assumes various human and animal disguises to obtain illicit sexual favors.

In one series of the Raven stories, an old fisherman tricks Raven into stealing bait from a hook, and he loses his beak in the escapade. He sulks shamefaced around the man's village, a blanket covering his face, until he recovers the beak. In some of the more risqué tales, Raven's penis is so long that he has to coil it over his shoulder like a lasso. In a few of these adventures Raven succeeds in seducing various beautiful women (and men); in others, his amorous ruses are sometimes humiliatingly and sometimes painfully exposed. Tales of humiliation and triumph, of noble and foolish behavior, of reverence and irreverence, Raven stories illuminate the fundamental paradoxes of human life.

■ Water Creatures

The waters of the Northwest Coast provide the wealth of food, as well as awesome and often invisible dangers of the unpredictable and ever-changing watery environments. What better place to discover monumental monsters?

Among the northern tribes there is a powerful sea being called *Gonaquadet* among the Tlingit, *Ginaxcame'tk* among the Tsimshian and *Wasgo* or *Su'san* among the Haida. A wealth-bringing *Gonaguadet* and his ilk can assume any shape.[52] These monsters often had toenails, claws, teeth, hair, canoes and other belongings made of copper, the regional symbol of wealth throughout the Northwest Coast area.

Many of the stories reveal that the *Gonaquadet* has given his skin to a human cultural hero, usually a misfit of some sort, who performs amazing supernatural feats, such as rescuing the village from certain starvation by providing his people with inexhaustible food supplies. The hero's reward is immortality. Clothed in the monster's skin, the hero is the mythological analogy for the spiritually enlightened and wealthy chief in Northwest Coast society. So, the distinctive emblems of chiefly power – the raven rattle, the Chilkat dancing robe, the frontlet headdress, and the chief's box to contain this potlatch paraphernalia – are all said to have originated with *Gonaquadet*.[53]

Kwakiutl stories describe the power of *Sisiutl*, a giant double-headed serpent with darting tongues and a human face in the center of its body. Each of the three foreheads of the *Sisiutl* are adorned with horns of power, like those found on the great Thunderbird, its major predator. Noted for swiftness and a voracious appetite, the *Sisiutl* is a daunting carnivore that looks like a serpent, swims like a fish, yet can travel on and under land. Seeing it, touching it or even its slimy trail, can turn people into stone or foam, or cause them to vanish altogether. The *Sisiutl* can transform itself into a variety of forms including a self-propelling canoe that must be fed seals. Yet when killed properly, the creature's skin can be worn as a belt. The owner of such a belt, usually a warrior, is protected from death. This awesome protective power of the *Sisiutl* is represented visually on many housefronts, masks, and dancing paraphernalia.[54]

HOLY PLACES, SACRED SITES

In western cultures, places for worship and sacred sites are distant from everyday lives. In traditional Northwest Coast cultures, sacred events are held in the places where people work and live, reflecting the comprehensive, holistic world view that connects the spiritual and the profane. Their clan houses, for example, are living spaces for most of the year, but for parts of the winter they become sacred sites as ceremonial settings and metaphorical containers of the cosmos.

Holy and sacred are not necessarily concepts tied to place, but may express a condition – as in the sacred time of the winter ceremonies. Or 'sacred' may describe a kind of event – as in the offering of tobacco dipped in the water on the end of an oar to placate Swell Woman who has made seas dangerously high. 'Sacred' may also designate places such as grave sites. Unlike those in the Western culture, these are not the sites of pilgrimages or places of homage. From a Native view, these are places where ghosts may reside, and most are not places that people revisit after fulfilling their duty to the deceased.

Understanding the three important realms of Northwest Coast consciousness – earth, sea and sky – will illuminate the Northwest Coast concepts of sacred places. These realms intersect and provide an axis of human interaction with the supernatural forces of the universe.

■ Earth

The Earth is a complex plane, basically divided into three sectors. The beach is the first, where powerful and dangerous creatures pose enticing threats to human sanity. The Land Otter Man of the Tlingit and *Pook-ubs* of the Nuu-chah-nulth were spirits of drowned men who appeared as humans on lonely beaches and were dreaded because of their great supernatural powers to entice humans, rob them of their senses and turn them into Land Otter spirits.[55]

The second Earth plane is the forest, dark and equally dangerous as the beach, full of perils and rewards known and unknown to the hunter. The Kwakiutl *Bukwus,* or Wild Man of the Woods, and the *Pu'gwis* of the Tshimshian are remarkably similar spirits of deep woods. Each has a human-like countenance, but with the skin and facial features of a corpse: stretched facial skin, lips curled back from the teeth, and the fleshy parts of the nose decayed to reveal large nasal passages. The danger of this creature is that it has the ability to imitate humans, and to seduce or capture them by rendering them senseless or foolish.

The woods are also the home of the mysterious *Tsonoqua* or *Dzonokwa,* the Wild Woman of the Woods. She is a cannibal woman known to the Kwakiutl and Bella Coola. Her lonely cry is heard in the woods as a low, long whistling sound:'u, hu, u, u.' The image of *Tsonoqua* is a black-faced, sleepy-eyed woman with pursed lips. She sometimes appears in the winter ceremonial, an ogress threatening to snatch away children. For all her fearsomeness, she is also known to bestow power and great wealth: the abundance of food at feasts and great shield-like coppers.[56]

Humans occupy the third Earth plane: that thin strip of habitable land between beach and forest, between sea and sky. In that humble position of liminal existence, they contemplate their own power in relation to the sacred spaces of the universe around them. It is there that they give voice, image and memory to the contemplation of that tenuous and fragile existence in the tension between the natural and the supernatural.

■ Sea

Before them, the sea provides the wealth of food and the dangers of an alienated ecology. People need the sea for survival, yet every day they risk their lives interacting with it. The wealth of the sea lures the people, and it is personified in numerous supernatural creatures. For example, the Kwakiutl tell of the great chief under the waters, *Qlo-mogua,* or Wealthy, the controller of all sea life and consequently of great wealth. he is sometimes referred to as Copper Maker and his masks are adorned with parts of sea animals: spines, fins, tentacles and suckers as well as with copper or images of coppers. He is generally a benevolent spirit, bestowing great gifts on those who encounter him.

■ Sky

Sky beings occupy the layers that make up the solid vault above the Earth and sea. Home of the all-powerful ones who figure in the creation stories, the sky is also home to the spirits of Wind, Rainbow, Cloud, Sun and Moon. This heavenly realm, where the Milky Way is known as the Seam of Heaven in Kwakiutl thought, is similar to the Earthly plane. There one finds the good life, freedom from pain and sorrow, and timelessness. Humans have been known to travel to and from this realm, and to receive messages from it via supernatural birds. Many Northwest cultures view this upper world as the place of origins, the dwelling place of creators; as well, it is the place of endings, the dwelling place of ghosts of the dearly departed.

REVERED ANIMALS

Earth, sea and sky are inhabited by powerful and revered animals in Northwest Coast story and ritual. Animal spirits appear in natural and personified forms to enter into states of supernatural reciprocity with humans. Some of the most important animals of the coast – salmon, whale, killer-whale, bear, wolf, eagle and raven – demonstrate this concept in stories that illuminate the cosmic balances and spiraling cycles of life. Many of the revered animals figure as ancestors and are thus celebrated in the songs, dances, stories and visual images that are the personal property of individuals and clans.

■ Killer-Whale

Interestingly, humans are not considered to be superior to animals. Neither is independent of the other, for supernatural ancestors of the people were often transformative animal spirits. The Tlingit and Haida, for example, regard the Killer-Whale People as a superior race of beings, even though the Tlingit maintain the first killer-whale was made by a man out of a piece of yellow cedar. Haida women would take children down to the surf generated by a passing *Orca* pod, and dip the children's feet into the water while uttering a prayer that the powerful Killer-Whale, or *Sga'na* – which also means 'shaman' and 'power' – would give them strength, good health and wealth.[57] The Kwakiutl prayed to it to give them food and placed mountain – goat tallow, cedar bark or, in later times, tobacco in the water. Tsimshian sea monsters use killer-whales for their canoes. Many of these seafaring peoples believe the souls of drowned relatives became killer-whales and live with the powerful beings in their village under the

329

sea. This may explain why killer-whales are never hunted for food.

■ Wolf and Bear

On land, revered animals included the wolf and the bear. The Nuu-chah-nulth describe the connection between the wolf and killer-whale as originating from the time when the sea mammal beached on the shore and its spirit transformed into Wolf, which explains why the wolf has the same black and white markings. Wolves are both admired and feared as canny relentless hunters, swift and skilled. Supernatural wolves are a prominent feature of the Nuu-shah-nulth winter ceremonial known as the *Klookwana,* where they are responsible for taking initiates to the forest to begin the ritual process of joining a secret society. In a similar Kwakiutl ritual, wolves bite and then greedily devour the initiate; later, the guilty supernatural wolves revive the dancer.[58]

Although wolves are not hunted for food, bears are. The grizzly bear, the Salmon-Eater, shares an important role with eagles and with humans as omnivorous hunters. All North American First Nations have a profound respect for the bear, and Northwest Coast people share with them many ceremonial aspects of bear-hunting. Hunters fast and abstain from sexual intercourse before the hunt, and prayers are said to the bear thanking him for giving his body for food. After the kill, the head and skin are positioned in the same manner as a human chief lying in state. The head is sometimes painted and anointed with red ochre and eagle down; the bones are handled carefully, not only that the bear might be reincarnated in perfect form but so that the dead bear's friends will not kill the hunter.

Most important food sources, plant or animal, are thanked in simple prayers, such as this Kwakiutle one to a slain grizzly bear which illustrates their special relationship:

'Thank you friend, that you did not make me walk about in vain. Now you have come to take pity on me so that I may obtain game, that I may inherit your power of getting easily with your hands the salmon that you catch . . . O Friend! Now we press together our working hands that you may give over to me your power of getting everything easily with your hands, friend!'[59]

Prayers often conclude with a request for the slain animal to tell all its relatives that it has been well-treated and they should continue to come to the people with their ultimate offering.

RITUALS AND CEREMONIES

Synthesizing the social, natural and supernatural worlds, the ritual and ceremonial practices of the Northwest Coast people make visible and memorable the social and supernatural worlds. In events that define, separate and
then unite the sacred and the profane, the movement of human spirits
between social and spiritual realms is marked by ritual births, deaths, trans-
formations and regenerations.

■ First Salmon Ceremony

Most Northwest Coast people hold First Salmon ceremonies in the spring,
thus beginning the harvest of their primary food source. Swimming from
their underwater villages to their natal streams every four or five years, the
Salmon People assume fish form. Complex and solemn rituals accompany
the first salmon to be taken from the river. The salmon is their gift of life
and accordingly the animal is honored with prayer, song and ceremony.
The Kawkiutl have a prayer to these great supernatural beings who are
addressed as 'Swimmers' or *me'mEƩyo'xwEn*:

> 'Oh Swimmers. This was the dream given by you, to be the way
> of my late grandfathers when they first caught you at your play. I do
> not club you twice, for I do not wish to club to death your souls so
> that you may go home to the place where you came from,
> Supernatural One, you givers of heavy weight [meaning
> wealth/supernatural power] . . . Now you will go.'[60]

The fish is then cut up by the chief's wife, who offers a special prayer of
thanks. The parts of the salmon are distributed to members of the group,
consumed and then all the bones are carefully collected and returned to the
water for the Salmon spirit to reflesh and regenerate. Enacting this 'ritual
of rightness' the people enable the reincarnated salmon to swim back to
their villages. The continuity of life, for the people and for the salmon, is
thus ensured.

■ Cannibal Ceremony

The First Salmon Ceremony marks the opening of the profane season of
food gathering and ritually sanctions the devouring of supernatural animals

by humans. The Kwakiutl *Hamatsa,* or Cannibal, Ceremony marks the devouring of humans by the supernatural . The *Hamatsa,* a secret society of the Kwakiutl and Bella Bella, is performed in the *Tseyka,* or sacred season of the winter ceremonials. Neighboring tribes have similar cannibal societies: the *U'lala* or *Wa'lala* of the Haida, and the *xg.edt* or *U'lala* of the Tsimshian.

In these societies, an initiate begins a spirit quest, separating himself from the villagers by going into the forest and fasting for several days. While in isolation, the initiate 'travels' spiritually to the house of *Bakbakwalanooksiwey,* Great Cannibal at the North End of the World, and is devoured. In the belly of this monster that has an insatiable hunger for human flesh, the initiate's cultural identity is metaphorically digested and the raw, natural human spirit is either vomited or excreted. The initiate, stripped of his cultural attributes, is naked, has no language or song, walks on all fours and has an appetite for human flesh; he is the protégé of the Man Eater. Eventually the *Hamatsa* is 'captured' by members of the society and returned to the winter ceremonial house where he performs dances.

First appearing with darkened face and wearing only hemlock boughs, the *Hamatsa* dances with the assistance of helpers. With trembling outstretched hands he moves around the fire. Sometimes he lunges at people, biting them; sometimes, he appears to devour the flesh of a corpse. Later, with shredded cedar bark covering most of his body, he wears one of the supernatural bird-like masks that represents the creatures in the household of *Bakbakwalanooksiwey.* The masks are striking in the raking firelight: first the Man-eating Raven, then *Galokwudzuwis,* or the Crooked Beak of Heaven, and finally the long-beaked *Hokhokw,* or Cannibal-bird, that crushes men's skulls. The dancers appear one by one, until up to four of the great supernatural birds are around the fire. When they depart, the initiate dances alone: upright, proud, the inspired frenzy vanquished. As the wildness leaves his body, he once again resumes a tame and cultured life. However, the dancer is always a *Hamatsa,* a human transformed in the belly of the great supernatural one. Forever changed, with a new name and a new identity, he is reintegrated into society with an elevated spiritual status.

Wealth and great spirituality are the coinage of power on the Northwest Coast. Myth and ritual help ensure that power is made visible and memorable. The synthesis of power between natural and supernatural realms is thus enacted and made viable for human spirits questing and dreaming through the universe.

ARTS AND CRAFTS

Sophisticated, vital and brilliant, the Northwest Coast visual arts have captivated the imagination and appreciation of foreign visitors for over 200 years. It is this time period Euro-Americans have designated as 'traditional' but which represents merely an epoch in an art tradition that has spanned hundreds, if not thousands of years. Contact with Euro-Americans resulted in a florescence in the art, and it is from about 1749 until the present, that our most impressive museum collections of Northwest Coast art derive. As with most non-Western cultures, the Northwest Coast languages did not have a word for 'art', though by no means did their culture lack esthetic values, principles or appreciation of the practice of the visual arts. Indeed, their culture had specialists in art production – both men and women – who enjoyed long careers and held intertribal reputations for excellence. Almost every aspect of their extensive material culture inventory was or could have been embellished by any number of the decorative arts. Art on the Northwest Coast was a fact of everyday life rather than simply reserved for the elite or in special locations.

The people and cultures of the Northwest Coast occupied the narrow strip of island-dotted land from Yukatat Bay in Alaska to the Columbia River in what is now the state of Washington. Facing the Pacific Ocean to the west and confined to the coastal waters by the towering and most impenetrable coastal range of mountains on the east, the people evolved a distinctive cultural response to their largely maritime environment. The northern groups were the Tlingit of the Alaskan coast, the Tsimshian of the inland coastal waterways of the Nass and Skeena Rivers, the Haida of the Queen Charlotte Islands, and their relatives, the Kaigani Haida of the Prince of Wales Archipelago. The Wakashan or central groups of the coast between the Tsimshian in the North and the Kwakiutl in the south were the Bella Bella (or Northern Wakashan), and the Salishan-speaking Bella Coola. On the north and eastern shores of Vancouver Island and adjoining mainland were the group of tribes known as the Kwakiutl. The west coast of Vancouver Island and the tip of the Olympic Peninsula were occupied by the Nuu-chah-nulth (formerly the Nootka or Westcoast) and their relatives the Makah. The southernmost tribe was the Coast Salish of the Puget Sound and lower mainland.

■ The Practice of Art

If we could take a journey back in time, travel by an elegant wooden canoe to our hosts' home, we would pull up on the pebble beach of the village's protected cove. The dense cedar forest rises dark, huge and formidable behind the row of houses glowing in the silver patina of their weathered cedar facades. Massive gabled houses lining the beaches and monumental crest poles creating a veritable curtain of images in front of the houses further diminish our human dimensions. Experience of the monumental is precisely the theme underlying the production of the material culture of these coastal cultures.[61] Harnessing the invisible forces of society, nature and the supernatural by making them visible was a task particularly relished by Northwest Coast artists. Challenged by the task, these artists translated the idea of monumental not only in the size of their artistic productions, but by the degree of spiritual and material complexity in their arts. The same theme of monumentality may be found in a giant crest pole or in a tiny ivory charm; the conception guiding the artist's eye and hand is larger than a single human life; the art makes visible the contemplation of the invisible.

Who were the artists? As a general observation, women were the weavers of the Coast while men were the carvers and painters. There were exceptions, but generally women wove the garments, baskets and mats to furnish the comfort of daily life and enrich the spectacle of ceremonial life.[62] Men carved primarily in wood, though also in stone, bone and ivory, often combining their three-dimensional art with two-dimensional painted designs. Their arts formed the massive structures found in the material culture as well as the smaller embellished instruments of the hunt, food preparation and ceremony. Not infrequently, the arts involved varying degrees of collaboration as the weaver's talents were combined with those of the carver.

There were distinct, though shared, artistic conventions on the Coast, each with their own principles of composition and aesthetic rules.

Northwest Coast artists' adherence to these rules over large geographic areas through the centuries is impressive – and forms a stunning chapter in world art history. Forging metals and making and firing pottery were virtually unknown in traditional times. Yet, with few and relatively simple tools, Northwest Coast artists employed a myriad of techniques to manipulate mostly wood and wood fibers into an astonishingly large inventory of cultural objects that served all the purposes of life.

Throughout the region, the visual images were almost entirely representations of animals or humans.[63] Though the exact meaning of an image might be restricted to those who know the artist's intent, learning the basic vocabulary of forms gives the viewer access to a visual syntax of tremendous depth. Conventionalized identifying features distinguish one animal from another: the long, slender straight beak of Raven differs from the heavy, sharply down-curved beak of Eagle; Killer-Whale's long, upright dorsal fin marked with a circle contrasts with the smaller, blunt dorsal of Gray Whale; Beaver's image is characterized by long incisor teeth and a cross-hatched tail (for the scales) whereas Grizzly Bear is known by a square snout and large-toothed mouth with prominent canines and a protruding tongue. The system of identification is relatively simple when the artist chooses a simple, naturalistic representation, but becomes more complex when these conventionalized features become hidden in the design or when the design itself is of a lesser known natural or supernatural creature. A sea-monster, for example may have a wolf or bear head, but dorsal fins on its back and flippers or fins on the joints of limbs that end in claws. Subtle variations in the depiction of an anatomical part such as a beak may identify the specific species of bird.[64]

Aesthetic considerations governed the arrangement of these conventional features of the subjects. Artists distorted, exaggerated and rearranged the anatomy of whatever was being portrayed to fit the design field. Artists composed designs through such conventions as x-ray imaging where ribs, backbones, organs and joints are made visible; split-representation where the body image is split to show the frontal and back views or both sides of a figure simultaneously; and visual punning where one ambiguous feature may result in an image being read as two different subjects. Complexity of form was matched by complexity of iconography. Recorded information about what the art meant to owner and carver is surprisingly meager.[65] We cannot always know the full constellation of meanings surrounding a given object; some levels of meaning were personal and specific to a particular time and place. Yet understanding only some of the fundamental forms, techniques and principles of design opens lenses to a richness and complexity in the practice of Northwest art that allows stirring insight into some of those meanings and into the potential for innovation, invention and excellence.

One of the most distinctive and sophisticated design elements known by northern artists was first academically analyzed by the art historian, Bill Holm, in his definitive work on northern two-dimensional design. Holm described the calligraphic-like line found in northern design as the 'formline', a broad line with a single pulse that started and finished with a tapered point. Elements of two-dimensional designs were unified by seemingly continuous formlines. The primary forms of the design were defined first in black and called primary formlines. Secondary formlines, in red, further elaborated the form. The remaining spaces were either unpainted background spaces or tertiary forms that were outlines with thin black or red lines or were sometimes painted blue. Formline design included distinctive elements given visually descriptive names by Holm: ovoids (and their elaboration, salmon-trout heads) to depict eyes and the joints of the body; U-forms (and the variation Split U-forms) to depict ears, flukes and fin shapes; and S-forms (and the variation Split S-forms) to depict ribs and feathers.[66]

Remarkably, this design system, given its economy of elements and conventions, permitted a limitless range of images and interpretive innovations. Though genres of objects – for example, spoons, boxes, dancing robes, frontlet headdresses – evolved specific design codes, individual artists varied their interpretation of the codes. Personal interpretation of the tradition resulted in the stylistic signatures of individual artists that can be identified from preliterate times.[67]

Less well-defined, but no less significant or impressive, are the Nuu-chah-nulth and Makah two-dimensional design systems. Though clearly related to the northern design conventions, there are other design elements unique to the area: curlicues, thin crosses and rows of dots, and discontinuous, though sensuous, thin lines of solid color. Figures tended to be less abstract, more representational and portrayed in dramatic profile with asymmetrical eyelid forms. Coast Salish design was primarily expressed in three dimensions. Arguably, the Coast Salish were influenced by the pervasive northern design, for ovoids and U-forms with conventionalized cuneiform-like gouges in their centers were sometimes employed in low

relief carvings, but their geometric compositions were freer in spatial organization than in the north. Usually, Salish three-dimensional design is
characterized by bold geometric elements, broad flat planes intersecting
one another and generalized, though fluid, limbs and torsos.

Unfortunately, we know much of this art only from the objects that rest
silently in museum and gallery collections; they serve as dramatic memories
of voices, times and places in the not-too-distant past. We connect and
reconnect the objects with the artists, the artists with the cultures, mindful
that our attempts to contextualize and reconstruct usually fall short of a
complete appreciation of that time of monumental achievements in making the social and the supernatural worlds visible. It will be useful to scan
some of these high achievements, these 'objects of bright pride', to glimpse
not only the tremendous power and elegance of their expression, but to
gather perspective on an art that was a way of life.

■ Houses – Containers of the Cosmos

Virtually all of the early Euro-American explorers on the northern Pacific
Coast were astonished and impressed by the huge dwellings of the
Northwest Coast peoples. The massive structures towered against the
forested stands, occupying the thin strips of beach on protected coves and
bays. Planked and gabled, the houses were made of cedar and were large
enough to hold several families. Usually arranged in a single row along the
beach, or two rows if the frontage property was restricted, the rectangular
structures imposed a built reality to the misty coast. Northwest Coast
people lived in these permanent villages almost year-round, sometimes
having a summer village location as well as a winter one.

Red cedar (*Thuja plicata*) was the material favored by Northwest Coast
builders. The huge trees were selected, harvested, prepared and assembled
by skilled craftsmen working under the directions of one or more specialists. In traditional Northwest Coast society, the building of these massive
structures was a complicated and expensive undertaking requiring the com-
missioning of a coordinating architect who supervised the selection, felling
and transportation of large cedar logs to the building site, the splitting of
planks and forming of posts and beams. The owner of the house fed, sheltered and compensated the workers at every stage of construction, from the
assembling of materials to the raising of the posts and beams. Frequently
artists were employed to embellish posts and beams with adzed flutes or
carved crest images of animal spirits. Wealthier house-owners commis-

sioned massive paintings representing clan figures that covered entire house fronts. In postcontact times almost every northern-style house had a huge carved 'totem' pole gracing its facade.

The final expense was the ceremonial occasion or potlatch that marked the completion of the structure with feasting and the naming of the house.[68] Some families took years to build a house, and only the wealthy could begin such a commission after assembling and committing the resources of all the members of their extended family. The labor was intensive, traditionally undertaken with simple tools and without the benefit of tack or pulleys. Using levers, fulcrums, ropes and raw human strength, posts were set into the ground, beams hoisted to their lofty summits and massive planks then attached to the structures. If the labor to build a house was based on brute strength, the resulting architecture was simple yet elegant in thought and form. Northwest Coast houses were not only functionally durable, but they were also ingeniously suited to the environmental, spiritual and social needs of the occupants.

Fundamentally there were two kinds of architectural constructions for the post and beam framed houses of the coast: the northern type with house planking that was integral to the structure and the southern type with planked walls structurally separate from the main framework.[69] The southern type had two variations: the shed-roofed house with rectangular posts, and the Wakashan house with posts supporting two eave beams and one or two larger central ridge beams. Typically found in southern areas including the Coast Salish, Southern Kwakiutl, Nuu-chah-nulth and Bella Coola, both the shed-roofed house and the Wakashan house had walls of wide horizontal planks hung and lashed between pairs of vertical poles placed along the outside of the house's frame posts.

The northern post-and-beam house built by the Tlingit, Haida, Tsimshian and Northern Wakashan people had gabled roofs formed by massive roof beams. In contrast to the southern-type houses, northern houses for the most part had thick vertical planks up to 2ft (60cm) wide whose tapered ends slotted into grooves in the roof beams and ground level sills.[70] The interior of the house was similar in concept to southern houses, with raised platforms for seating and sleeping. At least one house in every village, usually that of the village chief and therefore the largest house, had an excavated interior. Entry into these houses was at ground level with one or two levels of concentric platforms surrounding the subterranean central fire. The chief's family occupied the rear of the house, their quarters often separated from the rest of the house by a large screen of painted planks. Families of lesser rank were to the left and right of the screen, with those of the least rank next to the front door. The roof planks of these houses were often secured with rock-weighted boards and there was a movable opening in the roof to provide optimum ventilation for the central fire. Doors were traditionally at the front of the house, often through a central or portal house post. Other doors at the rear of the house were provided for emergency exits, and a special door was made in the rear of a house to remove the body of a deceased family member after the period of lying in state.

The house remains one of the most impressive of Northwest Coast artifacts, splendid in design and execution of its form, and astonishingly monumental in its concept and function. The wonder of the early travelers to the coast is mirrored by all those who encounter Northwest Coast houses for the first time. The structures were massive, made from massive materials. Strangers, after suffusing their wonderment, ask 'Why?'. Surely a people with such impressive technology for splitting and building shelters could have built smaller, single family dwellings. The answer is cultural rather than technological. From a sociological viewpoint, a Northwest Coast individual was part of an extended family, a lineage. As such, the house sheltered more than one's parents and children; it sheltered the lineage. In contemporary terms, the Northwest Coast house was more of a small apartment building than a nuclear family home. The house was for part of the year a profane place, site of the mundane stuff of everyday life: fish and game hung drying in its smoky rafters; people slept, ate and worked in its roomy shelter; interior platforms provided hidden storage space for clothing, foodstuffs, tools, hunting and ceremonial paraphernalia. Attached porches and semi-attached decks provided warm-weather spaces for gambling, gossiping and otherwise enjoying the company of others.

From a ritual and ceremonial viewpoint, the house was transformed in the dark months of winter into a site of sacred events. Figuratively and literally, the house became the center of the universe as the people gathered to witness the speeches, songs, dances, masked performances and rituals that enacted and validated their ancestral claims to the lineage's supernatural origins, property rights, wealth and traditions. Painted screens and interior houseposts carved with clan images heightened the sense of bringing together and making visible the social and the supernatural. New members of the lineage were thus socialized into the interrelationships of family and the supernatural; strangers and newcomers were educated to the valid claims of the lineage to supernatural ancestry and inherited social prerogatives that formed the exclusive property of the lineage. In this way lineages confirmed their relationship to every other lineage, to the larger clan units and ultimately to the cosmos. The names of some of the larger houses frequently referred to the vaunted position of the lineage's claims: The Monster House, House Split-in-Two-by-the-Sun, Thunder-Rolls-Upon-It, House-Chiefs-Peep-at-from-a-Distance and Mountain House. The names are fitting to the sizes of the houses, but also to the monumentality of their social and symbolic function in Northwest Coast cultural life.

As quickly as Northwest Coast technology and culture changed with exposure to Euro-American culture, innovations to housing also appeared. Grander houses featured European-style doors and windows, gingerbread gables and even picket fences. With missionization and the dramatic decimation of the population through disease in the late-19th and early-20th century, the building of large communal houses eventually gave way to smaller, though often no less grand, two-story frame houses. Some of the villages, such as those of the Haida at Ninstints, Tanu and Skedans, suffered such extreme losses that the villages were abandoned before the houses could ever be built. Posts, beams, and planks have decayed – melted back into the forest that gave them life. In one site, fluted house beams that once supported the roof of the cosmos, lie shrouded in the moss of the forest floor, giving new life to spruce. Skeletal is the wrong word to describe these fallen giants. For the Haida, they are fulfilling their destiny to complete the cycle of being first part of the natural world, then the cultural world, before returning – transformed and part of our memory – to nature.

■ Crest Poles – Heraldic Monuments in Cedar

The monumentality of the great planked houses of the Northwest Coast was complemented by the massive carved sculptures commonly but improperly called 'totem poles'.[71] The term 'crest poles' reflects what even the earliest Euro-American seamen knew: the images on the poles were never worshiped or part of religious ceremonies, but were a visual record of the owner's hereditary ancestors, a heraldic device that proclaimed for all to see the social positioning and antiquity of the family lineage.[72] Crest poles came in many forms and had various functions; generically, however, a pole was made from a large vertical cedar shaft and covered with interlocking images of supernatural clan ancestors.

There are various types of crest poles. The most frequently depicted is the free-standing singular crest pole. Depending on its function, the pole depicted the crests of a living family or commemorated the memory of a recently deceased person of high rank. Other memorial poles among the northern groups were sometimes simply tall cedar shafts, topped by a single massive crest animal, such as Thunderbird, Raven, Bear or Eagle. Crest poles were also features of house architecture. Some were attached directly to the front of a house. When these house frontal poles had an entrance carved in the lower portion of the pole – usually through the belly or mouth of the lowest creature – the pole was a house portal or entrance pole. Usually these kinds of entrances were considered highly symbolic as orifices of the house and were thus used only on ceremonial occasions. Separate doors were placed beside the pole for every day use. Corner posts and interior house posts were also appropriate spaces for crest carvings. Welcoming figures, such as those found among the Kwakiutl, were placed on the beach to welcome guests. These large human or animal forms were carved from a single log and had attached extended arms. Similar monumental sculptures have been recorded among the Haida as ridicule or shaming poles, where the purpose was not to welcome guests, but to humiliate them. Mortuary poles were most common among the Haida. The single mortuary pole had a cavity carved in the large end of the pole to receive a box containing the remains of the deceased. The tapered end of the pole was placed in the ground and a plank placed across the top of the pole to cover the opening. Double mortuary poles consisted of two poles with a platform between them to hold several burial boxes. As with the single pole, the covering plank was often carved in high relief and painted with the owner's crests.

Wealth was the key to demonstrating great social and supernatural power on the coast, and it was only the wealthy person who could afford the monumental sculptures adorning and surrounding the great houses. Crest poles were commissioned from recognized artists. Their reputations were well-known on the coast, and some traveled not only to other villages to fulfill commissions, but inter-tribally as well. As with house-building, every aspect of making a crest pole, from selection, felling and transportation of the log to the carving and raising of the pole, was paid for by the owner.[73] Compensation for this portion of the task was considerable.

Carving a crest pole was a lengthy process.[74] The prone log was stripped of bark and flattened on its back.[75] Large elbow adzes and chisels roughed out the preliminary shapes, and successively finer adzes and knives were used to refine the images. The artist used chisels to fashion mortise and tenon joints to attach appendages to the cylinder of emerging figures. Straight and curved knives completed the detail work: incised lines around the eyebrows and lids, cross-hatching on beaver tails and undercuts for claws and wings. Small adzes gave some texture to large expanses; carvers preferred the precise, rhythmic, parallel adzing marks over smooth 'unfinished' wood.[76] From early accounts, paint was used sparingly, if at all. Natural black, red, white and blue-green pigments were used to accent eyes, eye sockets, eyebrows, lips, tongues and nostrils. After glossy commercial marine paints became available, southern artists added other colors to their palettes – greens, blues, yellows and whites – and painted most of the surfaces of their poles with gusto.[77]

When the pole was finished, the owner hosted a substantial potlatch. Invited guests assembled to admire the pole, to witness and validate the owner's claims to the crests depicted in the carvings and the pole was carried to the site where it was to be erected by scores of men.[78] Drumbeats matched heartbeats as the pole inched up, dancing in the tension of ropes being pulled over the scaffolding and holding the unwieldly and precious column in balance. From a distance, the artist and his apprentices watched, their necks and waists circled with twisted cedar bark rings to which their carving tools have been attached. When the pole was up, the carvers danced at its base while those who hoisted on the ropes rested and celebrated the satisfaction of raising the pole and the triumph of its new owners.[79]

The florescence of crest-pole carving probably lasted less than a century, for eventually the wealth diminished and the death rate increased. By 1920 the art had all but vanished, though almost every major museum in the Western world boasted a huge 'totem pole' in their grand entry halls. Crest poles are again being made, some for important art commissions, others to serve the age-old practices of commemorating one's claims to ancient heraldic crests and prerogatives. From lofty heights, Eagles and Ravens, Killer-Whales and Wolves, Thunderbirds and Grizzly Bears, claim their places against the open skies and are cherished in the hearts of the people as emblems of a living culture.

■ Canoes – Monuments of the Seas

More than the principal means of transportation, the canoe was yet another feature of monumentality on the coast. Embellished with carving of prows and painted bows and sterns, the canoe was more than a functional object. A floating artistic statement of rare grace and brilliant design, it is little wonder that the canoe was one of the principal measurements, along with the house and the crest pole, of a family's material wealth. The finished canoes ranged in size from large ocean-going vessels 50 to 70ft (up to 21m) in length with beams of 6 to 10ft (up to 3m). Family canoes were smaller, in the 18 to 35ft (up to 10m) range and holding 15 to 20 people, while smaller canoes were constructed to be handled easily by as few as two people. From the Kwakiutl north, canoes were broad in the beam with both bow and stern ends swept upwards; a vertical fin under the bow cut the waves. Nuu-chah-nulth, Makah and Quilleute hunting and fishing canoes were generally flatter on the bottom, with low-rising vertical sterns and with concave prows which rose dramatically into a distinctive 'snout' that abstractly resembled the head of a wolf.[80] Both of these styles of canoes had a groove in the prow to hold masts or harpoons.[81]

Carved from single massive cedar trees, the canoe required much the same expertise and expense of houses and crest poles.[82] Deep in the forest, master carvers would select sound trees with few knots, and then rough out the top and narrow the ends of the canoe. With hull, bow and stern adzed into perfect symmetry, the unfinished canoe was left over the winter to season. The following spring the canoe was righted and the interior hollowed with chisels and adzes or, on some parts of the coast, excavated using controlled burning with rocks heated red-hot in a fire.

Precision was the hallmark of the master canoe-builder. Symmetry of the exterior was matched by the even thickness of the hull.[83] The final step in making large vessels was to fill the canoe with water, drop red-hot stones into it to boil the water, and gently spread the softened wood at the gunwales. On larger canoes, prow and stern extensions were carved then pegged or sewn into place. The final embellishment of a canoe was done by a master artist who painted crest designs on the vessel. Some canoes were painted red or white in the interior; some had exteriors painted black. Others were fitted with elaborately carved crested figures that were lashed to both sides of the bow and/or stern.

Canoes were highly valued possessions, carefully protected from the elements so they would not split, lovingly and effectively patched when damaged, and handled cautiously so that they would last a decade or more. As with houses, canoes were often given hereditary names. At a potlatch, a canoe was an extravagant gift and similarly the destruction of a canoe during a potlatch was an ostentatious display of conspicuous consumption that enhanced the owner's status. The value and grace of canoes inspired songs, and their elegance inspired myth images for the mind's eye of great wealth and power.

■ Bowls, Boxes and Baskets

Bowls of cedar, yew, alder, maple and other woods were sculpted into various geometric and anthropomorphic shapes using many of the same carving tools that were used to make canoes and crest poles. Wooden bowls could range in size from small personal feast dishes to enormous bowls used for potlatches that required several people to carry into the feast house. Animal-shaped bowls, bowls that imitated birch-bark containers, bowls with supernatural human and monster figures as well as bowls with geometric contours reminiscent of canoe shapes, were all part of the repertoire of Northwest Coast artists. Sometimes the rims of bowls were inlaid with opercula[84], sea-otter teeth or small pieces of abalone shell. Some wooden bowls were painted with crest designs, but most were not. Given the propensity of the wood to soak up the fish and sea mammal oils of foods served in the bowls, little more embellishment of the carved surfaces was needed. The glossy patina of well-used, oft-handled vessels was rich and mellow; the sensitive fit of the bowls' surfaces to the embrace of human palms was timeless.[85]

So different from the bowls that were carved from single pieces of wood, the bent box or bowl with its kerfed corners and inlaid base was perhaps one of the most distinctive aspects of the Northwest Coast people's culture and technology. Using bent-wood construction, men created containers from cedar planks for everything a person would use from cradle to coffin. The cedar bent-box technology was used for obvious constructions such as storage and furniture and less obvious functions such as drumming and cooking. Bent bowls were made in the same manner as boxes but begun with a plank that was pre-shaped with elegantly undulating rims and bulging contours with hollowed interiors. Boxes and chests were sometimes fitted with lids inlaid with opercula while bowls often had complex overhanging rims. Finishing touches to kerfed containers could include painted formline designs (flat or deeply incised), nearly three-dimensional carving in high relief and/or abalone shell inlay.

Sometimes the weight and rigidity of a box was more than necessary for containing the stuff of life. Baskets were woven by women to function in almost all the same ways a box was used.[86] Lighter than wooden boxes, baskets were no less durable. Some baskets were designed to be flexible and even collapsible when not in use. Some baskets were of a generalized form, others were created for specific tasks; elegance of form frequently matched the ingenuity of function. There were baskets for holding babies, for collecting shellfish, for cooking, storing and serving food stuffs,[87] for carrying the tools and implements of the hunt or the harvest, for holding treasures or for simply displaying the weaver's virtuosity. After contact with Euro-Americans and responding to a new market for their woven arts, women created basketry items that mimicked objects from the foreign culture: suitcases, dollies, lamp shades, bottles and lidded jars, plates and platters, and even tea cups and saucers.[88] Interestingly, though they were never intended for the indigenous use, these 'tourist' baskets nonetheless demonstrated some of the finest examples of the basket-makers' art. Within Northwest Coast culture, well-made basketry items were valued trade items and prestigious potlatch gifts; many baskets on the coast were found far from their places of origin.

Besides the ubiquitous cedar bark, withe and root, the Northwest Coast women harvested and used many natural materials for making their fine baskets. While no one fiber was specific to a given area of the coast, some groups had preferences. Spruce root was a favorite of northern weavers, especially the Tlingit and Haida. Nuu-chah-nulth women produced a very different kind of basketry from the many species of sedge grasses.[89] Cedar bark was an abundant and favorite construction material of the Coast Salish. Various grasses and reeds were employed by the weavers as foundation materials and for making the woven surface decoration on the baskets known as 'imbricating' where tucks of light grasses and shiny bark strips were caught under the stitches on the basket's outer surface. Another decorative technique was known as 'false embroidery' where bleached or dyed fibers were wrapped around the wefts at every stitch to form bands of geometric designs.[90]

The weavers used many techniques for basket making: coiling, plaiting, two- and three-strand twining, skip-stitch twining, twilled two-strand twining, warp twining, diagonal warp twining, and wrapped crossed warp, and flat weaving. While talented fingers did most of the work in creating the fine, regular surfaces of the baskets, the weaver's tool kit might also include a sharpened bone awl for piercing coiling strips, hard wood implements to press against smooth stones for flattening and smoothing the surface of twined strands, and bark splitting tools.[91]

Basketry designs were achieved with tremendous skill and dexterity. The catalogue of named designs seemed endless. Some representational designs included recognizable animal and human forms: wolf, merganser, man, dragonfly, butterfly. The Nuu-chah-nulth weavers frequently depicted whaling scenes showing a harpooner standing in a canoe, his line firmly attached to a gray whale. Other design terms are more enigmatic and seem to have a closer connection with the meanings given by the individual weaver rather than springing from a large, universal iconographic system. The names of the designs give some insight into the complex, precise woven arts that came from these consummate artists. The elegance of their artworks is matched by the poetry of the word images describing the design elements: Crow's shells, leaves of the fireweed, blanket border fancy picture, fern, porpoise, between-the-dice, double war club, mouth-rack of the woodworm, half the head of a salmonberry and fish flesh.[92]

■ Woven Clothing

If boxes and baskets were containers of life, then blankets were the containers of people. Northwest Coast women wove botanical and animal fibers on upright looms to create blankets, tunics and robes that graced the human form. Labor intensive from the gathering and processing of raw materials to the manufacturing process, weaving was a specialist art that took years to master and perfect.

Everyday clothing appropriate to the raincoast had to be water-repellent, comfortable to work in and warm. The ingenious response of all the Northwest Coast people was to turn again to the cedar tree.[93] Shredded bundles of yellow cedar were hung on an upright loom and the weaver twined them at intervals with wefts of cedar bark, nettle or wool string. Soft yet durable clothing was produced; its multi-layers were worked with oil to shed the water easily and wet surfaces could be dried quickly.[94] A versatile garment, the cedar bark robe could be fastened as a cape or skirt. Often adorned with fur or feathers, some had designs worked in dyed fibers and a few had edgings worked in mountain goat wool. Some robes were painted with elaborate crest images and were probably for ceremonial use by high-ranking individuals.[95]

On the northern Coast, Tlingit, Tsimshian and Haida women created ceremonial robes known as Chilkat blankets for high-ranking people.[96] Myth records the Chilkat blanket as originating with the Tsimshian,[97]

346

though it was developed by the Chilkat tribe of the Tlingit.[98] It took a master weaver a full year to complete the robe. Woven on an upright loom, on a warp of spun cedar bark and mountain goat wool with a weft of pure white, black, yellow and blue-green dyed mountain-goat wool, the five-sided blankets resembled the shape of an upside down house front.[99] Part of the sumptuous chiefly costume of frontlet headdress with its six foot train of ermine, raven rattle and dance apron, the Chilkat blanket had a deep double fringe that flared around the dancer's body.[100] As Bill Holm said of the blankets: 'No more royal robe ever draped a king. . . .'[101]

■ Masks and Ceremonial Paraphernalia

Without a doubt masks, headdresses and their associated ceremonial para-phernalia were and are one of the most distinctive cultural features of the Northwest Coast. The earliest explorers were struck by the elaboration and variety of the masking complex found all along the coast from the Salish in the south to the Tlingit in the north. Cognizant with every aspect of the art of mask-making and masked performance, the artists of the Northwest Coast explored the concept of making transformation visible and credible through the construction of elaborate hinged, movable and mutable masks. Masks that metamorphosed, grew, shrank, spoke, danced in thin air and were even destroyed and resurrected, were due to the skills of consummate master carvers. Appropriate to the ritual at hand, masks were accompanied by intricately carved rattles, puppets, speakers' staffs, headdresses, drums, whistles and other ceremonial paraphernalia to complete their presenta-tion. Consummate in the art of suspending disbelief, the artists restored and reinforced belief in the social, natural and supernatural.

The panoply of mask types was massive for each group along the Northwest Coast, except for the Nuu-chah-nulth and the Coast Salish. Cataloging that impressive array would be a monumental task. For every crest, for every lineage, for every ancestor, for every personal hereditary property or heraldic event, for each member of the culture, there could be, and probably was, at least one if not several artistic interpretations com-missioned by that lineage. The inventory was staggering if not infinite, bound only by our imagination – and that much can be concluded from museum collections alone. Museum collections, made mostly from the decades surrounding the turn of the century, contain mere samplings of what must have existed.[102]

From the Tlingit, powerful shaman's masks seem to freeze the human face in a moment of the healing trance.[103] The Haida were renowned for a kind of mask Euro-Americans have called the 'portrait' mask that depicted in wood with sensuous accuracy the skin stretched or wrinkled over the bones of the skull.[104] The *naxno'x* ceremony required masks of the Tsimshian carvers known as the *Git'sontk* or 'the People secluded' who created all the paraphernalia for the most sacred part of their potlatches.[105] From their hands, humanoid masks with movable eyes and mouths were exceptional and in the dim light of the fire, terrifying realistic. The Northern Wakashan and Bella Coola artists excelled in the creation of bold bird masks with sloped foreheads, large overhanging brows and piercing eyes: a stunning blend of stylized abstraction and naturalism.

The Kwakiutl's propensity for the theatrical and for flamboyance has been characterized by Holm as fundamental to their 'distinct and aggressive' culture.[106] The masks created for the *Hamatsa,* or Cannibal Society dances, fit the drama and prestige of portraying human encounters with the monumental supernatural birds at the edge of the universe.[107] The narrow elongated beaks of the *Hokhokw* were said to crush men's skulls; the beaks of some of these masks ranged in length from a modest two or three feet (60–90m) to up to ten (3m). These masks required the aid of a body harness and rigging, concealed by heavy fringes of shredded cedar bark, for the skillful dancer to carry the weight of the mask while snapping the movable mandibles of the supernatural birds. The neighboring Nuu-chah-nulth used a unique blend of smooth, spare sculptural form and decisive, abstract painted forms to create the subtle images of wolves with large nostrils, raptorial-beaked thunderbirds, and slender-nosed lightning snakes for the *Klookwana* ceremony.[108] The Coast Salish had but one mask, the *Sxwayxwey* that appeared always with three others of its kind. Huge and spectacular, the *Sxwayxwey* had large peg eyes that projected from the facial plane, with no lower mandible and a vertical flange below the nose.[109]

Frontlets were not masks. They were the individualized, exquisitely carved wooden portion attached to the front of headdress worn by high-ranking Tlingit, Tsimshian and Haida chiefs.[110] The headdress was almost always worn with the other prestigious items fitting the owner's high rank: a Chilkat blanket, dancing aprons and leggings, and the enigmatic, complex raven rattle. This impressive raiment, reportedly used in 'welcoming dances', representing the synthesis of the supernatural and social power of the chief. It was, in effect, the crown jewels and a bishop's miter all in one. In the ritual occasion for displaying the headdress, the chief acted as head of state and like a shaman: the roles were merging into a spectacular display of social and spiritual power.[111]

Increasingly, non-Native and Native people have discovered and rediscovered a fascination for these traditional arts and it is a fascination built not only on an appreciation of form. The images are timeless. They speak through the culture and across cultures, and hold our imagination. As anthropologist Wilson Duff observed, Northwest Coast art has this power because '[These] images seem to speak to the eye, but they are really addressed to the mind. They are ways of thinking, in the guise of ways of seeing. The eye can sometimes be satisfied with form alone, but the mind can only be satisfied with meaning, which can be contemplated, more consciously or less, after the eye is closed . . . The meaning is in the relationships being expressed . . . Images hold ideas apart so that they can be seen together.'[112]

■ The Tradition Continues

Living traditions change and develop and the visual art tradition of the Northwest Coast is no exception. The Euro-American trade brought new materials, new technologies and new wealth. The result was nothing short of a cultural revolution as social, economic, linguistic, religious, material and artistic ideas felt the impact of the foreigners. There were subtle changes in the art resulting in the decline of some forms and the rise of others.

The Northwest Coast people had skillfully hammered copper nuggets into items of personal adornment in precontact times, and after contact with Euro-Americans, they purchased commercial copper wire to make some of the same items: bracelets, anklets, earrings, nose-ornaments and beads. Engraving techniques were well-known to the early Haida and Tlingit artists, and when gold and silver coin was introduced to the Northwest Coast, these techniques were used on the new materials to create expertly crafted silver bracelets and other jewelry.[113] With a revival in the 1950s, the tradition continues to the present, with bold, finely carved formline designs sweeping across mirror-bright surfaces.

Unique to the Haida, a new art form emerged in the early-19th century: the carving of a slate-like, soft stone, argillite. In the early years of contact, argillite was much sought after by Euro-American seamen and commanded high prices, only to be scorned in later years as an art of acculturation. As Holm noted, 'In fact, some of the great masterpieces of Haida art as well as some of the most trite souvenirs' were produced by canny Haida artists who created and developed an exclusive market for this rare stone.[114] Carved with woodworking tools, argillite takes on a high luster. The earliest carvings were 'pipes' (though most could not be smoked) with clusters of Haida images and/or Euro-American ship motifs. Later new forms emerged as images of the people and materials from foreign visitors were faithfully, if not mockingly, carved in free-standing sculpture. A third period in the art, which occurred after 1865 when the Haida population was decimated by disease in less than a generation, marked a dramatic return to bold sculptural images of Haida life and mythology. The art failed to develop for a while, then was revived in the 1960s by Haida artists reestablishing connections to the past. Today, argillite sculpture is a flourishing art form, still created primarily for sale to non-Natives and still making dynamic artistic statements about all that it means to be Haida.

After contact, commercial blankets replaced cedar-bark clothing and the art all but disappeared. While plain commercial blankets were worn over Euro-American clothing, a new style of ceremonial blanket was developed with goods introduced shortly after the time of contact.[115] The spectacular robe was known as a 'button blanket' and it took the place of painted cedar bark, hide or sail canvas robes, replacing their use all over the coast by the turn of the century. Adapted to an older concept of a dancing robe with elaborate borders and a central crest figure rendered with an outline of abalone shell, the button blanket was constructed of dark blue or black Hudson's Bay Company blankets and a broad border of red melton cloth. Red cloth was used to create an appliqued crest image in the center of the blanket. Mother-of-pearl buttons were sewn along the edge of the red border and along the outlines of the appliqued formline design; sometimes buttons alone were used to render the crest figure. Great care was given to selecting buttons of regular size, color and shape. These elegant ceremonial robes, worn with the design at the back, flashed with the brilliance of a matador's 'coat of lights' in the firelight of the winter house.[116]

The renaissance of Northwest Coast art is wonderfully exemplified in the thriving serigraph studios in the Pacific Northwest.[117] This is an example of a new art form – the silk-screen print – being adapted to the tradition of two-dimensional formline design. Begun in the latter half of this century, this new tradition draws directly on earlier forms. With a vast visual library of published images, Northwest Coast serigraph artists have been able to draw inspiration from their prolific ancestors to create a body of work that reflects a continuity between past motifs and styles, and exciting innovations of contemporary minds.[118]

Of course all the other traditions of carving and now even weaving are alive and well – thanks to their resurrection by dedicated and innovative Northwest Coast artists and art schools such as the school of art at 'Ksan, Hazelton. In the dedication to their first art catalog, the artists have written:

'Walk on, walk on, walk on, on the breath of our grandfathers. These words follow the *wsinaax,* the songs we sing beside our dead. The words proclaim our strong sense of continuity, our belief in the constant reincarnation of thought, deed, and man; our knowledge of the presence of yesterday in today, of today in tomorrow.'[119]

REFERENCES

THE NORTHWEST COAST

1 For more discussion of this point, see Holm, 1983: 15-16. For more detailed information on Native methods of harvesting resources in their environment, see Stewart, 1973, 1977, 1984.
2 Duff, 1964: 38-9.
3 Jackson: 62-9.
4 For more discussion see Stewart, 1984.
5 Lobb: 21.
6 For more discussion of archaeology of the Northwest Coast, see Carlson ed., 1976; MacDonald and Inglis, 1976; Fladmark, 1986.
7 For a succinct discussion of social organization on the Northwest Coast, see Macnair *et al.,* 1984: 15-24; Bancroft-Hunt and Forman, 1979: 25-49. The discussion that follows is based on these sources.
8 Bancroft-Hunt, 1979: 37.
9 For more discussion of Tlingit social organization, see Jonaitis, 1986: 34-9; Holmberg, 1985: 10-11; de Laguna, 1972: 212-13.
10 Macnair *et al.,* 1984: 21.
11 Macnair *et al.,* 1984: 22.
12 Macnair *et al.,* 1984: 22.
13 For a succinct discussion of ceremonialism on the Northwest Coast, see Halpin, 1981: 6-15.
14 Brown, in Corey ed., 1987: 157-75.
15 Duff, 1975.
16 This style was analyzed in depth by Bill Holm in Holm, 1965. It was here that he defined the terminology 'Northern Formline'. A popularization of his technical discussion is provided in Stewart, 1979.
17 A clear and succinct discussion of these styles appears in Macnair *et al.,* 1984: 25-42.
18 A succinct description of the various cultural styles is found in Macnair *et al.,* 1984: 43-62.
19 These hats were discussed in Vaughan and Holm, 1982: 32-3.

20 For more detailed discussion of Salish weaving, see Gustafson, 1980.

21 For more discussion of Chilkat blankets, see Samuel, 1982.

22 Halpin, 1981: 16-23.

23 Halpin, 1981: 7-12; Holm, 1987: 84, 100.

24 Holm, 1987: 100; Macnair *et al.*, 1984: 50-51, 96; Holm, 1983: 86-7. The discussion of the Tseyka is based on these works.

25 Holm, 1987: 84.

26 Holm, 1987: 48-9.

27 Macnair *et al.*, 1984: 52-3, 62.

28 A classic example is the Haida wood bowl illustrated and described in Macnair *et al.*, 1984: 46-7, 50. The bowl is in the collections of the Royal British Columbia Museum, Victoria, B.C.

29 For more discussion of the interactions between Northwest Coast Indians and European explorers and maritime fur traders, see Gunther, 1972; Pethick, 1973; Cook, 1973.

30 For more discussion of the maritime fur trade, see Duff, 1964: 53-60; Fisher, 1977; Vaughan and Holm, 1983; Wyatt, 1984.

31 For a comprehensive discussion of government policies toward Native lands in British Columbia, see Tennant, 1990. Policies are also discussed in Duff, 1964: 60-74; Fisher, 1977.

32 For more more discussion of missionaries, see Duff, 1964: 87-101; LaViolette, 1973; Fisher, 1977: 119-45; and Fisher in Veillette and White, 1977: 1-11.

33 For more discussion of Native involvement in wage-labor industries, see Knight, 1978; and Wyatt in *Pacific Northwest Quarterly* 78 (1-2): 43-9.

34 For discussion of opposition to the potlatch, see LaViolette, 1973; Sewid-Smith, 1979; Hou, undated; Halliday, 1935. A book on the potlatch prohibition, written by Cole and Chaikin, is soon to be published by the University of Washington Press.

35 Hinckley, 1982: 249-53.

36 Hinckley, 1982: pp.251-3.

37 Duff, 1964: 40-44.

38 For a discussion of arrests made following a potlatch in 1921, see Sewid-Smith, 1979.

39 For more discussion of collecting, see Cole, 1985.

40 Holm, 1965: vii.

41 Spiritual thought in the region might be viewed as a quest to understand 'power' – the power that drives the universe and human existence within it. In the stories, songs and rituals there are continual references to the order and chaos of power, the acquisition and loss of power, the taming or control of power, and the alignment of protective or guardian power with human lives. Thus their lives were predicated on the natural cycles of physical and spiritual existence, and in Northwest Coast thought, reincarnation and transformation were the means by which human, natural and supernatural beings spiraled through cycles of life, death and renewal.

42 Boas, 1891:14 and 1898:29–30; Kennedy and Bouchard, 1977:4.

43 de Laguna, 1972:816; Swanton, 1905 (b):108–110 and 1970:454.

44 Kennedy and Bouchard, 1977:4.

45 Swanton, 1905 (a):74.

46 Boas, 1966:42.

47 Boast, 1970:584

48 Barnett, 1955:296

49 Swanton, 1970:454

50 Stewart, 1979:65

51 The central roof beam of a Kwakiutl house, for example, was said to represent the Milky Way.

52 The *Gonaquadet* appears to some people as a huge copper house, to others as a great painted house front rising out of the ocean swells, a great bear with sea-lion fins, a giant sea-wolf who carries

whales in his curly tail and between his enormous ears, or as a monster several miles in length with many children running along his back. Swanton, 1908:460 and 612–623; Waterman, 1923:450; Sheehan McLaren, 1977:197–229.

53 The potlatch is the major ceremonial on the coast and at it the chief follows *Gonaquadet*'s example and distributes his wealth to all who attend.

54 *Sisiutl*'s image is prolific in art, song and legend. It may be found not only in Earthly realms but in the sky world and the under world. In one region of the cosmos a *Sisiutl* mask is worn by the Sun; in the opposite, farthest region a *Sisiutl* design is found on a settee in the house of ghosts. Boas, 1935 (b):147–148.

55 For the Tlingit, placing tobacco, iron or lead into the mouth counteracted the spirit's influences.

56 Copper Woman and Woman-at-the-Head-of-the-Rivers among the Haida parallel the wealth-giving aspects of *Tsonoqua*, while Frog Woman and Volcano Woman among the Tsimshian share her attributes of great and vengeful power.

57 Swanton, 1905 (a):13

58 Boas, 1935 (b):156

59 Boas, 1930:193

60 Boas, 1966:155

61 Ryan and Sheehan, 1988.

62 Blackman (1982) records that Florence Davidson painted canoes carved by her husband Robert.

63 Sometimes plant, insect, celestial phenomena, tides and even the wind were represented; frequently they were given personified forms, though pure formline design elements could be used to portray their natural forms.

64 Frank Boas was one of the first ethnographers to publish the vocabulary of visual forms enabling Euro-Americans to 'read', at a pre-iconographic level, the fundamental images in Northwest Coast art, 1951:183-298. For a contemporary version of his interpretations see Stewart, 1979.

65 Fortunately, there were a few such as Marius Barbeau who made a special effort to identify artists not only by name, but by their works. Barbeau, 1929 and 1957.

66 Three-dimensional design of the north is strongly two-dimensional in concept: in some works, essentially flat design was wrapped around a form and carved in high relief. Some objects were more sculptural in concept, though still decorated with formline designs. Southern Kwakiutl and Bella Coola artists used a somewhat more flamboyant version of the northern formline design system. Holm, 1965, has the most in-depth analysis.

67 Again, Holm and his students have been at the forefront in the identification of individual Northwest artists through their stylistic signatures. Holm, 1983.

68 Some Haida named the individual beams and posts as well; in some instances a house could have more than one name.

69 / For house types see Stewart, 1984:60-75

70 Sometimes the Tsimshian houses used the slotted plank technology to create horizontal house planking between vertical, squared timber posts.

71 The antiquity of crest poles has long been debated. Scholars do know that the early European visitors to the coast recorded the presence of large house frontal poles and massive free standing carved poles, though their mention is sporadic. It is likely that with increased contact, and access to technology and wealth, there was a flourishing of crest-pole carving. Barbeau, 1929 and 1990; Inverarity, 1950; Keithahn, 1963; Halpin, 1981; Macdonald, 1983.

72 The concept of *totemism* acknowledges a special relationship between humans and animals marked by an avoidance of the animal for food or even for interactions. Totemism implies animal worship by humans. This cultural practice was not found on the Northwest Coast.

73 Physically the undertaking was complex and required the services of many experienced men to harvest a 60-80ft (18-24m) red cedar. The trees most suitable for poles (as well as houses and

canoes) were deep in the forest, straight and free from knots. Stewart, 1990.

74 Selection of the artist alone was a complicated matter. Initially a family member (usually from another lineage) might be given the hereditary honor of carving the pole though his involvement was nominal and in fact the actual carving was carried out by a professional artist. Maquettes, or miniatures of the pole, were sometimes carved and submitted to the patron for approval. Given artistic license in interpreting the crests, the artist nonetheless followed the conventions of three-dimensional representation and formline design.

75 Particularly if the sculpture was to be a house frontal or portal pole, the log's heartwood was excavated from the back of the pole, leaving it 'C'-shaped in the cross-section. This made it possible to use very large logs for poles, as they were considerably lighter without the heartwood and, moreover, were less likely to rot, split or check.

76 House planks were adzed in a similar manner, the builders claiming that the long parallel rows of adze marks gave a 'finished' appearance.

77 The northern artists, maintaining a traditional restraint, were far less flamboyant than their southern colleagues who sometimes painted rather than carved some of the crest details.

78 The method of raising a pole has not changed over the centuries – even contemporary poles are raised in the age-old manner. The heel of the pole was placed into the hole and ropes tied to the upper portion were strung over a crossbar supported by sturdy scaffolding. Under the direction of an experienced person counting time with a drum, the pole was slowly raised by dozens of people hauling and pulling.

79 Few poles ever fell, but if they did, they were left where they lay, for to raise the pole again would require the same level of potlatching it would take to raise a new pole. Economics and practical wisdom opted for the new pole.

80 Smaller canoes were constructed using the same methods as the larger ones, but were not steamed and usually lacked prow and stern additions.

81 Holm notes that there is considerable debate on whether or not Northwest Coast mariners 'sailed' before Euro-American contact. He believes the debate is a matter of semantics. Holm, 1987:98

82 Stewart, 1984:52-60; Duff, 1976; Arima, 1975.

83 Small holes were drilled in the roughed-out hull and filled with measured pegs of darkened wood or lighter yellow cedar. The carver then removed wood from the inside of the hull to the uniform depth of the pegs, creating an even thickness.

84 An operculum is the small white shell 'trap door' on the opening of the red turban snail.

85 Sturtevant, 1974.

86 Gender bias in traditional ethnographies has perhaps robbed women of full credit for this ingenious and elegant art which was as prevalent as men's woodworking arts and just as highly prized by their society.

87 Cooking baskets were woven with such tight construction methods that they could be used for stewing and steaming in much the same way as bent-wood boxes.

88 Holm, 1987:222

89 Stewart, 1984:128

90 Cherry bark, horsetail-fern roots, cattail leaves, leaves of beargrass, reed canary grass and swamp grass, to name a few, were employed in the construction and embellishment of baskets.

91 All of these techniques and materials are discussed with photographs in Lobb, 1978.

92 Emmons, 1903; Kaplan, 1986; Holm, 1987.

93 In the spring, after the offering of appropriate prayers, long strips of bark were taken from tall, living trees. (Taking the strips did not kill the tree.) The inner bark was separated from the outer and beaten to soften and separate layers.

94 Early mariners reported that the people wore two pieces of bark clothing, loose blankets or capes about the shoulders covering a blanket or skirt belted on the lower body.

95 A splendid painted cedar-bark robe is in the British Museum. Likely Nuu-chah-nulth, it was collected by Capt. Cook in 1780. (See King, 1979.)

96 Chilkat weaving was also used to produce tailored sleeved or sleeveless tunics, dance aprons, leggings and shamans' headgear.

97 See Dawson, 1880:120; 127-128. Samuel's monumental work *The Chilkat Dancing Blanket* remains the authority on the history and construction techniques. Samuel 1982.

98 Holm notes that 'Classic Chilkat blankets date only to the beginning of the 19th century. Their predecessors were geometrically patterned tined robes of which only a handful have survived.' Holm, 1987:182; Samuel, 1987.

99 'The blanket is shaped like a house worn upside down. Metaphorically, the house-shaped blanket which engulfs the dancer is *GonaquAde'ts* under-world house.' Sheehan, 1977:226-227.

100 In Tsimshian, all the words connected with this dancer have the same root word, *halait*, which roughly translates as 'dancer', 'shaman' 'power' and 'sacred'; the dancer is *Wihalait*, the blanket, *Gweshalait*; the frontlet headdress, *amhalait*; and the Raven rattle as *Hasem semhalait*. All are stored in a Chief's box or '*anda amhalait*. Halpin, 1973:213

101 Holm, 1984:182

102 Fane, et al, 1991; Holm, 1987; Gunther, 1966; Kaplan, 1986; Dempsey, 1991; Jonaitas, 1988.

103 Jonaitas, 1986.

104 Emmons, 1914, was one of the first to discuss 'portraiture' on the coast, though the Euro-American concept of portraiture may not have the same connotation. See also the discussion of portrait 'masks' by Haida artist Charles Gwaytihl in Macnair, et al. 1984:70-71; and King, 1979.

105 Halpin, 1973:75

106 Holm, 1984:89

107 A photographed account of a 20th century Hamatsa ceremony may be seen in Macnair, 1984.

108 For descriptions of the Kwakiutl masks see Hawthorn, 1967 and 1979; and Holm 1972.

109 The nose of the *Sxwayxwey* was either a head of a bird or it merely had skeletal nasal passages; two birds with elongated necks rose over the forehead of the *Sxwayxwey*. A wide ruff circled the mask and long reeds with tips of downy feathers bobbed from the perimeter. The four dancers, on a healing mission, carried hooped rattles hung with huge Pacific sea scallop shells. Salish art is described in Kew, 1980, and Suttles, 1982, describes the masks of the Halkomelem (Coast Salish) *Sxwayxwey*.

110 In the early-19th century, the hereditary right to this headdress was passed by marriage to a Kwakiutl family, the Hunts, where it is worn to this day. Later, it was also obtained by some Northern Wakashan and Bella Coola tribes.

111 Sheehan, 1977.

112 Duff, 1975:12

113 Euro-American motifs such as floral patterns and the American eagle were used along with traditional formline designs prior to 1900. Harris, 1983: 132-136.

114 Holm, 1983:106

115 Holm, 1984:186.

116 Jensen 1986. Innovating on appliquéd blankets, Haida artist Dorothy Grant has created contemporary fashions. Blackman, 1992.

117 Hall, et al 1981.

118 Blackman & Hall, 1982:30-39

119 Guédon and MacDonald, 1972.

THE SUBARCTIC

This vast area spans the whole continent of North America from the Labrador peninsula in the east (including Newfoundland) and dipping to the south of Hudson Bay then west to Alaska. It encompasses some two million square miles (3,219,000sq km) inhabited by perhaps no more than 60,000 Athapaskan or Algonquian-speaking people.

Although the climatic features in the Subarctic tend to be uniform over large areas, the terrain is varied. Most dominant, however, is open woodland tundra of scattered coniferous trees, which is bordered in the north by an Arctic-alpine tundra and to the south by boreal forest, or Parkland, consisting of broadleaf trees scattered on wide expanses of grassland.

Approximately west of the Churchill River on the Manitoba shore of Hudson Bay were the Athapaskan-speaking people, and to the east the Algonquians. For successful fishing and hunting, small groups of extended families who were united by a common dialect lived together and followed the movements of the game animals; only for a comparatively short period during the summer months did these various groups briefly rendezvous, hence expressing a form of tribal solidarity. The Athapaskan speakers included the Tanaina, Tanana, Kutchin, Han, Inland Tlingit, Tahltan, Hare and Mountain Indians in the northwest and the Yellowknife, Dogrib, Slavey, Beaver and Chipewyan in the east and to the south of the Great Bear and Great Slave lakes. The Algonquians, such as the Strongwoods Cree, Western Woods Cree and Rocky Cree, were east and south of the Slave and Athabasca rivers. A broad sweep eastwards beyond Lake Winnipeg in present-day Manitoba included the Swampy Cree, Northern Ojibwa, Saulteaux and West Main Cree whose territory bordered the shores of the Hudson and James bays. East of these bays and north of the St. Lawrence River were the East Cree, Attikamek, Naskapi and

Montagnais, the territory of the two latter tribes extending to the Labrador Sea. Because of the extensive area encompassed by the Subarctic region, it has been further divided into smaller regions – the Yukon, Mackenzie, Central (bordering the south of the Hudson Bay) and Eastern on the Labrador peninsula, and while the overall lifestyle of the people was similar, none, for example, practiced agriculture; they were all hunters and fishermen and tribal cohesion was minimal. However, the type of dwelling used, the mode of transportation, subsistence patterns, care of the elderly and warfare patterns were often markedly different.

The emphasis on local band affiliation was a characteristic feature of much of the Subarctic social organization. Such bands readily adapted to the annual migrations and seasonal foraging ranges. They had a high degree of continuity, but a fluidity of composition, and one scholar of the Chipewyan has recently pointed out the great value of such organization in maintaining identity in a variety of traditional and modern environments. For example, while the nomadic herds of caribou were generally predictable in their movements, any erratic or unusual changes could be accommodated by the spatial distribution of the bands facilitating a communication network which could 'report on the direction of movement, dispersal and concentration of the caribou'.[1]

The total population of the scattered bands, which constituted a loose-knit tribe, was generally small; that for the Montagnais-Naskapi, for example, was some four thousand in the mid-nineteenth century occupying a vast territorial range of at least four hundred thousand square miles. The statistics for the Chipewyan are similar: thus, a population density of about one person per one hundred square miles was not uncommon in both Athapaskan and Algonquian territory.

A marked social characteristic of the Subarctic people was the great emphasis placed on personal autonomy, and this gave rise to largely non-aggressive behavior in interpersonal relationships, thus respecting others' freedom of action and avoiding domination. Parents extended such behavior toward their children which led to the development of independent personalities with a high degree of self-reliance and personal initiative, traits so essential for maintaining harmonious life in the small extended family bands. However, a built-in symbolic warning that the independence must not be carried too far was another Subarctic trait; its message was conveyed in tribal mythology which warned of the dangers of extreme isolation from communal life and referred to lone forest prowlers, such as the Cree and

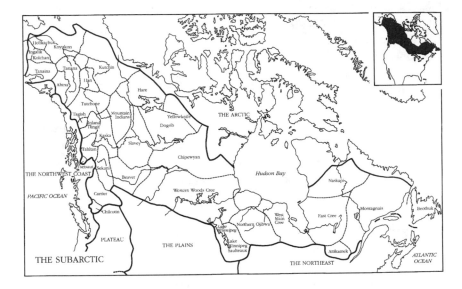

ABOVE: *This map shows approximate territories of tribes and language groups in about 1850, and somewhat earlier in a large region west of Hudson Bay. After that, many tribes lost territory and others moved.*

Saulteaux Windigo (cannibal) and the Kutchin's 'bush men'.

The immense self-reliance and personal initiative displayed by the Subarctic people was underlined by a remarkable episode related early in the history of the Canadian fur trade and reported on in 1770 by Samuel Hearne, who led an expedition from the Hudson's Bay post of Fort Churchill in search of the Coppermine River east of the Great Slave Lake. On their return journey, they came across a Dogrib woman who had escaped from Cree captors; alone for some seven months, she had not only built herself a small shelter, made snares to trap hares (the so-called snowshoe rabbit), fabricated snowshoes and begun work on a fish-net in anticipation of the spring melt, but had decorated her fur clothing. Hearne, obviously greatly impressed by this resourceful, brave woman, reported: 'It is scarcely possible to conceive that a person in her forlorn situation could be so composed . . . all her clothing, besides being calculated for real service, shewed great taste, and exhibited no little variety of ornament . . . as to make the whole of her garb have a very pleasing . . . appearance.'

Hearne's journal also gives an interesting perspective relating to the woman's lot in Subarctic culture at the time of early contact. Befriended by the influential Chipewyan chief, Mattonabee, Hearne was lectured on his misfortunes which were due, the Chief said, to the lack of women in Hearne's party. Women, he emphasized, were 'made for labor'; one of them, he maintained, could carry or haul as much as two men. They could also pitch the tents and keep up the fires at night. Further, he pointed out, although they did everything, they could be maintained at a trifling expense and, with wry humor added, that as they also acted as cooks, the 'very licking of their fingers' in scarce times would be quite sufficient for their subsistence.

The most common form of habitation was the conical tent – the 'wigwam' of the Algonquian-speaking groups – resembling the Plains tipi and covered with moose or caribou hides on the tundra, and bark in the forest regions. On occasions, the Cree used domed-shaped lodges covered with sheets of birch bark while the Kutchin, who had limited access to birch bark, utilized similarly constructed domed dwellings, but covered them with skins. In both the conical and dome-shaped lodges, the fireplace was located at the center; an exception to this was the East Cree *shabúktowan*, 'the house that you walk right through', which resembled two wigwams that were joined together with a fire at each end and a smoke hole above each. In constructing the conical lodge, two poles were laid on the ground

ABOVE: *Lower Ahtna Indians, the daughters of Chief Stickwan, c.1902, probably near the Lower Tonsin or Taral. They demonstrate the use of tumplines in the carrying of camp equipment.*

in the form of a cross; these were bound together at their intersection and set upright, a third pole was then placed into the crotch and this too was lashed in. By drawing the tripod closer together at the base, the top was elevated and the sides made steeper. Other poles were then laid into the foundation to support the covering of skin or bark. In the latter case, the bark was in rolls about 3ft (1m) wide and varying in length depending on its position on the conical frame. Once the bark was in place, more poles were laid upon it, thus anchoring the cover. Skin wigwams were similarly constructed, thus markedly differing from the Plains tipi which was generally of a single sewn cover and devoid of any external anchoring poles.

Wigwams were clearly not primitive dwellings, as a cursory inspection may suggest: the sewing of the bark rolls, the varying lengths, the shingle-like overlapping and the painted ornamentation referring, in the case of the East Cree, to property marks, point to a well-constructed and habitable dwelling suited to the environment and the nomadic lifestyle of the people. Likewise, wigwam organization and etiquette was well-developed, poles being tied across the interior some 6 to 8ft (1.8–2.4m) from the ground from which moccasins and utensils could be hung, and it was not uncommon also to hang fish on this cross-piece directly above the fire for slow curing, while the place of honor for guests was recognized as directly opposite the door.

Caribou and moose, the most important large food animals, were the Barren Ground caribou of the northern transitional forest and the adjacent tundra, while to the south and throughout the boreal forests were the woodland caribou, moose and a few woods buffalo.

The Chipewyan technique of hunting caribou was to drive them into the mouth of a chute consisting of bush or poles set some 50–65ft (15-20m) apart, which led to a circular pound, up to a third of a mile in diameter; this pound enclosed a complex maze of bush hedging between which snares were set. Entangled caribou were despatched with spears while the remaining loose ones were shot with arrows.

In contrast, the enormous moose did not move in herds and a different technique had to be adopted, a method which was based on the close observation of the behavioral characteristics of the animal. In order to catch the scent of any following predator, a moose generally doubles back after feeding, resting at a spot downwind of its earlier trail. Responding to this behavioral characteristic, the Indian hunter avoids following the trail of the moose, but instead makes semi-circular loops downwind; when the

ABOVE: *Northern Ojibwa camp, probably around 1900. The woman (right) heats water in a metal trade kettle. Note headscarves worn against swarms of mosquitoes.*

ABOVE: *Cree hunting camp. The hide (or bark) covered conical wigwams have extra protective poles on the outside, a commonly used technique where the cover was of several pieces of material.*

moose's trail loops back, the hunter can accurately locate it. During the rutting season, moose could be attracted by use of a birch-bark calling horn and in late winter immobilized by drawing them into deep snow, where they could be speared.

The main meat diet of the caribou and moose was supplemented by that from smaller animals such as beaver, hare, rabbit, muskrat and squirrel, which could be trapped with deadfalls or snares. The Subarctic areas required large quantities of food to support families, it being estimated that at least four pounds of flesh could be consumed daily by each adult. It was essential that a high proportion of this flesh was fat in order to ensure the necessary calorie and fatty acid intake, thus the *type* of flesh eaten was important. Rabbits, for example, were little valued by some groups as sustaining food, since most of the year they had limited body fat, a common native adage being that one could 'starve to death on rabbits'! One Hudson's Bay Company trader has pointed out that to these Subarctic people, the beaver – and this would be particularly applicable to the Cree in whose territory the animal abounded – was to a large extent what the seal was to the Eskimo. The beaver, in contrast to the snowshoe rabbit, carries a large amount of fat upon its body; it was, the Indians claimed, 'just as necessary to their well-being in the cold of winter as was bacon and butter to the white men'.

The availability of food resources varied with the season and in order to maintain a balancedeach family had to preserve diet a good deal of meat and fish. On occasions during the winter, sometimes flesh was frozen, but the most common methods were to smoke or sun-dry. One observer described the manner of smoking moose meat for quick preservation during traveling, as being accomplished 'by drying up the juice of the flesh by the heat from the fire'. The flesh was sliced up and placed on a scaffold formed of four upright sticks of green wood driven into the ground in the shape of a rectangle and at a height of about 3ft (1m); longitudinal bars were then lashed on the long sides and these supported the green-wood grill over which the thin strips were hung. A sizeable fire cured the meat within two to three hours – sufficient to preserve it for a few days – but the method required that the meat be constantly turned toward the fire and, if traveling for some time, it was necessary to repeat the process by stopping earlier in the day. An alternative technique, which gave more permanent preservation, was to smoke it on a frame built of three poles which were fastened together with cross bars near the top; the meat was hung on these bars and

ABOVE: *Ingalik man holding a pick and scoop used in fishing, Anvik, Alaska, c.1923. These implements were used in winter fishing for cutting a hole in and clearing the ice.*

364

smoked for several days. Enormous quantities of fish were often preserved in a similar way, particularly by those groups such as the Kutchin, some of the Hare bands, Tanana and Tanaina; indeed, in the case of the latter, salmon was the very basis of their subsistence.

Hide-tanning was a crucial part of Subarctic technology and, in the case of the Chipewyans, the caribou was a central component to their whole material culture complex and while the animal was hunted, skinned and butchered by men, the exhausting tanning process was carried out by women. Unlike the tanning of buffalo and moose hides, which were stretched or pegged out, Chipewyan women stretched the 'green' hide over a log and defleshed the inner side with a bone tool with a serrated edge. The hide was then soaked in water for several days, which loosened the hair so that it could be more easily removed with a bone beamer. The brain from a caribou skull was removed and mixed with water to produce a soup-like substance which was worked into the hide by alternately soaking and rubbing. It was necessary to carry out this step in the process with great care, ensuring that all the hide was thoroughly soaked, because it was at this stage that the chemical reaction led to the preservation of the hide and prevented subsequent deterioration. The hide was then stretched out to dry, often aided by freezing, and then soaked in water to wash out the unreacted tanning solution. It was then made pliable during the final period of drying by pulling it over a pole and working it by hand. An attractive brown color could be imparted to the hide by smoking it on a tripod over a hardwood fire which was smothered with moss; the process had the added advantages of partially waterproofing the hide – due to resin impregnation – and of repelling mosquitoes and flies.

Although there were some differences in the above process (some groups, such as the Dogrib for example, used urine to remove fat surplus in the hide), the basic technique of the tanning process was the same throughout the Subarctic region – defleshing, perhaps dehairing, tanning with fatty substances and rigorous mechanical handling during the final drying sequences.

While there were considerable variations within the Subarctic region in naming of seasons and months, the annual cycle is fairly typical, putting emphasis on important seasonal events – the budding, blooming, leafing and fruiting of vegetation, molting, migrating and pairing of animals and birds, and the freezing of the rivers. Many of the tribes would refer to the winter as the 'old fellow' which caused the pine needles to drop, forming a covering on the snow just as pine boughs were laid on the floor of a wig-wam to be used as bedding, an action referred to as 'spreading the brush'. The Cree divided the year into eight seasons with twelve months or moons, producing a clearly defined annual cycle.

Group activities related to seasonal changes were determined by the relative abundance of fish or big game in a particular area. For example, in the case of the Tanana on the downstream sections of the major rivers which had heavy concentrations of salmon, there was an emphasis on fish-ing for their subsistence and they were the least mobile with a compara-tively high population density. In contrast, those Tanana on the headwaters of the same rivers – perhaps less than two hundred miles away – put emphasis on hunting caribou, supplemented in July and August by the trapping of whitefish. Such groups were among the most mobile fol-lowing the caribou herds and had lower population densities. The general pattern was the same throughout the Subarctic region. Life was compara-tively sedentary during the summer months when local bands ren-dezvoused along the shores of the rivers and lakes, an environment which afforded some protection from the great swarms of mosquitoes and black-flies. This was a time when social and family ties were reinforced and plans made for the coming winter.

By early autumn, the gatherings began to disperse, each band departing by canoe; at this time, the big game were in prime condition – the hides were at their best and the animals had an abundance of fat. Hunting was now a major activity and each band moved to its winter locality and brought along enough meat and fish provision for the long winter months. The trapping of fur-bearing animals took place in November and December when the furs were of the best quality. The pelts and hides were processed during the severest months of January and February when out-side activities were virtually impossible due to the intense cold and extended hours of darkness.

It was during these enforced periods of inactivity that the story-makers recounted legends and perpetuated the tribal oral literature, while Montagnais-Naskapi hunters or shamans might assess their prospects, interpret dreams or organize discussion through the rituals of scapulimancy where moose, caribou or hare shoulder-blade bones were held over a fire; the heat cracks, blackened spots and breaks were then interpreted in direct proportion to the ingeniousness of the practitioner. The custom was ancient and has been sustained. It was reported on by the Jesuit missionary

Paul Le Jeune who wintered with a group of Montagnais in 1633–4 and it was *filmed* by Hugh Brody in Pien Penashue's camp of Eastern Montagnais on the Goose Bay, Newfoundland, during the autumn of 1989.

In addition to the tales of lone spirit woodland prowlers – the cannibals and bush men – it was also said that the spirits crossed the skies. In describing his travels with two Swampy Cree companions, one experienced observer reported that on witnessing the Aurora Borealis one remarked 'The *Choepi* [Ghosts] are having a good time to-night! . . . Look how the spirits of our departed friends are dancing . . . we call that *Pahkuk-kar-nemichik* – "The Dance of the Spirits!".']

In dealing with the supernatural, the East Cree, in common with most groups in the Subarctic, gave recognition to the enormous dependence on the products of the chase; this manifested itself in the form of sacrifices to propitiate the animals which they had to kill in order to survive. A widespread ethos recognized that a close bond existed between animals and human beings. Every animal was considered to have a spirit whose favor had to be sought, otherwise it could exert its influence to stop its species being killed by the hunters. Thus, the bones of beaver were carefully cleaned and cast into running water, while the heads of geese and ducks, the teeth of caribou and moose, and the claws and skull of the bear, were cleaned and saved, serving not only as talismans and tallies, but also and, primarily, as an offering to the spirit of the respective animal. Bears, in particular, were highly honored, their skulls being carefully cleaned, dried and painted with stripes or dots[2] in red vermilion. They were then placed in trees, out of respect to the animal.

At close quarters, the bear was a formidable opponent; nevertheless, because the bow was not considered powerful enough, they were hunted with club and knife. Crees reported that both the black and polar bears were particularly vulnerable when standing like a man, as they found difficulty in turning on the right side, thus an agile hunter was able to run in close and stab them in the heart. The creature was often likened to man and it was thought that they understood all that was said to them; as the hunter approached, he apologized and explained that the lack of food was the only motive for killing him and begged that the bear spirits would not be angry. At times, the bear was the winner, but the Cree explained that under these circumstances the powerful animal could show his own compassion, such as in the case of a hunter who on attacking a bear was 'horribly scarred and mangled' but was eventually set free when he pleaded with it for mercy.

In addition, the Subarctic people appealed to the powers of nature to help them with their great struggle for existence.[3] The winds were considered to be four brothers, the oldest and the most powerful being the north wind which brought the cold and had the power to punish evil doers. The other wind directions also had their distinctive characteristics and attributions.

For fast and effective travel, snowshoes were vital during the winter months; the style of snowshow varied, generally being described by reference to the frame shape. As a generalization, broad oval, sometimes almost circular frames, were typical of the Montagnais-Naskapi, while the narrow elongated shape was used further west. Virtually all such snowshoes were of a wooden frame which was netted with rawhide thong generally referred to as *babiche*, which universally took the place of vegetable cordage, almost absent in these regions. Finely cut rawhide strips were made into snares and netted game bags, while the heavier strips were used for burden straps, towlines and sometimes even extensive fencing when driving caribou into the pound. The snowshoes were not uncommonly embellished with tufts of colored trade wool which enabled them to be located in deep snow, while the *babiche* netting was colored, generally red and black, and patterns were produced by additional lacing at the toe and heel sections.

In this vast area, clothing tended to become increasingly elaborate from south to north. Widespread was the use of leggings or trousers with attached fur- or grass-lined moccasins and a semi-tailored dress or hide shirt. Some of the exceptional everyday and ceremonial clothing from such tribes as the Kutchin and Dogrib now resides in the Royal Scottish Museum, Edinburgh, having been collected by the Hudson's Bay chief trader, Bernard Rogan Ross, in 1859 and 1860. Collected just prior to the white man's all-pervading influence, they provide a variety of invaluable basic data for any Subarctic material culture studies. In the case of the Dogrib clothing, the woman's costume consists of a smoked caribou-skin dress sewn with sinew and decorated with red and white porcupine quills and red flannel, with a red and white quilled belt; tube-like leggings are also made of smoked caribou skin sewn with sinew, as are the separate straight center front seam-'T' back-seam moccasins. The man's costume is similarly constructed, which may have a slight hint of white influence, exhibiting as it does a curious military collar.

Similar everyday clothing for the East Cree was described by the explorer Alexander Mackenzie three-quarters of a century earlier, while

Skinner describes a fine hooded coat worn by hunters which was made of caribou skin and had retained the hair, 'somewhat resembling Eskimo parkas'. Of particular interest is that these items were painted *inside* by outlining on the skin, the eyes and mouth of the animal, symbolically stating that the power of the living animal – its speed, endurance or cunning – was possessed by the garment and could actually be transmitted to the wearer.

Ceremonial regalia was an elaboration of everyday clothing, generally embellished with porcupine quillwork, dentalium shells or painted. The quillwork was later combined with trade beads which ultimately virtually displaced the indigenous quillwork. Several garments are particularly distinctive within these areas. The Naskapi, for example, were well-known for use of clothing which was painted in intricate patterns with tools of bone or wood, the main colors being red and yellow, but pigments were also mixed to obtain varying hues. Extended parallel lines were produced by the use of a multiple prong tool while fine lines were drawn with a curved paint stick; many of the designs were geometrical, but the so-called double curve motif was also commonly used.

The work reached its fullest development on men's robes and summer coats, one specimen in the National Museum of Canada, Ottawa, dating as early as 1740. This particular piece is made of soft caribou hide with fringed edges which were once wrapped with red porcupine quills. It is embellished with scores of double curve motifs in addition to straight lines, triangular figures and dots in a three-fold division, which one scholar has suggested symbolize the three cosmic zones which only a shaman, wearing the robe, could actually penetrate. Recent research has led to the speculation that such robes represented a religious microcosm and that, in donning the robe, the wearer entered into contact with the spirit world, abolishing time and entering into a primordial state. It is contended that his symbolic rebirth achieved with the robe 'was synonymous with the return of the sun, the renewal of the world, the rebirth of his people and almost certainly the return of the caribou'.

Some of the earliest depictions of the magnificent prestige garments worn by the Athapaskan-speaking Kutchin to the northwest were made by Alexander Murray in his *Journal of the Yukon*, 1847-48. The distinctive pointed tailored shirts or tunics were often tailored in a complex pattern of many separate pieces of skin, although the main body was generally made up of large pieces, front and back. The same style had also been traditionally worn by the Chipewyans who inhabited the country to the southeast. Indeed, the name Chipewyan, it has been suggested, was derived from the Cree name for this tribe, *Chepau-Wayanuk*, which meant 'pointed skins'.[4]

Prior to the introduction of beads, such garments were embellished with bands of porcupine quillwork, perhaps 2 to 2½in (5–6cm) in width, which extended across the chest and over the shoulders; similar bands were sometimes attached to the cuffs. There were variations in the quill techniques employed; in some instances the quills were held to the surface by two rows of stitches, the thread of sinew being caught into the surface of the skin between each fold of the quills. Alternatively, a markedly different appearance was obtained by a variation in the technique of folding the quills so that the quills crossed diagonally, producing a double sawtooth-like pattern. Five to six lanes of such work produced the full-width bands, with patterns consisting of triangles, simple crosses and bands predominately in red, white and blue. In addition, the lower edges were generally embellished with a buckskin fringe completely wrapped with quills near the point of attachment, for some 2½in (6cm), and then changing to alternate wrapped and unwrapped sections for another 2½in or so, finally terminating to a free fringe. The whole – sewn band and wrapped fringe – greatly enhanced the overall appearance of this prestigious and valuable garment.

An alternative quill technique was a type of surface weaving where quills were applied direct to the hide. This was originally described by Orchard about the Tlingit, but now is rather firmly associated with the Alaskan Tanaina, the quills are laid lengthwise side by side on the hide surface. Spot stitches are concealed beneath the ends of the quills and at regular intervals a stitch is made across the surface of the quills; initially caught into the skin and under the quill on the outside edge of the decorative band, it then runs over the next quill and into the hide, running under the third quill and so on across the entire width of the band and acting as a type of weft. At the commencement of the second row of stitches, the surface of the *first* quill is crossed, then under the second, over the third, under the fourth, over the fifth, repeating the sequence to the opposite edge. Additional quills were spliced in by bending the end of the previous quill together with the new one under the nearest spot stitch.

A variant of this technique was to use a weft sinew such that, except for the outside quills, each rectangular exposed portion of quill was surrounded by a sinew thread. While patterns were predominately made up of stripes, the techniques did lend themselves to the production of curvilinear motifs and, particularly in the older specimens, the colors were a distinctive yellow/orange, black/brown and natural white.

Such bands were also utilized to embellish *mukluks* (combined moccasins and leggings), knife sheaths and mittens.[5] In the two latter cases, the quills were applied directly to the object, but for larger items – such as leggings and tunics – it was not unusual to work the quills onto a separate band and then sew them to the garment.

Separate woven quilled bands were, and still are, very much a speciality of the Slave and to a lesser extent, the Dogrib, who lived in the vicinity of the Great Slave Lake, North West Territories. Unlike the Tanaina work just described, this is done on a wooden bow loom. The warp threads are attached at each end of a green sapling, the tension bending the sapling into a bow shape so giving ample space below the threads for the work to be carried out unimpeded. A weft thread is now attached to the outer warp and then made to pass over and under the warp to the other side and back again; flattened quills are at the same time woven between the warp and weft threads. As the work proceeds, and each time a row is completed, the quills are pushed together so that the cross threads are hidden. Geometrical designs are produced by adding colored quills at various intervals. When the work is finished, the protruding underside ends of the quills are cut off for easy attachment of the band to an object. The finished piece has the appearance of fine cylindrical elements creating an impression that the quills themselves have been cut into short lengths and then woven in – as one could do with beads of a similar size and shape. The patterns produced in such work are wholly geometrical, commonly consisting of a series of repeated diamonds outlined in red, green, blue and orange quills. A notable feature of such work is the delicacy and repetition of the design patterns, in marked contrast to loom quillwork of some of the more southerly Algonquians such as the Cree and Métis (people of mixed Indian and French-Canadian blood) of the Red River area, where the patterns are bolder, design motifs are not quite so repetitive and larger quills are used.

A further feature of Slave woven quillwork is the occasional employment of moosehair in conjunction with the quills. Here, a number of hairs – perhaps four or five and equal to the width of a quill – are introduced in place of a quill, so building up the stepped diamond patterns. Although commonly used as belts, bands of such quillwork were also attached to moosehide jackets, game bags and gun cases. This type of quilling required great skill and patience, and was much coveted, as Hudson's Bay Company factor Bernard Ross reported in 1862: 'The quantity done in a day by a skillful operative is about 2½ inches [6cm] of belt size – and one of these articles is completed in about a fortnight, when it would be bartered for about 8 £-worth of goods.'

The impact of trade goods on the Subarctic tribes was considerable. When Alexander Hunter Murray, a senior clerk of the Hudson's Bay Company, established Fort Yukon on the Porcupine River in 1847,[6] he made reference to the great importance of acquiring beads for trading to the Kutchin Indians, remarking 'Without *beads* and plenty of them you can do little or no good here . . . To trade here successfully, there ought to be for one year's outfit four boxes of common white beads, one box of red (same size) and one box of fancy.' Beads were clearly a sign of wealth and prestige. 'I may here remark that all the chiefs hereabouts are young men, . . . none are considered a chief until they have 200 skins worth of beads . . . There is one man of the upper band who has between 90 and 100 skins in martens and beaver which he is keeping *all* for beads on our return.' Murray further reported a competition with the Russian traders and expressed concern at the time it took to get suitable goods to the distant trading posts – perhaps up to *seven* years after the request. He also refers to the high value placed by the local Indians on the dentalium shells[7] and requests more for trading: 'They are most valuable, every Indian wears them, as nose and ear ornaments, for hair bands, etc.'

Beads and dentalium shells were greatly favored by the Kutchin, and Murray was impressed by the large quantities which they procured to embellish their clothing. His on-the-spot pen and ink sketches illustrate their early and extensive use as well as giving a wealth of ethnological detail which, although lacking some of the finer points relating to bead motifs, are found to be largely reliable when compared to actual specimens. The beaded bands which were attached to the garments resembled the earlier woven quillwork, the string of beads following the long axis of the band. Just as in the lanes of quillwork, patterns too were not uncommonly made up of striped rectangular figures, similar to quillwork; colors differed, however: blue, red, as well as black and white, dominated and preferences changed, sometimes remarkably quickly.[8] Actual examination of specimens reveals the use of large round-ended cylindrical shaped beads about .15–.2in (4–5mm) in length and diameter to be common on mid-century and earlier pieces, while the slightly smaller and more rounded variety (generally referred to as 'pony beads' as previously mentioned, were more popular less than a quarter of a century later, possibly reflecting a change in trade patterns.

The coveted dentalium shell, while popular in the form of necklaces and carrying straps, was also combined with black or blue pony beads and sewn to the tunic or dress, generally following the contours of the shoulder cape. While large areas could be covered comparatively quickly by the use of these shells, they were an exceedingly expensive embellishment. Murray, reporting from Fort Yukon in 1847, states 'these are traded in this country 6 and 8 for a beaver or 3 martens, a box of these shells here would be worth over *two thousand pounds*'.

By the 1850s, a smaller type of bead was gaining popularity in the Subarctic region. Generally referred to as a 'seed' bead, which ranged approximately 1 to 2mm in diameter and came in a wide variety of colors, it was frequently used in combination with red and black cloth to embellish a wide variety of objects, considerably extending on the earlier artwork which had largely been restricted due to the scarcity of natural materials.

About the same time, silk and cotton threads were being introduced, particularly in the Lake Winnipeg region, with outlets at such Hudson's Bay Trading Posts as Norway House, located on the northern shore of that great lake. Embroidering with such threads was particularly popular with the Cree, Saulteaux and Métis people of that region and, on a smaller scale, to the north and west, among the Chipewyan, Slave and Dogrib, who wrapped horsehair[9] fillers with colored threads, or used silk and colored ribbons or tape largely as decoration around the edge of moccasin vamps.

As was discussed earlier, while some of the pony beadwork patterns can sometimes be related to those found in the earlier quillwork, this is not the case with embroidery or seed beadwork, the dominant motifs being floral and most highly developed in the Great Slave Lake–Mackenzie River region among those tribes – particularly Chipewyan, Slave and Dogrib – who had firm contacts with the Hudson's Bay Company Trading Posts such as Fort Chipewyan on Lake Athabasca, and Forts Resolution, Rae and Providence, on the Great Slave Lake. The new media allowed greater freedom in the development of design motifs which had previously been largely confined to the geometrical in porcupine quillwork. Further, there were considerable outside influences, not least the missionaries, who after establishing a religious community on the Red River among the Plains Cree and Chippewa (Ojibwa) in 1818, expanded north to Lake Athabasca and the Great Slave Lake in 1849. It is almost certain that floral vestments, altar cloths and church paintings became the inspiration for these new design motifs. Certainly in the case of the church paintings, one Mother Superior reported: 'The native women, who enjoy silk thread, bead and quill embroidery . . . came to copy these designs from the Cathedral.'[10]

Initial efforts at producing floral patterns could result in attractive but stiff designs but, in largely dispensing with a beaded background, which tended to crowd the decorative field, the motifs expand into dynamic semi-realistic, generally stemmed, patterns, which became the characteristic of much Athapaskan beadwork produced in the latter years of the nineteenth and early twentieth centuries. This ready adoption of European technology epitomized the flexibility of Athapaskan society, developed over the centuries in order to survive in a frequently hostile and often unpredictable environment and where the natural materials required for ornamentation were difficult to obtain and use. It also became a source of revenue for the often impoverished families whose womenfolk turned their hands to the production of wall pockets, dog blankets, pouches, moccasins, mittens, gauntlets, jackets and even shelf valances, all magnificently embellished with beads and to a lesser extent, thread embroidery.[11] Much of the raw materials were supplied by 'The Bay' which, since its foundation and Royal Charter from Charles II in 1670, encouraged the Indian people of the Subarctic to hunt and trap such creatures as the beaver, mink, ermine, fox, wolf, bear and otter, often with brutal metal traps supplied by 'The Company': all this to satisfy the demands of the European markets for exotic animal pelts. Clearly, by seemingly reconciling the ancient beliefs where animals were treated with respect and killed only for survival, Indian people expanded their hunting activities, thus obtaining some relief from the harsh Subarctic environment – expressed in utterances by the people themselves such as the Chipewyan eternal cry, 'Dow-diddla! dow-diddla!', meaning 'It is hard! it is hard!' and the Montagnais' sentiment, 'We are poor, . . . and we live among the trees, but we have our children.'

But for this a price was to be paid because, as with the decimation of the immense buffalo herds on the Great Plains to the south in the last quarter of the nineteenth century, so too with the fur-bearing animals of these northlands.

The immense number of animals which were slaughtered solely for their furs is illustrated by the Annual Reports of the fur companies. For instance, the returns of the North West Company,[12] c.1800, in a single season were reported as:

Beaver	106,000
Bear	21,000
Fox	15,000
Kit Fox	40,000
Otter	46,000
Marten	32,000

While trade values obviously varied, particularly when there was competition, the profits could be enormous. For example, when Alexander Murray set up a trading post in Kutchin territory in 1847 (as mentioned earlier), he reported that the Russian traders gave ten blue beads 'a little larger than a garden pea' for one beaver skin. The slaughter continued, virtually unabated, for a century. Over a nine-year period (1920–29), the average number of pelts returned per year by the Canadian provinces was:

Beaver	137,400
Red Fox	56,030
White Fox	39,688
Marten	43,480

The following year, however, saw a dramatic drop to less than fifty thousand in returns on the beaver, an animal generally considered emblematic of the fur trade, and which to several Subarctic tribes, as already mentioned, was as important to their territorial lifeway as the seal was to the Inuit. The enormous profits which could be made, as with the buffalo hunters some sixty years previously, caused the influx of white trappers who not infrequently employed hunting methods which gave scant regard for a basic woodland law which decreed that female animals were left undisturbed during the breeding season. In this, they were encouraged by traders because, although the pelts at this time were poor in quality, they were still accepted by all 'except the Hudson's Bay Company'.

The Dogrib and Slaves north of the Peace River, incensed at the white trappers encroachment, retaliated by starting forest fires in an effort to drive out the white invaders. To the south and east, in traditional Chippewa and Montagnais-Naskapi territory, full-bloods and Métis all reported the same tale: 'The beaver were going fast; in large areas they were already gone.'

On the Subarctic–Woodland boundary north of Lake Nipissing, one Indian hunter in the winter of 1925-6 had 'twelve white men trapping on his family hunting territory . . . As the white newcomers trapped an area until it became barren, to protect themselves from exploitation, the Indians began to do the same.'[13]

European diseases, and in some cases poor diet, also weakened resistance. As with the Plains tribes, smallpox had decimated many of the northern tribes in 1791-2 and again in 1837-8, while the influenza epidemics, against which the indigenous populations had little resistance, caused havoc. Skinner, for example, found that owing to the great mortality during the influenza epidemic which swept through Northern Quebec and Ontario in the winter of 1908-9, it was almost impossible to find anyone who was able to relate the myths and legends of the East Cree. Again, in 1917, it wiped out forty per cent of the Lake Nipigon Chippewa/Cree and, in the winter of 1927, most of the Prophet River band of Sekani.

By the 1930s, the great Subarctic was witnessing a fast vanishing frontier, with several parallels to events in the United States less than a half-century before. It would, however, be too simplistic to suggest that in this case it was largely dominated by avarice because this exploitation needs to be appreciated in the context of the times. The Great Depression of the 1920s caused the influx of large numbers of white trappers and traders. Lured by dreams of wealth, they tried their hand at trapping, often with little regard for any form of conservation or humane killing. It was a desperate attempt to 'escape the joblessness and despair of the Great Depression.' Traditional techniques of trapping by the indigenous people rotated trapping areas; the experienced hunter specifically designed his trap set so that only particular animals were guided to the trap and thus few unwanted and unnecessary catches were made.

By the beginning of the 1940s the economic effects of the Depression and World War were felt in the north: markets collapsed, and fur prices plummeted. While a few white traders and trappers stayed, most left, almost as suddenly as they had appeared and the fur trade reverted to the Dene, Métis and other indigenous groups of the Subarctic. The change came only just in time and today (1990s) it is claimed that no commercially trapped fur-bearing species is endangered or threatened with extinction, and the animal depletions which occurred during the early part of the twentieth century have now been restored and the fur-bearing animals are 'as abundant as they ever were.'

A new threat, however, confronts the Subarctic people as they now face the great anti-killing campaigns which stigmatize their very lifestyle. Living

376

in a land which does not lend itself to agriculture and in a land where oil, gas and mining developments are enormously expensive, they have been hardest hit by such campaigns, and they are becoming a serious threat to a long-standing and sound way of life which has adapted to and produced a balanced environment.[14] It has been suggested that the Subarctic people must assert their right to manage their ancestral lands and animals based not on imposed standards but on inherited principles.

MYTHS AND LEGENDS

S ubarctic mythology reflects the precariousness of human existence in a harsh, often hostile environment. Myths and legends provided reference and reassurance for the inexplicable or unpredictable aspects of daily life. They also provided a source and explanation for the multitude of rules which governed people's behavior. Such rules ranged from specific prohibitions, like that against women scraping skins at night, to complex instructions for the ritual treatment of a killed wolverine. Taken together, myths equipped their listeners with the means of understanding the natural world and their own place in it and established a code of proper behavior toward the environment and its resources.

ORIGIN MYTHS

All Subarctic communities have a vast repertoire of myths and legends relating to the origin of the world and everything in it. They are set in a remote primordial world and describe, often at great length and in great detail, how the present order of things was established.

■ The Distant Time

The Koyukon name for this series of myths is *Kkadontsidnee*, meaning Distant Time. In the Distant Time, all living things – people, animals and birds, trees and plants – were related. They all had human form, spoke the same language and lived in the same way. The stories explain how these human beings were transformed into the animal and plant species we know today. Certain trees, for example, were once women who were told of the deaths of their husbands. One cried and pinched her skin and was changed into the spruce tree with its rough and pinched bark. Another cried and slit her skin with a knife, and became the poplar with its deeply cut bark. Such stories, attractive in themselves, have a deeper purpose, for they remind people that even trees have spirits and need to be shown respect before they are 'killed' by being cut down.

The scope of Distant Time stories ranges from the cosmological to the minute. They explain the origins of the Sun, Moon and stars, winds and thunderstorms, mountains and lakes, as well as those of mosquitoes. The Northern Lights, for example, was once a hunter who broke his bow shooting at caribou and was burned up in a fire.

■ The Raven Trickster

The central figure in this ancient world is the trickster, known as Raven or Crow to tribes like the Tanaina, Kutchin, Inland Tlingit and Kaska, as *Wisakedjak* to the Cree, as *Nanabush* to the Ojibwa and as *Djokabish* to the Naskapi. Whatever his name, he is the same wonderfully contradictory figure – at one moment he is a creator, transformer and manipulator of the forces of nature, at the next a mischief-maker, buffoon, coward, thief and glutton. It was Raven, for example, who first created human beings out of stone, but then finding that they never died, recreated them from dust so that they became mortal as they are today.

Predictably perhaps, most Distant Time stories relate to animals. In their simplest form, the stories explain, often in a comical way, how an animal's present physical appearance came about. For example, a Tanaina myth describes how the beaver and muskrat originally had each other's tails, but decided to exchange them. The Koyukon said a lynx's black-tipped tail resulted from its having been burned, while the wolf received his dark markings when Raven tricked him, by throwing caribou innards in his face.

Other stories refer to the ceremonial treatment accorded to certain animals after they have been killed. One of these tells how two powerful chiefs went on a long and unsuccessful hunting expedition. As they wandered on and one, they became thin and their clothes ragged. Their skins tanned and their hair grew long. Finally they began to live like animals and they were transformed, one into a wolf and the other into a wolverine. This is why, traditionally, whenever these animals were killed, they were hailed as great chiefs and given the place of honor at a funeral feast, 'remembering their hardships long ago.'

Each tribe or group of tribes also had myths relating to their own origins. For example, several tribes, including the Chipewyan, Dogrib,

Hare, Slavey and Yellowknife, shared a mythical ancestry from a woman who married a dog which turned into a man at night. It is this story which probably gave rise to the Chipewyans and other Athapaskans being designated by early European travelers as 'dog-sided' or 'dog-ribbed.' It may also be related to the taboos against eating dogs.

■ Codes of Conduct

Origin myths were not told simply as entertainment, they also established the rules governing the interaction between human beings and the natural world. These rules were based upon a vast range of taboos against behaving in a particular way toward animate and inanimate elements in nature. Although they seldom contain explicit moralizing, myths were often told for moral effect. Thus myths served as a code of conduct and a medium of instruction.

ALL-POWERFUL SPIRITS

An elderly Cree in the James Bay area in the 1930s stated that *Manitou* had created everything. This appears to be at odds with the many origin myths in which the work of creation is credited to the trickster figure, as represented by Raven, *Wisakedjak, Nanabush* and so on. In contrast to the trickster, *Manitou* or *Kitche Manitou* – the Algonquian Great Spirit – is presented as a remote, mysterious and omniscient being, playing no role in traditional myths and not represented or personified in ceremonies.

■ Christian Influence

In seeking to rationalize such contradictions, it must be remembered that, as with other cultural areas, most Subarctic groups have been in contact with Christian missionaries since at least the middle of the 19th century, and, in the case of some groups, even earlier. This has not necessarily meant the loss of traditional beliefs, since Subarctic culture is characterized by a relativism which allows for the coexistence of different belief systems. Nevertheless, the intermingling of ideas which has undoubtedly taken place does tend to blur any reconstruction of the belief system which existed prior to the coming of Christianity. For example, the question of whether or not the concept of a supreme being (such as *Kitche Manitou*) is an indigenous one has been much debated.

It is true that, in the role of creator and transformer, beings such as Raven, *Wisakedjak* and *Nanabush* do display attributes of an all-powerful spirit and supreme being. However, there were no cults or ceremonies associated with them nor is there any suggestion that they were regarded as deities. Indeed, it is clear from the myths themselves that the trickster figure could in no way be equated with the supreme being of Judaic-Christian tradition. Among the present-day Kaska, for example, creation is attributed to God who is called *Tenatiia*, a term designating a rich and powerful person. In their traditional creation myths, a major active role was taken by Crow, but no one regards Crow and God as identical.

■ The Power of Many

Indeed, as far as the Athapaskans are concerned there is no indication in their mythology of the existence of a supreme being. Rather, there was a concept of an impersonal imminent power in the universe which could be tapped by people in order to gain food, health, long life or whatever was required. The same concept also existed among the Algonquians who believed all things were inhabited by a *Manitou* spirit, good or bad. *Kitche Manitou*, on the other hand, has been identified as a supreme beneficent force, dispenser of life and death, rewarder of goodness, and punisher of evil.

Those who argue that this concept was aboriginal point to 18th century references for support. David Thompson, the late-18th century trader and explorer, records a narrative in which *Wisakedjak* was instructed by *Kitche Manitou* to show men and animals how to live peaceably together. *Wisakedjak* disobeyed and spread dissent and confusion instead. In anger, *Kitche Manitou* destroyed all creation in a flood, only *Wisakedjak*, a beaver, a muskrat and an otter surviving. When the waters eventually subsided, man and all other life-forms were re-made, but *Wisakedjak* was stripped of his former authority and reduced to being only a trickster and deceiver. Whether or not the supreme being concept was traditional, it has to be said that this narrative and the characteristics ascribed to *Kitche Manitou* suggest more than a hint of Christian influence.

What seems more likely to be indigenous is the host of minor *Manitous* termed 'owners', 'masters', 'keepers' or, latterly, (in a borrowing from modern lumber camps) 'bosses' of game. This concept was based on the view, already described, that everything in the universe was animate. Every fish, animal and plant species functioned in a society which was parallel in all respects to that of mankind. Every species had a spiritual 'owner' or 'boss' who controlled the individuals of that species. Thus, bears had an 'owner', as did beavers, caribou, otters and so on. For a hunter to be successful, he had to win the help and favor of the owner of the game. Without this, individual animals could not be caught. If the owner of a species was insulted or alienated, the hunter would not be allowed to kill or even find a member of that species. For this reason, hunters treated the animals they killed with care and respect. The Athapaskan legend of the Game Mother reflected similar concerns. Failure by hunters to show proper respect would result in the animals being recalled to her home.

Subarctic religion was thus highly functional. While concepts of little immediate relevance remained poorly defined, those intimately bound up with the subsistence quest and physical survival tended to be much more elaborate.

HERO CREATURES AND MONSTERS

The archetypal culture hero is presented as a poor boy, perhaps an orphan or one abandoned by his friends and relatives, who aided by his spirit helper, has a series of adventures in which he overcomes many obstacles and gains wealth and power. The myth cycle relating to the Beaver culture hero *Saya* or *Usakindji* is typical. It begins with a young boy being abandoned on an uninhabited island by his father. He receives spirit help in a dream and with ingenuity and determination is able to survive the winter. Eventually he escapes from the island and travels around the world destroying the giant animals which at that time preyed on people, and transforming them into the smaller animals which exist today.

Saya's adventures are replicated in the stories recounted by other tribes about their culture heroes – the Kutchin *Ataachookai*, for example, the Kaska *Kliatata*, the Chipewyan *Segalaze* and *Eredk'ali*. All are represented as benefactors who passed on to others the knowledge which they acquired during their travels. Saya taught people how to make arrows. *Kliatata* gave them bows and showshoes and taught them to make fishing nets from willow bark.

■ Superhuman *Segalaze*

In carrying out their exploits, heroes often display strength and speed of superhuman proportions as in this story about *Segalaze*, recorded in the 1970s:

'Another time the people were walking up a big hill. When they got to the top there were two grizzly bears there. The people were scared but *Segalaze* was in back again. He loosened up his cape and he ran ahead to those grizzly bears and ran around them real fast. Pretty soon all you could see was just dust. He must have had some kind of medicine for that because there was no dirt there. And when the dust cleared away those bears were dead.'[15]

It is interesting to note that in modern renditions these traditional heroes are compared with comic book characters such as Superman or with real-life contemporary heroes like boxers or athletes. This is entirely logical for, as well as being told for entertainment, culture-hero stories were also a medium for instruction with the hero as role model. The story of *Saya* on the island, for example, is the story of a vision quest, something which all boys were expected to undertake. His adventures as a whole promote a philosophy of life in which self-reliance is combined with dependence on spiritual support.

■ The Malevolent

It is this instructional role which distinguishes the culture hero from the trickster. While Raven or *Nanabush* frequently perform feats appropriate to a hero, their heroic aspects are diminished by their corresponding failings. The culture hero helps and protects people in need; the trickster is more likely to take advantage of their weakness.

Many of the culture hero's exploits involve struggles with monsters, such as the giant man-eating animals destroyed by *Saya*. Monsters and malevolent beings of all kinds loom large in Subarctic mythology, reflecting the anxieties of people conscious of their vulnerability in an unpredictable and threatening environment.

Strange noises heard at night were attributed by the Athapaskans to the *Nakhani*, sometimes called the 'bush man' or 'brush man'. This was a monstrous giant who lurked in the undergrowth around summer camps, waiting to kidnap children. Most feared by the Algonquians was the *Windigo*, a man-eating giant with a heart of ice who haunted winter forests and devoured anyone who crossed his path. Other beings included the 'whistlers' who lived in the mountains, the 'tree people' who came out of the trees at night waving their arms, and the 'dog from the earth' which could be heard barking but which was never seen.

Like the culture hero myths, tales of giants and cannibals were also instructional. Mothers used them to frighten their children to prevent them from straying. For adults, too, they contained warnings to be on guard against the dangers of the forest, not only the unseen terrors of the *Nakhani*, but also the very real risks of becoming lost or falling prey to wild animals.

HOLY PLACES, SACRED SITES

For the traditional peoples of the Subarctic, the spirit world and the natural world were inseparable. Spirits were everywhere in the landscape, although not all were possessed of equal power. Certain natural features – waterfalls, lakes and streams, ancient trees and strangely shaped rocks – might have special powers which needed to be placated or shown deference. Others might have dangerous or hostile presences which needed to be avoided. Iliamna Lake in southwestern Alaska, for example, is said to be home to Big Fish, monsters powerful enough to bite the bottoms out of boats.

Sites with particular historical or mythological associations were also imbued with spiritual power. Abandoned villages and old campsites were places of danger, since the spirits of those who had lived and died there still inhabited them. For this reason, no one would think of remaining in such potentially terrifying places after dark.

■ The Landscape

Distant Time stories often account for the origin of particular geographical features. Iliamna Lake was created by giants from the north according to Tanaina myth, while Mount McKinley, the highest peak in North America, was created by Raven. The story goes that, while paddling his canoe across a lake, Raven found himself threatened by huge waves and they turned into mountains, the largest wave becoming Mount McKinley. Another story explains the presence of large depressions in an area of sand dunes around the upper reaches of the Nulitna River in Alaska. Here, it is said, two giants once fought for possession of the dunes, leaving their footprints in the sand as they wrestled.

The earth itself was a source of power and had to be treated with respect. Digging in the earth was not an action to be taken lightly. Earth had its ceremonial uses. It was used, for example, by shamans as medicine in treating illness, and earth pigments were used for body paint and for decorating clothing and equipment. The several locations along the Yukon and Konukuk rivers where deposits of red ochre occurred were regarded as sacred by the Kutchin and other western Athapaskan groups, and offerings were left when the pigment was extracted.

■ Ceremonial Shelter

As far as group ceremonialism was concerned, temples as such did not exist. The traditionally nomadic lifestyle of Subarctic peoples meant that most structures were either portable or capable of being erected quickly using readily available materials. It is true that Alaskan groups like the Ingalik did construct substantial wood and turf buildings in their winter villages, where the *kashim*, a large rectangular semi-subterranean structure, served as a men's meeting house and as an arena for a number of ceremonies.

In general, special shelters and enclosures were built to order for ceremonies, feasts and dances, and were usually destroyed after use. For the widespread Algonquian phenomenon known as the Shaking Tent ritual, for example, a cylindrical open-topped tent was constructed under the direction of the shaman engaged to perform the ritual. During it, the shaman conversed with a number of visiting spirits, whose presence caused the tent to shake violently despite its sturdy construction. The ritual was not associated with a particular site or sites, but was held where an individual or community required the services of a shaman to solve a particular problem.

A number of sacred sites in and around Lake Winnipeg were associated with the ceremonies of the *Midewiwin*, or Grand Medicine Society. The *Midewiwin*, an organization dedicated to curing the sick, was a major religious institution in the traditional culture of the Lake Winnipeg Saulteaux from the 18th century until the early years of the 20th century. Whether the sites were regarded as sacred because of their association with the *Midewiwin*, or whether they were chosen for the *Midewiwin* because of their existing sacred significance, is a moot point.

The name of one site, Dog Head, on the eastern side of the narrows, may be derived from the dog sacrifice which formed part of the *Midewiwin* ceremonies. (Note the similarity to the ceremonies and culture of the adjoining Northeast region.) Another site where the *Midewiwin* was regularly held during the 19th century was Black Island, at the southern end of Lake Winnipeg. The island was regarded as a sacred place on account of the mysterious reverberations or drumming sounds said to be heard there and it may have been for this reason that it was chosen as a spot particularly suited for the performance of the *Midewiwin* Ceremony.

REVERED ANIMALS

The single most consistent feature of northern Athapaskan belief systems was the reciprocal relationship which existed between human beings and the animals on which they depended for their livelihood. There was a widespread belief in reincarnation in animal form which blurred the distinction between men and animals. In addition, animals were thought to retain many of the human characteristics which they had had in Distant Time. They still understood human speech, they had spirits, often very powerful ones, and they had to be treated according to a strict code of moral and social etiquette. Game animals could punish people who breached this code simply by shunning them and thereby condemning them to starvation. People often accounted for the decline in particular species by identifying offenses committed against them in the past. This point is illustrated in the story of a conversation between Bear and Lynx. Bear said that if a human mistreated him, that person would get no more bears until his hair turned gray. But Lynx declared that people who mistreated him would never get another lynx as long as they lived.

■ The Rules of Respect

Koyukon hunters avoided pointing at animals, because it showed disrespect, 'like pointing or staring at a stranger.' When discussing animals, they chose their words with great care, avoiding boastful talk about hunting or trapping exploits. Bears were so powerful that they were never referred to directly. Hunting therefore involved far more than simply tracking and killing an animal. There were taboos associated with every aspect of hunting – the weapons and equipment used, the approach to the animals hunted, the treatment of the food which they supplied. Nearly all were designed to propitiate the animals' spirits and to ensure that game remained plentiful in the future. There was also a sense that, because of what they gave, animals were inherently deserving of such respect and homage.

There were also a large number of prescribed procedures and rituals for the butchering of game and the disposing of the bones and uneaten or inedible parts. Procedures related not only to animals important for subsistence, such as caribou or salmon, but also to those respected and feared for their power, like the wolf and bear.

■ The Power of the Bear

Bears commanded particular consideration, and there were elaborate rules surrounding the way in which they were killed and their carcasses disposed of. Sanction for these rules can be found in such myths as the Inland Tlingit's The Girl Who Married A Bear and the Cree's The Boy Kept by A Bear. Both describe how human beings who have spent some time in the animal world return home bringing with them the knowledge of how bears should be treated after death.

After a bear had been killed, it was laid on its back, thanked by the hunter and an offering of tobacco placed on its chest. A feast was held to which all the men of the hunting group were invited and small portions of the meat were placed in the fire as offerings to ensure the success of future hunts. The painted skull of the bear and its forelegs, wrapped in birchbark or cloth, were tied to a tree and left as a permanent display when the group moved camp.

Other animal remains were accorded similar treatment. Moose and caribou antlers were often decorated with ribbons and placed on an elevated platform specially built to keep them and other animal bones out of reach of the camp dogs. The bones of water animals, like the beaver and muskrat, were returned to the lake or river with the request, 'Be made again in the water.' Cree hunters in particular often kept parts of certain animals as personal trophies or amulets. These included such items as a bear's chin and the dried and stuffed head of a goose, both decorated and beaded, and ceremonial caribou hides.

■ Feast of Animals' Souls

The most elaborate rituals were those carried out by the more settled groups of the western Subarctic. The Ingalik held a whole series of animal ceremonies, such as the Mask Dance and the Feast of the Animals' Souls, which were intended to placate the animals and ensure their increase, but which were also great social occasions. During these ceremonies, dancers wearing colorful masks to represent the various animal species, performed to the accompaniment of songs and drumming.

RITUALS AND CEREMONIES

Personal power was a vital element in the religious life of the Subarctic people. Spirits came in dreams or were deliberately sought in visions. As elsewhere in North America, the components of the vision quest were isolation, fasting and meditation. The vision usually came in the form of an animal or bird, who then became the individual's guardian spirit or spirit helper.

■ Shaman Power

Those who acquired greater power and learned how best to control spirit forces became shamans. Each shaman – who might be male or female – formed special associations with a number of familiar (usually animal) spirits. Some of these were inherited, but most were found through dreams and visions. Shamans summoned their spirit helpers to direct them when they were called upon to exercise their powers. Often, in a trance-like state, they spoke through these spirits and claimed to travel over the world. A Naskapi story tells how, during a famine, a shaman visited the Master of the Caribou at his home inside a hollow mountain in the far north, from where he controls the caribou herds. The shaman persuaded him to release some of the caribou, thus relieving the famine.

The most important shamanistic activity lay in diagnosing and curing illness and disease. Curing usually involved the extraction, by sucking or blowing, of an object such as a stone, bullet, or piece of string which was considered to be the source of the patient's problem. The prevention of disease involved frightening away the spirit through a shamanistic performance. Apart from curing, the shaman also located game, predicted the weather and foretold the future.

The accouterments of shamans included special amulets, representing the various spirits they controlled, skins of their animal helpers, special cups, tubes and spoons used in curing rituals, and the skin blankets under which they performed. Shamans also 'owned' a number of songs and used drums and rattles for accompaniment when singing them. Tanaina shamans possessed considerable paraphernalia, including an elaborate caribou-skin parka decorated with appendages made of beaks and claws which rattled impressively when the wearer danced.

■ The Shaking Tent

The Shaking Tent ritual was a public performance which took place at dusk and often lasted well into the night. The shaman entered the tent and the arrival of the spirits was signaled by violent movement, strange lights and cries. The onlookers seated outside could hear conversations and often joined in by shouting questions. The performance had no set form, but depended on the individual shaman and the particular purpose for which the ceremony was being held.

As well as being a form of mediation with the spirits, the ceremony was also a form of community entertainment. In the Cree version of the ceremony, the first spirit to arrive was said to be *Mistaapew*, sometimes described as the 'boss' of the shaking tent, who acts as host or master of ceremonies. He was said to be a great joker who liked to make people, particularly women, laugh. A common feature of the ceremony was the part in which *Mistaapew* had a fight with the spirit of the bears. The presence of the bear inside the tent was revealed by the impression of a claw, which could be seen through the tent cover by the onlookers. *Mistaapew's* victory indicated that men would be able to kill bears in future.

■ Divination and Festivals

Scapulimancy was the single most common form of divination and could be done by anyone. It involved heating over a fire a flat bone (such as the shoulder-bone of an animal or the breast-bone of a bird) and interpreting the resulting scorch marks and cracks to determine the whereabouts of game or people. The reading was based on individual interpretations rather than on formalized rules.

Although individual practices predominated, community ceremonials were held by several western Athapaskan groups. The most elaborate were those performed by the Ingalik in their *kashims*. Seven 'great ceremonies' were held, four of which involved invitations to neighboring villages for feasting, dancing, ceremonial exchange and gift-giving. The Partner's Potlatch was an occasion for fun and could be held at any time of the year. The Death Potlatch was the year's most solemn occasion and was held in midwinter.

Other group activities included trading festivals, winter solstice festivals, feats and ceremonies to celebrate events such as a marriage, a boy's first kill, a girl's first menstruation, the first salmon run or a hunter's killing of a wolf or wolverine. Such occasions also provided opportunities for singing and dancing, racing, gambling and games of strength and skill.

ARTS AND CRAFTS

Although documentary sources for precontact life are meager, limited to the relatively few accounts by early travelers, fur traders and missionaries, there can be little doubt that the artistic traditions which, in many cases, only began to be recorded in the 18th century, had been an integral part of Subarctic life for centuries.

Unfortunately, at many sites, any organic matter has been destroyed by the acidity of the soil so that, while stone tools for working skin, bone, antler and wood have survived, the materials for which they were intended have not. There are a few exceptions where unusual conditions have led to a greater degree of preservation. For example, bone tools engraved with plain or ticked parallel lines have been excavated from prehistoric sites in northern Yukon. One of the most attractive objects recovered is a carved fish effigy – probably a fishing lure. Whether the engraved lines were intended simply as ownership marks or whether they should be regarded as symbolic – perhaps as stylized representations of animals or natural phenomena – remains a matter for conjecture.[17]

Sites around copper deposits, such as those on Lake Superior and in the Copper River area, have produced a range of objects hammered from copper nuggets in the form of arrowheads, knives, fishhooks, awls, chisels, beads and other ornaments. Evidence from sites elsewhere shows that such items were widely traded throughout the Subarctic.[18]

The shards of decorated pottery which also appear in prehistoric sites point to the development of a distinctive pottery-making tradition in Manitoba and Ontario.[19] In western Alaska the pottery made around the time of historic contact by the ancestors of the Ingalik and Koyukon reflects the influence of their Eskimo neighbours.[20]

Changes to traditional Algonquian culture began early in the 16th century when British, French and Portuguese fishermen came ashore to process the fish they had caught on the Newfoundland Banks. Trading metal knives, hatchets and kettles for meat and furs, they soon attracted hundreds of Indians to the north shore of the Gulf of the St. Lawrence every summer. As a result, tools and utensils of iron and brass came to replace stone and bone over much of northeastern America during the 16th and 17th centuries.

European contact began for the Athapaskans in the late-17th century with the establishment of trading forts on the southwestern shores of Hudson Bay. During the 18th century trapping and trading activities extended westwards, with the Cree, Chipewyan, Yellowknife and Dogrib acting as intermediaries between the traders and the northwestern groups. By the early-19th century the fur trade had reached the Tanaina, Tanana and western and northern Kutchin, although some Alaskan Dene on the uppermost reaches of the major rivers did not actually set eyes on a white man until about 1900.[21]

While the disruption caused to traditional society by imported diseases and missionary activity contributed to the discarding of old ideas and activities, practical considerations should not be underestimated. There can be little doubt that the advent of European technology greatly eased the workload of Indian women. The merchandise offered by traders – metal tools and cooking pots, woven textiles and ready-made clothing, decorative materials like beads, silk thread and ribbons – was both attractive and labor-saving. Moreover, the possession of trade goods and the wearing of fur-trade fashions conferred considerable social status and prestige. It is hardly surprising that by the end of the 18th century Sir Alexander Mackenzie was able to report of the Cree: 'They are fond of European articles and prefer them to their own native commodities.'[22]

WOOD AND BARK

It was from the forests that people, quite literally, built their lives. The forests supplied the materials for building shelters, whether substantial log houses or simple pole frameworks covered with skin or bark. They supplied materials for transport – for sleds, toboggans and snowshoe frames, and for canoes made of sheets of bark fitted over a wooden frame, the seams stitched with spruce root and caulked with spruce gum.

Bark and roots, as well as wood, were used for hunting and fishing equipment. Fishing lines and nets, for example, were made from willow bast, cut while green and torn into strips, then rolled on the naked thigh to produce a strong and durable twine. A fishing net made from willow twine could last a year or more.

Dishes, ladles and cups were carved from solid pieces of wood and decorated with notching or with incised or painted designs. In some areas, water buckets or cups were made from thin wooden slats (usually of spruce or larch) steamed and bent into circular or oval shapes. The overlapping edges were stitched with split spruce root and pieces of wood were cut and fitted in order to form the bases.

Not all woodwork was so utilitarian. For their winter ceremonials, the Ingalik of Alaska carved elaborate wooden masks, often painted and decorated with feathers and beads. Some had moveable appendages with which the wearer could imitate the movements of the being represented. Both the style of the masks and the ceremonies in which they were worn were greatly influenced by those of the neighboring Eskimo.

Baskets, both for cooking and storage, were made from sheets of birch bark and from twined spruce root (*watape*). Sir Alexander Mackenzie spoke approvingly of the spruce root baskets made by the Sekani in the late-18th century: 'Their kettles are also made of *watape*, which is so closely woven that they never leak, and they heat water in them by putting red hot coals into it.'[23]

Bark was cut from the tree in spring, while it was still flexible enough to be folded into the desired shape. The sides of the basket were stitched with strips of spruce root, which was also used to bind the rim. Baskets for cooking or for storing liquids were made watertight by applying spruce gum to the seams. Those intended to hold trinkets and other small objects sometimes had a buckskin top, closed with a drawstring.

Regional differences are apparent in both the shape and the decoration of bark containers. Those made in the Yukon and interior Alaska took the form of a bucket with a curved rim. Decoration consisted of horizontal or diagonal bands of lines and triangles, formed by scraping away the dark outer layer of bark to expose the paler bark underneath.[24]

Elsewhere in the Subarctic, bark baskets (referred to as *mococks*) had rectangular bases, sloping sides and oval rims. The sides (and lid, if one was attached) were often decorated with stylized plant or naturalistic animal motifs. In this case, decoration was achieved by scraping away the background, leaving the design in dark relief.[25]

■ Skindressing

According to the 18th century explorer Samuel Hearne, the making of a complete set of Chipewyan winter clothing could take as many as eleven caribou hides.[26] A hunter required a new set of clothing at least once a year and a new pair of moccasins every two to three weeks. It is small wonder then that for Indian women dressing skins was a constant occupation.

It was also a laborious occupation, involving de-hairing (if the skin was to be used for summer clothing), along with repeated scraping, soaking, stretching and rubbing with animal fat and brains. Finally, the skin was often smoked over a smoldering fire to give it a golden brown color. This last process also helped to make the skin waterproof and items like tent covers and moccasins were always produced out of smoke-tanned skin.

A whole range of items, including gun cases, quivers, tump-lines, baby carriers, dog packs and bags of various forms, were made from skins. *Babiche*, thin-cut lines of rawhide, was (and still is) one of the most versatile of traditional resources. It was used for snares, for snowshoe lacings and for infilling ice-scoops, for making strong, yet light, netted bags and for fastenings and lashings of all kinds. When modern technology fails, it has been used to make running repairs to chainsaws and outboard motors.[27]

The most important use of skins, however, was in the manufacture of clothing. Everyday clothing was similar for both sexes – a shirt or parka (generally longer for women), leggings or trousers, and moccasins. Some western groups like the Kutchin wore trousers with footwear attached. A cap or hood, mittens and a fur-lined robe or coat were added in cold weather.

The skins were cut up with a sharp flint or obsidian (later metal) knife and the pieces stitched together with sinew threaded through small holes punched along the seam lines with an awl.[28] Different types or parts of skin were preferred for different items of clothing – leg skins for mittens and moccasin uppers, for example, and calfskin for undergarments. When large game was scarce, shirts and robes might be made from rabbit skins, cut into strips and woven to make a warm fur fabric.[29] Fish skin was used in some parts of Alaska, where the Kolchan, for example, wore rain capes made of salmon skin.

With the establishment of trading posts, people increasingly came into contact with European manufactures, including ready-made clothing of wool and cotton. As early as 1809, David Harmon, a trader among the

Beaver, noted that 'the greater part of them are now clothed with European goods'.[30] By the beginning of the 20th century traditional everyday skin clothing, apart from a few items like mittens and moccasins, had more or less disappeared, replaced by garments of European style and fabric.[31]

■ Painting

Paint, most commonly red and black, was used to decorate a variety of objects, including snowshoes, sleds, canoe gunwales, drums, dishes and garments, particularly along the seams. Red, the most popular color, was originally obtained from local earth pigments, but vermilion, brighter and clearer, was supplied by traders from the earliest period of contact. Black was probably derived from burned bones or charcoal.

Designs tended to be highly symbolic. In the early 1770s Samuel Hearne watched Chipewyan warriors painting their shields with red and black designs in preparation for battle –

> ' . . . some with the figure of the sun, others with that of the moon, several with different kinds of birds and beasts of prey and many with the images of imaginary beings . . . I learned that each man painted his shield with the image of that being on which he relied most for success in the intended engagement.'[32]

Perhaps the best-known examples of Subarctic painted decoration are to be found on the caribou-skin coats worn by Montagnais-Naskapi hunters at least from the 18th century until the 1930s.[33] Part of their interest lies in the way in which they reflect the changing styles of European fashion during this period. In fact they illustrate a trend found all over the Subarctic (generally not until the 19th century) whereby garments, while continuing to be made from traditional materials, began to borrow European stylistic features such as center front openings, collars and cuffs.

The main significance of the Montagnais-Naskapi coats, however, lies with the designs, for these coats were made and worn in order to enlist supernatural aid in hunting the all-important caribou. A hunter received instructions in dreams concerning the symbols which would give him the special power he needed. He passed the dream instructions to his wife, who translated them into visual form by painting the skin.[34]

The designs themselves – intricate combinations of double curves, crosses, dots, lozenges, triangles, leaf- and heart-shaped motifs, among others – were applied to the coats with tools made of caribou antler or bone. The pigments used were yellow (derived from sucker-fish roe), red (locally obtained hematite or vermilion), black (possibly burned bone) and blue (indigo supplied by traders and, from the mid-19th century, laundry blue).[35]

The layout of the painted designs is remarkably standard and clearly subscribes to established tradition, the main pattern areas being the hem, the center back and fronts, and the collar. The most important constant feature of the coats is the back gusset, a narrow triangle of skin inserted where another triangle of skin has been cut out. As Dorothy Burnham has suggested, this painted area is almost certainly the symbolic center of the coat's power, representing 'the Magical Mountain where the Lord of The Caribou lived and from the fastness of which the caribou were released to give themselves to the hunter'.[36]

■ Quill and Hair Embroidery

Although very few precontact examples survive, quillwork was among the very earliest artifacts collected by European explorers, and from their comments it is evident that quill weaving and embroidery were already well-developed and sophisticated crafts by the time of contact.

Mackenzie, at the end of the 18th century, expressed admiration for the work done by Slavey and Dogrib women:

'They make their Clothing of the Rein or Moos Deer well dressed . . . some of which they embroider very neatly with Porcupine Quills & the Hair of the Moos Deer painted Red, Black, Yellow & White . . . The cinctures of garters are of Porcupine Quills wove with Sinews & are the neatest thing of the kind that ever I saw . . .'[37]

Quills included both porcupine and split bird quills, usually goose, and hair included moose and caribou, although where both were available the former was preferred. All these materials could be colored with dyes derived from plant or mineral sources, but the natural colors were used as required. Quills were sometimes dyed black or dark brown by being tied up and boiled with lichen. A later variant of this technique was to boil quills with blue or red trade cloth so that they absorbed the color. In modern times crepe paper has been used in the same way to produce red, green and yellow quills.

There were various ways of using quills, the most straightforward being to lay them in parallel rows, each being held by a stitch in the middle and at either end. This was the method applied to the stiffer, less malleable bird quills and was used for items like belts and tump-lines.

The simplest method of decorating clothing was by wrapping flattened porcupine quills around thong fringes. More complex techniques involved folding the quills over and under one or two sinew threads to produce lines or bands of color which could be combined to make patterns of rectangular blocks, stepped triangles and crosses. However, undoubtedly the finest porcupine quillwork was that which was woven either on a bow loom or directly onto the skin ground on a sinew cross-weft. Almost certainly, it was woven quillwork which so impressed Mackenzie.

Traditional woven and applied quillwork produced intricate geometric patterns, but during the 19th century curvilinear and floral patterns, first produced in eastern Canada via the European embroidery tradition, moved rapidly westwards.[38] By 1850 Dr. John Rae had acquired, probably from the Cree, a guncase decorated with double-curve moosehair scrolls.[39] Ten years later Andrew Flett of the Hudson's Bay Company collected for the Industrial Museum of Scotland a pair of Kutchin mooseskin moccasins embroidered with a floral motif in red and blue porcupine quills edged with moosehair.[40]

By that time, too, Indian women had acquired steel needles and silk thread and, influenced by fort life and mission schools, were producing skin moccasins, mittens, gloves, bags and other items decorated with silk floral embroidery entirely in the European tradition.[41] When both silks and quills are used to decorate the same object, the stiffness and formality of the quillwork is in striking contrast to the exuberance of the embroidery. Although quillwork continued to be used to decorate clothing, it is clear that Indian craftswomen had come to recognize its limitations and that, as European materials became more freely available, it would increasingly be relegated to a secondary position.

■ Beadwork

Beads made of bone, shell, copper, seeds and dried berries were used as jewelry and to decorate clothing in precontact times and into the Historic Period. After European contact, imported glass beads and metal ornaments began to be found alongside native materials. As Lieutenant Zagoskin wrote in the 1840s when visiting the mouth of the Yukon River:

'All the natives of the interior, are passionately fond of finery and bright colors. They have contrived to adorn their simple clothing by sewing on porcupine quills, deer hair, borders of threaded beads, shells, pendants cut out of copper, little bells and so on . . .'[42]

Glass beads came in a range of colors and sizes. The large beads supplied by Russian traders on the North Pacific coast from the end of the 18th century varied from 'necklace' beads (7mm or more in diameter), to 'pony' beads (3-4mm). Further east 'seed' beads (2mm or less) were in use by the mid-18th century, becoming widespread by the second half of the 19th century.[43] Faceted metal beads became popular towards the end of the 19th century, the 'silver' beads being polished iron and the 'gold' ones brass or copper.

As beads became more readily available in the 19th century, they were incorporated into the established geometric design tradition and it is possible to trace the continuity from quilled designs to very similar ones produced with beads or by combinations of beads and dentalia shells.[44] Kutchin garments and accessories collected in the 1860s show dentalia and glass beads being used in equal proportion to produce checkered bands of color on the yoke seams and cuffs of dresses and shirts and down the seams of leggings.

Beads were attached to skin and cloth using a two-thread couching technique, whereby the beads, strung on one thread, are stitched to the surface at intervals by a second thread passing between every two or three beads. This technique allowed the beadworker greater flexibility of design since the strung beads could be turned in any direction desired and this, together with the introduction of steel needles and cotton thread, led to the great development of floral beadwork throughout most of the Subarctic region in the latter half of the 19th century.

Some of the far western groups like the Tahltan did retain more geometric patterns adapted from quillwork and basketry and their bold, rectilinear beadwork designs are in strong contrast to the conventionalized floral and curvilinear designs being produced elsewhere. The woven beadwork in some areas also retained the rectilinear designs necessitated by the weaving technique.

Present-day beadworkers continue to practice and develop floral beadwork, although always within the established design tradition, because 'that is how it is done'. The respect for technical quality remains, with emphasis on matching beads for size and color, even stitching and symmetry of design. It is these qualities which Indian craftswomen find aesthetically pleasing – in the words of a modern beadworker, Minnie Peter of Fort Yukon, – 'I like to make something bright. If I want to sew, I like to make something pretty.'[45]

REFERENCES

THE SUBARCTIC

1 Band communication clearly led to efficient exploitation strategies: while living in a severe environment, Smith points out, the Chipewyan 'do not have myths and legends which emphasize starvation' (Smith, 1978:68).

2 Frank G. Speck has discussed the distribution and symbolism of dot ornamentation on both Inuit and Indian objects (Speck, 1925:151-72).

3 See epigraph to this chapter.

4 A close observer of the Chipewyans commented on the large number of caribou hides required to make a complete outfit for one hunter – ten to twelve – and 'an even larger number to supply him with lodge, lines, snares and nets' (Godsell, 1938:246-7).

5 Speyer, 1968:Abb.2 and 4

6 This was actually *within* Russian territory. As Burpee observes, Murray seemed to have deliberately invaded the ground of his rivals, but it was 'all in the game of the fur trade, and that game was a rough-and-tumble affair at the best' (Murray, Burpee ed., 1910:5).

7 Petroff refers to the very high value placed on these shells in 1802: 'The price of one pair of these shells was a whole parka of squirrel skins' (ibid:71).

8 Duncan reports that a Hudson's Bay Company trade list refers to 'amber and crystal beads, both unsalable five years earlier, are listed as now acceptable' (Duncan, 1989:44).

9 Horsehair was another valuable trade item (Turner, 1955:64).

10 I am appreciative of discussions with Katherine Pettipas of the Manitoba Museum of Man and Nature, who first drew my attention to such influences in the summer of 1977.

11 The influence of some particularly active Métis women on such artwork was commented on by Agnes Cameron, a journalist who visited Fort Chipewyan in 1909. Of Mrs. Loutit, a Métis lady of mixed Chipewyan, Cree and Scottish blood, Bell reported 'She weaves fantastic belts of beads and sets the fashion for the whole North' (Cameron, 1912:321).

12 The most powerful of all the Hudson's Bay Company's rivals.

13 The great efforts of the English-born, Archibald Belaney – better known as Grey Owl – in the 1930s to reintroduce the beaver and his emphasis on conservation were to earn him the title, 'Father of Canadian Conservation'.

14 The Canadian director of Greenpeace recently observed: 'Greenpeace, of course, is opposed at a philosophical level to the inflicting of pain on any wildlife at all for any purpose. But . . . where you still have a semblance of the natural ecosystem and where you still have an abundance of the wildlife species . . . I don't see any reason not to attempt, at least, to retain some kind of balance between the original peoples there and the wildlife resources and the plant resources that they have depended on for so many centuries' (Bourque, 1986:11).

16 Many explorers and traders found, often after initial skepticism, that native technology had much to commend it. Dr John Rae, who explored the western shores of Hudson Bay in the 1840s, wrote: 'At first I could not be persuaded that a person could walk better with such great clumsy looking

things as snowshoes on his feet crunching knee deep in snow, but it did not require very long practice to decide this question in favour of the snowshoes'. Quoted in Idiens & Wilson, 1993:80.

17 It has been suggested that the decoration of ritual equipment with incised lines (for example, items used during periods of puberty seclusion or mourning) may imply that at least some of this was more than merely decorative. (Thompson, 1987:146).

18 None of the Native peoples lived in isolation prior to European contact. All were part of an elaborate and long-established inter-tribal trading network.

19 According to the archaeologist J. V. Wright, 'It has been somewhat of a problem to determine from where this pottery came. It is not part of any of the ceramic complexes to the south, and there exists a broad zone to the northwest completely lacking in and thereby precluding a possible Asiatic origin. The only reasonable alternative is that the idea of pottery was adopted from the south via stimulus diffusion and that the Archaic populations of the Shield evolved a distinctive ceramic complex after they had acquired the essential techniques of manufacture.' (Helm, 1981:89)

20 Koyukon and Ingalik continued to make clay lamps and cooking pots into the Historic Period and into the 20th century.

21 The effect of Europeans was felt long before they actually appeared and western manufactured goods were traded through the existing aboriginal networks to become part of the cultural inventory of groups far from the point of source.

22 Mackenzie, 1970:133

23 Mackenzie, 1970:291 A traditional method of cooking was to fill a container with food and water and drop in heated stones until the water boiled.

24 It has been suggested that this style of decoration may in fact pre-date European contact because of its similarity to the earliest known woven quillwork, although the few bark trays so far recovered are undecorated. (Duncan, 1989:26).

25 Perhaps the most unusual method of decorating bark is that still practiced today by Cree women in Manitoba and Saskatchewan. By folding a piece of bark and biting it, a skilled worker can create a range of intricate patterns which is revealed when the bark is unfolded.

26 Quoted in McMillan, 1988:219-220.

27 Savishinsky, 1974:21.

28 Eyed needles for sewing appear to have been unknown in the Subarctic until introduced by traders, although eyed needles for lacing snowshoes have been recovered from prehistoric sites.

29 Whole rabbit skins were too flimsy for clothing.

30 Quoted in Duncan, 1989: 38. It was, of course, in the trader's interest that people should bring him their furs and dressed skins rather than turn them into clothing for themselves. When Alexander Murray established Fort Yukon in 1847, he reported, 'Blankets, axes, knives, powder horns and files went off rapidly enough, but it was hard to dispose of the clothing as they consider their own dresses much superior to ours both in beauty and durability, and they are partly right, although I endeavoured to persuade them to the contrary.' Quoted in Nelson, 1973:205.

31 There are still certain areas where traditional materials triumph. The anthropologist Joel Savishinsky records a Hare hunter comparing the skin slippers made by his wife with a pair of store-bought woolen socks: 'Two weeks ago all I had were those lousy woolen ones from the store, but they weren't worth a damn. It was forty or fifty below and my feet were freezing. Then I had Lena make me these. That's some difference I'll tell you. I put these on and I don't care if it's sixty below – it's like I don't feel anything and my feet never hurt.' Quoted in Savishinsky, 1974:21.

32 Quoted in Thompson, 1987:147.

33 Because the style and decoration of these painted coats proved attractive to travelers and collectors, a number have survived from quite an early date. Several of those now in European museums have been dated as early as 1700 – largely on stylistic grounds, since documentation is often lacking.

34 While the designs clearly had very powerful symbolic meaning for the hunter who dreamed them

and had them painted on his coat, it is impossible at this remove even to guess what that meaning might have been. (Burnham,1992:59).

35 It has been noted that, in general, the earlier coats display finer, more detailed painting. Dorothy Burnham has suggested that, before the arrival of Christian missionaries, when hunters were able to have several wives, one might have been released from her other duties to concentrate on painting her husband's coat. (Burnham, 1992:3).

36 While in coats of similar European cut, gussets are introduced to give added fullness to the skirts, this is not necessarily the case with these painted skin coats. On some of the later coats, the insert is actually narrower than the piece it replaced. Thus, the influence of contemporary European fashion, although strong, is more visual than structural. (Burnham, 1992:11-12).

37 Mackenzie, 1970:184.

38 The floral designs which have dominated Subarctic art since the mid-19th century are entirely European in origin.

39 National Museums of Scotland L.304.127.

40 National Museums of Scotland 563.1.

41 White women who exerted influence on native communities – nuns, schoolteachers, the wives of clergymen and traders – actively encouraged Indian women to learn European domestic crafts such as embroidery and lace-making, which they regarded as having a civilizing effect.

42 Quoted in Duncan, 1989:38. Zagoskin is, of course, describing ceremonial or 'dress' clothing. Everyday wear in this area, as elsewhere, was not decorated apart from a few fringes and perhaps a patterned belt. Because such costume was everyday, it was rarely commented on or collected.

43 Venice had the monopoly of glass-bead production until the 1880s, when Bohemian (Czech) beads became available and were imported.

44 The shells mentioned by Zagoskin were almost certainly dentalia or 'tooth shells', which were widely traded from the Pacific coast all over the interior. They were highly prized as decoration and as a form of currency and conspicuous wealth.

45 Quoted in Duncan & Carney, 1988:34.

THE ARCTIC

The Arctic conjures up romantic images of an untamed land of ice and snow, a land of mystery and grandeur. The Arctic is also seen as a harsh, unforgiving environment where any wrong choice is the difference between life and death. The Northwest Passage is one of many places where imagination and reality come together. Explorers have long tested themselves against the Arctic and continue to do so in the twentieth century. Nowadays, the Arctic is frequently envisioned as a refugium, one of the last pristine environments on the planet.

The Arctic is not a vast, uninhabited land. It is the homeland of three separate linguistic groups: the Aleut, the Yup'ik, and the Inuit-Inupiaq. In fact, not all of these groups live in the Arctic as defined by geographers. The Arctic is usually regarded as the region north of the treeline, the mean 50°F (10°C) July isotherm, and/or the line of continuous permafrost. Depending on the definition, some speakers of each of these groups do not live in the Arctic. However, these people are all regarded as the descendants of a common ancestral group, the Eskimo-Aleuts, and therefore they are all regarded as inhabitants of the Arctic by anthropologists.

Archaeologists hypothesize that the Eskimo-Aleuts migrated across the Bering Straits some 8-10,000 years ago. As they spread across the North the three linguistic groups evolved. First, Aleut separated from the Eskimo-Aleut stock and then Yup'ik and Inuit-Inupiaq split. Eventually these people colonized the area from Prince William Sound in southern Alaska to eastern Greenland. The peoples of the Arctic have many diverse cultures. They have never remained static and today they continue to change and adapt to new social, political and economic situations. A 19th-century Aleut love song proclaimed:

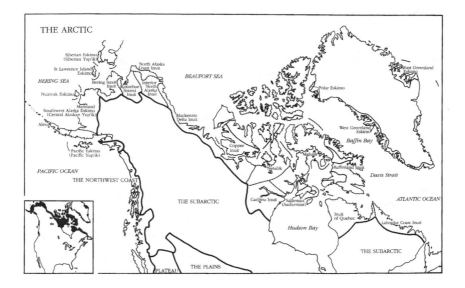

ABOVE: *This map shows the approximate territories of tribes and language groups in about 1850 over most of the region, but somewhat earlier in northwest Alaska and coastal Labrador, and somewhater later for south Alaska and Greenland. After that, many groups lost territory and some disappeared.*

My breath, I have it here
My bones, I have them here
My flesh, I have it here
With it I seek you,
With it I find you,
But speak to me
Say something nice to me.

In 1741 Aleut culture was changed irrevocably by the visit of two Russian ships. Captains Bering and Chirikov, on a voyage of discovery, became the first Europeans to visit the Aleutian Islands. Although Bering later died on the Commander Islands, following a shipwreck, many of his crew returned to Russia with a cargo of sea-otter pelts. These pelts, highly prized by the Chinese Emperor and his court, were virtually unobtainable because sea otters had been hunted almost to extinction in the waters of the western Pacific. The discovery of a new land rich in sea otters led Russian fur traders, known as the *promyshlenniki*, to build boats and set sail for Alaska.

To the Aleuts, the visit of strangers in ships was an oddity but not a unique event. Steller, the naturalist on Bering's ship, noted the presence of iron among the Aleuts:

'Two had, in the fashion of Russian peasants, a long iron knife of very poor workmanship, which may be their own and no European fabrication . . . From a distance, I observed very exactly the quality of this knife, when one of the Americans unsheathed it and cut a bladder in two with it, and I saw . . . that it did not resemble any European workmanship.'

This iron may have come through the growing trade from the Northeast, or more likely it was recovered from Japanese fishing boats blown off course and wrecked on the foggy islands. These contacts with strangers were rare and their impacts on the Aleut society proved to be minimal.

In the early 1700s Aleut society was still expanding. The population for this period has been estimated at 12,000 to 15,000 spread throughout the entire 1,200-mile Aleutian archipelago, a chain of active volcanic islands strung like a pearl necklace across the northern Pacific. The majority of

RIGHT: *Bering Strait Inuit man using a bow drill to make an ivory cribbage board, c.1902. This group produced a great deal of artwork, notably wooden and ivory sculptures.*

BELOW: *Iglulik woman inside an igloo softening a skin by chewing. This could also be carried out by using a stone scraper.*

Aleuts lived on the islands closest to the Alaskan mainland, but even the Near Islands (those nearest Russia) were inhabited. Archaeologists believe that the Aleutians were first occupied about 8,000 years ago with people reaching the Near Islands about 1,000 years ago. This vast region can be divided into two based on dialect: Eastern and Western Aleut. Within these regions there were many village-level societies each of which had their own territorial boundaries and their own leaders.

Relations between villages were generally cordial. Trade goods such as pine bark and birch bark were exchanged from the mainland to the treeless islands. Villagers visited each other for feasts and masked dances usually held in December. However, relations between the various groups were not always harmonious; murders, witchcraft and insults led to stealthy and deadly raids. Captives became slaves, and the raiders would quickly dismember those killed. Dismemberment dissipated the power contained within the deceased, preventing it from harming the attackers.

Aleut homes were dug into the ground to a depth of 5 to 6½ft (1.5-2m). They were then roofed with whale bones and driftwood and covered with sod, '. . . when they have stood for some time they become overgrown with grass, so that a village has the appearance of a European church-yard full of graves'. Some of these houses were single-family dwellings, others were multi-family longhouses 40 to 65ft (12-20m) long and 20 to 33ft (6-10m) wide.

Houses were oriented along an east-west axis and the location of families within a house mirrored the importance of the East in Aleut cosmology where the east was viewed as the home of the creator. The longhouses had a central passageway on either side of which were individual family compartments. All the families living within a longhouse were related. The headman and his family occupied the easternmost compartment while the slaves lived at the western end. Entrance into these houses was through one or two holes in the roof; a notched log provided access from the entrance to the floor.

These holes were the only means of entering and exiting houses. This left the occupants easy prey for surprise attacks. The Aleuts employed three means to counteract this problem. Firstly, villages were usually located on isthmuses or narrow necks of land with dual sea access to provide a means of escape. Secondly, lookouts were posted to watch for unexpected and unwanted arrivals. Thirdly, secret compartments were excavated into house walls. During an attack, people could escape detection by taking shelter in these compartments.

ABOVE: *Men from Icy Cape, Arctic Ocean, Alaska, c.1880. They wear labrets – ornaments of bone and ivory – in holes pierced through the lips at puberty.*

ABOVE: *Copper Inuit caribou hunters. Caribou were mainly hunted with bow and arrow, the former generally composite with sections joined together with sinew.*

Raids were rarely over territory. They were most often retaliatory feuds. The Aleuts had no need to fight over territory as the sea and land provided them with a bounty of resources. Starvation was almost unknown although March was often a lean time. There were very few land mammals on the Aleutians, but this lack of terrestrial fauna was compensated for by the variety of flora, marine fauna and bird life. The starchy roots of several plants were made into a thick gruel; the greens of fiddleheads, mountain sorrel, cress, cowslip and others were eaten, and some herbs and roots were gathered for medicinal purposes. Berries, including crow berries, salmon berries and cloud berries were both consumed fresh and stored for winter use. The beach grass (*Elymus mollis*) was used to produce the exceptionally fine baskets and mats made by Aleut women. Grasses were split into thin strands by fingernails and then twined. Baskets with over 1,000 stitches per square inch were made. This quality of workmanship and attention to detail was characteristic of items created by Aleut women. Finally, monkshood was known to be poisonous and aconite was probably used for whaling. The gathering of these plants, with the exception of monkshood and some medicinal plants, was women's work. The women would store these seasonal plants for use throughout the year in pokes made from seals or seal-lion stomachs.

Every spring flocks of waterfowl migrate to the Aleutians. Ducks, geese, swans, murres, puffins and many others lay eggs, raise their young and then fly south in the fall. The Aleuts gathered the eggs and hunted the different species, adapting hunting methods to the habits of the birds. For example, puffins nest in burrows, therefore the hunters placed snares over the entrance holes thereby strangling the puffins as they left their burrows in the morning. Another example was the hunting of albatross: 'The people sail out to catch them when the weather is quiet and foggy, because in such weather the birds cannot fly so well. The hunters move against them, since they know that the birds always fly up against the wind.'

The intertidal zone provided shellfish, octopus and seaweeds, foods that were gathered easily by women, children and the elderly. The availability of these resources gave widows a freedom to choose their own future rather than remarrying immediately as was the case among other northern peoples. They also saw people through the lean times when stores ran low and it was too rough to go out hunting.

Salmon were harvested throughout the summer and early autumn when they migrated up the short Aleutian rivers to spawn. Although many were

407

caught and dried for winter use, the staples of the Aleut diet were the marine mammals, especially sea lions. These mammals were hunted by men from their *baidarkas* (the Russian name for the Aleut kayak). Sea lions, seals and sea otters were hunted with darts thrown overhand using throwing boards. All men hunted these species. For a successful hunt a man had to prepare himself both physically and spiritually. Included in his hunting equipment were amulets to attract the animals and appease their spirits. 'Their preparation and place of preservation are kept secret, one observer noted, otherwise the amulets will lose their power. It is necessary to protect them from wetness; if an amulet becomes wet its owner will rot.'

Only a few men who had undergone special training would hunt whales. The hunt began on shore with the collection of the whaler's amulets and the preparation of a special potion used to coat the dart and poison the whale. Some of the amulets used included hematite, feathers of a rosy finch and fluids from mummified bodies of dead hunters. The latter were considered extremely powerful amulets but the owner of such an amulet would lead a short life. When a whale was sighted a single hunter would set out to sea in his baidarka, then he would throw his dart into the whale and immediately return home, where he would enter an isolation hut and lie under a blanket for three days while remaining motionless. 'He behaved, . . . like a sick man and thus by sympathetic magic attempted to persuade the whale to be sick,' wrote W.S. Laughlin. On the third day he would rise when the whale was seen to be dying. The people dispatched the whale and brought it to shore. It is not known how successful this method of hunting was. If the whale did not drift into your particular territory it might end up as the bounty of another village.

All of these dangerous hunts were undertaken in the baidarka, a watercraft renowned for its speed and its ability to withstand the rough waters of the Gulf of Alaska. The Aleut baidarka was unique among kayaks as it had a bifurcated prow and a straight stern. These design elements are thought to have allowed the baidarka to ride over waves and to counteract ' . . . the lift created when the bow meets waves' respectively. In the event of a sudden storm, Aleut would strap their baidarkas together, thus creating a more stable craft.

Boys began learning kayaking skills from an early age. They had their tendons and ligaments stretched to allow them to sit in the baidarka for hours. They also played games mimicking hunting from a baidarka and practiced with a baidarka in calm waters. Later, they would venture out in a two-hatched baidarka with an experienced hunter, often a maternal uncle. By late teens a boy would become a man by building his own baidarka. He was then considered to be ready for marriage.

Constructing a baidarka was extremely complex. First, driftwood was collected for the frame. Then the baidarka was crafted to the exact measurement of its owner. Many of the construction techniques were jealously guarded secrets passed from the father or uncle to the boy. According to one observer:

> 'In some places, where the different pieces of the skeleton are fastened together, two flat bones are bound cross-ways over the joint inside, and this the chief assured me was of the greatest use in stormy weather. As the fastenings are apt to be loosened by the shock of the waves, these bones contribute essentially towards preventing such an inconvenience; but this art is not known to all, and is kept very much secret by those who possess it.'

Finally, women would cover the baidarka with the skins of sea lions. The women had to be careful that none of their hairs were caught in the seams or a sea lion, enraged by this female contamination, would bite a hole in it.

The Russian interest in the Aleuts is as much due to the versatility of the baidarka as to the presence of the sea otters in the region. When the promyshlenniki first visited the Aleutians, they hunted by themselves. The Aleuts were regarded simply as useful trading partners. Then the Russians realized the potential of the baidarka for sea-otter hunting. They began exploiting the Aleut hunters, forcing their villages to hunt by capturing hostages who were then returned at the end of the hunting season.

In the early 1760s the eastern Aleuts tried to rebel but they were crushed. In one incident, the Russian Soloviev lined up a dozen men from Kashega and fired his musket at point-blank range to see how many Aleuts one bullet would kill. The answer was nine. The Aleut recognized their inability to succeed against the guns of the Russians. Introduced diseases further reduced their numbers and by 1799 only an eighth of the pre-contact population remained.

The Russian American Company (RAC) was established in 1799 and granted monopoly trading rights by the Russian crown. For most Aleuts this charter meant they became vassals of the company. The RAC was allowed to employ half the able-bodied men of a village and need only pay them a fifth of the wages of a Russian although often even these provisions were ignored by the company. This led to complaints by the Aleuts to the crown and a revision of the RAC charter in 1821. The change allowed the company to employ half the able-bodied men of a village for a period no longer than three years. By the 1800s Aleuts had been settled on the Commander and Pribilof Islands (the breeding grounds of the northern fur seal) by the RAC and Aleut hunters were located in Sitka and at the company's post, Fort Ross, on the California coast. One song in particular captures the loneliness of an Aleut hunter a long way from home.

Oh, what is it going to be?
What is he going to say?
Not expecting to be like this,
I entered again the end of it.
My islands, my dear islands there east!
Above them the clouds will be light in
*   the morning.*
Over there it will be like that, too, in the morning.
If I live on like this, endless, unceasing.
This boredom, this grief!

Under the 1821 revision to its charter the RAC had to provide schooling, health services, churches and missionaries. The schools provided instruction not only in reading and writing but also in trades including shipbuilding, carpentry and metal-working. Many of the students attending these schools were the offspring of Russian-Aleut unions, known as creoles. These unions led to a new class of people. At the top were the Russians, followed by the creoles and at the bottom the Aleuts. Health care was rudimentary; however, it did include a massive vaccination program following the devastating smallpox epidemic of 1838.

Most Aleuts were converted to the Russian (Orthodox) Church by lay preachers who also built small churches. In 1824 the first missionary, Father Veniaminov, arrived in the Aleutians. This priest, beloved by his Alaskan parishioners, later became the Metropolitan of the church and is now Saint Innokenti. Another of the early priests was the creole Father Netsvetov, who had been educated in Russia. Why did the Aleuts embrace Christianity so readily? Part of the answer may lie in the church's ability to provide hope and succour. Another part may lie in the god-parenting of Aleuts by Russians creating kin and economic ties of benefit to both groups.

By 1867 Aleut society had adapted to the Russian presence. The population showed signs of recovery, many Aleut children received some schooling and everyone belonged to the Russian Orthodox faith. However, the Opium Wars had caused the sea-otter market to collapse and RAC efforts to diversify the Alaskan economy had proved unsuccessful. Also, Russian America was a very long way from Moscow. Therefore, the Russian empire accepted an American offer to purchase Alaska for $7.2 million in gold.

Once again, without warning, life changed for the Aleut. The RAC was gone, the schools were closed, as were the health clinics, and many educated creoles chose to move to Russia. All that remained of the Russian presence was the church whose ministers were permitted to stay. The Aleuts were still vassals but they had lost power. The Russians had needed the Aleuts and the relationship had become symbiotic. The days of the sea-otter hunt were gone and the Aleuts no longer had access to the trade goods on which they depended. The Aleutian Islands became a far flung and forgotten corner of the USA. Not until 1885, eighteen years after the departure of the RAC, was a mission with a school established.

Gradually, Americans began to discover and exploit their new colony. A San Francisco concern purchased the assets of the RAC and then renamed it the Alaska Commercial Company (ACC). The ACC, interested in profits, concentrated on the lucrative Pribilof Island seal industry. The Americans expanded both the seal and sea-otter hunts, removing all quotas implemented by the RAC to protect these populations. By the 1880s the seal population exhibited signs of overhunting and the sea otter population was on the verge of extinction. In 1911 an international treaty curtailed the hunting of sea otter and placed strict quotas on the seal hunt.

Foxes were indigenous to a few of the Aleutian Islands and some had been introduced by the Russians. Independent American trappers and traders began leasing entire islands from the government in 1880. With no predators and abundant waterfowl the foxes prospered and so did some of the independents. However, the collapse of the fur market in 1941 spelled the end of this industry. This boom-and-bust economy characterized other industries on the Aleutians prior to the Second World War. A gold mine brought a flurry of activity from 1886 to 1908. A cod-salting station was built in 1876 and was soon followed by salmon canneries and the establishment of a Norwegian shore-based whaling station. This station operated from 1907 until 1939 taking an average 100 whales per season.

The beginnings of the Second World War saw a collapse in the never stable economy of the Aleutian Islands. The Aleuts found themselves in the position described by Leo Moses:

Only the mind
will make a person
continue on,
only his will to follow
those who are successful,
Will bring him finally to his goal.
Great wealth will not bring him all that
*   way*
only his will to follow those who are
*   successful.*
Whoever has very little
must aspire to do
as others around him who are more
*   successful do.*

He must try to imitate, follow, and
*   listen*
to those he wants to be like, and only
in this way can he succeed in life.

Speakers of Yup'ik languages have lived for centuries on both sides of the Bering Strait. Across this narrow waterway they traded, visited and occasionally fought. The many items traded from Siberia to Alaska included iron, tobacco and the skins of domestic reindeer. The mottled, variated domestic reindeer skins were especially valued by the Yup'ik of southwestern Alaska as they were more colorful than the coats of the wild Alaskan caribou. Tobacco, another prized commodity, almost circumnavigated the globe from its homeland in eastern North America to Alaska. Despite these ties, the differences between Yup'ik-speaking groups are vast. There are five separate Yup'ik languages: Sireniski, Central Siberian Yup'ik, Naukanski (Siberian Eskimo), Central Alaskan Yup'ik (Mainland

Southwest Alaskan Eskimo) and Pacific Yup'ik (Pacific Eskimo). In fact, the Siberian Yup'ik (Siberian Eskimo) are actually more similar to their Maritime Chukchi neighbors than to their American relatives. This diversity extends from language to economy, social organization, belief systems and contact history. For our purposes, only one language group will be discussed: the Central Alaskan Yup'ik, who inhabit the mainland of southwestern Alaska.

The pre-contact social organization of the Yup'ik centered on the family, as did the Aleut, although it was not as hierarchial, nor were slaves kept. Village societies maintained territories large enough to support their needs. The Yukon–Kuskokwim Delta teems with wildlife although much of it – the birds, anadromous fish and caribou – is migratory. This abundance enabled the Yup'ik to live in permanent villages located along river banks. During the spring, summer and fall they would travel into the country to intercept migrating wildlife.

Each village consisted of many single-family homes and one or two *qasgiq*, or communal men's house. Single-family dwellings belonged to the women and were their domain. This is where they would sew, cook and raise their children. At around the age of six a boy would move from his mother's home to the *qasgiq*. This large dwelling had an important place in the lives of the men for it was where they ate, worked, played, held ceremonies, took sweat baths and slept. The transition to the *qasgiq* signaled the beginning of a boy's training for manhood. Joseph Eriday of Chevak said in 1978:

> 'It was good for us to hear the admonitions of those in the *qasgiq* who did the speaking there, though we did not always think so. Poor me! Sometimes I thought they could see right through into me, into my life, when they spoke. It was chilling, I tingled all over. How could they know me so well . . . Their instructions on how to live come up again, and again . . . It is true, the *qasgiq* is a place of instruction, the only place where the necessary instruction can be given in full.'

These instructions were extremely important. It was not enough for the youth to gain technical skills; they had to learn their place in the universe. In Yup'ik cosmology the universe consisted of many different layers held in a delicate balance. The ill-considered actions of people could offend the spirits thus upsetting this balance. The result could be illness, poor hunting or stormy weather.

Therefore, a necessary part of growing up was learning correct behavior. For example, the relatives of a dead person could not use any sharp tools in case they accidentally cut the deceased's spirit. If a spirit was cut, 'it would become very angry and bring sickness or death to the people'. While boys learned in the communal men's houser, girls learned from their mothers and female relatives.

The Yup'ik also believed in two different worlds: the visible and the invisible. These two worlds occupied the same physical space although the spirits of the latter were seldom visible to the occupants of the former. The extensive boundary between these worlds was permeable, however, and at times of transition such as birth, death or puberty it was most transparent.

At these times accordance with proper ritual was crucial or *tunghat*, generally malevolent spirits, could be released and would harm the people.

All objects, animate and inanimate, had spirits or *yuas* of human form. In the past all animals had the ability to transmute at will. In *Adventures of a Young Girl*, Ella Lewis wrote:

> 'After a while she saw a fierce old wolf coming over the rise on the bank of the lake. His red tongue hung out. When he came down he went over to the girl and prodded her on her side with his nose. Then he stood up beside her and was transformed into a big husky man in his prime. He wore nothing but a cape of wolfskin.'

By the time of contact, animals had lost this power.

Occasionally, a hunter would still glimpse a human face in the eye of an animal he was pursuing and know that he had seen its *yua*. He would then carve a mask of his vision and at the next festival he would sing of his encounter while dancing with the mask. Shamans had similar experiences with *tunghat* which only they could see.

The following dance was witnessed by Lieutenant Zagoskin in the early 1840s:

> 'But now the skylight opens, and quickly, in a flash, a dancer slides down a strap and with a quick leap is on the stage; two pairs of women take their places beside him. He is wearing a mask representing a fantastic raven's head, and there he goes jumping about on

the stage, calling like a raven; the drums sound their rhythmic beat, the singers strike up a song. The dancer at one time represents a raven perching and hopping like bird; at another time he represents the familiar actions of a man who is unsuccessful in everything. The content of the dance is explained in the words of the song and may briefly be described as follows. A shaman is living in his trail camp. He is hungry, and he notices that wherever he goes a raven goes with him and gets in his way. If the game he is pursuing is a deer, the raven from some place or other caws, startles the deer, and makes it impossible to creep up within a bowshot of it. If the man sets a noose for hare or partridge, the raven tangles it or runs off with it. If he sets a fish-trap for imagnat, there too the raven finds a way to do him harm. "Who are you?" cries the shaman at last. The spirit in the form of the raven smiles and answers: "Your evil fate." '

Shamans were holistic healers, treating their patients' physical, psychological and spiritual symptoms. Gifted individuals, they could devine the cause of ill health or poor hunting. When the infractions of people upset the universe the shaman would fly to the spirit world and mediate with the spirits in an effort to restore the balance.

Shamans and elders were responsible for the yearly ceremonial cycle. There were four major annual festivals: the Asking Festival (*Petugtaq*), the Feast of the Dead (*Merr'aq*), the Bladder Festival (*Nakaciuq*) and the Inviting-in Festival (*Kelek/Itruka'ar*). The Asking Festival was an intra-village event where kin relationships, particularly cross-cousin ties, were reinforced through the exchange of requested gifts. The Feast of the Dead ensured that the deceased would have food, drink and clothing in the after-world. At the Bladder Festival the bladders of all seals caught during the year were inflated, painted and hung in the *qasgiq*. The souls of the seals lived in the bladders and for several days they were offered food, song and dances. Finally, the bladders and the souls were returned to the water. If the seals had been treated with respect they would allow themselves to be recaptured. The final festival of the year was the Inviting-in Feast. For this ceremony, held when food was scarcest, the people invited the spirits to share in what they had left. By inviting the spirits, the people hoped to ensure successful hunting for the coming year.

Other festivals were held at different intervals. One of these was the Great Feast of the Dead. At this festival, often held ten years after the death, gifts were given away to honor the deceased. During the festival the spirit of the deceased was believed to enter its namesake. Many gifts and clothing were given to the namesake and were therefore also given to the deceased.

Once this festival had been held, it was no longer necessary to remember the individuals at the annual Feast of the Dead. Words to the deceased, as recorded by E.W. Nelson in the 1896-97 Bureau of American Ethnology *Annual Report*, included:

> *My children, where are you?*
> *Ai-ya-ya-yai.*
> *Come back to us, our children,*
> *We are lonely and sad.*
> *Ai-ya-ya-yai.*
> *For our children are gone,*
> *While those of our friends remain*
> *Ai-ya-ya-yai.*
> *Come back, nephew, come back, we*
> *   miss you;*
> *Ai-ya-ya-yai.*
> *Come back to us our lost ones,*
> *We have presents for you,*
> *Ai-ya-ya-yai.*

The importance of the spirit world was not confined to rules of behavior and ceremonies, it permeated all aspects of Yup'ik life. Hunting equipment was exquisitely fashioned to please the *yua* of the prey, thus persuading it to give itself to the hunter. By carving bears, wolves and otters onto his weapons, the hunter appropriated the qualities of these predators. These disparate concepts, spiritual appeasement and appropriation of spiritual power, were also incorporated into the clothing that was sewn by women.

Very complex concepts were contained in the Yup'ik symbols on clothing and tools. A hole placed in the palm of a thumbless hand symbolized the game that the *tunghat* had allowed to escape from the skyworld for consumption by people. One simple symbol, the circle and dot motif, represented the Yup'ik world view. Like the universe, it had several layers of meaning: it stood for the all-seeing eye, the world and the layers of the universe, and the crucial passageway from one world into the next.

The first direct contact the Central Alaskan Yup'ik had with Europeans was with the Russians. This contact began following the establishment of the RAC's trading monopoly in 1799. The Russians explored southern Alaska and realized that beaver were available on the mainland. As the sea-otter populations declined Russian interest in the beaver increased. The RAC constructed several trading posts on the mainland in the early 1800s. By 1845 Russian Orthodox missionaries had established themselves at most of these posts. The Yup'ik, however, maintained their independence from the RAC and some were even able to resist conversion to Christianity.

Following the sale of Alaska to the United States, the RAC was replaced by the Alaska Commercial Company with very little impact on the population except an increase in quantity and variety of trade goods. However, Yup'ik desire for trading goods led to a gradual change in their economy. Individuals who spent more time trapping beavers had proportionally less time available for subsistence hunting. Eventually, this led to a dependence on the trading posts. In many communities, however, the subsistence economy with its seasonal hunting and gathering cycle was hardly disturbed at all.

The Russian Orthodox church continued to play an important role in Yup'ik daily life. Missionaries of other faiths attempted to convert the Yup'ik but they proved to be mostly unsuccessful. The work of a powerful Inuit minister led to the founding of a successful Moravian mission in Bethel in 1885.

The 'rich man's route' to the Klondike gold rush was up the Yukon River by paddle steamer from Saint Michael, Alaska. However, no gold was found in the Yup'ik territory and so the thousands of miners pouring into the Yukon Territory from 1896 to 1899 had almost no impact on the local population.

In 1883 the first salmon cannery opened in the area and was quickly followed by others. At first these canneries employed Euro-American and Philippino workers, but by the 1920s many of the workers were Native Alaskans. Seasonal job opportunities in the canneries were responsible for an out-migration from some of the more northern and interior communities into Bristol Bay. These canneries and the trapping industry soon became the main employers of Yup'ik prior to the Second World War.

Other than Christianity and clapboard above-ground homes, Yup'ik culture prior to the war was similar to the pre-contact culture. The last masked dance ceremonies were performed in the 1930s. Recently, this

417

tradition as well as others have been undergoing a revival. A mother's poem spoke of the peaceful joy of being:

> It is so still in the house,
> There is calm in the house;
> The snowstorm wails out there,
> And the dogs are rolled up with snouts
>   under the tail.
> My little boy is sleeping on the ledge,
> On his back he lives, breathing through
>   his open mouth.
> His little stomach is bulging round -
> Is it strange if I start to cry with joy?

Speakers of Inuit-Inupiaq live in four countries – the U.S.S.R., the United States of America, Canada and Greenland (formerly part of Denmark). Despite the thousands of miles involved, Inuit-Inupiaq is regarded by linguists as a single language with many separate dialects. The cohesiveness of the language stems from a relatively recent migration from northern Alaska to Greenland in about AD 1,000. Northern Canada and Greenland were both inhabited as early as 2,500 BC, however this population was then overpowered and assimilated by the later migrants who adopted their culture and language.

The patient fur-clad man poised over a seal breathing hole. The smiling baby peeking out from its mother's parka. A howling wind sweeping over dogs and an igloo. A man paddling a kayak. These images form the stereotype of the Inuit – a smiling, friendly people eking out a marginal existence in a harsh environment. This stereotype ignores the diversity and complexity of Inuit societies. The Nuvugmiut (a subgroup of the North Alaska Coast Inuit) of northern Alaska were whale hunters and lived in semi-subterranean log houses in large permanent villages. They rarely used kayaks and only made snowhouses if caught on the land in a snowstorm. Their society was highly structured with special status accorded to the *umialik*, owner of a whale-hunting boat. In contrast, the Padlirmiut (a subgroup of the Caribou Inuit) lived a nomadic lifestyle on the west coast of Hudson Bay. In spring they hunted seals basking on the ice; however, the rest of the year was spent in the interior hunting caribou and musk oxen. Padlirmiut society was strongly egalitarian; knowledgeable individuals were asked for advice but each person was free to reach his or her own decisions.

British explorers' descriptions of the Central Inuit, the people of the Canadian Arctic, are the origin of the Eskimo stereotype. There are many divisions within the Central Inuit; one of these is the Iglulik Inuit. The Iglulik Inuit consist of four societies: the Tununirusirmiut (of northern Baffin Island), the Tununirmuit (of northern Baffin Island), the Iglulingmiut (of northern Foxe Basin) and the Aivilingmiut (of the north-west coast of Hudson Bay). In this section the culture and contact history of one of the Iglulik societies – the Aivilingmiut – will be considered in more detail.

While reading about the Aivilingmiut it is necessary to realize that generalizations are being made. There are myriad ecological niches across the north, each one providing Inuit with the challenge of discovering its complexities and designing hunting strategies to exploit its resources. Inuit oral history contains accounts of individuals or groups who migrated into new regions and starved because they were unfamiliar with local conditions. In one particular incident, a murderer and his extended family (Tununirusirmiut) fled their home in order to escape revenge. They found an uninhabited island with abundant marine life and decided to settle. All winter they waited for the ice to freeze solid. It never did and eventually they all starved to death except one woman. In this region the local population (Iglulingmiut) had learned to hunt on the shifting ice flows and thin elastic ice (only a few centimeters thick). The migrants, ignorant of this particular technique, eventually starved to death, surrounded by a sea of plenty.

Inuit-Inupiaq, in common with Aleut and Yup'ik, is an agglutinative language. For instance, the name Aivilingmiut is composed of *aivik* (walrus), -*lik* (place) and -*miut* (people of); it means, people of the place of walrus. The Aivilingmiut were renowned for their walrus-hunting and their concomitantly strong dog teams. These teams enabled people to travel long distances to hunt, to visit relatives and, later, to visit trading posts. Long voyages occurred in spring when the days were lengthening and warming, migratory birds were returning to their breeding grounds and basking seals provided relatively easy prey.

As the summer approached the hunters would move to the floe edge for walrus hunting. Walrus were harpooned either from the floe edge or from kayaks. The prow of the kayak was made narrow in order that the hunter could aim it directly between the tusks of an enraged walrus, thus preventing the walrus from ripping the skin of the kayak and drowning its occupant.

Once caught, the walrus was butchered and most of it cached for future use. Some parts were eaten immediately, either raw or cooked over a bone and oil fire. The Inuit diet is almost entirely meat. Meat contains all the nutrients required for life as long as both the fat and meat are consumed and a significant portion of the meat is eaten raw.

In autumn, people would split into smaller groups, which were often no larger than one or two families and travel to their summer hunting grounds. These families had areas they visited habitually and, while there was no individual ownership of land, if others wished to hunt in these areas it was only polite to ask permission. Autumn hunting varied. Generally, older men stayed on the coast hunting walrus, seals and whales until the sea ice formed. Younger men, on the other hand, often hunted caribou in the interior.

Caribou were hunted in many different ways. In some cases hunters would sneak up on the caribou raising their hands above their heads as if antlers. In other cases stone hunting blinds were built beside caribou trails. Yet another method required the participation of the entire family. A series of *inukshuit* (means: 'look like people') of stone were built along a caribou trail. Caribou mistook these cairns for people and were channeled into either a river or narrow valley. This method of corralling allowed people to take many caribou in a short time. The caribou provided not only sustenance but also bone and antler for tools, and fur for clothing. Caribou taken in September and October were preferred for clothing. Those taken later in the year, when the caribou had longer hair, were used for bedding.

When the sea froze (usually in the middle of September) the older men and their families would also go caribou hunting. At this time of the year, Arctic char were caught using leisters at stone weirs. Some were dried and could easily be carried when the family moved camp. Others were cached and collected later by dog team.

In January/February the Aivilingmiut congregated in large villages of snowhouses. Snow is a versatile building material; not only is it plastic but it is also a good insulator. When traveling the Aivilingmiut built simple one-room snowhouses. In winter villages the houses could last several months. These complex houses had entrance passages and side chambers for clothes and meat storage. Sometimes houses were connected so that people could visit without going outside.

In winter, when the weather was bad, the people would live on their cached supplies. However, they took advantage of calm days to hunt seals at their breathing holes. Seals keep many breathing holes open and the Aivilingmiut practiced several methods to increase their chances of success. Usually a group of hunters would go out together and each stand at a breathing hole. Sometimes, the women and children would scare the seal away from its other breathing holes, thereby forcing it to the hole where the hunter waited. At other times a boy would drive a dog team in a wide circle around the hole occupied by the hunter thereby frightening the seal toward it.

Winter was also a time for socializing, telling stories and renewing friendships and alliances. A single family's home was too small for a community gathering: consequently a large snowhouse, an architectural marvel, sometimes over 23ft (7m) in diameter was constructed. In this building drum dances and shamanic seances were held. At the dances people would sing their personal songs. The following is the song of a great hunter and modest man:

> *It is a time of hunger,*
> *But I don't feel like hunting.*
> *I don't care for the advice of old people,*
> *I only care for dreaming, wishing, nothing else.*
> *I only care for gossip;*
> *I am fond of young caribou, the age they*
> *   start getting their antlers.*
> *Nobody is like me,*
> *I am too lazy, simply too lazy,*
> *I just can't bring myself to go and get*
> *   some meat.*

Aivilingmiut beliefs were quite similar to those of the Yup'ik. When the weather was poor or game disappeared, the shaman would hold a seance to divine the cause. During seances such as these, shamans transformed into bears and visited Uiniyumayuittuq (literally 'one who does not want a husband'), from whose hands sprang all sea mammals and who therefore controlled them. The shaman would comb her hair and ask forgiveness for the transgressions of the people. As one hunter said:

That woman down there beneath the
  sea,
She wants to hide the seals from us.
These hunters in the dance-house,
They cannot right matters.
They cannot mend matters.
Into the spirit world
Will go I,
Where no humans dwell.
Set matters right will I.
Set matters right will I.

Shamans were highly regarded individuals but they were not viewed as leaders. Likewise elders were respected and their opinions sought. Also, skilled individuals were consulted. A man who combined several of these functions was known as an *isumataq* (literally 'one who thinks'). He had the ability to command individuals and create new camps. This position was held through general acknowledgement not through coercion or heredity.

Aivilingmiut society was fairly flexible; people could come and go as they pleased. This flexibility was extremely important in an unpredictable environment. When an unexpected environmental crisis occurred and starvation appeared, imminent camps dispersed. At these times a network additional to, and reinforcing, the kinship network was required. The Aivilingmiut maintained an elaborate alliance system that operated at many levels. Some of these alliances or fictive kin relationships were namesakes, joking partners, singing partners, trading partners, adoption and spouse exchange partners (often incorrectly called wife exchange). The perfect Eskimo alliance was an extensive network made up of real kinships and fictive kinships. During normal times these partnerships were fun and made travel to new areas easy. In times of stress, however, they carried the obligation of aid which was usually provided as shelter and food.

This obligation was often unrecognized by the Euro-Americans when they participated in unequal spouse-exchange alliances. In a spouse exchange the couples agreed to exchange partners for a short time. The result of this spouse exchange was a mutual obligation for support in the future. It was also trans-generational; that is, the offspring of the couples, whether related by blood or not, would regard each other as siblings. This is a very different type of arrangement from that described by most Euro-Americans.

The earliest contact the Aivilingmiut had with Europeans was an indirect one. They were unaffected by the first British voyages in search of the Northwest Passage (1570s-1630s). In 1670 the British Crown granted the Hudson's Bay Company monopoly trading rights in Rupert's Land. The Company then established forts in the 'bottom of the bay'. There were no beaver to the north and the Company was rarely interested in venturing into this area; they tried a whale fishery in Padlirmiut territory on the west coast of the Bay (1765-72) and sent out the occasional exploratory expedition when their monopoly was challenged. By the early 1800s Inuit from the west coast of Hudson Bay were traveling regularly to the Company post at Churchill to trade seals. As far as we know, these were not Aivilingmiut but, by 1821, when the first British explorers Parry and Lyon visited them, they already had acquired iron knives and copper kettles. Such possessions were most likely attained through trade with their southern neighbors.

Parry and Lyon were searching for the Northwest Passage by following the continental coast of North America. After two years' attempts to traverse Fury and Hecla Strait, they returned to Britain and correctly reported that no viable route existed following the mainland. As a result, the Aivilingmiut remained undisturbed until 1860 when American whalers expanded their whaling into Hudson Bay. This led to a migration of Aivilingmiut southwards as they congregated around the whalers and took jobs working as crew members.

Inuit crews were not paid wages by the whalers, instead they received goods and food. If a hunter killed a whale he might be given a wooden whaling boat. Other rewards for service included shirts, guns, ammunition and knives. Women also worked for the whalers, scrubbing decks, cleaning clothes and sewing winter clothing. Their remuneration included dresses, knives, scissors, needles and beads.

The whalers wintered over in Hudson Bay. As the sea ice formed they would allow the ship to be frozen in. A 'house' was built on the deck and became the venue for dances and theatricals. The Aivilingmiut built their villages beside the ship and went on board for meals and entertainment. During the winter the Aivilingmiut supplied the ship with fresh meat.

The presence of the whalers changed Aivilingmiut life in many ways. Guns and whale boats displaced the bow and arrow, and kayak. Supplying the whalers with fresh meat depleted local wildlife. The whalers introduced new foods including alcohol. Also, other Inuit groups, some former enemies of the Aivilingmiut, migrated into the region to work for the whalers. The tensions between these groups sometimes eruped into fist fights.

As in all contact situations, disease took its toll on the Native population. Syphilis and tuberculosis were perhaps the most insidious problems, but even common diseases could have disastrous effects. In 1902 the Scottish whaler *Active* carried a sailor ill with dysentery into the region. This disease was so virulent that the Aivilingmiut of Lyon Inlet felt they had been bewitched by their neighbors. This same epidemic resulted in the virtual extinction of the aboriginal occupants of Southampton Island, the Sadlermiut (Sallirmuit). The deserted island was later repopulated by the Aivilingmiut.

Many of the impacts of whaling were not negative, however; the Aivilingmiut and other Inuit who participated remember this period with fondness. It was a time of excitement, new things and of great hunters. When the last whaling ship sailed away in 1915 never to reappear, the people were sad. One, Leah Arnaujaq, later recalled:

> 'We wondered, but we never really knew why the whalers didn't come back. We were kind of regretful because we remembered how good their food had tasted and we remembered everybody getting together like a big family. When the whalers left, that big family feeling was gone.'

The Royal Canadian Mounted Police (RCMP) established their first eastern Arctic post in 1903 among the Aivilingmiut. Its purpose was to ensure Canadian sovereignty over the area and to collect duty from the American whalers. When the whalers left, the RCMP remained to bring law and order to the North.

The Hudson's Bay Company, now interested in seals and white fox, moved in to fill the void left by the whalers. With the Company came the Catholic and Anglican missionaries. The Company, Royal Canadian Mounted Police and missionaries sought to change Inuit culture. The Company depended on the hunters to bring in furs and fostered a dependence on the goods already introduced by the whalers. They realigned, but did not radically alter Inuit subsistence economy. The missionaries sought to replace Inuit cosmology with Christianity. While they succeeded in converting the people and deposing the shamans, they were less successful in altering the people's fundamental beliefs about their world.

Finally, the RCMP were in the north as agents of the Canadian government. It was their role to ensure that justice was done. Their imposition of an unknown legal system was confusing to a people who had their own system of customary law. Although the Company, RCMP and missions were paternalistic and autocratic institutions, they had relatively few representatives in the North. As a result of this lack of representation, their impact was limited. It was only after the Second World War that most Canadian Inuit groups became more exposed to southern Canadian education and at last began to benefit from regular health services and social services.

MYTHS AND LEGENDS

The 4,000 miles (6,437km) of the Arctic coastline from eastern Siberia to Greenland form the very fringes of the habitable world. The landscape varies from the flat coastal plains of Alaska and the Mackenzie Delta to the rocky terrain of the interior barren grounds west of Hudson Bay and the high granite mountains and deeply cut fiords of the eastern islands. The one constant feature is the lack of trees.

During the long cold winter – nine months or more each year – the sea and lakes are frozen solid. Darkness reigns uninterrupted for weeks in midwinter, with only a brief twilight at midday. The brief summer restores life and color to the landscape with varieties of moss, grass, wild flowers and berries. Days are long, sunny and pleasantly warm with a period near midsummer when the Sun never sets.

Traditional settlements were usually small, consisting of one or two extended families, although at certain times several groups might come together for communal hunting, trading, or religious ceremonies. People depended for survival both on sea creatures, such as seal, walrus, and whale, and on land animals, like caribou and musk ox. Fishing played a major part in the economy of most groups. Birds were also hunted and their eggs collected.

Nevertheless, starvation was an ever-present threat in this desolate environment. The successful food quest required strict observance of taboos and special care had to be taken not to offend game food animals. The belief that the products of land and sea should not be mixed was a widespread one throughout the Arctic. To break this taboo, by example, cooking seal and caribou meat together, was to risk supernatural retribution in the form of storms or sickness – or even death itself. (In some instances, amulets did offer a degree of personal protection.)

Indeed, the taboo system was the cornerstone of religious life. In a world controlled by supernatural beings – openly dangerous or potentially so – it was only through references to taboos that the stress and unpredictability of daily life could be made explicable and acceptable. Myths and legends also provided reassurance by validating taboos and by offering structure and meaning to the spirit world.

ORIGIN MYTHS

In the primeval world there was no difference between people and animals. A human being could become an animal at will and vice versa. All spoke the same language and lived in identical fashion. In many other ways this was a world quite different from the present one. It was a world where snow burned, houses flew through the air, tools and weapons moved of their own accord and forests grew at the bottom of the sea. (This served to explain the presence of driftwood on the sea shore.) As one Iglulik story-teller explained, 'These stories were made when all unbelievable things could happen.'[1]

■ The Creation of Light

Origin myths relate how present order was created out of this chaotic, topsy-turvy world. In the beginning, for example, there was no light on Earth. Fox argued for the continuance of everlasting darkness, since it provided him with cover under which to raid hunters' caches. Hare, on the other hand, called for the light of day to help him find food. Hare's words proved the more powerful and so it was that day came to alternate with night. According to another myth, it was Raven who won the argument with Fox, and it was Raven's cry of 'qua! qua!' (meaning light or dawn) which brought daylight to mankind.

■ Origin of Indians and White Men

A widespread myth tells of the origin of Indians and white men and, in its telling, reveals how the Inuit regarded these two groups. The Caribou Inuit version describes how a man, angered by his daughter's refusal to take a husband, forced her to marry his dog and banished the pair to a distant island. Here the woman gave birth to a litter of puppies. To revenge herself on her father, the woman sent her dog-children to drown him by overturning his kayak. The women then cut the soles from her *kamiks* (boots) and set them at the water's edge. She placed some of her dog-children on

427

one sole, telling them to be skillful in all things. As the dogs drifted away from the island, the sole turned into a ship and they sailed away to the land of the white men. From those dogs, it is said, all the white men came. The woman placed the remaining dogs on the other sole and, reminding them of how they had killed their grandfather, exhorted them to treat all human beings they met in a similarly murderous manner. This sole also drifted out from the island and washed up on a distant shore. The dogs wandered off up country and became the ancestors of the Indians, the traditional enemies of the Inuit.

■ The Animals

Many myths describe how various animals came to have their present form. Willow grouse, for example, were children who were so frightened by a sudden noise that they grew wings and flew up into the sky. Similarly, gulls were once women who had been abandoned by their traveling companions, whom they continue to seek with their mournful cries.

Other animal myths have a comical quality, like the tale of the raven and the loon. In the days when all the birds were white, these two agreed to tattoo one another using soot. Unfortunately, the loon was so dissatisfied with the pattern produced by the raven that he threw the soot at him, thus causing all the ravens to be black to this day. In his turn, the enraged raven beat the loon so severely that he was unable to walk. That is why loons now walk so awkwardly.

■ Sun, Moon, Thunder, and Lightning

In several myths, an evil action or breach of taboo is shown as the catalyst by which a human being is transformed into a supernatural being.

A Caribou Inuit tale recounts the story of how *Tatqeq* and his sister *Siqiniq* were surprised in an incestuous relationship. Overwhelmed with shame, they rose up from Earth into the sky. It was winter and dark and both carried flaming torches. *Tatqeq* rushed into the sky with such speed that his torch went out. He became the Moon, giving light but no heat from the embers of his torch. His sister rose more slowly. Her torch remained burning, and she became the Sun, giving out both light and warmth to the world.

Another story tells how there was no theft in the world until a brother and sister stole a caribou skin and a firestone (iron pyrites). No sooner had they done so than they were stricken with guilt. At first they talked of changing into animals to escape retribution, but always they were afraid of being killed. Finally, they decided to turn into thunder and lightning so that people could not catch them. Now when thunder rolls and lightning flashes in the heavens, it is because the brother is rattling the dry caribou skin, while his sister strikes sparks from the firestone.

ALL-POWERFUL SPIRITS

For those who inhabited the inhospitable vastness of the Arctic, supernatural beings were everywhere. The most powerful and dangerous of all was the Sea Spirit, known variously among different groups from central Canada to east Greenland as *Sedna, Nuliajuk, Takanaksaluk* ('the terrible one down there'), or *Immap Ukuua* ('mother of the sea'). Her power was based on the fact that, in a region where the struggle for human survival was perhaps more desperate than anywhere else on Earth, she exercised control over the major source of food – the sea.

■ The Sea Spirit

The myth concerning the Sea Spirit tells of a young woman – sometimes described as a friendless orphan, by others as a rejected daughter – who was thrown into the sea by her traveling companions during a storm. As she attempted to climb back into the boat, those on board sought to dislodge her by hacking off the first joints of her fingers. These fell into the sea and turned into seals. Still the woman clung to the side of the boat and this time the rest of her fingers were cut off, becoming walruses. Finally, her hands were struck off at the wrists and became whales. The woman sank to the bottom of the sea, where she became the Sea Spirit.

Because of their cruelty to her, *Sedna* had little love for human beings. In her home at the bottom of the ocean, she jealously guarded the animals which came from her hands. (In some areas she was believed to control the land animals too.) She demanded respect and strict observance of all taboos relating to animals and hunting. Violations enraged her and in revenge she shut the animals away or raised storms to prevent hunting. At such times it was necessary for a shaman, in a trance, to visit *Sedna* to placate her by promising that people would confess and repent their wrongdoings.

A great ceremonial was performed on Baffin Island each summer during which a shaman battled with *Sedna,* harpooning her like a seal and killing her, thus liberating the seals for the coming hunting season. Since *Sedna* subsequently came to life again, the ceremony had to be repeated the following year.

■ Omnipresent *Pinga*

To some of the inland groups who had no direct contact with the coast, the Sea Spirit had, of course, no significance. Among the Caribou Inuit, for example, the supreme being was *Pinga,* who corresponded to *Sedna* in many ways but lived in the air. *Pinga* was feared as an omnipresent spirit, watching over people's actions, particularly as regards their treatment of game animals – in this case, of caribou. Although not credited with exercising the same control over caribou as did *Sedna* over seals, she nevertheless demanded that they be treated with respect and dignity.

■ Master of Weather

Next in power and importance to the Sea Spirit was *Narssuk* or *Sila,* controller of the weather, master of wind, rain and snow, who could raise a storm at any moment and render hunting impossible. He was envisaged as a giant baby, wrapped in caribou skins tied with thongs. When the thongs were loosened, he was free to move and blizzards swept the country. Then the disembodied spirits of shamans had to fly up in the air and fight to refasten the thongs.

■ The Moon Spirit

Tatqeq, the Moon Spirit, was generally regarded as better-disposed toward mankind. Through his influence over tides and currents, he was thought to bring good luck to hunters. He was also believed by the Central Inuit to control fertility in women and to enforce the taboos concerning childbirth. In some areas, however, he was greatly feared. Greenlanders believed that he kept a special watch over human behavior and punished disobedience, while around the Bering Strait it was he, and not the Sea Spirit, who ruled the game animals. In this area also it was believed that diseases emanated from the Moon and a lunar eclipse was said to presage an epidemic.

HERO CREATURES AND MONSTERS

The adventures of the culture hero *Kivioq* are familiar throughout the Arctic region, from Alaska to Greenland, although often they are told as separate stories, rather than as linked episodes in an epic cycle that would be familiar to readers of the Icelandic Sagas.

■ Tales of *Kivioq*

Typically, *Kivioq* undertakes a series of long and dangerous journeys to distant lands, where he overcomes fearful obstacles, battles with monsters and has numerous narrow escapes before finally achieving great wealth and importance among his people. The stories are set in a primeval time when animals were larger and stronger than they are now and shared the same traits as humans. During the course of his adventures, *Kivioq* takes several animal wives, including a wolf, a fox and a goose, is attacked by giant caterpillars and mussels, and is carried part of his way on the back of a salmon.

Elements of various forms of myth, in particular origin myths, are contained within the cycle. However, unlike the actions of culture heroes in other areas, the changes which *Kivioq* is credited with bringing about do not appear to be particularly beneficial to mankind. While living among the wolves, for example, he taught them to run down caribou. Now, thanks to *Kivioq* all wolves have learned to hunt caribou.

In another adventure, *Kivioq* was pursued by a cannibalistic witch. In an attempt to prevent him escaping in his kayak, the witch hurled her *ulu* (knife) at him. She missed and the *ulu* skimmed over the sea and turned into an ice floe. Until then, according to the myth, the sea had been open all the year round. Now it began to freeze over in winter and people had to learn to hunt seals at their breathing holes in the ice.

Another origin myth, which is also reminiscent of trickster tales, has *Kivioq* hiding in a meat cache in order to catch the thief who has been raiding it. The culprit, a bear in human form, threw *Kivioq* over his shoulder and carried him home, believing him to be a seal carcass. The story describes several comic scenes at the bear's house, with *Kivioq* pretending to be frozen and the bear's wife laying him out to thaw, and the bear-children catching sight of the supposed dead seal opening his eyes. When the bear attempted to cut him up, *Kivioq* hit him with an ax and escaped. He was pursued by the wife in bear form, and in an attempt to throw her off his trail, caused a fast-flowing river to well up between them. The bear-woman attempted to cross the river by drinking it dry and, as a result, burst. All the water in her stomach rose up in the form of a white mist and thus created the first fog.

Finally, in the traditional style of the epic hero, *Kivioq* returns home, rich and powerful. It is interesting to note that, in a Netsilik version recorded in the 1920s, he only finds success by leaving the Inuit and going 'to the land of the white man . . . (who) made him a great man with great possessions. It has been said that he has five ships . . .'[2]

Another form of hero is the orphan boy – poor, friendless and mistreated – who receives help, usually from a supernatural source and thereby becomes strong and powerful. Typical is the story of *Kajjajuk,* who is temporarily transformed into a giant by the sympathetic Moon Spirit and thus able to take revenge on those who had abused and tormented him.

■ Beings to Fear

Unlike *Tatqeq,* the Moon Spirit, most supernatural beings appear malevolent and dangerous toward human beings. Stories abound of man-eating giants, dwarfs, ghosts and bloodthirsty monsters of all kinds. Alaskan myths tell of the *Amikuk,* a sea-serpent which dragged unwary hunters from their kayaks, and the *Aziwugum,* a creature like a dog, but with a scaly body and a tail so powerful that one blow from it could kill. The Central Inuit feared the *Amayersuk,* a giant woman who carried children away, and the man-eating *Nakasungnaikut,* who had no leg bones and had to crawl instead of walking.

People lived in great fear of such beings, especially during the long dark winter months. They heard their voices howling in the wind, saw their tracks in the snow and glimpsed them lurking under the ice. 'Invisible beings, something we cannot see, sometimes murder and kill; it is terrible and almost intolerable.'[3]

HOLY PLACES, SACRED SITES

The people of the Arctic believed that almost everything in the universe had a soul or spirit which could be pleased or angered by the actions of human beings. This belief also extended to inanimate objects and places so that a rock, an island or a stream was regarded as having a kind of soul or *inua* – a power and vitality of its own. Those crossing dangerous glaciers or stretches of water, where they might encounter treacherous currents or whirlpools, often made a small offering, such as a piece of meat or blubber, in order to pacify the *inua* of that particular locality.

■ Power in the Landscape

The people of Cumberland Sound left offerings at the places where they quarried steatite for the making of lamps and dishes. Failure to do so, it was believed, would render the stone hard and unworkable. Certain structures were also associated with supernatural beings. A small stone house near Netsilik Lake was said to be the home of the thunder spirits. Those entering it had to exercise great care, for it was believed that if they or their clothing touched the walls they would die within the year.

Most important of all were the places associated with food resources. There were certain spots, for example, which were regarded as sacred simply because they appeared to be particularly attractive to caribou or because they regularly provided good fishing.

The Caribou Inuit, who each summer camped on Sentry Island in Hudson Bay to hunt seals, regarded a certain boulder there as sacred and hung it with gifts of food, tobacco and trinkets in order to bring good luck in hunting. According to the Netsilik, a similar rock, to which offerings of small stones were made, was originally a woman who turned to stone because she refused to marry. People believed that the stone woman was fond of playing with pebbles and so offered these to her in the hope that she would give them game in return.

■ Hunting Sites

Taboos and observances which applied to hunting also applied to hunting sites, so that they acquired a kind of holy status. Most Central Inuit observed very strict taboos at fishing weirs and at the river-crossings where caribou were hunted. These related to the important rules separating land and sea animals. Thus it was forbidden to sleep with seal meat in one's tent or to work seal and walrus skins in caribou hunting camps. Indeed the Caribou Inuit made a very sharp distinction between what belonged to the interior and what came from the 'salt-water people'. In their eyes, all trade goods obtained from the coast had to be treated with the utmost caution in the vicinity of caribou crossing places.

Restrictions also applied to all men's and women's work at fishing weirs. When a man was required to make essential repairs to his fishing gear, it was necessary for him to leave the river bank and hide behind a rock in order to do so.

Part of the sacred character of these hunting places derived from their links with the *Tunrit,* a quasi-mythical, superhuman race of giants who, according to legends told throughout much of the central and eastern Arctic, were the original inhabitants of the area. They were skillful hunters who constructed the stone cairns, which led the caribou herds to the crossing places, as well as the stone fishing weirs. Whatever the historical significance of the *Tunrit* (who can probably be identified with the pre-historic Dorset people), they were regarded by the Inuit as supernatural beings and offerings were made at sites and structures associated with them.

■ Graves and Cairns

Ancestral graves and memorial cairns could also acquire a sacred character. Offerings and prayers were sometimes made at such places so that the dead could assist the living by bringing fine weather or ensuring good hunting. A poignant Netsilik legend describes the origin of a series of cairns found at Kamigluk on Simpson Strait. They commemorated a group of women who were drowned when the ice from which they were fishing broke up and carried them out to sea. Their grieving husbands set up the cairns on the shore, one for each woman lost, so that their souls could return to dry land instead of remaining in the restless sea.

REVERED ANIMALS

The concept that animals possessed souls influenced almost every aspect of daily life. Since the regular killing of game animals was essential for human survival, the maintenance of a harmonious relationship between the hunters and the hunted was of paramount importance. To this end, it was necessary for a hunter to show honor and respect to the animal he killed by observing a number of rigorous taboos. One of the most important taboos banned contact between land animals and those of the sea. Thus it was forbidden to eat caribou and seal meat on the same day, or to sew caribou skin clothing while hunting for seal and walrus.

Proper observance of such rules, it was believed, pleased the soul of the dead animal so that it would allow itself to be reincarnated and hunted again. On the other hand, failure to carry out the prescribed procedures could lead to a dearth of game and turn the animal soul into a dangerous spirit. In other words, it was possible for the very food upon which people depended to become a source of evil. The taboo system allowed the killing of animals to become a safe activity, and ensured successful future hunting.

In that the motivating force in both cases was the conciliation of the departed soul, the treatment accorded to dead animals bore many similarities to the funeral and mourning observances for human beings. For example, just as in the case of a human death, no work was permitted for several days after the capture of a seal, walrus, caribou or bear.

Another widespread practice was that of offering dead seals and whales a drink by pouring water into the animal's mouth or sprinkling some over its head. On whaling expeditions, Point Barrow Inuit carried a supply of water for this very purpose. Seals and whales were believed to be thirsty creatures and the intention was to provide comfort for the animal's soul.

◼ The Caribou

The souls of caribou were thought to be particularly sensitive and required special care and attention. It was forbidden to do any work on caribou skins while the animal was being hunted. Scraping the skin was considered particularly dangerous since it could offend and drive away the grazing herds before they could be hunted. The Caribou Inuit, who had only the caribou to live on, had to exercise the greatest caution in handling the dead animal. When a caribou was butchered, everything that was not carried home had to be covered up. To fail to do so was regarded as disrespectful to the soul of the caribou and could incur the anger of *Pinga.*

◼ The Seal

As perhaps the most important food animal, seals were also treated with great respect. If a seal carcass was brought indoors for butchering, it was never placed directly on the floor, since it was thought to be offensive to the seal to lie where women had been walking. When people moved camp in winter, the skulls of the seals caught at the old site were laid out facing in the direction of the new one so that their soul could accompany the hunters on their way.

◼ The Bear

The bear's soul was regarded as most powerful and dangerous of all. It was believed that after a bear had been killed, its soul remained on the tip of the hunter's spear for four or five days. During this period, certain procedures had to be followed if the bear was not to turn into an evil spirit. All work in the house was forbidden. The bear's skin was hung outside and surrounded by tools (women's tools for a female bear, men's tools for a male). In addition, gifts and offerings to the soul of the bear were placed on the skin.

◼ Feasts and Festivals

The most elaborate rites were those held by the Yup'ik-speaking people of the western Arctic. The Inviting-In Feast was a masked ceremonial held in January to appeal to the spirits for success in hunting during the coming year. The Bladder Festival, held in November and December, was intended to placate the animals slain during the previous year. At the start of the five-day ceremony, each hunter hung up in the *kashim,* or meeting house, the inflated bladders of all the seals, walruses, whales and bears which he had killed. Food and drink were offered to the bladders, which represented the souls of the animals. After several days of ceremonies and dancing, the bladders where taken down, burst and thrust into holes in the ice. In this way the animals' souls were returned to the sea to enter the unborn.

RITUALS AND CEREMONIES
In addition to the taboos and practices governing hunting, there was also a series of equally exacting observances relating to the critical phases of human life, such as birth, puberty and, of course, death.

■ Mourning the Dead
Those relating to death were particularly important. A death was normally followed by a mourning period of four or five days, during which time all work in the household ceased. Everyone within the camp was banned from cutting their nails or combing their hair, eating certain foods or undertaking certain activities, such as cleaning lamps or gathering fuel. After the funeral, the camp was moved to a new site. If these things were not done correctly, there was a danger that the soul of the deceased might become an evil spirit, as happened to *Qubliusaq* in this Netsilik story:

> '. . .And when they came to the snow hut were the body had been left, they found *Qubliusaq* all alive . . .they could just see her on the platform, where she was already turning ugly, unrecognisable and terrible as a ghost. She was sitting at her lamp boiling blood . . . People were stricken with terror and now, too late, repented that they had not given her the full death taboo. Happily, among the men there was a great shaman who was accustomed to overcoming ghosts . . .If she had not been killed in time she would certainly have persecuted her old neighbours and either stricken them with disease or frightened them all to death.'[4]

In Alaska, where ceremonial life was most developed, an annual Feast of the Dead was held to which the spirits of the dead were invited and offered gifts of food, drink and clothing.

436

A more elaborate version of this ceremony, the Great Feast of the Dead, was held every 10 or 15 years, depending on the ability of the surviving relatives to accumulate sufficient property to honor the dead. The ceremony was similar to a potlatch. During several days of singing, dancing and drumming, vast quantities of food, clothing, skins and other valuables were distributed to those present.

■ Amulets

Personal protection from ghosts and evil spirits was provided by amulets. Most men and women carried several, stitched into their clothing or hung on a special belt. Almost any small object could serve as an amulet, since its power derived from the spirit resident within rather than from any physical property. Children were given amulets as soon as they were born and one Netsilik child was found to have as many as 80 sewn up in various parts of his clothing.

Each amulet generally had a specific purpose. *Pilarqaq,* a young Netsilik hunter, had six amulets stitched into his coat. These consisted of seal teeth to bring him luck in sealing, the head of a tern to bring him luck in fishing, an ermine skin to make him a good runner, two miniature snow beaters to protect him from evil spirits and a small kayak cleaner intended to help him to paddle faster.

■ The Shaman

The *angatok,* or shaman, occupied an extremely important position in society. Shamans, both male and female, provided protection, both for the individual and the community as a whole, by acting as mediators between human beings and the spirit world.

They used their powers to cure sickness, attract game, control the weather and locate lost people or property. Sickness, for example, was always regarded as having been caused by evil ghosts and spirits. It was for the shaman to identify the reason for the sickness (usually a breach of taboo) and then, with the aid of his spirit helpers, to drive the evil spirits from the patient's body and kill them. In public performances or seances the shaman fell into a trance, communicating with his audience through his spirit helpers, usually in an archaic or incomprehensible language. At such times his disembodied spirit traveled to the spirit world, to the Moon or below the sea, in order to discover the causes of people's misfortunes and to intercede with the spirits on their behalf.

Shamanism thus operated as a form of social control, enforcing taboos and thereby establishing harmony and balance between the physical and spiritual worlds.

ARTS AND CRAFTS

The North American Arctic features a surprisingly varied land mass with distinct ecological and cultural zones. The extensive coastline and tundra interior encourages mixed maritime and inland hunting economies. Major river systems penetrate the interior; their fertile deltas provide rich feeding grounds for fish, seals and small mammals. In Alaska and on Baffin Island, ranges of snow-capped mountains rise majestically from low-lying coastal plains. The treeline marks a meandering route staying within 250 miles (402km) of coastal Alaska but sloping sharply south beyond the Mackenzie Delta. Marked with patches of dwarf willow, the central Canadian Arctic features a seemingly boundless expanse of tundra. Rich in vegetation, the tundra provides summer grazing land for herds of caribou and musk oxen, as well as migratory wildfowl.

For over 2,000 years, Aleutian, Yup'ik and Inuit-Inupiaq peoples, descendants of the Eskimo-Aleut linguistic family, have skillfully exploited local resources, sustaining a remarkably productive life in a wide range of environmental conditions.[5] At the time of contact with Russian explorers in 1741, the Unangan (Aleuts) occupied the Aleutian archipelago, clusters of islands which extend from the Alaskan peninsula 1,300 miles (2,092km) toward Asia. With scarce land resources, Aleutian hunters pursued whales, sea lions, fur seals and sea otters by baidarka (kayak) in coastal waters. Fish, nesting birds and marine life collected on beaches, provided additional food and raw material.

The Yup'ik-speaking cultures of southwestern Alaska constructed villages of semi-subterranean houses on the Bering Sea coast and off-shore islands, as well as along the Yukon and Kuskokwim Rivers. The Yukon–Kuskokwim Delta, a crescent-shaped area extending from Norton Sound to Kuskokwim Bay (and 200 miles inland), is the heartland of

Central Yup'ik country.[6] The river deltas provide rich sealing areas while the rivers and their tributaries offer access to fish and wildlife resources in the interior.

The Inuit-Inupiaq peoples of northern Alaska, Arctic Canada and Greenland share a common language with a continuum of regional dialects. Scattered in camps and villages across an extensive territorial range, they too developed distinctly regional hunting economies. During the spring migration of bowhead whales, Inupiat in northwestern Alaska, for example, conducted a highly ceremonialized form of whalehunting under the direction of *umialit*, whaling captains.[7] Across the Canadian Arctic, Inuit families lived in camps of extended kin, shifting location in response to the seasonal movement of game. From coastal communities on Baffin Island and along the west coast of Hudson Bay, kayak hunters pursued whales, walrus and narwhal. They seal-hunted at breathing holes in winter and hunted caribou inland in spring and fall. Fish (fresh, frozen or dried) provided an important food source throughout the year.

In tandem with extreme winter temperatures, the Arctic experiences a dramatic seasonal change in light and animal resources. As the sun disappears in early fall, caribou, whales, geese and ducks abandon the North. They return each spring to give birth and nurture their young. This annual cycle of light and dark, scarcity and abundance, makes the Arctic a land of sharp contrasts. In winter families relied on available game and reserves of stored food. Through social gatherings and ritual ceremonies, they appeased spirit forces which controlled the supply of animals. The sun's reappearance in spring, accompanied by the return of the whales, migratory birds and thundering herds of caribou, heralded a period of regeneration and renewal.

■ Historical Art Forms

Flawlessly designed implements, produced from wood, bone, antler, ivory and stone, comprised the remarkably efficient toolkit that enabled hunters to procure game on land or sea. With ingenuity and technical expertise, women used sewing skills to fashion objects necessary for everyday use. Animal hides and furs furnished women with raw material for clothing, tents, umiak and kayak covers, quivers, storage bags and various hunting and domestic equipment.

Despite clear regional differences in language, dialect, hunting pursuits and social practices, Arctic cultures shared broadly similar ideological concerns which imbued the production of traditional art forms. These are an intimate physical and metaphysical relationship between humans and animals; a profound awareness of the tenuous nature of human existence; a firm respect for craftsmanship with social prestige vested in skill and productivity; and a deep love of children and desire to impart the knowledge and skills necessary for them to achieve a productive life in an exacting, and often, unforgiving environment.

Arctic peoples believed that well-crafted objects pleased spirit forces and secured goodwill toward the maker and his/her family.[8] Impeccably tailored clothing and finely carved hunting tools, provide evidence of the value placed on the artistic combination of form and function. Today, well-made, skillfully decorated clothing remains a treasured gift from a seamstress to her husband, daughter-in-law or grandchild.

■ Clothing as Art

'A parka is a beautiful art form. It is our cultural heirloom, which we call *paitaq*. The parka is pieced together from the animals of our area. . . . It's all the life forms coming together through the hands and skills of a seamstress.'[9]

Throughout the Arctic, extraordinary time, skill and talent were invested in clothing production. Women possessed expert knowledge in treating animal skins to maximize warmth or waterproof garments. Rendered from animal products, clothing underscored human dependence on the animal. Clothing design was functional as well as symbolic. Since clothing styles were regional, they served as an important sign of social identity and collective cohesion.[10]

Waterproof garments made from sea-mammal intestine were used for maritime hunting throughout the Aleutians, coastal Alaska, St. Lawrence Island and the eastern Canadian Arctic.[11] Yards of tubular intestines were scraped, inflated and dried. Treated as such, the gutskin appears as translucent parchment, seemingly fragile but surprisingly resilient when oiled. On St. Lawrence Island, gutskins were bleached in freezing temperatures to achieve their creamy color and soft texture. To fashion the parka, bands of gutskin were laid in horizontal tiers or vertical columns. The seams were folded over and stitched without fully penetrating the skin. Whale or walrus sinew was often used for thread; it swelled when wet, helping to seal the hole.

Gutskin garments were frequently decorated with alder-dyed hair of unborn seals, cormorant feather tufts or tiny auklet crowns, inserted at regular intervals in the seams. Such decoration was both visually pleasing and profoundly symbolic. Cormorant feathers alluded to the bird's diving and fishing ability; the hair of unborn seals symbolized the propagation of the species. Women, as well as men, wore exquisitely decorated gutskin parkas. These served a utilitarian function as rain cover, but were also featured in ceremonial contexts.[12] In the wake of European contact and trade, bits of red, blue and green yarn replaced traditional forms of decoration.

Although apparently regarded as a poor man's clothing choice, bird skins provided an important source of parka material, particularly in areas of limited resources. Eider duck, emperor goose, murre, puffin, squaw duck, loon and cormorant skins made lightweight and water-repellent parkas. Certainly, the doll of a Yup'ik hunter, dressed in a cormorant parka with elaborate personal adornment, presents an image of affluence and prestige.

In general, Yup'ik seamstresses preferred ground squirrel (marmot), mink, otter and muskrat furs for parka material. Flensed, dried and scraped to soften, the small pelts were laid in horizontal rows, sometimes with tails intact. Traditionally, Yup'ik parkas were long, dress-like garments, often hoodless with a high standing collar. Today, women's parkas (*atkupiaq*) are hooded with a 'sunburst' trim of wolverine and wolf similar to hood styles in northern Alaska.[13] Plates of white calfskin (formerly *pukiq*, white caribou fur) are fixed with wolverine, otter or mink tassles and attached in horizontal tiers across the parka front and back. They are highlighted with decorative stitching (*kelurqut*) on thin strips of black or red painted skin. 'The red earth paint is called *uiteraq* or *kavirun*. It is the representation of the blood of our ancestral mother *An'gaqtar*. *An'gaqtar*, who some people say is the daughter of Raven, the Creator, left pockets of her menstrual blood in various [sacred] places in southwest Alaska.'[14]

Caribou fur and ground squirrel were preferred by the Inupiaq of northern Alaska. Men's parkas were thigh-length with slightly rounded hems in front and back. Trousers and boots completed the outfit. The creamy white mottled fur of domesticated Siberian reindeer, obtained from itinerant Chuckchi traders or St. Lawrence Island middlemen, was considered extremely valuable.[15] Wolverine or wolf tails, an eagle feather or loon's head were often attached to the parka back, evoking respect for the subject's predatory skill and serving as a talisman for the wearer.[16]

Caribou fur provides exceptional hypothermal protection and was favored by Inuit throughout Arctic Canada.[17] While traveling or hunting in winter, the parka was worn in two layers. The uniform design of the outer parka signified one's regional and gender identity while the inner parka was decorated with amulets which alluded to the wearer's personal relationship with spirit forces.[18]

Sealskin parkas were prevalent in Greenland, Baffin Island and Labrador. Lightweight and water-repellent, they were worn especially during the wet spring and warm summer months. The sealskin was scraped on the inside, stretched and laced to a drying rack to air dry. For parkas and trousers, the hair was left intact. Women took great pride in contrasting the skin's silver tone with dark decorative inserts. As Lucien Turner notes, 'The woman may be several years in getting the right kind [of sealskin] and may have effected many exchanges before being suited with the quality and color.'[19]

Clothing styles contained specific design elements which identified the wearer as male or female. Inuit women's parkas, for example, were identified by a back pouch (*amaut*) used to carry a baby. The *amaut* emphasized the woman's maternal role on both a functional and symbolic level.[20]

Trade played a prominent role in the design of clothing and personal adornment. Blue trade beads from China, purchased from itinerant Siberian traders, decorated labrets, clothing, needlecases and hunting implements.[21] Russian and European explorers, whalers and traders introduced manufactured cloth and beads. Tartan shawls, wool berets and calico covers became the height of fashion in different areas. In Greenland, women devised an elaborately netted collar of colored beads in bold geometric patterns. Strands of beads formed variegated color bands that were draped from shoulder to shoulder on women's parkas on Baffin Island and in northern Quebec. In the central Arctic, seamstresses created narrative and abstract designs by sewing seed beads to a stroud backing attached over the chest, shoulders, wrists and hood. The woman adhered to regional design norms, but the pictorial images were the creation of each seamstress.[22]

■ Carving and Graphic Arts

While women's art was primarily demonstrated through sewing,[23] men were proficient in producing hunting equipment and household implements. As noted earlier, superior craftsmanship was believed to please the souls of prey and enhance the efficacy of an object. Moreover, Arctic cultures believed that animals possessed a soul (Yup'ik: *yua*; Inupiaq: *inua*). In response to the respect paid to the animal and its spirit, animals allowed themselves to be captured. A hunter demonstrated his respect for the animal by virtue of his moral character, personal appearance and the care taken in producing and maintaining hunting equipment.

Hunting equipment was often designed to attract prey. Ivory fishing-hooks were carved as fish with precious blue trade beads for eyes. Arrow straighteners took the form of complacent caribou. Passing repeatedly through the device, the arrow became used to the caribou's body while the animal learned to accept the hunter's weapon.[24]

In Alaska, hunting gear was stored in covered wooden boxes. The interior was often painted with hunting trophies, mythological beings and explicit sexual images. The sexual energy conveyed in these pictographs also empowered the hunter. In fact, the hunt itself was frequently perceived in sexual terms. Sexual abstinence was encouraged, for a woman's smell was believed to be abhorrent to the animal. Young men were discouraged from looking at women in order to preserve and intensify their hunting vision.[25]

Meat trays with painted pictographs also combined pragmatic and spiritual functions. The wood was carved, steamed, bent and fitted. Seams were stitched with spruce root. Trays and ladles were painted with mythological images in the early fall and accompanied men in the ritual sweatbath in order to fix the pigment.[26] Food contained in these trays fed spirits, deceased ancestors and other guests. The painted images alluded to spirit forces and animal procreation. For example, a bentwood tray shows two figures, a male caribou and its *inua*, energized by a mystical power line. The exposed penis sexually charges the image, emphasizing the fecundity of the species. A delicately carved snuff box takes the form of a mother sea otter, playfully carrying her offspring on her belly. The pair are incised with skeletal markings studded with white trade beads, a design recalling the practice of marking joints, the site of souls, with nucleated circles.[27] Its function as a snuff box also demonstrates the hunter's generosity in sharing his valuables and serves as a form of spirit propitiation.

In the central Arctic, Inuit were reluctant to accumulate unnecessary personal possessions. Moving seasonally from camp to camp, families used caches, marked by stone formations known as *inukshuit*, to store food and unneeded seasonal goods. Wood, a scarce commodity, was reserved for kayak and umiak frames, sleds, tent poles and essential hunting equipment. In its place, Inuit relied heavily on stone, bone, antler, ivory and animal skins. Among the Copper Inuit, musk-ox horn was boiled, carved and shaped into ladles; bone marrow picks were handsomely rendered with decorative finials; seal hide, bird skins and ducks' feet were sewn into exquisitely designed containers. Families traveled widely to trade and to obtain raw materials. Indigenous names for places and social groups often derived from the most prominent resource available in a region.

■ Dolls and Models

Throughout the Arctic, parents fashioned ivory, wood and skin figures, as well as model umiaks, kayaks and hunting and domestic equipment for the entertainment and instruction of children. Ivory storyknives, carved by male relatives in the *qasgi* (men's house), were used by Yup'ik girls to depict mythological and historical epics, and to relate personal narratives.[28] More than an entertaining pastime, these stories served a key educational function. Similarly, girls learned the pattern designs (and decorative codes) of adult clothing by sewing miniature replicas for their dolls. Model-building allowed an older generation to convey details of large-scale construction to children and grandchildren.[29]

Thus, child-scale equipment was produced with exceptional care. The future hunter's quiver and visor replicated their full-scale counterpart, even in details of magico-religious decoration.[30] As well, time was reserved in social gatherings for children to demonstrate their novice skills. This practice continues today and serves as an important occasion of social pride in the physical and cultural development of a new generation.

■ Magico-Religious Art

Arctic cultures acknowledged their dependence on spirit forces through an annual cycle of ritual ceremonies. Their complex cosmology demanded that respect be paid to celestial beings, the spirit of animals and deceased ancestors. Festival gatherings, ritual or secular in nature, consisted of appropriate combinations of songs, dances, social play, comic scenes and dramatically staged masked performances.

The extensive resources and large settled populations in the Yup'ik area supported an impressive ceremonial cycle. Ceremonies included food offerings made to children (*Qaariitaaq*), gift exchanges between men and women (*Petugtaq*), formal thanks for the annual harvest of seals (*Nakaciuq*), memorial celebrations dedicated to the spirits of the deceased (*Elriq*), elaborate gift distributions in honor of a child's first catch (*Kevgiq*)

445

and ritual feasts (*Keleq*) directed by shamans for ensuring a 'time of plenty'.[31] The *qasgi* (men's house) served as the ritual center in which ancestor and animal spirits were hosted by those present. New clothing, bentwood trays and ladles were made in early fall at the start of the ceremonial calendar.[32]

Nakaciuq, the Bladder Festival, took place over a five-day period in December, known as *cauyarvik* (time for drumming).[33] Hunters reserved the bladders of seals they had caught throughout the year. Bladders lost or destroyed by dogs were replaced by the stomach or other organ. Participants washed in urine, rinsing their bodies in the snow. During *Nakaciuq* the inflated bladders were displayed in the men's house; their souls (*yua*) were feted with food, song, oratory and dance. At dawn following the full moon, the hunters returned the bladders to the sea through a hole chipped in the ice. Confident of being well-treated, the seal's spirit, contained in the bladder, returned to the hunter the following season.

During *Elriq* namesakes received gifts of food and clothing presented to honor the deceased. Bits of food were dropped through the floorboards to ancestor spirits gathered beneath. For *Keleq*, the Inviting-In Feast, one village hosted another with several days of masked performances staged to please animal spirits and thus ensure a plentiful hunt. Masks, commissioned from carvers, were often made under the direction of shamans. The masks illustrated supernatural visions, personal narratives or symbolized the relationship between a participant and an animal *yua*.[34] Bird feathers often surrounded the mask. In ritual contexts birds served as messengers between the natural and supernatural worlds. Large-scale *tunghak* masks were grotesque impersonations of the spirit force which controlled the supply of animals. Frequently depicted with a leering grin, the *tunghak*'s hands were characteristically pierced with an unopposable thumb, signaling its benign authority in releasing animals to the hunter.[35] Wooden carvings of select species were placed tauntingly about the *tunghak*'s face.

An assembly of seated male drummers accompanied the dancers. The drum covering was struck with a long narrow baton. When women danced, they performed with downcast eyes, holding a pair of finger masks which served as their surrogate eyes.[36]

Dance styles between the South and North differed radically. In the early-20th century, Hawkes contrasted the 'raw vigor' of northern dance with the graceful, fluid motions used in the South.[37] Moreover, the material richness of festivals in the western Arctic contrasted sharply with the more austere gatherings of Inuit in Arctic Canada.

In the eastern Canadian Arctic, early ethnographic accounts provide some evidence of communal ceremonies with skin masks, transsexual costuming and the formal propitiation of animal spirits.[38] However, few references fully describe annual ritual cycles. Social gatherings provided a context for shamanistic performances in which the shaman (*angakuq*) was called upon to heal the sick, locate game, predict or change the weather, and ascertain metaphysical causes for any disaster confronting the community. Dances were held to greet visitors and to establish relationships between hosts and guests. Accompanied by the resounding pulse of the large skin-covered drum almost 3 feet (1m), a male or female dancer performed stylized movements of birds and animals, sang songs of hunting exploits and personal experiences, or lampooned themselves or a joking-partner.

■ Transformations in Artistic Expression

From the early-20th century, and particularly following the Second World War, Arctic peoples have faced an increasingly cash-dependent economy with few employment opportunities for unilingual individuals. In this context, one cannot underestimate the economic importance of independent artmaking or community-based, often government-supported, art and craft programs. Yet it is only now that we are beginning to appreciate their cultural and historical importance. For example, small ivory carvings once produced for whalers, missionaries and traders are often dismissed as nothing more than 'souvenir art'. A ivory model of a bidarka, however, embodies significant historical and cultural information. The center hole carries a European-dressed figure lighting his pipe while two Aleuts paddle. There is humor and irony in this depiction, particularly in a cultural setting that places a high value on self-sufficiency and deplores indolence and pretentious authority.

The work of contemporary sculptors, printmakers, and textile and graphic artists throughout Alaska, Arctic Canada and Greenland comprises a valuable source of personal and collective history. Stone and wood carvings, works on paper, and textile art offer perceptive, first-hand insights into the social, spiritual, economic and intellectual life of northern peoples.[39] Research among elders by native and non-native ethnographers affirms that the rich mythological and cosmological traditions of Arctic societies remain a vital cultural force.[40] Furthermore, scholars point out that despite centuries of trade and culture contact, imported materials were often syncretically adopted, bringing about superficial rather than substantive changes in material culture.[41] Thus, as Aleutian, Yup'ik and Inuit-Inupiaq peoples seek to rediscover and reclaim cultural traditions as a vital source of knowledge, the testimony of elders, the witness of museum artifacts and the creative work of contemporary artists, all serve as essential resources in ensuring the continuing strength of indigenous Arctic cultures.

REFERENCES

THE ARCTIC

1 Rasmussen, 1929:257
2 Rasmussen, 1931:376
3 Rasmussen, 1931:239
4 Rasmussen, 1931:240
5 For a full discussion of the prehistoric and historical development of Arctic cultures, see Damas (ed.), 1984
6 Burch, 1984:5
7 Lantis, 1947; Lowenstein, 1993; Spencer, 1959: 332-353; Fitzhugh and Crowell, 1988
8 Rasmussen, 1929; Fitzhugh and Kaplan, 1982; Fienup-Riordan, 1990:167
9 Meade, 1990:230
10 Driscoll, 1987: 176-187
11 For a description of gutskin parkas and treatment, as well as examples of extant garments, see: Nelson, 1983; Turner, 1976 (1894):56-58; Moore, 1923; Jochelson, 1933; Collins, et al., 1973; Fitzhugh and Kaplan, 1982; Hickman, 1987; Bockstoce, 1977; Black and Liapunova in Fitzhugh and Crowell, 1988; Chaussonnet in Fitzhugh and Crowell, 1988.
12 Morrow, 1984:125, 137
13 Meade, 1990:231
14 Meade, 1990:231-234
15 Fitzhugh and Kaplan, 1982:220; Nelson, 1899: 228-232
16 Driscoll, 1987: 176-182
17 See Stenton, 1991, for an excellent description of the hypothermal qualities of caribou clothing.
18 Driscoll, 1987
19 Turner, 1976 (1884):49
20 Driscoll, 1980, 1987
21 For artifact examples, see: Ray, 1977, 1981; Fitzhugh and Kaplan, 1982; Driscoll, 1987 (Vol. 2)
22 Driscoll, 1987:193-199
23 Aleutian women were especially known for their production of finely woven grass baskets, an area outside the scope of this chapter. See, for example, Ray, 1981; Black, 1982.
24 Fitzhugh and Kaplan, 1982:56, 107
25 Fienup-Riordan, 1994:168
26 Morrow, 1984:124
27 See Morrow quoted in Fienup-Riordan, 1990:53; see also Fitzhugh and Kaplan, 1982:166.
28 Ager, 1974; Fitzhugh and Kaplan, 1982:156-159
29 See also Laughlin, 1980; Fienup-Riordan, 1994.

30 See, especially, Black, 1991, for analysis of the symbolic implications of hunting-hat decoration.

31 Morrow, 1984, offers an excellent summary of Yup'ik ceremonialism based on research among elders collected by Elsie Mather, a native Yup'ik speaker.

32 Morrow, 1984:124

33 Morrow, 1984:123-127

34 Hawkes, 1914

35 Fitzhugh and Kaplan, 1982:202-205

36 Fienup-Riordan, 1990:49-67

37 Hawkes, 1914

38 Boas 1964:197

39 For a comprehensive discussion of the development of Inuit art in the Canadian Arctic, see Swinton, 1992; for an exceptional analysis of a specific theme in contemporary Canadian Inuit art, see Blodgett, 1979.

40 Morrow, 1984; Fienup-Riordan, 1990, 1994

41 Black, 1981

THE NORTHEAST

The geographic area here under discussion, conveniently referred to as the Northeast, stretches approximately from the northwestern shore of Lake Superior south to the confluence of the Ohio and Cumberland Rivers and then east to the Atlantic coast. Its northern border runs just south of the Lake of the Woods and the area extends as far south as the Virginia–North Carolina coastal plain. Newfoundland, once inhabited by the now-extinct Beothuks, is included in the Subarctic chapter.

While it is useful to consider the concept of cultural areas in North America suggesting an internal homogeneity, it is important to stress that – and this particularly applies to the Northeast – there was great variation in lifestyle and, while dominated by Algonquian- and Iroquoian-speaking people, some Siouan in the west – *possibly* east as well – were also represented. Recognizing the difficulties of applying an all-embracing cultural description, recent studies have subdivided the area into three further geographic regions – Coastal, Saint Lawrence Lowlands and Great Lakes-Riverine – and, while even this tripartite division has its shortcomings, it more accurately delineates common lifestyles. For example, the Saint Lawrence Lowlands was the traditional home of the powerful and famous Iroquois Confederacy – the 'People of the Longhouse' – who shared similar cultural patterns which were based on fishing and horticulture, residence in mostly fortified villages, ritual sacrifice of prisoners, similar ceremonials and a matrilineal kinship system.

The Coastal region encompassed the Eastern Algonquian linguistic group, the Saint Lawrence Lowlands were home to the Northern Iroquoian-speakers and the Great Lakes–Riverine area was occupied by the Central Algonquian linguistic group.

In terms of population, tribes or groups were small, certainly no more than sixteen thousand for the Iroquois in the late seventeenth century, twenty thousand for the Huron prior to the smallpox epidemic during the winter of 1639-40 which reduced the population by one-half, and some twenty-five thousand for the Chippewa in 1760. These, however, are but estimates since, in early days, only limited numbers of the various tribes actually came into contact with whites at any particular period, such as in the case of the Chippewa whose settlement pattern in the early Historic Period was that of many widely scattered and small bands. The fortunes of the Indian tribes, the changes in their lifestyles and population, can be illustrated by reference to one tribe – the Micmac – who were among the first to encounter Europeans.

It has been estimated that the population of these Algonquian-speaking people was about four thousand prior to white contact. Their territory was the area to the south and west of the Gulf of Saint Lawrence, the Gaspé Peninsula and the Maritime Provinces. This is a heavily forested region with many lakes and rivers and natural harbors along the extended coastline. By use of the canoe, scattered bands maintained their strong ethnic identity between the seven districts traditionally observed by the Micmac.[1] Because the winters were so severe, only tobacco was cultivated and the subsistence was predominately one firmly based on an annual cycle of hunting and fishing.

One of the most comprehensive reports on the Micmac (which undoubtedly closely describes a lifestyle which had been established and little changed for centuries) comes from the writings of the missionary, Pierre Biard (*c.* 1616). Describing those groups associated with southern Nova Scotia, he refers to a two-phase-type annual cycle now classified as 'diffuse' and 'compact' settlements.

In the first phase, which coincided with the winter season, the population was widely scattered throughout the seven districts; the main activities at this time were the hunting of beaver, otter, moose, caribou and bear, which occupied the months of January to March. At the onset of spring, 'After the smelt comes the herring at the end of April; and at the same time bustards [Canada geese] . . . sturgeon, and salmon, and the great search through the Islets for [waterfowl] eggs. . . From the month of May up to the middle of September, they are free from all anxiety about their food; for the cod are upon the coast, and all kinds of fish and shellfish. . .'.

At these abundant times, large groups – the 'compact settlements' – gathered at favorite camping sites along the coast or rivers. It was a time

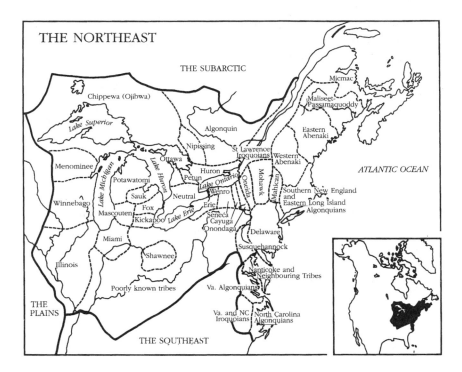

THE NORTHEAST

THE SUBARCTIC

Micmac

Chippewa (Ojibwa)

Maliseet-
Passamaquoddy

Lake Superior

Algonquin

Nipissing

Eastern
Abenaki

St Lawrence
Iroquoians

Western
Abenaki

ATLANTIC OCEAN

Menominee

Ottawa

Huron

Lake Michigan

Lake Huron

Potawatomi

Petun

Lake Ontario

Oneida

Mahican

Winnebago

Sauk

Neutral

Wenro

Southern New England
and
Eastern Long Island
Algonquians

Mascouten

Fox

Erie

Seneca

Cayuga

Delaware

Kickapoo

Lake Erie

Onondaga

Miami

Susquehannock

Illinois

Shawnee

Nanticoke and
Neighbouring Tribes

Poorly known tribes

Va. Algonquians

THE
PLAINS

Va. and NC
Iroquoians

North Carolina
Algonquians

THE SOUTHEAST

ABOVE: *This map shows approximate territories of tribes and language groups in the seventeenth century. After that, all tribes lost territory, some disappeared, some moved and a few new tribes arose.*

when friendships were renewed or made and, particularly, when the many elements of tribal solidarity were recognized. As Biard reported, it was principally at this time that 'they pay visits and hold their State Councils; I mean that several Sagamores [Chiefs] come together and consult . . . about peace and war, treaties of friendship and treaties for the common good.'

The French were greatly impressed by the Micmac and many found their way of life far more agreeable than that which they had experienced in their native land. French youths readily adapted to the Indian lifestyle and language, encouraged by the early French traders, who thus gained efficient interpreters and agents for the lucrative fur trade. The French found the Micmac a vigorous, handsome and healthy race, who were disdainful of those among the French who were squint or one-eyed, flat-nosed and hairy. The Micmac had few diseases; they knew nothing of fevers, gout or rheumatism, and the French were impressed by their knowledge of plants, 'for wounds and other mischances'. Thus, the Micmac formed strong friendships with the French[2] and they became increasingly dependent on trade goods, particularly such things as axes, metal knives and kettles. This improvement in their material possessions, however, was increasingly offset by rapid decreases in their population, due to smallpox and other diseases against which the indigenous populations had little resistance, and their numbers, it has been estimated, decreased to some two thousand by the early eighteenth century.

The period 1610 to about 1760 saw an increasing dependence on the fur trade – mainly carried on with the French – and, while Acadia[3] was ceded to the English by the Treaty of Utrecht in 1713, the new owners found it impossible to gain control of the fur trade which had been monopolized by the French for so long; any attempted changes were fiercely opposed by the Micmac and not until 1779 did the difficulties that the English have with the Micmac actually cease.

The English trait of colonization was rapidly put into effect, the Micmac being confined to reservations and the old free hunting and fishing economy gone forever. The subsequent exploitation – further loss of lands, loss of water resources and the offer of only seasonal jobs at subsistence wages – is a shameful chapter in the settling of Acadia, but it did demonstrate the great resilience of the people. Adapting to the rapid changes, the men took to fabricating wooden craft items and baskets, while the women, utilizing some of their traditional knowledge and skills, together with those indirectly acquired from the Ursuline Nuns of Quebec,

ABOVE: *Keokuk, a distinguished Sauk chief and able leader who was poisoned by one of his own band. He wears a necklace of bear claws on an otterskin collar.*

produced greatly prized souvenirs which were embellished with quillwork, moosehair and beads. Thus, unlike the Beothuk of Newfoundland who were all but brutally exterminated by 1830, the Micmac population – much to the surprise of those whites who concerned themselves with Micmac welfare – actually progressively increased and by 1900 it again approached four thousand.

At least three basic central principles were shared by both the Algonquian and Iroquoian people who lived in this vast region. The first emphasized and defined the rights of the individual such that all actions of individuals were based on their own decisions and all group actions pivoted on the consensus of the participants. The second was that everybody shared, and in times of want the well-being of all was to be taken into account; charity and generosity were considered paramount principles by which all should abide. The third was that man was part of nature – not outside it – he was but part of the web of the natural world, and the earth and woodlands could be neither owned nor exploited.

One notable scholar, Cleland, managed to express this last principle particularly well:

'Thus a man is born and for a time becomes a cannibal, eating and taking energy from his fellow creatures; when his soul and shadow leave his body, Earth Mother takes it back to nourish the plants which in turn feed both animals and men. His debt is repayed, his spirit freed, and the cycle of life complete.'

These central principles were incorporated in the famed Confederacy of the League of the Iroquois, the founding of which is still celebrated today. According to Iroquois tradition, the League was founded by the prophet Deganawida[4] who had a vision of a great spruce tree which reached through the sky to communicate with the Master of Life. The tree was considered the sisterhood of all tribes while its roots represented the five Iroquoian tribes – Seneca, Cayuga, Onondaga, Oneida and Mohawk – who make up the Confederacy.[5] The names which each had for themselves, such as 'The great hill people' for the Seneca and 'The possessors of the flint' for the Mohawk, give interesting insights.

The League was founded in about 1570 in response to the state of continual war which existed between the tribes of the region and had a double purpose: the establishment and enforcement of peace and the acquisition

RIGHT: *Ne Shiw Shkak and Wis Ki gete, Potawatomi. Fine ribbon appliqué decoration is in evidence on the leggings worn by Wis Ki gete.*

BELOW: *A traditional Micmac wigwam of poles and branches bound with cedar bark fiber and covered with overlapping strips of birch bark and grass matting.*

of strength to oppose any would-be intruders. An eagle perched at the top of the great spruce tree in Deganawida's vision was a symbolic reference to a state of vigilance against any enemy who might break the peace. The League was governed by a carefully worked out constitution, the laws and regulations of which were transmitted orally from one generation to another by selected leaders. At the time of its establishment, the centrally placed Onondagas were chosen as both the 'firekeepers' and 'wampum keepers' of the League. As firekeepers of the League, it was the Onondagas' responsibility to call yearly councils at which the constitution and laws were rehearsed and differences resolved.

At its foundation, the League took into account the established clan system which had been used by the five tribes from ancient times; each clan owned several personal names which served to define roles within the tribes, while the fifty chiefs who made up the 'Roll Call of Chiefs' were each elected from the appropriate clan members. Thus, the ancient social organization was maintained, giving stability and unification to the League, which would not have otherwise been obtained had the old social structure been discarded.[6]

The Iroquois clan system was matrilineal, emphasized by the custom of a child receiving a name belonging to the mother's clan. Of great interest is the power which the woman had in the selection of the clan chiefs: 'When one of these "federal" chiefs died, the clan mother (senior woman of the clan, that is, the "aged sensible" women recognized as such) in consultation with other women belonging to that clan in the same tribe, chose the man who would assume that name and hence become successor to the deceased chief. Often she chose a man of her lineage (and of the lineage of the deceased chief), but if there was not a suitable man of this lineage, a man of another lineage in the clan might be chosen. If the clan did not have a suitable candidate, the name might be "loaned" to another clan, that is, the name given to a man belonging to another clan with the understanding that at his death the name would then return to the clan that had loaned it.' Therefore, although the League of the Iroquois had the appearance of a government consisting exclusively of males, each member of that governing body was in reality answerable to the women of his maternal family, which in fact consisted only of one female, the 'aged sensible' woman. There is little doubt that this power wielded by the women had its foundation in the Iroquoian subsistence patterns which were highly dependent on horticulture.

Maize, beans and squashes were the three major sources of nourishment to the Iroquois, and these were regarded as sacred gifts from the Creator; called 'the three sisters', these foods played an important part in the ceremonials, particularly those associated with the spirit of gratitude. At the gathering and storing of these crops, the communities celebrated the completion of the cycle: 'The "three sisters" are happy because they are home again from their summer in the fields.'[7] A survey of Iroquois horticultural achievements, together with their knowledge of wild plants, leaves little doubt that, as with their northern neighbors, the Huron, meat was of fairly limited importance to their subsistence. Up to seventeen distinct varieties of maize were produced, some sixty varieties of beans and some seven squashes. Additionally, they collected thirty-four wild fruits, eleven species of nuts, twelve types of edible roots, thirty-eight varieties of bark, stem and leaf products, and six fungi. They also produced some twelve beverages and eleven infusions from parts of plants as occasional drinks, and while salt was little used, maple sap was very popular, being used to flavor corn meal, sweeten mush and as a beverage. Little wonder that culture statisticians have given the Indians of the Eastern Woodlands 'a high rating in the ratio of food discoveries' when the Old and New World peoples are compared.

Iroquois villages were composed of bark-covered houses averaging perhaps 65ft (20m) in length, 20ft (6m) wide and 20ft high. The Iroquois referred to these as *ganonh'sees*, the 'longhouse', which, depending on its size, could accommodate between five and twenty families. There were only two doors, one at each end and lengthwise down the center ran a passageway 6½–10ft (2–3m) in width, either side of which and raised 1½ft (45cm) from the ground ran a platform which served as both seats and beds. Above this, perhaps 8ft (2.5m) from the ground, was a second platform which could be used for storage and, if necessary, additional beds. The longhouse was divided into family apartments some 10ft (3m) wide and either side of the passage, two families were served by a small fire set at intervals along the length of the house. In the roof were openings to allow for the escape of smoke and to give light to the interior; as necessary, openings could be shut off by use of a slab of roof bark. The longhouse was warm and weatherproof, but unlike the Plains tipi there was no direct control over the rising smoke. However, the large doors at each end undoubtedly produced a useful forced convection effect, expelling smoke through the roof apertures.

The longhouse was made from a basic framework of upright posts set into the ground and enclosing a rectangular floor area. Attached to the tops of the posts were flexible poles which were bent over to produce the roof frame. Slabs of bark about 5ft wide by 6½ft in length (1.5 × 2m), preferably elm although basswood, ash, hemlock or cedar were also used, were then attached to the frame in an overlapping fashion with strips of the inner bark of hickory or basswood trees. As with the clearing of the fields the work was carried out by the men but longhouses were considered the property of the women.

Although similar houses were used by other tribes in the region – for example by the Huron to the north (who favored cedar rather than elm bark) – the longhouse was the most conspicuous feature of Iroquois villages and each was a microcosm of the whole community becoming a symbol of identity, thus the common description for themselves – with some variations – strongly conveyed the idea of them being 'The people of the longhouse'.

By the end of the eighteenth century, there was a gradual abandonment of the longhouse in favor of single family dwellings. However, the longhouse has now become the council house of the communities; while today the longhouse often resembles a modern building, symbolically it states tribal unity and is the center which perpetuates the teachings of the Seneca prophet 'Handsome Lake' who, in 1799, recognizing the social disorganization which was occurring, urged then return to the ancient annual ceremonials of the Iroquois. The so-called 'Longhouse Religion' has thus become a 'continued assertion of the integrity of an Iroquois ethnic identity'.

Early descriptions of Iroquois villages refer to elaborate fortifications consisting of a stockade and sometimes a moat. In illustrating his attack on the Onondaga in 1615, the French explorer Samual Champlain showed massive palisades which the Iroquois had constructed by driving two rows of tree trunks into the ground, inclining each pair so that they crossed some 16½ft (5m) from the ground, the space between being filled with logs. The trunks were bound together at their point of crossing and horizontal beams were laid into the Vs, thus forming a narrow walkway that was protected on the outer side with bark slabs. Notched poles on the inner part of the palisade were used as rough ladders giving the defenders access to the protected walkway. They were formidable forts and, even with the use of a cavalier,[8] the Onondaga held off the gun-armed French and their Huron allies for nearly a week until the attackers abandoned the action, much, it must be said, to Champlain's discredit in the eyes of both friend and enemy.[9]

Other than the supporting French, the raid on the Onondaga village was typical of intertribal warfare between Iroquoian-speaking tribes. Indeed, such was the nature of the Iroquoian warfare pattern, it is unlikely that the Huron would have considered the Onondaga siege a failure because hostile encounters were not generally a struggle for hunting territory or land, but a test of a warrior's bravery, to take a scalp or two and perhaps prisoners for torture.

Prior to an expedition against the enemy and agreement having been reached in council, the Hurons traditionally had a war feast which was prepared by the women. The origin of the feast – and it also went some way to explain the warlike nature of the Iroquoians – was attributed in their mythology to a giant whom a number of Hurons had encountered on the shore of a large lake. When the giant failed to reply politely to his greeting, one of the Hurons wounded him in the forehead. In punishment, the giant sowed the seeds of discord among the Huron, but before he disappeared into the earth he recommended the war and *Ononharoia* feasts and the use of the war cry, *wiiiiii*. The feast was accompanied by singing and dancing by the young warriors who uttered abuse against the enemy with promises of victory and as they moved from one end of the longhouse to the other, 'under the pretext of doing it in jest, [they] would knock down others whom they did not like'.

It was not unusual for several hundred Huron warriors to lay siege to an Iroquois village, generally the Seneca who lived closest to Huron territory. Such expeditions usually took place in the summer, when there was plenty of leaf cover, and often had an air of an outing, as Champlain commented on the prelude to one Huron-Iroquois battle: 'This war had much of the character of an organized sport', the men traveling slowly toward enemy country, fishing and hunting along the way. On crossing Lake Ontario by canoe to the south shore, they would then hide, split up into smaller groups and then travel on foot to the Iroquois villages. Women and children were not infrequently captured before the village itself was put to siege. The principal weapon used in pre- or early contact times was the stone-headed or wooden ball-headed club. The latter was a formidable weapon at close range; commonly made of ironwood and up to 2ft (60cm) in length, it had a large knob or ball at the head, some 4½–10in (12–25cm) in diameter which was often carved with animal figures, perhaps emblematic of the owner's personal totem and protective power.[10] The ball-headed club was later superseded by the trade metal-pipe tomahawk, and, likewise, the bow and arrow was eventually replaced by the gun, the latter having a particular impact on warfare tactics, for example the abandonment of wooden body armor, and change in battle formation.[11]

In all cases, casualties were usually few in number, the young aspiring warriors laying emphasis on performing acts of daring. Generally, after a few injuries and deaths the attackers withdrew to their temporary forts which they commonly built near the enemy village. Pitched battles tended to be avoided and if reinforcements from other settlements were imminent, the attackers left for home.

The wounded were carried home in a makeshift basket sling, on the backs of their companions and, while it was a practical means of transport through the heavily wooded forest, it was appallingly uncomfortable for the injured. Champlain, who was himself wounded in the leg and knee by two Iroquois arrows, describes how the Huron men fabricated the frame of hickory or elm, attaching a seat with straps of hide or of the plaited inner bark of elm. The frame and burden were supported by a tump-line across the carrier's forehead and the wounded warrior sat on the seat, his legs under his chin and tightly bound in position. Champlain described his ordeal – undoubtedly an extremely unpleasant one experienced by many an immobilized Iroquoian warrior:

'It was impossible to move any more than a little child in its swaddling clothes[un]. . . and this causes the wounded great and extreme pain. I can say this indeed from my own case, having been carried for several days because I was unable to stand, chiefly on account of the arrow-wound I had received in my knee, for never did I find myself in such a hell as during this time; for the pain I suffered from the wound in my knee was nothing in comparison with what I endured tied and bound on the back of one of our savages. . .'

Such journeys subjected the helpless incumbent to endless tossing, buffeting and whipping by the tree branches and half, sometimes complete, immersion in water as the bearer made his way through forests and streams, but it was greatly preferable to falling into the hands of Iroquois enemies.

Early explorers found much to admire in Iroquoian society; they describe, for example, the superb physique of the men and the beauty of the young women. There was surprisingly little internal conflict within the crowded villages and all were fond of laughter and jokes, applied good sense and justice in their affairs, showed great hospitality and, at times, great kindness. They had an acuteness of sense, great courage, endurance and were stoic to pain.

The Iroquoian treatment of prisoners was, however, another matter and many whites were stunned and appalled by what they saw. In Iroquoian war ethos, nothing was considered more desirable than to be credited with the capture of prisoners and more particularly the capture of an enemy warrior. On occasions, if several men claimed the capture of a particular prisoner, the prisoner himself would be requested to designate his official captor. In so doing, wily captured Iroquoians, who were well versed in the psychology of intertribal warfare, not infrequently named another who was less involved in his capture. In so doing, he struck a note of discord among his captors and sometimes, rather than allow the honor to go to the wrong man, he was helped to escape. While women and children might be slain on the spot or taken back for adoption, male prisoners – unless there were too many of them – were taken back to the villages. On some occasions, men were formally adopted, receiving the name of a lost relative which 'served to dry the tears of the bereaved', but most often they were subjected to ritual torture which for some unexplained reason was part of Iroquois and Huron psychology and far less practiced by the Algonquian tribes.

The historian Francis Parkman has described in great detail the fate of one Iroquois prisoner who was captured by Hurons during the savage Iroquois-Huron war of 1648-50.[12] *Saouandanancous* was brought in by his Huron captors and adopted by an elderly chief who, having lost a son, had hoped that *Saouandanancous* might take his place; the prisoner's hands, however, had been seriously injured[13] and because of this, although treated with courtesy and an outward show of genuine affection, he was condemned to die. He was put to death by fire so carefully applied that it took him over twelve hours to die. Astoundingly, his tormentors showed no signs of lack of self-control and as each applied his particular torture they spoke to the prisoner in a kindly way. Equally extraordinary is that *Saouandanancous* demonstrated the courage and endurance expected of an Iroquois warrior: during intervals between the torture he not only reported on Hurons who had been adopted into his tribe, but sang as well. When he finally expired, he was cut up and small pieces of his flesh distributed for eating.

In 1609, Champlain described a similar episode; after the battle at

Ticonderoga, one of the dozen or so prisoners was selected for torture. The Huron harangued him with the cruelties which he and members of his tribe had practiced on them and that he should prepare himself to experience as much. They told him to sing 'if he had the heart' and Champlain reports that he did 'but it was a very sad song to hear'.

Although it has been reported that on occasions the body of the dead man was burned as a sacrifice to the most powerful of the Huron supernaturals, *Oki*, 'the sky',[14] the ritually tortured prisoners were probably symbols of the tribe represented; as one anthropologist has recently explained it, the prisoners became a 'hate object on whom the frustrations of life and past wrongs could be expended'.

West and north of Huronia was the domain of an equally powerful, but politically considerably less coordinated, tribe – the Algonquian-speaking Chippewa – who occupied much of what is now the state of Wisconsin, southwest Ontario and northeastern Minnesota. Unlike the Iroquois, who were too far south and so had largely to resort to elm bark for building their longhouses and fabricating utensils and canoes, the Chippewa had easy access to a superior natural material – birch bark – and, in further contrast, depended to a far lesser degree on horticulture, the maize of their southern neighbors being largely replaced by superb wild 'rice' which grew in abundance in the countless streams and lakes so characteristic of the Mississippi headwaters region.

Wild 'rice' (*Zizania aquatica*) was not in actuality a true rice but an aquatic grass. Early explorers were greatly impressed by its nutritious value and it was an important component in the diet of the Western Great Lakes people, particularly the Chippewa and Menominee, whose tribal name was derived from the Chippewa for wild 'rice', *manomini*. It was the chief vegetal food for that tribe although for religious reasons they never attempted to cultivate it, seemingly as part of their unwillingness to 'wound their mother, the earth'.

The rice was collected in late August or early September[15] with the people working in groups; certain areas were recognized as being the property of certain families, and it was a right that was seldom disputed. Often the growth was so dense that the areas gave the appearance of enormous green meadows and the canoes needed to be poled through the torpid streams or shallow lakes, generally by a male member of the group, while the women gathered. Two sticks about 2ft (60cm) long were used in the harvesting process; the women sat in the stern of the canoe and bent down the stalks, which could be over 20ft (6m) high, with one stick and struck the kernel with the other; the process was continued until the canoe was full. On return to the temporary lake-shore camp, the gatherers laid out the 'rice' on sheets of birch bark for drying; it was then poured into a lined hole in the ground and pounded with long pestles, or curved sticks, to loosen the husks, perhaps several women participating in this part of the work. Finally, the 'rice' was winnowed by pouring it from one special large bark tray to another. The quality, size and taste differed and it was recognized that certain areas produced particularly good crops, 'kernels there are small and better tasting than the ones around here', and the kernels on the La Pointe Reservation were 'finer than the ones at Red Lake'. Nevertheless, whatever its type, as with the tapping for maple syrup in the spring, it was an opportunity for group activities and joyous gatherings.

The collecting of maple sugar was an activity of great importance as it was used in feasts and ceremonials and everyone was expected to eat all that was set before them. The sugar was used on fruits, vegetables, cereals and even fish. Although the collecting of maple sugar – which generally commenced in March – was a time of work, it was also one of pleasure, and special wigwams were retained from year to year in certain areas. It was an opportunity for social and ceremonial gatherings and a chance to catch up on the previous year's tribal gossip.

The maple trees were tapped by making a gash in the trunk 3ft (1m meter) or so above the ground. A cedar spike was pounded into the tree at an angle to allow the sap to drip down into a birch-bark bucket placed on the ground. The sap was boiled and when it hung in strings from the stirring paddle it was considered ready; it was then strained through a basswood-fiber matting and transferred to a granulating trough. It was worked as it cooled and the granulated sugar which resulted was pulverized into finer granules. Some of the sugar was packed into molds to make little cakes, but most was put into *makuks* – special birch-bark storage containers – and carried home for use throughout the rest of the year. In addition to its use as a highly nutritious food source, it was also mixed with water to make a refreshing drink. A small amount of the sugar was always offered to Manito[16] and this type of ceremonial – the offering of the first fruit or game – was observed with the first preparation of each seasonal food.

The vast woodland areas had an abundance of wild foods, such as cranberries, gooseberries, blueberries, black and red raspberries, cherries and grapes, hickory, hazel, beech and butternuts and also wild onions and potatoes, the former being particular favorites. Later in the summer when plants were fully developed, special attention was given to gathering herbs for medicine. The person gathering the herbs would offer tobacco to the four directions as well as to the sky and earth. Prayers were made in a low voice with promises that no more would be taken than was necessary, while hope was expressed that the mysterious powers would make their use successful. After being gathered, the various plants were dried, each variety being separately stored. While most of the herbs were used as remedies for sore eyes, abdominal problems, skin and lung troubles, some were also used as hunting charms; powdered or in the form of fine roots, they were mixed with tobacco or red willow and smoked in a pipe. During the course of tracking the deer, men occasionally sat down and smoked one of the herbs 'and it is said that before long the deer came toward them sniffing the air'. For so many of these subsistence activities – the canoe to collect the wild 'rice' and the winnowing trays used to separate it, the *makuk* for collecting berries, the leak-proof containers for collecting the maple syrup and water, and the fabrication of their habitations – the Chippewa very much depended on one natural and remarkable material, *wigass*, or 'birch bark'; it was the very basis of their material culture.

Although the time varied in different localities, the Chippewa knew when they could remove the bark without destroying the tree, but generally it was between the end of spring and the early summer. The process of removing the bark was demonstrated by a Lac Courte (Wisconsin) Chippewa lady to Sister Inez Hilger: clutching her pocket knife in her right hand and 'with blade extending beyond her little finger [she] carefully cut the outer bark (only the outer bark is removed) from a place as high as she could reach, down to the root. In removing the bark she moved clockwise around the tree, loosening it carefully with both hands so as not to break it'. It was later explained that when very large pieces of bark were needed, such as were used in making canoes, trees were felled and then all the bark stripped off. The bark was then rolled or folded and tied up with a basswood fiber and transported on the back of the gatherer; rolls or folded batches of birch bark were common in or close to the wigwams, ready for use. The actual thickness of the bark determined the use to which it could be put: that removed from the large trees could have up to nine separate layers and was suitable for making canoes; some, however, was as thin and pliable as tissue paper, but so tough and durable that it was used for wrapping. Between these extremes were several other grades, mainly used for containers and trays; that which was three or more layers in thickness was suitable for peaked or domed winter wigwams, while two layers for the conical summer lodge would suffice.

The domed wigwam consisted of a framework made of flexible poles or saplings of ironwood or elm which were pushed into the ground and then bent over, producing a series of arches. Horizontal encircling poles were then lashed to the vertical poles with basswood fiber producing a net-like framework. The sheets of bark, perhaps over 6ft long and 3ft wide (about 2 × 1m) wide, were then laid on a lining of woven cattail (*Typha latifolia*) mats, overlapping as one would shingle a roof; a smoke hole was left at the top. The fire was small and provided by several dry logs which radiated from the central hearth, and as the logs burned they were pushed inward. By careful selection of the wood, the flame could be made virtually smokeless. The permanent lodges generally had a platform about 1½ft (45cm) extending part way around the interior, which served both as seats and beds; many had a medicine pole, perhaps 20ft (6m) high, attached to the top of which was a small sacrifice to the mysterious and unfathomable potentials and powers of life and the universe – the Manito.

One observer, Frances Densmore, who spent over twenty years studying the life of the Chippewa, came to view these people with enormous respect. She was moved by the beauty of the northern woodlands, familiar with its changing seasons, the material abundance and inspiration, giving, she concluded, the poetry and the spiritual essence of Chippewa culture. Densmore captured in words the special warmth and beauty of the winter wigwam, where the 'winter evenings were social and pleasant. The fire burned brightly, but no work was done which placed a strain on the eyes. A favorite pastime was the making of birch-bark transparencies. The women made basswood cord or fish nets, and sometimes they made birch-bark *makuks* or dishes. The young men reclined in the wigwam and always had a drum conveniently near them. . . the winter was the time for story-telling, and many old women were experts in this art. One old woman used to act out her stories, running around the fire and acting while she talked.'

Because the Great Lakes region was dotted with lakes and laced with streams and rivers, a great deal depended on transportation by canoe, the best being made of the versatile birch bark.[17] In common with most tribes inhabiting this area, the Chippewa were considered to be expert canoemen and builders, employing one of at least three styles although it is probable that the so-called 'high-ended' type was the old tribal form resembling that of the Algonquin further east. This particular type of canoe was still used by the Chippewa on Lake Nipigon in Ontario and also by the Menominee in Wisconsin in the nineteenth century. The artist and explorer George Catlin was particularly impressed with the Chippewa canoe, and the consummate skill with which it was fashioned, observing:

'The bark canoe of the Chippeways is, perhaps, the most beautiful and light model of all the water crafts that ever were invented. They are . . . so ingeniously shaped and sewed together, with roots of the tamarack, . . . that they . . . ride upon the water, as light as a cork.'

The immense skill required in handling these bark canoes was not lost on Catlin:

'They gracefully lean and dodge about, under the skillful balance of an Indian, . . . but like everything wild, are timid and treacherous under the guidance of white man; and, if he be not an experienced equilibrist, he is sure to get two or three times soused, in his first endeavors at familiar acquaintance with them.'

While the size of the canoe varied depending on its use, the typical model was just under 16ft (5m) in length, 3ft (1m) wide at the middle, and 1½ft (45cm) deep. Such a canoe could carry about six adults. All measurements were based on the distances between various parts of the human body, although one basic unit employed by many good canoe makers was the 'hand spread' or span from the end of middle finger to the tip of the thumb. It took great skill to fabricate these crafts; the women generally prepared the ground, bark and pitch, while the men shaped the wood for the floor, ribs, stern and bow. The whole process was customarily supervised by a highly respected, skilled canoe-maker, such expertise not uncommonly passing from father to son so that the traditional skills could indeed be maintained.

In one description of the fabrication of a birch-bark canoe, it was reported that it took about a week to gather all the materials together and make the craft. All the materials came from trees; the framework and lining was of lightweight cedar, the cords used to keep the frame and other parts together was of spruce root and the pitch for the seams was made from spruce gum, which was generally boiled to thicken it (that which was to be used on the main seams being mixed with powdered charcoal which not only made the resin less brittle when it dried, but gave an ornamental appearance to the caulking). Often, the ground on which the canoe was to be fabricated was covered with a layer of sand so as to shape the canoe bottom, then long sheets of thick bark with the inner side of the bark to the outside were weighted down with a flat frame, which defined the approximate length and width of the canoe; large stones ensured that the frame and bark were held firmly in place. Seven or eight pairs of short poles were now driven into the ground, slightly inclined to the vertical, conforming to the shape of the lower frame and perhaps 3ft (1m) or so apart at the middle; as the posts were positioned they eased the bark up at an angle and the canoe now began to take shape. The gunwales were now placed in lengthwise and the bark sewn in place with the spruce root; the gunwale gave shape and strength to the upper edges of the canoe and was prepared beforehand so as to have the correct shape and curve as were the sections of cedar for the bow and stern which were eased between the bark at each end. This was then trimmed, conforming to an approved outline. All the final sewing was carried out by the women, traditionally using a bone awl, the finer being done with split and soaked spruce root. Several women could probably complete the required sewing on an average canoe in one day; some of the stitching was deliberately of uneven length, particularly at the ends, to reduce the likelihood of the bark splitting.

It was important that all overlapping edges of the bark were toward the stern of the canoe so as to ensure streamline flow around its contours, and that all the gores and laps were firmly stuck together with spruce gum. Ribs were now cut to length and shape and eased into place with a lining of thin strips of cedar placed between the ribs and the bark as the work proceeded; this protected the floor and sides of the canoe. Ribs, lining and bark were all kept moist, but the varying width crosspieces which permanently shaped the top of the canoe were sewn in dry.

The canoe was now left to dry for several days and, if necessary, pulled into correct shape by tying it between end stakes. It was then inverted and the seams sealed with the black spruce pitch.

Paddles were of birch or cedar, some 4ft (1.2m) in length, approximately half being the blade which was 4½ or 6in (12 or 15cm) wide. Both men and women rowed, generally with the man seated in the prow and the woman in the stern; however, for fast travel, up to four men might paddle at one time.

A good serviceable canoe would last a family perhaps a year or so; some men were especially known for making and supplying canoes, and a typical price in the late nineteenth century would be a three-point Hudson's Bay blanket.

There is little wonder that, given the great value of birch bark in the life of the woodland tribes, there are references to it as sacred material. The Abenaki, for example, named the birch *Gluskabe* which was one of their hero gods who, it is recorded, asked the tree 'to take care of the Indians'. A widespread mythological tale explains the migrations of birds back to the northern forests after the intense winters. The birds are caged in birch-bark containers which are torn open by animal-men volunteers from the North, freeing the birds who fly north bringing the summer warmth and regrowth; symbolically, life emerges from the birch container, hence the patterns, produced by a scraping technique (sgraffito), of birds, plants and shrubs embellished on their outer surface.[18]

The spiritual life of the Western Lakes tribes, which has been so eloquently captured in the writings of Frances Densmore on the Chippewa and referred to earlier, centered around the ceremonials of the *Midewiwin*,[19] or Grand Medicine Society, which has been particularly well-documented for the Chippewa. The existence of the *Midewiwin* was not recorded by the Jesuit Relations (covering the period 1640 to 1700). However, it has been suggested that special efforts were made by the ritualists to conceal this religious rite which was in direct conflict with the missionary message.[20] The probable antiquity of the *Midewiwin* is suggested by its extensive distribution in the Western Great Lakes region, being practiced by the Potawatomi, Menominee, Winnebago, Sauk, Fox and Kickapoo from 'early historic times'.

While there were regional variations in the *Midewiwin* ceremony, the principles of ethical conduct, the desire for attainment of a long life, the interpretation of dreams and the phenomena of the natural world, permeated the activities of the Society. The basic ethics of the *Midewiwin* were that rectitude of conduct produced length of life and that, conversely, evil conduct would eventually react on the offender. Stealing and lying and the use of alcohol were strictly forbidden, while respect toward women was emphasized. Male members of the *Midewiwin* were taught to be quiet in manner and moderate in speech and not hasty in action. As Densmore observed, 'this directed [my] attention to the gentle voices, the patience, and the courtesy of the old people who had been trained in the Midewiwin'.

The initiation ceremony was designed to inject a spirit power into the candidate, achieved by pointing a special medicine bag whereupon the candidate fell to the ground unconscious. The bags were made of animal or bird skins being distinctive of one of the four orders of degrees which could be attained in *Midewiwin* membership. The initiation of one candidate who was seated in the middle of the Grand Medicine Lodge, was described by one observer:

> 'The medicine men, four or five of them, came dancing in, carrying pouches. The pouches were made of the skins of beaver, otter, white martin or weasel – all elongated like snake skins. The dancers danced along the path of the wigwam and when they came near my uncle they threw their pouches at him. The "medicine" in them was so strong that he fell over and fainted. Each man then picked up his pouch and laid it on him, and he came to.'

The *Midewiwin* medicine bags held a special small white shell called the *migis*;[21] this was considered the sacred symbol of the Society and traditionally associated with immortality. It was also the *migis* which transmitted the spirit power, as noted in the *Midewiwin* initiation songs:

> *Here it is*
> *Here it is*
> *The weasel skin* [medicine bag]
> *Through it I shoot the white shells.*
>
> *It never fails*
> *The shell*
> *Goes toward them*
> *And they fall.*

The ceremony was one of curing a sick individual or responding to a dream that directed application for membership should be made. The *Midewiwin* was generally an annual affair that was held in the late spring or early fall and lasted for up to five days, depending on the number of candidates. A possible reason for its popularity with the Chippewa is that they have been identified by one anthropologist as having an unusual preoccupation with health, a manifestation of this concern being their assortment of different roots and herbs which were used for medicinal purposes, gaining a knowledge of which was one of the major objectives of the members of the *Midewiwin*.

A notable component associated with the Society was the use of bark rolls inscribed with pictographs, which referred to the instructions to be given to its members; they also recorded the songs and teachings of the *Midewiwin*. The rolls were some 2½ft in length by 1ft wide (75 × 30cm), the pictographs being engraved with a bone stylus. To the uninitiated, they were virtually meaningless, but to those with the esoteric knowledge the figures were invaluable memory aids. The records were passed down through successive generations, the aged keepers initiating younger men in regard to the meaning of each pictograph. Such pictographic records in the Woodland region were by no means unique to the Chippewa alone, but because of their close association with religious concepts of these people, they have been extensively reported on.

Studies have shown that there were similarities between birch-bark pictographs of all the Algonquian stock from the northeastern seaboard to west of the Great Lakes, and the Abenaki in Maine even modified the ancient pictographic techniques when, in the late nineteenth century, they became 'engaged in civilized industries in which they have found it necessary to keep accounts'.

Extending on the nineteenth-century studies of Mallery, W.C. Sturtevant has recently demonstrated that Iroquois hieroglyphics[22] could convey extensive and sophisticated ideas to those familiar with the glyphs. Such pictographic work was perhaps the nearest approach to writing by the indigenous population of North America,[23] but the influx of Europeans caused the abandonment of these hieroglyphics before further development took place.

'Had the whites delayed their coming for another century, . . . these Indians might have succeeded in establishing an enduring State based on the six foundation stones of the League – health, happiness, righteousness, justice, power and strength of character.'[24]

MYTHS AND LEGENDS

In overtly simple terms, a quote by the Shawnee, Tecumseh, reveals the very essence of native philosophy and cosmology among the tribes of the Northeast Woodlands and Great Lakes: 'The Sun is my father, and the Earth is my mother. I will repose upon her bosom.' The mythological origins of the people, arising as they did from the union of Sun and Earth, had, and continues to have, a profound effect on their lives.

The diverse Northeast Woodlands and Great Lakes area was united by a number of common cosmological beliefs. Central to these beliefs was a reverence for the three cosmic zones of Upper World (sky and Sun), Earth and Under World (water or beneath the earth), and the recognition of a continuum that encompasses human persons to other-than-human persons. Included, too, was the understanding that features of the landscape and the forces of nature, as well as animals and vegetation, possessed spiritual power in the form of *Orenda* for the Iroquoians, *Maintou* for the Algonquians, and *Wakan* for the Siouans. Paramount was the gaining of personal power through dreams, visions and the acquision of spirit helpers. Shamans were efficacious in curing and concerns effecting group wellbeing. Common to all were ritual obligations of propitiation to these powers, often in the form of tobacco offerings and prayers.

Evidence of their cosmological beliefs has been made manifest in a number of material forms. At times the human body itself has been the canvas for ritual painting and permanent tattooing. Sacred items range from clothing and personal adornment to items such as drums, rattles and wands used in ceremonies, and weapons used in war. Vision quests, shamanic experience and guidelines for the litany of certain healing ceremonies are recorded in pictographic form on rock formations, wooden prayer sticks, and birch-bark scrolls. For each society these tangible items metonymically revealed the depth of their being.

Within the culture area, three cultural 'zones' based on language affiliation, geographic distribution and subsistence are apparent. A Coastal Zone that included the eastern Algonquian tribes of Micmac, Maliseet-Passamoquoddy, Abenaki, Delaware, Nanticoke, and Powhatan followed a maritime foraging subsistence with agriculture in the southern portion. In the Saint Lawrence Lowlands and below the Great Lakes, the northern Iroquoian speakers were represented by the Saint Lawrence Iroquoians, Mohawk, Oneida, Onondaga, Cayuga, Seneca, Tuscarora, Huron, Erie and Susquehannock. The practice of intensive horticulture augmented by fishing and hunting permitted increased social complexity. In the third zone the central Algonquian linguistic group of the Great Lakes–Riverine region embraced the Chippewa (Ojibwa in Canada), Ottawa, Potawatomi, Menominee, Sauk and Fox, Kickapoo, Miami, Illinois and Shawnee. Contiguous with these Algonquian tribes were the Siouan-speaking Winnebago. Their culture resembled that of their Algonquian neighbors.

ORIGIN MYTHS
The strength of origin stories in the form of myths and legends that continue to be passed down from generation to generation serve to preserve traditions and instill cultural values.

■ The Origin of Stories
This myth reveals how the Senecas acquired their knowledge of the world before this one. It all began with young Orphan Boy who had become very successful at hunting birds. One day when deep in the woods pursuing birds, he sat down on a flat-topped round stone. As he began to repair his arrow, a voice near him asked, 'Shall I tell you stories?' Looking around he saw no one. However, when the voice repeated the question, Orphan Boy asked, 'What is that? What does it mean to tell stories?' The stone responded that it meant telling what happened a long time ago. In exchange for the boy's birds, the stone told story after story about the world before the present. Each day Orphan Boy would bring birds in exchange for more stories. One day he was joined by an older boy, then by two men, all of whom listened to the origin stories related by the stone. Eventually the stone requested that all the villagers should come to listen. Each person brought a gift of food in exchange for the stories. And from then on, following the instructions of the rock, these stories were to be told to

generation after generation as long as the world lasts.

◪ The World on the Turtle's Back

This tale relates the origins of the Iroquoians which began in the sky with the uprooting of the Celestial Tree of Light. *Ataentsic,* or Sky Woman, slipped through the hole and began to fall through the air to the ocean below. As she fell, the geese spread out their wings to catch her. Seeing this, Great Turtle entreated the other aquatic creatures to dive to the bottom of the sea to gather earth to place on his back. One by one the diving birds and animals tried without success until finally Muskrat, more dead than alive, returned to the surface clutching some soil in his paw. Placing it on the turtle's back, the soil expanded to form an island, and Sky Woman was placed upon it. And so the Earth came into being.

■ Children of the Rising Sun

The Wabenaki, living on the shores of the Atlantic Ocean, considered themselves to be the children of the rising Sun. According to an early myth, the Sun first created the entire universe and then, with the power of his penetrating rays, impregnated Mother Earth, and the people were brought forth into this world. At the dawn of each new day, the Wabenaki directed their prayers of respect and adoration to their father, the Rising Sun, and invoked his blessings. At sunset these rituals were repeated.

■ Great Tree of Peace

This signifies the legendary founding of the Confederacy or League of the Five Nations of the Iroquois. The vision of bringing together the warring Iroquoian tribes into a peaceful alliance is attributed to *Deganawidah,* culture hero and prophet, and was brought to fruition by the eloquent and persuasive speech-making of his co-worker, *Hiawatha.* Initial efforts were obstructed by Onondaga Chief *Thadodaho,* who represented all that was repugnant, anti-social and profane to the ideals of the proposed Iroquois League. By combing out these snakes, *Hiawatha* brought about a transformation from repulsive creature to the epitome of ideal leader, holder of the prestigious position of Keeper of the League's Sacred Fire. To symbolize the formation of the League, *Deganawidah* planted the Tree of Peace in Onondaga territory as the center of the League, its roots of peace reaching to the four corners of the Earth, its branches reaching into the sky. Placed on the top of the tree was the 'Eagle who Sees Afar', and in a cavity below the roots, were buried all the weapons of strife.

■ Origin of the Medicine Society

The rituals of the Medicine Society were given to the Great Lakes people by the culture hero *Manabus,* or *Nanabojo,* to save them from certain extinction by a deadly disease. In the Upper World, the Upper and Lower powers worked together to make a lodge for *Manabus.* It was in this specially constructed lodge that he received instructions for curing. Here he was taught the use of medicines found on Earth, the specific rites to be performed and to revere the Earthly forms of the Sacred Otter, the Bear and the Megis shells as powerful medicines. Descending to Earth with his medicine bag, *Manabus* instructed the people and initiated them into the society's mysteries.

ALL-POWERFUL SPIRITS

It is no surprise to find the Sun with an important position in regional culture, a feature of so many belief systems. Another common but more intriguing concept is that of the duality of good and bad and their constant struggles against each other for supremacy.

■ The Sun

In his various guises as Grandfather, Elder Brother, Good Twin, Honored Chief, Great Warrior and War God, the Sun played a paramount role in the early times for all groups. Certainly, the Sun was regarded as eternal, all-seeing and all-penetrating, source of growth and vigor, father and master of all life and bringer of daylight. The extent and variety of this Sun veneration (including his Earthly representation as fire) acknowledges the antiquity and importance of the Sun's role.[25]

The Great Lakes peoples (as did the ancient Micmacs) also associated the Sun with war. In his guise as Great Warrior and Patron of War, the Sun was honored with scalp-taking, ritual torture and sacrificial burning of war captives. Those Menomiee warriors who dreamed of the Sun were believed to benefit from his protection in war, and they signified this power by roaching their hair and suspending an amulet-like figure of the Sun over their chests.

■ *Manabus*

This semi-divine culture hero of the Algonquians (also known as *Nanabojo*) has a lively and somewhat enigmatic personality. The old stories cast him as the endower and master of life, and as introducer of technological inventions – the making of fire, clothing, snares, traps, nets – who instructed the people in their use. His teachings also provided each of the floral and faunal species with ways to protect themselves from enemies. And in his capacity as intermediary between the Creator and the people, *Manabus* brought the life-prolonging powers of the *Midewiwin* to the Earth world.

However, *Manabus* has become renowned as a trickster, deceiving and playing pranks on humans. Coupled with this is his ability to transform into a number of corporal forms, including that of a hare. These numerous impersonations of diverse personalities strongly suggest that *Manabus* is the quintessential embodiment of the concept of Life.

■ Earthmaker

The Creator or Great Spirit of the Winnebago created the spirits who live above the Earth, those who live on the Earth and those who live below the Earth and in the water. Thus, it was he who created the world and all that exists in it and who sent their great transformer heroes, Trickster, Turtle and Hare. In this Winnebago pantheon, Earthmaker, as a deity of peace, serves as the antithesis to the violence and force pre-eminent in ceremonies devoted to enhancing warriors and warfare.

After creating tobacco, Earthmaker entrusted its power to the people so they would have a desirous item to exchange with the spirits in return for their favors. Often described as being anthropomorphic, Earthmaker was symbolized by a cross representative of the four cardinal points.

■ *Glooskap*

Similar to *Manabus, Glooskap*'s position in the case of pantheonic characters of the eastern Algonquians was paradoxical. His divinity, established in some accounts as being the creation of the Great Spirit, was recognized in *Glooskap*'s special spiritual and physical powers. It is *Glooskap*, as protagonist, who competed with the Creator in a power of wills to give existence to things. At other times he was portrayed as the Good Twin constantly thwarting the destructive powers of his evil brother, *Malsum*. Even in his capacity as a trickster, *Glooskap* continues to exude benevolence.

■ The Theme of Twins

According to Iroquian mythology, Sky Woman (or, variously, her daughter) gave birth to twin boys named *Iouskeha,* the Good-minded Twin, and *Tawiscaron,* the Evil-minded Twin. The Good-minded Twin was born in the normal manner while his twin brother burst forth from their mother's armpit, killing her in the process.

Iouskeha, possessing the ability to create constructively, made the plants, animals, birds and mankind, while *Tawiscaron,* controlling the destructive forces, tried to destroy his brother's work. Together they established a world simultaneously divided and yet balanced. However, a last relentless contest left the Evil-minded Twin dead and sent the Good-minded Twin to the Sky World or Upper World as the Master of Life.

This motif of twins, giving corporal form to the powers of good and bad, is prevalent among other Northeast groups, and in other regions too. In the eastern regions *Glooskap* and his twin brother, *Malsum,* or Wolf, entered the world in the same way with similar results as the Iroquoian twins. Tales of their escapades reinforce the concept of an inherent dualism in the structuring of the cultures and the on-going battle between good and evil principles. This also holds true among the Chippewa/Ojibwa, Potawatomi and Ottawa who provide *Nanabojo* with a brother. In these alternative versions, it is the brother who is represented as a hare.

HERO CREATURES AND MONSTERS
Many of the Northeast's themes are familiar from other regions – serpents, underwater monsters and so on – and draw from the diversity of nature. Familiar, too, are feared anthropomorphic beings – cannibals, little people, and disembodied heads – that become sources of power and medicine. A more novel concept is that of the Iroquoian False Faces, although even they have some parallels elsewhere.

■ Thunderbird
A super-eagle (Winnebago) or hawk (Chippewa/Ojibwa) with lightning flashing from its eyes and thunder rumbling with the beat of its wings, lived in the Upper World. It was customary to give the Thunderbird and his assistants a ceremonial smoke directed to the four directions whenever they were heard to cry. As an ally and protector of the people, Thunderbird aided cultivation by watering the land with rain, and rendered the Earth safer by terrorizing and ultimately consuming the much-feared Horned Water Snake of the Under World. Seeking the benevolent power of the Thunderbird as guardian spirit was a common visionary quest of youths

477

and men. Those who received such visions were blessed with victory in war and protection in life. Capable of transforming into human form with a large beak, the Thunderbird was often depicted in either manifestation in native art.

■ **Underwater Monster**

Among the Great Lakes tribes, this was a wide-spread supernatural force appearing in variations of two major forms, mammalian and serpentine. In mammalian form, the monster occurred as an underwater panther, lynx or bear, with such anomalous characteristics as horns, dragon-like spikes, scales or copper tails. In its serpentine form, its flesh was pure copper and it possessed horns, a hairy body and, occasionally, legs. This evil force continually sought to destroy man both in the water and on the earth. Success was rare due, to the unrelenting efforts of the Thunderbird. A single clap of thunder was sufficient to send the monster to seek the depths of the Under World.

■ **False Faces**

These supernatural beings of the Iroquois were bodiless flying heads with long streaming hair and huge eyes who sought to frighten the unwary. Manifested in masks carved from living trees by the Iroquois, the False Faces were used in curing rites performed by the False Face Society. Each class of mask has its own origin story, the most important of these being Old Broken Nose whose twisted features resulted when he dared to contest the supremacy of the Creator. As a consequence of this confrontation, he became known as the Great Doctor destined to wander the rim of the Earth healing and curing the people. The power of all False Faces to cure is acquired and renewed through the performance of the society's rites and the masks' ritual association with the sacred fire, the turtle rattle and the Cosmic Tree. When not in use, their spiritual power must be kept alive with frequent feedings of tobacco.

■ **Little People**

The Algonquian *May-may-gway-shi* were the Little People who lived in caves or crevices in waterside rock faces. Exceedingly fond of fish, they resorted to stealing them from Indian nets. If sighted or pursued, these hairy-faced little men would paddle their stone canoes straight into the rock face and disappear. *May-may-gway-shi* are credited with carving and painting the petroglyphs and pictographs, and in some places reaching their hands out of the water to leave red hand prints on the rock. They were thought to have strong spirit power but only the most gifted shamans were able to enter the rock to exchange tobacco for this extremely potent rock medicine.

■ Giants

These loom large in myths and legends. Among the Iroquois and Chippewa/Ojibwa, giants were fearsome creatures displaying undesirable traits, the foremost being the consumption of human flesh. The Stone Giants of the Iroquois, man-like and covered with coats of flint, were ravenous cannibals who devoured all they encountered on their journey from the West.[26] The cannibal giant of the Chippewa/Ojibwa came from the North, killing and consuming all those who showed him kindness. In one village along the way, one little boy escaped and when he grew into manhood he sought revenge. He appealed to the spirits for power and they sent 100 winged men to assist him. The ploy they devised was to entice the cannibal giant with a feast of his favorite white bear meat. Eagerly succumbing to this invitation, he afterward became lethargic and the winged spirit people clubbed him to death. His body was then devoured by a host of small animals and his bones consumed by fire. The ashes, scattered by the four winds, became the birds of the air.

HOLY PLACES, SACRED SITES

A Chippewa/Ojibwa shaman once said the visual images depicted in pictographs and petroglyphs on rock faces in the Upper Great Lakes area were 'like shorthand'. This form of visual expression is found in many locations throughout the entire culture area. Located on dramatic rock formations, vertical cliffs rising out of the water, or hidden in rocky caverns, the red ochre painting and carved glyphs serve as both testimony and supplication to the spirits. Revered as sacred sites by shamans and vision-seekers as well as for individual rites and group ceremonials, it is here that communion with the supernatural occurs. The presence of tobacco and other offerings attests to their continued sanctity.

■ Lake Superior

At the Agawa Rock site on the northeastern shore of Lake Superior, the soaring cliff provides a dramatic contrast to the surrounding landscape.

With the mythological *Michipeshu* housed in the watery depths of Lake Superior and Thunderbird nests on its highest reaches, this stone shrine is the uniting force between the cosmic powers of the Under World and the Upper World.

At Agawa Rock over 100 images of indeterminate age record the supernatural and natural worlds of the Great Lakes Algonquians. Of especial significance are the pictographs of *Michipeshu* with lynx-like tufts of cheek fur, incurving horns on his head and spiny protrusions on his back and tail. Always depicted with serpents, fish and canoes as evidence of *Michipeshu's* Under-World powers, the pictograph association at this particular site becomes an apt metaphor for the unpredictable and dangerously powerful tempests of Lake Superior.

Some miles to the east there are over 900 glyphs engraved into the white crystalline limestone of the Peterborough Petroglyphs site.

■ Niagara Falls

These were created following a conflict between the Thunderer and the Great Snake Monster. Long, long ago a beautiful Seneca maiden, escaping from an undesirable marriage, launched her canoe into the swift-flowing Niagara River. From his cave behind the rushing waters the Thunderer spotted the maiden's impending peril as her canoe was dashed against the rocks. Spreading out his wings, he caught her just as her canoe splintered into innumerable pieces.

During the following weeks, the Thunderer taught the girl many things. For one, the source of illness among her people was caused by the Snake Monster coiled beneath their village. However, a move to a new village site closer to the great lake was soon discovered by the snake. Once again coming to the assistance of the Seneca, the Thunderer hurled lightning bolts at the monster until its enormous dead body lay wedged in the rocks. The Niagara River was forced to rise above it and then fall in a magnificent cascade, a permanent reminder to mankind of the victorious contest of good over evil.

■ The Longhouse

In contrast to the permanency of sacred rocks, microcosmic structures were erected and dissembled in response to a society's needs. Wherever built, these structures replicated the cosmology in material form.

After the formation of the League of Five Nations, the Iroquois

Confederacy was referred to as a Longhouse. The Mohawks guarded the eastern door while the Senecas became the keepers of the western door. In the center of the Longhouse was the territory of the Onondagas who, as keepers of the fire, were said to stand directly beneath the Longhouse's central smoke-hole. Inside the northern and southern walls, respectively, lived the Cayugas and Oneidas. Clan leaders were the supporting braces and the tribal chiefs served as posts. Communication and mutual defense were hastened by means of the Iroquois Trail, the symbolic central aisle. As a collective symbol, the Longhouse retains its potency as an Iroquois institution to this day.

■ The Big House

This sacred structure of the Delawares symbolized their universe. A gable-ended log structure, the dirt floor represented the earth, the roof the sky, the four walls the four sides of the horizon. Painted carved faces on the supporting posts and sacred center pole represented the *Manitous* of the 12 layers of the Delaware cosmos.

■ *Midewigan*

The *midewigan* of the *Midewiwin* (Grand Medicine Society), was a long bower-like enclosure formed from ritually harvested saplings. Within this structure, members of the Great Lakes tribes followed rites inscribed in pictographs on sacred birch-bark scrolls. Once the ceremonies were completed, the *midewigan* was left to decay.

■ The Tree of Life

Common to all groups was the Tree of Life or World Tree, further recognized as the Cosmic Axis, located at the center of the world and serving as the pathway connecting the various layers of the cosmos. For the Great Lakes tribes and the Delaware, the Tree of Life and Cosmic Axis are symbolized by the ceremonial posts in their respective sacred structures. For the Iroquoians, this Tree of Life encompasses many levels of meaning. Integrated with the concept of Cosmic Axis is the Great Tree of Peace arising from the back of the primal turtle, its branches piercing the sky and its top surmounted by an eagle; its roots spreading to the four directions serve to connect the cosmic regions.

■ Revered Animals

Of all the other-than-human persons, animals play an enormous role in native spiritual life. As *Manitous,* mediators and protagonists, animals do indeed 'tell the grand story'.

■ The Turtle

As Earth-holder, Turtle bears the colossal weight of Iroquian creation on his back and serves to both separate and mediate between the Sky and the Under Worlds. This protective role of the turtle continues with the healing powers of the snapping turtle rattle used by the Great Doctor, its powers renewed by rubbing it on pine tree trunks. Turtle's strengths were such that he presided over one of the four worlds of the Winnebago and in his land-turtle form he supported the four sacred poles of each Medicine Society member's *tipi* on his paws. Acting as a messenger to the spirits, Turtle often appeared as one of the many *Midewiwin* patrons. To both Iroquoians and Algonquians the turtle was one of the most important *Manitous,* a metaphoric symbol for the Earth and, by extension, a symbol of fertility. Among the Ottawa it is believed that Mackinac Island, between Lake Huron and Lake Michigan, was formed when the Great Turtle froze to death on his pilgrimage northward.

■ The Bear

Bear, in his many guises and on each of the cosmic levels, was revered as the embodied source of shamanic medicine. Human-like in his Earthly form, Bear was treated as a wise and honored guest, powerful in his curative abilities and Grandfather to all. These curative powers, including success in hunting, were bound up in a form of complex ceremonialism designed to honor and propitiate the revered spirit of the bear.

In the Sky World of the Micmac, the Great Bear (Ursa Major) exemplified cyclic renewal, replicating the winter hibernation and spring awakening of the bear's Earthly form. In the world above, Bear was chased by three avian hunters who finally succeeded in mid-autumn. Once the flesh was consumed, the skeleton lay on its back in the winter sky to be revitalized once again each spring. And the cycle continued.

The White Bear of the Great Lakes, intimate with the Great Spirit and assistant to Shell, brought forth the *Midewiwin* from below, along the Cosmic Axis to the people on the Earth. As guardian of the *Mide* Ceremony, Bear opens the eastern door of the *Mide* Lodge admitting only those who are ritually prepared. Partial preparation entailed purification rites within the sanctity and protection of Grandfather Bear's sweat lodge constructed from his ribs (bent branches) and covered with his skin.

■ Eagle

Revered as chief of the birds, Eagle soars the highest, is the bravest, possesses keen sight, looks straight into the eye of the Sun and serves as mediator between Earth and Sun. The mythological Dew Eagle of Iroquian tradition was believed to inhabit the uppermost level in the sky, was suffused with *Orenda,* and held restorative powers to cure illness. It was further believed that the Dew Eagle, as the Thunderbird, was capable of transforming from bird to human at will. In his role as the 'Eagle who Sees Afar' perched on the topmost branch of the Tree of Peace, the eagle was the terrestrial counterpart of the orb or ball of light on the topmost branch of the celestial Tree of Light. Algonquian speakers held similar concepts emphasizing the eagle's superior strengths as a fighter.

■ Animals as Mediators

Certain animals, such as birds and serpents, are venerated for their mastery of more than one cosmic zone and the additional powers thus gained by communication with the supernatural. This ability to cross cosmic thresholds is best exemplified by waterfowl as they move from water to land to air, or directly from the Under World to the Sky World. As mediators between these zones, the waterfowl played a significant role in Iroquoian mythology by intercepting Sky Woman's precipitous fall into the watery Under World until the Earth could be formed.

Otter's roll as mediator is revealed in the origin myth of the *Mide* Ceremony. When the *Mide* lodge was finished, the Upper World Powers, or Grandfathers, sent a hawk with the message for *Manabus* to enter. Only when Otter, as representative of the Under World Powers, delivered the message would *Manabus* accept the invitation. During the Grandfathers' ensuing presentation of protective powers and medicines, *Manabus* was given an otter-skin medicine bag with its own song. Otter, as embodied by the skin bag, dispenses medicine and symbolically restores the life of initiates during the ceremony.

Similar beliefs in the mediating and curing abilities of the otter were demonstrated by the Otter Society. The otter, chief of the small water animals, was a powerful medicine animal controlling the health, fortunes and destinies of the people. The Otter Society possessed no songs or dances but was organized to retain the favors of the water animals. Failure to express gratitude would result in illness.

Also mediating between the Under World and the Earth, snakes carry messages from one cosmic zone to another by entering and emerging through holes in the ground, and by transporting souls to the world beyond. While connections with the Under World were reflected by their relationship with powers of darkness and evil, snakes also signified regeneration through both their winter dormancy and spring rejuvenation, and the shedding of their old skin. These features meant that reptiles were abhorred yet widely accepted as powerful *Manitous.*

RITUALS AND CEREMONIES

Drumbeats are the heartbeats of the people summoning the *Manitous* to participate in the ceremonies. For centuries the drum has been identified with the spiritual and cultural lives of the Indians, its very rhythm profoundly affecting all ceremonial activity. The importance of drums and drumming to the Chippewa identity is instilled in young babies before they are able to walk. Ceremonies may involve a single shaman drumming in his conjuring tent for a few hours, the ritual drumming in the *Mide* Lodge or the four-day ceremony of the Drum Dance[27] with several drums following the *Midewiwin.*

■ The Midwinter Festival

Held in the Iroquian longhouse this was considered to be the most important of the calendric ceremonies. In ancient times this ceremonial had been a winter solstice rite whose purpose was to bring back the Sun from its nadir. Handsome Lake's addition of the Four Sacred Rituals in the early 1800s had little effect on the earlier Sun veneration, for many of the rituals continued to focus on the power of the Sun. For instance, the ceremonial climax, the Creator's own Feather Dance, symbolized the diurnal journey of the Sun. Similarly, the Bowl Game dedicated to the Great Warrior, the Sun, who determined the results of the game, supported the theme of renewal. In earlier times, arrows had been shot at the Sun, each volley accompanied by a chorus of war cries to call back the Sun. More recently, participants attired in their finery carried wooden Sun disc wands painted with Sun motifs surrounded with down and eagle feathers signifying the Sun's corona as metonymic reminders to ensure the Sun's return.

■ The White Dog Sacrifice

At one time throughout the entire Woodlands and Great Lakes area, this sacrificial rite had taken place throughout the year. By the 1800s it, too, had become one of the rituals of the Iroquoian Midwinter Ceremony. This ritual necessitated the selection of a pure white dog free of blemishes and imperfections. Ritually prepared, its hair was combed, its face painted to represent *Teharonhiawagon* (Sky God or Sun), and its legs wound spirally with red ribbon. Strangled without shedding blood, the dog was sacrificed to *Areskoue,* the Sun in his guise as God of War. Designed to secure the continued protection of the Sun and to sustain the cycle of life for another year, it was the most sacred and emotional moment of the entire Midwinter Ceremony.

■ Initiation

For all the tribes scalp-taking was recognized as a rite of passage marking social puberty and the incorporation of youths into the warrior status. Following a regime of ritual purification and the sanctification of their weapons by dancing, the youth and his sponsors undertook a foray. With the acquision of a scalp, the youth was given instructions for its ritual preparation. Offered first to the Sun for its blessing, the flesh was then removed, the skin and hair were sewn on to a hoop and the inner side painted with motifs associated with the Sun: a face, a sunburst, or concentric circles. Mounted on a slender pole, the scalp was carried home where a Scalp Dance formally incorporated the youth into the society.

■ Acquiring Power

According to Menominee elders, power is an invisible force that emits bright light. The much-desired acquisition of power began in early childhood with short periods of fasting and instructions on the appropriateness of humble behavior. Puberty was marked by the Great Fast when a boy or girl blackened his or her face and retreated into the woods. There, in seclusion, the power-seeker remained alone without food for periods of up to 10 days, all the while focusing on receiving a vision and, through that, the source of power. Appearance of the Golden Eagle, White Bear or any other of the Upper World spirits indicated success, while visions of Under World creatures such as the Horned Snake marked an unsuccessful attempt. If success was not attained after four tries, the power-seeker was doomed to life thereafter as a witch.

■ The Arrival of Strangers

Many of these traditions changed with the coming of the Europeans. It is fitting, therefore, to conclude with the Micmac legend relating the arrival of these strange beings. While *Glooskap* is the protagonist in some versions and in others a young woman dreams about the event, the details are similar. A small island was seen to be drifting toward the land. It was covered with tall trees with a number of bear-like creatures climbing in the branches. As the floating island came closer it was seen that these bears were men with white skins and hair on their faces. These strangers brought items of great curiosity that excited the people. And changes began to take place . . .

ARTS AND CRAFTS

With a few words, a Mesquakie (Fox) artist, Adeline Wanatee, establishes the significance of arts and crafts in the Northeast woodlands and Great Lakes: 'We are like the trees who have a visible form above the ground and an equal part which is out of sight beneath the surface. This is what my mother and aunt told me.' Not only do the words exemplify the Native understanding of the complementary halves of reality and spirituality, of the visible and the invisible, of the past and the present, but they also reflect the reality of two separate, yet strongly interactive worlds of Indians and Europeans. While we, as non-Natives, may see the visible part presented in the tangible forms of Native arts and crafts, much still remains hidden from view, evoking a desire to learn more. Wanatee's final words also attest to the role that tribal women held, and continue to hold, in the transference of cultural knowledge through material expression.

The Northeast Woodlands and Great Lakes area, extending from the shores of the Atlantic Ocean in the east to the western shores of the Great Lakes, was the first region to be exposed to continuous European contact. Beginning in the early 1500s, Basque fishermen were soon followed by traders, missionaries, French and British officials and adventure-seekers. With them came trade goods to be exchanged, first for furs and then for exotic items. A historical overview of indigenous arts and crafts reflects the impact of this early interaction. The ability of the various groups to adapt Native materials and techniques to provide satisfactorily the exotic and the practical to fulfill European perceptions of aesthetics and requirements, attests to the flexibility and fluidity of Native culture and establishes an innate entrepreneurial spirit. At the same time, Native Americans continued to create material objects to fulfill their own needs, aesthetic values and religious expression. It was through this transformation of intangibles into dynamic and symbolic aspects of material culture that both individual tribes and broader culture areas established and maintained their identity.

Despite overlaps of art forms, techniques and materials, there is often a distinctive art tradition that has become associated with a specific group and/or area. Differences can be attributed to divergent subsistence economies, access to materials restricted by environmental features, encroachment of Europeans onto Indian lands and any number of social, economic and political circumstances. Examples presented here underscore several of these elements. Certainly economic necessity and a local non-Native market stimulated the expansion of the traditional woodsplint basketry craft among the Algonquian-speaking New England tribes on the southeastern Atlantic Coast. Farther up the Atlantic Coast, the Micmac (also Algonquian) shifted their porcupine quillwork techniques from decorating native birch-bark objects to decorating forms more acceptable to European tastes. In the St. Lawrence Lowlands, Iroquois, Huron and Abenaki, having been taught the fundamentals of true embroidery using indigenous materials by the French Ursuline nuns, refined this skill into the production of a made-for-trade commodity. To the south of the Great Lakes, the horticultural Iroquois carved wooden masks for performance in public and private tribal rituals. As the Chippewa moved westward into the northern Great Lakes area, they adapted quillwork techniques to create elaborate beadwork items. The tribes of the Great Lakes region, comprising both Algonquian and Siouan speakers, continued to twine fiber bags according to prehistoric traditions. Concurrently, these same groups adeptly transformed European trade textiles into a distinctly Native art form.

Thus each and every art and craft form voiced the Native aesthetics, innovations, creativity and complementary roles of men and women that constitute the essence of dynamic artistic expression.

■ Birch-Bark Biting

Creating pictures on folded sheets of very thin layers of birch bark with the teeth was a ubiquitous art form wherever the white birch tree (*Betula papyrifera*) grew. Historical accounts from the 17th, 18th and 19th centuries establish the antiquity of this unusual craft and ethnographic accounts of the early-20th century continue to record the practice.[28] More recently, recognition of birch-bark dental pictographs as both an entirely

Native and an endangered art form has prompted collectors and museum curators to acquire the work of the very few contemporary artists who possess the ability to create these bitten-bark transparencies.

According to current knowledge, bark is collected in the spring when the sap first starts to run. Criteria for the selection of the perfect tree entail the color (which should be pure white), the correct age and size and freedom from imperfections and knots. From this living source the bark (the best is ten layers thick) is removed and is then painstakingly peeled into fine paper-like pieces, of which only half may be suitable. The sharpest pictures result by biting the prepared bark while it is still fresh. However, written accounts of frozen birch logs releasing tissue-thin layers of bark as they thawed by the fire and of warming pieces of bark from dried logs would have ensured a winter supply as well.[29]

Various folding procedures determine the configuration of the designs. Most of the bark is folded in half to make an oblong and in half again to form a square, and finally folded from corner to corner to form a triangle. Holding the folded bark with the fingers, the point is inserted into the mouth. Using the incisor and canine teeth to make impressions in the folded bark, the piece is moved about in the mouth with the help of fingers and tongue. After the biting is completed, the bark is unfolded to reveal an intricate symmetrical design formed in the translucent medium. A second method of folding begins with a rectangular piece folded in half lengthwise, the upper third folded down and then diagonally to form a triangle. Teeth impressions are made along the hypotenuse thus formed. The bottom third of the oblong is folded only once on an oblique angle. The result resembles similar patterns of flowers with leaves and stems worked on moccasin vamps. By leaving the bark unfolded and biting it according to the position of the artist's fingers, single realistic and/or asymmetrical figures can be produced. Those with expertise can, by regulating the force of the bite, produce a shaded effect. In a matter of minutes a pattern emerges that may be geometric, abstract or representative of particular life forms, handsomely revealed when the pieces of bark are held up to sunlight or campfire light.

Several recorded accounts suggest that dental pictographs were made purely for pleasure.[30] Certainly as a diversion around the camp fire or stove, women and children (and occasionally men) derived great pleasure from this creative activity. By imitating their mothers, aunts and grandmothers, children learned new skills and absorbed new ideas and cultural values. Although results varied in artistic quality depending on expertise, most if not all efforts were consumed by the fire. If, as some researchers have suggested, these bitten patterns were used as guides for making beadwork designs and scraped patterns on birch bark, a few would have been kept.[31]

Bitten-bark designs constitute a truly ephemeral art, providing pleasure only for the moment. However, the implications that arise are significant. It has been considered by some to be the only example of 'art for art's sake' among Native North Americans.[32] As an art form, it demonstrates the multiplicity of designs possible, and lends itself to design experimentation. More importantly, it affords insights into the cognitive skills that utilize mental templates in the designing of an artifact. 'A woman never copied one pattern from another – it was original work, and a peculiarity was that **the pattern was clear in the mind of the worker before she made her first fold**. She said that she knew how the finished work would look before she began to work . . .'[33] The 'portability' of such a capacity was of supreme value to earlier hunting and foraging groups who, out of necessity, carried their worldly goods with them. The capability to recreate objects using 'the mind's eye' diminished the burden of excess material culture.

In its own small way, this art form establishes Native creativity and innovation to set the stage for other forms of arts and crafts utilizing either indigenous or foreign materials for personal use or for exchange purposes.

■ Woodsplint Basketry

Prevalent throughout the Northeast Woodlands, it was among the New England tribes of the eastern Maritime regions that woodsplint basketry attained its greatest expression. First developed through an intimate knowledge of the woodland environment, basketry became an integral aspect of maize horticulture and the related preparation of maize foods. Baskets also served traditional needs as eel and fish traps, containers for berry-picking and for a multitude of uses as storage containers. Later, basketry skills provided necessary products for early European settlers and, as such, continued as a source of subsistence income for the Indians. Within the Native community, basketry, as a means of communication, became a source for regional, ethnic, family and individual identity.

The processes involved in creating a basket begin with the initial steps of preparing the flat sturdy strips of wood splints, usually undertaken by a man. Selection of the preferred black ash (*Fraximus nigra* Marsh), or 'basket' tree, growing in bogs and along streams, is done in the spring when the sap is running. Tobacco offerings propitiate the spirit of this slow-growing hardwood as it stands straight, its trunk marred by few knots, before it is cut down. Once felled and the bark removed, the entire circumference of the log is pounded with overlapping strokes using a wooden maul. This releases anywhere from one to six annual growth layers, called grains, six to ten inches (15–25cm) in width at one time.[34] This process is continued until the heartwood is reached. As black ash is a ring-porous hardwood, the cells laid down during the rapid growth period in the spring are coarser and less dense than those laid down during the summer. When the log is pounded, these coarser cells collapse allowing the grains to separate easily.[35] The rough, grainy remains of the soft cellular tissue between each ring are scraped off to reveal smooth, light wood. These splints can be separated further into finer splints, and then divided into widths appropriate for the type and size of basket desired. Specialty, but non-essential, tools in the form of splitters, scrapers, basket gauges and forms introduced during the mid-19th century, continued to ease the preparation process and establish uniformity in materials.

Prepared splints are then transformed into baskets of innumerable shapes, sizes and purposes, decorated and plain. Primarily three weaving techniques were used: 'checker' in which the warp and weft have the same thickness and pliability and are woven one over, one under; 'twill' in which the warp and weft alternate at a ratio other than one-to-one, creating a diagonal pattern; and 'wicker' in which flexible, narrow splints are woven onto a wide and inflexible warp in a basic one-over, one-under pattern. Occasionally 'twining' is used in which two or more flexible wefts are twisted around individual warps.

The addition of color in various ways comprised early decorative applications. Splints could be completely permeated by dyes, swabbed on one side with color before weaving, block-stamped with designs cut from potatoes, turnips or wood and dipped into pigment, or hand-painted with a brush or chewed twig on the finished basket. Textural patterns, generated by alternating scraped and unscraped splints, or those created by using narrow and wide wefts, were also intentional decorative devices. Greater texture and shadow were added when basket weavers began to incorporate secondary twisted or 'curlicue' wefts into their baskets. In this latter technique the outermost of a pair of wefts is twisted to form patterns of loops or curls commonly referred to as 'porcupine', 'shell' and 'diamond'.

Regional, cultural, individual and blended styles can be distinguished through materials, techniques, form, decoration and function during specific time periods. Regional styles are composites of ideas and techniques used by two or more contiguous groups living in an area. Cultural styles reveal the ethnic identity of specific groups. Imbedded within these styles are individual or family expressions recognized through certain features or innovations. An overlapping or combining of traits from two styles is called blended.

By way of illustration, baskets made by the Schaghticoke, Mahican and Paugusett peoples of the southwestern New England region during the 18th and 19th centuries were woven with both wide and narrow wefts of black ash and decorated by swabbing and/or stamping. In contrast, during the same period, the baskets of the southeastern New England Mohegan, Pequot, Niantic, Nipmuck and Wampanoag were constructed with wide wefts of white oak enhanced with elaborate, painted designs. From the late-19th century onward, both regions began to produce virtually identical undecorated narrow-weft splint baskets.

Cultural styles such as those evident in the painted designs of the Mohegan, also reveal temporal changes reflecting native reactions to changing political and social environments. During the period of forced removal from their lands, the Mohegans recorded their resistence with basket decoration that enclosed a traditional four-domed medallion or rosette symbolizing the Mohegan people inside a boundary or enclosure. Outside the ancestral lands, Mohegans were often represented as a strawberry or a flower. Thus, through continued use of symbols on their basketry, Mohegans maintained their sense of ethnic identity and documented their grief.

Individuals and families of basket-makers gained recognition with the intensification of their skills in response to an increasing tourist market. As specialty tools (gauges, splitters and blocks) became commonplace, weavers transformed the exceedingly fine narrow splints into elaborate Victorian-inspired styles eagerly purchased as souvenirs. With the development of summer tourist resorts certain individuals or families retained rights to these areas to sell their winter's production.[36] Elaboration was expressed in both the form of the baskets, encompassing everything from novelty items to fancy household items to serviceable shopping bags, and in the decorative elements of ingeniously twisted and curled splint. Children learned the craft through observation, producing small rimless baskets and developing their marketing skills by selling these for five cents during the early-20th century.

492

■ Micmac Quillwork

Unique to the Micmac of the Atlantic provinces is the decorative insertion of dyed porcupine quills into birch bark found primarily on covered boxes. The fairly complete chronological sequence for this quillwork affords insights into the development of forms, styles, decorative techniques, motifs and functions. While early historic documentation establishes that the Micmac used five different techniques of quillwork, by the beginning of the 17th century all but insertion appears to have fallen from use.[37] It was this fast and easy technique that became the basis for the Native entrepreneurial spirit. The Micmac response to the 18th century European desire for souvenirs and curiosities was to continue to use Native materials in the production and decoration of European forms. By 1750 a distinctive Micmac style was already evident in the round and rectangular lidded containers completely covered with dyed quills. As the Victorian mania for tourist items took hold over the following century, the repertoire of forms expanded to include such novelty items as tea cosies, lamp shades, fire screens, fans, cigar cases, purses and chair seats.

Materials were birch bark, porcupine quills, spruce roots and the occasional use of thin wooden box liners. The bark of *B. papyrifera,* or white birch, was harvested by the men from the living tree during the latter days of July when the bark is pliable.[38] Porcupine quills, actually modified hairs with tiny barbs on the points, are plucked from the dead animal's back by the women, separated from the other hair and sorted according to size.[39] Coarser tail quills were also used for specific finishing details. Prior to the 1860s quills were dyed predominantly red, yellow, black or white (the natural quill color) from vegetal sources. Additional sources provided blue and violet. After that time, inorganic aniline dyes from trade sources expanded the color palette but increased the susceptibility to color fading. From the black spruce (*Picea mariana*) came long slender roots split lengthwise into fibers for sewing birch bark and for decorative applications. The colors of dyed spruce roots faded rapidly, producing a more or less uniform soft brown tone. In the production of quilled boxes and purses, the softwood of pine, spruce or cedar was used for bases, pegs, linings, handles and hoops. The addition of sweetgrass (*Hierochloe odorata*) as a finishing edging imparted a sweet, long-lasting fragrance.

Round and oval lidded boxes, the most frequently encountered forms, are also the simplest to construct. A piece of birch bark cut to shape is rolled into a cylinder, the ends held together with quills. Once quilled this cylinder is stitched with spruce root to a bark base or pegged to a wooden base. Into this is inserted a bark liner (or for rectangular boxes, a thin wooden liner) extending above the box height equal to the depth of the box lid. The sides of the lid were then flush with those of the box. The lid itself was composed of a top of quilled bark sewn to a root-wrapped or quill-worked bark ring side. For some boxes the bark liner served as the foundation over which root-wrapped rings were built up to form the exterior.

The insertion of the dyed quills into the birch bark to produce the typically vibrant mosaic patterns entailed a number of steps. Both bark and quills were worked while slightly damp, the bark being dipped into warm water before beginning and the quills moistened as needed. A tiny insertion hole was made from the outer side of the bark with a beaver incisor or bone awl (and more recently with a darning needle). Once the quill was inserted into the hole, the bark contracted as it dried holding the quill tightly in place. The process was repeated for either end of each quill until the desired area was covered with closely inserted parallel rows. On the underside the barbed ends of the quills were burned and all remaining ends were cut flush with the surface.[40]

Further steps in the design process built upon the basic principles of running quills all one way within a single color area and by contrasting colors or design areas by placing quills at angles to other sections. The break created by these placements was filled in first with a single quill-width, then two, and eventually this 'fill' developed into a complete design element such as that used to divide a pattern into four quarters. Also possibly introduced during the 19th century were designs of flattened quills overlaid on solidly quilled areas. Readily recognizable is the lattice-like design first used as an overlay but which evolved into being used alone on bare bark. Checkered patterns on root-wrapped rings were obtained by weaving natural colored quills into the vertical warp of the roots. Border edges were often finished with lengths of flattened tail quills or bundles of sweetgrass with fine spruce roots.

Similar to other groups, early Micmac dream-inspired designs rendered tangibly on material items provided protection, healing and power. The symbolic meaning of these designs has become lost over the years and all of the traditional names forgotten, except for an eight-pointed star called *gogwit* or *kagwet* (Eight-Legged Starfish) and a fan-shaped motif called *waegardisk* (Northern Lights). The earliest dated design of 1760 has a double two-dimensional arch or rainbow which by the 20th century had degenerated into a token arched line incorporated into a central design element. Often found in combination with this double rainbow is a stepped design. The most common motif is the chevron (and the variant, half-chevron) traditionally found on the sides of lids and boxes.[41] Over time the visual dominance of the chevron pattern gave way to zig-zag lines created visually through the use of color. The chevron also occurs in a half-form as well as integrated with diamonds and triangles. Circles, crosses, stars, double curves, squares, 'fylfot', and several realistic forms comprise the majority of the design elements.[42] With the introduction of aniline dyes, the intricacy of earlier designs was replaced with stronger ones placed on a white background to accentuate the brilliant colors.

Although virtually all the quillwork produced over the centuries was for trade, this art form is so strongly identified with the Micmac nation that they themselves have come to regard it as a traditional form.[43]

■ Moosehair Embroidery

The use of animal hair – moose, caribou and reindeer – as a widespread medium of artistic expression among northern aboriginal groups became the medium of instruction used by the Ursuline nuns to demonstrate French embroidery techniques to young Native girls. By the early 1700s in the St. Lawrence River Lowlands, Iroquoian (most notably the Huron) and Algonquian artists had become adept at creating exquisite floral designs and pictorial depictions of Native life. These moosehair masterpieces, embroidered on to black tanned hide,[44] trade cloth and birch bark, formed the basis of a strong commercial venture.[45]

Moosehair, the primary decorative material, was procured from the winter pelage of the moose (*Alces alces*). Fine white hairs, four to five inches in length with long tapering black tips, removed from the dead animal's cheeks, mane, rump and 'bell' were washed and then dyed. Initially, the dyeing process involved steeping the hair in hot vegetal infusions to acquire various shades of red, blue and yellow to be used in combination with the natural white ones. These indigenous organic ones were quickly replaced when the introduction of aniline dyes offered an easier process and a wider selection of colors. Tied into bundles for storing, dyed hairs merely required moistening in the mouth to be ready for use.

Three precontact techniques of line-work (spot stitching or appliquéing bundles of the moosehair into straight, curved or zig-zag lines onto a background), loom weaving and false embroidery were supplemented by the

495

European introduction of true embroidery which relied upon steel needles threaded with a filament (in this case, moosehair). The continued use of line-work can be recognized by the distinctive bead-like effect created by the slight twisting of the hair bundle just before the couching thread is pulled tight. However, with the new technique of needle embroidery, depth, shading and further three-dimensional texture were achieved through color variation and various embroidery stitches. Simple patterns soon became elaborated into complex designs and earlier non-representational motifs became dominated by floral ones.

By the beginning of the 19th century, Huron floral-decorated items epitomized the height of this expression. Rich colors and intricate designs accentuated by their background of black, tanned hide were rendered on mittens, moccasins, pouches and leggings. Cloth panels enhanced with floral designs were sewn to collars, cuffs, epaulettes, lapels and borders of hide and cloth coats. Similar decorations appeared on 'pockets' formed from the lower legs of moose and caribou, knife sheaths, belts, garters and bandoleers. Although long considered as items made solely for the tourist market, their native forms suggest probable indigenous functions as well.

A second genre, well-developed by the first half of the 19th century, was moosehair embroidery on birch bark items. This souvenir work was either entirely floral in design or depicted narrative vignettes of native life enhanced with flowers and trees. Traditionally garbed Indians were embroidered in romanticized settings in canoes, in front of wigwams, smoking peace pipes, hunting in the forest, juxtaposed with larger-than-life flowers and berries, all designed to appeal to the then current European notion of the Noble Savage. Imbedded within these images, however, are invaluable iconographic details of Native ideals concerning the environment, establishing individual and group identity through clothing, and such symbolic referents as strawberries with their association of an idyllic afterworld. Decorated with either flowers or pictorials, the forms of this second genre are non-traditional containers, boxes, whimsies, cigar cases, bases for women's reticules and so on, designed specifically for trade and as gifts for foreign dignitaries.

■ Iroquoian Masks

Two types of Iroquoian masks, classified according to materials used, are carved wooden ones associated with the False Face Society, and those woven of cornhusks for the Husk Face or Bushy-heads' Society.

Individually each form reflects one half of the complementary features that comprise the synergistic whole of Iroquoian culture. False Faces are carved by men from the material of the forest domain while Husk Faces are woven by women from products of their horticultural endeavors. Together, the False Face and Husk Face Societies, men and women, hunting and horticultural, function to ensure the health and well-being of the society.

Origins of the False Face masks arose as a result of a mythic contest between the Great Creator and the First *Hodo'win,* the most powerful of the Forest Faces.[46] To test the strength of their powers they each attempted to summon a mountain to them; success would acknowledge supremacy. The first to try, *Hodo'win,* achieved only partial success. So anxious was he to see what the Creator was achieving, *Hodo'win* turned sharply, striking his face on the mountain which had appeared directly behind him. The impact broke his nose; his mouth twisted from the pain. The successful Creator, recognizing the strength of the loser, entrusted him to assist humans to combat illness and other evil influences. Henceforth, as the Great Doctor, it became *Hodo'win's* responsibility to instruct men in the art of carving masks and in the ceremonies in which they were to be used.

As a mask was carved from a living tree to acquire the earth power and sky power imbued within this cosmic axis, this necessitated ritual preparation of both carver and tree. In order to retain the potency and spirit of the basswood or other softwood tree, three days were spent ceremonially feeding tobacco (*Nicotiana rustica*) and tobacco smoke to the Tree Spirit and entreating forgiveness for the impending injury. Appeased, the Tree Spirit requested that its life spirit be continued in the mask to be carved and hewn from its trunk.

Before the introduction of steel tools, woodworking was accomplished by burning the area and scraping away the charred wood. With steel tools, carving was performed directly on the wood. Once the bark was removed, the face was roughed out and only when the carving was nearly completed was the mask released from the tree. The finished mask was smoothed inside and out, metal eye rings were attached, the face was painted and long hair inserted into holes. If the carving of the mask was begun in the morning, it was painted red; black was indicative of an afternoon start. These colors represented the belief that the daily journey of the first False Face followed the sun; therefore his face appeared red in the morning as he came from the east, and black in the evening as he looked back from the west. A mask painted half-red and half-black represented a divided being – half-human, half-supernatural – whose body was split in two and who stood facing south, his red cheek to the east, black one to the west.

The features of masks vary according to their intended function, dream visions experienced by the carvers, and local styles. Generally, the masks possess deep-set eyes accentuated with metal 'whites', large noses bent in imitation of the Great Doctor's, and often a deeply creased forehead. The mouth is the most variable feature, leading to contemporary classifications based solely on this feature.[47] The twisted mouth of the Great Doctor is replaced alternatively with a smile, a grimace with teeth showing, a pucker as if whistling and a pucker with spoon-like lips or with lips distended to blow ashes. A number display protruding tongues.[48]

Sanctification of completed masks consisted of a number of steps. A tiny bag filled with tobacco was attached to the forehead of the mask; its face was rubbed with sunflower oil to feed it; and then it was placed near the fire, and tobacco was thrown into the fire. As the mask became suffused by wood and tobacco smoke, the carver told the mask what it was supposed to do.[49] The mask was then ready to perform in curing rituals. Periodic feeding of sunflower oil and tobacco continued to maintain the strength of the mask as long as it was used. Boys learned to carve by first making small masks.

Visually and tactilely pleasing, the significance of the masks rests, however, in their power which is especially efficacious in healing rites. The best-known, although not the most important, curing rituals were performed by the False Face Society. When a person fell ill, the members of the Society would don their masks and creep towards the sick person's home. There they scraped their snapping turtle rattles against the wooden door frame before entering the house, shaking the rattles all the while.[50] Using sacred ashes and tobacco in specific rites, the masked healers effected a cure. Once cured, the patient became a member of the Society along with anyone who had an appropriate visionary dream. Although most curing sessions were held privately, the False Faces also performed curing rituals during the public Midwinter Festival.

The Society of Husk Faces or Bushy-heads are earthbound spirits, who in their capacity as messengers of the Three Sisters – corn, beans and squash – taught agricultural practices to humans. Although not as integrated or prominent as their counterparts, the False Faces, they shared certain functions. Under a condition of remaining mute, members of this group, nevertheless, possessed their own tobacco invocation, a medicine song and the power to cure by blowing ashes. Wearing cornhusk masks, they appeared at the Midwinter Festival to dance with the people and beg for food.

The fabrication of these masks by the women is based on an ancient craft technique wherein cornhusks are shredded and braided. Two different methods are used to give them the desired shape: sewing of coiled husk braids and twining. In the first, long strips of cornhusk braid are sewn into three coils to form the eyes and mouth and the nose (which is often a sheathed corncob attached), and then the fringe is added. Twined masks were begun at the nose with eight warps which were later extended by twisting on new elements. A pair of wefts was twisted around each warp until the rim was reached. At first sight there appears to be little variety in these faces, which are always surrounded by husk streamers, but closer inspection reveals much individuality. Paint was only occasionally applied to these masks.[51]

■ Beadwork

A kaleidoscope of colors and patterns dominates Chippewa/Ojibwa beadwork. With the introduction of glass trade beads early in the 17th century, techniques already in use for porcupine quillwork were easily adapted to accommodate this exciting new medium of artistic expression. First 'pony' beads and later tiny 'seed' beads, pinpoints of light and color, readily lent themselves to the complex forms of woven and appliquéd beadwork. Through the subtle blending of vividly colored transparent, translucent and opaque, round or faceted seed beads, artistic masterpieces emerged. For more than two centuries beadwork was a major artistic focus for the Chippewa and continues to gain them as much recognition from within their own culture area as it does from non-Native audiences.

Loom-weaving produced beadwork in which the fibers carrying the beads are also the sole foundation of the finished item. The earliest loom was the bow loom, a flexible stick with birch bark or hide heddles to hold and separate the sinew warps fastened at each end. Exchanging beads for porcupine quill, women wove beaded bands suitable for garters, belts, headbands and decorative strips to be sewn onto articles of clothing. Limitations in length and width of finished pieces led to the development of the simple rectangular box loom devised of four pieces of wood fastened together at the corners. On this loom one continuous warp thread is strung evenly spaced around the frame, including one warp row more than the number of beads required for the width of the pattern. To weave the beads on either loom requires a long, fine beading needle, threaded and with one end tied to an outside warp. The appropriate number of beads for one width are strung onto this weft thread. First the threaded and bead-strung needle is passed under the warp to the opposite side. Holding the thread tight, each of the beads is pushed up between a pair of the warp threads all the way across so that the holes in them are above the level of the warp threads. The threaded needle is then passed back through all the beads while they are in this position, thus weaving the first row. All subsequent rows follow this procedure. Loose ends are woven back into the beadwork to produce a stronger foundation. Sometimes the warp threads are braided or woven into fringes. The introduction of the box loom expanded the earlier repertoire of beadwork with longer and wider forms. Wider pieces were sewn whole onto bandoleer bags and smaller pouches. Understandably, this technique of square weaving dominates design, creating motifs and patterns which are basically geometric. Even floral motifs are reduced to the artificial 'curves' of tiny square steps.[52]

Appliquéd beadwork involves the stitching of beads to another material such as hide or cloth which serves as the foundation. Basically, a line of sinew-threaded beads is sewn to the foundation by means of a second thread tacking (spot stitching or couching) the first one after every two or three beads. In contrast to woven beadwork, this beadwork application permits the design to dominate the technique. As a result, a wide range of decorative possibilities abound: curves pose no problem; both outline patterns and solid areas are beaded with equal ease; and colors can be changed at will. Great examples appear on clothing, ceremonial items, cradle boards and bags.

Both types of beadwork appear together on bandoleer bags, 'the apex of the beadworker's art'.[53] A shoulder strap or 'baldric' of woven or appliqued beadwork was attached to a rectangular pouch of heavy floral appliqué work and to the bottom of this was stitched either a fringe or a wide loom-woven panel. Asymmetrical patterns on the strap with motifs and configurations changing at mid-point in the length, serve as an identifying feature. These ornate bags, worn cross-wise over each shoulder in ceremonies and dances, once served as fire bags carrying smoking pipes and tobacco. As their significance and popularity increased, aesthetic properties supplanted practical ones and the bags were made without true pouches. Ultimately they became a symbol of wealth with an individual wearing anywhere from the usual one or two to as many as 12 or more. Sometimes referred to as

'Friendship Bags', bandoleer bags were presentation gifts at tribal and inter-tribal gatherings, enhancing the prestige of artist, donor and recipient alike.

■ Twined Fiber Bags

All the Great Lakes and Northeast Woodlands tribes were proficient at twining fiber bags for their own use. Regional evidence dating from at least AD 300 establishes this craft's relationship to widespread ancient finger-weaving techniques which no machine can duplicate.[54] It is the people of the Great Lakes area – Fox, Sauk, Menominee, Winnebago, Potawatomi, Ottawa – whose inventory of materials and finger-weaving techniques showed the greatest variety. Decoration, somewhat limited by the twining technique, was restricted to patterns formed through the use of contrasting color fibers and complex methods of twining. Stripes, geometric shapes and stylized birds, felines, deer and humans constituted the basis of the imagery. While coarser utilitarian bags that functioned as harvesting and storage containers were sometimes decorated with colored patterns, it is the smaller, softer bags that have received greater attention.[55]

These softer bags were made of fine *Apocynum* fibers.[56] The stalks of this plant were first soaked in stagnant water until the fleshy parts could be beaten off, leaving fibers three or four feet (1_1.2m) in length. Rolling these fibers into an S twist on the knee yielded strands then twisted together to produce the two-ply cords preferred for weaving. Dark brown buffalo wool was sometimes used for natural color contrast. As trade with the Europeans, increased, these native fibers were replaced with colored yarns.

To twine the bags, prepared warp elements are hung over a stick sus-pended horizontally. Beginning closest to the stick, two weft cords are passed one in front of a warp element and one behind it and then twined (twisted) at each crossing. This procedure is continued from left to right in a continuous spiral around the loose-hanging warps. Weaving is discontin-ued four or five inches from the ends of the warp elements. These ends are braided horizontally to form the opening of the bag. By removing the stick from between the warps, a seamless bag results.

Decorative elements are created by setting up double warps of light and dark contrasting colors. Whichever of these two warp colors is pulled for-ward during the weaving is the one that appears at that point on the sur-face of the bag. Due to the limitations of the twining technique, motifs tend to be angular, with representational figures rendered in a stylized manner.

The imagery on a number of bags reflects the cosmology of the Great Lakes area. Birds and felines appearing on opposite sides of these bags are interpreted, respectively, as depictions of the mythical Thunderbird and the Underwater Panther. The Thunderbird is most often depicted as two triangles joined to form a stylized hourglass shape to which down-thrust wings are attached. In some versions the hourglass is filled with concentric triangles, chevrons or diamonds. A central diamond on the torso indicates the heart. Often associated with a large central Thunderbird figure are smaller Thunderbirds and recurrent geometric patterns in the form of parallel zig-zag lines representing lightning or thunderbolts. On the other side of the bag the Underwater Panther (or group of Panthers), as the key figure, is depicted with horns, ribs, dorsal scales and an exceedingly long tail coiled around the cat-like body. Associated with this figure are elongated hexagonal forms identified as representing sacrifices of food in bark dishes as well as zig-zag, wavy or castellated lines interpreted as wavy or roiled water.[57] These associated geometric designs become significant in the absence of life figures on some bags; for wherever these non-representational geometric designs are present, they can be construed as symbolic of *manitous*.

Both the Thunderbird and the Underwater Panther were extremely powerful *manitous* who, respectively, controlled the Sky World and the Under World. The power of each was manifested in both beneficent and malevolent aspects with the Thunderbird responsible for rain and victory in war but who also caused devastating storms. Balancing the Underwater Panther's malevolent forces that roiled the waters and drowned the unwary were its curative powers that could heal and prolong life. Mythic accounts place them as opponents in a continuing battle. Conflicts of power and strength between these two opposing *manitous* are mediated by elements of the Earth zone represented by the vegetal and animal fibers of the bag. By this means a balanced tri-partite cosmos is rendered tangible in these fiber bags.

Twined bags functioned within the societies as containers for individual personal medicines or as components of larger medicine bundles. Intriguing are those bags that were 'rigged with internal mechanical devices and used by medicine men to perform spectacular tricks in public performances, such as the appearance or disappearance of seemingly live but actually wooden snakes or puppets'.[58] Only after their power was no longer efficacious were these personally significant Native-made bags of indigenous materials acquired by non-Natives.

■ Ribbonwork

Ribbonwork is the art of cutting and sewing brightly colored silk ribbon to trade cloth for decorative purposes on clothing and other paraphernalia. The technique, first developed in the early-18th century, initially had a wide distribution throughout the entire cultural region. However, it is among the Great Lakes tribes that it reached its apogee and continues there today as an important art form. While the development of this art form was entirely dependent upon the introduction of trade goods – cloth, ribbon, thread, scissors or knives, and needles – the origins, forms, motifs, color selection and intended use are totally Indian.

Silk ribbons, first presented as gifts to the Indians, continued to be available through trade. Early ribbons were narrow, often only one-half to one-and one-half inches (1.2–4cm) in width. Later ones reached widths of three and four inches (up to 10cm). Woolen trade cloth, providing backgrounds of black, dark blue or red, was fashioned into women's blankets (shawls) and skirts, men's shirts, leggings, moccasins and other miscellaneous items.

In its simplest form, the ribbonwork technique consists of cutting a design into a silk ribbon of one color and hand-sewing it onto a background panel of another color and then stitching the panel to the fabric of the garment. Mirror images, repetition and asymmetrical designs are typical. Positive and negative styles are identified by pairs of ribbons sewn to produce a bilaterally symmetrical four-ribbon strip. The distinguishing feature is determined by the layer in which the figure is created. Positive style is identified by the cut and sewn top layer which is perceived to be the design. Negative style is created when the top parts of the ribbon are cut away to reveal the bilaterally symmetrical figure on the bottom layer of ribbons.[59] Around 1850 these basic styles became elaborated with design units larger, more varied and more complicated in shape and incorporating several layers of various colored ribbons. Simple geometric designs in earlier work were later augmented with intricate curvilinear ones. Patterns to create these designs were cut from birch bark or paper, and a collection of these became a woman's most treasured personal possession.[60]

Preference in ribbon colors was given to those with symbolic meaning in addition to their aesthetic value. For the Menominee, colors from the realm of Sky Woman were associated with the cardinal points: red for east; white and yellow for south; blue for west; and black for north.[61] For Mesquakie Ada Old Bear, red signified the Fox clan and black was associated with spiritual enlightenment and prayer.[62] Color selection performs as an integral aspect of the interplay between foreground and background, between dark and light, and between pattern form and color. This interplay and the tensions of mirror images and pattern reversals creates a dynamic vitality, the carefully balanced designs changing as the perspectives of the viewer shift. Creativity, innovation and a common regional aesthetic of these Native artists is superbly demonstrated through this manipulation of non-Native textiles.

It is fitting that many contemporary examples of ribbonwork shirts and skirts are made especially to accompany the dead,[63] for in this way the metaphor of duality, of a whole being split – half in this world, half in the spirit world – is brought to life as the corporeal body transforms into the spiritual one, as the past world becomes the new world.

REFERENCES

THE NORTHEAST

1 Cape Breton district, called *Onamag* by the Micmac, was – and still is – considered the residence of the head chief.
2 Although contacts with England may have occurred as early as 1497 when Sebastian Cabot was said to have taken three Micmac Indians to England, the rapport which the French developed contrasted markedly with the attitude of superiority which characterized most of the English colonists.
3 The early name for the areas of Nova Scotia and New Brunswick.
4 Deganawida was possibly of Huron descent. Closely associated with Deganawida was the Iroquois chief, Hiawatha, and the renowned woman chief of the Neutral Nation, Djigonsasen.
5 The Tuscarora joined in about 1720.
6 It has been suggested that the ideals underlying the founding of the League inspired the forming of the American Constitution because it is known that a number of the main writers of the Constitution were thoroughly familiar with the structure of the League.
7 Iroquois women's celebration song
8 In this context, a moveable tower, overtopping the palisade.
9 This battle has been described as one of the most decisive in American history, it being suggested that had the Hurons and French won the land of the Iroquois, 'Iroquoia', would have been dominated by the French, displacing the Dutch, and the course of colonial history changed (Bishop, 1949:240).
10 One particularly fine Iroquoian ball-headed club is in the collections of Skokloster Castle, Sweden (Ryden, 1963:114-15). A similar club also with a lizard-like creature carved at the top of the handle is in the Museum of Mankind, London (King, 1982:85).
11 Champlain vividly describes the battle between the Huron and Iroquois in which he participated in 1609 and demonstrates the useless protection which 'shields made of cotton thread woven together and wood' afforded against guns (Bishop, 1949:148).
12 War between Iroquois and Hurons dated from prior to colonial times; this particular conflict, however, finally destroyed the Huron Confederacy.
13 As soon as the Huron had an enemy in their power they tore out his finger-nails and bit or cut off

the fingers which he used to draw the string of a bow. While often causing serious infection, it rarely resulted in the prisoner dying before he reached the Huron settlements; indeed, he was well fed to ensure that he could 'better endure the tortures that awaited him' (Trigger, 1969:48).

14 Shamans and powerful warriors were also referred to as *Oki*. For a graphic 1616 description of a Huron *Oki*, see Bishop (1949:252).

15 This was just before the rice matured; if attempts were made to gather it later, a great deal was lost.

16 Manito, variants of which were manitto, manetto, manitoa and, more popularly as it has now been taken into the English language, manitou. It may be described as the 'mysterious and unknown potencies and powers of life and of the universe' (Hodge ed., 1907-10:800).

17 In comparison, although the Iroquois were great travelers, they were essentially landsmen, having only limited access to birch bark. While they used canoes, these were fabricated of elm bark which has been described as 'a clumsy craft unsuited to long voyages, dangerous for crossing lakes, and suicide in white water' (Fenton, Trigger ed., 1978:303). The more northerly Huron (Wyandot), however, lived within easier range of birch-bark country and mastered both technique of manufacture and use from their Algonquian neighbors. (See particularly Adney and Chapelle, 1964:214-15 for more details on Iroquois styles of canoe, and their characteristics.)

18 With acknowledgement to Alika Webber (1978:57-61). The author wishes to emphasize here that there is no suggestion meant that such designs were necessarily universally read and understood; however, the roots of the symbolism could well be elucidated by tribal shamans in the mythological terms described.

19 In recording Chippewa language, vowels are indicated as: a, as pronounced in father; e, as in they; ĕ, as in met; i, as in marine; ĭ, as in mint; o, as in note; u, as in rule; û, as in but (acknowledgement to Densmore, 1929:10).

20 The diplomacy of the Algonquians was clearly not matched by the more volatile Iroquoians. It will be recalled that the missionaries' well-intentioned but zealous thrust among the Huron and Iroquois led to the martyrdom of several priests.

21 Hoffman states that the *migis* may consist of any white shell; a cowrie shell was used in one tradition (Hoffman, 1891:167) and Ritzenthaler, who observed the ceremony in the 1940s, also refers to a cowrie shell, *'mikiss'* (Ritzenthaler, Trigger ed., 1978:754).

22 American Indian Workshop, Vienna, April 1989

23 It should be emphasized here that the reference is to peoples north of Mexico. For a discussion on writing in Mesoamerica, see Brotherston (1979:15-19). The Cree writing (referred to in the Subarctic chapter) was developed by the missionary James Evans in about 1840, while the mixed-blood Cherokee, Sequoyah, developed an alphabet in 1821.

Both developments, however, appear to have had their inspiration from European, rather than indigenous American, roots.

24 Observations on the League of the Iroquois, Palmer, 1949:102-3.

25 The Moon, as the celestial Nocturnal Orb of Light, complements the Sun's diurnal role. As Our Grandmother among the Iroquois and Winnebago, the Moon has various names relating to specific phases and functions. While the Sun oversaw daily life, it was the Moon, with her mysterious powers, who regulated the calendric cycle with its attendant ceremonials and seasonality. Strongly associated with women's reproductive powers, the Moon's powers also provided the men with luck in hunting – this last blessing an extrapolation of the notion of reproduction, with the animals' fertility providing an abundance. The Menominee explanation for the Moon's monthly disappearance is based upon the Moon's search for her brother, the Sun, who has gone forth to hunt. For 20 days she follows his trail without success and then dies. Four days pass when nothing is seen of her. At the end of this time, she is given new life to renew her quest once again.

26 In one legendary version it is only the kind intervention of the West Wind that finally freed the Iroquois by sending these giants to a watery death.

27 Although the actual origins are shrouded with uncertainty, the Drum Dance was given to a woman by the Great Spirit. Acording to legend, she hid from the white soldiers for several days. In a vision the Great Spirit instructed her to make a large dance drum and taught her the songs and rituals for the ceremony. An organization of members belonged to each drum, and the major portion of the ceremony consisted of singing and dancing to the beat of this instrument of peace.

28 In the autumn of 1687, Jesuit Father Beschefer sent 'Pieces of bark, on which figures have been marked by the teeth' to France (Thwaites 1959:287).

29 For example, Friedl, 1944:150

30 See Speck 1937:74-80. He also suggests that these dental pictographs might have been a source for what he calls 'phytomorphic' (literally, plant forms) art decorations (Speck, 1937:77-78).

31 Davidson, 1928; Moody, 1957; Speck, 1937; and innumerable others have suggested this and yet there is no concrete evidence.

32 For instance, William H. Holmes, as cited by Densmore 1941:679

33 Densmore, 1941:679 (emphasis added). A number of other sources reinforce this ability.

34 Bardwell, 1986:54

35 Wetherbee, 1980:197

36 Speck (1947:22) lists several individuals and their rights to specific resorts in New England. Mason (1904: Plate 120) provides a photograph of Caroline Masta, an Abenaki who made baskets at Belmar, New Jersey, from splints and sweet grass supplied by her family in Quebec (Canada). These she sold at Asbury Park and Boardwalk in New Jersey (Pelletier, 1982:6).

37 R. H. Whitehead (1982) provides the definitive study and analysis of Micmac quillwork from the historical evidence to the current situation.

38 If the bark is removed properly at the correct time, the tree is not killed.

39 When possible, the quills were taken during the spring before they became filled with an oily fluid as the summer progressed.

40 The burning of the barbed end turns the quill into ash, effectively removing it from being caught on the hands or bare feet (Whitehead, 1982:100n3).

41 Whitehead suggests that this might have been considered a conventionalized representation of a fir tree (1982:146n304)

42 Whitehead (1982:193) uses this term to distinguish the motif from the right-angled swastika. However, linguist Peter Bakker (1991:21), recognizing the motif as identical to the Basque national symbol, calls it by the Basque term *lauburu.*

43 It is important to note here that Ursuline nuns located in Quebec convents are known to have produced similar quillwork from circa 1773 until the 1830s. Poor quality and differences in motifs serve to differentiate these from the work of the Micmac.

44 Once a hide had been scraped, it was soaked overnight in a solution of butternut shells or alder bark before tanning. Although there are some indications that this was done for 'special' garments, it was most assuredly an aesthetic intent.

45 Native people first taught the nuns how to work in birch bark and moosehair. However, not only did the nuns utilize these materials to provide instruction in European methods of embroidery, they also commercially exploited this bark and moosehair art form by producing and selling similar wares themselves for a brief period of time (Phillips, 1991:22).

46 Forest Faces were mythological semi-human beings appearing as disembodied heads with long, snapping hair who darted from tree to tree in the forest. They are constantly hungry for tobacco.

47 Fenton (1987) has suggested a classification scheme which not all Iroquoianists accept.

48 Another set of wooden masks represents a variety of forms from pigs to clowns and for specialized societies.

49 Fenton, 1987:177-178

50 This replicates the action of the Great Doctor who scraped his rattle on the cosmic (World) tree

to absorb its strength.

51 Fenton, 1987:54-59
52 Bowdoin Gil, 1977:50
53 Pohrt, 1990:25
54 Whiteford, 1977:52
55 See, for example, Feest 1984; Phillips 1989; Whiteford 1977; Wilson 1982.
56 One species used is the Spreading Dogbane (*A. androsaemi folium*) and the other, Indian Hemp (*A. cannibinum*).
57 Skinner, 1921:260n3
58 Feest, 1984:15
59 Abbass, 1986
60 Hartman, 1988:41; Torrence and Hobbs, 1989:18
61 Skinner, 1921
62 Torrence and Hobbs, 1989:19
63 Torrence and Hobbs, 1989:49

INDEX

510

The publisher is grateful to the following for permission to reproduce photographs.

Courtesy of NAA, Smithsonian Institution, Washington, DC: 18, 20, 70, 72, 74, 76, 130, 134, 198, 200, 252, 254, 256, 302, 306, 360, 364, 404 (top), 454, 456 (top).

Courtesy Department Library Services, American Museum of Natural History, New York: 362, 404 (bottom).

Pitt Rivers Museum, Oxford: 456 (bottom).